Toyota Camry Automotive Repair Manual

by Ken Freund and John H Haynes
Member of the Guild of Motoring Writers

Models covered:
All Toyota Camry models with gasoline engines
1983 through 1991
Does not include diesel engine information

(6H19 - 92005)
(1023)

ABCDE
FGHIJ
KLMNO
PQ
3

AUTOMOTIVE
PARTS &
ACCESSORIES
ASSOCIATION
MEMBER

Haynes Publishing Group
Sparkford Nr Yeovil
Somerset BA22 7JJ England

Haynes North America, Inc
861 Lawrence Drive
Newbury Park
California 91320 USA

About this manual

Its purpose

The purpose of this manual is to help you get the best value from your vehicle. It can do so in several ways. It can help you decide what work must be done, even if you choose to have it done by a dealer service department or a repair shop; it provides information and procedures for routine maintenance and servicing; and it offers diagnostic and repair procedures to follow when trouble occurs.

We hope you use the manual to tackle the work yourself. For many simpler jobs, doing it yourself may be quicker than arranging an appointment to get the vehicle into a shop and making the trips to leave it and pick it up. More importantly, a lot of money can be saved by avoiding the expense the shop must pass on to you to cover its labor and overhead costs. An added benefit is the sense of satisfaction and accomplishment that you feel after doing the job yourself.

Using the manual

The manual is divided into Chapters. Each Chapter is divided into numbered Sections, which are headed in bold type between horizontal lines. Each Section consists of consecutively numbered paragraphs.

At the beginning of each numbered Section you will be referred to any illustrations which apply to the procedures in that Section. The reference numbers used in illustration captions pinpoint the pertinent Section and the Step within that Section. That is, illustration 3.2 means the illustration refers to Section 3 and Step (or paragraph) 2 within that Section.

Procedures, once described in the text, are not normally repeated. When it's necessary to refer to another Chapter, the reference will be given as Chapter and Section number. Cross references given without use of the word "Chapter" apply to Sections and/or paragraphs in the same Chapter. For example, "see Section 8" means in the same Chapter.

References to the left or right side of the vehicle assume you are sitting in the driver's seat, facing forward.

Even though we have prepared this manual with extreme care, neither the publisher nor the author can accept responsibility for any errors in, or omissions from, the information given.

NOTE

A **Note** provides information necessary to properly complete a procedure or information which will make the procedure easier to understand.

CAUTION

A **Caution** provides a special procedure or special steps which must be taken while completing the procedure where the Caution is found. Not heeding a Caution can result in damage to the assembly being worked on.

WARNING

A **Warning** provides a special procedure or special steps which must be taken while completing the procedure where the Warning is found. Not heeding a Warning can result in personal injury.

© **Haynes North America, Inc. 1989, 1990, 1992, 1999**

With permission from J.H. Haynes & Co. Ltd.

A book in the Haynes Automotive Repair Manual Series

Printed in the U.S.A.

ISBN 1 56392 030 1

Library of Congress Catalog Card Number 92-70524

Contents

1986 Toyota Camry 4-door sedan

Introduction to the Toyota Camry

Toyota Camry models are available in 4-door sedan, liftback and station wagon body styles.

The transversely mounted inline four-cylinder or V6 engines used in these models are equipped with electronic fuel injection. Later model four-cylinder engines are equipped with double overhead cams and four valves per cylinder.

The engine drives the front wheels through either a 5-speed manual or 4-speed automatic transaxle via independent driveaxles. On all-wheel drive models, a transfer case is used to drive the rear wheels through a driveshaft, rear differential and driveaxles.

Independent suspension, featuring coil spring/strut damper units, is used on all four wheels. The power assisted rack and pinion steering unit is mounted behind the engine.

The brakes are disc at the front with either drum or discs at the rear, depending on model, with power assist standard.

Vehicle identification numbers

Modifications are a continuing and unpublicized process in vehicle manufacturing. Since spare parts manuals and lists are compiled on a numerical basis, the individual vehicle numbers are essential to correctly identify the component required.

Vehicle Identification Number (VIN)

This very important identification number is stamped on the firewall in the engine compartment and on a plate attached to the dashboard inside the windshield on the driver's side of the vehicle (see illustration). The VIN also appears on the Vehicle Certificate of Title and Registration. It contains information such as where and when the vehicle was manufactured, the model year and the body style.

Manufacturer's plate

The manufacturer's plate is attached to the firewall in the engine compartment (see illustration). The plate contains the name of the manufacturer, the month and year of production, the Gross Vehicle Weight Rating

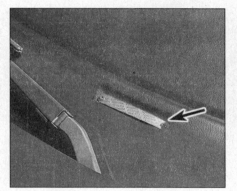

The VIN number plate is attached to the dashboard on the driver's side of the vehicle

(GVWR), the Gross Axle Weight Rating (GAWR) and the certification statement.

Engine numbers

The engine code numbers can be found in a variety of locations, depending on engine type (see illustrations).

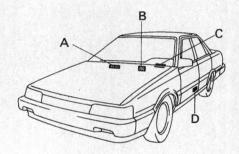

Important ID numbers and other information can be found in several locations on the vehicle

A   Vehicle Identification Number (stamped on firewall)
B   Manufacturer s plate
C   Vehicle Identification Number (visible through the drivers side windshield)
D   Certification regulation plate

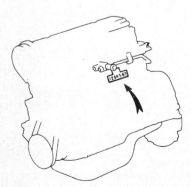

1983 through 1986 four-cylinder engine code number location

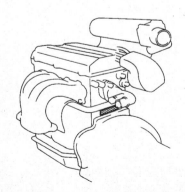

On 1987 and later four-cylinder engines, the code number is on the rear of the block, just below the cylinder head

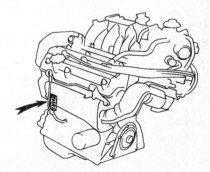

V6 engine code number location

Buying parts

Replacement parts are available from many sources, which generally fall into one of two categories - authorized dealer parts departments and independent retail auto parts stores. Our advice concerning these parts is as follows:

Retail auto parts stores: Good auto parts stores will stock frequently needed components which wear out relatively fast, such as clutch components, exhaust systems, brake parts, tune-up parts, etc. These stores often supply new or reconditioned parts on an exchange basis, which can save a considerable amount of money. Discount auto parts stores are often very good places to buy materials and parts needed for general vehicle maintenance such as oil, grease, filters, spark plugs, belts, touch-up paint, bulbs, etc. They also usually sell tools and general accessories, have convenient hours, charge lower prices and can often be found not far from home.

Authorized dealer parts department: This is the best source for parts which are unique to the vehicle and not generally available elsewhere (such as major engine parts, transmission parts, trim pieces, etc.).

Warranty information: If the vehicle is still covered under warranty, be sure that any replacement parts purchased - regardless of the source - do not invalidate the warranty!

To be sure of obtaining the correct parts, have engine and chassis numbers available and, if possible, take the old parts along for positive identification.

Maintenance techniques, tools and working facilities

Maintenance techniques

There are a number of techniques involved in maintenance and repair that will be referred to throughout this manual. Application of these techniques will enable the home mechanic to be more efficient, better organized and capable of performing the various tasks properly, which will ensure that the repair job is thorough and complete.

Fasteners

Fasteners are nuts, bolts, studs and screws used to hold two or more parts together. There are a few things to keep in mind when working with fasteners. Almost all of them use a locking device of some type, either a lockwasher, locknut, locking tab or thread adhesive. All threaded fasteners should be clean and straight, with undamaged threads and undamaged corners on the hex head where the wrench fits. Develop the habit of replacing all damaged nuts and bolts with new ones. Special locknuts with nylon or fiber inserts can only be used once. If they are removed, they lose their locking ability and must be replaced with new ones.

Rusted nuts and bolts should be treated with a penetrating fluid to ease removal and prevent breakage. Some mechanics use turpentine in a spout-type oil can, which works quite well. After applying the rust penetrant, let it work for a few minutes before trying to loosen the nut or bolt. Badly rusted fasteners may have to be chiseled or sawed off or removed with a special nut breaker, available at tool stores.

If a bolt or stud breaks off in an assembly, it can be drilled and removed with a special tool commonly available for this purpose.

Most automotive machine shops can perform this task, as well as other repair procedures, such as the repair of threaded holes that have been stripped out.

Flat washers and lockwashers, when removed from an assembly, should always be replaced exactly as removed. Replace any damaged washers with new ones. Never use a lockwasher on any soft metal surface (such as aluminum), thin sheet metal or plastic.

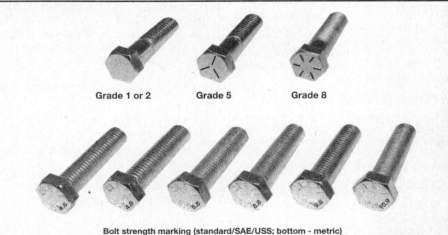

Grade 1 or 2   Grade 5   Grade 8

Bolt strength marking (standard/SAE/USS; bottom - metric)

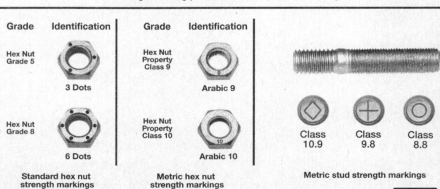

Standard hex nut strength markings

Metric hex nut strength markings

Metric stud strength markings

00-1 HAYNES

Fastener sizes

For a number of reasons, automobile manufacturers are making wider and wider use of metric fasteners. Therefore, it is important to be able to tell the difference between standard (sometimes called U.S. or SAE) and metric hardware, since they cannot be interchanged.

All bolts, whether standard or metric, are sized according to diameter, thread pitch and length. For example, a standard 1/2 - 13 x 1 bolt is 1/2 inch in diameter, has 13 threads per inch and is 1 inch long. An M12 - 1.75 x 25 metric bolt is 12 mm in diameter, has a thread pitch of 1.75 mm (the distance between threads) and is 25 mm long. The two bolts are nearly identical, and easily confused, but they are not interchangeable.

In addition to the differences in diameter, thread pitch and length, metric and standard bolts can also be distinguished by examining the bolt heads. To begin with, the distance across the flats on a standard bolt head is measured in inches, while the same dimension on a metric bolt is sized in millimeters (the same is true for nuts). As a result, a standard wrench should not be used on a metric bolt and a metric wrench should not be used on a standard bolt. Also, most standard bolts have slashes radiating out from the center of the head to denote the grade or strength of the bolt, which is an indication of the amount of torque that can be applied to it. The greater the number of slashes, the greater the strength of the bolt. Grades 0 through 5 are commonly used on automobiles. Metric bolts have a property class (grade) number, rather than a slash, molded into their heads to indicate bolt strength. In this case, the higher the number, the stronger the bolt. Property class numbers 8.8, 9.8 and 10.9 are commonly used on automobiles.

Strength markings can also be used to distinguish standard hex nuts from metric hex nuts. Many standard nuts have dots stamped into one side, while metric nuts are marked with a number. The greater the number of dots, or the higher the number, the greater the strength of the nut.

Metric studs are also marked on their ends according to property class (grade). Larger studs are numbered (the same as metric bolts), while smaller studs carry a geometric code to denote grade.

It should be noted that many fasteners, especially Grades 0 through 2, have no distinguishing marks on them. When such is the case, the only way to determine whether it is standard or metric is to measure the thread pitch or compare it to a known fastener of the same size.

Standard fasteners are often referred to as SAE, as opposed to metric. However, it should be noted that SAE technically refers to a non-metric fine thread fastener only. Coarse thread non-metric fasteners are referred to as USS sizes.

Since fasteners of the same size (both standard and metric) may have different

Metric thread sizes	Ft-lbs	Nm
M-6	6 to 9	9 to 12
M-8	14 to 21	19 to 28
M-10	28 to 40	38 to 54
M-12	50 to 71	68 to 96
M-14	80 to 140	109 to 154
Pipe thread sizes		
1/8	5 to 8	7 to 10
1/4	12 to 18	17 to 24
3/8	22 to 33	30 to 44
1/2	25 to 35	34 to 47
U.S. thread sizes		
1/4 - 20	6 to 9	9 to 12
5/16 - 18	12 to 18	17 to 24
5/16 - 24	14 to 20	19 to 27
3/8 - 16	22 to 32	30 to 43
3/8 - 24	27 to 38	37 to 51
7/16 - 14	40 to 55	55 to 74
7/16 - 20	40 to 60	55 to 81
1/2 - 13	55 to 80	75 to 108

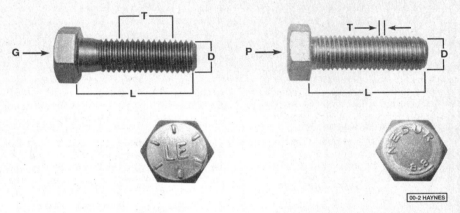

Standard (SAE and USS) bolt dimensions/grade marks

G   Grade marks (bolt strength)
L   Length (in inches)
T   Thread pitch (number of threads per inch)
D   Nominal diameter (in inches)

Metric bolt dimensions/grade marks

P   Property class (bolt strength)
L   Length (in millimeters)
T   Thread pitch (distance between threads in millimeters)
D   Diameter

strength ratings, be sure to reinstall any bolts, studs or nuts removed from your vehicle in their original locations. Also, when replacing a fastener with a new one, make sure that the new one has a strength rating equal to or greater than the original.

Tightening sequences and procedures

Most threaded fasteners should be tightened to a specific torque value (torque is the twisting force applied to a threaded component such as a nut or bolt). Overtightening the fastener can weaken it and cause it to break, while undertightening can cause it to eventually come loose. Bolts, screws and studs, depending on the material they are

made of and their thread diameters, have specific torque values, many of which are noted in the Specifications at the beginning of each Chapter. Be sure to follow the torque recommendations closely. For fasteners not assigned a specific torque, a general torque value chart is presented here as a guide. These torque values are for dry (unlubricated) fasteners threaded into steel or cast iron (not aluminum). As was previously mentioned, the size and grade of a fastener determine the amount of torque that can safely be applied to it. The figures listed here are approximate for Grade 2 and Grade 3 fasteners. Higher grades can tolerate higher torque values.

Fasteners laid out in a pattern, such as cylinder head bolts, oil pan bolts, differential cover bolts, etc., must be loosened or tight-

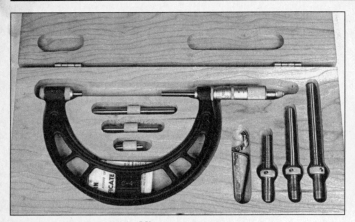

Micrometer set

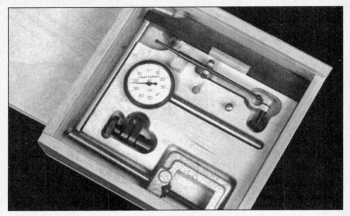

Dial indicator set

ened in sequence to avoid warping the component. This sequence will normally be shown in the appropriate Chapter. If a specific pattern is not given, the following procedures can be used to prevent warping.

Initially, the bolts or nuts should be assembled finger-tight only. Next, they should be tightened one full turn each, in a criss-cross or diagonal pattern. After each one has been tightened one full turn, return to the first one and tighten them all one-half turn, following the same pattern. Finally, tighten each of them one-quarter turn at a time until each fastener has been tightened to the proper torque. To loosen and remove the fasteners, the procedure would be reversed.

Component disassembly

Component disassembly should be done with care and purpose to help ensure that the parts go back together properly. Always keep track of the sequence in which parts are removed. Make note of special characteristics or marks on parts that can be installed more than one way, such as a grooved thrust washer on a shaft. It is a good idea to lay the disassembled parts out on a clean surface in the order that they were removed. It may also be helpful to make sketches or take instant photos of components before removal.

When removing fasteners from a component, keep track of their locations. Sometimes threading a bolt back in a part, or putting the washers and nut back on a stud, can prevent mix-ups later. If nuts and bolts cannot be returned to their original locations, they should be kept in a compartmented box or a series of small boxes. A cupcake or muffin tin is ideal for this purpose, since each cavity can hold the bolts and nuts from a particular area (i.e. oil pan bolts, valve cover bolts, engine mount bolts, etc.). A pan of this type is especially helpful when working on assemblies with very small parts, such as the carburetor, alternator, valve train or interior dash and trim pieces. The cavities can be marked with paint or tape to identify the contents.

Whenever wiring looms, harnesses or connectors are separated, it is a good idea to identify the two halves with numbered pieces of masking tape so they can be easily reconnected.

Gasket sealing surfaces

Throughout any vehicle, gaskets are used to seal the mating surfaces between two parts and keep lubricants, fluids, vacuum or pressure contained in an assembly.

Many times these gaskets are coated with a liquid or paste-type gasket sealing compound before assembly. Age, heat and pressure can sometimes cause the two parts to stick together so tightly that they are very difficult to separate. Often, the assembly can be loosened by striking it with a soft-face hammer near the mating surfaces. A regular hammer can be used if a block of wood is placed between the hammer and the part. Do not hammer on cast parts or parts that could be easily damaged. With any particularly stubborn part, always recheck to make sure that every fastener has been removed.

Avoid using a screwdriver or bar to pry apart an assembly, as they can easily mar the gasket sealing surfaces of the parts, which must remain smooth. If prying is absolutely necessary, use an old broom handle, but keep in mind that extra clean up will be necessary if the wood splinters.

After the parts are separated, the old gasket must be carefully scraped off and the gasket surfaces cleaned. Stubborn gasket material can be soaked with rust penetrant or treated with a special chemical to soften it so it can be easily scraped off. A scraper can be fashioned from a piece of copper tubing by flattening and sharpening one end. Copper is recommended because it is usually softer than the surfaces to be scraped, which reduces the chance of gouging the part. Some gaskets can be removed with a wire brush, but regardless of the method used, the mating surfaces must be left clean and smooth. If for some reason the gasket surface is gouged, then a gasket sealer thick enough to fill scratches will have to be used during reassembly of the components. For most applications, a non-drying (or semi-drying) gasket sealer should be used.

Hose removal tips

Warning: *If the vehicle is equipped with air conditioning, do not disconnect any of the A/C hoses without first having the system depressurized by a dealer service department or a service station.*

Hose removal precautions closely parallel gasket removal precautions. Avoid scratching or gouging the surface that the hose mates against or the connection may leak. This is especially true for radiator hoses. Because of various chemical reactions, the rubber in hoses can bond itself to the metal spigot that the hose fits over. To remove a hose, first loosen the hose clamps that secure it to the spigot. Then, with slip-joint pliers, grab the hose at the clamp and rotate it around the spigot. Work it back and forth until it is completely free, then pull it off. Silicone or other lubricants will ease removal if they can be applied between the hose and the outside of the spigot. Apply the same lubricant to the inside of the hose and the outside of the spigot to simplify installation.

As a last resort (and if the hose is to be replaced with a new one anyway), the rubber can be slit with a knife and the hose peeled from the spigot. If this must be done, be careful that the metal connection is not damaged.

If a hose clamp is broken or damaged, do not reuse it. Wire-type clamps usually weaken with age, so it is a good idea to replace them with screw-type clamps whenever a hose is removed.

Tools

A selection of good tools is a basic requirement for anyone who plans to maintain and repair his or her own vehicle. For the owner who has few tools, the initial investment might seem high, but when compared to the spiraling costs of professional auto maintenance and repair, it is a wise one.

To help the owner decide which tools are needed to perform the tasks detailed in this manual, the following tool lists are offered: *Maintenance and minor repair, Repair/overhaul* and *Special.*

The newcomer to practical mechanics

Dial caliper

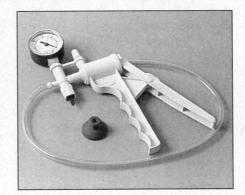

Hand-operated vacuum pump

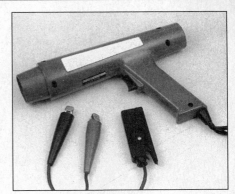

Timing light

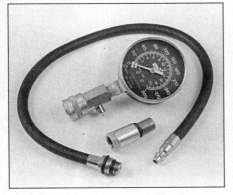

Compression gauge with spark plug
hole adapter

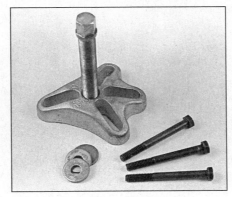

Damper/steering wheel puller

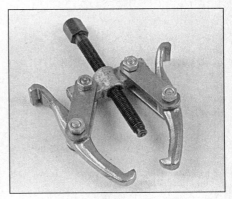

General purpose puller

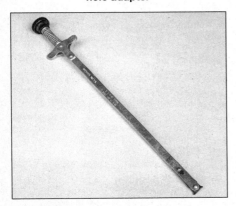

Hydraulic lifter removal tool

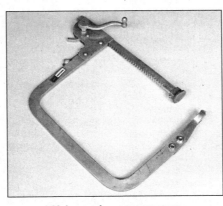

Valve spring compressor

Valve spring compressor

Ridge reamer

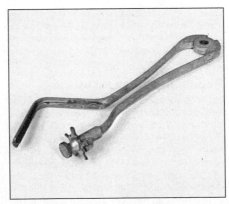

Piston ring groove cleaning tool

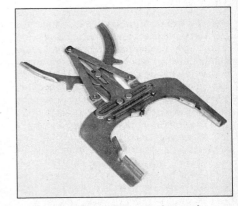

Ring removal/installation tool

Ring compressor

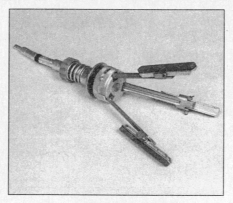

Cylinder hone

Brake hold-down spring tool

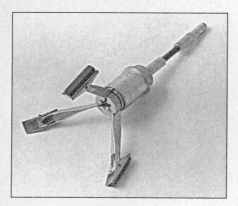

Brake cylinder hone

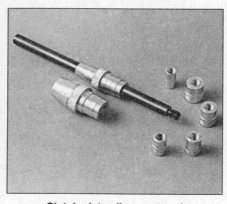

Clutch plate alignment tool

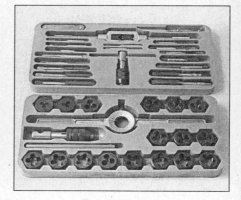

Tap and die set

should start off with the *maintenance and minor repair* tool kit, which is adequate for the simpler jobs performed on a vehicle. Then, as confidence and experience grow, the owner can tackle more difficult tasks, buying additional tools as they are needed. Eventually the basic kit will be expanded into the *repair and overhaul* tool set. Over a period of time, the experienced do-it-yourselfer will assemble a tool set complete enough for most repair and overhaul procedures and will add tools from the special category when it is felt that the expense is justified by the frequency of use.

Maintenance and minor repair tool kit

The tools in this list should be considered the minimum required for performance of routine maintenance, servicing and minor repair work. We recommend the purchase of combination wrenches (box-end and open-end combined in one wrench). While more expensive than open end wrenches, they offer the advantages of both types of wrench.

*Combination wrench set (1/4-inch to
    1 inch or 6 mm to 19 mm)*
Adjustable wrench, 8 inch
Spark plug wrench with rubber insert
Spark plug gap adjusting tool
Feeler gauge set
Brake bleeder wrench
*Standard screwdriver (5/16-inch x
    6 inch)*

Phillips screwdriver (No. 2 x 6 inch)
Combination pliers - 6 inch
Hacksaw and assortment of blades
Tire pressure gauge
Grease gun
Oil can
Fine emery cloth
Wire brush
Battery post and cable cleaning tool
Oil filter wrench
Funnel (medium size)
Safety goggles
Jackstands (2)
Drain pan

Note: *If basic tune-ups are going to be part of routine maintenance, it will be necessary to purchase a good quality stroboscopic timing light and combination tachometer/dwell meter. Although they are included in the list of special tools, it is mentioned here because they are absolutely necessary for tuning most vehicles properly.*

Repair and overhaul tool set

These tools are essential for anyone who plans to perform major repairs and are in addition to those in the maintenance and minor repair tool kit. Included is a comprehensive set of sockets which, though expensive, are invaluable because of their versatility, especially when various extensions and drives are available. We recommend the 1/2-inch drive over the 3/8-inch drive. Although the larger drive is bulky and more expensive,

it has the capacity of accepting a very wide range of large sockets. Ideally, however, the mechanic should have a 3/8-inch drive set and a 1/2-inch drive set.

Socket set(s)
Reversible ratchet
Extension - 10 inch
Universal joint
*Torque wrench (same size drive as
    sockets)*
Ball peen hammer - 8 ounce
Soft-face hammer (plastic/rubber)
Standard screwdriver (1/4-inch x 6 inch)
*Standard screwdriver (stubby -
    5/16-inch)*
Phillips screwdriver (No. 3 x 8 inch)
Phillips screwdriver (stubby - No. 2)
Pliers - vise grip
Pliers - lineman's
Pliers - needle nose
Pliers - snap-ring (internal and external)
Cold chisel - 1/2-inch
Scribe
*Scraper (made from flattened copper
    tubing)*
Centerpunch
Pin punches (1/16, 1/8, 3/16-inch)
Steel rule/straightedge - 12 inch
*Allen wrench set (1/8 to 3/8-inch or
    4 mm to 10 mm)*
A selection of files
Wire brush (large)
Jackstands (second set)
Jack (scissor or hydraulic type)

Note: *Another tool which is often useful is an electric drill with a chuck capacity of 3/8-inch and a set of good quality drill bits.*

Special tools

The tools in this list include those which are not used regularly, are expensive to buy, or which need to be used in accordance with their manufacturer's instructions. Unless these tools will be used frequently, it is not very economical to purchase many of them. A consideration would be to split the cost and use between yourself and a friend or friends. In addition, most of these tools can be obtained from a tool rental shop on a temporary basis.

This list primarily contains only those tools and instruments widely available to the public, and not those special tools produced by the vehicle manufacturer for distribution to dealer service departments. Occasionally, references to the manufacturer's special tools are included in the text of this manual. Generally, an alternative method of doing the job without the special tool is offered. However, sometimes there is no alternative to their use. Where this is the case, and the tool cannot be purchased or borrowed, the work should be turned over to the dealer service department or an automotive repair shop.

> *Valve spring compressor*
> *Piston ring groove cleaning tool*
> *Piston ring compressor*
> *Piston ring installation tool*
> *Cylinder compression gauge*
> *Cylinder ridge reamer*
> *Cylinder surfacing hone*
> *Cylinder bore gauge*
> *Micrometers and/or dial calipers*
> *Hydraulic lifter removal tool*
> *Balljoint separator*
> *Universal-type puller*
> *Impact screwdriver*
> *Dial indicator set*
> *Stroboscopic timing light (inductive pick-up)*
> *Hand operated vacuum/pressure pump*
> *Tachometer/dwell meter*
> *Universal electrical multimeter*
> *Cable hoist*
> *Brake spring removal and installation tools*
> *Floor jack*

Buying tools

For the do-it-yourselfer who is just starting to get involved in vehicle maintenance and repair, there are a number of options available when purchasing tools. If maintenance and minor repair is the extent of the work to be done, the purchase of individual tools is satisfactory. If, on the other hand, extensive work is planned, it would be a good idea to purchase a modest tool set from one of the large retail chain stores. A set can usually be bought at a substantial savings over the individual tool prices, and they often come with a tool box. As additional tools are

needed, add-on sets, individual tools and a larger tool box can be purchased to expand the tool selection. Building a tool set gradually allows the cost of the tools to be spread over a longer period of time and gives the mechanic the freedom to choose only those tools that will actually be used.

Tool stores will often be the only source of some of the special tools that are needed, but regardless of where tools are bought, try to avoid cheap ones, especially when buying screwdrivers and sockets, because they won't last very long. The expense involved in replacing cheap tools will eventually be greater than the initial cost of quality tools.

Care and maintenance of tools

Good tools are expensive, so it makes sense to treat them with respect. Keep them clean and in usable condition and store them properly when not in use. Always wipe off any dirt, grease or metal chips before putting them away. Never leave tools lying around in the work area. Upon completion of a job, always check closely under the hood for tools that may have been left there so they won't get lost during a test drive.

Some tools, such as screwdrivers, pliers, wrenches and sockets, can be hung on a panel mounted on the garage or workshop wall, while others should be kept in a tool box or tray. Measuring instruments, gauges, meters, etc. must be carefully stored where they cannot be damaged by weather or impact from other tools.

When tools are used with care and stored properly, they will last a very long time. Even with the best of care, though, tools will wear out if used frequently. When a tool is damaged or worn out, replace it. Subsequent jobs will be safer and more enjoyable if you do.

How to repair damaged threads

Sometimes, the internal threads of a nut or bolt hole can become stripped, usually from overtightening. Stripping threads is an all-too-common occurrence, especially when working with aluminum parts, because aluminum is so soft that it easily strips out.

Usually, external or internal threads are only partially stripped. After they've been cleaned up with a tap or die, they'll still work. Sometimes, however, threads are badly damaged. When this happens, you've got three choices:

1) *Drill and tap the hole to the next suitable oversize and install a larger diameter bolt, screw or stud.*
2) *Drill and tap the hole to accept a threaded plug, then drill and tap the plug to the original screw size. You can also buy a plug already threaded to the original size. Then you simply drill a hole to the specified size, then run the threaded plug into the hole with a bolt and jam*

nut. Once the plug is fully seated, remove the jam nut and bolt.
3) *The third method uses a patented thread repair kit like Heli-Coil or Slimsert. These easy-to-use kits are designed to repair damaged threads in straight-through holes and blind holes. Both are available as kits which can handle a variety of sizes and thread patterns. Drill the hole, then tap it with the special included tap. Install the Heli-Coil and the hole is back to its original diameter and thread pitch.*

Regardless of which method you use, be sure to proceed calmly and carefully. A little impatience or carelessness during one of these relatively simple procedures can ruin your whole day's work and cost you a bundle if you wreck an expensive part.

Working facilities

Not to be overlooked when discussing tools is the workshop. If anything more than routine maintenance is to be carried out, some sort of suitable work area is essential.

It is understood, and appreciated, that many home mechanics do not have a good workshop or garage available, and end up removing an engine or doing major repairs outside. It is recommended, however, that the overhaul or repair be completed under the cover of a roof.

A clean, flat workbench or table of comfortable working height is an absolute necessity. The workbench should be equipped with a vise that has a jaw opening of at least four inches.

As mentioned previously, some clean, dry storage space is also required for tools, as well as the lubricants, fluids, cleaning solvents, etc. which soon become necessary.

Sometimes waste oil and fluids, drained from the engine or cooling system during normal maintenance or repairs, present a disposal problem. To avoid pouring them on the ground or into a sewage system, pour the used fluids into large containers, seal them with caps and take them to an authorized disposal site or recycling center. Plastic jugs, such as old antifreeze containers, are ideal for this purpose.

Always keep a supply of old newspapers and clean rags available. Old towels are excellent for mopping up spills. Many mechanics use rolls of paper towels for most work because they are readily available and disposable. To help keep the area under the vehicle clean, a large cardboard box can be cut open and flattened to protect the garage or shop floor.

Whenever working over a painted surface, such as when leaning over a fender to service something under the hood, always cover it with an old blanket or bedspread to protect the finish. Vinyl covered pads, made especially for this purpose, are available at auto parts stores.

Booster battery (jump) starting

Observe these precautions when using a booster battery to start a vehicle:

a) *Before connecting the booster battery, make sure the ignition switch is in the Off position.*
b) *Turn off the lights, heater and other electrical loads.*
c) *Your eyes should be shielded. Safety goggles are a good idea.*
d) *Make sure the booster battery is the same voltage as the dead one in the vehicle.*
e) *The two vehicles MUST NOT TOUCH each other!*
f) *Make sure the transaxle is in Neutral (manual) or Park (automatic).*
g) *If the booster battery is not a maintenance-free type, remove the vent caps and lay a cloth over the vent holes.*

Connect the red jumper cable to the positive (+) terminals of each battery **(see illustration)**.

Connect one end of the black jumper cable to the negative (-) terminal of the booster battery. The other end of this cable should be connected to a good ground on the vehicle to be started, such as a bolt or bracket on the body.

Start the engine using the booster battery, then, with the engine running at idle speed, disconnect the jumper cables in the reverse order of connection.

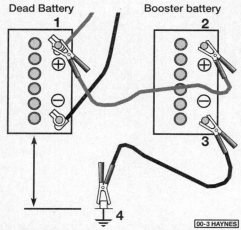

Make the booster battery cable connections in the numerical order shown (note that the negative cable of the booster battery is NOT attached to the negative terminal of the dead battery)

Jacking and towing

Jacking

Warning: *The jack supplied with the vehicle should only be used for changing a tire or placing jackstands under the frame. Never work under the vehicle or start the engine while this jack is being used as the only means of support.*

The vehicle should be on level ground. Place the shift lever in Park, if you have an automatic, or Reverse if you have a manual transaxle. Block the wheel diagonally opposite the wheel being changed. Set the parking brake.

Remove the spare tire and jack from stowage. Remove the wheel cover and trim ring (if so equipped) with the tapered end of the lug nut wrench by inserting and twisting the handle and then prying against the back of the wheel cover. On aluminum wheels, tap the back side of the wheel hub cover after removing the wheel (do not attempt to pull off the wheel hub cover by hand). Loosen, but do not remove, the lug nuts (one-half turn is sufficient).

Place the scissors-type jack under the side of the vehicle and adjust the jack height until it fits between the notches in the vertical rocker panel flange nearest the wheel to be changed. There is a front and rear jacking point on each side of the vehicle **(see illustration)**.

Turn the jack handle clockwise until the tire clears the ground. Remove the lug nuts and pull the wheel off. Replace it with the spare.

Replace the lug nuts with the beveled edges facing in. Tighten them snugly. Don't attempt to tighten them completely until the vehicle is lowered or it could slip off the jack.

Turn the jack handle counterclockwise to lower the vehicle. Remove the jack and tighten the lug nuts in a criss-cross pattern.

Install the cover (and trim ring, if used) and be sure it's snapped into place all the way around.

Stow the tire, jack and wrench. Unblock the wheels.

Towing

All-Trac/4WD models

All-Trac models can be towed in one of two ways - never use any other method! One way is to place the rear wheels on a dolly and raise the front wheels off the ground with a towing sling (the method most tow trucks would use). They can also be towed with all four wheels on the ground if the parking brake is released, the transmission is in Neutral and the ignition key is in the ACC position. If the vehicle has a center differential lock button, the center differential must be unlocked (the indicator light must be off with the ignition key on). **Note:** *Don't tow the vehicle with the key removed or in the LOCK position. The steering lock mechanism isn't strong enough to hold the front wheels straight while towing.*

FWD models

As a general rule, the vehicle should be towed with the front (drive) wheels off the ground. If they can't be raised, place them on a dolly. The ignition key must be in the ACC position, since the steering lock mechanism isn't strong enough to hold the front wheels straight while towing.

Vehicles equipped with an automatic transaxle can be towed from the front only with all four wheels on the ground, provided that speeds don't exceed 30 mph and the distance is not over 50 miles. Before towing, check the transmission fluid level (see Chapter 1). If the level is below the HOT line on the dipstick, add fluid or use a towing dolly. Release the parking brake, put the transaxle in Neutral and place the ignition key in the ACC position. Caution: Never tow a vehicle with an automatic transaxle from the rear with the front wheels on the ground.

Equipment specifically designed for towing should be used. It should be attached to the main structural members of the vehicle, not the bumpers or brackets.

Safety is a major consideration when towing and all applicable state and local laws must be obeyed. A safety chain system must be used at all times. Remember that power steering and power brakes will not work with the engine off.

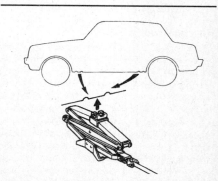

The jack fits over the rocker panel flange, between the two notches (there are two jacking points on each side of the vehicle)

Automotive chemicals and lubricants

A number of automotive chemicals and lubricants are available for use during vehicle maintenance and repair. They include a wide variety of products ranging from cleaning solvents and degreasers to lubricants and protective sprays for rubber, plastic and vinyl.

Cleaners

Carburetor cleaner and choke cleaner is a strong solvent for gum, varnish and carbon. Most carburetor cleaners leave a dry-type lubricant film which will not harden or gum up. Because of this film it is not recommended for use on electrical components.

Brake system cleaner is used to remove grease and brake fluid from the brake system, where clean surfaces are absolutely necessary. It leaves no residue and often eliminates brake squeal caused by contaminants.

Electrical cleaner removes oxidation, corrosion and carbon deposits from electrical contacts, restoring full current flow. It can also be used to clean spark plugs, carburetor jets, voltage regulators and other parts where an oil-free surface is desired.

Demoisturants remove water and moisture from electrical components such as alternators, voltage regulators, electrical connectors and fuse blocks. They are non-conductive, non-corrosive and non-flammable.

Degreasers are heavy-duty solvents used to remove grease from the outside of the engine and from chassis components. They can be sprayed or brushed on and, depending on the type, are rinsed off either with water or solvent.

Lubricants

Motor oil is the lubricant formulated for use in engines. It normally contains a wide variety of additives to prevent corrosion and reduce foaming and wear. Motor oil comes in various weights (viscosity ratings) from 0 to 50. The recommended weight of the oil depends on the season, temperature and the demands on the engine. Light oil is used in cold climates and under light load conditions. Heavy oil is used in hot climates and where high loads are encountered. Multi-viscosity oils are designed to have characteristics of both light and heavy oils and are available in a number of weights from 5W-20 to 20W-50.

Gear oil is designed to be used in differentials, manual transmissions and other areas where high-temperature lubrication is required.

Chassis and wheel bearing grease is a heavy grease used where increased loads and friction are encountered, such as for wheel bearings, balljoints, tie-rod ends and universal joints.

High-temperature wheel bearing grease is designed to withstand the extreme temperatures encountered by wheel bearings in disc brake equipped vehicles. It usually contains molybdenum disulfide (moly), which is a dry-type lubricant.

White grease is a heavy grease for metal-to-metal applications where water is a problem. White grease stays soft under both low and high temperatures (usually from -100 to +190-degrees F), and will not wash off or dilute in the presence of water.

Assembly lube is a special extreme pressure lubricant, usually containing moly, used to lubricate high-load parts (such as main and rod bearings and cam lobes) for initial start-up of a new engine. The assembly lube lubricates the parts without being squeezed out or washed away until the engine oiling system begins to function.

Silicone lubricants are used to protect rubber, plastic, vinyl and nylon parts.

Graphite lubricants are used where oils cannot be used due to contamination problems, such as in locks. The dry graphite will lubricate metal parts while remaining uncontaminated by dirt, water, oil or acids. It is electrically conductive and will not foul electrical contacts in locks such as the ignition switch.

Moly penetrants loosen and lubricate frozen, rusted and corroded fasteners and prevent future rusting or freezing.

Heat-sink grease is a special electrically non-conductive grease that is used for mounting electronic ignition modules where it is essential that heat is transferred away from the module.

Sealants

RTV sealant is one of the most widely used gasket compounds. Made from silicone, RTV is air curing, it seals, bonds, waterproofs, fills surface irregularities, remains flexible, doesn't shrink, is relatively easy to remove, and is used as a supplementary sealer with almost all low and medium temperature gaskets.

Anaerobic sealant is much like RTV in that it can be used either to seal gaskets or to form gaskets by itself. It remains flexible, is solvent resistant and fills surface imperfections. The difference between an anaerobic sealant and an RTV-type sealant is in the curing. RTV cures when exposed to air, while an anaerobic sealant cures only in the absence of air. This means that an anaerobic sealant cures only after the assembly of parts, sealing them together.

Thread and pipe sealant is used for sealing hydraulic and pneumatic fittings and vacuum lines. It is usually made from a Teflon compound, and comes in a spray, a paint-on liquid and as a wrap-around tape.

Chemicals

Anti-seize compound prevents seizing, galling, cold welding, rust and corrosion in fasteners. High-temperature ant-seize, usually made with copper and graphite lubricants, is used for exhaust system and exhaust manifold bolts.

Anaerobic locking compounds are used to keep fasteners from vibrating or working loose and cure only after installation, in the absence of air. Medium strength locking compound is used for small nuts, bolts and screws that may be removed later. High-strength locking compound is for large nuts, bolts and studs which aren't removed on a regular basis.

Oil additives range from viscosity index improvers to chemical treatments that claim to reduce internal engine friction. It should be noted that most oil manufacturers caution against using additives with their oils.

Gas additives perform several functions, depending on their chemical makeup. They usually contain solvents that help dissolve gum and varnish that build up on carburetor, fuel injection and intake parts. They also serve to break down carbon deposits that form on the inside surfaces of the combustion chambers. Some additives contain upper cylinder lubricants for valves and piston rings, and others contain chemicals to remove condensation from the gas tank.

Miscellaneous

Brake fluid is specially formulated hydraulic fluid that can withstand the heat and pressure encountered in brake systems. Care must be taken so this fluid does not come in contact with painted surfaces or plastics. An opened container should always be resealed to prevent contamination by water or dirt.

Weatherstrip adhesive is used to bond weatherstripping around doors, windows and trunk lids. It is sometimes used to attach trim pieces.

Undercoating is a petroleum-based, tar-like substance that is designed to protect metal surfaces on the underside of the vehicle from corrosion. It also acts as a sound-deadening agent by insulating the bottom of the vehicle.

Waxes and polishes are used to help protect painted and plated surfaces from the weather. Different types of paint may require the use of different types of wax and polish. Some polishes utilize a chemical or abrasive cleaner to help remove the top layer of oxidized (dull) paint on older vehicles. In recent years many non-wax polishes that contain a wide variety of chemicals such as polymers and silicones have been introduced. These non-wax polishes are usually easier to apply and last longer than conventional waxes and polishes.

Conversion factors

Length (distance)

Inches (in)	X	25.4	= Millimetres (mm)	X 0.0394	= Inches (in)
Feet (ft)	X	0.305	= Metres (m)	X 3.281	= Feet (ft)
Miles	X	1.609	= Kilometres (km)	X 0.621	= Miles

Volume (capacity)

Cubic inches (cu in; in^3)	X	16.387	= Cubic centimetres (cc; cm^3)	X 0.061	= Cubic inches (cu in; in^3)
Imperial pints (Imp pt)	X	0.568	= Litres (l)	X 1.76	= Imperial pints (Imp pt)
Imperial quarts (Imp qt)	X	1.137	= Litres (l)	X 0.88	= Imperial quarts (Imp qt)
Imperial quarts (Imp qt)	X	1.201	= US quarts (US qt)	X 0.833	= Imperial quarts (Imp qt)
US quarts (US qt)	X	0.946	= Litres (l)	X 1.057	= US quarts (US qt)
Imperial gallons (Imp gal)	X	4.546	= Litres (l)	X 0.22	= Imperial gallons (Imp gal)
Imperial gallons (Imp gal)	X	1.201	= US gallons (US gal)	X 0.833	= Imperial gallons (Imp gal)
US gallons (US gal)	X	3.785	= Litres (l)	X 0.264	= US gallons (US gal)

Mass (weight)

Ounces (oz)	X	28.35	= Grams (g)	X 0.035	= Ounces (oz)
Pounds (lb)	X	0.454	= Kilograms (kg)	X 2.205	= Pounds (lb)

Force

Ounces-force (ozf; oz)	X	0.278	= Newtons (N)	X 3.6	= Ounces-force (ozf; oz)
Pounds-force (lbf; lb)	X	4.448	= Newtons (N)	X 0.225	= Pounds-force (lbf; lb)
Newtons (N)	X	0.1	= Kilograms-force (kgf; kg)	X 9.81	= Newtons (N)

Pressure

Pounds-force per square inch (psi; lbf/in^2; lb/in^2)	X	0.070	= Kilograms-force per square centimetre (kgf/cm^2; kg/cm^2)	X 14.223	= Pounds-force per square inch (psi; lbf/in^2; lb/in^2)
Pounds-force per square inch (psi; lbf/in^2; lb/in^2)	X	0.068	= Atmospheres (atm)	X 14.696	= Pounds-force per square inch (psi; lbf/in^2; lb/in^2)
Pounds-force per square inch (psi; lbf/in^2; lb/in^2)	X	0.069	= Bars	X 14.5	= Pounds-force per square inch (psi; lbf/in^2; lb/in^2)
Pounds-force per square inch (psi; lbf/in^2; lb/in^2)	X	6.895	= Kilopascals (kPa)	X 0.145	= Pounds-force per square inch (psi; lbf/in^2; lb/in^2)
Kilopascals (kPa)	X	0.01	= Kilograms-force per square centimetre (kgf/cm^2; kg/cm^2)	X 98.1	= Kilopascals (kPa)

Torque (moment of force)

Pounds-force inches (lbf in; lb in)	X	1.152	= Kilograms-force centimetre (kgf cm; kg cm)	X 0.868	= Pounds-force inches (lbf in; lb in)
Pounds-force inches (lbf in; lb in)	X	0.113	= Newton metres (Nm)	X 8.85	= Pounds-force inches (lbf in; lb in)
Pounds-force inches (lbf in; lb in)	X	0.083	= Pounds-force feet (lbf ft; lb ft)	X 12	= Pounds-force inches (lbf in; lb in)
Pounds-force feet (lbf ft; lb ft)	X	0.138	= Kilograms-force metres (kgf m; kg m)	X 7.233	= Pounds-force feet (lbf ft; lb ft)
Pounds-force feet (lbf ft; lb ft)	X	1.356	= Newton metres (Nm)	X 0.738	= Pounds-force feet (lbf ft; lb ft)
Newton metres (Nm)	X	0.102	= Kilograms-force metres (kgf m; kg m)	X 9.804	= Newton metres (Nm)

Vacuum

Inches mercury (in. Hg)	X	3.377	= Kilopascals (kPa)	X 0.2961	= Inches mercury
Inches mercury (in. Hg)	X	25.4	= Millimeters mercury (mm Hg)	X 0.0394	= Inches mercury

Power

Horsepower (hp)	X	745.7	= Watts (W)	X 0.0013	= Horsepower (hp)

Velocity (speed)

Miles per hour (miles/hr; mph)	X	1.609	= Kilometres per hour (km/hr; kph)	X 0.621	= Miles per hour (miles/hr; mph)

Fuel consumption*

Miles per gallon, Imperial (mpg)	X	0.354	= Kilometres per litre (km/l)	X 2.825	= Miles per gallon, Imperial (mpg)
Miles per gallon, US (mpg)	X	0.425	= Kilometres per litre (km/l)	X 2.352	= Miles per gallon, US (mpg)

Temperature

Degrees Fahrenheit = (°C x 1.8) + 32   Degrees Celsius (Degrees Centigrade; °C) = (°F - 32) x 0.56

*It is common practice to convert from miles per gallon (mpg) to litres/100 kilometres (l/100km), where mpg (Imperial) x l/100 km = 282 and mpg (US) x l/100 km = 235

Safety first!

Regardless of how enthusiastic you may be about getting on with the job at hand, take the time to ensure that your safety is not jeopardized. A moment's lack of attention can result in an accident, as can failure to observe certain simple safety precautions. The possibility of an accident will always exist, and the following points should not be considered a comprehensive list of all dangers. Rather, they are intended to make you aware of the risks and to encourage a safety conscious approach to all work you carry out on your vehicle.

Essential DOs and DON'Ts

DON'T rely on a jack when working under the vehicle. Always use approved jackstands to support the weight of the vehicle and place them under the recommended lift or support points.

DON'T attempt to loosen extremely tight fasteners (i.e. wheel lug nuts) while the vehicle is on a jack - it may fall.

DON'T start the engine without first making sure that the transmission is in Neutral (or Park where applicable) and the parking brake is set.

DON'T remove the radiator cap from a hot cooling system - let it cool or cover it with a cloth and release the pressure gradually.

DON'T attempt to drain the engine oil until you are sure it has cooled to the point that it will not burn you.

DON'T touch any part of the engine or exhaust system until it has cooled sufficiently to avoid burns.

DON'T siphon toxic liquids such as gasoline, antifreeze and brake fluid by mouth, or allow them to remain on your skin.

DON'T inhale brake lining dust - it is potentially hazardous (see *Asbestos* below).

DON'T allow spilled oil or grease to remain on the floor - wipe it up before someone slips on it.

DON'T use loose fitting wrenches or other tools which may slip and cause injury.

DON'T push on wrenches when loosening or tightening nuts or bolts. Always try to pull the wrench toward you. If the situation calls for pushing the wrench away, push with an open hand to avoid scraped knuckles if the wrench should slip.

DON'T attempt to lift a heavy component alone - get someone to help you.

DON'T rush or take unsafe shortcuts to finish a job.

DON'T allow children or animals in or around the vehicle while you are working on it.

DO wear eye protection when using power tools such as a drill, sander, bench grinder, etc. and when working under a vehicle.

DO keep loose clothing and long hair well out of the way of moving parts.

DO make sure that any hoist used has a safe working load rating adequate for the job.

DO get someone to check on you periodically when working alone on a vehicle.

DO carry out work in a logical sequence and make sure that everything is correctly assembled and tightened.

DO keep chemicals and fluids tightly capped and out of the reach of children and pets.

DO remember that your vehicle's safety affects that of yourself and others. If in doubt on any point, get professional advice.

Asbestos

Certain friction, insulating, sealing, and other products - such as brake linings, brake bands, clutch linings, torque converters, gaskets, etc. - may contain asbestos. Extreme care must be taken to avoid inhalation of dust from such products, since it is hazardous to health. If in doubt, assume that they do contain asbestos.

Fire

Remember at all times that gasoline is highly flammable. Never smoke or have any kind of open flame around when working on a vehicle. But the risk does not end there. A spark caused by an electrical short circuit, by two metal surfaces contacting each other, or even by static electricity built up in your body under certain conditions, can ignite gasoline vapors, which in a confined space are highly explosive. Do not, under any circumstances, use gasoline for cleaning parts. Use an approved safety solvent.

Always disconnect the battery ground (-) cable at the battery before working on any part of the fuel system or electrical system. Never risk spilling fuel on a hot engine or exhaust component. It is strongly recommended that a fire extinguisher suitable for use on fuel and electrical fires be kept handy in the garage or workshop at all times. Never try to extinguish a fuel or electrical fire with water.

Fumes

Certain fumes are highly toxic and can quickly cause unconsciousness and even death if inhaled to any extent. Gasoline vapor falls into this category, as do the vapors from some cleaning solvents. Any draining or pouring of such volatile fluids should be done in a well ventilated area.

When using cleaning fluids and solvents, read the instructions on the container carefully. Never use materials from unmarked containers.

Never run the engine in an enclosed space, such as a garage. Exhaust fumes contain carbon monoxide, which is extremely poisonous. If you need to run the engine, always do so in the open air, or at least have the rear of the vehicle outside the work area.

If you are fortunate enough to have the use of an inspection pit, never drain or pour gasoline and never run the engine while the vehicle is over the pit. The fumes, being heavier than air, will concentrate in the pit with possibly lethal results.

The battery

Never create a spark or allow a bare light bulb near a battery. They normally give off a certain amount of hydrogen gas, which is highly explosive.

Always disconnect the battery ground (-) cable at the battery before working on the fuel or electrical systems.

If possible, loosen the filler caps or cover when charging the battery from an external source (this does not apply to sealed or maintenance-free batteries). Do not charge at an excessive rate or the battery may burst.

Take care when adding water to a non maintenance-free battery and when carrying a battery. The electrolyte, even when diluted, is very corrosive and should not be allowed to contact clothing or skin.

Always wear eye protection when cleaning the battery to prevent the caustic deposits from entering your eyes.

Household current

When using an electric power tool, inspection light, etc., which operates on household current, always make sure that the tool is correctly connected to its plug and that, where necessary, it is properly grounded. Do not use such items in damp conditions and, again, do not create a spark or apply excessive heat in the vicinity of fuel or fuel vapor.

Secondary ignition system voltage

A severe electric shock can result from touching certain parts of the ignition system (such as the spark plug wires) when the engine is running or being cranked, particularly if components are damp or the insulation is defective. In the case of an electronic ignition system, the secondary system voltage is much higher and could prove fatal.

Troubleshooting

Contents

This section provides an easy reference guide to the more common problems which may occur during the operation of your vehicle. These problems and their possible causes are grouped under headings denoting various components or systems, such as Engine, Cooling system, etc. They also refer you to the chapter and/or section which deals with the problem.

Remember that successful troubleshooting is not a mysterious black art practiced only by professional mechanics. It is simply the result of the right knowledge combined with an intelligent, systematic approach to the problem. Always work by a process of elimination, starting with the simplest solution and working through to the most complex - and never overlook the obvious. Anyone can run the gas tank dry or leave the lights on overnight, so don't assume that you are exempt from such oversights.

Finally, always establish a clear idea of why a problem has occurred and take steps to ensure that it doesn't happen again. If the electrical system fails because of a poor connection, check the other connections in the system to make sure that they don't fail as well. If a particular fuse continues to blow, find out why - don't just replace one fuse after another. Remember, failure of a small component can often be indicative of potential failure or incorrect functioning of a more important component or system.

Engine

1 Engine will not rotate when attempting to start

1   Battery terminal connections loose or corroded (Chapter 1).
2   Battery discharged or faulty (Chapter 1).
3   Automatic transmission not completely engaged in Park (Chapter 7) or clutch not completely depressed (Chapter 8).
4   Broken, loose or disconnected wiring in the starting circuit (Chapters 5 and 12).
5   Starter motor pinion jammed in flywheel ring gear (Chapter 5).
6   Starter solenoid faulty (Chapter 5).
7   Starter motor faulty (Chapter 5).
8   Ignition switch faulty (Chapter 12).
9   Starter pinion or flywheel teeth worn or broken (Chapter 5).

2 Engine rotates but will not start

1   Fuel tank empty.
2   Battery discharged (engine rotates slowly) (Chapter 5).
3   Battery terminal connections loose or corroded (Chapter 1).
4   Leaking fuel injector(s), faulty cold start valve, fuel pump, pressure regulator, etc.

(Chapter 4).
5   Fuel not reaching fuel rail (Chapter 4).
6   Ignition components damp or damaged (Chapter 5).
7   Worn, faulty or incorrectly gapped spark plugs (Chapter 1).
8   Broken, loose or disconnected wiring in the starting circuit (Chapter 5).
9   Loose distributor is changing ignition timing (Chapter 5).
10   Broken, loose or disconnected wires at the ignition coil or faulty coil (Chapter 5).

3 Engine hard to start when cold

1   Battery discharged or low (Chapter 1).
2   Malfunctioning fuel system (Chapter 4).
3   Faulty cold start injector (Chapter 4).
4   Injector(s) leaking (Chapter 4).
5   Distributor rotor carbon tracked (Chapter 5).

4 Engine hard to start when hot

1   Air filter clogged (Chapter 1).
2   Fuel not reaching the fuel injection system (Chapter 4).
3   Corroded battery connections, especially ground (Chapter 1).

5 Starter motor noisy or excessively rough in engagement

1   Pinion or flywheel gear teeth worn or broken (Chapter 5).
2   Starter motor mounting bolts loose or missing (Chapter 5).

6 Engine starts but stops immediately

1   Loose or faulty electrical connections at distributor, coil or alternator (Chapter 5).
2   Insufficient fuel reaching the fuel injector(s) (Chapters 1 and 4).
3   Vacuum leak at the gasket between the intake manifold/plenum and throttle body (Chapters 1 and 4).

7 Oil puddle under engine

1   Oil pan gasket and/or oil pan drain bolt washer leaking (Chapter 2).
2   Oil pressure sending unit leaking (Chapter 2).
3   Cylinder head covers leaking (Chapter 2).
4   Engine oil seals leaking (Chapter 2).
5   Oil pump housing leaking (Chapter 2).

8 Engine lopes while idling or idles erratically

1   Vacuum leakage (Chapters 2 and 4).
2   Leaking EGR valve (Chapter 6).
3   Air filter clogged (Chapter 1).
4   Fuel pump not delivering sufficient fuel to the fuel injection system (Chapter 4).
5   Leaking head gasket (Chapter 2).
6   Timing belt and/or pulleys worn (Chapter 2).
7   Camshaft lobes worn (Chapter 2).

9 Engine misses at idle speed

1   Spark plugs worn or not gapped properly (Chapter 1).
2   Faulty spark plug wires (Chapter 1).
3   Vacuum leaks (Chapter 1).
4   Incorrect ignition timing (Chapter 1).
5   Uneven or low compression (Chapter 2).

10 Engine misses throughout driving speed range

1   Fuel filter clogged and/or impurities in the fuel system (Chapter 1).
2   Low fuel output at the injector(s) (Chapter 4).
3   Faulty or incorrectly gapped spark plugs (Chapter 1).
4   Incorrect ignition timing (Chapter 5).
5   Cracked distributor cap, disconnected distributor wires or damaged distributor components (Chapters 1 and 5).
6   Leaking spark plug wires (Chapters 1 or 5).
7   Faulty emission system components (Chapter 6).
8   Low or uneven cylinder compression pressures (Chapter 2).
9   Weak or faulty ignition system (Chapter 5).
10   Vacuum leak in fuel injection system, intake manifold, air control valve or vacuum hoses (Chapter 4).

11 Engine stumbles on acceleration

1   Spark plugs fouled (Chapter 1).
2   Fuel injection system needs adjustment or repair (Chapter 4).
3   Fuel filter clogged (Chapters 1 and 4).
4   Incorrect ignition timing (Chapter 5).
5   Intake manifold air leak (Chapters 2 and 4).

12 Engine surges while holding accelerator steady

1   Intake air leak (Chapter 4).

2   Fuel pump faulty (Chapter 4).
3   Loose fuel injector wire harness connectors (Chapter 4).
4   Defective ECU (Chapter 6).

13 Engine stalls

1   Idle speed incorrect (Chapter 1).
2   Fuel filter clogged and/or water and impurities in the fuel system (Chapters 1 and 4).
3   Distributor components damp or damaged (Chapter 5).
4   Faulty emissions system components (Chapter 6).
5   Faulty or incorrectly gapped spark plugs (Chapter 1).
6   Faulty spark plug wires (Chapter 1).
7   Vacuum leak in the fuel injection system, intake manifold or vacuum hoses (Chapters 2 and 4).
8   Valve clearances incorrectly set (Chapter 1).

14 Engine lacks power

1   Incorrect ignition timing (Chapter 5).
2   Excessive play in distributor shaft (Chapter 5).
3   Worn rotor, distributor cap or wires (Chapters 1 and 5).
4   Faulty or incorrectly gapped spark plugs (Chapter 1).
5   Fuel injection system out of adjustment or excessively worn (Chapter 4).
6   Faulty coil (Chapter 5).
7   Brakes binding (Chapter 9).
8   Automatic transaxle fluid level incorrect (Chapter 1).
9   Clutch slipping (Chapter 8).
10   Fuel filter clogged and/or impurities in the fuel system (Chapters 1 and 4).
11   Emission control system not functioning properly (Chapter 6).
12   Low or uneven cylinder compression pressures (Chapter 2).

15 Engine backfires

1   Emission control system not functioning properly (Chapter 6).
2   Ignition timing incorrect (Chapter 5).
3   Faulty secondary ignition system (cracked spark plug insulator, faulty plug wires, distributor cap and/or rotor) (Chapters 1 and 5).
4   Fuel injection system in need of adjustment or worn excessively (Chapter 4).
5   Vacuum leak at fuel injector(s), intake manifold, air control valve or vacuum hoses (Chapters 2 and 4).
6   Valve clearances incorrectly set and/or valves sticking (Chapter 1).

16 Pinging or knocking engine sounds during acceleration or uphill

1   Incorrect grade of fuel.
2   Ignition timing incorrect (Chapter 5).
3   Fuel injection system in need of adjustment (Chapter 4).
4   Improper or damaged spark plugs or wires (Chapter 1).
5   Worn or damaged distributor components (Chapter 5).
6   Faulty emission system (Chapter 6).
7   Vacuum leak (Chapters 2 and 4).

17 Engine runs with oil pressure light on

1   Low oil level (Chapter 1).
2   Idle rpm below specification (Chapter 1).
3   Short in wiring circuit (Chapter 12).
4   Faulty oil pressure sender (Chapter 2).
5   Worn engine bearings and/or oil pump (Chapter 2).

18 Engine diesels (continues to run) after switching off

1   Idle speed too high (Chapter 1).
2   Excessive engine operating temperature (Chapter 3).

Engine electrical system

19 Battery will not hold a charge

1   Alternator drivebelt defective or not adjusted properly (Chapter 1).
2   Battery electrolyte level low (Chapter 1).
3   Battery terminals loose or corroded (Chapter 1).
4   Alternator not charging properly (Chapter 5).
5   Loose, broken or faulty wiring in the charging circuit (Chapter 5).
6   Short in vehicle wiring (Chapter 12).
7   Internally defective battery (Chapters 1 and 5).

20 Alternator light fails to go out

1   Faulty alternator or charging circuit (Chapter 5).
2   Alternator drivebelt defective or out of adjustment (Chapter 1).
3   Alternator voltage regulator inoperative (Chapter 5).

21 Alternator light fails to come on when key is turned on

1   Warning light bulb defective (Chapter 12).
2   Fault in the printed circuit, dash wiring or bulb holder (Chapter 12).

Fuel system

22 Excessive fuel consumption

1   Dirty or clogged air filter element (Chapter 1).
2   Incorrectly set ignition timing (Chapter 5).
3   Emissions system not functioning properly (Chapter 6).
4   Fuel injection internal parts excessively worn or damaged (Chapter 4).
5   Low tire pressure or incorrect tire size (Chapter 1).

23 Fuel leakage and/or fuel odor

1   Leaking fuel feed or return line (Chapters 1 and 4).
2   Tank overfilled.
3   Evaporative canister filter clogged (Chapters 1 and 6).
4   Fuel injector internal parts excessively worn (Chapter 4).

Cooling system

24 Overheating

1   Insufficient coolant in system (Chapter 1).
2   Water pump drivebelt defective or out of adjustment (Chapter 1).
3   Radiator core blocked or grille restricted (Chapter 3).
4   Thermostat faulty (Chapter 3).
5   Electric coolant fan blades broken or cracked (Chapter 3).
6   Radiator cap not maintaining proper pressure (Chapter 3).
7   Ignition timing incorrect (Chapter 5).

25 Overcooling

1   Faulty thermostat (Chapter 3).
2   Inaccurate temperature gauge sending unit (Chapter 3)

26 External coolant leakage

1   Deteriorated/damaged hoses; loose

clamps (Chapters 1 and 3).
2 Water pump seal defective (Chapter 3).
3 Leakage from radiator core or coolant reservoir bottle (Chapter 3).
4 Engine drain or water jacket core plugs leaking (Chapter 2).

27 Internal coolant leakage

1 Leaking cylinder head gasket (Chapter 2).
2 Cracked cylinder bore or cylinder head (Chapter 2).

28 Coolant loss

1 Too much coolant in system (Chapter 1).
2 Coolant boiling away because of overheating (Chapter 3).
3 Internal or external leakage (Chapter 3).
4 Faulty radiator cap (Chapter 3).

29 Poor coolant circulation

1 Inoperative water pump (Chapter 3).
2 Restriction in cooling system (Chapters 1 and 3).
3 Water pump drivebelt defective/out of adjustment (Chapter 1).
4 Thermostat sticking (Chapter 3).

Clutch

30 Pedal travels to floor - no pressure or very little resistance

1 Master or release cylinder faulty (Chapter 8).
2 Hose/pipe burst or leaking (Chapter 8).
3 Connections leaking (Chapter 8).
4 No fluid in reservoir (Chapter 8).
5 If fluid level in reservoir rises as pedal is depressed, master cylinder center valve seal is faulty (Chapter 8).
6 If there is fluid on dust seal at master cylinder, piston primary seal is leaking (Chapter 8).
7 Broken release bearing or fork (Chapter 8).

31 Fluid in area of master cylinder dust cover and on pedal

Rear seal failure in master cylinder (Chapter 8).

32 Fluid on release cylinder

Release cylinder plunger seal faulty (Chapter 8).

33 Pedal feels spongy when depressed

Air in system (Chapter 8).

34 Unable to select gears

1 Faulty transaxle (Chapter 7).
2 Faulty clutch disc (Chapter 8).
3 Fork and bearing not assembled properly (Chapter 8).
4 Faulty pressure plate (Chapter 8).
5 Pressure plate-to-flywheel bolts loose (Chapter 8).

35 Clutch slips (engine speed increases with no increase in vehicle speed)

1 Clutch plate worn (Chapter 8).
2 Clutch plate is oil soaked by leaking rear main seal (Chapter 8).
3 Clutch plate not seated. It may take 30 or 40 normal starts for a new one to seat.
4 Warped pressure plate or flywheel (Chapter 8).
5 Weak diaphragm spring (Chapter 8).
6 Clutch plate overheated. Allow to cool.

36 Grabbing (chattering) as clutch is engaged

1 Oil on clutch plate lining, burned or glazed facings (Chapter 8).
2 Worn or loose engine or transaxle mounts (Chapters 2 and 7).
3 Worn splines on clutch plate hub (Chapter 8).
4 Warped pressure plate or flywheel (Chapter 8).
5 Burned or smeared resin on flywheel or pressure plate (Chapter 8).

37 Transaxle rattling (clicking)

1 Release fork loose (Chapter 8).
2 Clutch plate damper spring failure (Chapter 8).
3 Low engine idle speed (Chapter 1).

38 Noise in clutch area

1 Fork shaft improperly installed (Chapter 8).
2 Faulty bearing (Chapter 8).

39 Clutch pedal stays on floor

1 Piston binding in bore (Chapter 8).

2 Broken release bearing or fork (Chapter 8).

40 High pedal effort

1 Piston binding in bore (Chapter 8).
2 Pressure plate faulty (Chapter 8).
3 Incorrect size master or release cylinder (Chapter 8).

Manual transaxle

41 Knocking noise at low speeds

1 Worn driveaxle constant velocity (CV) joints (Chapter 8).
2 Worn side gear shaft counterbore in differential case (Chapter 7A).*

42 Noise most pronounced when turning

Differential gear noise (Chapter 7A).*

43 Clunk on acceleration or deceleration

1 Loose engine or transaxle mounts (Chapters 2 and 7A).
2 Worn differential pinion shaft in case.*
3 Worn side gear shaft counterbore in differential case (Chapter 7A).*
4 Worn or damaged driveaxle inboard CV joints (Chapter 8).

44 Clicking noise in turns

Worn or damaged outboard CV joint (Chapter 8).

45 Vibration

1 Rough wheel bearing (Chapters 1 and 10).
2 Damaged driveaxle (Chapter 8).
3 Out of round tires (Chapter 1).
4 Tire out of balance (Chapters 1 and 10).
5 Worn CV joint (Chapter 8).

46 Noisy in neutral with engine running

1 Damaged input gear bearing (Chapter 7A).*
2 Damaged clutch release bearing (Chapter 8).

47   Noisy in one particular gear

1   Damaged or worn constant mesh gears (Chapter 7A).*
2   Damaged or worn synchronizers (Chapter 7A).*
3   Bent reverse fork (Chapter 7A).*
4   Damaged fourth speed gear or output gear (Chapter 7A).*
5   Worn or damaged reverse idler gear or idler bushing (Chapter 7A).*

48   Noisy in all gears

1   Insufficient lubricant (Chapter 7A).
2   Damaged or worn bearings (Chapter 7A).*
3   Worn or damaged input gear shaft and/or output gear shaft (Chapter 7A).*

49   Slips out of gear

1   Worn or improperly adjusted linkage (Chapter 7A).
2   Transaxle loose on engine (Chapter 7A).
3   Shift linkage does not work freely, binds (Chapter 7A).
4   Input gear bearing retainer broken or loose (Chapter 7A).*
5   Dirt between clutch cover and engine housing (Chapter 7A).
6   Worn shift fork (Chapter 7A).*

50   Leaks lubricant

1   Side gear shaft seals worn (Chapter 8).
2   Excessive amount of lubricant in transaxle (Chapters 1 and 7A).
3   Loose or broken input gear shaft bearing retainer (Chapter 7A).
4   Input gear bearing retainer O-ring and/or lip seal damaged (Chapter 7A).*

51   Locked in second gear

Lock pin or interlock pin missing (Chapter 7A).*
* Although the corrective action necessary to remedy the symptoms described is beyond the scope of the home mechanic, the above information should be helpful in isolating the cause of the condition so that the owner can communicate clearly with a professional mechanic.

Automatic transaxle

Note: *Due to the complexity of the automatic transaxle, it is difficult for the home mechanic to properly diagnose and service this component. For problems other than the following, the vehicle should be taken to a dealer or transmission shop.*

52   Fluid leakage

1   Automatic transmission fluid is a deep red color. Fluid leaks should not be confused with engine oil, which can easily be blown onto the transaxle by air flow.
2   To pinpoint a leak, first remove all built-up dirt and grime from the transaxle housing with degreasing agents and/or steam cleaning. Then drive the vehicle at low speeds so air flow will not blow the leak far from its source. Raise the vehicle and determine where the leak is coming from. Common areas of leakage are:
  a) *Pan (Chapters 1 and 7)*
  b) *Dipstick tube (Chapters 1 and 7)*
  c) *Transaxle oil lines (Chapter 7)*
  d) *Speed sensor (Chapter 7)*

53   Transaxle fluid brown or has a burned smell

Transaxle fluid burned (Chapter 1).

54   General shift mechanism problems

1   Chapter 7, Part B, deals with checking and adjusting the shift linkage on automatic transaxles. Common problems which may be attributed to poorly adjusted linkage are:
  a) *Engine starting in gears other than Park or Neutral.*
  b) *Indicator on shifter pointing to a gear other than the one actually being used.*
  c) *Vehicle moves when in Park.*
2   Refer to Chapter 7B for the shift linkage adjustment procedure.

55   Transaxle will not downshift with accelerator pedal pressed to the floor

Throttle valve cable out of adjustment (Chapter 7B).

56   Engine will start in gears other than Park or Neutral

Neutral start switch malfunctioning (Chapter 7B).

57   Transaxle slips, shifts roughly, is noisy or has no drive in forward or reverse gears

There are many probable causes for the above problems, but the home mechanic should be concerned with only one possibility - fluid level. Before taking the vehicle to a

repair shop, check the level and condition of the fluid as described in Chapter 1. Correct the fluid level as necessary or change the fluid and filter if needed. If the problem persists, have a professional diagnose the cause.

Driveaxles

58   Clicking noise in turns

Worn or damaged outboard CV joint (Chapter 8).

59   Shudder or vibration during acceleration

1   Excessive toe-in (Chapter 10).
2   Incorrect spring heights (Chapter 10).
3   Worn or damaged inboard or outboard CV joints (Chapter 8).
4   Sticking inboard CV joint assembly (Chapter 8).

60   Vibration at highway speeds

1   Out of balance front wheels and/or tires (Chapters 1 and 10).
2   Out of round front tires (Chapters 1 and 10).
3   Worn CV joint(s) (Chapter 8).

Brakes

Note: *Before assuming that a brake problem exists, make sure that:*
  a) *The tires are in good condition and properly inflated (Chapter 1).*
  b) *The front end alignment is correct (Chapter 10).*
  c) *The vehicle is not loaded with weight in an unequal manner.*

61   Vehicle pulls to one side during braking

1   Incorrect tire pressures (Chapter 1).
2   Front end out of line (have the front end aligned).
3   Front, or rear, tires not matched to one another.
4   Restricted brake lines or hoses (Chapter 9).
5   Malfunctioning drum brake or caliper assembly (Chapter 9).
6   Loose suspension parts (Chapter 10).
7   Loose calipers (Chapter 9).
8   Excessive wear of brake shoe or pad material or disc/drum on one side.

62 Noise (high-pitched squeal when the brakes are applied)

Front and/or rear disc brake pads worn out. The noise comes from the wear sensor rubbing against the disc (does not apply to all vehicles). Replace pads with new ones immediately (Chapter 9).

63 Brake roughness or chatter (pedal pulsates)

1   Excessive lateral runout (Chapter 9).
2   Uneven pad wear (Chapter 9).
3   Defective rotor (Chapter 9).

64 Excessive brake pedal effort required to stop vehicle

1   Malfunctioning power brake booster (Chapter 9).
2   Partial system failure (Chapter 9).
3   Excessively worn pads or shoes (Chapter 9).
4   Piston in caliper or wheel cylinder stuck or sluggish (Chapter 9).
5   Brake pads or shoes contaminated with oil or grease (Chapter 9).
6   New pads or shoes installed and not yet seated. It will take a while for the new material to seat against the rotor or drum.

65 Excessive brake pedal travel

1   Partial brake system failure (Chapter 9).
2   Insufficient fluid in master cylinder (Chapters 1 and 9).
3   Air trapped in system (Chapters 1 and 9).

66 Dragging brakes

1   Incorrect adjustment of brake light switch (Chapter 9).
2   Master cylinder pistons not returning correctly (Chapter 9).
3   Restricted brakes lines or hoses (Chapters 1 and 9).
4   Incorrect parking brake adjustment (Chapter 9).

67 Grabbing or uneven braking action

1   Malfunction of proportioning valve (Chapter 9).
2   Malfunction of power brake booster unit (Chapter 9).
3   Binding brake pedal mechanism (Chapter 9).

68 Brake pedal feels spongy when depressed

1   Air in hydraulic lines (Chapter 9).
2   Master cylinder mounting bolts loose (Chapter 9).
3   Master cylinder defective (Chapter 9).

69 Brake pedal travels to the floor with little resistance

1   Little or no fluid in the master cylinder reservoir caused by leaking caliper piston(s) (Chapter 9).
2   Loose, damaged or disconnected brake lines (Chapter 9).

70 Parking brake does not hold

Parking brake linkage improperly adjusted (Chapters 1 and 9).

Suspension and steering systems

Note: *Before attempting to diagnose the suspension and steering systems, perform the following preliminary checks:*
a) *Tires for wrong pressure and uneven wear.*
b) *Steering universal joints from the column to the rack and pinion for loose connectors or wear.*
c) *Front and rear suspension and the rack and pinion assembly for loose or damaged parts.*
d) *Out-of-round or out-of-balance tires, bent rims and loose and/or rough wheel bearings.*

71 Vehicle pulls to one side

1   Mismatched or uneven tires (Chapter 10).
2   Broken or sagging springs (Chapter 10).
3   Wheel alignment (Chapter 10).
4   Front brake dragging (Chapter 9).

72 Abnormal or excessive tire wear

1   Wheel alignment (Chapter 10).
2   Sagging or broken springs (Chapter 10).
3   Tire out of balance (Chapter 10).
4   Worn strut damper (Chapter 10).
5   Overloaded vehicle.
6   Tires not rotated regularly.

73 Wheel makes a thumping noise

1   Blister or bump on tire (Chapter 10).
2   Improper strut damper action (Chapter 10).

74 Shimmy, shake or vibration

1   Tire or wheel out-of-balance or out-of-round (Chapter 10).
2   Loose or worn wheel bearings (Chapters 1, 8 and 10).
3   Worn tie-rod ends (Chapter 10).
4   Worn lower balljoints (Chapters 1 and 10).
5   Excessive wheel runout (Chapter 10).
6   Blister or bump on tire (Chapter 10).

75 Hard steering

1   Lack of lubrication at balljoints, tie-rod ends and rack and pinion assembly (Chapter 10).
2   Front wheel alignment (Chapter 10).
3   Low tire pressure(s) (Chapters 1 and 10).

76 Poor returnability of steering to center

1   Lack of lubrication at balljoints and tie-rod ends (Chapter 10).
2   Binding in balljoints (Chapter 10).
3   Binding in steering column (Chapter 10).
4   Lack of lubricant in rack and pinion assembly (Chapter 10).
5   Front wheel alignment (Chapter 10).

77 Abnormal noise at the front end

1   Lack of lubrication at balljoints and tie-rod ends (Chapters 1 and 10).
2   Damaged strut mounting (Chapter 10).
3   Worn control arm bushings or tie-rod ends (Chapter 10).
4   Loose stabilizer bar (Chapter 10).
5   Loose wheel nuts (Chapters 1 and 10).
6   Loose suspension bolts (Chapter 10).

78 Wander or poor steering stability

1   Mismatched or uneven tires (Chapter 10).
2   Lack of lubrication at balljoints and tie-rod ends (Chapters 1 and 10).
3   Worn strut assemblies (Chapter 10).
4   Loose stabilizer bar (Chapter 10).
5   Broken or sagging springs (Chapter 10).
6   Wheel alignment (Chapter 10).

79 Erratic steering when braking

1   Wheel bearings worn (Chapter 10).
2   Broken or sagging springs (Chapter 10).
3   Leaking wheel cylinder or caliper (Chapter 10).
4   Warped rotors or drums (Chapter 10).

80   Excessive pitching and/or rolling around corners or during braking

1   Loose stabilizer bar (Chapter 10).
2   Worn strut dampers or mountings (Chapter 10).
3   Broken or sagging springs (Chapter 10).
4   Overloaded vehicle.

81   Suspension bottoms

1   Overloaded vehicle.
2   Worn strut dampers (Chapter 10).
3   Incorrect, broken or sagging springs (Chapter 10).

82   Cupped tires

1   Front wheel or rear wheel alignment (Chapter 10).
2   Worn strut dampers (Chapter 10).
3   Wheel bearings worn (Chapter 10).

4   Excessive tire or wheel runout (Chapter 10).
5   Worn balljoints (Chapter 10).

83   Excessive tire wear on outside edge

1   Inflation pressures incorrect (Chapter 1).
2   Excessive speed in turns.
3   Front end alignment incorrect (excessive toe-in). Have professionally aligned.
4   Suspension arm bent or twisted (Chapter 10).

84   Excessive tire wear on inside edge

1   Inflation pressures incorrect (Chapter 1).
2   Front end alignment incorrect (toe-out). Have professionally aligned.
3   Loose or damaged steering components (Chapter 10).

85   Tire tread worn in one place

1   Tires out of balance.
2   Damaged or buckled wheel. Inspect and replace if necessary.
3   Defective tire (Chapter 1).

86   Excessive play or looseness in steering system

1   Wheel bearing(s) worn (Chapter 10).
2   Tie-rod end loose (Chapter 10).
3   Rack and pinion loose (Chapter 10).
4   Worn or loose steering intermediate shaft (Chapter 10).

87   Rattling or clicking noise in rack and pinion

1   Insufficient or improper lubricant in rack and pinion assembly (Chapter 10).
2   Rack and pinion attachment loose (Chapter 10).

Chapter 1
Tune-up and routine maintenance

Contents

Specifications

Recommended lubricants and fluids

Note: *Listed here are manufacturer recommendations at the time this manual was written. Manufacturers occasionally upgrade their fluid and lubricant specifications, so check with your local auto parts store for current recommendations.*

Engine oil type	API grade "certified for gasoline engines"
Viscosity	See accompanying chart
Fuel	Unleaded gasoline, 87 octane or higher
Automatic transaxle fluid type	Dexron II automatic transmission fluid
Automatic transaxle differential fluid type	Dexron II automatic transmission fluid
Manual transaxle lubricant type	
Front wheel drive models	
Four-cylinder engines	Dexron II automatic transmission fluid
V6 engine	API GL-5 SAE 75W90W or 80W90W gear oil
All-wheel drive models	API GL-5 SAE 75W90W or 80W90W gear oil
All-wheel drive transfer case lubricant type	API GL-5 SAE 75W90W or 80W90W gear oil
All-wheel drive rear differential oil type	API GL-5 SAE 75W90W or 80W90W gear oil
Brake fluid type	DOT 3 brake fluid
Clutch fluid type	DOT 3 brake fluid
Power steering system fluid	Dexron II automatic transmission fluid

---

Recommended SAE viscosity grades for engine oils and manual transaxle lubricants

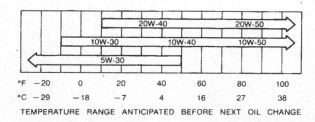

For best fuel economy and cold starting, select the lowest numbered SAE viscosity grade oil for the expected temperature range

Ignition system

Spark plug type and gap
1983 through 1986 .... ND W16EXR-U11 @ 0.043 in
1987 through 1991 .... ND Q16R-U11 @ 0.043 in.
Spark plug wire resistance .... Less than 25000 ohms
Ignition timing .... Refer to the emission control information label
in the engine compartment

Engine firing order
Four-cylinder engine 1-3-4-2
V6 engine.. 1-2-3-4-5-6

Cooling system

Thermostat rating
Starts to open.. 190-degrees F (88-degrees C)
Fully open .... 212-degrees F (100-degrees C)

Accessory drivebelt tension (with Burroughs BTG-20 95506-00020 or Nippondenso BT-33-73F tension gauge) - used belt

Four-cylinder engine
Power steering pump .... 80 (20 lbs
Alternator .... 125 (25 lbs
Air conditioning compressor .... 95 (20 lbs
V6 engine
Power steering pump .... 80 (20 lbs
Alternator .... 115 (20 lbs
Air conditioning compressor .... 95 (20 lbs

Clutch

Clutch pedal
Free play.. 0.2 to 0.6 in (5 to 15 mm)
Pedal height .... 7.5 to 7.8 in (191 to 201 mm)
Pushrod play at pedal top (1987 on) .... 0.39 to 0.197 in (1.0 to 5.0 mm)

Brakes

Disc brake pad lining thickness (minimum) .... 0.040 in (1 mm)
Drum brake shoe lining thickness (minimum)........... 0.040 in (1 mm)
Parking brake adjustment.. 5 to 8 clicks

Suspension and steering

Steering wheel free play limit.................................. 1.18 in (30 mm)
Balljoint allowable movement .... 0 in (0 mm)

Ground clearance	Front	Rear
1983 through 1986	8.54 in (217 mm)	10.28 in (261 mm)
1987 on		
Sedan	9.17 in (233 mm)	10.24 in (260 mm)
Wagon	9.09 in (231 mm)	11.42 in (290 mm)

Wheel runout limit
1983 through 1986 .... 0.047 in (1.2 mm)
1987 on... .... 0.039 in (1.0 mm)

General

Valve clearances (engine cold)
Intake valve
Four-cylinder engine .... 0.007 to 0.011 in (0.19 to 0.29 mm)
V6 engine.. 0.005 to 0.009 in (0.13 to 0.23 mm)
Exhaust valve
Four-cylinder engine .... 0.011 to 0.015 in (0.28 to 0.38 mm)
V6 engine.. 0.011 to 0.015 in (0.28 to 0.38 mm)

Torque specifications

Ft-lbs

Automatic transaxle
Pan bolts 4
Filter bolt 7
Drain plug 36
Manual transaxle drain and filler plugs.................... 36
Engine mounting center member bolt
1983 through 1986 29
1987 on 45

FRONT

2S-E engine

FRONT   **3S-F/3S-FE**

V6 engine

FRONT

Cylinder location and distributor rotation

The blackened terminal shown on the distributor cap indicates the Number One spark plug wire position

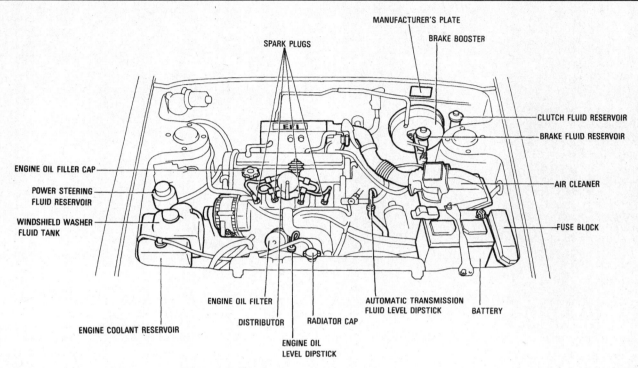

1983 through 1986 model engine compartment

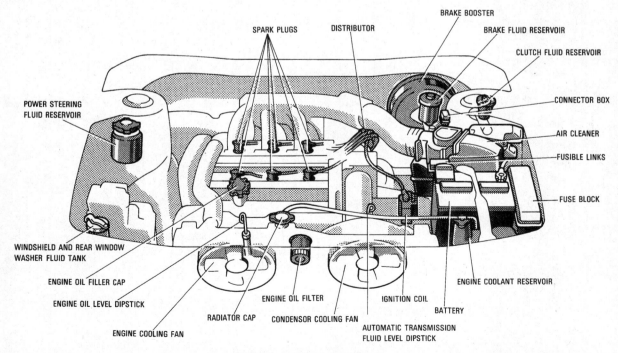

V6 engine compartment

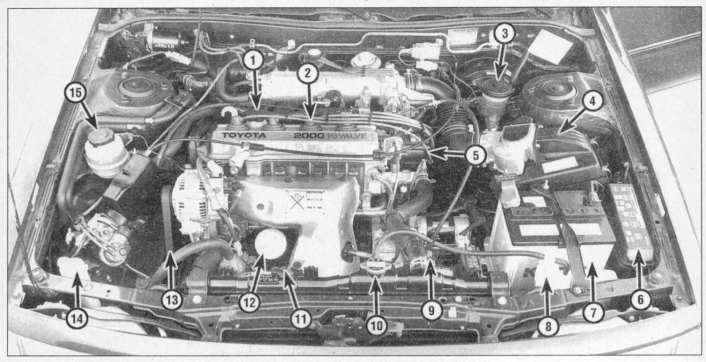

1987 and later model engine compartment

1 Oil filler cap	6 Fuse block	11 Engine oil dipstick
2 Spark plugs	7 Battery	12 Engine oil filter
3 Brake fluid reservoir	8 Coolant reservoir	13 Alternator drivebelt
4 Air cleaner assembly	9 Automatic transaxle dipstick	14 Windshield washer fluid reservoir
5 Distributor	10 Radiator cap	15 Power steering fluid reservoir

Typical engine compartment under side components

1 Steering arm boot	4 Automatic transaxle differential fill plug	8 Driveaxle boot
2 Suspension crossmember bolt	5 Exhaust pipe	9 Brake hose
3 Automatic transaxle differential drain plug	6 Engine oil drain plug	10 Brake caliper
	7 Automatic transaxle drain plug	

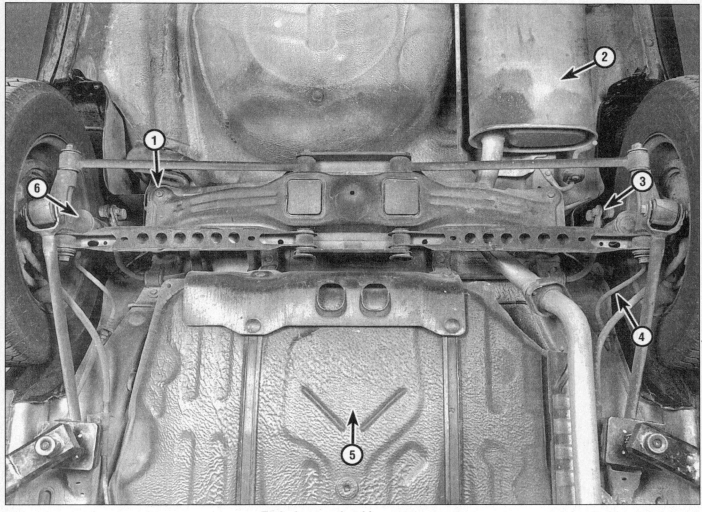

Typical rear under side components

1	Rear suspension crossmember bolt	3	Sway bar link	5	Gas tank
2	Muffler	4	Brake hose	6	Suspension shock strut

1   Introduction

This chapter is designed to help the home mechanic maintain the Toyota Camry for peak performance, economy, safety and long life.

On the following pages is a master maintenance schedule, followed by sections dealing specifically with each item on the schedule. Visual checks, adjustments, component replacement and other helpful items are included. Refer to the accompanying illustrations of the engine compartment and the underside of the vehicle for the location of various components.

Servicing your Camry in accordance with the mileage/time maintenance schedule and the following Sections will provide it with a planned maintenance program that should result in a long and reliable service life. This is a comprehensive plan, so maintaining some items but not others at the specified service intervals will not produce the same results.

As you service your Camry, you will discover that many of the procedures can - and should - be grouped together because of the nature of the particular procedure you're performing or because of the close proximity of two otherwise unrelated components to one another.

For example, if the vehicle is raised for chassis lubrication, you should inspect the exhaust, suspension, steering and fuel systems while you're under the vehicle. When you're rotating the tires, it makes good sense to check the brakes and wheel bearings since the wheels are already removed.

Finally, let's suppose you have to borrow or rent a torque wrench. Even if you only need to tighten the spark plugs, you might as well check the torque of as many critical fasteners as time allows.

The first step of this maintenance program is to prepare yourself before the actual work begins. Read through all sections pertinent to the procedures you're planning to do, then make a list of and gather together all the parts and tools you will need to do the job. If it looks as if you might run into problems during a particular segment of some procedure, seek advice from your local parts man or dealer service department.

2 Toyota Camry Maintenance schedule

The maintenance intervals in this manual are provided with the assumption that you, not the dealer, will be doing the work. These are the minimum maintenance intervals recommended by the factory for Camrys that are driven daily. If you wish to keep your vehicle in peak condition at all times, you may wish to perform some of these procedures even more often. Because frequent maintenance enhances the efficiency, performance and resale value of your car, we encourage you to do so. If you drive in dusty areas, tow a trailer, idle or drive at low speeds for extended periods or drive for short distances (less than four miles) in below freezing temperatures, shorter intervals are also recommended.

When your vehicle is new, it should be serviced by a factory authorized dealer service department to protect the factory warranty. In many cases, the initial maintenance check is done at no cost to the owner.

Every 250 miles or weekly, whichever comes first

Check the engine oil level (Section 4)
Check the engine coolant level (Section 4)
Check the windshield washer fluid level (Section 4)
Check the brake and clutch fluid levels (Section 4)
Check the tires and tire pressures (Section 5)

Every 3000 miles or 3 months, whichever comes first

All items listed above plus:
Check the power steering fluid level (Section 6)
Check the automatic transaxle fluid level (Section 7)
Change the engine oil and oil filter (Section 8)

Every 6000 miles or 6 months, whichever comes first

Inspect and replace if necessary the windshield wiper
    blades (Section 9)
Check the clutch pedal for proper free play (Section 10)
Check and service the battery (Section 11)
Check and adjust if necessary the engine drivebelts
    (Section 12)
Inspect and replace if necessary all underhood hoses
    (Section 13)
Check the cooling system (Section 14)
Rotate the tires (Section 15)

Every 15,000 miles or 12 months, whichever comes first

All items listed above plus:
Inspect the brake system (Section 16)*
Replace the air filter (Section 17)
Inspect the fuel system (Section 18)
Replace the fuel filter (Section 19)
Check and replace if necessary the spark plugs
    (Section 20)

Inspect and replace if necessary the spark plug wires, distributor cap and rotor (Section 21)
Check and adjust if necessary the engine idle speed
    (Section 22)
Check the automatic transaxle differential oil level
    (Section 23)*
Check the manual transaxle lubricant level (Section 24)*
Check the rear differential oil level (all-wheel drive models)
    (Section 25)
Inspect the suspension and steering components
    (Section 26)*
Check the driveaxle boots (Section 27)

Every 30,000 miles or 24 months, whichever comes first

Service the cooling system (drain, flush and refill)
    (Section 28)
Inspect the evaporative emissions control system
    (Section 29)
Inspect the exhaust system (Section 30)
Change the automatic transaxle fluid and filter and differential oil (Section 31) **
Change the manual transaxle lubricant (Section 32)
Change the rear differential oil (all-wheel drive models)
    (Section 33)
Check and tighten critical chassis and body fasteners
    (Section 34)

Every 60,000 miles or 24 months, whichever comes first

Inspect and if necessary adjust the valve
    clearance (1987 and later models) (Section 35)
Replace the timing belt (Chapter 2) ***
Replace the fuel tank cap gasket (Section 36)
* This item is affected by "severe" operating conditions as
    described below. If your vehicle is operated under
    "severe" conditions, perform all maintenance indicated
    with an asterisk (*) at 3000 mile/3 month intervals.
Severe conditions are indicated if you mainly operate your
    vehicle under one or more of the following conditions:
Operating in dusty areas
Towing a trailer
Idling for extended periods and/or low speed operation
Operating when outside temperatures remain below
    freezing and when most trips are less than 4 miles
** If operated under one or more of the following
    *conditions,*change the automatic transaxle fluid and differential lubricant every 15,000 miles:
In heavy city traffic where the outside temperature regularly
reaches 90-degrees F (32-degrees C) or higher
In hilly or mountainous terrain
Frequent trailer pulling
*** Replace the timing belt at 60,000 miles only if operated
    under severe conditions.

4.2 The engine oil dipstick (arrow) is located on the front side of the engine. behind the radiator

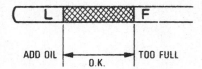

4.4 The oil level should be at or near the F mark - if it isn't add enough oil to bring the level to or near the F mark (it takes one full quart to raise the level from the L to the F mark)

4.6 The threaded oil filler cap is located on the camshaft cover (rear cover on V6 engine) - always make sure the area around the opening is clean before unscrewing the cap to prevent dirt from contaminating the engine

3   Tune-up general information

The term tune-up is used in this manual to represent a combination of individual operations rather than one specific procedure.

If, from the time the vehicle is new, the routine maintenance schedule is followed closely and frequent checks are made of fluid levels and high wear items, as suggested throughout this manual, the engine will be kept in relatively good running condition and the need for additional work will be minimized.

More likely than not, however, there will be times when the engine is running poorly due to lack of regular maintenance. This is even more likely if a used vehicle, which has not received regular and frequent maintenance checks, is purchased. In such cases, an engine tune-up will be needed outside of the regular routine maintenance intervals.

The first step in any tune-up or engine diagnosis to help correct a poor running engine would be a cylinder compression check. A check of the engine compression (Chapter 2 Part C) will give valuable information regarding the overall performance of many internal components and should be used as a basis for tune-up and repair procedures. If, for instance, a compression check indicates serious internal engine wear, a conventional tune-up will not help the running condition of the engine and would be a waste of time and money. Because of its importance, compression checking should be performed by someone with the proper compression testing gauge and the knowledge to use it properly.

The following series of operations are those most often needed to bring a generally poor running engine back into a proper state of tune.

Minor tune-up

Clean, inspect and test the battery
Check all engine related fluids
Check and adjust the drivebelts

Replace the spark plugs
Inspect the distributor cap and rotor
Inspect the spark plug and coil wires
Check and adjust the idle speed
Check the air filter
Check the cooling system
Check all underhood hoses

Major tune-up

All items listed under minor tune-up, plus...
Check the EGR system
Check the ignition system
Check the charging system
Check the fuel system
Replace the air filter
Replace the distributor cap and rotor
Replace the spark plug wires

4   Fluid level checks

1   Fluids are an essential part of the lubrication, cooling, brake, clutch and other systems. Because these fluids gradually become depleted and/or contaminated during normal operation of the vehicle, they must be periodically replenished. See *Recommended lubricants, fluids and capacities* at the beginning of this Chapter before adding fluid to any of the following components. **Note:** *The vehicle must be on level ground before fluid levels can be checked.*

Engine oil

Refer to illustrations 4.2, 4.4 and 4.6
2   The engine oil level is checked with a dipstick located at the front side of the engine **(see illustration)**. The dipstick extends through a metal tube from which it protrudes down into the engine oil pan.
3   The oil level should be checked before the vehicle has been driven, or about 15 minutes after the engine has been shut off. If the oil is checked immediately after driving the vehicle, some of the oil will remain in the upper engine components, producing an inaccurate reading on the dipstick.
4   Pull the dipstick from the tube and wipe all the oil from the end with a clean rag or paper towel. Insert the clean dipstick all the way back into its metal tube and pull it out again. Observe the oil at the end of the dip-

stick. At its highest point, the level should be between the L and F marks (see illustration).
5   It takes one quart of oil to raise the level from the L mark to the F mark on the dipstick. Do not allow the level to drop below the L mark or oil starvation may cause engine damage. Conversely, overfilling the engine (adding oil above the F mark) may cause oil fouled spark plugs, oil leaks or oil seal failures.
6   Remove the threaded cap from the camshaft cover to add oil **(see illustration)**. Use an oil can spout or funnel to prevent spills. After adding the oil, install the filler cap hand tight. Start the engine and look carefully for any small leaks around the oil filter or drain plug. Stop the engine and check the oil level again after it has had sufficient time to drain from the upper block and cylinder head galleys.
7   Checking the oil level is an important preventive maintenance step. A continually dropping oil level indicates oil leakage through damaged seals, from loose connections, or past worn rings or valve guides. If the oil looks milky in color or has water droplets in it, a cylinder head gasket may be blown. The engine should be checked immediately. The condition of the oil should also be checked. Each time you check the oil level, slide your thumb and index finger up the dipstick before wiping off the oil. If you see small dirt or metal particles clinging to the dipstick, the oil should be changed (Section 8).

Engine coolant

Refer to illustration 4.9
Note: *Do not use an alcohol-based antifreeze solution.*
8   All vehicles covered by this manual are equipped with a pressurized coolant recovery system. A white coolant reservoir located in the left rear corner of the engine compart-

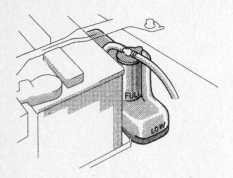

4.9 Make sure that the coolant level in the reservoir is between the Low and Full marks

4.14 The windshield washer fluid reservoir tank is located in the right front corner of the engine compartment - fluid can be added after flipping up the cap

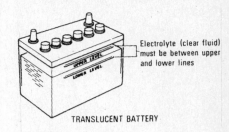

4.15 Keep the electrolyte level of all the cells in the battery between the Upper and Lower levels - use only distilled water to replenish a cell and never overfill it or electrolyte may squirt out of the battery during periods of heavy charging

ment is connected by a hose to the base of the coolant filler cap. If the coolant heats up during engine operation, coolant can escape through a pressurized filler cap, then through a connecting hose into the reservoir. As the engine cools, the coolant is automatically drawn back into the cooling system to maintain the correct level.

9   The coolant level should be checked regularly. It must be between the Full and Low lines on the tank **(see illustration)**. The level will vary with the temperature of the engine. When the engine is cold, the coolant level should be at or slightly above the Low mark on the tank. Once the engine has warmed up, the level should be at or near the Full mark. If it isn't, allow the fluid in the tank to cool, then remove the cap from the reservoir and add coolant to bring the level up to the Full line. Use only ethylene/glycol type coolant and water in the mixture ratio recommended by your owner's manual. Do not use supplemental inhibitors or additives. If only a small amount of coolant is required to bring the system up to the proper level, water can be used. However, repeated additions of water will dilute the recommended antifreeze and water solution. In order to maintain the proper ratio of antifreeze and water, it is advisable to top up the coolant level with the correct mixture. Refer to your owner's manual for the recommended ratio.

10   If the coolant level drops within a short time after replenishment, there may be a leak in the system. Inspect the radiator, hoses, engine coolant filler cap, drain plugs, air bleeder plugs and water pump. If no leak is evident, have the radiator cap pressure tested by your dealer. **Warning:** *Never remove the radiator cap or the coolant recovery reservoir cap when the engine is running or has just been shut down, because the cooling system is hot. Escaping steam and scalding liquid could cause serious injury.*

11   If it is necessary to open the radiator cap, wait until the system has cooled completely, then wrap a thick cloth around the cap and turn it to the first stop. If any steam escapes, wait until the system has cooled further, then remove the cap.

12   When checking the coolant level, always note its condition. It should be relatively clear. If it is brown or rust colored, the system should be drained, flushed and refilled. Even if the coolant appears to be normal, the corrosion inhibitors wear out with use, so it must be replaced at the specified intervals.

13   Do not allow antifreeze to come in contact with your skin or painted surfaces of the vehicle. Flush contacted areas immediately with plenty of water.

Windshield washer fluid

Refer to illustration 4.14

14   Fluid for the windshield washer system is stored in a plastic reservoir which is located at the right front corner of the engine compartment **(see illustration)**. In milder climates, plain water can be used to top up the reservoir, but the reservoir should be kept no more than 2/3 full to allow for expansion should the water freeze. In colder climates, the use of a specially designed windshield washer fluid, available at your dealer and any auto parts store, will help lower the freezing point of the fluid. Mix the solution with water in accordance with the manufacturer's directions on the container. Do not use regular antifreeze. It will damage the vehicle's paint.

Battery electrolyte

Refer to illustration 4.15

15   Check the electrolyte level of all six battery cells. It must be between the upper and lower levels **(see illustration)**. If the level is low, unscrew the filler/vent cap and add distilled water. Install and securely retighten the cap. **Caution:** *Overfilling the cells may cause electrolyte to spill over during periods of heavy charging, causing corrosion or damage.*

Brake and clutch fluid

Refer to illustrations 4.16 and 4.17

16   The brake master cylinder is mounted on the front of the power booster unit in the engine compartment **(see illustration)**. The clutch cylinder used on manual transaxles is located next to the master cylinder.

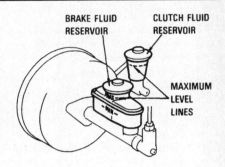

4.16 The brake and (if equipped) clutch master cylinder reservoirs are located in the left rear corner of the engine compartment - the brake reservoir is the larger one closer to the center of the vehicle

4.17 The brake fluid level should be kept between the MIN and MAX marks on the translucent plastic reservoir - lift up the cap to add fluid

17   To check the fluid level of the brake master cylinder reservoir, simply look at the MAX and MIN marks on the reservoir **(see illustration)**. To check the fluid level of the clutch master cylinder reservoir, note whether the fluid level is even with the maxi-

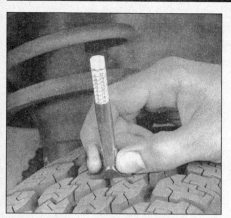

5.2 A tire tread depth indicator should be used to monitor tire wear - they are available at auto parts stores and service stations and cost very little

mum level line. The level should be within the specified distance from the maximum fill line for both reservoirs.

18 If the level is low for either reservoir, wipe the top of the reservoir cover with a clean rag to prevent contamination of the brake or clutch system before lifting the cover.

19 Add only the specified brake fluid to the brake or clutch reservoir (refer to *Recommended lubricants, fluids and capacities* at the front of this chapter or to your owner's manual). Mixing different types of brake fluid can damage the system. Fill the brake master cylinder reservoir only to the dotted line - this brings the fluid to the correct level when you put the cover back on. **Warning:** *Use caution when filling either reservoir- brake fluid can harm your eyes and damage painted surfaces. Do not use brake fluid that has been opened for more than one year or has been left open. Brake fluid absorbs moisture from the air. Excess moisture can cause a dangerous loss of braking.*

20 While the reservoir cap is removed, inspect the master cylinder reservoir for contamination. If deposits, dirt particles or water droplets are present, the system should be drained and refilled (see Chapter 8 for clutch reservoir or Chapter 9 for brake reservoir).

21 After filling the reservoir to the proper level, make sure the lid is properly seated to prevent fluid leakage and/or system pressure loss.

22 The brake fluid in the master cylinder will drop slightly as the brake pads at each wheel wear down during normal operation. If the master cylinder requires repeated replenishing to keep it at the proper level, this is an indication of leakage in the brake system, which should be corrected immediately. Check all brake lines and connections, along with the wheel cylinders and booster (see Section 16 for more information).

23 If, upon checking the master cylinder fluid level, you discover one or both reservoirs empty or nearly empty, the brake system should be bled (Chapter 9).

---

5   Tire and tire pressure checks

Refer to illustrations 5.2, 5.3, 5.4a, 5.4b, 5.8a and 5.8b

1 Periodic inspection of the tires may spare you from the inconvenience of being stranded with a flat tire. It can also provide you with vital information regarding possible problems in the steering and suspension systems before major damage occurs.

2 Normal tread wear can be monitored with a simple, inexpensive device known as a tread depth indicator **(see illustration)**. When the tread depth reaches the specified minimum, replace the tire(s).

3 Note any abnormal tread wear **(see illustration)**. Tread pattern irregularities such as cupping, flat spots and more wear on one side than the other are indications of front end alignment and/or balance problems. If

UNDERINFLATION

INCORRECT TOE-IN OR EXTREME CAMBER

CUPPING

Cupping may be caused by:
- **Underinflation and/or mechanical irregularities such as out-of-balance condition of wheel and/or tire, and bent or damaged wheel.**
- **Loose or worn steering tie-rod or steering idler arm.**
- **Loose, damaged or worn front suspension parts.**

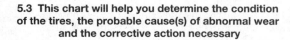

5.3 This chart will help you determine the condition of the tires, the probable cause(s) of abnormal wear and the corrective action necessary

OVERINFLATION

FEATHERING DUE TO MISALIGNMENT

5.4a If a tire loses air on a steady basis, check the valve core first to make sure it's snug (special inexpensive wrenches are commonly available at auto parts stores)

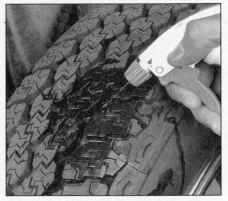

5.4b If the valve core is tight, raise the corner of the vehicle with the low tire and spray a soapy water solution onto the tread as the tire is turned slowly - leaks will cause small bubbles to appear

5.8a To extend the life of the tires, check the air pressure at least once a week with an accurate gauge (don't forget the spare!)

5.8b The tire pressures are listed on the driver's door

6.2 The power steering fluid filler cap/dipstick is located on the right side of the engine compartment - unscrew the cap to add fluid

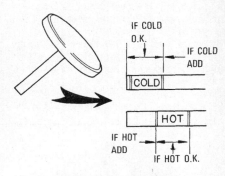

6.6 On earlier models the power steering fluid is checked with a dipstick which is part of the cap - the fluid level varies with temperature, so the dipstick is marked accordingly

any of these conditions are noted, take the vehicle to a tire shop or service station to correct the problem.

4   Look closely for cuts, punctures and embedded nails or tacks. Sometimes a tire will hold its air pressure for a short time or leak down very slowly even after a nail has embedded itself into the tread. If a slow leak persists, check the valve stem core to make sure it is tight **(see illustration)**. Examine the tread for an object that may have embedded itself into the tire or for a "plug" that may have begun to leak (radial tire punctures are repaired with a plug that is installed in a puncture). If a puncture is suspected, it can be easily verified by spraying a solution of soapy water onto the puncture area **(see illustration)**. The soapy solution will bubble if there is a leak. Unless the puncture is inordinately large, a tire shop or gas station can usually repair the punctured tire.

5   Carefully inspect the inboard sidewall of each tire for evidence of brake fluid leakage. If you see any, inspect the brakes immediately.

6   Correct tire air pressure adds miles to the lifespan of the tires, improves mileage and enhances overall ride quality. Tire pressure cannot be accurately estimated by looking at a tire, particularly if it is a radial. A tire

pressure gauge is therefore essential. Keep an accurate gauge in the glovebox. The pressure gauges fitted to the nozzles of air hoses at gas stations are often inaccurate.

7   Always check tire pressure when the tires are cold. "Cold," in this case, means the vehicle has not been driven over a mile in the three hours preceding a tire pressure check. A pressure rise of four to eight pounds is not uncommon once the tires are warm.

8   Unscrew the valve cap protruding from the wheel or hubcap and push the gauge firmly onto the valve **(see illustration)**. Note the reading on the gauge and compare this figure to the recommended tire pressure shown on the tire placard on the left door **(see illustration)**. Be sure to reinstall the valve cap to keep dirt and moisture out of the valve stem mechanism. Check all four tires and, if necessary, add enough air to bring them up to the recommended pressure levels.

9   Don't forget to keep the spare tire inflated to the specified pressure (consult your owner's manual). Note that the air pressure specified for the compact spare is significantly higher than the pressure of the regular tires.

6   Power steering fluid level check

All models

Refer to illustration 6.2

1   Unlike manual steering, the power steering system relies on fluid which may, over a period of time, require replenishing.

2   The fluid reservoir for the power steering pump is located on the inner fender panel near the front of the engine **(see illustration)**.

3   For the check, the front wheels should be pointed straight ahead and the engine should be off.

1983 through 1986 models

Refer to illustration 6.6

4   Use a clean rag to wipe off the reservoir cap and the area around the cap. This will help prevent any foreign matter from entering the reservoir during the check.

5   Twist off the cap and check the temperature of the fluid at the end of the dipstick with your finger.

6   Wipe off the fluid with a clean rag, reinsert it, then withdraw it and read the fluid level. The level should be at the HOT mark if

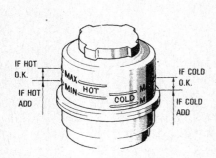

6.7 On later models, the power steering fluid reservoir is translucent so the fluid level can be checked without removing the cap

7.4a The automatic transmission dipstick (arrow) is located in a long tube which extends back from behind the radiator to the transaxle

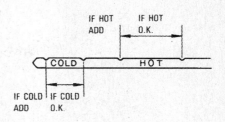

7.4b If the automatic transmission fluid is cold, the level should be between the two lower notches; if it's at operating temperature, the level should be between the two upper notches

the fluid was hot to the touch **(see illustration)**. It should be at the COLD mark if the fluid was cool to the touch. Note that the marks (HOT and COLD) are on opposite sides of the dipstick. At no time should the fluid level drop below the upper mark for each heat range.

1987 and later models

Refer to illustration 6.7
7   On these models the reservoir is translucent plastic and the fluid level can be checked visually **(see illustration)**.

All models

8   If additional fluid is required, pour the specified type directly into the reservoir, using a funnel to prevent spills.
9   If the reservoir requires frequent fluid additions, all power steering hoses, hose connections, the power steering pump and the rack and pinion assembly should be carefully checked for leaks.

7   Automatic transaxle fluid level check

Refer to illustrations 7.4a and 7.4b
1   The level of the automatic transaxle fluid should be carefully maintained. Low fluid level can lead to slipping or loss of drive, while overfilling can cause foaming, loss of fluid and transaxle damage.
2   The transaxle fluid level should only be checked when the transaxle is hot (at its normal operating temperature). If the vehicle has just been driven over 10 miles (15 miles in a frigid climate), and the fluid temperature is 160-175 degrees F, the transaxle is hot. **Caution:** If the vehicle has just been driven for a long time at high speed or in city traffic in hot weather, or if it has been pulling a trailer, an accurate fluid level reading cannot be obtained. Allow the fluid to cool down for about 30 minutes.
3   If the vehicle has not just been driven, park the vehicle on level ground, set the park-

ing brake and start the engine. While the engine is idling, depress the brake pedal and move the selector lever through all the gear ranges, beginning and ending in Park.
4   With the engine still idling, remove the dipstick from its tube **(see illustration)**. Check the level of the fluid on the dipstick **(see illustration)** and note its condition.
5   Wipe the fluid from the dipstick with a clean rag and reinsert it back into the filler tube until the cap seats.
6   Pull the dipstick out again and note the fluid level. If the transaxle is cold, the level should be in the COLD or COOL range on the dipstick. If it is hot, the fluid level should be in the HOT range. If the level is at the low side of either range, add the specified automatic transmission fluid through the dipstick tube with a funnel.
7   Add just enough of the recommended fluid to fill the transaxle to the proper level. It takes about one pint to raise the level from the low mark to the high mark when the fluid is hot, so add the fluid a little at a time and keep checking the level until it is correct.
8   The condition of the fluid should also be checked along with the level. If the fluid at the end of the dipstick is black or a dark reddish brown color, or if it emits a burned smell, the fluid should be changed (Section 31). If you are in doubt about the condition of the fluid, purchase some new fluid and compare the two for color and smell.

8   Engine oil and oil filter change

Refer to illustrations 8.2, 8.7, 8.12 and 8.14
1   Frequent oil changes are the best preventive maintenance the home mechanic can give the engine, because aging oil becomes diluted and contaminated, which leads to premature engine wear.
2   Make sure that you have all the necessary tools before you begin this procedure **(see illustration)**. You should also have plenty of rags or newspapers handy for mopping up any spills.

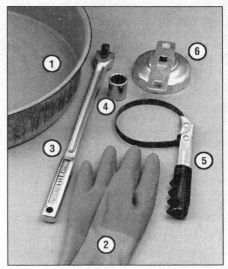

8.2 These tools are required when changing the engine oil and filter

1   **Drain pan** - It should be fairly shallow in depth, but wide to prevent spills
2   **Rubber gloves** - When removing the drain plug and filter, you will get oil on your hands (the gloves will prevent burns)
3   **Breaker bar** - Sometimes the oil drain plug is tight, and a long breaker bar is needed to loosen it
4   **Socket** - To be used with the breaker bar or a ratchet (must be the correct size to fit the drain plug - six-point preferred)
5   **Filter wrench** - This is a metal band-type wrench, which requires clearance around the filter to be effective
6   **Filter wrench** - This type fits on the bottom of the filter and can be turned with a ratchet or breaker bar (different-size wrenches are available for different types of filters)

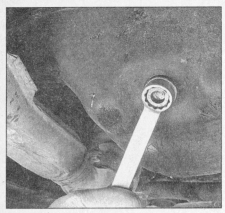

8.7 Use the proper size box end wrench or six-point socket to remove the oil drain plug to prevent rounding it off

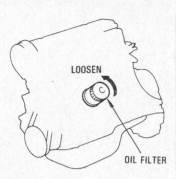

8.12 The oil filter is usually on very tight and will require a special wrench for removal - DO NOT use the wrench to tighten the new filter

8.14 Lubricate the gasket with clean oil before installing the filter on the engine

3   Access to the underside of the vehicle is greatly improved if the vehicle can be lifted on a hoist, driven onto ramps or supported by jackstands. **Warning:** *Do not work under a vehicle which is supported only by a bumper, hydraulic or scissors-type jack.*

4   If this is your first oil change, get under the vehicle and familiarize yourself with the locations of the oil drain plug and the oil filter. The engine and exhaust components will be warm during the actual work, so try to anticipate any potential problems before the engine and accessories are hot.

5   Park the vehicle on a level spot. Start the engine and allow it to reach its normal operating temperature (the needle on the temperature gauge should be at least above the bottom mark). Warm oil and sludge will flow out more easily. Turn off the engine when it's warmed up. Remove the filler cap in the rear cam cover.

6   Raise the vehicle and support it on jack-stands. **Warning:** *To avoid personal injury, never get beneath the vehicle when it is supported by only by a jack. The jack provided with your vehicle is designed solely for raising the vehicle to remove and replace the wheels. Always use jackstands to support the vehicle when it becomes necessary to place your body underneath the vehicle.*

7   Being careful not to touch the hot exhaust components, place the drain pan under the drain plug in the bottom of the pan and remove the plug **(see illustration)**. You may want to wear gloves while unscrewing the plug the final few turns if the engine is really hot.

8   Allow the old oil to drain into the pan. It may be necessary to move the pan farther under the engine as the oil flow slows to a trickle. Inspect the old oil for the presence of metal shavings and chips.

9   After all the oil has drained, wipe off the drain plug with a clean rag. Even minute metal particles clinging to the plug would immediately contaminate the new oil.

10   Clean the area around the drain plug opening, reinstall the plug and tighten it

securely, but do not strip the threads.

11   Move the drain pan into position under the oil filter.

12   Loosen the oil filter **(see illustration)** by turning it counterclockwise with the filter wrench. Any standard filter wrench will work. Sometimes the oil filter is screwed on so tightly that it cannot be loosened. If this situation occurs, punch a metal bar or long screwdriver directly through the side of the canister and use it as a T-bar to turn the filter. Be prepared for oil to spurt out of the canister as it is punctured. Once the filter is loose, use your hands to unscrew it from the block. Just as the filter is detached from the block, immediately tilt the open end up to prevent the oil inside the filter from spilling out. **Warning:** *The engine exhaust manifold may still be hot, so be careful.*

13   With a clean rag, wipe off the mounting surface on the block. If a residue of old oil is allowed to remain, it will smoke when the block is heated up. It will also prevent the new filter from seating properly. Also make sure that the none of the old gasket remains stuck to the mounting surface. It can be removed with a scraper if necessary.

14   Compare the old filter with the new one to make sure they are the same type. Smear some engine oil on the rubber gasket of the new filter and screw it into place **(see illustration)**. Because overtightening the filter will damage the gasket, do not use a filter wrench to tighten the filter. Tighten it by hand until the gasket contacts the seating surface. Then seat the filter by giving it an additional 3/4-turn.

15   Remove all tools, rags, etc. from under the vehicle, being careful not to spill the oil in the drain pan, then lower the vehicle.

16   Add new oil to the engine through the oil filler cap in the rear cam cover. Use a spout or funnel to prevent oil from spilling onto the top of the engine. Pour three quarts of fresh oil into the engine. Wait a few minutes to allow the oil to drain into the pan, then check the level on the oil dipstick (see Section 4 if necessary). If the oil level is at or near the F

mark, install the filler cap hand tight, start the engine and allow the new oil to circulate.

17   Allow the engine to run for about a minute. While the engine is running, look under the vehicle and check for leaks at the oil pan drain plug and around the oil filter. If either is leaking, stop the engine and tighten the plug or filter slightly.

18   Wait a few minutes to allow the oil to trickle down into the pan, then recheck the level on the dipstick and, if necessary, add enough oil to bring the level to the F mark.

19   During the first few trips after an oil change, make it a point to check frequently for leaks and proper oil level.

20   The old oil drained from the engine cannot be reused in its present state and should be discarded. Oil reclamation centers, auto repair shops and gas stations will normally accept the oil, which can be refined and used again. After the oil has cooled, it can be drained into a suitable container (capped plastic jugs, topped bottles, milk cartons, etc.) for transport to one of these disposal sites.

9   Windshield wiper blade inspection and replacement

Refer to illustrations 9.5a, 9.5b and 9.7

1   The windshield wiper and blade assembly should be inspected periodically for damage, loose components and cracked or worn blade elements.

2   Road film can build up on the wiper blades and affect their efficiency, so they should be washed regularly with a mild detergent solution.

3   The action of the wiping mechanism can loosen bolts, nuts and fasteners, so they should be checked and tightened, as necessary, at the same time the wiper blades are checked.

4   If the wiper blade elements are cracked, worn or warped, or no longer clean adequately, they should be replaced with new ones.

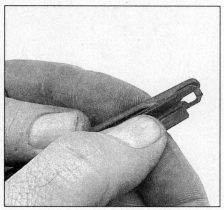

9.5a To remove the old wiper blade element, pull the top end of the element down until you can see the replacement hole in the frame . . .

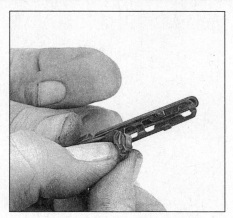

9.5b . . . then pull the element tab out of the hole (note the relationship to the frame) and slide the element from the frame

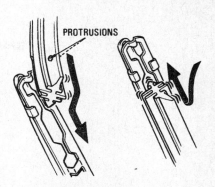

9.7 To install a new element, insert the end of the blade with the small protrusions into the replacement hole and work the rubber along the slot in the blade frame - once all the rubber is in the frame slot, allow it to expand and fill in the end

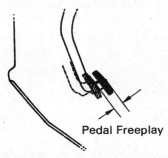

10.1 To check clutch pedal free play, measure the distance between the natural resting place of the pedal and the point at which you encounter resistance

5   Lift the arm assembly away from the glass for clearance and pull the top end of the rubber blade element inward **(see illustrations)** until the rubber blade is free of the end slot and you can see the replacement hole.

6   Remove the rubber blade from the frame and discard it.

7   To install a new rubber wiper element, insert the end with the small protrusions **(see illustration)** into the replacement hole and work the rubber along the slot in the blade frame.

8   Once all the rubber is in the frame slot, allow it to expand and fill in the end.

10   Clutch pedal free play check and adjustment

Refer to illustrations 10.1, 10.2a and 10.2b

1   Press down lightly on the clutch pedal and, with a small steel ruler, measure the distance that it moves freely before the clutch resistance is felt **(see illustration)**. The free play should be within the specified limits. If it isn't, it must be adjusted.

2   Loosen the locknut on the pedal end of the clutch pushrod **(see illustrations)**.

3   Turn the pushrod until pedal free play and push rod free play are correct.

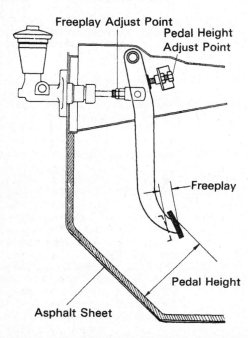

10.2a Clutch pedal height and free play adjustment details (1983 through 1986 models)

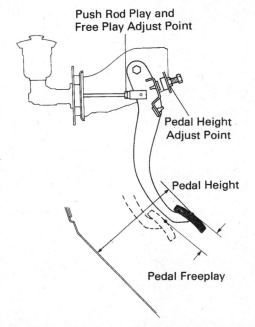

10.2b The clutch pedal pushrod play, pedal height and free play adjustments are made by loosening the locknut and turning the threaded adjuster (1987 and later models)

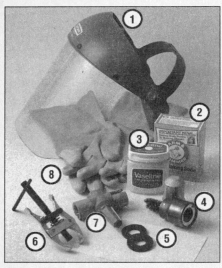

11.1 Tools and materials required for battery maintenance

1   *Face shield/safety goggles* - *When removing corrosion with a brush, the acidic particles can easily fly up into your eyes*

2   *Baking soda* - *A solution of baking soda and water can be used to neutralize corrosion*

3   *Petroleum jelly* - *A layer of this on the battery posts will help prevent corrosion*

4   *Battery post/cable cleaner* - *This wire brush cleaning tool will remove all traces of corrosion from the battery posts and cable clamps*

5   *Treated felt washers* - *Placing one of these on each post, directly under the cable clamps, will help prevent corrosion*

6   *Puller* - *Sometimes the cable clamps are very difficult to pull off the posts, even after the nut/bolt has been completely loosened. This tool pulls the clamp straight up and off the post without damage*

7   *Battery post/cable cleaner* - *Here is another cleaning tool which is a slightly different version of Number 4 above, but it does the same thing*

8   *Rubber gloves* - *Another safety item to consider when servicing the battery; remember that's acid inside the battery!*

4   Tighten the locknut.

5   After adjusting the pedal free play, check the pedal height.

6   If pedal height is incorrect, loosen the locknut and turn the stopper bolt until the height is correct. Tighten the locknut.

11 Battery check and maintenance

Refer to illustrations 11.1, 11.6a, 11.6b, 11.7a and 11.7b

1   A routine preventive maintenance program for the battery in your vehicle is the only

11.6a Battery terminal corrosion usually appears as light, fluffy powder

11.7a When cleaning the cable clamps, all corrosion must be removed (the inside of the clamp is tapered to match the taper on the post, so don't remove too much material)

way to ensure quick and reliable starts. But before performing any battery maintenance, make sure that you have the proper equipment necessary to work safely around the battery **(see illustration)**.

2   There are also several precautions that should be taken whenever battery maintenance is performed. Before servicing the battery, always turn the engine and all accessories off and disconnect the cable from the negative terminal of the battery.

3   The battery produces hydrogen gas, which is both flammable and explosive. Never create a spark, smoke or light a match around the battery. Always charge the battery in a ventilated area.

4   Electrolyte contains poisonous and corrosive sulfuric acid. Do not allow it to get in your eyes, on your skin on your clothes. Never ingest it. Wear protective safety glasses when working near the battery. Keep children away from the battery.

5   Note the external condition of the battery. If the positive terminal and cable clamp on your vehicle's battery is equipped with a rubber protector, make sure that it's not torn or damaged. It should completely cover the

11.6b Removing the cable from a battery post with a wrench - sometimes special battery pliers are required for this procedure if corrosion has caused deterioration of the nut hex (always remove the ground cable first and hook it up last!)

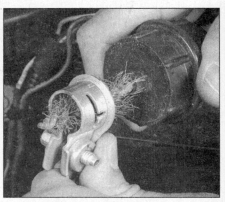

11.7b Regardless of the type of tool used on the battery posts, a clean, shiny surface should be the result

terminal. Look for any corroded or loose connections, cracks in the case or cover or loose hold-down clamps. Also check the entire length of each cable for cracks and frayed conductors.

6   If corrosion, which looks like white, fluffy deposits **(see illustration)** is evident, particularly around the terminals, the battery should be removed for cleaning. Loosen the cable clamp bolts with a wrench, being careful to remove the ground cable first, and slide them off the terminals **(see illustration)**. Then disconnect the hold-down clamp bolt and nut, remove the clamp and lift the battery from the engine compartment.

7   Clean the cable clamps thoroughly with a battery brush or a terminal cleaner and a solution of warm water and baking soda **(see illustration)**. Wash the terminals and the top of the battery case with the same solution but make sure that the solution doesn't get into the battery. When cleaning the cables, terminals and battery top, wear safety goggles and rubber gloves to prevent any solution from

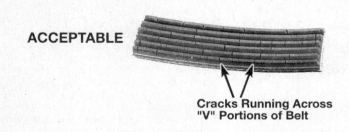

ACCEPTABLE

Cracks Running Across
"V" Portions of Belt

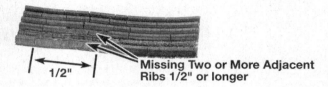

1/2"

Missing Two or More Adjacent
Ribs 1/2" or longer

UNACCEPTABLE

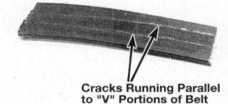

Cracks Running Parallel
to "V" Portions of Belt

12.3 Check the V-ribbed belt for signs of wear like these -
if the belt looks worn, replace it

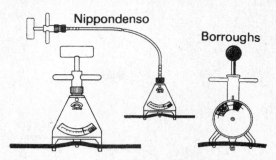

Nippondenso

Borroughs

12.4 If you are able to borrow either a Nippondenso or
Burroughs belt tension gauge, this is how it's installed on the
belt - compare the reading on the scale with the specified
drivebelt tension

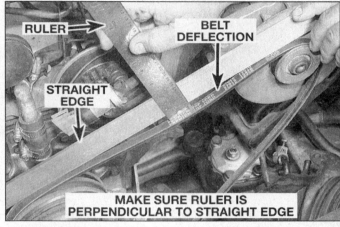

RULER

BELT
DEFLECTION

STRAIGHT
EDGE

MAKE SURE RULER IS
PERPENDICULAR TO STRAIGHT EDGE

12.5 Measuring drivebelt deflection with a straightedge and ruler

coming in contact with your eyes or hands. Wear old clothes too - even diluted, sulfuric acid splashed onto clothes will burn holes in them. If the terminals have been extensively corroded, clean them up with a terminal cleaner **(see illustration)**. Thoroughly wash all cleaned areas with plain water.

8   Before reinstalling the battery into the engine compartment, inspect the plastic battery carrier. If it's dirty or covered with corrosion, remove it and clean it in the same solution of warm water and baking soda. Inspect the metal brackets which support the carrier to make sure that they are not covered with corrosion. If they are, wash them off. If corrosion is extensive, sand the brackets down to bare metal and spray them with a zinc-based primer (available in spray cans at auto paint and body supply stores).

9   Reinstall the battery carrier and the battery back into the engine compartment. Make sure that no parts or wires are laying on the carrier during installation of the battery.

10   Install a pair of specially treated felt washers around the terminals (available at auto parts stores), then coat the terminals and the cable clamps with petroleum jelly or grease to prevent further corrosion. Install the cable clamps and tighten the bolts, being careful to install the negative cable last.

11   Install the hold-down clamp and bolts. Tighten the bolts only enough to hold the bat-

tery firmly in place. Overtightening these bolts can crack the battery case.

12   Further information on the battery, charging and jump starting can be found in Chapter 5 and at the front of this manual.

12   Drivebelt check, adjustment and replacement

Refer to illustrations 12.3, 12.4, 12.5, 12.6 and 12.10

Check

1   The alternator and air conditioning compressor drivebelts, also referred to as V-ribbed belts or simply "fan" belts, are located at the right end of the engine. The good condition and proper adjustment of the alternator belt is critical to the operation of the engine. Because of their composition and the high stresses to which they are subjected, drivebelts stretch and deteriorate as they get older. They must therefore be periodically inspected.

2   The number of belts used on a particular vehicle depends on the accessories installed. One belt transmits power from the crankshaft to the alternator and water pump. If your vehicle is equipped with air conditioning, the A/C compressor is driven by another belt.

3   With the engine off, open the hood and locate the drivebelts at the left end of the engine. With a flashlight, check each belt for separation of the adhesive rubber on both sides of the core, core separation from the belt side, a severed core, separation of the ribs from the adhesive rubber, cracking or separation of the ribs, and torn or worn ribs or cracks in the inner ridges of the ribs **(see illustration)**. Also check for fraying and glazing, which gives the belt a shiny appearance. Both sides of the belt should be inspected, which means you will have to twist the belt to check the underside. Use your fingers to feel the belt where you can't see it. If any of the above conditions are evident, replace the belt (go to Step 8).

4   To check the tension of each belt in accordance with factory specifications, install either a Nippondenso or Burroughs belt tension gauge on the belt **(see illustration)**. Measure the tension in accordance with the manufacturer's instructions and compare your measurement to the specified drive belt tension for either a used or new belt. **Note:** *A "used" belt is defined as any belt which has been operated more than five minutes on the engine; a "new" belt is one that has been used for less than five minutes.*

5   If you don't have either of the above tools, and cannot borrow one, the following rule of thumb method is recommended: Push

12.6 After loosening the pivot bolt (A) and locking bolt (B), a socket with an extension can be used to turn the adjusting bolt (C)

firmly on the belt with your thumb at a distance halfway between the pulleys and note how far the belt can be pushed (deflected). Measure this deflection with a ruler **(see illustration)**. The belt should deflect 1/4-inch if the distance from pulley center to pulley center is between 7 and 11 inches; the belt should deflect 1/2-inch if the distance from pulley center to pulley center is between 12 and 16 inches.

Adjustment

6   If the alternator belt must be adjusted on earlier models, loosen the adjustment bolt that secures the alternator to its slotted bracket and pivot the alternator (away from the engine block to tighten the belt, toward the block to loosen the belt). It's helpful to lever the alternator with a large pry bar when adjusting the belt because the pry bar enables you to precisely position the alternator until the adjuster bolt is tightened. Be very careful not to damage the aluminum housing of the alternator. Recheck the belt tension using one of the above methods. Repeat this Step until the alternator drivebelt tension is correct. On later models, the alternator drivebelt is adjusted by loosening the pivot bolt and locking bolt and turning the adjusting bolt with a wrench or socket and ratchet to tension the belt **(see illustration)**.

7   If the air conditioner compressor drivebelt must be adjusted, locate the idler pulley on the front right corner of the block, just above the compressor. Turn the idler pulley adjuster bolt (clockwise to tighten the belt and counterclockwise to loosen it). Measure the belt tension in accordance with one of the above methods. Repeat this step until the air conditioning compressor drivebelt is adjusted.

Replacement

8   To replace a belt, follow the above procedures for drivebelt adjustment but slip the belt off the crankshaft pulley and remove it. If

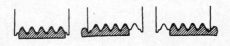

CORRECT   WRONG   WRONG

12.10 When installing a V-ribbed belt, make sure that it is centered - it must not overlap either edge of the pulley

you are replacing the alternator belt, you will have to remove the air conditioning compressor belt first because of the way they are arranged on the crankshaft pulley. Because of this and because belts tend to wear out more or less together, it is a good idea to replace both belts at the same time. Mark each belt and its appropriate pulley groove so the replacement belts can be installed in their proper positions.

9   Take the old belts to the parts store in order to make a direct comparison for length, width and design.

10   After replacing the drivebelt, make sure that it fits properly in the ribbed grooves in the pulleys **(see illustration)**. It is essential that the belt be properly centered.

11   Adjust the belt(s) in accordance with the procedure outlined above.

13   Underhood hose check and replacement

Caution: *Replacement of air conditioning hoses must be left to a dealer service department or air conditioning shop that has the equipment to depressurize the system safely. Never remove air conditioning components or hoses until the system has been depressurized.*

General

1   High temperatures in the engine compartment can cause the deterioration of the rubber and plastic hoses used for engine, accessory and emission systems operation. Periodic inspection should be made for cracks, loose clamps, material hardening and leaks.

2   Information specific to the cooling system hoses can be found in Section 14.

3   Some, but not all, hoses are secured to the fittings with clamps. Where clamps are used, check to be sure they haven't lost their tension, allowing the hose to leak. If clamps aren't used, make sure the hose has not expanded and/or hardened where it slips over the fitting, allowing it to leak.

Vacuum hoses

4   It's quite common for vacuum hoses, especially those in the emissions system, to be color coded or identified by colored stripes molded into them. Various systems

require hoses with different wall thicknesses, collapse resistance and temperature resistance. When replacing hoses, be sure the new ones are made of the same material.

5   Often the only effective way to check a hose is to remove it completely from the vehicle. If more than one hose is removed, be sure to label the hoses and fittings to ensure correct installation.

6   When checking vacuum hoses, be sure to include any plastic T-fittings in the check. Inspect the fittings for cracks and the hose where it fits over the fitting for distortion, which could cause leakage.

7   A small piece of vacuum hose (1/4-inch inside diameter) can be used as a stethoscope to detect vacuum leaks. Hold one end of the hose to your ear and probe around vacuum hoses and fittings, listening for the "hissing" sound characteristic of a vacuum leak. **Warning:** *When probing with the vacuum hose stethoscope, be very careful not to come into contact with moving engine components such as the drivebelts, cooling fan, etc.*

Fuel hose

Warning: *There are certain precautions which must be taken when inspecting or servicing fuel system components. Work in a well ventilated area and do not allow open flames (cigarettes, appliance pilot lights, etc.) or bare light bulbs near the work area. Mop up any spills immediately and do not store fuel soaked rags where they could ignite. On vehicles equipped with fuel injection, the fuel system is under pressure, so if any fuel lines are to be disconnected, the pressure in the system must be relieved first (see Chapter 4 for more information).*

8   Check all rubber fuel lines for deterioration and chafing. Check especially for cracks in areas where the hose bends and just before fittings, such as where a hose attaches to the fuel filter.

9   High quality fuel line, usually identified by the word Fluroelastomer printed on the hose, should be used for fuel line replacement. Never, under any circumstances, use unreinforced vacuum line, clear plastic tubing or water hose for fuel lines.

10   Spring-type clamps are commonly used on fuel lines. These clamps often lose their tension over a period of time, and can be "sprung" during removal. Replace all spring-type clamps with screw clamps whenever a hose is replaced.

Metal lines

11   Sections of metal line are often used for fuel line between the fuel pump and fuel injection unit. Check carefully to be sure the line has not been bent or crimped and that cracks have not started in the line.

12   If a section of metal fuel line must be replaced, only seamless steel tubing should be used, since copper and aluminum tubing don't have the strength necessary to withstand normal engine vibration.

Check for a chafed area that could fail prematurely.

Check for a soft area indicating the hose has deteriorated inside.

Overtightening the clamp on a hardened hose will damage the hose and cause a leak.

Check each hose for swelling and oil-soaked ends. Cracks and breaks can be located by squeezing the hose.

14.4 Hoses, like drivebelts, have a habit of failing at the worst possible time - to prevent the inconvenience of a blown radiator or heater hose, inspect them carefully as shown here

13   Check the metal brake lines where they enter the master cylinder and brake proportioning unit (if used) for cracks in the lines or loose fittings. Any sign of brake fluid leakage calls for an immediate thorough inspection of the brake system.

14 Cooling system check

Refer to illustration 14.4
1   Many major engine failures can be attributed to a faulty cooling system. If the vehicle is equipped with an automatic transmission, the cooling system also cools the transmission fluid and thus plays an important role in prolonging transmission life.
2   The cooling system should be checked with the engine cold.

Do this before the vehicle is driven for the day or after the engine has been shut off for at least three hours.
3   Remove the radiator cap by turning it to the left until it reaches a stop. If you hear a hissing sound (indicating there is still pressure in the system), wait until it stops. Now press down on the cap with the palm of your hand and continue turning to the left until the cap can be removed. Thoroughly clean the cap, inside and out, with clean water. Also clean the filler neck on the radiator. All traces of corrosion should be removed. The coolant inside the radiator should be relatively transparent. If it's rust colored, the system should be drained and refilled (Section 28). If the coolant level isn't up to the top, add additional antifreeze/coolant mixture (see Section 4).
4   Carefully check the large upper and lower radiator hoses along with the smaller diameter heater hoses which run from the engine to the firewall. Inspect each hose along its entire length, replacing any hose which is cracked, swollen or shows signs of deterioration. Cracks may become more apparent if the hose is squeezed **(see illustration)**. Regardless of condition, it's a good idea to replace hoses with new ones every two years.
5   Make sure that all hose connections are tight. A leak in the cooling system will usually show up as white or rust colored deposits on the areas adjoining the leak. If wire-type clamps are used at the ends of the hoses, it may be a good idea to replace them with more secure screw-type clamps.
6   Use compressed air or a soft brush to remove bugs, leaves, etc. from the front of the radiator or air conditioning condenser. Be careful not to damage the delicate cooling fins or cut yourself on them.
7   Every other inspection, or at the first indication of cooling system problems, have the cap and system pressure tested. If you don't have a pressure tester, most gas stations and repair shops will do this for a minimal charge.

15 Tire rotation

Refer to illustration 15.2
1   The tires should be rotated at the specified intervals and whenever uneven wear is noticed. Since the vehicle will be raised and the tires removed anyway, check the brakes (Section 16) at this time.
2   Radial tires must be rotated in a specific pattern **(see illustration)**.
3   Refer to the information in Jacking and towing at the front of this manual for the proper procedures to follow when raising the vehicle and changing a tire. If the brakes are to be checked, do not apply the parking brake as stated. Make sure the tires are blocked to prevent the vehicle from rolling.
4   Preferably, the entire vehicle should be

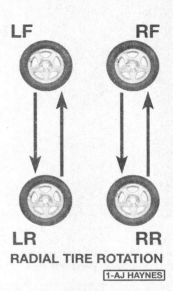

15.2 The recommended tire rotation pattern

raised at the same time. This can be done on a hoist or by jacking up each corner and then lowering the vehicle onto jackstands placed under the frame rails. Always use four jackstands and make sure the vehicle is firmly supported.
5   After rotation, check and adjust the tire pressures as necessary and be sure to check the lug nut tightness.
6   For further information on the wheels and tires, refer to Chapter 10.

16 Brake check

Note: *For detailed photographs of the brake system, refer to Chapter 9.*
1   In addition to the specified intervals, the brakes should be inspected every time the wheels are removed or whenever a defect is suspected. Any of the following symptoms could indicate a potential brake system defect: The vehicle pulls to one side when the brake pedal is depressed; the brakes make squealing or dragging noises when applied; brake travel is excessive; the pedal pulsates; brake fluid leaks, usually onto the inside of the tire or wheel.
2   The disc brake pads have built-in wear indicators which should make a high pitched squealing or scraping noise when they are worn to the replacement point. When you hear this noise, replace the pads immediately or expensive damage to the rotors can result.
3   Loosen the wheel lug nuts.
4   Raise the vehicle and place it securely on jackstands.
5   Remove the wheels (see *Jacking and towing* at the front of this book, or your owner's manual, if necessary).

16.6 You will find an inspection hole like this in each caliper - placing a steel ruler across the hole should enable you to determine the thickness of remaining pad material for both inner and outer pads

16.11 Always inspect the brake hoses before installing the wheels - look for cracks, leaks and damage of any kind

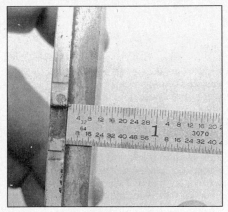

16.9 If a more precise measurement of pad thickness is necessary, the pads must be removed from the caliper and measured like this - spraying the pads with brake cleaner will help you determine where the pad material ends and the steel backing material begins

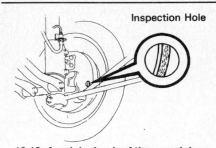

16.13 A quick check of the remaining drum brake shoe lining material can be made by removing the rubber plug in the backing plate and looking through the inspection hole

16.10 Measure the rotor thickness with a micrometer or a vernier caliper - even if the rotor has some service life remaining, inspect it for grooves, score marks and burned spots

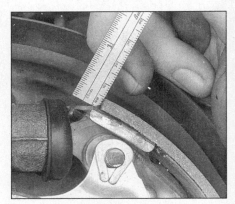

16.16 The rear brake shoe lining thickness is measured from the outer surface of the lining to the metal shoe

Disc brakes

Refer to illustrations 16.6, 16.9, 16.10 and 16.11

6   There are two pads - an outer and an inner - in each caliper. The pads are visible through small inspection holes in each caliper **(see illustration)** .

7   Check the pad thickness by looking at each end of the caliper and through the inspection hole in the caliper body. If the lining material is less than the specified thickness, replace the pads. **Note:** *Keep in mind that the lining material is riveted or bonded to a metal backing plate and the metal portion is not included in this measurement.*

8   If it is difficult to determine the exact thickness of the remaining pad material by the above method, or if you are at all concerned about the condition of the pads, remove the caliper(s), then remove the pads from the calipers for further inspection (refer to Chapter 9).

9   Once the pads are removed from the calipers, clean them with brake cleaner and remeasure them with a small steel pocket ruler **(see illustration)** or a vernier caliper.

10   Measure the disc rotor thickness with a

micrometer **(see illustration)** to make sure that it still has service life remaining. If any disc is thinner than the specified minimum thickness, replace it (refer to Chapter 9). Even if the rotor has service life remaining, check its condition. Look for scoring, gouging and burned spots. If these conditions exist, remove the rotor and have it resurfaced (refer to Chapter 9).

11   Before installing the wheels, check all brake lines and hoses for damage, wear, deformation, cracks, corrosion, leakage, bends and twists, particularly in the vicinity of the rubber hoses at the calipers **(see illustra-tion)**. Check the clamps for tightness and·the connections for leakage. Make sure that all hoses and lines are clear of sharp edges, moving parts and the exhaust system. If any of the above conditions are noted, repair, reroute or replace the lines and/or fittings as necessary (refer to Chapter 9).

12   Later models are equipped with disc brakes on the rear wheels which incorporate drum-type parking brakes into the rear discs. The inspection procedure for these parking brakes is the same as for the rear drum brakes described below.

Rear drum brakes

Refer to illustrations 16.13, 16.16 and 16.18

13   To check the brake shoe lining thickness without removing the brake drums, remove the rubber plug from the backing plate and use a flashlight to inspect the linings **(see illustration)**. For a more thorough brake inspection, follow the procedure below.

14   Refer to Chapter 9 and remove the rear brake drums.

15   **Warning:** *Brake dust produced by lining wear and deposited on brake components contains asbestos, which is hazardous to your health. DO NOT blow it out with compressed air and DO NOT inhale it! DO NOT use gasoline or solvents to remove the dust. Brake system cleaner should be used to flush the dust into a drain pan. After the brake components are wiped clean with a damp rag, dispose of the contaminated rag(s) and solvent in a covered and labeled container. Try to use non-asbestos replacement parts whenever possible.*

16   Note the thickness of the lining material on the rear brake shoes **(see illustration)** and look for signs of contamination by brake fluid

16.18 Carefully peel back the wheel cylinder boot and check for leaking fluid indicating that the cylinder must be replaced or rebuilt

17.2 Hold the cover up out of the way while lifting the filter element out

and grease. If the lining material is within 1/16-inch of the recessed rivets or metal shoes, replace the brake shoes with new ones. The shoes should also be replaced if they are cracked, glazed (shiny lining surfaces) or contaminated with brake fluid or grease. See Chapter 9 for the replacement procedure.

17   Check the shoe return and hold-down springs and the adjusting mechanism to make sure they're installed correctly and in good condition. Deteriorated or distorted springs, if not replaced, could allow the linings to drag and wear prematurely.

18   Check the wheel cylinders for leakage by carefully peeling back the rubber boots **(see illustration)**. If brake fluid is noted behind the boots, the wheel cylinders must be replaced (see Chapter 9).

19   Check the drums for cracks, score marks, deep scratches and hard spots, which will appear as small discolored areas. If imperfections cannot be removed with emery cloth, the drums must be resurfaced by an automotive machine shop (see Chapter 9 for more detailed information).

20   Refer to Chapter 9 and install the brake drums.

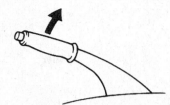

16.30 Slowly pull up on the parking brake and count the number of clicks you hear - if the handle reaches its maximum travel in more or fewer than the specified number of clicks, adjust the parking brake cable

21   Install the wheels and snug the wheel lug nuts finger tight.
22   Remove the jackstands and lower the vehicle.
23   Tighten the wheel lug nuts to the specified torque.

Brake booster check

24   Sit in the driver's seat and perform the following sequence of tests.
25   With the brake fully depressed, start the engine - the pedal should move down a little when the engine starts.
26   With the engine running, depress the brake pedal several times- the travel distance should not change.
27   Depress the brake, stop the engine and hold the pedal in for about 30 seconds - the pedal should neither sink nor rise.
28   Restart the engine, run it for about a minute and turn it off. Then firmly depress the brake several times - the pedal travel should decrease with each application.
29   If your brakes do not operate as described above when the preceding tests are performed, the brake booster is either in need of repair or has failed. Refer to Chapter 9 for the removal procedure.

Parking brake

Refer to illustration 16.30
30   Slowly pull up on the parking brake and count the number of clicks you hear until the handle is up as far as it will go **(see illustration)**. The adjustment is correct if you hear the specified number of clicks. If you hear more or fewer clicks, it's time to adjust the parking brake (refer to Chapter 9).
31   An alternative method of checking the parking brake is to park the vehicle on a steep hill with the parking brake set and the transmission in Neutral. If the parking brake cannot prevent the vehicle from rolling, it is in need of adjustment (see Chapter 9).

17   Air filter replacement

Refer to illustrations 17.1 and 17.2
1   The air filter is located inside a housing at the left side of the engine compartment. To remove the air filter, release the four spring

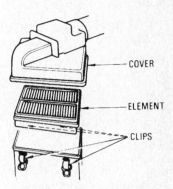

17.1 Two clips on the top and two on the bottom hold the two halves of the air cleaner housing together - they can be pried loose with a screwdriver

clips that keep the two halves of the air cleaner housing together **(see illustration)**.
2   Lift the cover up and remove the air filter element **(see illustration)**.
3   Inspect the outer surface of the filter element. If it is dirty, replace it. If it is only moderately dusty, it can be reused by blowing it clean from the back to the front surface with compressed air. Because it is a pleated paper type filter, it cannot be washed or oiled. If it cannot be cleaned satisfactorily with compressed air, discard and replace it. **Caution:** *Never drive the vehicle with the air cleaner removed. Excessive engine wear could result and backfiring could even cause a fire under the hood.*
4   Installation is the reverse of removal.

18   Fuel system check

Warning: *Certain precautions should be observed when inspecting or servicing the fuel system components. Work in a well ventilated area and do not allow open flames (cigarettes, appliance pilot lights, etc.) near the work area. Mop up spills immediately and do not store fuel soaked rags where they could ignite. It is a good idea to keep a dry chemical (Class B) fire extinguisher near the work area any time the fuel system is being serviced.*

1   If you smell gasoline while driving or after the vehicle has been sitting in the sun, inspect the fuel system immediately.
2   Remove the gas filler cap and inspect if for damage and corrosion. The gasket should have an unbroken sealing imprint. If the gasket is damaged or corroded, remove it and install a new one (Section 36).
3   Inspect the fuel feed and return lines for cracks. Make sure that the threaded flare nut type connectors which secure the metal fuel lines to the fuel injection system and the banjo bolts which secure the banjo fittings to the in-line fuel filter are tight. **Warning:** *It is necessary to relieve the fuel system pressure*

19.3 The fuel filter assembly is held in place by two bracket bolts (arrows)

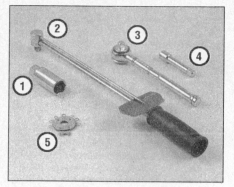

20.1 Tools required for changing spark plugs

1   **Spark plug socket** - This will have special padding inside to protect the spark plug's porcelain insulator
2   **Torque wrench** - Although not mandatory, using this tool is the best way to ensure the plugs are tightened properly
3   **Ratchet** - Standard hand tool to fit the spark plug socket
4   **Extension** - Depending on model and accessories, you may need special extensions and universal joints to reach one or more of the plugs
5   **Spark plug gap gauge** - This gauge for checking the gap comes in a variety of styles. Make sure the gap for your engine is included

20.4a Spark plug manufacturers recommend using a wire-type gauge when checking the gap - if the wire does not slide between the electrodes with a slight drag, adjustment is required

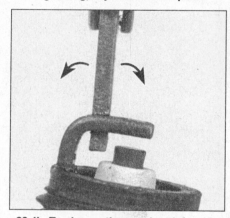

20.4b To change the gap, bend the side electrode only, as indicated by the arrows, and be very careful not to crack or chip the porcelain insulator surrounding the center electrode

before servicing fuel system components. The correct procedures for fuel system pressure relief are outlined in Chapter 4.

4   Since some components of the fuel system - the fuel tank and part of the fuel feed and return lines, for example - are underneath the vehicle, they can be inspected more easily with the vehicle raised on a hoist. If that's not possible, raise the vehicle and secure it on jackstands.

5   With the vehicle raised and safely supported, inspect the gas tank and filler neck for punctures, cracks and other damage. The connection between the filler neck and the tank is particularly critical. Sometimes a rubber filler neck will leak because of loose clamps or deteriorated rubber. These are problems a home mechanic can usually rectify. **Warning:** *Do not, under any circumstances, try to repair a fuel tank (except rubber components). A welding torch or any open flame can easily cause fuel vapors inside the tank to explode.*

6   Carefully check all rubber hoses and metal lines leading away from the fuel tank. Check for loose connections, deteriorated hoses, crimped lines and other damage. Carefully inspect the lines from the tank to the fuel injection system. Repair or replace damaged sections as necessary

19 Fuel filter replacement

Refer to illustration 19.3
Warning: *Before removing the fuel filter, the fuel system pressure must be relieved. Refer to Chapter 4 for the procedure.*
1   Remove the air cleaner duct.
2   Loosen the threaded banjo fittings on both ends of the fuel filter with a flare nut wrench (use a backup wrench on the fitting at the filter bottom). Disconnect both ends.
3   Remove both bracket bolts from the fender well and remove the old filter and the filter support bracket (see illustration).
4   Remove the filter clamp bolt and separate the old filter from the bracket. Note that the inlet and outlet pipes are clearly labeled

on their respective ends of the filter and that the flanged end of the filter faces down.
5   Install the new filter and bracket assembly and tighten the bracket bolts securely. Make sure that the new filter is installed so that it's facing the proper direction as noted above. When correctly installed, the filter should be installed so that the outlet pipe faces up and the inlet pipe faces down.
6   Using the new crush washers provided by the filter manufacturer, install the inlet and outlet banjo fittings and tighten them securely.
7   The remainder of installation is the reverse of the removal procedure.

20 Spark plug check and replacement

Refer to illustrations 20.1, 20.4a, 20.4b, 20.6, 20.8 and 20.10
1   Spark plug replacement requires a spark plug socket which fits onto a ratchet wrench. This socket is lined with a rubber grommet to protect the porcelain insulator of the spark plug and to hold the plug while you insert it into the spark plug hole. You will also need a wire-type feeler gauge to check and adjust the spark plug gap and a torque wrench to tighten the new plugs to the specified torque (see illustration).
2   If you are replacing the plugs, purchase

the new plugs, adjust them to the proper gap and then replace each plug one at a time. **Note:** *When buying new spark plugs, it's essential that you obtain the correct plugs for your specific vehicle. This information can be found on the Vehicle Emissions Control Information (VECI) label located on the underside of the hood or in the owner's manual. If these two sources specify different plugs, purchase the spark plug type specified on the VECI label because that information is provided specifically for your engine.*
3   Inspect each of the new plugs for defects. If there are any signs of cracks in the porcelain insulator of a plug, don't use it.
4   Check the electrode gaps of the new plugs. Check the gap by inserting the wire gauge of the proper thickness between the electrodes at the tip of the plug (see illustration). The gap between the electrodes should be identical to that specified on the VECI label. If the gap is incorrect, use the notched adjuster on the feeler gauge body to bend the curved side electrode slightly (see illustration).

20.6 When removing the spark plug wires, pull only on the boot and use a twisting/pulling motion

20.8 Use a socket wrench with a long extension to remove the spark plug

20.10 A length of 3/16-inch ID rubber hose will save time and prevent damaged threads when installing the spark plugs

5   If the side electrode is not exactly over the center electrode, use the notched adjuster to align them. **Caution:** *If the gap of a new plug must be adjusted, bend only the base of the ground electrode do not touch the tip.*

Removal

6   To prevent the possibility of mixing up spark plug wires, work on one spark plug at a time. Remove the wire and boot from one spark plug. Grasp the boot - not the cable - as shown, give it a half twisting motion and pull straight up **(see illustration)**.

7   If compressed air is available, blow any dirt or foreign material away from the spark plug area before proceeding (a common bicycle pump will also work).

8   Remove the spark plug **(see illustration)**.

9   Whether you are replacing the plugs at this time or intend to reuse the old plugs, compare each old spark plug with those shown in the photos on the inside back cover of this manual to determine the overall running condition of the engine.

Installation

10   It's often difficult to insert spark plugs into their holes without cross-threading them. To avoid this possibility, fit a short piece of 3/16-inch ID rubber hose over the end of the spark plug **(see illustration)**. The flexible hose acts as a universal joint to help align the plug with the plug hole. Should the plug begin to cross-thread, the hose will slip on the spark plug, preventing thread damage. Tighten the plug securely.

11   Attach the plug wire to the new spark plug, again using a twisting motion on the boot until it is firmly seated on the end of the spark plug.

12   Follow the above procedure for the remaining spark plugs, replacing them one at a time to prevent mixing up the spark plug wires.

21   Spark plug wire, distributor cap and rotor check and replacement

Refer to illustrations 21.11, 21.12 and 21.13

1   The spark plug wires should be checked whenever new spark plugs are installed.

2   Begin this procedure by making a visual check of the spark plug wires while the engine is running. In a darkened garage (make sure there is ventilation) start the engine and observe each plug wire. Be careful not to come into contact with any moving engine parts. If there is a break in the wire, you will see arcing or a small spark at the damaged area. If arcing is noticed, make a note to obtain new wires, then allow the engine to cool and check the distributor cap and rotor.

3   The spark plug wires should be inspected one at a time to prevent mixing up the order, which is essential for proper engine operation. Each original plug wire should be numbered to help identify its location. If the number is illegible, a piece of tape can be marked with the correct number and

wrapped around the plug wire.

4   Disconnect the plug wire from the spark plug. A removal tool can be used for this purpose or you can grasp the rubber boot, twist the boot half a turn and pull the boot free. Do not pull on the wire itself.

5   Check inside the boot for corrosion, which will look like a white crusty powder.

6   Push the wire and boot back onto the end of the spark plug. It should fit tightly onto the end of the plug. If it doesn't, remove the wire and use pliers to carefully crimp the metal connector inside the wire boot until the fit is snug.

7   Using a clean rag, wipe the entire length of the wire to remove built-up dirt and grease. Once the wire is clean, check for burns, cracks and other damage. Do not bend the wire sharply, because the conductor might break.

8   Disconnect the wire from the distributor. Again, pull only on the rubber boot. Check for corrosion and a tight fit. Replace the wire in the distributor.

9   Inspect the remaining spark plug wires, making sure that each one is securely fastened at the distributor and spark plug when the check is complete.

10   If new spark plug wires are required, purchase a set for your specific engine model. Pre-cut wire sets with the boots already installed are available. Remove and replace the wires one at a time to avoid mix-ups in the firing order.

11   Detach the distributor cap by removing the two cap retaining bolts. Look inside it for cracks, carbon tracks and worn, burned or loose contacts **(see illustration)**.

12   Pull the rotor off the distributor shaft and examine it for cracks and carbon tracks **(see illustration)**. Replace the cap and rotor if any damage or defects are noted.

13   It is common practice to install a new cap and rotor whenever new spark plug wires are installed, but if you wish to continue using the old cap, check the resistance between the spark plug wires and the cap first **(see**

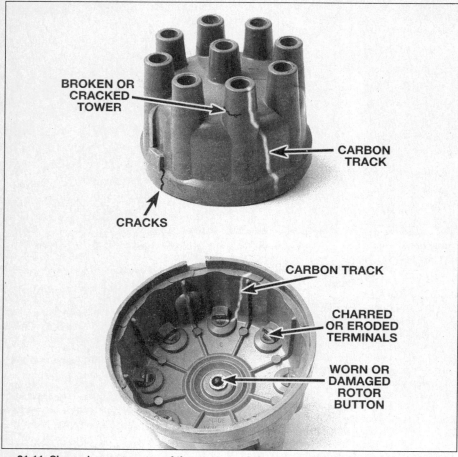

21.11 Shown here are some of the common defects to look for when inspecting the distributor cap (if in doubt about its condition, install a new one)

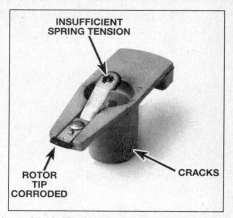

21.12 The ignition rotor should be checked for wear and corrosion as indicated here (if in doubt about its condition, buy a new one)

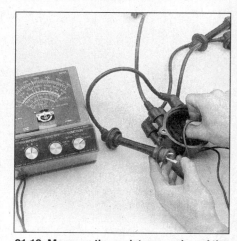

21.13 Measure the resistance value of the distributor cap and the spark plug wires - if it exceeds the specified maximum value, replace either the cap, or the wires, or both

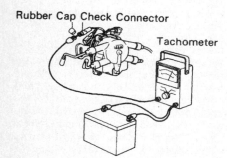

22.3 Make sure that the tachometer is hooked up to the distributor check connector

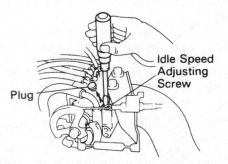

22.5 The idle speed adjusting screw is on the rear side of the throttle body - note that the idle speed is quite sensitive to even the slightest turn of this screw

22   Engine idle speed check and adjustment (1983 through 1986 models)

Refer to illustrations 22.3 and 22.5

1   Engine idle speed is the speed at which the engine operates when no accelerator pedal pressure is applied, as when stopped

illustration). If the indicated resistance is more than the specified maximum value, replace the cap and/or wires.

14   When installing a new cap, remove the wires from the old cap one at a time and attach them to the new cap in the exact same location - do not simultaneously remove all the wires from the old cap or firing order mix-ups may occur.

at a traffic light. This speed is critical to the performance of the engine itself, as well as many engine subsystems.

2   Set the parking brake firmly set and block the wheels to prevent the vehicle from rolling. Put the transaxle in Neutral.

3   Hook up a hand held tachometer (**see illustration**). **Caution:** *Some tachometers may not be compatible with this ignition system. It is recommended that you consult with the manufacturer. Do not allow the tachometer to touch ground or it could result in damage to the igniter and/or the ignition coil.*

4   Start the engine and race it at 2,500 rpm for about two minutes to warm it up.

5   Allow the engine to idle. On 1986 models, disconnect the vacuum switching valve from the idle speed control. Note the indicated idle rpm on the tachometer and, if the idle speed is too low or too high, adjust it by removing the plastic plug from the adjusting screw bore and turning the idle speed adjusting screw (**see illustration**).

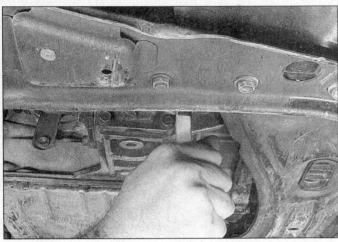

23.2 Because of the tight clearance, use a thin open end wrench to remove the differential check/fill plug - reach up and check the lubricant level with your finger

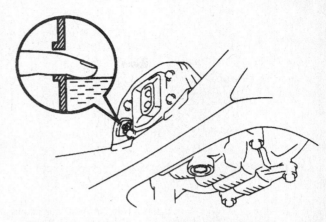

25.3 Check the differential lubricant with your finger to make sure the level is even with the bottom of the filler hole

6   Turn off the engine, disconnect the tachometer and reconnect the vacuum switching valve (1986 models).

23   Automatic transaxle differential lubricant level check

Refer to illustration 23.2

1   The automatic transaxle differential has a check/fill plug which must be removed to check the lubricant level. If the vehicle is raised to gain access to the plug, be sure to support it safely on jackstands - DO NOT crawl under the vehicle when it's supported only by the jack.
2   Remove the check/fill plug from the front of the differential **(see illustration)**.
3   Use your little finger as a dipstick to make sure the lubricant level is even with the bottom of the plug hole. If not, use a syringe to add the recommended lubricant until it just starts to run out of the opening.
4   Install the plug and tighten it securely.

24   Manual transaxle lubricant level check

Refer to illustration 24.1

1   The manual transaxle does not have a dipstick. To check the fluid level, raise the vehicle and support it securely on jackstands. On the lower front side of the transaxle housing, you will see a plug **(see illustration)**. Remove it. If the lubricant level is correct, it should be up to the lower edge of the hole.
2   If the transaxle needs more lubricant (if the level is not up to the hole), use a syringe to add more. Stop filling the transaxle when the lubricant begins to run out the hole.
3   Install the plug and tighten it securely. Drive the vehicle a short distance, then check for leaks.

25   All-wheel drive rear differential lubricant level check

Refer to illustration 25.3

1   The differential has a check/fill plug

which must be removed to check the lubricant level. If the vehicle is raised to gain access to the plug, be sure to support it safely on jackstands - DO NOT crawl under the vehicle when it's supported only by a jack.
2   Remove the check/fill plug from the differential.
3   The lubricant level should be at the bottom of the plug opening **(see illustration)**. If not, use a syringe to add the recommended lubricant until it just starts to run out of the opening.
4   Install the plug and tighten it securely.

26   Steering and suspension check

Refer to illustrations 26.1, 26.6 26.8 and 26.9
Note: *For detailed illustrations of the steering and suspension components, refer to Chapter 10.*

With the wheels on the ground

1   With the vehicle stopped and the front wheels pointed straight ahead, rock the steering wheel gently back and forth. If free play **(see illustration)** is excessive , a front wheel bearing, main shaft yoke, intermediate shaft yoke, lower arm balljoint or steering system joint is worn or the steering gear is out of adjustment or broken. Refer to Chapter 10 for the appropriate repair procedure.
2   Other symptoms, such as excessive vehicle body movement over rough roads, swaying (leaning) around corners and binding as the steering wheel is turned, may indicate faulty steering and/or suspension components.
3   Check the shock absorbers by pushing down and releasing the vehicle several times at each corner. If the vehicle does not come back to a level position within one or two bounces, the shocks/struts are worn and must be replaced. When bouncing the vehicle up and down, listen for squeaks and noises from the suspension components.

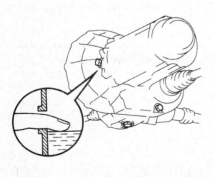

24.1 The manual transaxle filler plug is located on the side of the case - remove it with a socket and ratchet

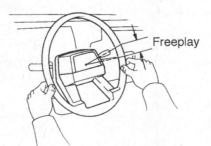

Freeplay

26.1 Steering wheel free play is the amount of travel between an initial steering input and the point at which the front wheels begin to turn (indicated by a slight resistance)

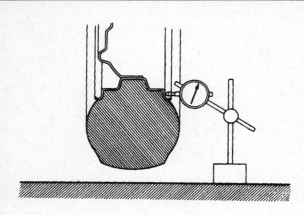

26.6 If you have a dial gauge, you can easily pinpoint lateral wheel runout - set it up like this with the pointer against the bead flange of the wheel, then slowly spin the wheel

26.9 Push on the balljoint boot to check for damage

Additional information on suspension components can be found in Chapter 10.

4   Measure the front and rear chassis clearance (the height of the vehicle above the ground) by measuring the distance from the ground to the center of the control arm bolts. Also note whether the vehicle looks canted to one side or corner. If the clearance of the vehicle is not as specified or if it is canted to one side or corner, try to level it by rocking it down. If this doesn't work, look for bad springs or worn or loose suspension parts.

Under the vehicle

5   Raise the vehicle with a floor jack and support it securely on jackstands. See Jacking and towing at the front of this book for the proper jacking points.

6   Check the tires for irregular wear patterns (see Section 5) and proper inflation. If you have a dial gauge and base, check the

26.8 To check a balljoint for wear, raise the vehicle, and support it on jackstands, place a 71/2-inch thick block of wood under the tire, block the wheel with chocks and lower the jack until there is about half a load on the coil spring - then move the lower arm up and down with a prybar to make sure there is no play in the balljoint (if there is, replace it)

lateral runout of the wheels **(see illustration)**. If lateral runout is not within specification, the tires are worn or improperly inflated, the wheels are out of balance or the wheel bearings are worn. See Section 5 in this chapter for information regarding tire wear and Chapter 10 for the wheel bearing replacement procedures.

7   Inspect the universal joint between the steering shaft and the steering gear housing. Check the steering gear housing for grease leakage or oozing. Make sure that the dust seals and boots are not damaged and that the boot clamps are not loose. Check the steering linkage for looseness or damage. Check the tie-rod ends for excessive play. Look for loose bolts, broken or disconnected parts and deteriorated rubber bushings on all suspension and steering components. While an assistant turns the steering wheel from side to side, check the steering components for free movement, chafing and binding. If the steering components do not seem to be reacting with the movement of the steering wheel, try to determine where the slack is located.

8   Check the balljoints for wear by placing

27.2 Flex the driveaxle boots by hand to check for cracks and/or leaking grease

a 7-1/2-inch thick wooden block under each tire. Lower the jack until there is about half a load on the coil spring. Make sure that the front wheels are in a straight forward position and block the wheel with chocks. Move each lower arm up and down with a pry bar **(see illustration)** to ensure that its balljoint has no play. If any balljoint does have play, replace it. Refer to Chapter 10 for the front balljoint replacement procedure.

9   Inspect the balljoint boots for damage and leaking grease **(see illustration)**. Replace the boots with new ones if they are damaged (Chapter 10).

---

27   Driveaxle boot check

Refer to illustration 27.2

The driveaxle boots are very important because they prevent dirt, water and foreign material from entering and damaging the constant velocity (CV) joints. Oil and grease can cause the boot material to deteriorate prematurely, so it's a good idea to wash the boots with soap and water.

2   Inspect the boots for tears and cracks as well as loose clamps **(see illustration)**. If there is any evidence of cracks or leaking lubricant, they must be replaced as described in Chapter 8.

---

28   Cooling system servicing (draining, flushing and refilling)

Warning: *Antifreeze is a corrosive and poisonous solution, so be careful not to spill any of the coolant mixture on the vehicle's paint or your skin. If this happens, rinse immediately with plenty of clean water. Consult local authorities regarding proper disposal procedures for antifreeze before draining the cooling system. In many areas, reclamation centers have been established to collect used oil and coolant mixtures.*

28.4 On most models you will have to remove a cover for access to the radiator drain fitting located at the bottom of the radiator - before opening the valve, push a short section of 3/8-inch ID hose onto the plastic fitting (some models are already equipped with one) to prevent the coolant from splashing as it drains

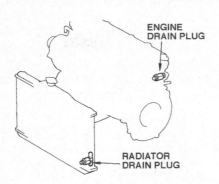

28.5a Four-cylinder model radiator and engine drain locations

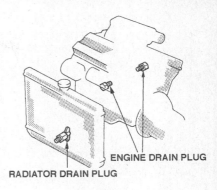

28.5b V6 model radiator and engine drain locations

1   Periodically, the cooling system should be drained, flushed and refilled to replenish the antifreeze mixture and prevent formation of rust and corrosion, which can impair the performance of the cooling system and cause engine damage. When the cooling system is serviced, all hoses and the radiator cap should be checked and replaced if necessary.

Draining

Refer to illustrations 28.4, 28.5a and 28.5b
2   Apply the parking brake and block the wheels. If the vehicle has just been driven, wait several hours to allow the engine to cool down before beginning this procedure.
3   Once the engine is completely cool, remove the radiator cap.
4   Move a large container under the radiator drain to catch the coolant. Attach a 3/8-inch inner diameter hose to the drain fitting to direct the coolant into the container (some models are already equipped with a hose), then open the drain fitting (a pair of pliers may be required to turn it) **(see illustration)**.
5   After the coolant stops flowing out of the radiator, move the container under the engine block drain plug(s) **(see illustrations)**. Loosen the plug(s) and allow the coolant in the block to drain.
6   While the coolant is draining, check the condition of the radiator hoses, heater hoses and clamps (refer to Section 13 if necessary).
7   Replace any damaged clamps or hoses (refer to Chapter 3 for detailed replacement procedures).

Flushing

8   Once the system is completely drained, flush the radiator with fresh water from a garden hose until water runs clear at the drain. The flushing action of the water will remove sediments from the radiator but will not

remove rust and scale from the engine and cooling tube surfaces.
9   These deposits can be removed by the chemical action of a cleaner. Follow the procedure outlined in the manufacturer's instructions. If the radiator is severely corroded, damaged or leaking, it should be removed (Chapter 3) and taken to a radiator repair shop.
10   Remove the overflow hose from the coolant recovery reservoir. Drain the reservoir and flush it with clean water, then reconnect the hose.

Refilling

11   Close and tighten the radiator drain. Install and tighten the block drain plug(s).
12   Place the heater temperature control in the maximum heat position.

Four-cylinder engine

13   Slowly add new coolant (a 50/50 mixture of water and antifreeze) to the radiator until it's full. Add coolant to the reservoir up to the lower mark.
14   Leave the radiator cap off and run the engine in a well-ventilated area until the thermostat opens (coolant will begin flowing through the radiator and the upper radiator hose will become hot).
15   Turn the engine off and let it cool. Add more coolant mixture to bring the level back up to the lip on the radiator filler neck.
16   Squeeze the upper radiator hose to expel air, then add more coolant mixture if necessary. Replace the radiator cap.
17   Start the engine, allow it to reach normal operating temperature and check for leaks.

V6 engine

Refer to illustration 28.18
18   Loosen the air bleeder plug in the water outlet housing until the holes are visible **(see illustration)**.
19   Fill the radiator with a 50/50 solution of water and antifreeze. Add coolant to the reservoir up to the lower mark. Tighten the bleeder plug.
20   Install the radiator cap and run the engine until the thermostat opens (the upper

radiator hose becomes hot).
21   Shut the engine off and allow it to cool. Open the bleeder plug. Add more coolant if necessary.
22   Repeat the procedure until the air is bled from the system (no bubbles issue from the coolant when the bleeder plug is opened).

29   Evaporative emissions control system check

Refer to illustrations 29.3a and 29.3b
1   The function of the Fuel Evaporative Emission Control (EVAP) System is to store fuel vapors from the fuel tank in a charcoal canister until they can be routed to the intake manifold where they mix with incoming air before being burned in the cylinder combustion chambers.
2   The most common symptom of a faulty evaporative emissions system is a strong fuel odor in the engine compartment. If a fuel odor is detected, inspect the charcoal canister, located on the left side of the engine compartment, and the EVAP system hoses.
3   To perform a simple check of system operation, label and disconnect the hoses. Inspect the canister for cracks or damage

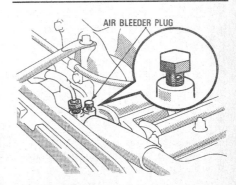

28.18 V6 engine air bleeder plug details - it must be opened during the refilling process to bleed air out of the system

Air should flow through freely
and no charcoal should come out

**29.3a 1983 and 1984 model EVAP canister
check details**

Air should flow through freely
and no charcoal should come out

**29.3b 1985 through 1988 model EVAP
canister checking details**

**31.7 Use an Allen wrench to remove the
transaxle drain plug**

before beginning the following tests. Check for a clogged filter and/or stuck check valve by blowing out the tank pipe with no more than 43 psi (294 kPa) of compressed air while plugging the other upper canister pipe with a finger **(see illustrations)**. Air should flow freely through the canister and no charcoal should issue from it. If the canister is clogged or leaking charcoal, replace it.

4   The evaporative emissions control system is explained in more detail in Chapter 6.

30 Exhaust system check

1   With the engine cold (at least three hours after the vehicle has been driven), check the complete exhaust system from its starting point at the engine to the end of the tailpipe. This should be done on a hoist where unrestricted access is available.

2   Check the pipes and connections for evidence of leaks, severe corrosion or damage. Make sure that all brackets and hangers are in good condition and tight.

3   At the same time, inspect the underside of the body for holes, corrosion, open seams, etc. which may allow exhaust gases to enter the passenger compartment. Seal all body openings with silicone or body putty.

4   Rattles and other noises can often be traced to the exhaust system, especially the mounts and hangers. Try to move the pipes, muffler and catalytic converter. If the components can come in contact with the body or suspension parts, secure the exhaust system with new mounts.

5   Check the running condition of the engine by inspecting inside the end of the tailpipe. The exhaust deposits here are an indication of engine state-of-tune. If the pipe is black and sooty or coated with white deposits, the engine is in need of a tune-up, including a thorough fuel system inspection and adjustment.

31 Automatic transaxle/differential fluid and filter change

Refer to illustrations 31.7, 31.9, 31.11 and 31.13

1   At the specified time intervals, the automatic transaxle and differential fluid should be drained and replaced.

2   Before beginning work, purchase the specified transmission fluid (see *Recommended fluids and lubricants* at the front of this chapter).

3   Other tools necessary for this job

include jackstands to support the vehicle in a raised position, a 10 mm Allen wrench, a drain pan capable of holding at least eight pints, newspapers and clean rags.

4   The fluid should be drained immediately after the vehicle has been driven. Hot fluid is more effective than cold fluid at removing built up sediment. **Caution:** *Fluid temperature can exceed 350-degrees in a hot transaxle. Wear protective gloves.*

5   After the vehicle has been driven to warm up the fluid, raise it and place it on jackstands for access to the transaxle and differential drain plugs.

6   Move the necessary equipment under the vehicle, being careful not to touch any of the hot exhaust components.

7   Place the drain pan under the drain plug in the transaxle pan **(see illustration)** and remove the drain plug with the Allen wrench. Be sure the drain pan is in position, as fluid will come out with some force. Once the fluid is drained, reinstall the drain plug securely.

8   Remove the transaxle pan bolts, carefully pry the pan loose with a screwdriver and remove it.

9   Remove the three filter retaining bolts, disconnect the clip and lower the filter from the transaxle **(see illustration)**. Be careful when lowering the filter as it contains residual fluid.

**31.9 Remove the filter bolts (arrows) (note the lengths because
one bolt is longer), swing back the clip (arrow) and lower the filter
- be careful, there will be some residual fluid**

**31.11 Noting their locations, remove the magnets and wash them
and the pan in solvent before reinstalling them**

31.13 Use an Allen wrench to remove the differential drain plug

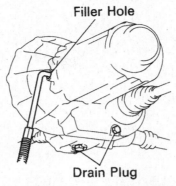

32.3 Fill the manual transaxle until lubricant starts to come out of the filler hole

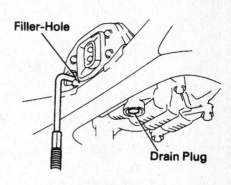

33.7 Use a pump or funnel to fill the differential

10   Place the new filter in position and install the bolts. Tighten the bolts to the specified torque. Connect the clip.

11   Carefully clean the gasket surfaces of the fluid pan, removing all traces of old gasket material. Wash the pan in clean solvent and dry it with compressed air. Be sure to clean and reinstall the magnets **(see illustration)**.

12   Install a new gasket, place the fluid pan in position and install the bolts in their original positions (the single bolt at the front of the filter is usually longer than the two rear bolts). Tighten the bolts to the specified torque.

13   Find the differential drain plug **(see illustration)**. Place the drain pan underneath the plug, remove it with the Allen wrench and drain the fluid. When the differential fluid has drained, reinstall the plug securely.

14   Add new fluid to the differential until it begins to run out of the filler hole (see *Recommended lubricants and fluids* at the beginning of this Chapter for the specified fluid type and capacity). **Caution:** *Do not overfill. The automatic transaxle and the differential are separate units.*

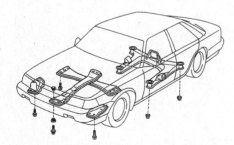

34.1 The mounting bolts for the front seat, the bolts and nuts that attach the front and rear suspension members, and the nuts and bolts attaching the strut bar brackets to the body are critical fasteners that must be periodically checked and tightened

15   Lower the vehicle.

16   With the engine off, add new fluid to the transaxle through the dipstick tube (see *Recommended fluids and lubricants* for the recommended fluid type). Use a funnel to prevent spills. It is best to add a little fluid at a time, continually checking the level with the dipstick (Section 7). Allow the fluid time to drain into the pan.

17   Start the engine and shift the selector into all positions from P through L, then shift into P and apply the parking brake.

18   With the engine idling, check the fluid level. Add fluid up to the Cool level on the dipstick.

32   Manual transaxle lubricant change

Refer to illustration 32.3

1   Remove the drain plug(s) and drain the fluid.

2   Reinstall the drain plug(s) securely.

3   Add new fluid until it begins to run out of the filler hole (Section 24) **(see illustration)**. See *Recommended lubricants and fluids* for the specified lubricant type.

33   All-wheel drive rear differential lubricant change

Refer to illustration 33.7

1   Drive the vehicle for several miles to warm up the differential oil, then raise the vehicle and support it securely on jackstands.

2   Move a drain pan, rags, newspapers and a 1/2-inch drive breaker bar or ratchet with an extension and socket under the vehicle.

3   With the drain pan under the differential, use the breaker bar or ratchet and socket to loosen the drain plug.

4   Once loosened, carefully unscrew it with your fingers until you can remove it from the case.

5   Allow all of the oil to drain into the pan,

then replace the drain plug and tighten it to the specified torque.

6   Feel with your hands along the bottom of the drain pan for any metal bits that may have come out with the oil. If there are any, it's a sign of excessive wear, indicating that the internal components should be carefully inspected in the near future.

7   Remove the differential check/fill plug located above the drain plug. Using a hand pump, syringe or funnel, fill the differential with the correct amount and grade of oil (see the Specifications) until the level is just at the bottom of the plug hole **(see illustration)**.

8   Reinstall the plug and tighten it securely.

9   Lower the vehicle. Check for leaks at the drain plug after the first few miles of driving.

34   Chassis and body fastener check

Refer to illustration 34.1

Tighten the following parts securely: front seat mounting bolts, front suspension member-to-body mounting bolts and nuts and strut bar bracket-to-body mounting bolts (left and right sides) **(see illustration)**.

35   Valve clearance check and adjustment (DOHC engines only)

Refer to illustrations 35.6a, 35.6b, 35.6c, 35.7, 35.8a, 35.8b, 35.10a, 35.10b and 35.11 **Note:** *The following procedure requires the use of a special valve lifter tool. It is impossible to perform this task without it.*

1   Disconnect the negative cable from the battery. Place the cable out of the way so it cannot accidentally come in contact with the negative terminal of the battery, as this would once again allow power into the electrical system of the vehicle.

2   Disconnect the cruise control cable, air cleaner duct or other components which will interfere with cylinder head cover removal.

3   Remove the cylinder head cover(s) (refer to Chapter 2).

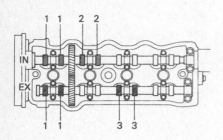

35.6a On four-cylinder engines, when the no. 1 piston is at TDC on the compression stroke, the valve clearances for the no. 1 and no. 3 exhaust valves and the no. 1 and no. 2 intake valves can be measured

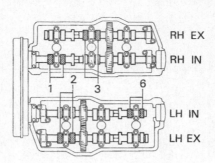

35.6b On V6 engines, when the no. 1 piston is at TDC on the compression stroke, the clearances for the valves indicated can be measured

35.6c Measure the clearance for each valve with a feeler gauge of the specified thickness - if the clearance is correct, you should feel a slight drag on the gauge as you pull it out

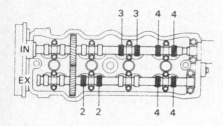

35.7 On four-cylinder engines, when the no. 4 piston is at TDC on the compression stroke, the valve clearances for the no. 2 and no. 4 exhaust valves and the no. 3 and no. 4 intake valves can be measured

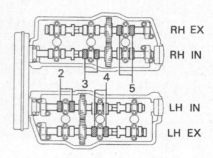

35.8a On V6 engines, make sure the no. 1 piston is at TDC on the compression stroke, then rotate the engine 2/3 of a revolution (240°) and measure the clearances for the valves indicated

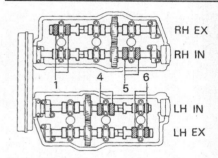

35.8b Rotate the crankshaft an additional 2/3-turn (240°) and measure the valve clearances for the remaining valves

4   Blow out the recessed area between the camshafts with compressed air, if available, to remove any debris that might fall into the cylinders, then remove the spark plugs (Section 20).

5   Refer to Chapter 2 and position the number 1 piston at TDC on the compression stroke.

6   Measure the clearances of the indicated valves with a feeler gauge of the specified thickness **(see illustrations)**. Record the measurements which are out of specification. They will be used later to determine the required replacement shims.

7   On the four-cylinder engine, turn the crankshaft one complete revolution and realign the timing marks. Measure the remaining valves **(see illustration)**.

8   On V6 engines, turn the crankshaft 2/3-turn (240 degrees), align the timing marks and measure the valve clearances shown **(see illustration)**. Turn the crankshaft a further 2/3-turn and measure the remaining valves **(see illustration)**.

9   After all the valve clearances have been measured, turn the crankshaft pulley until the camshaft lobe above the first valve which you intend to adjust is pointing upward, away from the shim.

10   Position the notch in the valve lifter

toward the spark plug. Then press down the valve lifter with the special valve lifter tool **(see illustration)**. Place the special valve lifter tool in position as shown, with the longer jaw of the tool gripping the lower edge of the cast lifter boss and the upper, shorter jaw gripping the upper edge of the lifter itself. Press down the valve lifter by squeezing the

35.10a Install the valve lifter tool as shown and squeeze the handles together to lower the valve lifter so the shim can be removed

handles of the valve lifter tool together and remove the adjusting shim with a small screwdriver or a pair of tweezers **(see illustration)**. Note that the wire hook on the end of one valve lifter tool handle can be used to clamp both handles together to keep the lifter depressed while the shim is removed.

35.10b Remove the shim with a small screwdriver, a pair of tweezers or a magnet

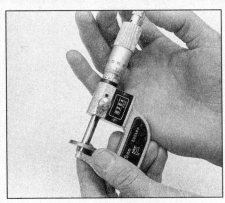

35.11 Measure the shim thickness with a micrometer

11   Measure the thickness of the shim with a micrometer **(see illustration)**. To calculate the correct thickness of a replacement shim that will place the valve clearance within the specified value, use the following formula:

Four cylinder engine

Intake: N = T + (A-0.24 mm[0/009 inch])
Exhaust: N + T + (A-0.33 mm [0.013 inch])

V6 engine

Intake: N = T + (A-0.18 mm [0.007 inch])
Exhaust: N + T + (A-0.32 mm [0.013 inch])

T = Thickness of original shim
A = Measured value clearance
N = Thickness of new shim

12   Select a shim with a thickness as close as possible to the valve clearance calculated. Shims, which are available in 17 sizes in increments of 0.050 mm (0.0020 in), range in size from 2.500 mm (0.0984 in) to 3.300 mm (0.1299 in). **Note**: *Through careful analysis of the shim sizes needed to bring all the out-of-specification valve clearances within specification, it is often possible to simply move a shim that has to come out anyway to another valve lifter requiring a shim of that particular size, thereby reducing the number of new shims that must be purchased.*

13   Place the special valve lifter tool in position as shown in illustration 35.10a, with the longer jaw of the tool gripping the lower edge of the cast lifter boss and the upper, shorter jaw gripping the upper edge of the lifter itself, press down the valve lifter by squeezing the handles of the valve lifter tool together and install the new adjusting shim (note that the

wire hook on the end of one valve lifter tool hand can be used to clamp the handles together to keep the lifter depressed while the shim is inserted). Measure the clearance with a feeler gauge to make sure that your calculations are correct.

14   Repeat this procedure until all the valves which are out of clearance have been corrected.

15   Installation of the spark plugs, cylinder head cover(s), center cover, spark plug wires and boots, accelerator cable bracket, etc. is the reverse of removal.

36 Fuel tank cap gasket replacement

1   Obtain a new gasket.
2   Remove the tank cap and carefully pry the old gasket out of the recess. Be very careful not to damage the sealing surface inside the cap.
3   Work the new gasket into the cap recess.
4   Install the cap, then remove it and make sure the gasket seals all the way around.

Notes

Chapter 2 Part A
Four-cylinder engines

Contents

Specifications

General

Engine type
- 2S-E ... SOHC, two valves per cylinder
- 3S-FE ... DOHC, four valves per cylinder

Cylinder numbers (drivebelt end-to-transaxle end) ... 1-2-3-4
Firing order ... 1-3-4-2

The blackened terminal shown on the distributor cap indicates the Number One spark plug wire position

FRONT — 2S-E engine

FRONT — 3S-FE engine
Cylinder location and distributor rotation

Warpage limits

Cylinder head-to-block surface	0.020 in (0.50 mm)
Intake and exhaust manifolds	0.012 in (0.30 mm)
Cylinder head camshaft housing surface (2S-E engine only)	0.002 in (0.05 mm)
Camshaft housing warpage limit (2S-E engine only)	0.0031 in (0.08 mm)

Timing belt

Idler pulley spring tension
- 2S-E engine (at 51 mm) ... 16 to 19 lbs
- 3S-FE engine (at 46.1 mm) ... 13.2 to 15.4 lbs

Idler pulley spring free length
- 2S-E engine ... 2.01 in (51 mm)
- 3S-FE engine ... 1.815 in (46.1 mm)

Camshaft thrust clearance (end play)

2S-E engine
- Standard ... 0.0031 to 0.0091 in (0.08 to 0.23 mm)
- Service limit ... 0.0138 in (0.35 mm)

3S-FE engine
- Intake camshaft
  - Standard ... 0.0018 to 0.0039 in (0.045 to 0.100 mm)
  - Service limit ... 0.0047 in (0.12 mm)
- Exhaust camshaft
  - Standard ... 0.0012 to 0.0033 in (0.030 to 0.084 mm)
  - Service limit ... 0.0039 in (0.10 mm)

Camshaft

Journal diameter
- 2S-E engine
  - No.1 ... 1.8291 to 1.8297 in (46.459 to 46.475 mm)
  - No.2 ... 1.8192 to 1.8199 in (46.209 to 46.225 mm)
  - No.3 ... 1.8094 to 1.8100 in (45.959 to 45.975 mm)

Camshaft (continued)

2S-E engine
No.4 .... 1.7996 to 1.8002 in (45.709 to 45.729 mm)
No.5 .... 1.7897 to 1.7904 in (45.459 to 45.475 mm)
No.6 .... 1.7799 to 1.7805 in (45.209 to 45.225 mm)
S-FE engine (all journals) .... 1.0614 to 1.0620 in (26.959 to 26.975 mm)
Bearing oil clearance
2S-E engine
Standard .... 0.0010 to 0.0026 in (0.025 to 0.067 mm)
Service limit... 0.0039 in (0.10 mm)
3S-FE engine
Standard .... 0.0010 to 0.0024 in (0.025 to 0.062 mm)
Service limit... 0.0039 in (0.10 mm)
Runout limit .... 0.016 in (0.40 mm)
Lobe height
2S-E engine
Standard .... 1.5325 to 1.5365 in (38.926 to 39.026 mm)
Service limit... 1.5268 in (38.78 mm)
3S-FE engine
Intake camshaft
Standard .... 1.3744 to 1.3783 in (34.910 to 35.010 mm)
Service limit... 1.3701 in (34.80 mm)
Exhaust camshaft
Standard .... 1.4000 to 1.4039 in (35.560 to 35.660 mm)
Service limit.. 1.3957 in (35.45 mm)
Camshaft gear spring free length (3S-FE engine only)............................ 0.886 to 0.902 in (22.5 to 22.9 mm
Camshaft gear backlash (3S-FE engine only)
Standard .... 0.0008 to 0.0079 in (0.020 to 0.200 mm)
Service limit.. 0.0188 in (0.30 mm)
Valve lifter (3S-FE engine only)
Diameter .... 1.1014 to 1.1018 in (27.975 to 27.985 mm)
Bore diameter.. 1.1024 to 1.1032 in (28.000 to 28.021 mm)
Lifter oil clearance
Standard .... 0.0005 to 0.0018 in (0.015 to 0.046 mm)
Service limit... 0.0028 in (0.07 mm)

Oil pump

Driven rotor-to-case clearance
1983 through 1985 .... 0.0039 to 0.0067 in (0.10 to 0.17 mm)
1986 on .... 0.0039 to 0.0063 in (0.10 to 0.16 mm)
Rotor tip clearance .... 0.0016 to 0.0063 in (0.04 to 0.16 mm)
Wear limit .... 0.0079 in (0.20 mm)

Torque specifications

Ft-lbs (unless otherwise indicated)

Intake manifold
2S-E engine.. 31
3S-FE engine.. 14
Intake manifold brace
12 mm bolt 14
14 mm bolt 31
Exhaust manifold 31
Crankshaft pulley-to-crankshaft bolt
1983 .... 73 to 86
1984 on 80
Flywheel/driveplate bolts
1983 through 1985.. 72
1986 on ....
Flywheel 72
Driveplate... 61
Idler pulley bolts
1983 .... 26 to 36
1984 on 31
Cylinder head bolts
1983 .... 44 to 50
1984 on 47
Camshaft housing-to-head bolts (2S-E engine only) .... 9 to 13
Camshaft bearing cap bolts (3S-FE engine only) 14
Camshaft cover nuts
2S-E engine.. 11
3S-FE engine.. 13
Camshaft pulley bolt... 40

Oil pump bolts

1983	65 to 100 in-lbs
1984 on	82 in-lbs

Oil pump pulley nut ... 20

Oil pick-up (strainer) nuts/bolts

1983	35 to 60 in-lbs
1984 on	48 in-lbs

Oil pan-to-block bolts

1983	35 to 60 in-lbs
1984 on	48 in-lbs

Rear crankshaft oil seal retainer bolts ... 75 in-lbs

1 General information

This Part of Chapter 2 is devoted to in-vehicle repair procedures for the four-cylinder engines. All information concerning engine removal and installation and engine block and cylinder head overhaul can be found in Part C of this Chapter.

The following repair procedures are based on the assumption that the engine is installed in the vehicle. If the engine has been removed from the vehicle and mounted on a stand, many of the Steps outlined in this Part of Chapter 2 will not apply.

The Specifications included in this Part of Chapter 2 apply only to the procedures contained in this Part. Part C of Chapter 2 contains the Specifications necessary for cylinder head and engine block rebuilding.

Two different four-cylinder gasoline engines were installed in the Camry during the years covered by this manual. The single overhead camshaft (SOHC), two valve per cylinder engine is designated the 2S-E by Toyota. The dual overhead camshaft (DOHC), four valve per cylinder engine is designated the 3S-FE.

2 Repair operations possible with the engine in the vehicle

Many major repair operations can be accomplished without removing the engine from the vehicle.

Clean the engine compartment and the exterior of the engine with some type of degreaser before any work is done. It will make the job easier and help keep dirt out of the internal areas of the engine.

Depending on the components involved, it may be helpful to remove the hood to improve access to the engine as repairs are performed (refer to Chapter 11 if necessary). Cover the fenders to prevent damage to the paint. Special pads are available, but an old bedspread or blanket will also work.

If vacuum, exhaust, oil or coolant leaks develop, indicating a need for gasket or seal replacement, the repairs can generally be made with the engine in the vehicle. The intake and exhaust manifold gaskets, oil pan gasket, crankshaft oil seals and cylinder head gasket are all accessible with the engine in place.

Exterior engine components, such as the intake and exhaust manifolds, the oil pan, the oil pump, the water pump, the starter motor, the alternator, the distributor and the fuel system components can be removed for repair with the engine in place.

Since the cylinder head can be removed without pulling the engine, camshaft and valve component servicing can also be accomplished with the engine in the vehicle. Replacement of the timing belt and pulleys is also possible with the engine in the vehicle.

In extreme cases caused by a lack of necessary equipment, repair or replacement of piston rings, pistons, connecting rods and rod bearings is possible with the engine in the vehicle. However, this practice is not recommended because of the cleaning and preparation work that must be done to the components involved.

3 Top Dead Center (TDC) for number one piston - locating

Refer to illustration 3.8

Note: *The following procedure is based on the assumption that the distributor is correctly installed. If you are trying to locate TDC to install the distributor correctly, piston position must be determined by feeling for compression at the number one spark plug hole, then aligning the ignition timing marks as described in Step 8.*

1 Top Dead Center (TDC) is the highest point in the cylinder that each piston reaches as it travels up-and-down when the crankshaft turns. Each piston reaches TDC on the compression stroke and again on the exhaust stroke, but TDC generally refers to piston position on the compression stroke.

2 Positioning the piston(s) at TDC is an essential part of many procedures such as camshaft and timing belt/pulley removal and distributor removal.

3 Before beginning this procedure, be sure to place the transmission in Neutral and apply the parking brake or block the rear wheels. Also, disable the ignition system by detaching the coil wire from the center terminal of the distributor cap and grounding it on the block with a jumper wire. Remove the spark plugs (see Chapter 1).

4 In order to bring any piston to TDC, the crankshaft must be turned using one of the methods outlined below. When looking at the front of the engine, normal crankshaft rotation is **clockwise**.

a) *The preferred method is to turn the crankshaft with a socket and ratchet attached to the bolt threaded into the front of the crankshaft.*

b) *A remote starter switch, which may save some time, can also be used. Follow the instructions included with the switch. Once the piston is close to TDC, use a socket and ratchet as described in the previous paragraph.*

c) *If an assistant is available to turn the ignition switch to the Start position in short bursts, you can get the piston close to TDC without a remote starter switch. Make sure your assistant is out of the vehicle, away from the ignition switch, then use a socket and ratchet as described in Paragraph a) to complete the procedure.*

5 Note the position of the terminal for the number one spark plug wire on the distributor cap. If the terminal isn't marked, follow the plug wire from the number one cylinder spark plug to the cap.

6 Use a felt-tip pen or chalk to make a mark on the distributor body directly under the terminal.

7 Detach the cap from the distributor and set it aside (see Chapter 1 if necessary).

8 Turn the crankshaft (see Paragraph 3 above) until the notch in the crankshaft pulley is aligned with the 0 on the timing plate (located at the front of the engine) **(see illustration)**.

9 Look at the distributor rotor - it should be pointing directly at the mark you made on the distributor body.

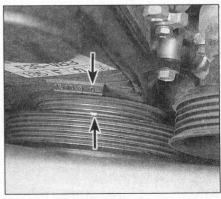

3.8 Align the crankshaft drivebelt pulley notch (arrow) with the 0 (zero) on the timing plate (3S-FE engine shown, 2S-E similar)

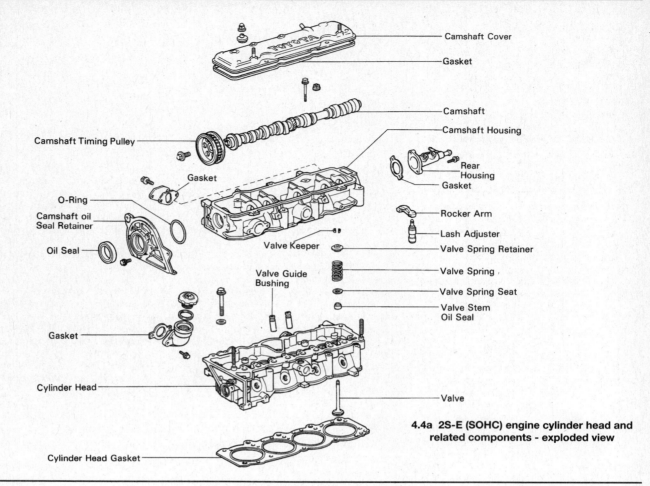

4.4a 2S-E (SOHC) engine cylinder head and related components - exploded view

10　If the rotor is 180-degrees off, the number one piston is at TDC on the exhaust stroke.

11　To get the piston to TDC on the compression stroke, turn the crankshaft one complete turn (360-degrees) clockwise. The rotor should now be pointing at the mark on the distributor. When the rotor is pointing at the number one spark plug wire terminal in the distributor cap and the ignition timing marks are aligned, the number one piston is at TDC on the compression stroke. **Note:** *If it's impossible to align the ignition timing marks when the rotor is pointing at the mark on the distributor body, the timing belt may have jumped the teeth on the pulleys or may have been installed incorrectly.*

12　After the number one piston has been positioned at TDC on the compression stroke, TDC for any of the remaining pistons can be located by turning the crankshaft and following the firing order. Mark the remaining spark plug wire terminal locations on the distributor body just like you did for the number one terminal, then number the marks to correspond with the cylinder numbers. As you turn the crankshaft, the rotor will also turn. When it's pointing directly at one of the marks on the distributor, the piston for that particular cylinder is at TDC on the compression stroke.

4　Camshaft cover - removal and installation

Refer to illustrations 4.4a, 4.4b, 4.4c, 4.6a and 4.6b

1　Disconnect the negative cable from the battery.

2　Detach the breather hose from the camshaft cover.

3　If you're working on a 3S-FE engine, remove the spark plug wires from the spark plugs.

4　Remove the mounting nuts and sealing washers, then detach the cover and gasket from the head. On the 3S-FE engine, the spark plug tube nuts are used to hold the cover in place **(see illustrations)**. If the cover is stuck to the head, bump the end with a block of wood and a hammer to jar it loose. If that doesn't work, try to slip a flexible putty knife between the head and cover to break the seal. **Caution:** *Don't pry at the cover-to-head joint or damage to the sealing surfaces may occur, leading to oil leaks after the cover is reinstalled.*

5　The mating surfaces of the housing or cylinder head and cover must be clean when the cover is installed. Use a gasket scraper to remove all traces of sealant and old gasket material, then clean the mating surfaces with lacquer thinner or acetone. If there's residue or oil on the mating surfaces when the cover is installed, oil leaks may develop.

6　If you're working on a 3S-FE engine, apply a thin, uniform layer of sealant to the gasket/seal joints **(see illustration)**. Install the spark plug tube grommets with the index marks facing the timing belt end of the engine **(see illustration)**.

7　Position a new gasket and seals (if used) on the cylinder head, then install the camshaft cover, sealing washers and nuts.

8　Tighten the nuts to the specified torque in three or four equal steps.

9　Reinstall the remaining parts, run the engine and check for oil leaks.

5　Intake manifold - removal and installation

Refer to illustrations 5.4a, 5.4b, 5.5 and 5.8

1　Disconnect the negative cable from the battery.

2　Drain the cooling system (see Chapter 1).

3　Remove the throttle body, fuel injectors and fuel rail (see Chapter 4).

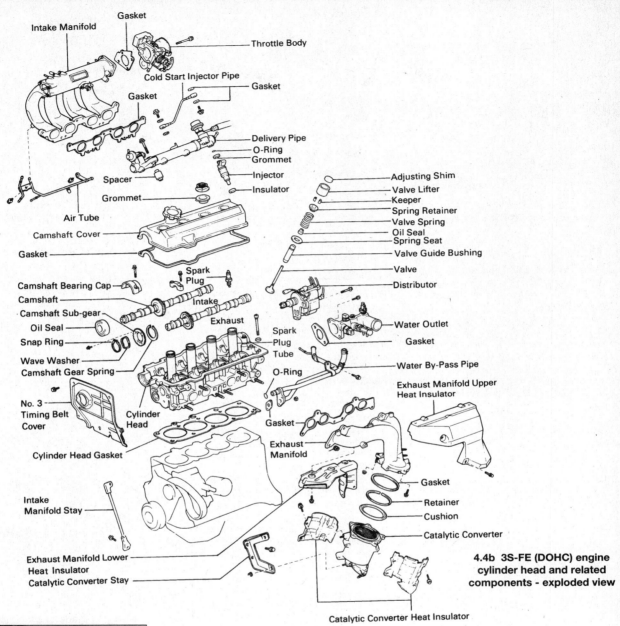

Intake Manifold
Gasket
Throttle Body
Cold Start Injector Pipe
Gasket
Gasket
Delivery Pipe
O-Ring
Grommet
Injector
Insulator
Spacer
Grommet
Air Tube
Camshaft Cover
Gasket
Spark Plug
Camshaft Bearing Cap
Camshaft
Intake
Camshaft Sub-gear
Oil Seal
Exhaust
Snap Ring
Wave Washer
Camshaft Gear Spring
No. 3 Timing Belt Cover
Cylinder Head
Cylinder Head Gasket
Intake Manifold Stay
Exhaust Manifold Lower Heat Insulator
Catalytic Converter Stay

Adjusting Shim
Valve Lifter
Keeper
Spring Retainer
Valve Spring
Oil Seal
Spring Seat
Valve Guide Bushing
Valve
Distributor
Water Outlet
Gasket
Spark Plug Tube
O-Ring
Water By-Pass Pipe
Exhaust Manifold Upper Heat Insulator
Gasket
Exhaust Manifold
Gasket
Retainer
Cushion
Catalytic Converter

4.4b 3S-FE (DOHC) engine cylinder head and related components - exploded view

Catalytic Converter Heat Insulator

4.4c On the 3S-FE engine. the camshaft cover is held in place by the large spark plug tube nuts (arrows)

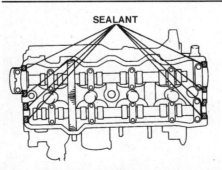

SEALANT

4.6a On the 3S-FE engine, apply sealant to the eight points indicated by the shaded areas before installing the camshaft cover

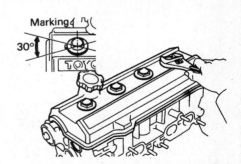

Marking
30°

4.6b Install the spark plug tube seals with the index marks facing the timing belt end of the engine (3S-FE engine)

5.4a The various hoses should be marked with paint to ensure correct reinstallation

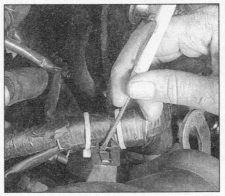

5.4b Press in on the clips to release the wiring harness retainers

5.5 Lift the wiring harness over the intake manifold (3S-FE engine)

4   Label and detach all wire harnesses, control cables and hoses still connected to the intake manifold **(see illustrations)**.

5   If you're working on a 3S-FE engine, carefully lift the wire harness over the manifold **(see illustration)**.

6   Unbolt any braces still in place.

7   Remove the eight mounting nuts/bolts, then detach the manifold from the engine.

8   Use a scraper to remove all traces of old gasket material and sealant from the manifold and cylinder head **(see illustration)**, then clean the mating surfaces with lacquer thinner or acetone. If the gasket was leaking, have the manifold checked for warpage at an automotive machine shop and resurfaced if necessary.

9   Install a new gasket, then position the manifold on the head and install the nuts/bolts.

10   Tighten the nuts/bolts in three or four equal steps to the specified torque. Work from the center out towards the ends to avoid warping the manifold.

11   Install the remaining parts in the reverse order of removal.

12   Before starting the engine, check the throttle linkage for smooth operation.

13   Run the engine and check for coolant and vacuum leaks.

14   Road test the vehicle and check for

proper operation of all accessories, including the cruise control system.

6   Exhaust manifold - removal and installation

Refer to illustrations 6.3, 6.6 and 6.8

Warning: *The engine must be completely cool before beginning this procedure.*

1   Disconnect the negative cable from the battery.

2   Unplug the oxygen sensor wire harness. If you're installing a new manifold, remove the sensor (see Chapter 6).

3   Remove the upper heat insulator from the manifold **(see illustration)**.

4   Apply penetrating oil to the exhaust manifold mounting nuts/bolts.

5   Disconnect the catalytic converter (3S-FE engine) or exhaust pipe (2S-E engine) from the exhaust manifold (see Chapter 4).

6   Remove the nuts/bolts and detach the manifold and gasket **(see illustration)**.

7   Use a scraper to remove all traces of old gasket material and carbon deposits from the manifold and cylinder head mating surfaces. If the gasket was leaking, have the manifold checked for warpage at an automotive machine shop and resurfaced if necessary.

8   Position a new gasket over the cylinder

head studs. **Note:** *The marks on the gasket should face out (away from the head) and the arrow should point toward the rear (transaxle end) of the engine* **(see illustration)**.

9   Install the manifold and thread the mounting nuts/bolts into place.

10   Working from the center out, tighten the nuts/bolts to the specified torque in three or four equal steps.

11   Reinstall the remaining parts in the reverse order of removal.

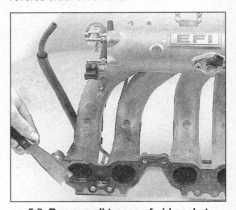

5.8 Remove all traces of old gasket material and sealant with a scraper - be careful not to gouge the manifold; itÕs made of aluminum

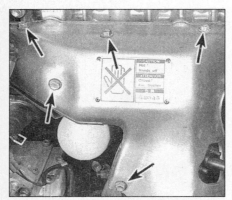

6.3 Remove the 3S-FE engine exhaust manifold heat insulator bolts (arrows)

6.6 Remove the oil filter to access the two nuts (arrows) above the oil filter boss (3S-FE engine shown)

6.8 Be sure the marks on the exhaust manifold gasket face out - the arrow must point toward the rear (transaxle end) of the engine

12   Run the engine and check for exhaust leaks.

7   Timing belt - removal, inspection and installation

Removal

Refer to illustrations 7.9a, 7.9b, 7.10a, 7.10b, 7.11a, 7.11b, 7.12, 7.13, 7.14, 7.15a, 7.15b, 7.16, 7.17, 7.18a and 7.18b

1   Disconnect the negative cable from the battery.
2   Block the rear wheels and set the parking brake.

3   Loosen the lug nuts on the right front wheel and raise the vehicle. Support the front of the vehicle securely on jackstands.
4   Remove the right front wheel and fender apron seal (see Chapter 11).
5   Remove the spark plugs and drivebelts (see Chapter 1).
6   Remove the alternator and bracket (see Chapter 5).
7   Unbolt the power steering reservoir and cruise control actuator (if equipped) and set them aside.
8   Support the engine and remove the right engine mount (see Section 18). **Note:** *If you're planning on removing the oil pan, in addition to the timing belt, support the engine*

with a hoist from above (see Chapter 2C - engine removal).
9   Remove the upper (no. 2) timing belt cover and gaskets **(see illustrations)**.
10   If you're working on a 2S-E (SOHC) engine, turn the crankshaft clockwise until the groove in the crankshaft pulley is aligned with the preset mark on the lower timing belt cover **(see illustration)**. This corresponds to 90-degrees BTDC on the number one piston compression stroke. Check to be sure the center of the small hole in the camshaft pulley is aligned with the preset mark on the camshaft oil seal retainer **(see illustration)**.
11   If you're working on a 3S-FE (DOHC) engine, position the number one piston at

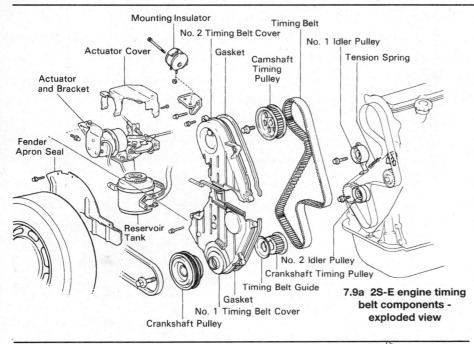

7.9a 2S-E engine timing belt components - exploded view

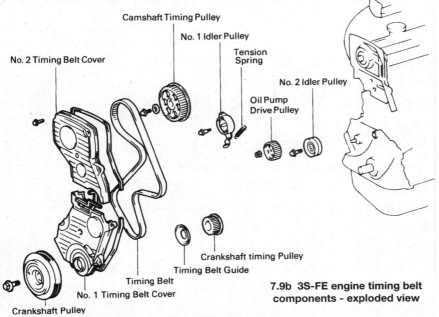

7.9b 3S-FE engine timing belt components - exploded view

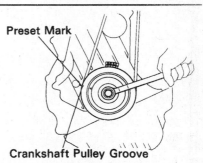

7.10a On the 2S-E engine, align the crankshaft pulley groove with the preset mark . . .

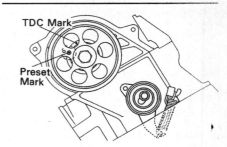

7.10b . . . and the preset mark on the oil seal retainer should be visible through the inspection hole in the camshaft pulley

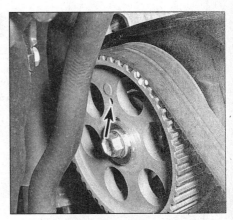

7.11a On 3S-FE models. rotate the crankshaft until the hole in the camshaft pulley (arrow) is at the top . . .

7.11b . . . and use a mirror to look into the hole to check for alignment of the bearing cap mark

7.12 If you intend to reuse the timing belt, paint match marks on the pulley and belt (arrow)

7.13 Loosen the upper idler pulley set bolt (arrow) and push the pulley down, against spring tension, to release the belt (note the arrow, indicating direction of belt travel)

TDC on the compression stroke (see Section 3). Make sure the small hole in the camshaft pulley is aligned with the TDC mark on the cam bearing cap **(see illustrations)**.

12   If you plan to reuse the timing belt, paint match marks on the pulley and belt and an arrow indicating direction of travel on the belt **(see illustration)**.

13   Loosen the upper (no. 1) idler pulley set bolt **(see illustration)** and push the pulley down (against spring tension) as far as it will go, then temporarily tighten it. Slip the timing belt off the pulley. If you're removing the belt for camshaft seal replacement or cylinder head removal, it isn't necessary to detach the belt from the crankshaft pulley.

14   If the camshaft pulley is worn or damaged, remove the camshaft cover, hold the rear (intake) camshaft with a large wrench and remove the bolt, then detach the pulley **(see illustration)**.

15   To proceed with timing belt removal, keep the crankshaft (accessory drivebelt) pulley from turning with a large Phillips screwdriver and a pry bar **(see illustration)**, remove the bolt and detach the pulley with a vibration damper puller **(see illustration)**. Do not use a gear puller! Sometimes the pulley can be removed by hand.

16   Remove the lower (no. 1) timing belt cover and gaskets **(see illustration)** and slip the belt guide off the crankshaft.

17   If you plan to reuse the timing belt, paint match marks on the pulley and belt **(see illustration)**.

7.15a Insert a Phillips screwdriver into one of the pulley holes, place a socket and breaker bar over the bolt head, wedge a screwdriver between the tools and loosen the crankshaft bolt - DO NOT use the timing belt tension to keep the pulley from turning!

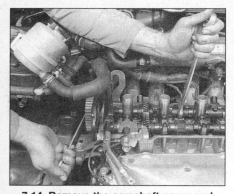

7.14 Remove the camshaft cover and hold the camshaft with a large wrench on the raised hex as the pulley bolt is loosened - DO NOT use the timing belt tension to keep the pulley from turning!

7.15b Use a puller that applies force to the hub only - don't use a gear puller to remove the pulley

7.16 Remove the lower timing belt cover bolts (arrows) and slip the cover and gaskets off the engine (3S-FE shown, 2S-E similar)

7.17 If you plan to reuse the timing belt, paint match marks (arrow) on the belt and pulleys

7.18a The pulley should slide off the crankshaft quite easily

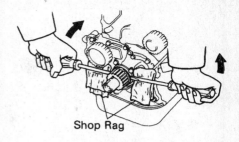

Shop Rag

7.18b If the crankshaft pulley is stuck, protect the oil pump case with rags and pry the pulley off with two screwdrivers

18 Slip the timing belt off the pulley and remove it. If the pulley is worn or damaged, or if you need to get at the front crankshaft oil seal, remove the pulley from the crankshaft **(see illustrations)**.

Inspection

Refer to illustrations 7.19, 7.21, 7.22 and 7.23
Caution: *Do not bend, twist or turn the timing belt inside out. Do not allow it to come in contact with oil, coolant or fuel. Do not utilize timing belt tension to keep the camshaft or crankshaft from turning when installing the pulley bolt(s). Do not turn the crankshaft or camshaft more than a few degrees (necessary for tooth alignment) while the timing belt is removed.*

19 Remove the idler pulleys and check the bearings for smooth operation and excessive play. Inspect the spring for damage and compare the free length to the Specifications **(see illustration)**.

20 If the timing belt broke during engine operation, the belt may have been contaminated or overtightened.

21 If the belt teeth are cracked or pulled off **(see illustration)**, the distributor, water pump, oil pump or camshaft(s) may have seized.

22 If there is noticeable wear or cracks in the belt, check to see if there are nicks or burrs on the pulleys **(see illustration)**.

23 If there is wear or damage on only one side of the belt, check the belt guide and the alignment of all pulleys **(see illustration)**.

24 Replace the timing belt with a new one if obvious wear or damage is noted or if it is the least bit questionable. Correct any problems which contributed to belt failure prior to belt installation.

Installation

Refer to illustrations 7.29, 7.30, 7.35a and 7.35b

25 Remove all dirt and oil from the timing belt area at the front of the engine.

26 If they were removed, install the idler pulleys and tension spring. The upper (no. 1) idler should be pulled back against spring

tension as far as possible and the bolt temporarily tightened.

27 Recheck the camshaft and crankshaft timing marks to be sure they are properly aligned (see Step 10 or 11).

28 Install the timing belt on the crankshaft, oil pump, water pump and idler pulleys. If the original belt is being reinstalled, align the marks made during removal.

29 Slip the belt guide onto the crankshaft with the cupped side facing out **(see illustration)**.

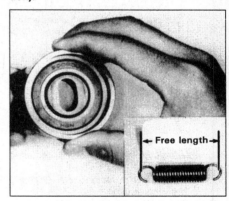

← Free length →

7.19 Check the idler pulley bearing for smooth operation and measure the free length of the tension spring for comparison to the Specifications

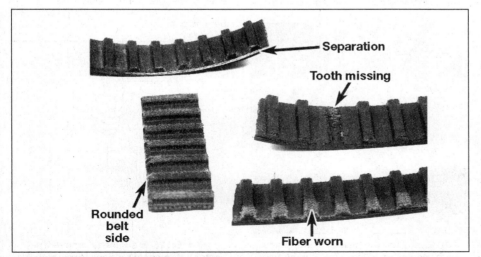

Separation

Tooth missing

Rounded belt side

Fiber worn

7.21 Check the timing belt for cracked and missing teeth. If the belt is cracked or worn, check the pulleys for nicks and burrs. Check the timing belt(s) for the conditions shown and replace as necessary.

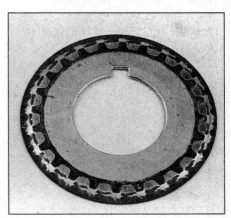

7.29 The belt guide should be installed with the tooth marks in contact with the timing belt and the cupped side out

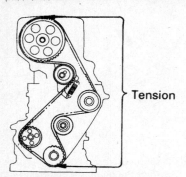

7.30 **There should be moderate tension on the side of the belt facing the front of the vehicle**

30   Slip the timing belt over the camshaft pulley. Keep tension on the side nearest the front of the vehicle **(see illustration)**. If the original belt is being reinstalled, align the marks made during removal.
31   Loosen the upper (no. 1) idler pulley bolt 1/2-turn, allowing the spring to apply pressure to the idler pulley.
32   On 2S-E engines only, turn the crankshaft clockwise 1/4-turn (90-degrees) to TDC, then tighten the upper (no. 1) idler pulley mounting bolt to the specified torque.
33   On all models, slowly turn the crankshaft clockwise two complete revolutions (720-degrees).
34   On 3S-FE engines, tighten the idler pulley mounting bolt to the specified torque.
35   Recheck the timing marks **(see illustrations)**. If the marks are not aligned exactly as shown, repeat the belt installation procedure. **Caution:** *DO NOT start the engine until you're absolutely certain that the timing belt is installed correctly. Serious and costly engine damage could occur if the belt is installed wrong.*
36   Reinstall the remaining parts in the reverse order of removal.
37   Run the engine and check for proper operation.

8.2 **Wrap tape around a screwdriver tip and carefully work the crankshaft front oil seal out of the bore - DO NOT nick or scratch the crankshaft!**

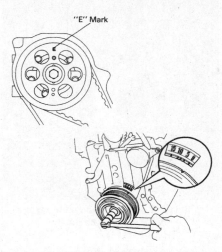

"E" Mark

7.35a **Correct valve timing mark alignment - 2S-E engine**

8   Front crankshaft oil seal - replacement

Refer to illustrations 8.2 and 8.4
1   Remove the timing belt and crankshaft pulley (see Section 7).
2   Note how far the seal is seated in the bore, then carefully pry it out of the oil pump housing with a screwdriver or seal removal tool **(see illustration)**. Don't scratch the housing bore or damage the crankshaft in the process (if the crankshaft is damaged, the new seal will end up leaking).
3   Clean the bore in the housing and coat the outer edge of the new seal with engine oil or multi-purpose grease. Apply moly-base grease to the seal lip.
4   Using a socket with an outside diameter slightly smaller than the outside diameter of the seal, carefully drive the new seal into place with a hammer **(see illustration)**. Make sure it's installed squarely and driven in to the

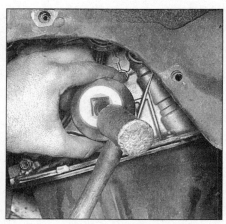

8.4 **Gently tap the new seal into place with the spring side toward the engine**

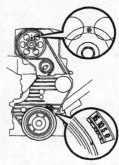

7.35b **On 3S-FE engines, the marks should align as shown at Top Dead Center**

same depth as the original. If a socket isn't available, a short section of large diameter pipe will also work. Check the seal after installation to make sure the garter spring didn't pop out of place.
5   Reinstall the crankshaft pulley and timing belt (see Section 7).
6   Run the engine and check for oil leaks at the front seal.

9   Camshaft oil seal - replacement

1   Remove the timing belt and camshaft pulley (see Section 7).

2S-E engine

Refer to illustrations 9.3 and 9.7
2   Remove the bolts and detach the camshaft oil seal retainer and O-ring from the head **(see illustration 4.4a)**.
3   Support the retainer on two blocks of wood and drive the old seal out from the back side **(see illustration)**.
4   Clean the retainer and cylinder head mating surfaces and the seal bore with lacquer thinner or acetone.
5   Coat the outer edge of the new seal with engine oil or multi-purpose grease.
6   Support the retainer as close to the seal bore as possible.

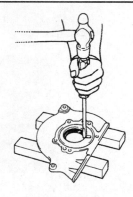

9.3 **On 2S-E engines, remove the camshaft oil seal retainer from the head and drive the old seal out from the back side**

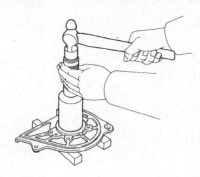

9.7 Tap the new seal into place with a large socket or piece of pipe and a hammer

9.12 On 3S-FE engines, carefully pry the camshaft seal out of the bore - DO NOT nick or scratch the camshaft journal

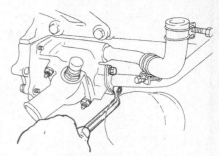

10.3 Disconnect the heater tube at the rear end housing (2S-E engine)

7   Using a socket with an outside diameter slightly smaller than the outside diameter of the seal, carefully drive the new seal into place with a hammer **(see illustration)**. Make sure it's installed squarely and check it after installation to make sure the garter spring didn't pop out of place. If a socket isn't available, a short section of large diameter pipe will also work.

8   Clean the bolt threads and apply sealant to the first three threads. Apply molybase grease to the seal lip.

9   Install a new O-ring, then position the retainer on the head and install the bolts. Tighten the bolts in a criss-cross pattern to the specified torque.

10   Proceed to Step 15.

3S-FE engine

Refer to illustration 9.12

11   Unbolt the upper timing belt rear cover.

12   Note how far the seal is seated in the bore, then carefully pry it out with a small screwdriver **(see illustration)**. Don't scratch the bore or damage the camshaft in the process (if the camshaft is damaged, the new seal will end up leaking).

13   Clean the bore and coat the outer edge of the new seal with engine oil or multi-purpose grease. Apply moly-base grease to the seal lip.

14   Using a socket with an outside diameter slightly smaller than the outside diameter of the seal, carefully drive the new seal into place with a hammer. Make sure it's installed

squarely and driven in to the same depth as the original. If a socket isn't available, a short section of pipe will also work.

Both engines

15   Reinstall the camshaft pulley and timing belt (see Section 7).

16   Run the engine and check for oil leaks at the camshaft seal.

10 Camshaft, rocker arms and lash adjusters - removal, inspection and installation (2S-E engine only)

Removal

Refer to illustrations 10.3, 10.7 and 10.8

1   Remove the negative cable from the battery and detach the air cleaner inlet duct.

2   Drain the cooling system (see Chapter 1).

3   Label and disconnect all hoses wires, linkages, tubes and brackets attached to the camshaft housing **(see illustration)**.

4   Unbolt and remove the rear end housing **(see illustration 4.4a)**.

5   Remove the timing belt and the camshaft pulley (see Section 7).

6   Remove the camshaft cover (see Section 4).

7   Remove the camshaft housing by loos-

ening each bolt a little at a time in the sequence shown **(see illustration)**.

8   With the camshaft still in the housing, use a dial indicator to check the end play. Attach the gauge to the end of the housing and move the camshaft all the way to the rear. Next, use a screwdriver to pry it all the way forward. If the end play exceeds the specified limit, replace the camshaft and/or the housing **(see illustration)**.

9   Remove the camshaft from the housing after detaching the camshaft oil seal retainer **(see illustration 4.4a)**.

10   Use a small screwdriver to pry the O-ring out of the retainer.

11   While turning the camshaft, slowly pull it out, being careful not to damage the bearings in the housing.

12   Remove the rocker arms by lifting them off the lash adjusters.

13   The lash adjusters can then be withdrawn by pulling them out of the cylinder head **(see illustration 4.4a)**. Keep the rocker arms and lash adjusters in order during removal to ensure that they are reinstalled in their original locations.

Inspection

Refer to illustrations 10.14a, 10.14b, 10.15, 10.16, 10.18 and 10.20

14   Visually examine the camshaft journals and rocker arms. Check for score marks, pitting and evidence of overheating (blue, discolored areas) **(see illustrations)**. If wear is

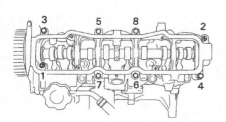

10.7 Camshaft housing bolt LOOSENING sequence (2S-E engine)

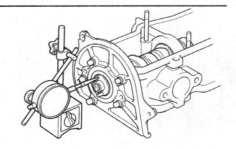

10.8 Mount a dial indicator as shown to measure camshaft end play

10.14a Check the cam lobes for pitting, wear and score marks - if scoring is excessive, as is the case here, replace the camshaft

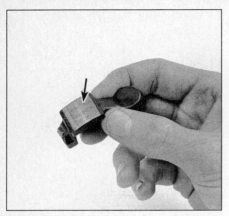

10.14b Check the rocker arm pads for wear and damage as well

10.15 Measure the lobe heights on each camshaft - if any lobe height is less than the specified allowable minimum, replace that camshaft

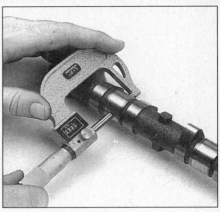

10.16 Measure each journal diameter with a micrometer (if any journal measures less than the specified limit, replace the camshaft)

10.18 Place each lash adjuster in a container of light oil, insert an appropriate size tool into the plunger hole and slide the plunger up-and-down several times

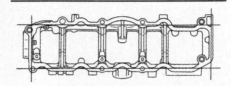

10.20 Using a straightedge and feeler gauges, check the camshaft housing surfaces for warpage and compare the results to the Specifications (2S-E engine)

excessive or damage is evident, the component will have to be replaced.

15   Using a micrometer, measure the cam lobe height and compare it to the Specifications. If the lobe height is less than the minimum allowable, the camshaft is worn and must be replaced **(see illustration)**.

16   Using a micrometer, measure the diameter of each journal and compare it to the Specifications **(see illustration)**. If the jour-

nals are worn or damaged, replace the camshaft.

17   Using an inside micrometer or a telescoping gauge, measure each housing bore. Subtract the journal diameter measurements from the housing bore measurements to determine the bearing oil clearance. Compare it to the Specifications. If the clearance is greater than the maximum, replace the camshaft and, if necessary, the housing.

18   Before being reinstalled, the lash adjusters must be bled. Immerse them, one at a time, in a container of light oil **(see illustration)**. Insert a pin punch into the plunger hole to depress the check valve and slide the plunger up-and-down several times while

pushing down lightly on the check ball.

19   Replace the lash adjuster with a new one if the plunger stroke exceeds 0.020-inch (0.5 mm) after bleeding. Do not disassemble the lash adjusters.

20   Check the camshaft housing for warpage. Using a precision straight-edge and feeler gauge, check the surface which contacts the cylinder head for warpage and compare it to the Specifications **(see illustration)**. If the warpage is greater than the maximum specified, replace the housing.

Installation

Refer to illustrations 10.22, 10.24 and 10.25

21   Installation is basically the reverse of the removal procedure. However, keep the following points in mind.

22   Apply engine assembly lube or moly-base grease to the camshaft lobes and journals **(see illustration)**. Also apply the same lubricant to the rocker arms and lash adjusters.

23   Insert the camshaft into the housing, then install a new O-ring and the oil seal retainer. The retainer bolts must have anaerobic sealer on the first two or three threads.

24   Before attaching the camshaft housing to the cylinder head, clean the mating surfaces with lacquer thinner or acetone, then apply a bead of sealer as shown **(see illustration)**.

10.22 Apply engine assembly lube or moly-base grease to the cam lobes and journals before installing the camshaft in the engine

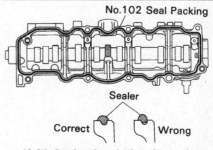

10.24 Apply a bead of sealer to the cylinder head side of the camshaft housing

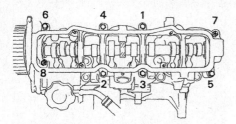

10.25 Camshaft housing bolt TIGHTENING sequence (2S-E engine)

11.6 Install a service bolt through the sub-gear, into the main gear (arrow)

25   Install the housing bolts and tighten them in three steps, in the sequence shown **(see illustration)**, to the specified torque.

---

11   Camshafts and valve lifters - removal, inspection and installation (3S-FE engine only)

Note: *Before beginning this procedure, obtain two 6 x 1.0 mm bolts 16 to 20 mm long. They will be referred to as service bolts in the text.*

Removal

Refer to illustrations 11.4, 11.5, 11.6, 11.11, 11.16, 11.17 and 11.18

1   Remove the camshaft cover as de-

11.17 Install a second service bolt in the unthreaded hole and rotate the sub-gear clockwise until the tension is released so the first bolt can be removed

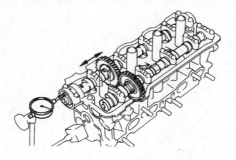

11.4 Position the dial indicator as shown, pry the camshaft back and forth with a screwdriver and note the end play (3S-FE engine)

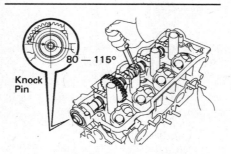

11.11 Turn the intake camshaft until the knock pin is 80- to 115-degrees to the left of vertical (12 o'clock position)

scribed in Section 4.
2   Remove the distributor (see Chapter 5).
3   Remove the timing belt and camshaft pulley (see Section 7).
4   Measure the camshaft thrust clearance (end play) with a dial indicator **(see illustration)**. If the clearance is greater than the specified maximum, replace the camshaft and/or the cylinder head.

Exhaust camshaft

5   Position the knock pin in the INTAKE camshaft at 10 to 45-degrees left of vertical **(see illustration)**. This will position the exhaust camshaft lobes so the camshaft will be pushed out evenly by the valve spring pressure.
6   Secure the exhaust camshaft sub-gear to the main gear with one of the service bolts **(see illustration)**.
7   Remove the rear (transaxle end) exhaust camshaft bearing cap bolts and detach the bearing cap.
8   Loosen the number 1, 2 and 4 exhaust camshaft bearing cap bolts in 1/4-turn increments until the bolts can be removed by hand. Lift off the first, second and fourth bearing caps. **Caution:** *DO NOT remove the center (no. 3) bearing cap bolts at this point!*
9   Finally, loosen the number 3 bearing cap bolts in 1/4-turn increments until they can be removed by hand, then detach the center (no. 3) cap. **Caution:** *As the center bearing cap bolts are being loosened, make sure the camshaft is moving up evenly. If one end or the other stops moving and the cam gets*

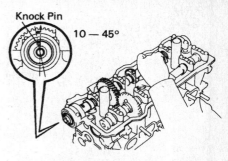

11.5 Turn the INTAKE camshaft until the knock pin is 10- to 45-degrees to the left of vertical (12 o'clock position)

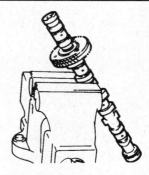

11.16 Grip the hex on the camshaft to hold it in the vise

cocked, start over by reinstalling the bearing caps and resetting the knock pin. DO NOT try to pry or force the camshaft out.
10   Lift the camshaft out of the head.

Intake camshaft

11   Position the knock pin in the intake camshaft at 80 to 115-degrees left of vertical **(see illustration)**.
12   Remove the front (timing belt end) intake camshaft bearing cap bolts and detach the bearing cap and oil seal. **Caution:** *Do not pry the cap off. If it doesn't come loose easily, leave it in place without bolts.*
13   Loosen the number 1, 3 and 4 intake camshaft bearing cap bolts in 1/4-turn increments until the bolts can be removed by hand. Lift off the first, third and fourth bearing caps. **Caution:** *DO NOT remove the center (no. 2) bearing cap bolts at this point!*
14   Finally, loosen the number 2 bearing cap bolts in 1/4-turn increments until they can be removed by hand, then detach the center (no. 2) cap. **Caution:** *As the center bearing cap bolts are being loosened, make sure the camshaft is moving up evenly. If one end or the other stops moving and the cam gets cocked, start over by reinstalling the bearing caps and resetting the knock pin. DO NOT try to pry or force the camshaft out.*
15   Lift the camshaft out of the head.
16   To disassemble the exhaust camshaft, mount it in a vise with the jaws gripping the large hex on the shaft **(see illustration)**.
17   Install a second service bolt in the

11.18 Remove the sub-gear snap-ring with a snap-ring pliers

11.22 Wipe off the oil and inspect each lifter for wear and scuffing

unthreaded hole in the camshaft sub-gear. Using a screwdriver positioned against the service bolt just installed, rotate the sub-gear clockwise and remove the first service bolt **(see illustration)**.

18   Remove the sub-gear snap-ring **(see illustration)**.

19   The wave washer, sub-gear and camshaft gear spring can now be removed from the camshaft **(see illustration 4.4b)**.

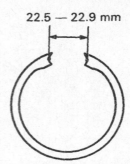

11.20 Measure the distance between the ends of the camshaft gear spring

22.5 — 22.9 mm

Inspection

Refer to illustrations 11.20, 11.21, 11.22, 11.23a, 11.23b, 11.28a, 11.28b and 11.30

20   Measure the free length (distance between the ends) of the camshaft gear spring **(see illustration)** and compare it to the Specifications.

21   Carefully label, then remove the valve lifters and shims **(see illustration)**.

22   Inspect each lifter for scuffing and score marks **(see illustration)**.

23   Measure the outside diameter of each lifter and the corresponding lifter bore inside diameter **(see illustrations)**. Subtract the lifter diameter from the lifter bore diameter to determine the oil clearance. Compare it to the Specifications. If the oil clearance is excessive, a new head and/or new lifters will be required.

24   Store the lifters in a clean box, separated from each other, so they won't be damaged. Make sure the shims stay with the lifters (don't mix them up).

25   Visually examine the cam lobes and bearing journals for score marks, pitting, galling and evidence of overheating (blue, discolored areas). Look for flaking away of the hardened surface layer of each lobe.

26   Using a micrometer, measure the height of each camshaft lobe **(see illustration 10.15)**. If the height for any one lobe is less than the specified minimum, replace the camshaft.

11.21 Wipe the oil off the valve shims and mark the intakes I and the exhausts E - a magnetic tool works well for re moving lifters

27   Using a micrometer, measure the diameter of each journal at several points **(see illustration 10.16)**. If the diameter of any one journal is less than specified, replace the camshaft.

28   Check the oil clearance for each camshaft journal as follows:

a) Clean the bearing caps and the camshaft journals with lacquer thinner or acetone.

b) Carefully lay the camshaft(s) in place in the head. Don't install the lifters and don't use any lubrication.

c) Lay a strip of Plastigage on each journal **(see illustration)**.

d) Install the bearing caps with the arrows pointing toward the front (timing belt end) of the engine.

e) Tighten the bolts to the specified torque in 1/4-turn increments. **Note:** *Don't turn the camshaft while the Plastigage is in place.*

f) Remove the bolts and detach the caps.

g) Compare the width of the crushed Plastigage (at its widest point) to the scale on the Plastigage envelope **(see illustration)**.

h) If the clearance is greater than specified, replace the camshaft and/or cylinder head.

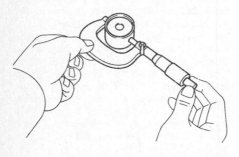

11.23a Use a micrometer to measure lifter diameter

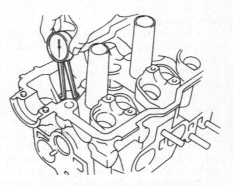

11.23b Use a telescoping gauge to measure the lifter bores

11.28a Lay a strip of Plastigage on each camshaft journal

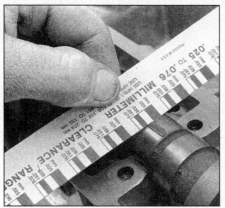

11.28b Compare the width of the crushed Plastigage to the scale on the envelope to determine the oil clearance

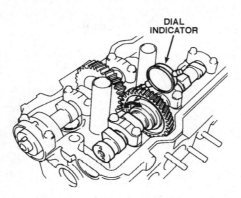

11.30 Position the dial indicator as shown here to measure gear backlash (free play) (3S-FE engine)

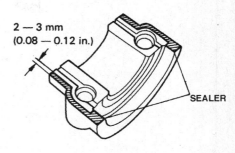

11.34 Apply sealer to the shaded areas of the front intake camshaft bearing cap (3S-FE engine)

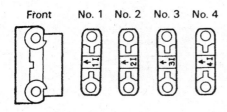

11.35 Intake camshaft bearing caps (3S-FE engine) - the arrows point toward the timing belt end of the engine

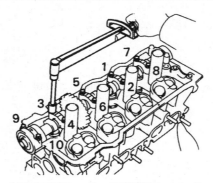

11.36 35-FE engine INTAKE camshaft bearing cap bolt tightening sequence

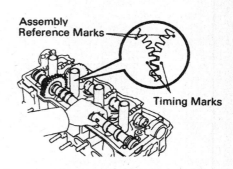

11.43 Align the camshaft gear timing marks as shown here

i)   *Scrape off the Plastigage with your fingernail or the edge of a credit card - don't scratch or nick the journals or bearing caps.*

29   Temporarily install the camshafts without installing the lifters or exhaust camshaft sub-gear.

30   Measure the gear backlash (the free play between the gear teeth) with a dial indicator **(see illustration)** and compare it to the Specifications.

Installation

Intake camshaft

Refer to illustrations 11.34, 11.35, 11.36, 11.43, 11.45 and 11.46

31   Apply moly-base grease or engine assembly lube to the lifters, then install them in their original locations. Make sure the valve adjustment shims are in place in the lifters.

32   Apply moly-base grease or engine assembly lube to the camshaft lobes and bearing journals.

33   Position the intake camshaft in the cylinder head with the knock pin 80-degrees to the left of vertical **(see illustration 11.11)**.

34   Apply a thin coat of sealer to the outer edge of the front bearing cap cylinder head mating surface **(see illustration)**. **Note:** *The cap must be installed immediately or the sealer will dry prematurely.*

35   Install the bearing caps in numerical order with the arrows pointing toward the timing belt end of the engine **(see illustration)**.

36   Tighten the bearing cap bolts in 1/4-turn increments until the specified torque is reached. Follow the factory recommended sequence **(see illustration)**.

37   Refer to Section 9 and install a new camshaft oil seal.

Exhaust camshaft

38   To reassemble the exhaust camshaft, install the cam gear spring, sub-gear and wave washer in the gear, then secure them with the snap-ring.

39   Reinstall the service bolt in the unthreaded hole, turn the sub-gear with a screwdriver and install the second service bolt in the threaded hole. Tighten it to clamp the sub-gear to the camshaft gear, then remove the first bolt.

40   Apply moly-base grease or engine assembly lube to the lifters, then install them in their original locations. Make sure the valve adjustment shims are in place in the lifters.

41   Apply moly-base grease or engine assembly lube to the camshaft lobes and bearing journals.

42   Rotate the INTAKE camshaft until the

knock pin is positioned 10-degrees to the left of vertical **(see illustration 11.5)**.

43   Align the exhaust camshaft gear with the intake camshaft gear by matching up the timing marks on the gears **(see illustration)**. **Caution:** *There are also assembly reference marks on each gear, above the timing marks - do not mistake them for the timing marks.*

44   Roll the exhaust camshaft down into position. Turn the intake camshaft back and forth a little until the exhaust camshaft sits in the bearings evenly.

45   Install the bearing caps in numerical order with the arrows pointing toward the timing belt end of the engine **(see illustration)**.

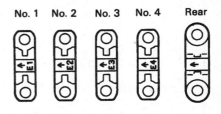

11.45 Exhaust camshaft bearing caps (3S-FE engine) - the arrows point toward the timing belt end of the engine

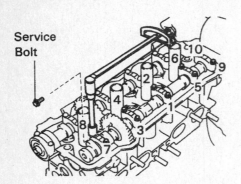

11.46 3S-FE engine EXHAUST camshaft bearing cap bolt tightening sequence

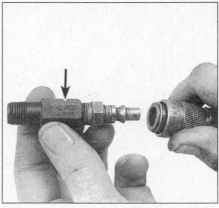

12.4 This is what the air hose adapter that threads into the spark plug hole looks like - they're commonly available from auto parts stores

12.17 Apply a small dab of grease to each keeper before installation to hold it in place on the valve stem until the spring is released

46   Tighten the bearing cap bolts in 1/4-turn increments until the specified torque is reached. Follow the factory recommended sequence **(see illustration)**.

47   Remove the service bolt from the camshaft gear.

48   Install the timing belt pulley on the intake camshaft and tighten the bolt to the specified torque. Prevent the camshaft from turning by holding it with a wrench on the large hex **(see illustration 7.14)**.

49   Install the timing belt (see Section 7).

50   The remainder of installation is the reverse of the removal procedure.

12   Valve springs, retainers and seals - replacement (2S-E engine only)

Refer to illustrations 12.4 and 12.17

Note: *Broken valve springs and defective valve stem seals can be replaced without removing the cylinder head. Two special tools and a compressed air source are normally required to perform this operation, so read through this Section carefully and rent or buy the tools before beginning the job. If compressed air isn't available, a length of nylon rope can be used to keep the valves from falling into the cylinder during this procedure.*

1   Refer to Section 10 and remove the camshaft and camshaft housing.

2   Remove the spark plug from the cylinder which has the defective component. If all of the valve stem seals are being replaced, all of the spark plugs should be removed.

3   Turn the crankshaft until the piston in the affected cylinder is at top dead center on the compression stroke (refer to Section 3 for instructions). If you're replacing all of the valve stem seals, begin with cylinder number one and work on the valves for one cylinder at a time. Move from cylinder-to-cylinder following the firing order sequence (see the Specifications).

4   Thread an adapter into the spark plug hole **(see illustration)** and connect an air hose from a compressed air source to it. Most auto parts stores can supply the air hose adapter. **Note:** *Many cylinder compres-*

sion gauges utilize a screw-in fitting that may work with your air hose quick-disconnect fitting.

5   Apply compressed air to the cylinder. **Warning:** *The piston may be forced down by compressed air, causing the crankshaft to turn suddenly. If the wrench used when positioning the number one piston at TDC is still attached to the bolt in the crankshaft nose, it could cause damage or injury when the crankshaft moves.*

6   The valves should be held in place by the air pressure. If the valve faces or seats are in poor condition, leaks may prevent air pressure from retaining the valves - refer to the alternative procedure below.

7   If you don't have access to compressed air, an alternative method can be used. Position the piston at a point just before TDC on the compression stroke, then feed a long piece of nylon rope through the spark plug hole until it fills the combustion chamber. Be sure to leave the end of the rope hanging out of the engine so it can be removed easily.

8   Use a large ratchet and socket to rotate the crankshaft in the normal direction of rotation (clockwise, viewed from the front) until slight resistance is felt.

9   Stuff shop rags into the cylinder head holes above and below the valves to prevent parts and tools from falling into the engine, then use a valve spring compressor to compress the spring. Remove the keepers with small needle-nose pliers or a magnet **(see illustration 4.4a)**. **Note:** *A couple of different types of tools are available for compressing the valve springs with the head in place. One type grips the lower spring coils and presses on the retainer as the knob is turned, while the other type utilizes a bolt or stud and nut for leverage. Both types work very well, although the lever type is usually less expensive.*

10   Remove the spring retainer and valve spring, then remove the stem oil seal. **Note:** *If air pressure fails to hold the valve in the closed position during this operation, the valve face and/or seat is probably damaged.*

If so, the cylinder head will have to be removed for additional repair operations.

11   Wrap a rubber band or tape around the top of the valve stem so the valve won't fall into the combustion chamber, then release the air pressure. **Note:** *If a rope was used instead of air pressure, turn the crankshaft slightly in the direction opposite normal rotation.*

12   Inspect the valve stem for damage. Rotate the valve in the guide and check the end for eccentric movement, which would indicate that the valve is bent.

13   Move the valve up-and-down in the guide and make sure it doesn't bind. If the valve stem binds, either the valve is bent or the guide is damaged. In either case, the head will have to be removed for repair.

14   Reapply air pressure to the cylinder to retain the valve in the closed position, then remove the tape or rubber band from the valve stem. If a rope was used instead of air pressure, rotate the crankshaft in the normal direction of rotation until **slight** resistance is felt.

15   Lubricate the valve stem with engine oil and install a new oil seal.

16   Install the spring in position over the valve. Be sure the closely wound coils are next to the head

17   Install the valve spring retainer. Compress the valve spring and carefully position the keepers in the groove. Apply a small dab of grease to the inside of each keeper to hold it in place if necessary **(see illustration)**.

18   Remove the pressure from the spring tool and make sure the keepers are seated.

19   Disconnect the air hose and remove the adapter from the spark plug hole. If a rope was used in place of air pressure, pull it out of the cylinder.

20   Refer to Section 10 and install the camshaft and housing.

21   Install the spark plug(s) and hook up the wire(s).

22   Start and run the engine, then check for oil leaks and unusual sounds coming from the camshaft cover area.

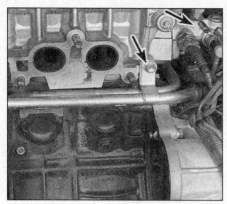

13.12 Remove the coolant tube bracket nut and the housing (arrows) (3S-FE engine)

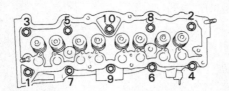

13.13 Cylinder head bolt LOOSENING sequence (2S-E engine shown, 3S-FE uses same sequence)

13.14 If the head is stuck, pry only at the overhang, not between the mating surfaces

13 Cylinder head - removal and installation

Note: *The engine must be completely cool before beginning this procedure.*

Removal

Refer to illustrations 13.12, 13.13 and 13.14

1 Disconnect the negative cable from the battery.
2 Drain the coolant from the engine block and radiator (see Chapter 1).
3 Drain the engine oil and remove the oil filter (see Chapter 1).
4 Remove the throttle body, the injectors and the fuel rails (see Chapter 4).
5 Remove the intake manifold (see Section 5).
6 Remove the exhaust manifold (see Section 6).
7 Remove the timing belt and upper idler pulley (see Section 7). On 3S-FE engines, remove the rear (no. 3) timing belt cover **(see illustration 4.4b)**.
8 On 2S-E engines, remove the camshaft and housing (see Section 10).
9 On 3S-FE engines, remove the camshafts and lifters (see Section 11).

10 Remove the alternator and distributor (see Chapter 5).
11 Unbolt the power steering pump and set it aside without disconnecting the hoses.
12 Check the cylinder head. Label and remove any remaining items, such as coolant fittings, tubes, cables, hoses or wires **(see illustration)**. At this point the head should be ready for removal.
13 Using an 8 mm Allen head socket and a breaker bar, loosen the cylinder head bolts in 1/4-turn increments until they can be removed by hand. Follow the recommended sequence **(see illustration)** to avoid warping or cracking the head.
14 Lift the cylinder head off the engine block. If it's stuck, very carefully pry up at the transaxle end, beyond the gasket surface **(see illustration)**.
15 Remove all external components from the head to allow for thorough cleaning and inspection. See Chapter 2, Part C, for cylinder head servicing procedures.

Installation

Refer to illustrations 13.17 and 13.25

16 The mating surfaces of the cylinder head and block must be perfectly clean when the head is installed.
17 Use a gasket scraper to remove all traces of carbon and old gasket material **(see illustration)**, then clean the mating surfaces with lacquer thinner or acetone. If there's oil on the mating surfaces when the head is

installed, the gasket may not seal correctly and leaks could develop. When working on the block, stuff the cylinders with clean shop rags to keep out debris. Use a vacuum cleaner to remove material that falls into the cylinders.
18 Check the block and head mating surfaces for nicks, deep scratches and other damage. If damage is slight, it can be removed with a file; if it's excessive, machining may be the only alternative.
19 Use a tap of the correct size to chase the threads in the head bolt holes, then clean the holes with compressed air - make sure that nothing remains in the holes. **Warning:** *Wear eye protection when using compressed air!*
20 Mount each bolt in a vise and run a die down the threads to remove corrosion and restore the threads. Dirt, corrosion, sealant and damaged threads will affect torque readings.
21 Install the components that were removed from the head.
22 Position the new gasket over the dowel pins in the block.
23 Carefully set the head on the block without disturbing the gasket.
24 Before installing the head bolts, apply a small amount of clean engine oil to the threads.
25 Install the bolts in their original locations and tighten them finger tight. Following the recommended sequence, tighten the bolts in several steps to the specified torque **(see illustration)**.

13.17 Remove all traces of old gasket material - the cylinder head and block mating surfaces must be perfectly clean to ensure a good gasket seal

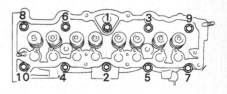

13.25 Cylinder head bolt TIGHTENING sequence (2S-E engine shown, 3S-FE uses same sequence)

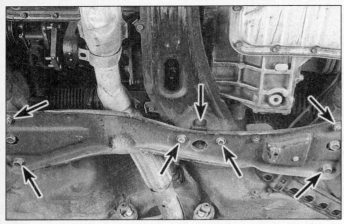

14.7a Unbolt the rear crossmember and remove the engine mount nuts (arrows)

14.7b Unbolt the front mount and remove the two front crossmember bolts (arrows)

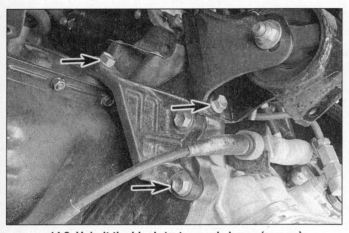

14.8 Unbolt the block-to-transaxle brace (arrows)

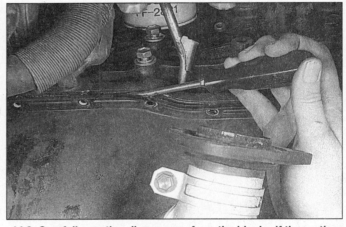

14.9 Carefully pry the oil pan away from the block - if the mating surfaces are damaged, oil leaks could develop

26   The remaining installation steps are the reverse of removal.
27   On 3S-FE engines, check and adjust the valves as necessary (see Chapter 1).
28   Refill the cooling system, install a new oil filter and add oil to the engine (see Chapter 1).
29   Run the engine and check for leaks. Set the ignition timing (see Chapter 5) and road test the vehicle.

14   Oil pan - removal and installation

Refer to illustrations 14.7a, 14.7b, 14.8, 14.9 and 14.14

1   Disconnect the negative cable from the battery.
2   Set the parking brake and block the rear wheels.
3   Raise the front of the vehicle and support it securely on jackstands.
4   Remove the splash shields under the engine, if equipped.
5   Drain the engine oil and remove the oil filter (see Chapter 1). Remove the oil dipstick.
6   Disconnect the front exhaust pipe from the engine and remove the clamp behind the

engine to allow the pipe to hang down.
7   Unbolt the crossmember which connects the lower suspension mounts, then remove the crossmember under the oil pan **(see illustrations)**.
8   Remove the block-to-transaxle brace **(see illustration)**.
9   Remove the bolts and detach the oil pan. If it's stuck, pry it loose very carefully with a small screwdriver or putty knife **(see illustration)**. Don't damage the mating surfaces of the pan and block or oil leaks could develop.
10   Use a scraper to remove all traces of old gasket material and sealant from the block and oil pan. Clean the mating surfaces with lacquer thinner or acetone.
11   Make sure the threaded bolt holes in the block are clean.
12   Check the oil pan flange for distortion, particularly around the bolt holes. If necessary, place the pan on a block of wood and use a hammer to flatten and restore the gasket surface.
13   Inspect the oil pump pick-up tube assembly for cracks and a blocked strainer. If the pick-up was removed, install it now, using a new O-ring or gasket. Tighten the fasteners to the specified torque.

14   Apply a 5 mm wide bead of sealer to the oil pan flange **(see illustration)**. **Note:** *The oil pan must be installed within 3 minutes once the sealer has been applied.*
15   Carefully position the oil pan on the engine block and install the bolts. Working

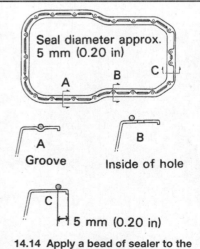

14.14 Apply a bead of sealer to the oil pan flange

15.2 The oil pick-up assembly and baffle plate are held in place with two nuts and two bolts (arrows)

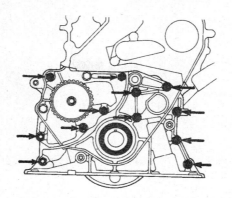

15.4 Remove the oil pump case-to-block bolts (arrows)

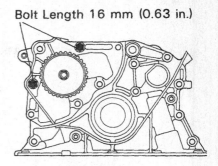

15.5a Remove the oil pump body-to-oil pump case bolts

from the center out, tighten them to the specified torque in three or four steps.

16 The remainder of installation is the reverse of removal. Be sure to add oil and install a new oil filter.

17 Run the engine and check for oil pressure and leaks.

15 Oil pump - removal, inspection and installation

Removal

Refer to illustrations 15.2, 15.4, 15.5a, 15.5b, 15.6 and 15.8

1 Remove the oil pan (see Section 14).

2 Remove the nuts/bolts and detach the oil pick-up tube assembly and baffle plate **(see illustration)**.

3 Remove the timing belt, lower idler pulley and crankshaft pulley (see Section 7). **Note:** *Since the oil pan has been removed, the engine must be supported securely from above when removing the following components.*

4 Remove the bolts and detach the oil pump case from the engine **(see illustration)**. You may have to pry carefully between the front main bearing cap and the pump case with a screwdriver.

5 Remove the two remaining bolts **(see illustration)** and separate the pump body from the case. Lift out the driven rotor and remove the O-ring **(see illustration)**.

6 Clamp the pump pulley in a well padded vise **(see illustration)** and remove the pulley nut. Take off the pulley and remove the drive rotor **(see illustration 15.5b)**.

7 Use a scraper to remove all traces of sealant and old gasket material from the pump case and engine block, then clean the mating surfaces with lacquer thinner or acetone.

8 Remove the oil pressure relief valve snap-ring **(see illustration)**, retainer, spring and piston **(see illustration 15.5b)**. **Warning:** *The spring is tightly compressed - be careful and wear eye protection.*

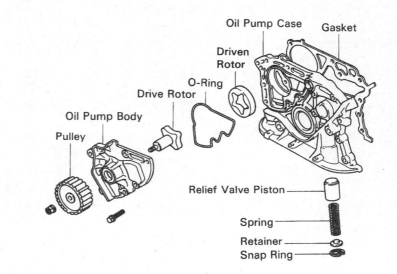
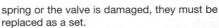

15.5b Oil pump components - exploded view

Inspection

Refer to illustrations 15.11a and 15.11b

9 Clean all components with solvent, then inspect them for wear and damage.

10 Check the oil pressure relief valve piston sliding surface and valve spring. If either the spring or the valve is damaged, they must be replaced as a set.

11 Check the driven rotor-to-case and drive rotor tip clearances with feeler gauges **(see illustrations)** and compare the results to the Specifications.

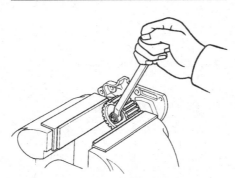

15.8 Remove the snap-ring to disassemble the oil pressure relief valve

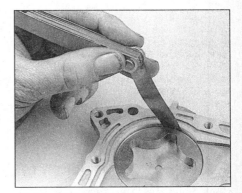

15.11a Measure the driven rotor-to-case clearance . . .

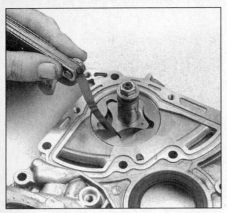

15.11b . . . and the rotor tip clearance with feeler gauges

15.12a Carefully pry the oil seal out of the pump body

15.12b Gently drive a new seal into place

15.14 Oil pump case ready for pump body installation - note that the seal is in place, the O-ring is in place and the mark on the driven rotor is facing out (arrow)

16.3 Mark the flywheel/driveplate and the crankshaft so they can be reassembled in the same relative positions

16.5 On vehicles with a spacer plate, note the position of the locating pin (arrow)

Installation

Refer to illustrations 15.12a, 15.12b and 15.14

12   Pry the old drive rotor shaft seal out with a screwdriver. Using a deep socket and a hammer, carefully drive a new seal into place **(see illustrations)**. Apply moly-base grease to the seal lip.

13   Install a new crankshaft seal using the same procedure as outlined in the previous Step. Apply moly-base grease to the seal lip.

14   Install a new O-ring, then lubricate the driven rotor with clean engine oil and place it in the pump case with the mark facing out **(see illustration)**.

15   Lubricate the shaft and install the drive rotor in the pump body, then reinstall the pulley and tighten the nut to the specified torque.

16   Pack the pump cavity with petroleum jelly and attach the pump body to the case with the 16 mm long bolts **(see illustration 15.5a)**.

17   Lubricate the oil pressure relief valve piston with clean engine oil and reinstall the valve components in the pump case.

18   Place a new gasket on the engine block (the dowel pins should hold it in place).

19   Position the pump against the block and install the mounting bolts.

20   Tighten the bolts to the specified torque in three or four steps. Follow a criss-cross pattern to avoid warping the case.

21   Using a new gasket or O-ring (whichever it came with), install the oil pick-up tube assembly and baffle plate. Tighten the fasteners to the specified torque.

22   Reinstall the remaining parts in the reverse order of removal.

23   Add oil, start the engine and check for oil pressure and leaks.

24   Recheck the engine oil level.

16   Flywheel/driveplate - removal and installation

Refer to illustrations 16.3 and 16.5

1   Raise the vehicle and support it securely on jackstands, then refer to Chapter 7 and remove the transaxle. If it's leaking, now would be a very good time to replace the front pump seal/O-ring (automatic transaxle only).

2   Remove the pressure plate and clutch disc (Chapter 8) (manual transaxle equipped

vehicles). Now is a good time to check/replace the clutch components and pilot bearing.

3   Use a center punch or paint to make alignment marks on the flywheel/driveplate and crankshaft to ensure correct alignment during reinstallation **(see illustration)**.

4   Remove the bolts that secure the flywheel/driveplate to the crankshaft. If the crankshaft turns, wedge a screwdriver in the ring gear teeth to jam the flywheel.

5   Remove the flywheel/driveplate from the crankshaft. Since the flywheel is fairly heavy, be sure to support it while removing the last bolt. Automatic transaxle equipped vehicles have spacers on both sides of the driveplate **(see illustration)**.

6   Clean the flywheel to remove grease and oil. Inspect the surface for cracks, rivet grooves, burned areas and score marks. Light scoring can be removed with emery cloth. Check for cracked and broken ring gear teeth. Lay the flywheel on a flat surface and use a straightedge to check for warpage.

7   Clean and inspect the mating surfaces of the flywheel/driveplate and the crankshaft. If the crankshaft rear seal is leaking, replace it before reinstalling the flywheel/driveplate.

17.2 The quick and dirty way to replace the rear crankshaft oil seal is to simply pry the old one out with a screwdriver, lubricate the crankshaft journal and the lip of the new seal with moly-base grease and push the new seal into place - the trouble is, the seal lip is pretty stiff and can be easily damaged during installation if you're not careful

17.5 After removing the retainer assembly from the block, support it on a couple of wood blocks and drive out the old seal with a screwdriver and hammer

17.6 Drive the new seal into the retainer with a block of wood or a section of pipe, if you have one large enough - make sure that you don't cock the seal in the retainer bore

8   Position the flywheel/driveplate against the crankshaft. Be sure to align the marks made during removal. Note that some engines have an alignment dowel or staggered bolt holes to ensure correct installation. Before installing the bolts, apply thread locking compound to the threads.

9   Wedge a screwdriver in the ring gear teeth to keep the flywheel/driveplate from turning as you tighten the bolts to the specified torque. Follow a criss-cross pattern and work up to the final torque in three or four steps.

10   The remainder of installation is the reverse of the removal procedure.

17   Rear crankshaft oil seal - replacement

Refer to illustrations 17.2, 17.5 and 17.6

1   The transaxle must be removed from the vehicle for this procedure (see Chapter 7).

2   The seal can be replaced without dropping the oil pan or removing the seal retainer. However, this method is not recommended because the lip of the seal is quite stiff and it's possible to cock the seal in the retainer bore or damage it during installation. If you want to take the chance, pry out the old seal with a screwdriver **(see illustration)**. Apply moly-base grease to the crankshaft seal journal and the lip of the new seal and carefully push the new seal into place. The lip is stiff so carefully work it onto the seal journal of the crankshaft with a smooth object like the end of an extension as you tap the seal into place. Don't rush it or you may damage the seal.

3   The following method is recommended but requires removal of the oil pan (see Section 14) and the seal retainer.

4   After the oil pan has been removed,

remove the bolts, detach the seal retainer and peel off all the old gasket material.

5   Position the seal and retainer assembly on a couple of wood blocks on a workbench and drive the old seal out from the back side with a screwdriver **(see illustration)**.

6   Drive the new seal into the retainer with a block of wood **(see illustration)** or a section of pipe slightly smaller in diameter than the outside diameter of the seal.

7   Lubricate the crankshaft seal journal and the lip of the new seal with moly-base grease. Position a new gasket on the engine block.

8   Slowly and carefully push the seal onto the crankshaft. The seal lip is stiff, so work it onto the crankshaft with a smooth object such as the end of an extension as you push the retainer against the block.

9   Install and tighten the retainer bolts to the specified torque. The bottom sealing flange of the retainer must not extend below the bottom sealing flange (oil pan rail) of the block.

10   The remaining steps are the reverse of removal.

18   Engine mounts - check and replacement

Refer to illustrations 18.8a, 18.8b, 18.10a and 18.10b

1   Engine mounts seldom require attention, but broken or deteriorated mounts should be replaced immediately or the added strain placed on the driveline components may cause damage or wear.

Check

2   During the check, the engine must be raised slightly to remove the weight from the mounts.

3   Raise the vehicle and support it securely on jackstands, then position a jack under the engine oil pan. Place a large block of wood between the jack head and the oil pan, then

carefully raise the engine just enough to take the weight off the mounts. **Warning:** *DO NOT place any part of your body under the engine when it's supported only by a jack!*

4   Check the mounts to see if the rubber is cracked, hardened or separated from the metal plates. Sometimes the rubber will split right down the center.

5   Check for relative movement between the mount plates and the engine or frame (use a large screwdriver or pry bar to attempt to move the mounts). If movement is noted, lower the engine and tighten the mount fasteners.

6   Rubber preservative should be applied to the mounts to slow deterioration.

Replacement

7   Disconnect the negative battery cable from the battery, then raise the vehicle and support it securely on jackstands (if not already done). Support the engine as described in Step 3.

8   To remove the right engine mount, remove the nut and withdraw the through-bolt from the frame bracket **(see illustrations)**.

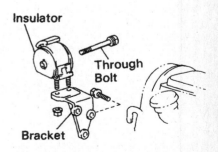

18.8a To remove the right engine mount, remove the through bolt and the two nuts under the insulator (2S-E engine shown)

18.8b The right engine mount on the 3S-FE engine has an additional stud (arrow) for a brace

18.10a To access the rear engine mount (shown from below) the crossmembers must be removed

18.10b Remove the mounting nuts (arrows)

9   Remove the mount-to-bracket nuts and detach the mount.
10   To remove the rear engine mount, detach the crossmembers as described in Section 14, then remove the nuts from the side of the mount **(see illustrations)** and lower the mount from the bracket. **Warning:** *Do not remove the crossmembers if the upper mounts are disconnected!*
11   Installation is the reverse of removal.

Use thread locking compound on the mount bolts/nuts and be sure to tighten them securely.
12   See Chapter 7 for transaxle mount replacement.

Chapter 2 Part B
V6 engine

Contents

Specifications

General

Cylinder numbers (timing belt end-to-transaxle end)
    Right (firewall) side 1-3-5
    Left (radiator) side 2-4-6
Firing order 1-2-3-4-5-6

The blackened terminal shown on the distributor cap indicates the Number One spark plug wire position

41710-2B-specs

Cylinder location and distributor rotation

Warpage limits

Cylinder head............... 0.0039 in (0.10 mm)
Intake manifold... .... 0.0039 in (0.10 mm)
Exhaust manifolds .... 0.0394 in (1.0 mm)

Camshaft and related components

Lifters

Outside diameter .... 1.1014 to 1.1018 in (27.975 to 27.985 mm)
Bore diameter .... 1.1024 to 1.1032 in (28.000 to 28.021 mm)
Lifter-to-bore (oil) clearance
    Standard............... 0.0005 to 0.0018 in (0.015 to 0.046 mm)
    Service limit .... 0.028 in (1.07 mm)

Camshaft

Valve clearances (engine cold)
    Intake............... 0.005 to 0.009 in (0.13 to 0.23 mm)
    Exhaust............... 0.011 to 0.015 in (0.27 to 0.37 mm)
Bearing journal diameter............... 1.0610 to 1.0616 in (26.949 to 26.965 mm)
Bearing oil clearance
    Standard............... 0.0014 to 0.0028 in (0.035 to 0.072 mm)
    Service limit .... 0.0039 in (0.10 mm)
Lobe height
    Intake
        Standard .... 1.5555 to 1.5594 in (39.51 to 39.61 mm)
        Service Limit .... 1.5496 in (39.36 mm)
    Exhaust
        Standard... .... 1.5339 to 1.5378 in (38.960 to 39.060 mm)
        Service limit............... 1.5279 in (38.81 mm)
End play
    Standard............... 0.0012 to 0.0031 in (0.030 to 0.080 mm)
    Service limit............... 0.0047 in (0.12 mm)
Runout limit (total indicator reading) .... 0.0024 in (0.06 mm)
Camshaft gear backlash
    Standard... .... 0.0008 to 0.0079 in (0.02 to 0.20 mm)
    Service limit............... 0.0188 (0.30 mm)
Camshaft gear spring free distance .... 0.712 to 0.740 in (18.2 to 18.8 mm)

Timing belt tensioner protrusion .... 0.413 to 0.453 in (10.5 to 11.5 mm)

Oil pump

Driven rotor-to-pump body clearance
    Standard.. 0.0039 to 0.0069 in (0.100 to 0.175 mm)
    Service limit .... 0.0118 in (0.30 mm)
Rotor tip clearance
    Standard.. 0.0043 to 0.0094 in (0.11 to 0.24 mm)
    Service limit .... 0.0138 in (0.35 mm)
Rotor side clearance
    Standard.. 0.0012 to 0.0035 in (0.03 to 0.09 mm)
    Service limit .... 0.0059 in (0.15 mm)

Torque specifications

	Ft-lbs (unless otherwise indicated)
Intake manifold bolts/nuts	13
Exhaust manifold nuts	29
Crankshaft pulley bolt	181
Timing belt cover bolts (no. 3)	65 in-lbs
Idler pulley bolts	
No. 1	25
No. 2	29
Timing belt tensioner bolts	20
Cylinder head cover nuts	52 in-lbs
Camshaft pulley bolts	80
Camshaft bearing cap bolts	12
Cylinder head bolts	
Step 1	25
Step 2	Turn an additional 90 (1/4-turn)
Step 3	Turn an additional 90-degrees (1/4-turn)
Cylinder head bolt (recessed)	13
Oil pan bolts	52 in-lbs
Oil pump mounting bolts	
12 mm bolt head	14
14 mm bolt head	30
Oil pick-up tube mounting bolts	61 in-lbs
Flywheel/driveplate bolts*	61
Rear crankshaft oil seal retainer mounting bolts	69 in-lbs

*Apply thread locking compound to the threads prior to installation

1 General information

This Part of Chapter 2 is devoted to in-vehicle repair procedures for the V6 engine. All information concerning engine removal and installation and engine block and cylinder head overhaul can be found in Part C of this Chapter.

The following repair procedures are based on the assumption that the engine is installed in the vehicle. If the engine has been removed from the vehicle and mounted on a stand, many of the steps outlined in this Part of Chapter 2 will not apply.

The Specifications included in this Part of Chapter 2 apply only to the procedures contained in this Part. Part C of Chapter 2 contains the Specifications necessary for cylinder head and engine block rebuilding.

2 Repair operations possible with the engine in the vehicle

Many major repair operations can be accomplished without removing the engine from the vehicle.

Clean the engine compartment and the exterior of the engine with some type of degreaser before any work is done. It will make the job easier and help keep dirt out of the internal areas of the engine.

Depending on the components involved, it may be helpful to remove the hood to improve access to the engine as repairs are performed (refer to Chapter 11 if necessary). Cover the fenders to prevent damage to the paint. Special pads are available, but an old bedspread or blanket will also work.

If vacuum, exhaust, oil or coolant leaks develop, indicating a need for gasket or seal replacement, the repairs can generally be made with the engine in the vehicle. The intake and exhaust manifold gaskets, oil pan gasket, crankshaft oil seals and cylinder head gaskets are all accessible with the engine in place.

Exterior engine components, such as the intake and exhaust manifolds, the oil pan, the oil pump, the water pump, the starter motor, the alternator, the distributor and the fuel system components can be removed for repair with the engine in place.

Since the cylinder heads can be removed without pulling the engine, valve component servicing can also be accomplished with the engine in the vehicle. Replacement of the camshafts, timing belt and pulleys is also possible with the engine in the vehicle.

In extreme cases caused by a lack of necessary equipment, repair or replacement

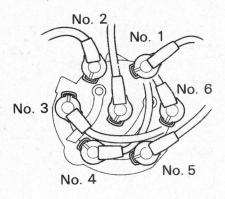

3.5 Make a mark on the distributor body, directly below the no. 1 spark plug wire terminal on the cap

3.8 Turn the crankshaft until the notch in the pulley aligns with the zero (0) on the timing plate

4.3 Remove the spark plug wires, the breather hose and the retaining nuts (arrows) to detach the cylinder head cover

of piston rings, pistons, connecting rods and rod bearings is possible with the engine in the vehicle. However, this practice is not recommended because of the cleaning and preparation work that must be done to the components involved.

3 Top Dead Center (TDC) for number one piston - locating

Refer to illustrations 3.5 and 3.8
Note: *The following procedure is based on the assumption that the distributor is correctly installed. If you are trying to locate TDC to install the distributor correctly, piston position must be determined by feeling for compression at the number one spark plug hole, then aligning the ignition timing marks as described in Step 8.*

1 Top Dead Center (TDC) is the highest point in the cylinder that each piston reaches as it travels up-and-down when the crankshaft turns. Each piston reaches TDC on the compression stroke and again on the exhaust stroke, but TDC generally refers to piston position on the compression stroke.

2 Positioning the piston(s) at TDC is an essential part of many procedures such as valve timing, camshaft and timing belt/pulley removal and distributor removal.

3 Before beginning this procedure, be sure to place the transaxle in Neutral and apply the parking brake or block the rear wheels. Also, disable the ignition system by detaching the coil wire from the center terminal of the distributor cap and grounding it on the block with a jumper wire. Remove the spark plugs (see Chapter 1).

4 In order to bring any piston to TDC, the crankshaft must be turned using one of the methods outlined below. When looking at the front of the engine, normal crankshaft rotation is clockwise.

  a) *The preferred method is to turn the crankshaft with a socket and ratchet attached to the bolt threaded into the front of the crankshaft.*

  b) *A remote starter switch, which may save some time, can also be used. Follow the instructions included with the switch. Once the piston is close to TDC, use a socket and ratchet as described in the previous paragraph.*

  c) *If an assistant is available to turn the ignition switch to the Start position in*

short bursts, you can get the piston close to TDC without a remote starter switch. Make sure your assistant is out of the vehicle, away from the ignition switch, then use a socket and ratchet as described in Paragraph a) to complete the procedure.

5 Note the position of the terminal for the number one spark plug wire on the distributor cap **(see illustration)**. If the terminal isn't marked, follow the plug wire from the number one cylinder spark plug to the cap.

6 Use a felt-tip pen or chalk to make a mark on the distributor body directly under the terminal.

7 Detach the cap from the distributor and set it aside (see Chapter 1 if necessary).

8 Turn the crankshaft (see Paragraph 3 above) until the notch in the crankshaft pulley is aligned with the 0 on the timing plate (located at the front of the engine) **(see illustration)**.

9 Look at the distributor rotor - it should be pointing directly at the mark you made on the distributor body.

10 If the rotor is 180-degrees off, the number one piston is at TDC on the exhaust stroke.

11 To get the piston to TDC on the compression stroke, turn the crankshaft one complete turn (360-degrees) clockwise. The rotor should now be pointing at the mark on the distributor. When the rotor is pointing at the number one spark plug wire terminal in the distributor cap and the ignition timing marks are aligned, the number one piston is at TDC on the compression stroke.

12 After the number one piston has been positioned at TDC on the compression stroke, TDC for any of the remaining pistons can be located by turning the crankshaft and following the firing order. Mark the remaining spark plug wire terminal locations on the distributor body just like you did for the number one terminal, then number the marks to correspond with the cylinder numbers. As you turn the crankshaft, the rotor will also turn. When it's pointing directly at one of the marks on the distributor, the piston for that particular cylinder is at TDC on the compression stroke.

4 Cylinder head covers - removal and installation

Refer to illustrations 4.3, 4.5 and 4.7
1 Disconnect the negative cable from the battery.

2 If you're removing the rear (firewall side) cover, remove the throttle body and air intake chamber (see Chapter 4).

3 If you're working on the front (radiator side) or both covers, remove the spark plug connectors and wires from the spark plugs **(see illustration)**.

4 Detach the breather hose from the cover fitting.

5 Remove the six retaining nuts and seal

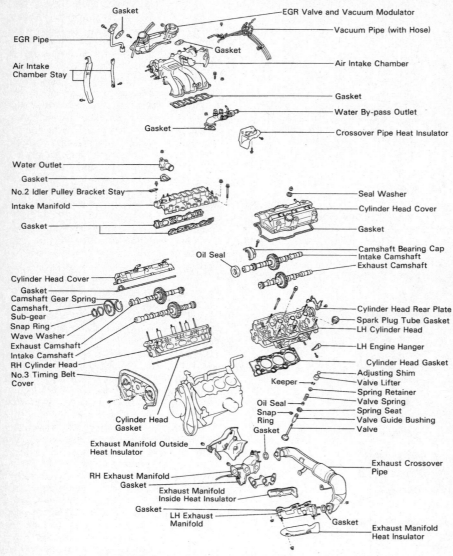

4.5 Cylinder heads and related components - exploded view

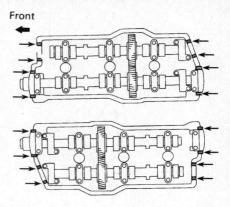

4.7 Apply sealer to the shaded areas (arrows) before installing the gasket and cylinder head cover

washers **(see illustration)**, then detach the cover. If the cover is stuck to the head, bump the end with a block of wood and a hammer to jar it loose. If that doesn't work, try to slip a flexible putty knife between the head and cover to break the seal. **Caution:** *Don't pry at the cover-to-head joint or damage to the sealing surfaces may occur, leading to oil leaks after the cover is reinstalled.*

6   The mating surfaces of the cylinder head and cover must be clean when the cover is installed. Use a gasket scraper to remove all traces of sealant and old gasket material, then clean the mating surfaces with lacquer thinner or acetone. If there's residue or oil on the mating surfaces when the cover is installed, oil leaks may develop.

7   Position new semi-circular seals (if needed) in the cylinder head cutouts, then apply a thin, uniform layer of gasket sealer to the gasket/seal joints **(see illustration)**.

8   Install new spark plug tube seals.

9   Position a new gasket on the cylinder head, then install the cover, sealing washers and nuts.

10   Tighten the nuts to the specified torque in three or four equal steps.

11   Reinstall the remaining parts, run the engine and check for oil leaks.

5   Intake manifold - removal and installation

1   Disconnect the negative cable from the battery.

2   Drain the coolant into a clean container (see Chapter 1).

3   Position the number one piston at Top Dead Center (see Section 3), remove the upper (no. 2) timing belt cover and loosen the

no. 1 timing belt idler pulley (see Section 7).

4   Remove the throttle body, fuel injectors and air intake chamber (see Chapter 4).

5   Remove the upper (no. 2) idler pulley bracket stay **(see illustration 4.5)**.

6   Clearly label, then detach all remaining wires, hoses and brackets still attached to the intake manifold and coolant outlets **(see illustration 4.5)**.

7   Remove the water outlet (thermostat housing) and water bypass outlet **(see illustration 4.5)**.

8   Remove the eight mounting nuts/bolts, then detach the manifold from the engine. If it's stuck, don't pry between the gasket mating surfaces or damage may result.

9   Use a scraper to remove all traces of old gasket material and sealant from the manifold and cylinder heads, then clean the mating surfaces with lacquer thinner or acetone.

10   Install new gaskets, then position the manifold on the engine. Make sure the gaskets haven't shifted and install the nuts/bolts.

11   Tighten the nuts/bolts, in three or four equal steps, to the specified torque. Work from the center out towards the ends to avoid warping the manifold.

12   Install the remaining parts in the reverse order of removal.

13   Refill the cooling system. Run the engine and check for fuel, vacuum and coolant leaks.

6   Exhaust manifolds - removal and installation

Note: *The engine must be completely cool when this procedure is done.*

1   Disconnect the negative cable from the battery.

2   Spray penetrating oil on the exhaust manifold fasteners and allow it to soak in.

3   Unbolt the heat insulators from the manifold(s) being removed **(see illustration 4.5)**.

4   Disconnect the exhaust crossover pipe (see Chapter 4).

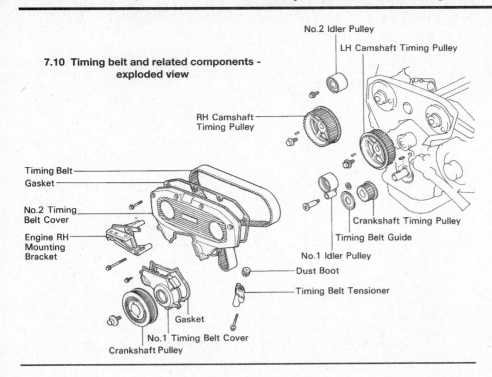

7.10 Timing belt and related components - exploded view

No.2 Idler Pulley
LH Camshaft Timing Pulley
RH Camshaft Timing Pulley
Timing Belt
Gasket
No.2 Timing Belt Cover
Engine RH Mounting Bracket
Crankshaft Timing Pulley
Timing Belt Guide
No.1 Idler Pulley
Dust Boot
Timing Belt Tensioner
Gasket
No.1 Timing Belt Cover
Crankshaft Pulley

manifold and cylinder head mating surfaces. If the gasket was leaking, have the manifold checked for warpage at an automotive machine shop and resurfaced if necessary.

10   Position a new gasket over the cylinder head studs.

11   Install the manifold and thread the mounting nuts into place.

12   Working from the center out, tighten the nuts to the specified torque in three or four equal steps.

13   Reinstall the remaining parts in the reverse order of removal. Use new gaskets when connecting the exhaust pipes.

14   Run the engine and check for exhaust leaks.

7   Timing belt and pulleys - removal, inspection and installation

Removal

Refer to illustrations 7.10, 7.13, 7.14, 7.15, 7.18, 7.21, 7.22, 7.23, 7.26 and 7.28

1   Disconnect the negative cable from the battery.

2   Remove the cruise control actuator and vacuum pump, if equipped.

3   Remove the power steering reservoir without disconnecting the hoses.

4   Loosen the lug nuts on the right front wheel, but don't remove them.

5   Raise the front of the vehicle and support it securely on jackstands. Apply the parking brake and block the rear wheels. Remove the right front wheel.

6   Remove the right front inner fender apron (see Chapter 11).

7   Remove the drivebelts from the alternator and power steering pump (see Chapter 1).

8   Support the engine and remove the right engine mount and braces (see Section 16). **Note:** *On ABS equipped models, remove the clamp bolts on the power steering cooling lines.*

9   Remove the spark plugs (see Chapter 1).

10   Remove the upper (no. 2) timing belt cover and gasket **(see illustration)**.

11   Remove the right side (RH) engine mounting bracket **(see illustration 7.10)**.

12   Position the number one piston at TDC (see Section 3).

13   Check to see if there are four installation marks on the timing belt **(see illustration)**. If you intend to reuse the belt and the marks have been obscured, make new ones.

14   Make sure the camshaft pulley timing marks are properly aligned **(see illustration)**.

15   Remove the timing belt tensioner **(see illustration)**.

16   Relieve the tension between the rear (RH) and front (LH) camshaft pulleys by turning the rear pulley slightly clockwise **(see illustration 7.10)**.

17   Remove the timing belt from the camshaft pulleys.

18   If you plan to reuse the timing belt and

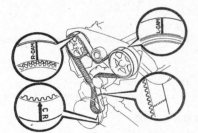

7.13 If you intend to reuse the belt and the installation marks shown here are obscured or missing, make new ones

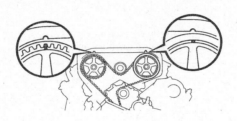

7.14 Both camshaft pulley timing marks should align with the marks on the rear cover

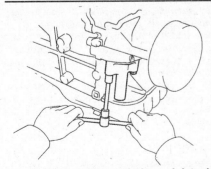

7.15 Remove the two bolts and detach the timing belt tensioner

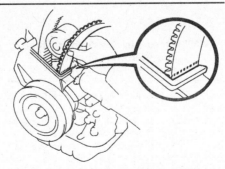

7.18 If you intend to reuse the belt and this mark is worn off, make a new one

Rear (firewall side) manifold only

5   Detach the exhaust pipe and oxygen sensor from the exhaust manifold (see Chapter 4).

6   Remove the EGR valve and pipe and vacuum modulator (see Chapter 6).

Both manifolds

7   Remove the nuts retaining the manifold to the cylinder head and slip it off the mounting studs.

8   Carefully inspect the manifold and fasteners for cracks and damage.

9   Use a scraper to remove all traces of old gasket material and carbon deposits from the

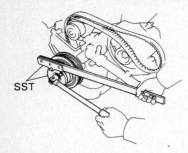

7.21 Keep the crankshaft from turning with a pin spanner wrench and loosen the bolt with a socket and breaker bar - the bolt is very tight, so use 1/2-inch drive tools

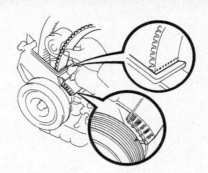

7.22 Recheck the position of the marks before proceeding

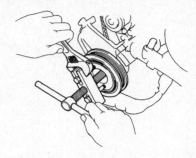

7.23 Use a vibration damper puller to remove the pulley from the crankshaft - don't use a gear puller that grips the outer edge of the pulley

7.26 There should be a mark on the belt next to the drilled mark on the pulley

7.28 Pad the front of the engine when prying off the pulley

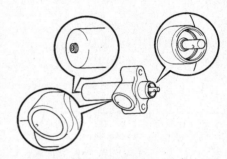

7.30 Check the belt tensioner for leakage in these areas

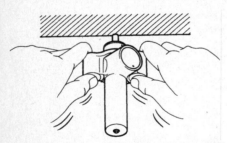

7.31 Check the tensioner for leakdown by forcing it against an immovable object

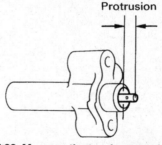

7.32 Measure the tensioner pushrod protrusion and compare it to the Specifications

the marks were worn off, place a new mark on the belt at the edge of the lower (no. 1) timing belt cover **(see illustration)**.
19   The camshaft pulleys can be removed at this point, if they are worn or damaged. Remove the cylinder head cover(s) (see Section 4) and hold the camshaft with a wrench on the cast-in hex while loosening the pulley bolt. Remove the bolt and detach the pulley.
20   Remove the upper (no. 2) idler pulley **(see illustration 7.10)**.
21   Remove the crankshaft (drivebelt) pulley bolt. Use a pin spanner to keep the crankshaft from turning **(see illustration)**. If a pin spanner isn't available, wedge a large screwdriver into the flywheel/driveplate ring gear teeth.
22   When the crankshaft pulley bolt is loosened, the position of the timing mark on the crankshaft pulley and the installation mark

may be disturbed. Check and align them again **(see illustration)**.
23   Using a vibration damper puller, remove the crankshaft pulley **(see illustration)**.
24   Remove the lower (no. 1) timing belt cover and gasket **(see illustration 7.10)**.
25   Slip the timing belt guide off the crankshaft **(see illustration 7.10)**.
26   If you're reusing the belt, check for a mark on the belt adjacent to the drilled mark on the crankshaft pulley **(see illustration)**. If the original mark is gone, make a new one, then slip the belt off the pulley.
27   Using an 8 mm Allen wrench, remove the no. 1 idler pulley and plate washer **(see illustration 7.10)**.
28   If it's worn or damaged, or if you're replacing the front crankshaft oil seal, the crankshaft timing pulley can now be

removed. If it won't come off by hand, lever it off with two screwdrivers **(see illustration)**.

Inspection

Refer to illustrations 7.30, 7.31 and 7.32
29   Refer to Chapter 2, Part A, Section 7 for the timing belt inspection procedures.
30   Check the belt tensioner for visible oil leakage **(see illustration)**. If there's only a faint trace of oil on the pushrod side, the tensioner seal is in satisfactory condition.
31   Hold the tensioner in both hands and push it forcefully against an immovable object **(see illustration)**. If the pushrod moves, replace the tensioner.
32   Measure the protrusion of the pushrod from the housing end **(see illustration)**. If the protrusion is not as specified, replace the tensioner.

Installation

Refer to illustrations 7.44, 7.45, 7.47, 7.49, 7.51 and 7.53
33   Remove all dirt and oil from the timing belt area at the front of the engine.
34   Align the crankshaft timing pulley keyway with the crankshaft key and install the pulley with the flange side up against the engine **(see illustration 7.10)**.
35   Apply thread locking compound to the first two or three threads on the lower (no. 1) idler pulley bolt, then position the idler pulley and washer and install the bolt. Tighten the bolt to the specified torque.

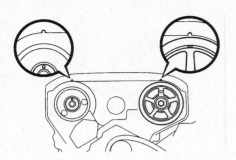

7.44 Align the camshaft knock pins with the timing marks on the rear cover

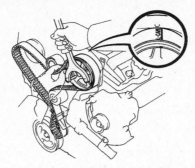

7.45 The mark on the timing belt must align with the camshaft pulley timing mark

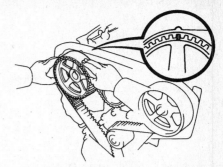

7.47 Align the marks on the belt, pulley and rear cover as you slip the belt onto the pulley

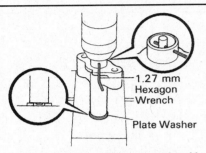

7.49 Restrain the tensioner pushrod by compressing the unit in a vise and holding it with a pin approximately 0.050-inch (1.27 mm) in diameter

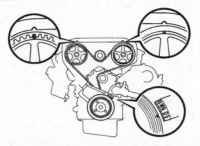

7.51 Starting at Top Dead Center for the number one piston, turn the crankshaft two complete revolutions (720°) and make sure the timing marks align

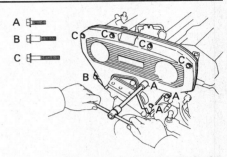

7.53 Install the various length bolts in the no. 2 timing belt cover as shown

36   Install the timing belt, starting at the crankshaft pulley. If you're reusing the original belt, align the marks on the belt with the marks on the pulleys and covers. Install the belt over the lower (no. 1) idler and water pump pulleys.

37   Slip the belt guide over the crankshaft with the cupped side facing out.

38   Install the lower (no. 1) timing belt cover and gasket **(see illustration 7.10)**.

39   Slip the crankshaft (drivebelt) pulley onto the crankshaft, aligning the pulley key-way with the crankshaft key. Install the bolt and tighten it to the specified torque. Use the method described in Step 21 to keep the crankshaft from turning.

40   Install the upper (no. 2) idler pulley. Tighten the bolt to the specified torque. Make sure the pulley turns smoothly.

41   Install the front (LH) camshaft pulley (if it was removed) on the camshaft with the flange side facing OUT. Align the pin hole in the pulley with the pin in the end of the camshaft.

42   Install the retaining bolt and tighten it to the specified torque. Use the method described in Step 19 to keep the camshaft from turning.

43   Recheck the timing marks to be sure the crankshaft hasn't turned **(see illustration 7.22)**. If you're reusing the original belt, the installation mark should line up as it did in Step 18. If not, change the position of the timing belt on the crankshaft pulley. The mark on the front (LH) camshaft pulley should be at the top (12 o'clock position), aligned with the

mark on the rear (no. 3) timing cover.

44   The rear (RH) camshaft knock pin hole should be at the top (12 o'clock position. If necessary, remove the camshaft cover and turn the camshaft slightly with a wrench to align it with the mark on the rear (no. 3) cover **(see illustration)**.

45   Turn the front (LH) camshaft pulley clockwise slightly (about one tooth) with a special tool, available at most auto parts stores **(see illustration)**. If the special tool isn't available, grip the hex on the camshaft with a wrench and turn it. If you're reusing the original belt, align the installation mark with the camshaft timing mark. Slip the belt onto the pulley, then turn the camshaft counter-clockwise, back to its original position. There should now be slight tension on the belt.

46   Install the rear (RH) camshaft pulley (if it was removed) on the camshaft with the flange side facing IN. Align the pin hole in the pulley with the knock pin in the end of the camshaft.

47   Install the retaining bolt and tighten it to the specified torque. Use the method described in Step 19 to keep the camshaft from turning. Be sure the timing mark is still aligned with the rear (no. 3) cover **(see illustration)**.

48   Slip the belt onto the pulley. If you're reusing the original belt, align the installation marks.

49   Using a press or vise, slowly compress the timing belt tensioner pushrod **(see illustration)**. Insert a metal pin or an Allen wrench through the holes in the pushrod and housing.

Release the pressure from the press or vise.

50   Install the timing belt tensioner and tighten the bolts to the specified torque. Remove the retaining pin or Allen wrench.

51   Using a socket and breaker bar on the crankshaft pulley bolt, turn the crankshaft slowly through two complete revolutions (720-degrees). Recheck the timing marks **(see illustration)**. **Caution:** *If the timing marks are not aligned exactly as shown, repeat the timing belt installation procedure. DO NOT start the engine until you're absolutely certain that the timing belt is installed correctly. Serious and costly engine damage could occur if the belt is installed wrong.*

52   Reinstall the right engine mounting bracket.

53   Install the upper (no. 2) timing belt cover and gasket. Three different length bolts are used **(see illustration)**.

54   Install the right engine mount and braces and tighten the bolts securely.

55   Reinstall the remaining parts in the reverse order of removal.

8   Front crankshaft oil seal - replacement

Refer to illustrations 8.3 and 8.5

1   Remove the timing belt and crankshaft timing pulley (see Section 7).

2   Note how far the seal is seated in the bore, then cut away the seal lip with a razor knife.

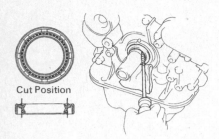

8.3 Cut away the crankshaft seal lip, wrap a screwdriver tip with tape and pry out the seal

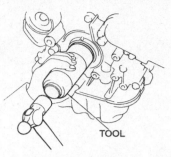

8.5 Lubricate the seal lip and tap the new crankshaft seal into place with a large socket or piece of pipe and a hammer

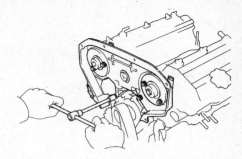

9.2 The rear timing belt cover must be removed to gain access to the camshaft oil seals

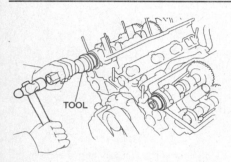

9.5 Lubricate the seal lip and tap the new camshaft seal into place with a large socket or piece of pipe and a hammer

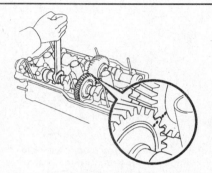

10.3 Align the timing marks on the camshaft gears

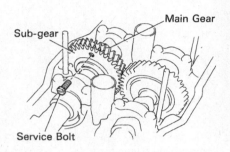

10.4 Install a service bolt through the sub-gear into the main gear

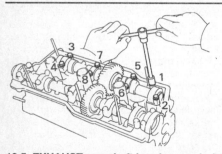

10.5 EXHAUST camshaft bearing cap bolt loosening sequence - rear cylinder head

3   Carefully pry the seal out of the engine with a screwdriver or seal removal tool **(see illustration)**. If you use a screwdriver, wrap tape around the tip - don't scratch the housing bore or damage the crankshaft (if the crankshaft is damaged, the new seal will end up leaking).

4   Clean the bore in the engine and coat the outer edge of the new seal with engine oil or multi-purpose grease. Apply moly-base grease to the seal lip.

5   Using a socket with an outside diameter slightly smaller than the outside diameter of the seal, carefully drive the new seal into place with a hammer **(see illustration)**. Make sure it's installed squarely and driven in to the same depth as the original. If a socket isn't available, a short section of large diameter pipe will also work. Check the seal after installation to make sure the garter spring didn't pop out of place.

6   Reinstall the crankshaft timing pulley and timing belt (see Section 7).

7   Run the engine and check for oil leaks at the front seal.

9   Camshaft oil seals - replacement

Refer to illustrations 9.2 and 9.5

1   Remove the timing belt and camshaft pulley(s) (see Section 7).

2   Remove the bolts and detach the rear (no. 3) timing belt cover **(see illustration)**.

3   Note how far the seal is seated in the bore, then carefully pry it out with a straight-slot screwdriver. Wrap the screwdriver tip with tape - don't scratch the bore or damage the camshaft (if the camshaft is damaged, the new seal will end up leaking).

4   Clean the bore and coat the outer edge of the new seal with engine oil or multi-purpose grease. Apply moly-base grease to the seal lip.

5   Using a socket with an outside diameter slightly smaller than the outside diameter of the seal, carefully drive the new seal into place with a hammer **(see illustration)**. Make sure it's installed squarely and driven in to the same depth as the original. If a socket isn't available, a short section of pipe will also work.

6   reinstall the rear timing belt cover and tighten the bolts.

7   Reinstall the camshaft pulley(s) and timing belt (see Section 7).

8   Run the engine and check for oil leaks at the camshaft seal.

10   Camshafts and lifters - removal, inspection and installation

Note: *Before beginning this procedure, obtain two 6 x 1.0 mm bolts 16 to 20 mm long. They will be referred to as service bolts in the text.*

Removal

Refer to illustrations 10.3, 10.4, 10.5, 10.7, 10.9, 10.10, 10.11, 10.13, 10.15a, 10.15b, 10.16, 10.17, 10.18 and 10.19

1   Remove the cylinder head covers (see Section 4) and the timing belt (see Section 7).

2   Remove the distributor (see Chapter 5).

Exhaust camshaft in rear (RH) cylinder head

3   Align the cam timing marks on the drive and driven gears **(see illustration)**. Turn the camshaft with a wrench if necessary.

4   Secure the exhaust camshaft sub-gear to the driven gear with a service bolt **(see illustration). Caution:** *Since the camshaft thrust clearance is minimal, the camshafts must be held level as they are being removed. If they aren't, the portion of the cylinder head next to the cam gears may crack or be damaged by the gear leverage. Before lifting a camshaft out of the head, make certain that the torsional spring force of the sub-gear has been eliminated by the service bolt.*

5   Loosen the camshaft bearing cap bolts in 1/4-turn increments until they can be removed by hand. Follow the factory recom-

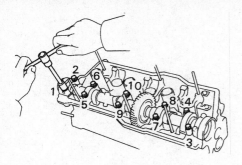

10.7 INTAKE camshaft bearing cap bolt loosening sequence - rear cylinder head

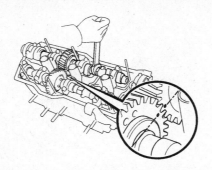

10.9 The front cylinder head camshaft gears have one dot for timing marks

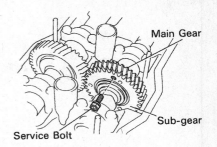

10.10 Install a service bolt through the sub-gear into the main gear

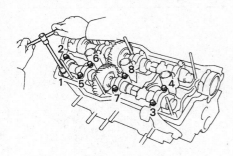

10.11 EXHAUST camshaft bearing cap bolt loosening sequence - front cylinder head

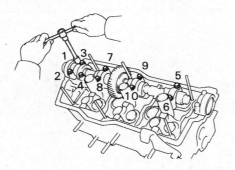

10.13 INTAKE camshaft bearing cap bolt loosening sequence - front cylinder head

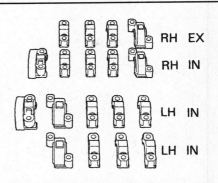

10.15a Store the bearing caps in the correct order

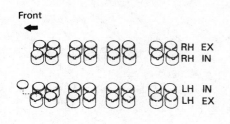

10.15b Keep the lifters in order and make sure the shims stay with the lifters

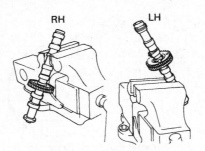

10.16 Clamp the camshaft in a padded vise

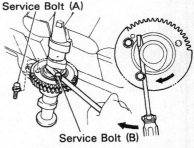

10.17 Align the holes, then install a second service bolt

mended sequence **(see illustration)**.

6   Remove the bearing caps and gently lift out the exhaust camshaft. Be sure to keep it level.

Intake camshaft in rear (RH) cylinder head

7   Loosen the camshaft bearing cap bolts in 1/4-turn increments until they can be removed by hand. Follow the recommended sequence **(see illustration)**.

8   Remove the bearing caps and oil seal and gently lift out the intake camshaft. Be sure to keep it level.

Exhaust camshaft in front (LH) cylinder head

9   Align the camshaft timing marks on the

drive and driven gears **(see illustration)**. Turn the camshaft with a wrench if necessary.

10   Secure the exhaust camshaft sub-gear to the driven gear with a service bolt **(see illustration)**.

11   Loosen the camshaft bearing cap bolts in 1/4-turn increments until they can be removed by hand. Follow the factory recommended sequence **(see illustration)**.

12   Remove the bearing caps and gently lift out the exhaust camshaft. Keep it level.

Intake camshaft in front (LH) cylinder head

13   Loosen the camshaft bearing cap bolts in 1/4-turn increments until they can be removed by hand. Follow the recommended sequence **(see illustration)**.

14   Remove the bearing caps and oil seal

and gently lift out the intake camshaft. Keep it level.

15   Store the bearing caps in the correct order **(see illustration)**. **Note:** *If necessary, the valve lifters and shims can be removed after the camshaft(s) by simply pulling up on them with a magnetic tool. Be sure to store them separately so they can be reinstalled in their original locations* **(see illustration)**.

16   To disassemble the exhaust camshafts, mount them in a vise, one at a time, with the jaws gripping the large hex on the shaft **(see illustration)**.

17   Install a second service bolt in the unthreaded hole in the camshaft sub-gear. Using a screwdriver positioned against the service bolt just installed, rotate the sub-gear clockwise and remove the first service bolt **(see illustration)**.

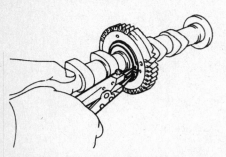

10.18 Remove the snap-ring with a pair of snap-ring pliers

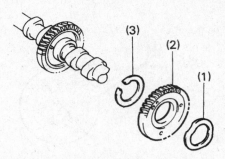

10.19 Remove the wave washer (1), the camshaft sub-gear (2) and the gear spring (3)

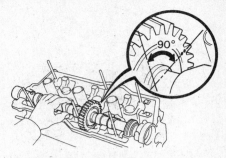

10.26 Set the rear cylinder head intake camshaft into place with the two dots at the 3 o'clock position (facing the exhaust camshaft)

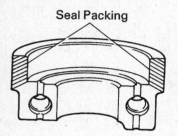

Seal Packing

10.27 Apply sealer to the shaded areas on the bearing cap

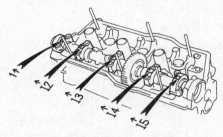

10.28 Install the rear cylinder head INTAKE camshaft bearing caps as shown with the arrows pointing toward the timing belt end of the engine

10.29 Rear cylinder head INTAKE camshaft bearing cap bolt tightening sequence

18   Remove the sub-gear snap-ring **(see illustration)**.

19   The wave washer, sub-gear and camshaft gear spring can now be removed from the camshaft **(see illustration)**. Be sure to keep the parts from the left side camshaft separate from the right side.

Inspection

20   Refer to Chapter 2, Part A, Section 11 for camshaft, lifter and related component checking procedures. Be sure to use the Specifications in this Part of Chapter 2 for the V6 engine.

Installation

Refer to illustrations 10.26, 10.27, 10.28, 10.29, 10.32, 10.33, 10.34, 10.37, 10.39, 10.40, 10.43, 10.44 and 10.45

21   Reassemble the exhaust camshafts by installing the camshaft gear spring, sub-gear, wave washer and snap-ring.

22   Mount each camshaft in a padded vise, just like during disassembly.

23   Insert a service bolt into the unthreaded hole in the camshaft subgear. Using a screwdriver, align the holes of the camshaft driven gear and sub-gear by turning the camshaft sub-gear clockwise. Install a second service bolt in the threaded hole and use it to clamp the gears together with the teeth aligned.

24   Apply moly-base grease or engine assembly lube to the lifters, then install them in their original locations in the heads. Make sure the valve adjustment shims are in place in the lifters.

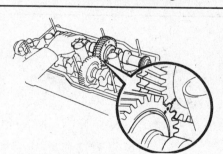

10.32 Install the rear cylinder head exhaust camshaft and align the marks on the gears

Intake camshaft in rear (RH) cylinder head

25   Apply moly-base grease or engine assembly lube to the camshaft lobes, bearing journals and gear thrust faces.

26   Set the intake camshaft in place in the rear cylinder head with the timing marks (two dots) facing the exhaust camshaft side of the head **(see illustration)**.

27   Apply a thin coat of sealer to the outer edges of the front bearing cap cylinder head mating surfaces **(see illustration)**.

28   Install the bearing caps in numerical order with the arrows pointing toward the TIMING BELT END of the engine **(see illustration)**.

29   Tighten the bearing cap bolts in 1/4-turn increments until the specified torque is reached. Follow the factory recommended

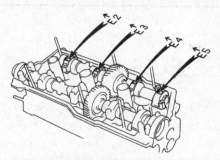

10.33 Install the rear cylinder head EXHAUST camshaft bearing caps as shown with the arrows pointing toward the timing belt end of the engine

sequence **(see illustration)**.

30   Refer to Section 9 and install a new camshaft oil seal.

Exhaust camshaft in rear (RH) cylinder head

31   Apply moly-base grease or engine assembly lube to the camshaft lobes, bearing journals and gear thrust faces.

32   Set the exhaust camshaft in place in the rear cylinder head with the timing marks (two dots) aligned with the intake camshaft timing marks **(see illustration)**.

33   Install the bearing caps in numerical order with the arrows pointing toward the TIMING BELT END of the engine **(see illustration)**.

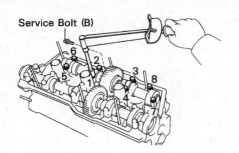

10.34 Rear cylinder head EXHAUST camshaft bearing cap bolt tightening sequence

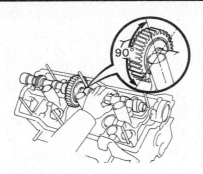

10.37 Set the front cylinder head intake camshaft into place with the one dot at the 3 o'clock position (facing the exhaust camshaft)

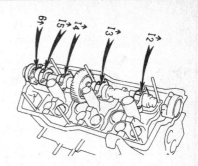

10.39 Install the front cylinder head INTAKE camshaft bearing caps as shown with the arrows pointing toward the transaxle end of the engine

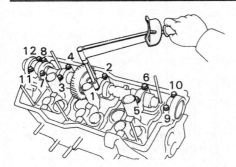

10.40 Front cylinder head INTAKE camshaft bearing cap bolt tightening sequence

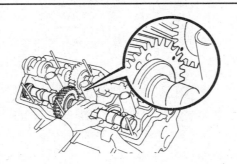

10.43 Install the front cylinder head exhaust camshaft and align the marks on the gears

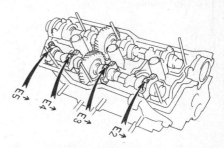

10.44 Install the front cylinder head EXHAUST camshaft bearing caps as shown with the arrows pointing toward the transaxle end of the engine

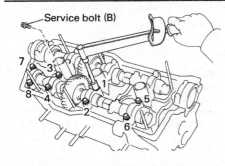

10.45 Front cylinder head EXHAUST camshaft bearing cap bolt tightening sequence

34 Tighten the bearing cap bolts in 1/4-turn increments until the specified torque is reached. Follow the factory recommended sequence **(see illustration)**.
35 Remove the service bolt.

Intake camshaft in front (LH) cylinder head

36 Apply moly-base grease or engine assembly lube to the camshaft lobes, bearing journals and gear thrust faces.
37 Set the intake camshaft in place in the front cylinder head with the timing mark (one dot) facing the exhaust camshaft side of the head **(see illustration)**.
38 Apply a thin coat of sealer to the outer edges of the front bearing cap cylinder head mating surfaces **(see illustration 10.27)**.
39 Install the bearing caps in numerical order with the arrows pointing toward the TRANSAXLE END of the engine **(see illustration)**.
40 Tighten the bearing cap bolts in 1/4-turn increments until the specified torque is reached. Follow the factory recommended sequence **(see illustration)**.
41 Refer to Section 9 and install a new camshaft oil seal.

Exhaust camshaft in front (LH) cylinder head

42 Apply moly-base grease or engine assembly lube to the camshaft lobes, bearing journals and gear thrust faces.
43 Set the exhaust camshaft in place in the front cylinder head with the timing mark (one dot) aligned with the intake camshaft timing mark **(see illustration)**.
44 Install the bearing caps in numerical order with the arrows pointing toward the TRANSAXLE END of the engine **(see illustration)**.
45 Tighten the bearing cap bolts in 1/4-turn increments until the specified torque is reached. Follow the factory recommended sequence **(see illustration)**.
46 Remove the service bolt.
47 Reinstall the timing belt (Section 7).

48 Reinstall the remaining components in the reverse order of removal.
49 Run the engine, then check for leaks and proper operation.

11 Cylinder heads - removal and installation

Removal

Refer to illustrations 11.10 and 11.11
1 Disconnect the negative cable from the battery.
2 Drain the cooling system, including both block drains (see Chapter 1).
3 Remove the air intake chamber, fuel delivery pipes and injectors (see Chapter 4).
4 Remove the exhaust manifold(s) (see Section 6).
5 Remove the alternator and distributor (see Chapter 5).
6 Remove the intake manifold (see Section 5).
7 Remove the timing belt, camshaft pulleys and upper idler pulley (see Section 7).
8 Remove the upper timing belt cover **(see illustration 9.2)**.
9 Remove the camshaft(s) from the head(s) you intend to remove (see Section 10).
10 Using an 8 mm Allen head socket,

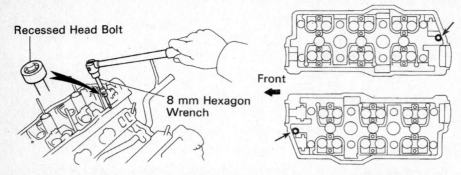

11.10 Remove the end (recessed) bolts (arrows) with an 8 mm Allen head socket

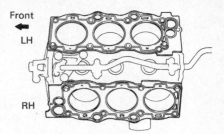

11.19 Be sure the new head gaskets are positioned right side up (check all holes and coolant passages for correct alignment)

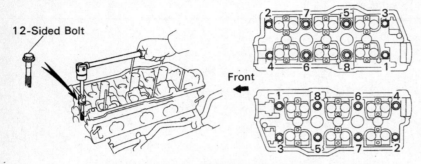

11.11 Cylinder head bolt LOOSENING sequence

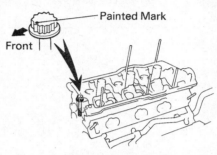

11.23 Apply a small dab of paint to the front of each cylinder head bolt . . .

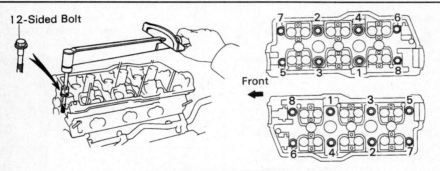

11.22 Cylinder head bolt TIGHTENING sequence

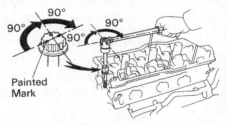

11.24 . . . then turn each bolt 1/4-turn (90-degrees) more, following the tightening sequence - as a final step, tighten each bolt an additional 1/4-turn in the same sequence, for a total of 180-degrees

remove the recessed head bolts (one in each head) **(see illustration)**.

11   Using a 12-point socket, loosen the rear cylinder head bolts in 1/4-turn increments until they can be removed by hand. Follow the factory recommended sequence **(see illustration)**.

12   Lift the rear cylinder head off the engine block. If the head is stuck, place a block of wood against it and strike the block with a hammer. **Caution:** *Don't pry between the head and block. The gasket surfaces may be damaged and leaks could result.*

13   Repeat the procedure for the front head.

Installation

Refer to illustrations 11.19, 11.22, 11.23 and 11.24

14   The mating surfaces of the cylinder heads and block must be perfectly clean when the heads are installed.

15   Use a gasket scraper to remove all traces of carbon and old gasket material, then clean the mating surfaces with lacquer thinner or acetone. If there's oil on the mating surfaces when the head is installed, the gasket may not seal correctly and leaks could develop. When working on the block, stuff the cylinders with clean shop rags to keep out debris. Use a vacuum cleaner to remove material that falls into the cylinders.

16   Check the block and head mating surfaces for nicks, deep scratches and other damage. If damage is slight, it can be removed with a file; if it's excessive, machining may be the only alternative.

17   Use a tap of the correct size to chase the threads in the head bolt holes, then clean the holes with compressed air - make sure that nothing remains in the holes. **Warning:** *Wear eye protection when using compressed air!*

18   Mount each bolt in a vise and run a die down the threads to remove corrosion and restore the threads. Dirt, corrosion, sealant and damaged threads will affect torque readings.

19   Position the new gaskets over the dowel pins in the block **(see illustration)**.

20   Carefully set the rear head on the block without disturbing the gasket.

21   Before installing the head bolts, apply a small amount of clean engine oil to the threads.

22   Install the bolts in their original locations and tighten them finger tight. Following the recommended sequence, tighten the bolts to the specified torque **(see illustration)**. Don't tighten the recessed bolt at this time.

23   Mark the front of each bolt head with paint **(see illustration)**.

24   Following the same sequence, tighten each bolt an additional 1/4-turn (90-degrees) **(see illustration)**.

25   Finally, tighten each bolt yet another 1/4-turn (90-degrees) following the same

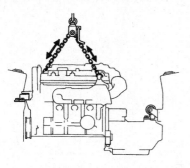

12.8 Connect a hoist chain to the lifting hooks and support the engine

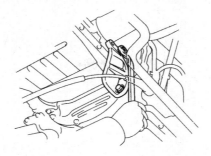

12.11 Unbolt the engine stiffener plate at the bellhousing

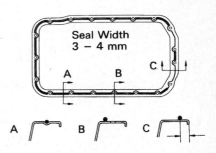

12.17 Apply the sealer toward the inside of the oil pan bolt holes as shown in B

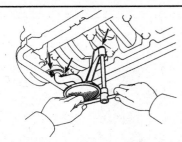

13.4 The oil pick-up tube is held in place with three fasteners (arrows)

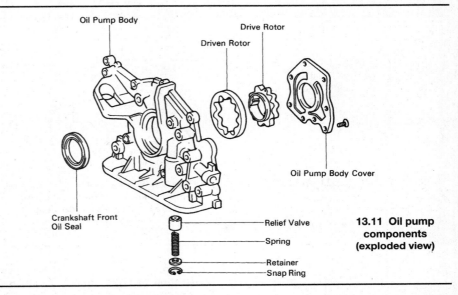

13.11 Oil pump components (exploded view)

sequence. The paint marks should now all be at the back of the bolt heads (180-degrees from the starting point).

26   Tighten the recessed bolt to the specified torque.

27   Repeat the entire procedure to install the front cylinder head.

28   The remaining installation steps are the reverse of removal.

29   Refill the cooling system, change the oil and filter (see Chapter 1), run the engine and check for leaks.

12 Oil pan - removal and installation

Note: *This procedure requires a hoist to lift the engine. Read through all the steps before beginning the job.*

Removal

Refer to illustrations 12.8 and 12.11

1   Remove the hood (see Chapter 11).
2   Disconnect the negative cable from the battery.
3   Raise the vehicle and support it securely on jackstands.
4   Remove the engine splash shields.
5   Drain the engine oil and remove the oil filter.
6   Remove the lower front suspension crossmember.
7   Disconnect the front exhaust pipe from the manifold (see Chapter 4).
8   Support the engine with a hoist having at least a 1000 pound capacity **(see illustration)**.
9   Remove the center engine mounting member.
10   Remove the front engine mount and bracket (see Section 17).

11   Remove the engine stiffener plate **(see illustration)**.
12   Remove the bolts and detach the oil pan. If it's stuck, pry it loose very carefully with a small screwdriver or putty knife. Don't damage the mating surfaces of the pan and block or oil leaks could develop.

Installation

Refer to illustration 12.17

13   Use a scraper to remove all traces of old sealant from the block and oil pan. Clean the mating surfaces with lacquer thinner or acetone.
14   Make sure the threaded bolt holes in the block are clean.
15   Check the oil pan flange for distortion, particularly around the bolt holes. If necessary, place the pan on a block of wood and use a hammer to flatten and restore the gasket surface.
16   Inspect the oil pump pick-up tube assembly for cracks and a blocked strainer. If the pick-up was removed, install it now, using a new gasket. Tighten the fasteners to the specified torque.
17   Apply a 3 to 4 mm wide bead of sealer to the oil pan flange **(see illustration)**. **Note:** *The oil pan must be installed within 3 minutes once the sealer has been applied.*

18   Carefully position the oil pan on the engine block and install the bolts. Working from the center out, tighten them to the specified torque in three or four steps.
19   The remainder of installation is the reverse of removal. Be sure to add oil and install a new oil filter.
20   Run the engine and check for oil pressure and leaks.

13 Oil pump - removal, inspection and installation

Removal

Refer to illustrations 13.4 and 13.11

1   Remove the oil pan (see Section 12).
2   Remove the timing belt (see Section 7) and lower timing belt idler pulley.
3   Remove the crankshaft timing pulley (see Section 7).
4   Remove the oil pick-up tube **(see illustration)**.
5   Remove the alternator (see Chapter 5) (air conditioning-equipped vehicles only).
6   Unbolt the air conditioner compressor and set it aside without disconnecting the refrigerant lines.
7   Remove the air conditioner compressor bracket.

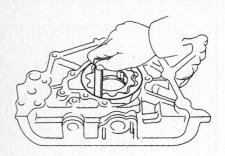

13.17a Measuring driven rotor-to-body clearance with a feeler gauge

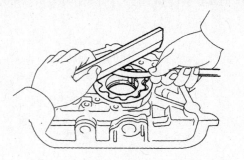

13.17b Measuring rotor side clearance with a precision straightedge and feeler gauge

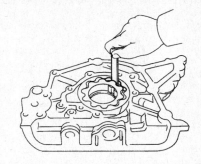

13.17c Measuring rotor tip clearance with a feeler gauge

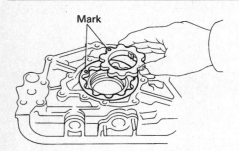

13.20 Install the rotors with the marks facing out (when the pump body cover is installed, the marks will be against the cover)

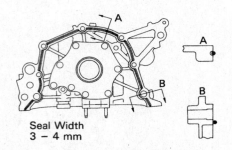

13.24 Apply a bead of sealer to the oil pump-to-block mating surface - make sure it's directed to the inside of each bolt hole

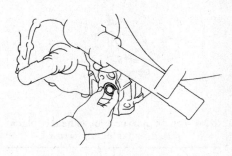

13.25 Be sure to install a new O-ring before bolting the pump to the block

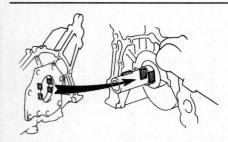

13.26 Be sure to align the drive rotor and the crankshaft as the oil pump is installed

8   Remove the power steering belt adjusting bar.
9   Remove the bolts and detach the oil pump from the engine. You may have to pry carefully between the front main bearing cap and the pump body with a screwdriver.
10   Remove the O-ring.
11   Use a large Phillips screwdriver to remove the eight screws holding the body cover to the rear of the oil pump **(see illustration)**.
12   Lift the cover off and remove the pump rotors.
13   Use a scraper to remove all traces of sealant and old gasket material from the pump body and engine block, then clean the mating surfaces with lacquer thinner or acetone.
14   Remove the oil pressure relief valve

snap-ring, retainer, spring and valve **(see illustration 13.11)**. **Warning:** *The spring is tightly compressed - be careful and wear eye protection.*

Inspection

Refer to illustrations 13.17a, 13.17b and 13.17c
15   Clean all components with solvent, then inspect them for wear and damage.
16   Check the oil pressure relief valve sliding surface and valve spring. If either the spring or the valve is damaged, they must be replaced as a set.
17   Check the following clearances with a feeler gauge **(see illustrations)** and compare the measurements to the Specifications:
    Driven rotor-to-oil pump body
    Rotor side clearance
    Rotor tip clearance

Installation

Refer to illustrations 13.20, 13.24, 13.25, 13.26 and 13.27
18   Pry the old crankshaft seal out with a screwdriver.
19   Apply multi-purpose grease or engine oil to the outer edge of the new seal and carefully drive it into place with a deep socket and a hammer. Apply moly-base grease to the seal lip.
20   Place the drive and driven rotors into the

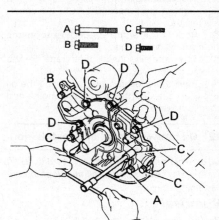

13.27 The oil pump bolts are different lengths and must be installed in the correct locations

pump body with the marks facing out **(see illustration)**.
21   Pack the pump cavity with petroleum jelly and install the cover. Tighten the screws securely following a criss-cross pattern.
22   Lubricate the oil pressure relief valve with engine oil and install the valve components in the pump body.
23   Use acetone or lacquer thinner and a clean rag to remove all traces of oil from the gasket surfaces.
24   Apply a 2 to 3 mm wide bead of sealer to the oil pump flange **(see illustration)**.

Avoid using excessive amount of sealer, especially around oil passages and bolt holes. Parts must be assembled within five minutes of sealer application, otherwise the material must be removed and reapplied.

25   Position a new O-ring on the block **(see illustration)**.

26   Engage the spline teeth on the oil pump drive rotor with the large teeth on the crankshaft and slide the pump into place **(see illustration)**.

27   Install the pump mounting bolts in their original locations **(see illustration)** and tighten them to the specified torque in a criss-cross pattern.

28   Using a new gasket, install the oil pick-up tube and tighten the fasteners to the specified torque.

29   Reinstall the remaining parts in the reverse order of removal.

30   Add oil, start the engine and check for oil leaks.

31   Recheck the engine oil level.

14   Flywheel/driveplate - removal and installation

Refer to Chapter 2, Part A, Section 16 for this procedure, but be sure to use the torque specifications in this Part of Chapter 2 for the V6 engine.

15   Rear crankshaft oil seal - replacement

Refer to illustration 15.1

Refer to Chapter 2, Part A, Section 17 for this procedure, but note that the V6 engine doesn't have a gasket between the seal retainer and the engine block. Instead, apply a 2 to 3 mm wide bead of sealer to the retainer flange **(see illustration)** before attaching the retainer to the block. Also, be sure to use the torque specifications in this Part of Chapter 2 for the V6 engine.

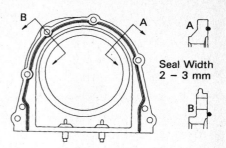

15.1 Apply sealer to the oil seal retainer-to-block mating surface

16   Engine mounts - check and replacement

Refer to Chapter 2, Part A, Section 18, but note that the V6 engine mounts are slightly different in ways that don't significantly affect the check and replacement procedures.

Notes

Chapter 2 Part C
General engine overhaul procedures

Contents

Specifications

Four-cylinder engines

General

Displacement	122 cu in (2.0 liters)
Cylinder compression pressure	
2S-E engine	
Standard	171 psi
Minimum	128 psi
3S-FE engine	
Standard	178 psi
Minimum	142 psi
Oil pressure (engine warm)	
At 3000 rpm	36 to 71 psi
At idle	4.3 psi minimum

Cylinder head warpage limits

2S-E engine	
Block surface	0.002 in (0.05 mm)
Camshaft housing surface	0.002 in (0.05 mm)
Manifold surfaces	0.0031 in (0.08 mm)
3S-FE engine	
Block surface	0.002 in (0.05 mm)
Manifold surfaces	0.0031 in (0.08 mm)

Valves and related components

Minimum valve margin width	
Intake	0.020 in (0.5 mm)
Exhaust	
2S-E engine	0.039 in (1.0 mm)
3S-FE engine	0.020 in (0.5 mm)
Intake valve	
Stem diameter	
2S-E engine	0.3138 to 0.3144 in (7.970 to 7.985 mm)
3S-FE engine	0.2350 to 0.2356 in (5.970 to 5.985 mm)
Valve stem-to-guide clearance	
Standard	0.0010 to 0.0024 in (0.025 to 0.060 mm)
Service limit	0.0031 in (0.08 mm)
Length	
2S-E engine	
Standard	4.319 in (109.7 mm)
Minimum	4.299 in (109.2 mm)

Four-cylinder engines

Valves and related components (continued)
3S-FE engine
    Standard.. 3.9606 in (100.60 mm)
    Minimum.. 3.9410 in (100.10 mm)
Exhaust valve
  Stem diameter
    2S-E engine .... 0.3136 to 0.3142 in (7.965 to 7.980 mm)
    3S-FE engine .... 0.2348 to 0.2354 in (5.965 to 5.980 mm)
  Valve stem-to-guide clearance
    Standard.. 0.0012 to 0.0026 in (0.030 to 0.065 mm)
    Service limit.. 0.0039 in (0.10 mm)
  Length
    2S-E engine
      Standard.. 4.303 in (109.3 mm)
      Minimum.. 4.283 in (108.8 mm)
    3S-FE engine
      Standard.. 3.9547 in (100.45 mm)
      Minimum.. 3.9370 in (100.0 mm)
Valve spring
  Out-of-square limit
    2S-E engine .... 0.079 in (2.0 mm)
    3S-FE engine .... 0.075 in (2.0 mm)
  Free length
    2S-E engine .... 1.839 in (46.71 mm)
    3S-FE engine .... 1.772 in (45.0 mm)
  Pressure/length
    2S-E engine .... 68.0 lbs at 1.555 in (30.8 kg at 39.55 mm)
    3S-FE engine .... 36.8 to 42.5 lbs at 1.366 in (16.7 to 19.3 kg at 34.7 mm)
  Installed height
    2S-E engine .... 1.555 in (39.5 mm)
    3S-FE engine .... 1.366 in (34.7 mm)

Engine block
Deck warpage limit .... 0.0020 in (0.05 mm)

Crankshaft and connecting rods
Connecting rod journal
  Diameter... 1.8892 to 1.8898 in (47.985 to 48.000 mm)
  Taper and out-of-round limits .... 0.0008 in (0.02 mm)
Bearing oil clearance
  Standard.. 0.0009 to 0.0022 in (0.024 to 0.055 mm)
  Service limit.. 0.0031 in (0.08 mm)
Connecting rod side clearance (end play)
  Standard
    2S-E engine .... 0.0063 to 0.0083 in (0.16 to 0.21 mm)
    3S-FE engine .... 0.0063 to 0.0123 in (0.160 to 0.312 mm)
  Service limit.. 0.012 in (0.35 mm)
Main bearing journal
  Diameter
    2S-E engine .... 2.1648 to 2.1654 in (54.985 to 55.000 mm)
    3S-FE engine
      Marked "0" .... 2.1652 to 2.1654 in (54.995 to 55.000 mm)
      Marked "1" .... 2.1650 to 2.1652 in (54.990 to 54.995 mm)
      Marked "2" .... 2.1648 to 2.1650 in (54.985 to 54.990 mm)
  Taper and out-of-round limits .... 0.0008 in (0.02 mm)
  Runout limit .... 0.0024 in (0.06 mm)
  Bearing oil clearance
    2S-E engine (standard)
      No. 3 (center) main .... 0.0012 to 0.0022 in (0.030 to 0.057 mm)
      All others.. 0.0008 to 0.0019 in (0.020 to 0.047 mm)
    3S-FE engine (standard)
      No. 3 (center) main .... 0.0011 to 0.0019 in (0.028 to 0.047 mm)
      All others.. 0.0007 to 0.0015 in (0.018 to 0.037 mm)
      Service limit.. 0.0031 in (0.08 mm)
Crankshaft end play
  Standard.. 0.0008 to 0.0087 in (0.020 to 0.220 mm)
  Service limit.. 0.0118 in (0.30 mm)
Thrust washer thickness... 0.0961 to 0.0980 in (2.440 to 2.490 mm)

Cylinder bore

Diameter	
2S-E engine	
Standard	3.3071 to 3.3083 in (84.00 to 84.03 mm)
Service limit	3.3181 in (84.28 mm)
3S-FE engine	
Standard	3.3858 to 3.3870 in (86.000 to 86.030 mm)
Service limit	3.3949 in (86.23 mm)
Taper and out-of-round limits	0.0008 in (0.020 mm)

Pistons and rings

Piston diameter	
2S-E engine	3.3061 to 3.3073 in (83.975 to 84.005 mm)
3S-FE engine	3.3836 to 3.3848 in (85.945 to 85.975 mm)
Piston-to-bore clearance	
2S-E engine	
Standard	0.0006 to 0.0014 in (0.015 to 0.035 mm)
Service limit	0.0020 in (0.05 mm)
3S-FE engine	
Standard	0.0018 to 0.0026 in (0.045 to 0.065 mm)
Service limit	0.0033 in (0.085 mm)
Piston ring end gap	
2S-E engine	
No. 1 (top)	0.0110 to 0.0209 in (0.28 to 0.53 mm)
No. 2 (middle)	0.0083 to 0.0189 in (0.21 to 0.48 mm)
Oil ring	0.0079 to 0.0323 in (0.20 to 0.82 mm)
3S-FE engine	
No. 1 (top)	0.0106 to 0.0205 in (0.270 to 0.520 mm)
No. 2 (middle)	0.0106 to 0.0209 in (0.270 to 0.520 mm)
Oil ring	0.0079 to 0.0323 in (0.200 to 0.820 mm)
Piston ring side clearance	0.0012 to 0.0028 in (0.030 to 0.070 mm)

Torque specifications*   **Ft-lbs**

Main bearing cap bolts	
1983	40 to 47
1984 on	43
Connecting rod cap nuts	
1983	33 to 39
1984 on	36

* **Note:** *Refer to Part A for additional torque specifications.*

V6 engine

General

Displacement	2.5 liters
Cylinder compression pressure at 250 rpm	
Standard	178 psi
Minimum	142 psi
Oil pressure (engine hot)	
At 3000 rpm	43 to 78 psi
At idle	4.3 psi minimum

Cylinder head warpage limit

Cylinder head warpage limit	0.0039 in (0.10 mm)

Valves and related components

Minimum valve margin width	0.020 in (0.5 mm)
Intake valve	
Stem diameter	0.2350 to 0.2356 in (5.970 to 5.985 mm)
Valve stem-to-guide clearance	
Standard	0.001 to 0.0024 in (0.025 to 0.060 mm)
Service limit	0.0031 in (0.08 mm)
Length	
Standard	3.783 in (96.1 mm)
Minimum	3.764 in (95.6 mm)
Exhaust valve	
Stem diameter	0.2348 to 0.2354 in (5.965 to 5.980 mm)
Valve stem-to-guide clearance	
Standard	0.0012 to 0.0026 in (0.030 to 0.065 mm)
Service limit	0.0039 in (0.10 mm)
Length	
Standard	3.787 in (96.2 mm)
Minimum	3.768 in (95.7 mm)

V6 engine (continued)

Valves and related components (continued)

Valve spring

Pressure .... 41.0 to 47.2 lbs at 1.33 in (182 to 210 N at 33.8 mm)

Free length .... 1.677 in (42.6 mm)

Out-of-square limit .... 0.075 in (2.0 mm)

Valve lifter

Diameter .... 1.1014 to 1.1018 in (27.975 to 27.985 mm)

Lifter bore diameter .... 1.1024 to 1.1032 in (28.000 to 28.021 mm)

Lifter-to-bore clearance

Standard .... 0.0005 to 0.0018 in (0.015 to 0.046 mm)

Service limit .... 0.0028 in (0.07 mm)

Crankshaft and connecting rods

Connecting rod journal

Diameter .... 1.8892 to 1.8898 in (47.987 to 48.000 mm)

Taper and out-of-round limits .... 0.0008 in (0.02 mm)

Bearing oil clearance

Standard .... 0.0011 to 0.0026 in (0.028 to 0.065 mm)

Service limit .... 0.0031 in (0.08 mm)

Connecting rod side clearance (end play)

Standard .... 0.0059 to 0.0130 in (0.150 to 0.330 mm)

Service limit .... 0.015 in (0.38 mm)

Connecting rod bolt outer diameter

Standard .... 0.3094 to 0.3150 in (7.860 to 8.000 mm)

Service limit .... 0.2992 in (7.60 mm)

Main bearing journal

Diameter

Marked "0" .... 2.5195 to 2.5197 in (63.996 to 64.000 mm)

Marked "1" .... 2.5193 to 2.5195 in (63.990 to 63.996 mm)

Marked "2" .... 2.5191 to 2.5193 in (63.985 to 63.990 mm)

Taper and out-of-round limits .... 0.0008 in (0.02 mm)

Bearing oil clearance

Standard .... 0.0011 to 0.0022 in (0.029 to 0.056 mm)

Service limit .... 0.0031 in (0.08 mm)

Crankshaft end play

Standard .... 0.0008 to 0.0087 in (0.020 to 0.220 mm)

Service limit .... 0.0118 in (0.30 mm)

Thrust washer thickness .... 0.0961 to 0.0980 in (2.440 to 2.490 mm)

Cylinder bore diameter

Standard .... 3.4449 to 3.4461 in (87.500 to 87.530 mm)

Service limit .... 3.4539 in (87.73 mm)

Pistons and rings

Piston diameter (standard) .... 3.4427 to 3.4439 in (87.445 to 87.475 mm)

Piston-to-bore clearance

Standard .... 0.0018 to 0.0026 in (0.045 to 0.065 mm)

Service limit .... 0.0033 in (0.085 mm)

Piston ring end gap

No. 1 (top) compression ring

Standard .... 0.0118 to 0.0213 in (0.300 to 0.540 mm)

Service limit .... 0.0449 in (1.14 mm)

No. 2 (middle) compression ring

Standard .... 0.0138 to 0.0244 in (0.350 to 0.620 mm)

Service limit .... 0.0480 in (1.22 mm)

Oil ring

Standard .... 0.0079 to 0.0224 in (0.200 to 0.570 mm)

Service limit .... 0.0461 in (1.17 mm)

Piston ring side clearance

No. 1 (top) compression ring .... 0.0004 to 0.0031 in (0.010 to 0.080 mm)

No. 2 (middle) compression ring .... 0.0012 to 0.0028 in (0.030 to 0.070 mm)

Torque specifications*

Ft-lbs

Main bearing cap assembly bolts

Step 1 45

Step 2 .... Turn an additional 90-degrees (1/4-turn)

Connecting rod cap nuts

Step 1 18

Step 2 .... Turn an additional 90-degrees (1/4-turn)

* **Note:** *Refer to Part B for additional torque specifications.*

1 General information

Included in this portion of Chapter 2 are the general overhaul procedures for the cylinder head(s) and internal engine components.

The information ranges from advice concerning preparation for an overhaul and the purchase of replacement parts to detailed, step-by-step procedures covering removal and installation of internal engine components and the inspection of parts.

The following Sections have been written based on the assumption that the engine has been removed from the vehicle. For information concerning in-vehicle engine repair, as well as removal and installation of the external components necessary for the overhaul, see Part A or B of this Chapter and Section 7 of this Part.

The Specifications included in this Part are only those necessary for the inspection and overhaul procedures which follow. Refer to Parts A and B for additional Specifications.

2 Engine overhaul - general information

Refer to illustrations 2.4a, 2.4b and 2.4c

It's not always easy to determine when, or if, an engine should be completely overhauled, as a number of factors must be considered.

High mileage is not necessarily an indication that an overhaul is needed, while low mileage doesn't preclude the need for an overhaul. Frequency of servicing is probably the most important consideration. An engine that's had regular and frequent oil and filter changes, as well as other required maintenance, will most likely give many thousands of miles of reliable service. Conversely, a neglected engine may require an overhaul very early in its life.

Excessive oil consumption is an indication that piston rings, valve seals and/or valve guides are in need of attention. Make sure that oil leaks aren't responsible before deciding that the rings and/or guides are bad. Perform a cylinder compression check to determine the extent of the work required (see Section 3).

Check the oil pressure with a gauge installed in place of the oil pressure sending unit **(see illustrations)** and compare it to the Specifications. If it's extremely low, the bearings and/or oil pump are probably worn out.

Loss of power, rough running, knocking or metallic engine noises, excessive valve train noise and high fuel consumption rates may also point to the need for an overhaul, especially if they're all present at the same time. If a complete tune-up doesn't remedy the situation, major mechanical work is the only solution.

An engine overhaul involves restoring the internal parts to the specifications of a new engine. During an overhaul, the piston

2.4a The oil pressure can be checked by removing the sending unit and installing a pressure gauge in the hole

2.4b On 3S-FE models, the oil pressure sending unit (arrow) is located on the left front corner of the cylinder head (on 2S-E engines, the sender is located in the left front corner of the engine block)

rings are replaced and the cylinder walls are reconditioned (rebored and/or honed). If a rebore is done by an automotive machine shop, new oversize pistons will also be installed. The main bearings, connecting rod bearings and camshaft bearings are generally replaced with new ones and, if necessary, the crankshaft may be reground to restore the journals. Generally, the valves are serviced as well, since they're usually in less-than-perfect condition at this point. While the engine is being overhauled, other components, such as the distributor, starter and alternator, can be rebuilt as well. The end result should be a like new engine that will give many trouble free miles. **Note:** *Critical cooling system components such as the hoses, drivebelts, thermostat and water pump MUST be replaced with new parts when an engine is overhauled. The radiator should be checked carefully to ensure that it isn't clogged or leaking (see Chapter 3). Also, we don't recommend overhauling the oil pump - always install a new one when an engine is rebuilt.*

Before beginning the engine overhaul, read through the entire procedure to familiarize yourself with the scope and requirements of the job. Overhauling an engine isn't difficult, but it is time consuming. Plan on the vehicle being tied up for a minimum of two weeks, especially if parts must be taken to an automotive machine shop for repair or reconditioning. Check on availability of parts and make sure that any necessary special tools and equipment are obtained in advance. Most work can be done with typical hand tools, although a number of precision measuring tools are required for inspecting parts to determine if they must be replaced. Often an automotive machine shop will handle the inspection of parts and offer advice concerning reconditioning and replacement. **Note:** *Always wait until the engine has been completely disassembled and all components, especially the engine block, have been inspected before deciding what service and repair operations must be performed by an automotive machine shop. Since the block's condition will be the major factor to consider*

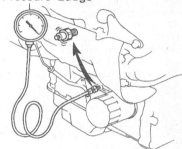

Oil Pressure Gauge

2.4c On V6 models, the sending unit is located adjacent to the oil filter

when determining whether to overhaul the original engine or buy a rebuilt one, never purchase parts or have machine work done on other components until the block has been thoroughly inspected. As a general rule, time is the primary cost of an overhaul, so it doesn't pay to install worn or substandard parts.

As a final note, to ensure maximum life and minimum trouble from a rebuilt engine, everything must be assembled with care in a spotlessly clean environment.

3 Cylinder compression check

Refer to illustration 3.6

1 A compression check will tell you what mechanical condition the upper end (pistons, rings, valves, head gasket[s]) of your engine is in. Specifically, it can tell you if the compression is down due to leakage caused by worn piston rings, defective valves and seats or a blown head gasket. **Note:** *The engine must be at normal operating temperature and the battery must be fully charged for this check.*

2 Begin by cleaning the area around the

3.6 A compression gauge with a threaded fitting for the spark plug hole is preferred over the type that requires hand pressure to maintain the seal - be sure to open the throttle valve as far as possible during the compression check!

spark plugs before you remove them (compressed air should be used, if available, otherwise a small brush or even a bicycle tire pump will work). The idea is to prevent dirt from getting into the cylinders as the compression check is being done.

3   Remove all of the spark plugs from the engine (Chapter 1).

4   Block the throttle wide open.

5   Detach the coil wire from the center of the distributor cap and ground it on the engine block. Use a jumper wire with alligator clips on each end to ensure a good ground. On EFI equipped vehicles, the fuel pump circuit should also be disabled (see Chapter 4).

6   Install the compression gauge in the spark plug hole (**see illustration**).

7   Crank the engine over at least seven compression strokes and watch the gauge. The compression should build up quickly in a healthy engine. Low compression on the first stroke, followed by gradually increasing pressure on successive strokes, indicates worn piston rings. A low compression reading on the first stroke, which doesn't build up during successive strokes, indicates leaking valves or a blown head gasket (a cracked head could also be the cause). Deposits on the undersides of the valve heads can also cause low compression. Record the highest gauge reading obtained.

8   Repeat the procedure for the remaining cylinders and compare the results to the Specifications.

9   Add some engine oil (about three squirts from a plunger-type oil can) to each cylinder, through the spark plug hole, and repeat the test.

10   If the compression increases after the oil is added, the piston rings are definitely worn. If the compression doesn't increase significantly, the leakage is occurring at the valves or head gasket. Leakage past the valves may be caused by burned valve seats and/or faces or warped, cracked or bent valves.

11   If two adjacent cylinders have equally low compression, there's a strong possibility that the head gasket between them is blown. The appearance of coolant in the combustion chambers or the crankcase would verify this condition.

12   If one cylinder is 20 percent lower than the others, and the engine has a slightly rough idle, a worn exhaust lobe on the camshaft could be the cause.

13   If the compression is unusually high, the combustion chambers are probably coated with carbon deposits. If that's the case, the cylinder head(s) should be removed and decarbonized.

14   If compression is way down or varies greatly between cylinders, it would be a good idea to have a leak-down test performed by an automotive repair shop. This test will pinpoint exactly where the leakage is occurring and how severe it is.

4   Engine removal - methods and precautions

If you've decided that an engine must be removed for overhaul or major repair work, several preliminary steps should be taken.

Locating a suitable place to work is extremely important. Adequate work space, along with storage space for the vehicle, will be needed. If a shop or garage isn't available, at the very least a flat, level, clean work surface made of concrete or asphalt is required.

Cleaning the engine compartment and engine before beginning the removal procedure will help keep tools clean and organized.

An engine hoist or A-frame will also be necessary. Make sure the equipment is rated in excess of the combined weight of the engine and transaxle. Safety is of primary importance, considering the potential hazards involved in lifting the engine out of the vehicle.

If the engine is being removed by a novice, a helper should be available. Advice and aid from someone more experienced would also be helpful. There are many instances when one person cannot simultaneously perform all of the operations required when lifting the engine out of the vehicle.

Plan the operation ahead of time. Arrange for or obtain all of the tools and equipment you'll need prior to beginning the job. Some of the equipment necessary to perform engine removal and installation safely and with relative ease are (in addition to an engine hoist) a heavy duty floor jack, complete sets of wrenches and sockets as described in the front of this manual, wooden blocks and plenty of rags and cleaning solvent for mopping up spilled oil, coolant and gasoline. If the hoist must be rented, make sure that you arrange for it in advance and perform all of the operations possible without it beforehand. This will save you money and time.

Plan for the vehicle to be out of use for quite a while. A machine shop will be required to perform some of the work which the do-it yourselfer can't accomplish without special equipment. These shops often have a busy schedule, so it would be a good idea to consult them before removing the engine in order to accurately estimate the amount of time required to rebuild or repair components that may need work.

Always be extremely careful when removing and installing the engine. Serious injury can result from careless actions. Plan ahead, take your time and a job of this nature, although major, can be accomplished successfully.

5   Engine - removal and installation

Refer to illustrations 5.6, 5.11, 5.14, 5.16a, 5.16b, 5.17a, 5.17b, 5.17c, 5.18 and 5.21

Note: *Read through the entire Section before beginning this procedure. The engine and transaxle are removed as a unit and then separated outside the vehicle.*

Removal

1   Relieve the fuel system pressure (see Chapter 4).

2   Disconnect the negative cable from the battery.

3   Place protective covers on the fenders and cowl and remove the hood (see Chapter 11).

4   Remove the air cleaner assembly (see Chapter 4).

5   Raise the vehicle and support it securely on jackstands. Drain the cooling system and engine oil and remove the drivebelts (see Chapter 1).

6   Clearly label, then disconnect all vacuum lines, coolant and emissions hoses, wiring harness connectors, ground straps and fuel lines. Masking tape and/or a touch up paint applicator work well for marking items (**see illustration**). Take instant photos or sketch the locations of components and brackets.

7   Remove the cooling fan(s), shroud(s) and radiator (see Chapter 3).

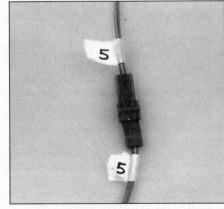

5.6 Label both ends of each wire before disconnecting it

5.11 Unbolt the air conditioning compressor and use wire or rope to tie it out of the way

5.14 Take up the slack in the hoist chain

5.16a If the transaxle mount throughbolt hits the fuel filter (arrow), unbolt the filter bracket and move it aside

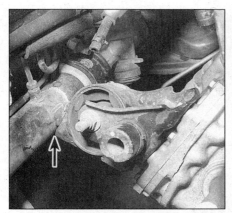

5.16b If you don't remove the rear transaxle mount it will catch on the steering rack (arrow) as you lift the engine

5.17a As the engine is lifted out, tilt it as shown

5.17b Be sure the upper transaxle mount separates from the bracket (arrow)

5.17c You may have to pry the mounts out of the frame brackets

5.18 Lift the engine/transaxle high enough to clear the vehicle, then move it away and lower the hoist

8 Release the residual fuel pressure in the tank by removing the gas cap, then undo the fuel lines connecting the engine to the chassis (see Chapter 4). Plug or cap all open fittings.

9 Disconnect the throttle linkage (and TV linkage and speed control cable, when equipped) from the engine (see Chapter 4).

10 On power steering equipped vehicles, unbolt the power steering pump. If clearance allows, tie the pump aside without disconnecting the hoses. If necessary, remove the pump (see Chapter 10).

11 On A/C equipped vehicles, unbolt the compressor and set it aside **(see illustration)**. Do not disconnect the refrigerant hoses.

12 Detach the exhaust pipe(s) from the manifold(s) (see Chapter 4).

13 Remove the driveaxles (see Chapter 8), wire harness, shift linkage and speedometer cable from the transaxle (see Chapter 7).

14 Attach a lifting sling to the brackets on the engine. Position a hoist and connect the sling to it. Take up the slack until there is slight tension on the hoist **(see illustration)**.

15 Recheck to be sure nothing except the mounts are still connecting the engine/transaxle to the vehicle. Disconnect anything still remaining.

16 Support the transaxle with a floor jack. Place a block of wood on the jack head to prevent damage to the transaxle. Remove the throughbolts from the engine and transaxle mounts **(see illustration)**. Unbolt the rear transaxle mount bracket from the transaxle (see Chapter 7) to prevent interference with the steering rack **(see illustration)**. **Warning:** *Do not place any part of your body under the engine/transaxle when it's supported only by a hoist or other lifting device.*

17 Slowly lift the engine/transaxle out of the vehicle. It may be necessary to pry the mounts away from the frame brackets **(see illustrations)**.

18 Move the engine/transaxle away from the vehicle and carefully lower the hoist until the transaxle is supported in a level position **(see illustration)**.

19 Remove the engine block-to-transaxle brace.

5.21 Remove the transaxle-to-engine bolts and separate the engine from the transaxle

20   On automatic transaxle equipped models, detach the torque converter dust shield from the lower bellhousing. Remove the torque converter-to-driveplate fasteners (see Chapter 7) and push the converter back slightly into the bellhousing.

21   Remove the engine-to-transaxle bolts and separate the engine from the transaxle **(see illustration)**. The torque converter should remain in the transaxle.

22   Place the engine on the floor or remove the flywheel/driveplate and mount the engine on an engine stand.

Installation

23   Check the engine/transaxle mounts. If they're worn or damaged, replace them.

24   On manual transaxle equipped models, inspect the clutch components (see Chapter 8) and on automatic models inspect the converter seal and bushing.

25   On manual transaxle equipped vehicles, apply a dab of high temperature grease to the pilot bearing.

26   On automatic transaxle equipped models, apply a dab of grease to the nose of the converter and to the seal lips.

27   Carefully guide the transaxle into place, following the procedure outlined in Chapter 7. **Caution:** *Do not use the bolts to force the engine and transaxle into alignment. It may crack or damage major components.*

28   Install the engine-to-transaxle bolts and tighten them securely.

29   Attach the hoist to the engine and carefully lower the engine/transaxle assembly into the engine compartment.

30   Install the mount bolts and tighten them securely.

31   Reinstall the remaining components and fasteners in the reverse order of removal.

32   Add coolant, oil, power steering and transmission fluids as needed (see Chapter 1).

33   Run the engine and check for proper operation and leaks. Shut off the engine and recheck the fluid levels.

6   Engine rebuilding alternatives

The do-it-yourselfer is faced with a number of options when performing an engine overhaul. The decision to replace the engine block, piston/connecting rod assemblies and crankshaft depends on a number of factors, with the number one consideration being the condition of the block. Other considerations are cost, access to machine shop facilities, parts availability, time required to complete the project and the extent of prior mechanical experience on the part of the do-it-yourselfer.

Some of the rebuilding alternatives include:

Individual parts - If the inspection procedures reveal that the engine block and most engine components are in reusable condition, purchasing individual parts may be the most economical alternative. The block, crankshaft and piston/connecting rod assemblies should all be inspected carefully. Even if the block shows little wear, the cylinder bores should be surface honed.

Short block - A short block consists of an engine block with a crankshaft and piston/connecting rod assemblies already installed. All new bearings are incorporated and all clearances will be correct. The existing camshaft, valve train components, cylinder head(s) and external parts can be bolted to the short block with little or no machine shop work necessary.

Long block - A long block consists of a short block plus an oil pump, oil pan, cylinder head(s), rocker arm cover(s), camshaft and valve train components, timing sprockets and chain or gears and timing cover. All components are installed with new bearings, seals and gaskets incorporated throughout. The installation of manifolds and external parts is

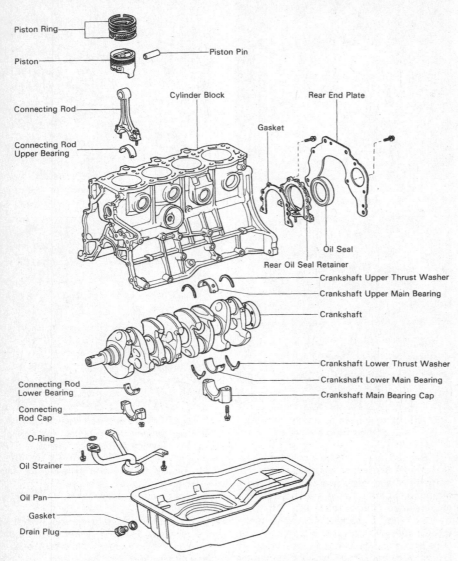

7.5a Four-cylinder engine lower end components - exploded view

all that's necessary.

Give careful thought to which alternative is best for you and discuss the situation with local automotive machine shops, auto parts dealers and experienced rebuilders before ordering or purchasing replacement parts.

7 Engine overhaul - disassembly sequence

Refer to illustrations 7.5a and 7.5b

1   It's much easier to disassemble and work on the engine if it's mounted on a portable engine stand. A stand can often be rented quite cheaply from an equipment rental yard. Before the engine is mounted on a stand, the flywheel/driveplate and rear oil seal retainer should be removed from the engine.

2   If a stand isn't available, it's possible to disassemble the engine with it blocked up on the floor. Be extra careful not to tip or drop the engine when working without a stand.

3   If you're going to obtain a rebuilt engine, all external components must come off first, to be transferred to the replacement engine, just as they will if you're doing a complete engine overhaul yourself. These include:

> Alternator and brackets
> Emissions control components
> Distributor, spark plug wires and spark plugs
> Thermostat and housing cover
> Water pump
> EFI components
> Intake/exhaust manifolds
> Oil filter
> Engine mounts
> Clutch and flywheel/driveplate
> Engine rear plate

Note: *When removing the external components from the engine, pay close attention to details that may be helpful or important during installation. Note the installed position of gaskets, seals, spacers, pins, brackets, washers, bolts and other small items.*

4   If you're obtaining a short block, which consists of the engine block, crankshaft, pistons and connecting rods all assembled, then the cylinder head(s), oil pan and oil pump will have to be removed as well. See *Engine rebuilding alternatives* for additional information regarding the different possibilities to be considered.

5   If you're planning a complete overhaul, the engine must be disassembled and the internal components removed in the following order **(see illustrations)**.

> Camshaft cover(s)
> Intake and exhaust manifolds
> Timing belt covers
> Timing belt and pulleys
> Cylinder head(s)
> Oil pan
> Oil pump
> Piston/connecting rod assemblies
> Crankshaft rear oil seal retainer
> Crankshaft and main bearings

6   Before beginning the disassembly and overhaul procedures, make sure the following items are available. Also, refer to *Engine overhaul - reassembly sequence* for a list of tools and materials needed for engine reassembly.

> Common hand tools
> Small cardboard boxes or plastic bags for storing parts
> Gasket scraper
> Ridge reamer
> Vibration damper puller
> Micrometers
> Telescoping gauges
> Dial indicator set
> Valve spring compressor
> Cylinder surfacing hone
> Piston ring groove cleaning tool
> Electric drill motor
> Tap and die set
> Wire brushes
> Oil gallery brushes
> Cleaning solvent

8 Cylinder head - disassembly

Refer to illustrations 8.2 and 8.3
Note: *New and rebuilt cylinder heads are commonly available for most engines at dealerships and auto parts stores. Due to the fact that some specialized tools are necessary for the disassembly and inspection procedures, and replacement parts may not be readily available, it may be more practical and economical for the home mechanic to purchase replacement head(s) rather than taking the time to disassemble, inspect and recondition the original(s).*

1   Cylinder head disassembly involves removal of the intake and exhaust valves and related components. It's assumed that the lifters or rocker arms and camshaft(s) have already been removed (see Part A or B as needed).

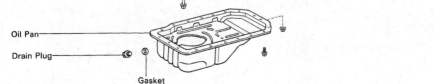

7.5b V6 engine lower end components - exploded view

8.2 A small plastic bag, with an appropriate label, can be used to store the valve train components so they can be kept together and reinstalled in the correct guide

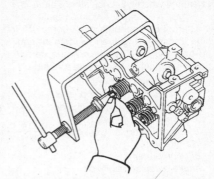

8.3 Compress the spring until the keepers can be removed

2   Before the valves are removed, arrange to label and store them, along with their related components, so they can be kept separate and reinstalled in the same valve guides they are removed from **(see illustration)**.

3   Compress the springs on the first valve with a spring compressor and remove the keepers **(see illustration)**. Carefully release the valve spring compressor and remove the retainer, the spring and the spring seat (if used). **Caution:** *If you're working on a 3S-FE or V6 engine, be very careful not to nick or otherwise damage the lifter bores when compressing the valve springs.*

4   Pull the valve out of the head, then remove the oil seal from the guide. If the valve binds in the guide (won't pull through), push it back into the head and deburr the area around the keeper groove with a fine file or whetstone.

5   Repeat the procedure for the remaining valves. Remember to keep all the parts for each valve together so they can be reinstalled in the same locations.

6   Once the valves and related components have been removed and stored in an organized manner, the head should be thoroughly cleaned and inspected. If a complete engine overhaul is being done, finish the engine disassembly procedures before

beginning the cylinder head cleaning and inspection process.

9   Cylinder head - cleaning and inspection

Refer to illustrations 9.12, 9.14, 9.16, 9.17 and 9.18

1   Thorough cleaning of the cylinder head(s) and related valve train components, followed by a detailed inspection, will enable you to decide how much valve service work must be done during the engine overhaul. **Note:** *If the engine was severely overheated, the cylinder head is probably warped (see Step 12).*

Cleaning

2   Scrape all traces of old gasket material and sealing compound off the head gasket, intake manifold and exhaust manifold sealing surfaces. Be very careful not to gouge the cylinder head. Special gasket removal solvents that soften gaskets and make removal much easier are available at auto parts stores.

3   Remove all built up scale from the coolant passages.

4   Run a stiff wire brush through the various holes to remove deposits that may have formed in them.

5   Run an appropriate size tap into each of

the threaded holes to remove corrosion and thread sealant that may be present. If compressed air is available, use it to clear the holes of debris produced by this operation. **Warning:** *Wear eye protection when using compressed air!*

6   Clean the exhaust and intake manifold stud threads with a wire brush.

7   Clean the cylinder head with solvent and dry it thoroughly. Compressed air will speed the drying process and ensure that all holes and recessed areas are clean. **Note:** *Decarbonizing chemicals are available and may prove very useful when cleaning cylinder heads and valve train components. They are very caustic and should be used with caution. Be sure to follow the instructions on the container.*

8   Clean the lifters and rocker arms (if used) with solvent and dry them thoroughly (don't mix them up during the cleaning process). Compressed air will speed the drying process and can be used to clean out the oil passages.

9   Clean all the valve springs, spring seats, keepers and retainers with solvent and dry them thoroughly. Do the components from one valve at a time to avoid mixing up the parts.

10   Scrape off any heavy deposits that may have formed on the valves, then use a motorized wire brush to remove deposits from the valve heads and stems. Again, make sure the valves don't get mixed up.

Inspection

Note: *Be sure to perform all of the following inspection procedures before concluding that machine shop work is required. Make a list of the items that need attention. The inspection procedures for the lifters and rocker arms, as well as the camshaft(s), can be found in Part A.*

Cylinder head

11   Inspect the head very carefully for cracks, evidence of coolant leakage and other damage. If cracks are found, check with an automotive machine shop concerning repair. If repair isn't possible, a new cylinder head should be obtained.

12   Using a straightedge and feeler gauge,

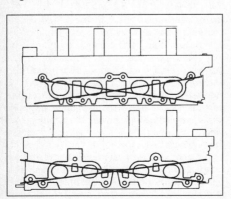

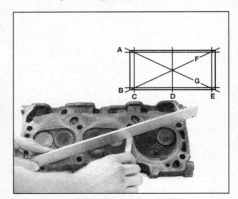

9.12 Check the cylinder head gasket surfaces for warpage by trying to slip a feeler gauge under the precision straightedge (see the Specifications for the maximum warpage allowed and use a feeler gauge of that thickness)

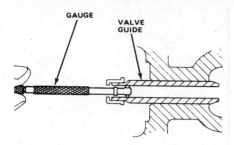

9.14 Use a small hole gauge to determine the inside diameter of the valve guides (the gauge is then measured with a micrometer)

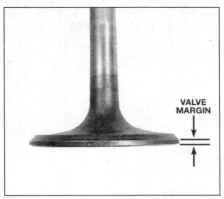

9.16 The margin width on each valve must be as specified (if no margin exists, the valve cannot be reused)

9.17 Measure the free length of each valve spring with a dial or vernier caliper

check the head gasket mating surface for warpage **(see illustration)**. If the warpage exceeds the specified limit, it can be resurfaced at an automotive machine shop. **Note:** *If the V6 engine heads are resurfaced, the intake manifold flanges will also require machining.*

13 Examine the valve seats in each of the combustion chambers. If they're pitted, cracked or burned, the head will require valve service that's beyond the scope of the home mechanic.

14 Check the valve stem-to-guide clearance with a small hole gauge and micrometer **(see illustration)**. Also, on the 2S-E engine, check the valve stem deflection crosswise (parallel to the rocker arm) with a dial indicator attached securely to the head. The valve must be in the guide and approximately 1/16-inch off the seat. The total valve stem movement indicated by the gauge needle must be noted. If it exceeds the specified stem-to-guide clearance limit, the valve guides should be replaced. After this is done, if there's still some doubt regarding the condition of the valve guides they should be checked by an automotive machine shop (the cost should be minimal).

Valves

15 Carefully inspect each valve face for uneven wear, deformation, cracks, pits and

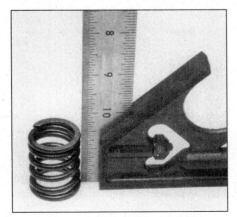

9.18 Check each valve spring for squareness

burned areas. Check the valve stem for scuffing and galling and the neck for cracks. Rotate the valve and check for any obvious indication that it's bent. Look for pits and excessive wear on the end of the stem. The presence of any of these conditions indicates the need for valve service by an automotive machine shop.

16 Measure the margin width on each valve **(see illustration)**. Any valve with a margin narrower than specified will have to be replaced with a new one.

Valve components

17 Check each valve spring for wear (on the ends) and pits. Measure the free length and compare it to the Specifications **(see illustration)**. Any springs that are shorter than specified have sagged and should not be reused. The tension of all springs should be checked with a special fixture before deciding that they're suitable for use in a rebuilt engine (take the springs to an automotive machine shop for this check).

18 Stand each spring on a flat surface and check it for squareness **(see illustration)**. If any of the springs are distorted or sagged, replace all of them with new parts.

19 Check the spring retainers and keepers for obvious wear and cracks. Any questionable parts should be replaced with new ones, as extensive damage will occur if they fail during engine operation.

20 Any damaged or excessively worn parts must be replaced with new ones.

21 If the inspection process indicates that the valve components are in generally poor condition and worn beyond the limits specified, which is usually the case in an engine that's being overhauled, reassemble the valves in the cylinder head and refer to Section 10 for valve servicing recommendations.

10 Valves - servicing

1 Because of the complex nature of the job and the special tools and equipment needed, servicing of the valves, the valve

seats and the valve guides, commonly known as a valve job, should be done by a professional.

2 The home mechanic can remove and disassemble the head, do the initial cleaning and inspection, then reassemble and deliver it to a dealer service department or an automotive machine shop for the actual service work. Doing the inspection will enable you to see what condition the head and valvetrain components are in and will ensure that you know what work and new parts are required when dealing with an automotive machine shop.

3 The dealer service department, or automotive machine shop, will remove the valves and springs, recondition or replace the valves and valve seats, recondition the valve guides, check and replace the valve springs, spring retainers and keepers (as necessary), replace the valve seals with new ones, reassemble the valve components and make sure the installed spring height is correct. The cylinder head gasket surface will also be resurfaced if it's warped.

4 After the valve job has been performed by a professional, the head will be in like new condition. When the head is returned, be sure to clean it again before installation on the engine to remove any metal particles and abrasive grit that may still be present from the valve service or head resurfacing operations. Use compressed air, if available, to blow out all the oil holes and passages.

11 Cylinder head - reassembly

Refer to illustration 11.3

1 Regardless of whether or not the head was sent to an automotive repair shop for valve servicing, make sure it's clean before beginning reassembly.

2 If the head was sent out for valve servicing, the valves and related components will already be in place. Begin the reassembly procedure with Step 8.

3 Install new seals on each of the valve guides. **Note:** *Intake and exhaust valves require different seals - DO NOT mix them up!*

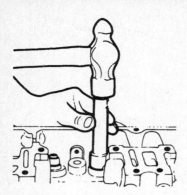

11.3 Gently tap the valve seals into place with a deep socket and hammer

12.1 A ridge reamer is required to remove the ridge from the top of each cylinder - do this before removing the pistons!

12.3 Check the connecting rod side clearance with a feeler gauge as shown here

Gently tap each intake valve seal into place until it's seated on the guide **(see illustration)**. **Caution:** *Don't hammer on the valve seals once they're seated or you may damage them. Don't twist or cock the seals during installation or they won't seat properly on the valve stems.*

4   Beginning at one end of the head, lubricate and install the first valve. Apply moly-base grease or clean engine oil to the valve stem.

5   Drop the spring seat or shim(s) over the valve guide and set the valve spring and retainer in place.

6   Compress the springs with a valve spring compressor and carefully install the keepers in the upper groove, then slowly release the compressor and make sure the keepers seat properly. Apply a small dab of grease to each keeper to hold it in place if necessary **(see illustration 12.17 in Part A)**.

7   Repeat the procedure for the remaining valves. Be sure to return the components to their original locations - don't mix them up!

8   Check the valve spring installed height with a dial or vernier caliper (2S-E engine only).

12   Pistons/connecting rods - removal

Refer to illustrations 12.1, 12.3, 12.4, and 12.6

Note: *Prior to removing the piston/connecting rod assemblies, remove the cylinder head(s), the oil pan and the oil pump pick-up tube by referring to the appropriate Sections in Chapter 2.*

1   Use your fingernail to feel if a ridge has formed at the upper limit of ring travel (about 1/4-inch down from the top of each cylinder). If carbon deposits or cylinder wear have produced ridges, they must be completely removed with a special tool **(see illustration)**. Follow the manufacturer's instructions provided with the tool. Failure to remove the ridges before attempting to remove the piston/connecting rod assemblies may result in piston breakage.

2   After the cylinder ridges have been removed, turn the engine upside-down so the crankshaft is facing up.

3   Before the connecting rods are removed, check the end play with feeler gauges. Slide them between the first connecting rod and the crankshaft throw until the play is removed **(see illustration)**. The end play is equal to the thickness of the feeler gauge(s). If the end play exceeds the service limit, new connecting rods will be required. If new rods (or a new crankshaft) are installed, the end play may fall under the specified minimum (if it does, the rods will have to be machined to restore it - consult an automotive machine shop for advice if necessary). Repeat the procedure for the remaining connecting rods.

4   Check the connecting rods and caps for identification marks. If they aren't plainly marked, use a small center punch to make the appropriate number of indentations on each rod and cap (1, 2, 3, etc., depending on the engine type and cylinder they're associated with) **(see illustration)**.

5   Loosen each of the connecting rod cap nuts 1/2-turn at a time until they can be

removed by hand. Remove the number one connecting rod cap and bearing insert. Don't drop the bearing insert out of the cap.

6   Slip a short length of plastic or rubber hose over each connecting rod cap bolt to protect the crankshaft journal and cylinder wall as the piston is removed **(see illustration)**.

7   Remove the bearing insert and push the connecting rod/piston assembly out through the top of the engine. Use a wooden hammer handle to push on the upper bearing surface in the connecting rod. If resistance is felt, double-check to make sure that all of the ridge was removed from the cylinder.

8   Repeat the procedure for the remaining cylinders.

9   After removal, reassemble the connecting rod caps and bearing inserts in their respective connecting rods and install the cap nuts finger tight. Leaving the old bearing inserts in place until reassembly will help prevent the connecting rod bearing surfaces from being accidentally nicked or gouged.

10   Don't separate the pistons from the connecting rods (see Section 17 for additional information).

12.4 The connecting rods and caps should be marked to indicate which cylinder they're installed in - if they aren't, mark them with a center punch to avoid confusion during reassembly

12.6 To prevent damage to the crankshaft journals and cylinder walls, slip sections of hose over the rod bolts before removing the pistons

13.1 Checking crankshaft end play with a dial indicator

13 Crankshaft - removal

Refer to illustrations 13.1, 13.3, 13.4a and 13.4b

Note: *The crankshaft can be removed only after the engine has been removed from the vehicle. It's assumed that the flywheel or driveplate, vibration damper, timing belt, oil pan, oil pick-up tube, oil pump and piston/connecting rod assemblies have already been removed. The rear main oil seal retainer must be unbolted and separated from the block before proceeding with crankshaft removal.*

1   Before the crankshaft is removed, check the end play. Mount a dial indicator with the stem in line with the crankshaft and just touching one of the crank throws **(see illustration)**.

2   Push the crankshaft all the way to the rear and zero the dial indicator. Next, pry the crankshaft to the front as far as possible and check the reading on the dial indicator. The distance that it moves is the end play. If it's greater than specified, check the crankshaft thrust surfaces for wear. If no wear is evident, new thrust washers should correct the end play.

3   If a dial indicator isn't available, feeler gauges can be used. Gently pry or push the crankshaft all the way to the front of the engine. Slip feeler gauges between the crankshaft and the front face of the thrust main bearing to determine the clearance **(see illustration)**. The thrust bearing on four-cylinder engines is number three (center), while on the V6 engine it's number two.

4   On four-cylinder engines, check the main bearing caps to see if they're marked to indicate their locations. They should be numbered consecutively from the front of the engine to the rear. If they aren't, mark them with number stamping dies or a center punch. Main bearing caps generally have a cast-in arrow, which points to the front of the engine. Loosen the main bearing cap bolts 1/4-turn at a time each, in the recommended sequence **(see illustrations)**, until they can be removed by hand. Note if any stud bolts are used and make sure they're returned to their original locations when the crankshaft is reinstalled.

5   Gently tap the caps with a soft-face hammer, then separate them from the engine block. If necessary, use the bolts as levers to remove the caps. Try not to drop the bearing inserts if they come out with the caps. The main bearing caps on the V6 engine are a one-piece assembly which may have to be carefully pried away from the block.

6   Carefully lift the crankshaft out of the engine. It may be a good idea to have an assistant available, since the crankshaft is quite heavy. With the bearing inserts in place in the engine block and main bearing caps or cap assembly, return the caps to their respective locations on the engine block and tighten the bolts finger tight.

14 Engine block - cleaning

Refer to illustrations 14.1, 14.8 and 14.10

Caution: *The core plugs (also known as freeze or soft plugs) may be difficult or impossible to retrieve if they're driven into the block coolant passages.*

1   Drill a small hole in the center of each core plug and pull them out with an auto body type dent puller **(see illustration)**.

2   Using a gasket scraper, remove all

13.3 Checking crankshaft end play with a feeler gauge

traces of gasket material from the engine block. Be very careful not to nick or gouge the gasket sealing surfaces.

3   Remove the main bearing caps or cap assembly and separate the bearing inserts from the caps and the engine block. Tag the bearings, indicating which cylinder they were removed from and whether they were in the cap or the block, then set them aside.

4   Remove all of the threaded oil gallery plugs from the block. The plugs are usually very tight - they may have to be drilled out and the holes retapped. Use new plugs when the engine is reassembled.

5   If the engine is extremely dirty it should be taken to an automotive machine shop to be steam cleaned or hot tanked.

6   After the block is returned, clean all oil holes and oil galleries one more time. Brushes specifically designed for this purpose are available at most auto parts stores. Flush the passages with warm water until the water runs clear, dry the block thoroughly and wipe all machined surfaces with a light, rust preventive oil. If you have access to compressed air, use it to speed the drying process and to blow out all the oil holes and galleries. **Warning:** *Wear eye protection when using compressed air!*

7   If the block isn't extremely dirty or sludged up, you can do an adequate cleaning job with hot soapy water and a stiff brush.

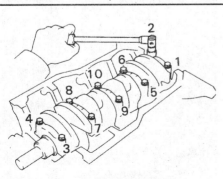

13.4a Loosen the main bearing cap bolts in this numerical sequence (four-cylinder engines only)

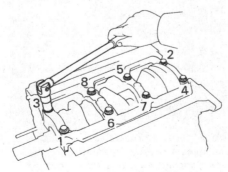

13.4b On V6 models, loosen the main bearing cap bolts in this numerical sequence

14.1 The core plugs should be removed with a puller - if they're driven into the block they may be impossible to retrieve

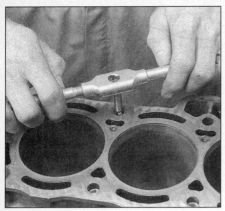

14.8 All bolt holes in the block - particularly the main bearing cap and head bolt holes - should be cleaned and restored with a tap (be sure to remove debris from the holes after this is done)

Take plenty of time and do a thorough job. Regardless of the cleaning method used, be sure to clean all oil holes and galleries very thoroughly, dry the block completely and coat all machined surfaces with light oil.

8   The threaded holes in the block must be clean to ensure accurate torque readings during reassembly. Run the proper size tap into each of the holes to remove rust, corrosion, thread sealant or sludge and restore damaged threads **(see illustration)**. If possible, use compressed air to clear the holes of debris produced by this operation. Now is a good time to clean the threads on the head bolts and the main bearing cap bolts as well.

9   Reinstall the main bearing caps and tighten the bolts finger tight.

10   After coating the sealing surfaces of the new core plugs with Permatex no. 2 sealant, install them in the engine block **(see illustration)**. Make sure they're driven in straight and seated properly or leakage could result. Spe-

14.10 A large socket on an extension can be used to drive the new core plugs into the bores

cial tools are available for this purpose, but a large socket, with an outside diameter that will just slip into the core plug, a 1/2-inch drive extension and a hammer will work just as well.

11   Apply non-hardening sealant (such as Permatex no. 2 or Teflon pipe sealant) to the new oil gallery plugs and thread them into the holes in the block. Make sure they're tightened securely.

12   If the engine isn't going to be reassembled right away, cover it with a large plastic trash bag to keep it clean.

15   Engine block - inspection

Refer to illustrations 15.4a, 15.4b, 15.4c, 15.12a and 15.12b

1   Before the block is inspected, it should be cleaned as described in Section 14.

2   Visually check the block for cracks, rust and corrosion. Look for stripped threads in the threaded holes. It's also a good idea to have the block checked for hidden cracks by an automotive machine shop that has the

special equipment to do this type of work. If defects are found, have the block repaired, if possible, or replaced.

3   Check the cylinder bores for scuffing and scoring.

4   Measure the diameter of each cylinder at the top (just under the ridge area), center and bottom of the cylinder bore, parallel to the crankshaft axis **(see illustrations)**.

5   Next, measure each cylinder's diameter at the same three locations across the crankshaft axis. Compare the results to the Specifications.

6   If the required precision measuring tools aren't available, the piston to-cylinder clearances can be obtained, though not quite as accurately, using feeler gauge stock. Feeler gauge stock comes in 12-inch lengths and various thicknesses and is generally available at auto parts stores.

7   To check the clearance, select a feeler gauge and slip it into the cylinder along with the matching piston. The piston must be positioned exactly as it normally would be. The feeler gauge must be between the piston and cylinder on one of the thrust faces (90 degrees to the piston pin bore).

8   The piston should slip through the cylinder (with the feeler gauge in place) with moderate pressure.

9   If it falls through or slides through easily, the clearance is excessive and a new piston will be required. If the piston binds at the lower end of the cylinder and is loose toward the top, the cylinder is tapered. If tight spots are encountered as the piston/feeler gauge is rotated in the cylinder, the cylinder is out-of-round.

10   Repeat the procedure for the remaining pistons and cylinders.

11   If the cylinder walls are badly scuffed or scored, or if they're out of-round or tapered beyond the limits given in the Specifications, have the engine block rebored and honed at an automotive machine shop. If a rebore is done, oversize pistons and rings will be required.

12   Using a precision straightedge and feeler gauge, check the block deck (the surface that mates with the cylinder head[s]) for distortion **(see illustrations)**. If it's distorted beyond the specified limit, it can be resur-

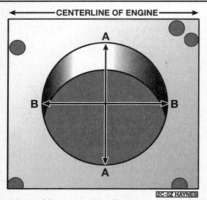

15.4a Measure the diameter of each cylinder at a right angle to the engine centerline (A), and parallel to the engine centerline (B) – out-of-round is the difference between A and B; taper is the difference between A and B at the top of the cylinder and A and B at the bottom of the cylinder

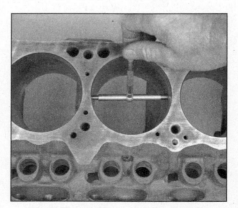

15.4b The ability to "feel" when the telescoping gauge is at the correct point will be developed over time, so work slowly and repeat the check until you're satisfied that the bore measurement is accurate

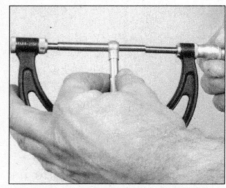

15.4c The gauge is then measured with a micrometer to determine the bore size

15.12a Check the block deck (both banks on a V6 engine) for distortion with a precision straightedge and feeler gauges

15.12b Lay the straightedge across the block, diagonally and from end-to-end when making the check

16.3a A "bottle brush" hone will produce better results if you have never done cylinder honing before

faced by an automotive machine shop.

13 If the cylinders are in reasonably good condition and not worn to the outside of the limits, and if the piston-to-cylinder clearances can be maintained properly, then they don't have to be rebored. Honing is all that's necessary (Section 16).

16 Cylinder honing

Refer to illustrations 16.3a and 16.3b

1 Prior to engine reassembly, the cylinder bores must be honed so the new piston rings will seat correctly and provide the best possible combustion chamber seal. **Note:** *If you don't have the tools or don't want to tackle the honing operation, most automotive machine shops will do it for a reasonable fee.*

2 Before honing the cylinders, install the main bearing caps or cap assembly (without bearing inserts) and tighten the bolts to the specified torque.

3 Two types of cylinder hones are commonly available - the flex hone or "bottle brush" type and the more traditional surfacing hone with spring-loaded stones. Both will do the job, but for the less experienced mechanic the "bottle brush" hone will probably be easier to use. You'll also need some

kerosene or honing oil, rags and an electric drill motor. Proceed as follows:

a) *Mount the hone in the drill motor, compress the stones and slip it into the first cylinder* **(see illustration)**. *Be sure to wear safety goggles or a face shield!*

b) *Lubricate the cylinder with plenty of honing oil, turn on the drill and move the hone up-and-down in the cylinder at a pace that will produce a fine crosshatch pattern on the cylinder walls. Ideally, the crosshatch lines should intersect at approximately a 60-degree angle* **(see illustration)**. *Be sure to use plenty of lubricant and don't take off any more material than is absolutely necessary to produce the desired finish.* **Note:** *Piston ring manufacturers may specify a smaller crosshatch angle than the traditional 60-degrees - read and follow any instructions included with the new rings.*

c) *Don't withdraw the hone from the cylinder while it's running. Instead, shut off the drill and continue moving the hone up-and-down in the cylinder until it comes to a complete stop, then compress the stones and withdraw the hone. If you're using a "bottle brush" type hone, stop the drill motor, then turn the chuck in the normal direction of rotation while withdrawing the hone from the cylinder.*

d) *Wipe the oil out of the cylinder and repeat the procedure for the remaining cylinders.*

4 After the honing job is complete, chamfer the top edges of the cylinder bores with a small file so the rings won't catch when the pistons are installed. **Be very careful not to nick the cylinder walls with the end of the file.**

5 The entire engine block must be washed again very thoroughly with warm, soapy water to remove all traces of the abrasive grit produced during the honing operation. **Note:** *The bores can be considered clean when a lint-free white cloth - dampened with clean engine oil- used to wipe them out doesn't pick up any more honing residue, which will show up as gray areas on the cloth.* Be sure to run a brush through all oil holes and galleries and flush them with running water.

6 After rinsing, dry the block and apply a

coat of light rust preventive oil to all machined surfaces. Wrap the block in a plastic trash bag to keep it clean and set it aside until reassembly.

17 Pistons/connecting rods - inspection

Refer to illustrations 17.4a, 17.4b, 17.10 and 17.11

1 Before the inspection process can be carried out, the piston/connecting rod assemblies must be cleaned and the original piston rings removed from the pistons. **Note:** *Always use new piston rings when the engine is reassembled.*

2 Using a piston ring installation tool, carefully remove the rings from the pistons. Be careful not to nick or gouge the pistons in the process.

3 Scrape all traces of carbon from the top of the piston. A hand-held wire brush or a piece of fine emery cloth can be used once the majority of the deposits have been scraped away. Do not, under any circumstances, use a wire brush mounted in a drill motor to remove deposits from the pistons. The piston material is soft and may be eroded away by the wire brush.

4 Use a piston ring groove cleaning tool to

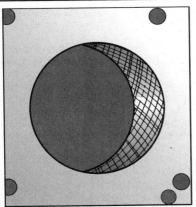

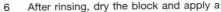

16.3b The cylinder hone should leave a smooth, crosshatch pattern with the lines intersecting at approximately a 60-degree angle

17.4a The piston ring grooves can be cleaned with a special tool, as shown here . . .

17.4b . . . or a section of a broken ring

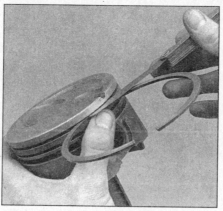

17.10 Check the ring side clearance with a feeler gauge at several points around the groove

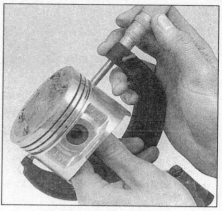

17.11 Measure the piston diameter at a 90-degree angle to the piston pin - depending on the model, the pistons must be measured at a precise point:

2S-E engine = 1.10 inch (28 mm) below the lower edge of the bottom groove
3S-FE engine = 1.00 inch (25.40 mm) below the top of the piston
V6 engine = 0.955 inch (24.25 mm) below the top of the piston

remove carbon deposits from the ring grooves. If a tool isn't available, a piece broken off the old ring will do the job. Be very careful to remove only the carbon deposits - don't remove any metal and do not nick or scratch the sides of the ring grooves **(see illustrations)**.

5   Once the deposits have been removed, clean the piston/rod assemblies with solvent and dry them with compressed air (if available). Make sure the oil return holes in the back sides of the ring grooves and the oil hole in the lower end of each rod are clear.

6   If the pistons and cylinder walls aren't damaged or worn excessively, and if the engine block is not rebored, new pistons won't be necessary. Normal piston wear appears as even vertical wear on the piston thrust surfaces and slight looseness of the top ring in its groove. New piston rings, however, should always be used when an engine is rebuilt.

7   Carefully inspect each piston for cracks around the skirt, at the pin bosses and at the ring lands.

8   Look for scoring and scuffing on the thrust faces of the skirt, holes in the piston crown and burned areas at the edge of the crown. If the skirt is scored or scuffed, the engine may have been suffering from overheating and/or abnormal combustion, which caused excessively high operating temperatures. The cooling and lubrication systems should be checked thoroughly. A hole in the piston crown is an indication that abnormal combustion (preignition) was occurring. Burned areas at the edge of the piston crown are usually evidence of spark knock (detonation). If any of the above problems exist, the causes must be corrected or the damage will occur again. The causes may include intake air leaks, incorrect fuel/air mixture, incorrect ignition timing and EGR system malfunctions.

9   Corrosion of the piston, in the form of small pits, indicates that coolant is leaking into the combustion chamber and/or the crankcase. Again, the cause must be corrected or the problem may persist in the rebuilt engine.

10   Measure the piston ring side clearance by laying a new piston ring in each ring groove and slipping a feeler gauge in beside it **(see illustration)**. Check the clearance at three or four locations around each groove. Be sure to use the correct ring for each groove - they are different. If the side clearance is greater than specified, new pistons will have to be used.

11   Check the piston-to-bore clearance by measuring the bore (see Section 15) and the piston diameter. Make sure the pistons and bores are correctly matched. Measure the piston across the skirt, at a 90-degree angle to the piston pin, the specified distance down from the top of the piston or the lower edge of the oil ring groove **(see illustration)**. Subtract the piston diameter from the bore diameter to obtain the clearance. If it's greater than specified, the block will have to be rebored and new pistons and rings installed.

12   Check the piston-to-rod clearance by twisting the piston and rod in opposite directions. Any noticeable play indicates excessive wear, which must be corrected. The piston/connecting rod assemblies should be taken to an automotive machine shop to have the pistons and rods resized and new pins installed.

13   If the pistons must be removed from the connecting rods for any reason, they should be taken to an automotive machine shop. While they are there have the connecting rods checked for bend and twist, since automotive machine shops have special equipment for this purpose. **Note:** *Unless new pistons and/or connecting rods must be installed, do not disassemble the pistons and connecting rods.*

14   If you're working on a V6 engine, see if the nut on each connecting rod bolt can be turned by hand all the way to the end of the threads. If not, measure the outer diameter of the bolt (over the threads) at a point 15 mm from the bolt end. If the bolt diameter is not as specified, use new nuts when the piston/connecting rod assemblies are installed and have an automotive machine shop install new rod bolts.

15   Check the connecting rods for cracks and other damage. Temporarily remove the rod caps, lift out the old bearing inserts, wipe the rod and cap bearing surfaces clean and inspect them for nicks, gouges and scratches. After checking the rods, replace the old bearings, slip the caps into place and tighten the nuts finger tight. **Note:** *If the engine is being rebuilt because of a connecting rod knock, be sure to install new rods.*

18   Crankshaft - inspection

Refer to illustration 18.6

1   Clean the crankshaft with solvent and dry it with compressed air (if available). Be sure to clean the oil holes with a stiff brush and flush them with solvent.

2   Check the main and connecting rod bearing journals for uneven wear, scoring, pits and cracks.

3   Rub a penny across each journal several times. If a journal picks up copper from the penny, it's too rough and must be reground.

4   Remove all burrs from the crankshaft oil holes with a stone, file or scraper.

5   Check the rest of the crankshaft for cracks and other damage. It should be magnafluxed to reveal hidden cracks - an automotive machine shop will handle the procedure.

6   Using a micrometer, measure the diameter of the main and connecting rod journals and compare the results to the Specifications **(see illustration)**. By measuring the diameter at a number of points around each journal's circumference, you'll be able to determine whether or not the journal is out-of-round. Take the measurement at each end of the journal, near the crank throws, to determine if

18.6 Measure the diameter of each crankshaft journal at several points to detect taper and out-of-round conditions

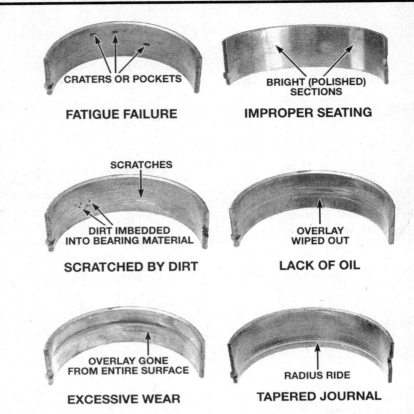

19.1 When inspecting the main and connecting rod bearings, look for these problems

the journal is tapered. Crankshaft runout should be checked also, but large V-blocks and a dial indicator are needed to do it correctly. If you don't have the equipment, have a machine shop check the runout.

7   If the crankshaft journals are damaged, tapered, out-of-round or worn beyond the limits given in the Specifications, have the crankshaft reground by an automotive machine shop. Be sure to use the correct size bearing inserts if the crankshaft is reconditioned.

8   Check the oil seal journals at each end of the crankshaft for wear and damage. If the seal has worn a groove in the journal, or if it's nicked or scratched, the new seal may leak when the engine is reassembled. In some cases, an automotive machine shop may be able to repair the journal by pressing on a thin sleeve. If repair isn't feasible, a new or different crankshaft should be installed.

9   Refer to Section 19 and examine the main and rod bearing inserts.

19   Main and connecting rod bearings - inspection and main bearing selection

Inspection

Refer to illustration 19.1

1   Even though the main and connecting rod bearings should be replaced with new ones during the engine overhaul, the old bearings should be retained for close examination, as they may reveal valuable information about the condition of the engine **(see illustration)**.

2   Bearing failure occurs because of lack of lubrication, the presence of dirt or other foreign particles, overloading the engine and corrosion. Regardless of the cause of bearing failure, it must be corrected before the engine is reassembled to prevent it from happening again.

3   When examining the bearings, remove them from the engine block, the main bearing caps, the connecting rods and the rod caps and lay them out on a clean surface in the same general position as their location in the engine. This will enable you to match any

bearing problems with the corresponding crankshaft journal.

4   Dirt and other foreign particles get into the engine in a variety of ways. It may be left in the engine during assembly, or it may pass through filters or the PCV system. It may get into the oil, and from there into the bearings. Metal chips from machining operations and normal engine wear are often present. Abrasives are sometimes left in engine components after reconditioning, especially when parts are not thoroughly cleaned using the proper cleaning methods. Whatever the source, these foreign objects often end up embedded in the soft bearing material and are easily recognized. Large particles will not embed in the bearing and will score or gouge the bearing and journal. The best prevention for this cause of bearing failure is to clean all parts thoroughly and keep everything spotlessly clean during engine assembly. Frequent and regular engine oil and filter changes are also recommended.

5   Lack of lubrication (or lubrication breakdown) has a number of interrelated causes. Excessive heat (which thins the oil), overloading (which squeezes the oil from the bearing face) and oil leakage or throw off (from excessive bearing clearances, worn oil pump or high engine speeds) all contribute to lubrication breakdown. Blocked oil passages, which usually are the result of misaligned oil holes in a bearing shell, will also oil starve a bearing and destroy it. When lack of lubrica-

tion is the cause of bearing failure, the bearing material is wiped or extruded from the steel backing of the bearing. Temperatures may increase to the point where the steel backing turns blue from overheating.

6   Driving habits can have a definite effect on bearing life. Full throttle, low speed operation (lugging the engine) puts very high loads on bearings, which tends to squeeze out the oil film. These loads cause the bearings to flex, which produces fine cracks in the bearing face (fatigue failure). Eventually the bearing material will loosen in pieces and tear away from the steel backing. Short trip driving leads to corrosion of bearings because insufficient engine heat is produced to drive off the condensed water and corrosive gases. These products collect in the engine oil, forming acid and sludge. As the oil is carried to the engine bearings, the acid attacks and corrodes the bearing material.

7   Incorrect bearing installation during engine assembly will lead to bearing failure as well. Tight fitting bearings leave insufficient bearing oil clearance and will result in oil starvation. Dirt or foreign particles trapped behind a bearing insert result in high spots on the bearing which lead to failure.

Selection

Refer to illustrations 19.10, 19.11a, 19.11b, 19.12a, 19.12b, 19.13 and 19.14

8   If the original bearings are worn or damaged, or if the oil clearances are incorrect

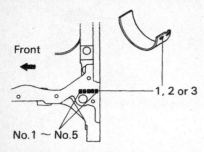

19.10 If the number on the original main bearing is not clear, install a new bearing with a number that matches the number stamped into the block - different journals may require different size bearings (2S-E engine only)

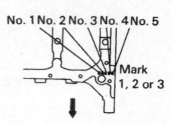

19.11a Main journal grade numbers are stamped into the oil pan mating surface on the block - there are 5 journals on the 3S-FE four-cylinder engine, so there are 5 numbers

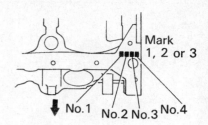

19.11b V6 main journal engine block grade numbers

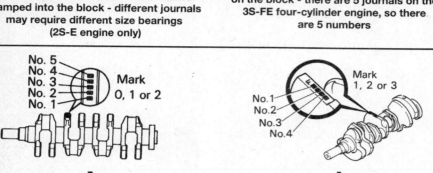

19.12a 3S-FE four-cylinder engine main journal crankshaft grade numbers

19.12b V6 engine main journal crankshaft grade numbers

	Number marked								
Cylinder block	1			2			3		
Crankshaft	0	1	2	0	1	2	0	1	2
Bearing	1	2	3	2	3	4	3	4	5

EXAMPLE: Cylinder block "2" + Crankshaft "1"
= Bearing "3"

19.13 3S-FE four-cylinder/V6 engine main bearing selection chart

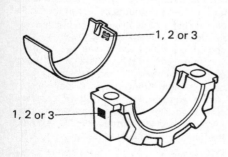

19.14 Connecting rod bearing cap mark location

ber locations).

10   If you're working on a 2S-E engine and the number on the original main bearing has been obscured, install one that has the same number as the number stamped into the block for the corresponding cap location **(see illustration)**.

11   If you're working on a 3S-FE four-cylinder or a V6 engine and the number on the original main bearing has been obscured, locate the main journal grade numbers stamped into the oil pan mating surface on the engine block **(see illustrations)**.

12   Locate the main journal grade numbers on the crankshaft as well **(see illustrations)**.

13   Use the accompanying chart to determine the correct bearings for each journal **(see illustration)**.

Connecting rod bearings

14   If you need to use a STANDARD size rod bearing, install one that has the same number as the number stamped into the connecting rod cap **(see illustration)**.

All bearings

15   Remember, the oil clearance is the final judge when selecting new bearing sizes. If you have any questions or are unsure which bearings to use, get help from a dealer parts or service department.

(Section 22 or 24), the following procedures should be used to select the correct new bearings for engine reassembly. However, if the crankshaft has been reground, new undersize bearings must be installed - **the following procedure should not be used if undersize bearings are required!** The automotive machine shop that reconditions the crankshaft will provide or help you select the correct size bearings. Regardless of how the bearing sizes are determined, use the oil clearance, measured with Plastigage, as a guide to ensure the bearings are the right size.

Main bearings

9   If you need to use a STANDARD size main bearing, install one that has the same number as the original bearing **(see illustrations 19.10 and 19.12b** for the bearing num-

20 Engine overhaul - reassembly sequence

1   Before beginning engine reassembly, make sure you have all the necessary new parts, gaskets and seals as well as the following items on hand:

Common hand tools
A 1/2-inch drive torque wrench
Piston ring installation tool
Piston ring compressor
Short lengths of rubber or plastic hose to fit over connecting rod bolts
Plastigage
Feeler gauges
A fine-tooth file
New engine oil
Engine assembly lube or moly-base grease
Gasket sealer
Thread locking compound

21.3 When checking piston ring end gap, the ring must be square in the cylinder bore (this is done by pushing the ring down with the top of a piston as shown)

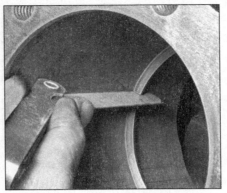

21.4 With the ring square in the cylinder, measure the end gap with a feeler gauge

21.9a Installing the spacer/expander in the oil control ring groove

21.9b DO NOT use a piston ring installation tool when installing the oil ring side rails

2   In order to save time and avoid problems, engine reassembly must be done in the following general order:

Four-cylinder engines

Piston rings (Part C)
Crankshaft and main bearings (Part C)
Piston/connecting rod assemblies (Part C)
Rear main (crankshaft) oil seal (Part C)
Cylinder head and rocker arms or lifters (Part A)
Camshaft (Part A)
Timing belt and pulleys (Part A)
Timing belt cover (Part A)
Oil pump (Part A)
Oil pick-up (Part A)
Oil pan (Part A)
Intake and exhaust manifolds (Part A)
Camshaft cover (Part A)
Flywheel/driveplate (Part A)

V6 engine

Piston rings (Part C)
Crankshaft and main bearings (Part C)
Piston/connecting rod assemblies (Part C)
Rear main oil seal/retainer (Part C)
Oil pump (Part B)
Oil pan (Part B)
Cylinder heads (Part B)
Camshafts and lifters (Part B)
Timing belt and pulleys (Part B)
Timing belt covers (Part B)
Intake and exhaust manifolds (Part B)
Cylinder head covers (Part B)
Flywheel/driveplate (Part B)

21 Piston rings - installation

Refer to illustrations 21.3, 21.4, 21.9a, 21.9b and 21.12

1   Before installing the new piston rings, the ring end gaps must be checked. It's assumed that the piston ring side clearance has been checked and verified correct (Section 17).

2   Lay out the piston/connecting rod assemblies and the new ring sets so the ring sets will be matched with the same piston and cylinder during the end gap measurement and engine assembly.

3   Insert the top (number one) ring into the first cylinder and square it up with the cylinder walls by pushing it in with the top of the piston **(see illustration)**. The ring should be near the bottom of the cylinder, at the lower limit of ring travel.

4   To measure the end gap, slip feeler gauges between the ends of the ring until a gauge equal to the gap width is found **(see illustration)**. The feeler gauge should slide between the ring ends with a slight amount of drag. Compare the measurement to the Specifications. If the gap is larger or smaller than specified, double-check to make sure you have the correct rings before proceeding.

5   If the gap is too small, replace the rings - DO NOT file the ends to increase the clearance.

6   Excess end gap isn't critical unless it's greater than 0.040-inch. Again, double-check to make sure you have the correct rings for your engine.

7   Repeat the procedure for each ring that will be installed in the first cylinder and for each ring in the remaining cylinders. Remember to keep rings, pistons and cylinders matched up.

8   Once the ring end gaps have been checked/corrected, the rings can be installed on the pistons.

9   The oil control ring (lowest one on the piston) is usually installed first. It's composed of three separate components. Slip the spacer/expander into the groove **(see illustration)**. If an anti-rotation tang is used, make sure it's inserted into the drilled hole in the ring groove. Next, install the lower side rail. Don't use a piston ring installation tool on the oil ring side rails, as they may be damaged. Instead, place one end of the side rail into the groove between the spacer/expander and the ring land, hold it firmly in place and slide a finger around the piston while pushing the rail into the groove **(see illustration)**. Next, install the upper side rail in the same manner.

10   After the three oil ring components have been installed, check to make sure that both the upper and lower side rails can be turned smoothly in the ring groove.

11   The number two (middle) ring is installed next. It's usually stamped with a mark which must face up, toward the top of the piston. **Note:** *Always follow the instructions printed on the ring package or box - different manufacturers may require different approaches. Do not mix up the top and middle rings, as they have different cross sections.*

12   Use a piston ring installation tool and make sure the identification mark is facing the top of the piston, then slip the ring into

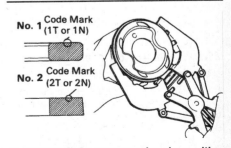

21.12 Install the compression rings with a ring expander - the mark must face up (four-cylinder engine shown - on V6 engines, top rings are marked 1R or T, second rings are marked 2R or T2)

22.10 Lay the Plastigage strips (arrow) on the main bearing journals, parallel to the crankshaft centerline

22.12a Main bearing cap bolt tightening sequence - four-cylinder engines

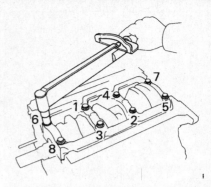

22.12b Main bearing cap assembly bolt tightening sequence - V6 engine

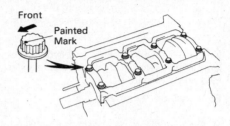

22.12c On V6 engines only, after reaching the specified torque, mark the front side of each bolt with paint as shown here . . .

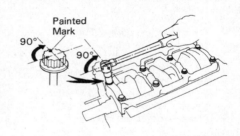

22.12d . . . then turn the bolts an additional 1/4-turn (90 degrees)

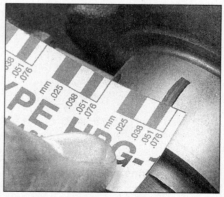

22.14 Compare the width of the crushed Plastigage to the scale on the envelope to determine the main bearing oil clearance (always take the measurement at the widest point of the Plastigage) - be sure to use the correct scale; standard and metric scales are included

the middle groove on the piston (**see illustration**). Don't expand the ring any more than necessary to slide it over the piston.

13   Install the number one (top) ring in the same manner. Make sure the mark is facing up. Be careful not to confuse the number one and number two rings.

14   Repeat the procedure for the remaining pistons and rings.

22   Crankshaft - installation and main bearing oil clearance check

Refer to illustrations 22.10, 22.12a, 22.12b, 22.12c, 22.12d, 22.14, 22.19a, 22.19b and 22.19c

1   Crankshaft installation is the first major step in engine reassembly. It's assumed at this point that the engine block and crankshaft have been cleaned, inspected and repaired or reconditioned.

2   Position the engine with the bottom facing up.

3   Remove the main bearing cap bolts and lift out the caps or cap assembly. Lay the caps out in the proper order to ensure correct installation (four-cylinder engine only).

4   If they're still in place, remove the old bearing inserts from the block and the main bearing caps. Wipe the main bearing surfaces of the block and caps with a clean, lint free cloth. They must be kept spotlessly clean!

Main bearing oil clearance check

5   Clean the back sides of the new main bearing inserts and lay the bearing half with the oil groove in each main bearing saddle in the block. Lay the other bearing half from each bearing set in the corresponding main bearing cap. Make sure the tab on each bearing insert fits into the recess in the block or cap. Also, the oil holes in the block must line up with the oil holes in the bearing insert. **Caution:** *Do not hammer the bearings into*

place and don't nick or gouge the bearing faces. No lubrication should be used at this time.

6   If you're working on a V6 engine, the thrust bearings (washers) must be installed in the number two cap and saddle. On four-cylinder engines, the thrust bearings (washers) must be installed in the number three (center) cap.

7   Clean the faces of the bearings in the block and the crankshaft main bearing journals with a clean, lint free cloth. Check or clean the oil holes in the crankshaft, as any dirt here can go only one way - straight through the new bearings.

8   Once you're certain the crankshaft is clean, carefully lay it in position in the main bearings.

9   Before the crankshaft can be permanently installed, the main bearing oil clearance **must** be checked.

10   Trim several pieces of the appropriate size Plastigage (they must be slightly shorter than the width of the main bearings) and place one piece on each crankshaft main bearing journal, parallel with the journal axis **(see illustration)**.

11   Clean the faces of the bearings in the caps and install the caps in their respective positions (don't mix them up) with the arrows pointing toward the front of the engine. If you're working on a V6 engine, carefully lay the main bearing cap assembly in place. Don't disturb the Plastigage. Apply a light coat of oil to the bolt threads and the under sides of the bolt heads, then install them.

12   Following the recommended sequence **(see illustrations)**, tighten the main bearing cap bolts, in three steps, to the specified torque. Don't rotate the crankshaft at any time during this operation! **Note:** *On V6 engines only, after reaching the specified torque, tighten each bolt an additional 90 degrees (1/4-turn)* **(see illustrations)**.

13   Remove the bolts and carefully lift off the main bearing caps or cap assembly. Keep them in order. Don't disturb the Plastigage or rotate the crankshaft. If any of the main bearing caps are difficult to remove, tap them gently from side-to-side with a soft-face hammer to loosen them.

14   Compare the width of the crushed Plastigage on each journal to the scale printed on the Plastigage envelope to obtain the main

22.19a Rotate the thrust washer into position on the number three crankshaft journal with the oil grooves facing OUT (four-cylinder engines only)

23.3 After removing the retainer from the block, support it on a couple of wood blocks and drive out the old seal with a punch or screwdriver and hammer

bearing oil clearance **(see illustration)**. Check the Specifications to make sure it's correct.

15   If the clearance is not as specified, the bearing inserts may be the wrong size (which means different ones will be required - see Section 19). Before deciding that different inserts are needed, make sure that no dirt or oil was between the bearing inserts and the caps or block when the clearance was measured. If the Plastigage is noticeably wider at one end than the other, the journal may be tapered (see Section 18).

16   Carefully scrape all traces of the Plastigage material off the main bearing journals and/or the bearing faces. Don't nick or scratch the bearing faces.

Final crankshaft installation

17   Carefully lift the crankshaft out of the engine. Clean the bearing faces in the block, then apply a thin, uniform layer of clean moly-base grease or engine assembly lube to each of the bearing surfaces. Coat the thrust washers as well.

18   Lubricate the crankshaft surfaces that

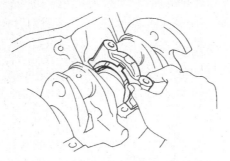

22.19b On four-cylinder engines, install the thrust washer in the number three cap with the oil grooves facing OUT

contact the oil seals with moly-base grease, engine assembly lube or clean engine oil.

19   Make sure the crankshaft journals are clean, then lay the crankshaft back in place in the block. Clean the faces of the bearings in the caps or cap assembly, then apply lubricant to them. Install the caps in their respective positions with the arrows pointing toward the front of the engine. **Note:** *Be sure to install the thrust washers* **(see illustrations)**.

20   Apply a light coat of oil to the bolt threads and the under sides of the bolt heads, then install them. On four-cylinder engines only, tighten all except the center (number three) cap bolts (the one with the thrust washers) to the specified torque (work from the center out and approach the final torque in three steps). Tighten the center cap bolts to 10-to-12 ft-lbs. Tap the ends of the crankshaft forward and backward with a lead or brass hammer to line up the thrust washer and crankshaft surfaces. Retighten all main bearing cap bolts to the specified torque, following the recommended sequence.

21   On manual transmission equipped models, install a new pilot bearing in the end of the crankshaft (see Chapter 8).

22   Rotate the crankshaft a number of times by hand to check for any obvious binding.

23   Check the crankshaft end play with a feeler gauge or a dial indicator as described in Section 13. The end play should be correct if the crankshaft thrust faces aren't worn or damaged and new thrust washers have been installed.

24   Install a new rear main oil seal, then bolt the retainer to the block (Section 23).

23   Rear main oil seal installation

Refer to illustrations 23.3 and 23.6

1   The crankshaft must be installed first and the main bearing caps or cap assembly bolted in place, then the new seal should be installed in the retainer and the retainer bolted to the block.

2   Check the seal contact surface on the crankshaft very carefully for scratches and nicks that could damage the new seal lip and cause oil leaks. If the crankshaft is damaged,

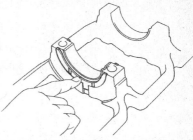

22.19c On V6 engines, install the thrust washers in the number two bearing cap and saddle with the tang in the notch in the main bearing cap assembly (be sure the oil grooves face OUT)

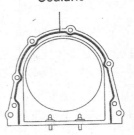

23.6 Apply sealant to the retainer before bolting it to the block

the only alternative is a new or different crankshaft.

3   The old seal can be removed from the retainer by driving it out from the back side with a hammer and punch **(see illustration)**. Be sure to note how far it's recessed into the bore before removing it; the new seal will have to be recessed an equal amount. Be very careful not to scratch or otherwise damage the bore in the retainer or oil leaks could develop.

4   Make sure the retainer is clean, then apply a thin coat of engine oil to the outer edge of the new seal. The seal must be pressed squarely into the bore, so hammering it into place isn't recommended. If you don't have access to a press, sandwich the housing and seal between two smooth pieces of wood and press the seal into place with the jaws of a large vise. The pieces of wood must be thick enough to distribute the force evenly around the entire circumference of the seal. Work slowly and make sure the seal enters the bore squarely.

5   As a last resort, the seal can be tapped into the retainer with a hammer. Use a block of wood to distribute the force evenly and make sure the seal is driven in squarely **(see illustration 17.6 in Part A)**.

6   The seal lips must be lubricated with clean engine oil or moly-based grease before the seal/retainer is slipped over the crankshaft and bolted to the block. On four-cylinder engines, use a new gasket - and sealant- and make sure the dowel pins are in place before installing the retainer. On V6

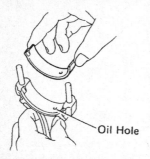

24.3 Align the oil hole in the bearing with the oil hole in the rod

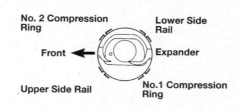

24.5 Stagger the ring end gaps before installing the pistons

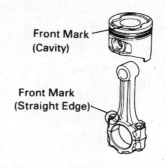

24.9a Check to be sure both the mark on the piston and the mark on the connecting rod are aligned as shown (four-cylinder engines)

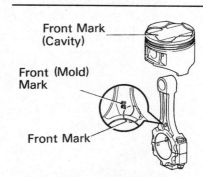

24.9b On V6 engines, both the mark on the piston and the mark on the connecting rod should face the timing belt end of the engine

engines, no gasket is required. Instead, apply a 2mm wide bead of sealant to the retainer-to-block surface **(see illustration)**.
7   Tighten the bolts a little at a time until they're all at the specified torque.

24 Pistons/connecting rods - installation and rod bearing oil clearance check

Refer to illustrations 24.3, 24.5, 24.9a, 24.9b, 24.11, 24.13, 24.14 and 24.17
1   Before installing the piston/connecting rod assemblies, the cylinder walls must be perfectly clean, the top edge of each cylinder must be chamfered, and the crankshaft must be in place.
2   Remove the cap from the end of the number one connecting rod (refer to the marks made during removal). Remove the original bearing inserts and wipe the bearing surfaces of the connecting rod and cap with a clean, lint-free cloth. They must be kept spotlessly clean.

Connecting rod bearing oil clearance check

3   Clean the back side of the new upper bearing insert, then lay it in place in the connecting rod. Make sure the tab on the bearing fits into the recess in the rod so the oil holes line up **(see illustration)**. Don't hammer the bearing insert into place and be very careful not to nick or gouge the bearing face. Don't lubricate the bearing at this time.
4   Clean the back side of the other bearing insert and install it in the rod cap. Again, make sure the tab on the bearing fits into the recess in the cap, and don't apply any lubricant. It's critically important that the mating surfaces of the bearing and connecting rod are perfectly clean and oil free when they're assembled.
5   Position the piston ring gaps at staggered intervals around the piston **(see illustration)**.
6   Slip a section of plastic or rubber hose over each connecting rod cap bolt.
7   Lubricate the piston and rings with clean engine oil and attach a piston ring compres-

sor to the piston. Leave the skirt protruding about 1/4-inch to guide the piston into the cylinder. The rings must be compressed until they're flush with the piston.
8   Rotate the crankshaft until the number one connecting rod journal is at BDC (bottom dead center) and apply a coat of engine oil to the cylinder walls.
9   With the dimple on top of the piston **(see illustrations)** facing the front of the engine, gently insert the piston/connecting rod assembly into the number one cylinder bore and rest the bottom edge of the ring compressor on the engine block.
10   Tap the top edge of the ring compressor to make sure it's contacting the block around its entire circumference.
11   Gently tap on the top of the piston with the end of a wooden hammer handle **(see illustration)** while guiding the end of the connecting rod into place on the crankshaft journal. The piston rings may try to pop out of the ring compressor just before entering the cylinder bore, so keep some downward pressure on the ring compressor. Work slowly, and if any resistance is felt as the piston enters the cylinder, stop immediately. Find out what's hanging up and fix it before proceeding. Do not, for any reason, force the piston into the cylinder - you might break a ring and/or the piston.
12   Once the piston/connecting rod assem-

bly is installed, the connecting rod bearing oil clearance must be checked before the rod cap is permanently bolted in place.
13   Cut a piece of the appropriate size Plastigage slightly shorter than the width of the connecting rod bearing and lay it in place on the number one connecting rod journal, parallel with the journal axis **(see illustration)**.
14   Clean the connecting rod cap bearing face, remove the protective hoses from the connecting rod bolts and install the rod cap. Make sure the mating mark on the cap is on

24.11 The piston can be driven (gently) into the cylinder bore with the end of a wooden or plastic hammer handle

24.13 Lay the Plastigage strips on each rod bearing journal, parallel to the crankshaft centerline

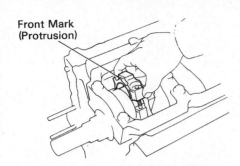

Front Mark
(Protrusion)

24.14 Install the connecting rod caps with the front mark facing the timing belt end of the engine

the same side as the mark on the connecting rod. If you're working on a late model four-cylinder or a V6 engine, check the cap to make sure the front mark is facing the timing belt end of the engine **(see illustration)**.

15 Apply a light coat of oil to the under sides of the nuts, then install and tighten them to the specified torque, working up to it in three steps. Use a thin-wall socket to avoid erroneous torque readings that can result if the socket is wedged between the rod cap and nut. If the socket tends to wedge itself between the nut and the cap, lift up on it slightly until it no longer contacts the cap. Do not rotate the crankshaft at any time during this operation. **Note:** *If you're working on a V6 engine, after reaching the specified torque, tighten each nut an additional 90 degrees (1/4-turn).*

16 Remove the nuts and detach the rod cap, being very careful not to disturb the Plastigage.

17 Compare the width of the crushed Plastigage to the scale printed on the Plastigage envelope to obtain the oil clearance **(see illustration)**. Compare it to the Specifications to make sure the clearance is correct.

18 If the clearance is not as specified, the bearing inserts may be the wrong size (which means different ones will be required). Before deciding that different inserts are needed, make sure that no dirt or oil was between the bearing inserts and the connecting rod or cap when the clearance was measured. Also, recheck the journal diameter. If the Plastigage was wider at one end than the other, the journal may be tapered (refer to Section 18).

Final connecting rod installation

19 Carefully scrape all traces of the Plastigage material off the rod journal and/or bear-

ing face. Be very careful not to scratch the bearing - use your fingernail or the edge of a credit card.

20 Make sure the bearing faces are perfectly clean, then apply a uniform layer of clean moly-base grease or engine assembly lube to both of them. You'll have to push the piston into the cylinder to expose the face of the bearing insert in the connecting rod - be sure to slip the protective hoses over the rod bolts first.

21 Slide the connecting rod back into place on the journal, remove the protective hoses from the rod cap bolts, install the rod cap and tighten the nuts to the specified torque. Again, work up to the torque in three steps.

22 Repeat the entire procedure for the remaining pistons/connecting rods.

23 The important points to remember are . .

a) *Keep the back sides of the bearing inserts and the insides of the connecting rods and caps perfectly clean when assembling them.*

b) *Make sure you have the correct piston/rod assembly for each cylinder.*

c) *The dimple on the piston must face the front of the engine.*

d) *Lubricate the cylinder walls with clean oil.*

e) *Lubricate the bearing faces when installing the rod caps after the oil clearance has been checked.*

24 After all the piston/connecting rod assemblies have been properly installed, rotate the crankshaft a number of times by hand to check for any obvious binding.

25 As a final step, the connecting rod end play must be checked. Refer to Section 12 for this procedure.

26 Compare the measured end play to the Specifications to make sure it's correct. If it was correct before disassembly and the original crankshaft and rods were reinstalled, it should still be right. If new rods or a new crankshaft were installed, the end play may be inadequate. If so, the rods will have to be removed and taken to an automotive machine shop for resizing.

25 Initial start-up and break-in after overhaul

Warning: *Have a fire extinguisher handy when starting the engine for the first time.*

1 Once the engine has been installed in the vehicle, double-check the engine oil and coolant levels.

2 With the spark plugs out of the engine

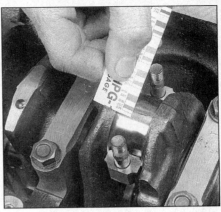

24.17 Measure the width of the crushed Plastigage to determine the rod bearing oil clearance (be sure to use the correct scale - standard and metric scales are included)

and the ignition system disabled (see Section 3), crank the engine until oil pressure registers on the gauge or the light goes out.

3 Install the spark plugs, hook up the plug wires and restore the ignition system functions (Section 3).

4 Start the engine. It may take a few moments for the fuel system to build up pressure, but the engine should start without a great deal of effort.

5 After the engine starts, it should be allowed to warm up to normal operating temperature. While the engine is warming up, make a thorough check for fuel, oil and coolant leaks.

6 Shut the engine off and recheck the engine oil and coolant levels.

7 Drive the vehicle to an area with minimum traffic, accelerate at full throttle from 30 to 50 mph, then allow the vehicle to slow to 30 mph with the throttle closed. Repeat the procedure 10 or 12 times. This will load the piston rings and cause them to seat properly against the cylinder walls. Check again for oil and coolant leaks.

8 Drive the vehicle gently for the first 500 miles (no sustained high speeds) and keep a constant check on the oil level. It is not unusual for an engine to use oil during the break-in period.

9 At approximately 500 to 600 miles, change the oil and filter.

10 For the next few hundred miles, drive the vehicle normally. Do not pamper it or abuse it.

11 After 2000 miles, change the oil and filter again and consider the engine broken in.

Notes

Chapter 3
Cooling, heating and air conditioning systems

Contents

Specifications

General

Radiator cap pressure rating	10.7 to 14.9 psi
Thermostat rating	See Chapter 1

Torque specifications

Ft-lbs (unless otherwise indicated)

Thermostat housing bolts	
Four-cylinder engines	14 to 21
V6 engine	14
Water pump-to-block bolts	
2S-E engine	78 in-lbs
3S-FE engine	82 in-lbs
V6 engine	14

1   General information

Engine cooling system

All vehicles covered by this manual employ a pressurized engine cooling system with thermostatically controlled coolant circulation. An impeller type water pump mounted on the front of the block pumps coolant through the engine. The coolant flows around each cylinder and toward the rear of the engine. Cast-in coolant passages direct coolant around the intake and exhaust ports, near the spark plug areas and in proximity to the exhaust valve guides.

A wax pellet type thermostat is located in the thermostat housing near the front of the engine. During warm up, the closed thermostat prevents coolant from circulating through the radiator. When the engine reaches normal operating temperature, the thermostat opens and allows hot coolant to travel through the radiator, where it is cooled before returning to the engine.

The cooling system is sealed by a pressure type radiator cap. This raises the boiling point of the coolant, and the higher boiling point of the coolant increases the cooling efficiency of the radiator. If the system pressure exceeds the cap pressure relief value, the excess pressure in the system forces the spring-loaded valve inside the cap off its seat and allows the coolant to escape through the overflow tube into a coolant reservoir. When the system cools, the excess coolant is automatically drawn from the reservoir back into the radiator.

The coolant reservoir does double duty as both the point at which fresh coolant is added to the cooling system to maintain the proper fluid level and as a holding tank for overheated coolant.

This type of cooling system is known as a closed design because coolant that escapes past the pressure cap is saved and reused.

Heating system

The heating system consists of a blower fan and heater core located within the heater box, the inlet and outlet hoses connecting the heater core to the engine cooling system and the heater/air conditioning control head on the dashboard. Hot engine coolant is circulated through the heater core. When the heater mode is activated, a flap door opens to expose the heater box to the passenger compartment. A fan switch on the control head activates the blower motor, which forces air through the core, heating the air.

Air conditioning system

The air conditioning system consists of a condenser mounted in front of the radiator, an evaporator mounted adjacent to the heater core, a compressor mounted on the engine, a filter-drier (accumulator) which contains a high pressure relief valve and the plumbing connecting all of the above.

A blower fan forces the warmer air of the passenger compartment through the evaporator core (sort of a radiator-in-reverse), transferring the heat from the air to the refrigerant. The liquid 3-13-1refrigerant boils off into low pressure vapor, taking the heat with it when it leaves the evaporator.

2   Antifreeze - general information

Warning: *Do not allow antifreeze to come in contact with your skin or painted surfaces of the vehicle. Flush contacted areas immediately with plenty of water. Antifreeze can be fatal to children and pets. Wipe up garage floor and drip pan coolant spills. Keep antifreeze containers covered and repair leaks in the cooling system immediately.*
Note: *Do not use an alcohol-based antifreeze solution.*

The cooling system should be filled with a water/ethylene glycol based antifreeze solution, which will prevent freezing down to at least -20 degrees F, or lower if local climate requires it. It also provides protection against corrosion and increases the coolant boiling point.

The cooling system should be drained, flushed and refilled at least every other year (see Chapter 1). The use of antifreeze solutions for periods of longer than two years is likely to cause damage and encourage the formation of rust and scale in the system. If your tap water is "hard", use distilled water with the antifreeze.

Before adding antifreeze to the system, check all hose connections, because antifreeze tends to search out and leak through very minute openings. Engines do not normally consume coolant. Therefore, if the level goes down find the cause and correct it.

The exact mixture of antifreeze-to-water which you should use depends on the relative weather conditions. The mixture should contain at least 50 percent antifreeze, but should never contain more than 70 percent antifreeze. Consult the mixture ratio chart on the antifreeze container before adding coolant. Hydrometers are available at most auto parts stores to test the ratio of antifreeze to water. Use antifreeze which meets the vehicle manufacturer's specifications.

3   Thermostat - check and replacement

Warning: *Do not attempt to remove the radiator cap, coolant or thermostat until the engine has cooled completely.*

Check

1   Before assuming the thermostat is to blame for a cooling system problem, check coolant level (Chapter 1), drivebelt tension (Chapter 1) and temperature gauge (or light) operation.
2   If the engine takes a long time to warm up (as indicated by the temperature gauge or heater operation), the thermostat is probably stuck open. Replace the thermostat with a new one.
3   If the engine runs hot, use your hand to check the temperature of the lower radiator hose. If the hose is not hot, but the engine is,

3.8 Disconnect the fan switch plug (3S-FE shown, 2S-E similar)

the thermostat is probably stuck in the closed position, preventing the coolant inside the engine from escaping to the radiator. Replace the thermostat. **Caution:** *Do not drive the vehicle without a thermostat. The computer may stay in open loop and emissions and fuel economy will suffer.*
4   If the lower radiator hose is hot, it means that the coolant is flowing and the thermostat is open. Consult the Troubleshooting Section at the front of this manual for further diagnosis.

Replacement

Refer to illustrations 3.8, 3.9, 3.10, 3.12 and 3.13

5   Disconnect the negative cable from the battery.
6   Drain the coolant from the radiator (see Chapter 1).
7   Remove the lower radiator hose from the thermostat housing (located on the water pump housing).
8   On four-cylinder models, disconnect the plug from the fan switch on the thermostat housing **(see illustration)**.
9   On V6 models, unbolt the water inlet pipe and remove the pipe and O-ring **(see illustration)**.
10   Remove the fasteners from the thermo-

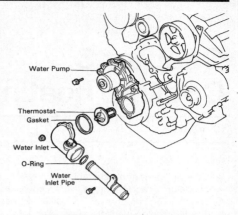

3.9 V6 thermostat and related components - exploded view

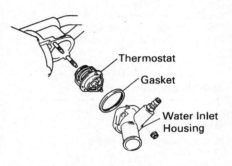

3.10 Four-cylinder thermostat and related components - exploded view

stat housing and detach the housing from the engine **(see illustration)**. Be prepared for some coolant to spill as the gasket seal is broken.
11   Remove the thermostat, noting the way it was mounted, and thoroughly clean the sealing surfaces.
12   Fit a new gasket onto the thermostat **(see illustration)**.
13   Install the thermostat and housing, making sure the jiggle pin is at the highest point **(see illustration)**.
14   Tighten the housing fasteners to the

3.12 The thermostat gasket fits over the edge of the thermostat

3.13 Install the thermostat with the jiggle pin (arrow) at the highest point (four-cylinder shown)

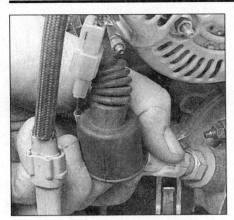

4.1a On four-cylinder models the water temperature sensor for the fan is located in the thermostat housing

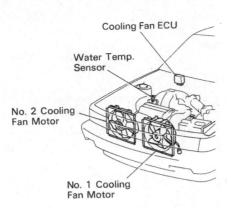

4.1b On V6 models, the water temperature sensor for the fan is located on the intake manifold

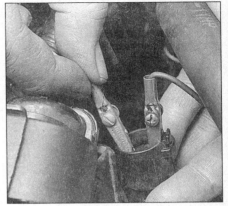

4.2 Disconnect the fan wiring plug and run jumper wires directly to the positive and negative terminals of the battery

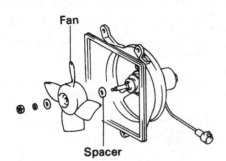

4.7 Remove the fan from the motor

specified torque and reinstall the remaining parts in the reverse order of removal. On V6 models, use a new O-ring on the water inlet pipe.

15 Refill the cooling system and on V6 models, bleed the air from the system (see Chapter 1). Run the engine and check for leaks and proper operation.

4 Engine cooling fan - check and replacement

Warning: *To avoid possible injury, keep clear of the fan blades, as they may start turning at any time!*

Check

Refer to illustrations 4.1a, 4.1b and 4.2

1 If the radiator fan won't shut off when the engine is cool, unplug the wiring connector from the water temperature sensor **(see illustrations)** and bridge the connector. If this shuts off the fan, replace the switch.

2 To test an inoperative fan motor (one that doesn't come on when the engine gets hot or when the air conditioner is on), first check the fuses and/or fusible links (see Chapter 12). Then unplug the electrical connector at the motor and use jumper wires to connect the fan directly to the battery **(see illustration)**. **Warning:** *Do not allow the test*

clips to contact each other or any metallic part of the vehicle. If the fan still does not work, replace the fan motor.

3 If the motor tested OK in the previous test but is still inoperative, then the fault lies in the relays, wiring or the cooling fan ECU. Due to the complexity and variety of circuits used, we recommend you take it to a dealer or other qualified repair facility for further diagnosis.

Replacement

Refer to illustration 4.7

4 Disconnect the negative battery cable.

5 Unplug the wiring connector at the fan motor.

6 Unbolt the fan shroud from the radiator and lift the fan/shroud assembly from the vehicle.

7 Hold the fan blades and remove the fan retaining nut (and spacer, if equipped) **(see illustration)**.

8 Unbolt the fan motor from the shroud.

9 Installation is the reverse of removal.

5 Radiator - removal and installation

Refer to illustrations 5.6, 5.7 and 5.11

1 With the engine cold, disconnect the battery cable.

2 Drain the coolant into a container (see Chapter 1).

3 Remove both the upper and lower radiator hoses.

4 Disconnect the reservoir hose from the radiator filler neck.

5 Remove the cooling fan (see Section 4).

6 If equipped with an automatic transaxle, disconnect the cooler lines from the radiator **(see illustration)**. Place a drip pan to catch the fluid and cap the fittings.

7 Remove the bolts that attach the radiator to its support **(see illustration)**.

8 Lift out the radiator. Be aware of dripping fluids and the sharp fins.

9 With the radiator removed, it can be inspected for leaks, damage and internal blockage. If in need of repairs, have a professional radiator shop or dealer service department perform the work as special techniques are required.

10 Bugs and dirt can be cleaned from the radiator with compressed air and a soft brush. Don't bend the cooling fins as this is done. **Warning:** *Wear eye protection.*

5.6 Remove the automatic transaxle cooler lines (arrows)

5.7 Remove the hold-down clamps from each end of the radiator (arrow)

5.11 The rubber mounts (arrow) must be in place when the radiator is reinstalled

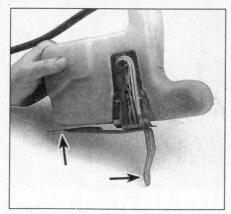

6.3 Typical coolant reservoir - removed to show bolt locations (arrows)

8.3 Remove the alternator adjusting bar (arrow)

11   Installation is the reverse of the removal procedure. Be sure the rubber mounts are in place **(see illustration)**.

12   After installation, fill the cooling system with the proper mixture of antifreeze and water. Refer to Chapter 1 if necessary.

13   Start the engine and check for leaks. Allow the engine to reach normal operating temperature, indicated by the upper radiator hose becoming hot. Recheck the coolant level and add more if required.

14   On automatic transmission equipped models, check and add fluid as needed.

6   Coolant reservoir - removal and installation

Refer to illustration 6.3
Warning: *The engine must be completely cool before removing the reservoir. Antifreeze/coolant is toxic; keep it away from children and pets.*

1   Disconnect the overflow hose from the radiator neck.

2   Remove the battery top brace if it blocks access to the reservoir.

3   Unbolt the reservoir **(see illustration)** and lift it out of the engine compartment.

4   Pour the coolant into a container. Wash out and inspect the reservoir for cracks and chafing. Replace if damaged.

5   Installation is the reverse of removal.

7   Water pump - check

1   A failure in the water pump can cause serious engine damage due to overheating.

2   With the engine running and warmed to normal operating temperature, squeeze the upper radiator hose. If the water pump is working properly, a pressure surge should be felt as the hose is released. **Warning:** *Keep hands away from fan blades!*

3   Water pumps are equipped with weep or vent holes. If a failure occurs in the pump seal, coolant will leak from this hole. In most cases it will be necessary to use a flashlight to find the hole on the water pump by looking through the space just below the pump to see evidence of leakage.

4   If the water pump shaft bearings fail there may be a howling sound at the front of the engine while it is running. Bearing wear

can be felt if the water pump pulley is rocked up and down. Do not mistake drivebelt slippage, which causes a squealing sound, for water pump failure. Spray automotive drivebelt dressing on the belts to eliminate them as a cause of noise.

8   Water pump - removal and installation

Four-cylinder engines

Refer to illustrations 8.3, 8.4, 8.6, 8.7, 8.9a and 8.9b

1   Disconnect the negative battery cable and drain the cooling system.

2   Remove the timing belt (see Chapter 2A).

3   Remove the alternator adjusting bar **(see illustration)**.

4   Remove the bolts from the water pump **(see illustration)**, noting the locations of the different length bolts. Remove the pump and O-ring. If necessary, tap the pump loose with a soft-face hammer.

5   To remove the pump cover (housing), follow this Step and Step 6. Disconnect the radiator hose and the fan temperature sensor wire at the water inlet (thermostat) housing.

6   Disconnect the coolant bypass hose from the water neck, then remove the two

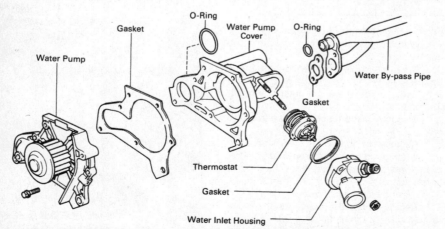

8.4 Typical four-cylinder engine water pump components - exploded view

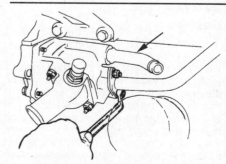

8.6 Disconnect the coolant bypass hose from the water neck (arrow) - the heater pipe is attached with two nuts

8.7 Scrape away all traces of the old gasket, but don't gouge the soft metal

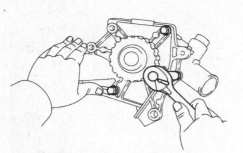

8.9a Install these bolts first . . .

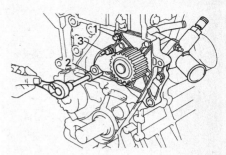

8.9b . . . then tighten these bolts in the order shown

nuts and heater pipe **(see illustration)** and lift out the pump cover (housing).

7   Thoroughly clean all sealing surfaces **(see illustration)**, removing all traces of old gaskets, sealer and O-rings.

8   Be sure to use new O-rings between the pump cover and engine block and also between the heater pipe and cover.

9   Using a new gasket, install the pump and bolts **(see illustrations)** and tighten them to the specified torque.

10   Install the remaining parts in the reverse order of removal.

11   Refill the cooling system (see Chapter 1), run the engine and check for leaks and proper operation.

V6 engines

Refer to illustrations 8.15 and 8.17

12   Disconnect the negative battery cable and drain the cooling system.

13   Remove the timing belt (see Chapter 2B).

14   Remove the water inlet pipe and thermostat (see Section 3).

15   Remove the seven water pump bolts **(see illustration)** and separate the pump from the engine.

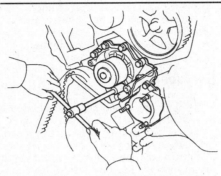

8.15 Remove the seven water pump bolts (V6)

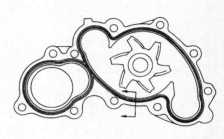

8.17 Apply a 2 to 3 mm wide bead of sealer to the water pump flange groove

16   Thoroughly clean all sealing surfaces, removing all traces of old gaskets, sealer and O-rings. Remove any traces of oil with acetone or lacquer thinner and a clean rag.

17   Apply sealer to the pump groove using a nozzle cut to a 2-3 mm opening **(see illustration)**. **Note:** *Parts must be assembled within five minutes to prevent the sealer from setting up.*

18   Reinstall the pump and the remaining parts in the reverse order of removal. Tighten the water pump bolts in several steps to the specified torque.

19   Refill the cooling system (see Chapter 1) and run the engine, checking for leaks and proper operation.

9   Coolant temperature sending unit - check and replacement

Warning: *The engine must be completely cool before removing the sending unit. Antifreeze/coolant is toxic; keep it away from children and pets.*

Note: *The following procedure applies only to the standard analog instruments. The optional digital panel diagnosis requires special equipment the home mechanic is not likely to have.*

Check

Refer to illustrations 9.3a, 9.3b and 9.3c

1   If the coolant temperature gauge is inoperative, check the fuses first (Chapter 12).

2   If the temperature gauge indicates excessive temperature after running a while, see the Troubleshooting Section in the front of the manual.

3   If the temperature gauge indicates Hot as soon as the engine is started cold, disconnect the wire at the coolant temperature sensor **(see illustrations)**. If the gauge reading drops, replace the sending unit. If the reading remains high, the wire to the gauge may be shorted to ground or the gauge is faulty.

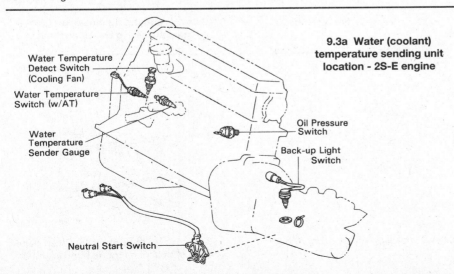

9.3a Water (coolant) temperature sending unit location - 2S-E engine

Water Temperature Detect Switch (Cooling Fan)

Water Temperature Switch (w/AT)

Water Temperature Sender Gauge

Oil Pressure Switch

Back-up Light Switch

Neutral Start Switch

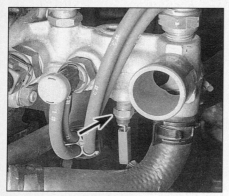

9.3b The coolant temperature sensor (arrow) on the 3S-FE engine is located under the bypass housing, above the starter (radiator hose removed for clarity)

9.3c On the V6 engine, the coolant temperature sensor is located under the bypass housing, above the exhaust crossover pipe - remove the heat shield bolts (arrows) and detach the shield for access

10.2a On early models, remove the right lower extension panel . . .

4 If the coolant temperature gauge fails to show any indication after the engine has been warmed up, (approx. 10 minutes) and the fuses checked out OK, shut off the engine. Disconnect the wire at the sending unit and, using a jumper wire, connect it to a clean ground on the engine. Briefly turn on the ignition without starting the engine. If the gauge now indicates Hot, replace the sending unit.

5 If the gauge still does not work, the circuit may be open or the gauge may be faulty - see Chapter 12 for additional information.

Replacement

6 Drain the coolant (see Chapter 1).
7 Unplug the wiring connector from the sending unit.
8 Using a deep socket or a wrench, unscrew the sending unit.
9 Install the new unit and tighten it securely. Do not use thread sealer as it may electrically insulate the sending unit.
10 Reconnect the wiring connector, refill the cooling system and check for coolant leakage and gauge function.

10 Blower unit - removal and installation

Refer to illustrations 10.2a, 10.2b, 10.2c, 10.2d, 10.2e, 10.2f, 10.2g and 10.4

1 Disconnect the negative cable from the battery.
2 Remove the glove compartment and right lower dash panel **(see illustrations)**.
3 The blower unit is located in the passenger compartment above the right front footwell.
4 Disconnect the flexible tube and wiring connector from the blower unit, then remove

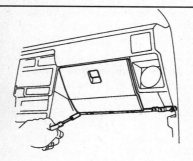

10.2b . . . unscrew the lower support . . .

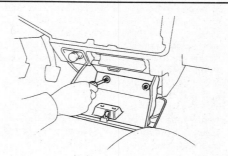

10.2c . . . remove the glove box . . .

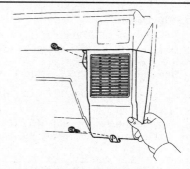

10.2d . . . and the right speaker grille to gain access to the blower unit

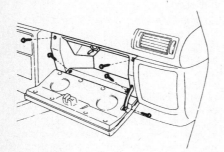

10.2e On later models, remove the glove compartment liner . . .

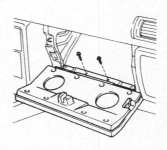

10.2f . . . the glove compartment door . . .

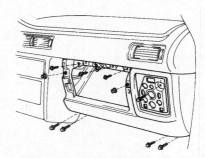

10.2g . . . and the right lower dash panel to gain access to the blower unit

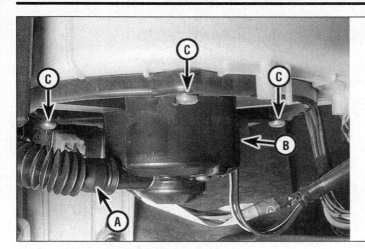

10.4 Blower unit

a) *Flexible tube*
b) *Wiring connector*
c) *Retaining screws*

11.6a On the left side above the gas pedal, disconnect the wires, controls and the mounting fasteners (arrows)

11.6b On the right side, detach the wiring, then unbolt the fastener (arrows)

8   Remove the screws and clips and separate the two halves of the housing. Take out the old heater core and install the new unit.
9   Reassemble the heater unit and check the operation of the air control flaps. If any parts bind, correct the problem before installation.
10   Reinstall the remaining parts in the reverse order of removal.
11   Refill the cooling system, reconnect the battery and run the engine. Check for leaks and proper system operation.

12   A/C and heater control assembly - removal and installation

Refer to illustrations 12.3, 12.4a, 12.4b, 12.6, 12.8a, 12.8b, 12.8c, 12.8d and 12.8e
Note: *This Section applies to the lever oper-*

ated controls. Due to the complexity of the electronic push-button system, we recommend that it be serviced only by a dealer service department.
1   Disconnect the negative cable from the battery.
2   Remove the radio (see Chapter 12).
3   Pull off the control knobs **(see illustration)**.
4   Remove the mounting screws located on the front of the control assembly **(see illustration)**. On 1987 and newer models with lever-type ventilation controls, remove the center dash console **(see illustration)** to access the control assembly.
5   Pull the control out slightly. On some models it will be necessary to disconnect the cables at the operating ends before this is possible.

the blower unit retaining screws **(see illustration)** and lower the unit from the housing.
5   If the motor is being replaced, transfer the fan to the new motor prior to installation.
6   Installation is the reverse of removal. Check for proper operation.

11   Heater core - removal and installation

Refer to illustrations 11.6a, 11.6b and 11.7
1   Disconnect the negative cable from the battery.
2   Drain the cooling system (see Chapter 1).
3   Working in the engine compartment, disconnect the heater hoses where they enter the firewall (below the heater valve).
4   Remove the instrument panel and the center console (see Chapter 11).
5   Remove the heater controls (see Section 12).
6   Label and detach the air ducts, wiring and controls still attached to the heater housing **(see illustrations)**.
7   Unbolt the heating unit **(see illustration)** and lift it from the vehicle.

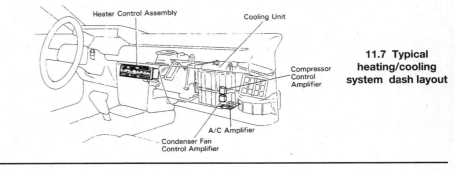

11.7 Typical heating/cooling system dash layout

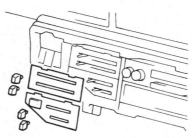

12.3 Pull the knobs off and, on early models, remove the face plates

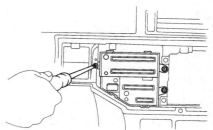

12.4a Removing early style heater controls

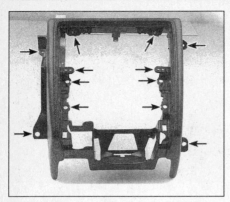

12.4b On late models, the center dash console must be removed (unit removed to show screw locations - arrows)

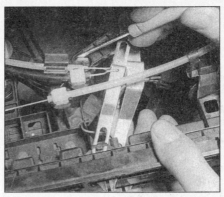

12.6 Press the ears together and push the cable clips through from the back side

6   Detach the cables and wiring from the control assembly **(see illustration)** and lift the assembly from the dash.

7   To install the unit, reverse the above procedure.

8   To adjust the cables, remove the adjustment clips at the operating ends, move the control levers to the positions indicated and position the dampers as shown **(see illustrations)**. Fasten the clips and check for stiffness or binding through the full range of operation.

9   Run the engine and check for proper functioning of the heater (and air conditioning, if equipped).

13   Air conditioning and heating system - check and maintenance

Air conditioning system

Refer to illustrations 13.5 and 13.7

Warning: The air conditioning system is under high pressure. Do not loosen any hose fittings or remove any components until after the system has been discharged by a dealer service department or an automotive air conditioning shop. Always wear eye protection when adding refrigerant or disconnecting air conditioning system fittings.

1   The following maintenance checks should be performed on a regular basis to ensure that the air conditioner continues to operate at peak efficiency.

a) Inspect the condition of the compressor drivebelt. If it is worn or deteriorated, replace it (see Chapter 1).

b) Check the drivebelt tension and, if necessary, adjust it (see Chapter 1).

c) Inspect the system hoses. Look for cracks, bubbles, hardening and deterioration. Inspect the hoses and all fittings for oil bubbles or seepage. If there is any evidence of wear, damage or leakage, replace the hose(s).

d) Inspect the condenser fins for leaves, bugs and any other foreign material that may have embedded itself in the fins. Use a "fin comb" or compressed air to remove debris from the condenser.

e) Make sure the system has the correct refrigerant charge.

2   It's a good idea to operate the system for about ten minutes at least once a month. This is particularly important during the winter months because long term non-use can cause hardening, and subsequent failure, of the seals.

3   Because of the complexity of the air conditioning system and the special equipment necessary to service it, in-depth troubleshooting and repairs are beyond the scope of this manual. However, simple component replacement procedures are provided in this Chapter.

4   The most common cause of poor cooling is simply a low system refrigerant charge. If a noticeable drop in system cooling ability occurs, one on the following quick checks will help you determine whether the refrigerant level is low.

5   Inspect the sight glass **(see illustration)**. If the refrigerant looks foamy, it's low.

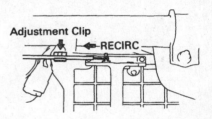

12.8a Set the air inlet damper and control lever to RECIRC

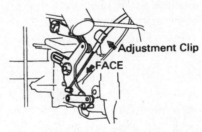

12.8b Set the mode selector damper and control lever to FACE

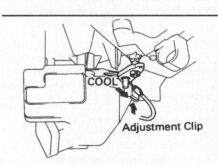

12.8c Set the air mix damper and control lever to COOL

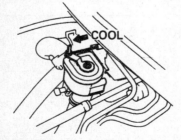

12.8d Set the water valve and control lever to COOL - place the water valve lever on COOL and while pushing the outer cable in the COOL direction, clamp the outer cable to the water valve bracket

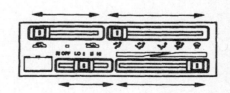

12.8e Move the control levers right and left and check for stiffness and binding through the full range of travel

13.5 The sight glass is located on the top of the receiver/drier (arrow)

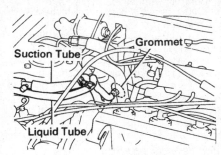

13.6 The charging kit must be connected to the suction tube (low pressure side) - the suction tube is larger in diameter than the liquid tube

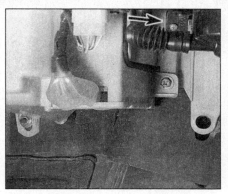

13.8 The blower motor resistor is located under the right side of the dash behind the blower motor (arrow)

14.3 The receiver/drier is located in the left front corner below the battery - once the pressure is discharged, the lines (arrows) may be disconnected

6   If there is no sight glass, feel the inlet and outlet pipes at the compressor. One side should be cold and one hot. If there is no perceptible difference between the two pipes, there is something wrong with the compressor or the system. It might be a low charge - it might be something else **(see illustration)**. Further testing of this type of system is beyond the scope of this manual. Take the vehicle to a dealer or automotive air conditioning shop.

Heating systems

Refer to illustration 13.8

7   If the air coming out of the heater vents isn't hot, the problem could stem from any of the following causes:

a) *The thermostat is stuck open, preventing the engine coolant from warming up enough to carry heat to the heater core. Replace the thermostat (see Section 3).*

b) *A heater hose is blocked, preventing the flow of coolant through the heater core. Feel both heater hoses at the firewall. They should be hot. If one of them is cold, there is an obstruction in one of the hoses or in the heater core, or the heater control valve is shut. Detach the hoses and back flush the heater core with a water hose. If the heater core is clear but circulation is impeded, remove the two hoses and flush them out with a water hose.*

c) *If flushing fails to remove the blockage from the heater core, the core must be replaced.*

8   If the blower motor speed does not correspond to the setting selected on the blower switch, the problem could be a bad fuse, circuit, switch, blower motor resistor or motor.

a) *Before checking the blower motor or circuit, always check the fuse first.*

b) *Using a test light or voltmeter, check the voltage at the motor.*

c) *Pull the heating/air conditioning control assembly (see Section 12) far enough from the dash to verify - with a test light or voltmeter - that current is reaching the blower switch on the control assembly. If the switch is not getting current, troubleshoot the circuit between the battery and the switch (see wiring diagrams at the end of this manual).*

d) *Locate the blower motor resistor behind the glove box* **(see illustration)**. *Check the resistor to make sure that it is getting current from the blower switch.*
1) *If the resistor is not getting current, check the wire.*
2) *If the wire is good, replace the switch (see Section 12).*

e) *Using a test light or voltmeter, verify that the blower motor is getting current. If the blower motor is not getting current, replace the resistor.*

9   If there isn't any air coming out of the vents:

a) *Turn the ignition ON and activate the fan control. Place your ear at the heating/air conditioning register (vent) and listen. Most motors are audible. Can you hear the motor running?*

b) *If you can't (and have already verified that the blower switch and the blower motor resistor are good), the blower motor itself is probably bad (see Section 10).* **Note:** *You can determine the motor's condition by hooking up a fused jumper wire directly between battery voltage and the blower motor.*

10   If the carpet under the heater core is damp, or if antifreeze vapor or steam is coming through the vents, the heater core is leaking. Remove it (see Section 11) and install a new unit (most radiator shops will not repair a leaking heater core).

14 Air conditioning receiver/drier - removal and installation

Refer to illustration 14.3

Warning: *For this operation, the system must be discharged by an air conditioning technician. Do not attempt to do this by yourself. The refrigerant is under high pressure and can cause serious injury and respiratory irritation.*

1   Have the refrigerant discharged by an air conditioning technician.

2   Remove the battery, igniter bracket (see Chapter 5) and coolant reservoir (see Section 6) as necessary to obtain access.

3   Disconnect the refrigerant lines **(see**

illustration) from the receiver/drier and cap the open fittings to prevent dirt and moisture entry.

4   Loosen the pinch bolt and slip the receiver/drier out of the bracket.

5   Installation is the reverse of removal.

6   Have the system evacuated, charged and leak tested by the shop that discharged it. If the receiver was replaced, have them add about 20cc (0.7 oz.) refrigeration oil to the compressor.

15 Air conditioning compressor - removal and installation

Refer to illustrations 15.4, 15.5, 15.6a and 15.6b
Warning: *For this operation, the system must be discharged by an air conditioning technician. Do not attempt to do this by yourself. The refrigerant is under high pressure and can cause serious injury and respiratory irritation.*

1   Have the refrigerant discharged by an automotive air conditioning technician.

2   Disconnect the negative cable from the battery.

3   Remove the drivebelt from the compressor (see Chapter 1).

4   Detach the wiring connectors **(see illustration)**.

15.4 Unplug the connectors (arrows)

15.5 Unbolt the flange (arrows) and detach the refrigerant lines

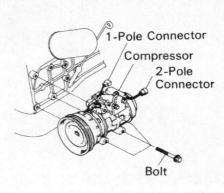

15.6a Four-cylinder engine compressor mounting details - exploded view

5   Disconnect the refrigerant lines **(see illustration)**.
6   Unbolt the compressor **(see illustrations)** and lift it from the vehicle.
7   If a new or rebuilt compressor is being installed, follow the directions which come with it regarding the proper level of oil prior to installation.
8   Installation is the reverse of removal. Replace any O-rings with new ones specifically made for the purpose and lubricate them with refrigerant oil.
9   Have the system evacuated, recharged and leak tested by the shop that discharged it.

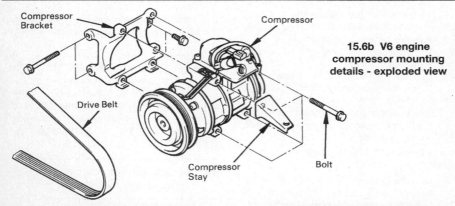

15.6b V6 engine compressor mounting details - exploded view

16 Air conditioning condenser - removal and installation

Refer to illustrations 16.4 and 16.5
Warning: *For this operation, the system must be discharged by an air conditioning technician. Do not attempt to do this by yourself. The refrigerant is under high pressure and can cause serious injury and respiratory irritation.*

1   Have the refrigerant discharged by an air conditioning technician.
2   Remove the radiator as described in Section 5.
3   Remove the battery and igniter bracket, if necessary.
4   Remove the grille for access (see Chapter 11) and disconnect the inlet and outlet fittings **(see illustration)**. Cap the open fittings immediately to keep moisture and dirt out of the system.
5   Remove the brackets **(see illustration)** and lift the condenser out.
6   Install the condenser, brackets and bolts, making sure the rubber cushions fit on the mounting points properly.
7   Reconnect the refrigerant lines, using new O-rings where needed.
8   Reinstall the remaining parts in the reverse order of removal.
9   Have the system evacuated, charged and leak tested by the shop that discharged it.

16.4 Disconnect the refrigerant lines by reaching through the grille opening - use two wrenches on fittings like this (arrow) to prevent twisting the tubing

16.5 Remove the bolt and condenser hold-down bracket on each side (arrow)

Chapter 4
Fuel and exhaust systems

Contents

Specifications

Fuel pressure

1983 and 1984	
Vacuum sensing hose detached	33 to 38 psi
Vacuum sensing hose attached	28 psi (approx.)
1985 and 1986	
Terminals +B and Fp bridged	33 to 38 psi
Vacuum sensing hose detached	33 to 38 psi
Vacuum sensing hose attached	27 to 31 psi
1987 on	
Terminals +B and Fp bridged	38 to 44 psi
Vacuum sensing hose detached	38 to 44 psi
Vacuum sensing hose attached	33 to 37 psi

Torque specifications

	Ft-lbs
Throttle body mounting bolts	
1983 through 1986	9
1987	N/A
1988 on	
Four-cylinder engines	14
V6 engines	9

1   Fuel injection system - general information

Refer to illustrations 1.1a and 1.1b

The engine is equipped with an Electronic Fuel Injection (EFI) system. The EFI system is composed of three basic sub systems: fuel system, air system and electronic control system **(see illustrations)**.

Fuel system

An electric fuel pump located inside the fuel tank supplies fuel under constant pressure to the fuel rail, which distributes fuel evenly to all injectors. From the fuel rail, fuel is injected into the intake ports, just above the intake valves, by four fuel injectors (six injectors on vehicles equipped with a V6 engine). The amount of fuel supplied by the injectors is precisely controlled by an Electronic Control Unit (ECU). An additional injector, known as the cold start injector, supplies extra fuel into the intake manifold for starting. A pressure regulator controls system pressure in relation to intake manifold vacuum. A fuel filter between the fuel pump and the fuel rail filters fuel to protect the components of the system.

Air system

The air system consists of an air filter housing, an air flow meter and a throttle body. The air flow meter is an information gathering device for the ECU. A potentiometer measures intake air flow and a temperature sensor measures intake air temperature. This information helps the ECU determine the amount (duration) of fuel to be injected by the injectors. The throttle plate inside the throttle body is controlled by the driver. As the throttle plate opens, the amount of air that can pass through the system increases, so the potentiometer opens further and the ECU signals the injectors to increase the amount of fuel delivered to the intake ports.

Electronic control system

The Toyota Computer Control System (TCCS) controls the EFI and other systems by means of an Electronic Control Unit (ECU), which employs a microcomputer. The ECU receives signals from a number of information sensors which monitor such variables as intake air volume, intake air temperature, coolant temperature, engine rpm, acceleration/deceleration and exhaust oxygen content. These signals help the ECU determine the injection duration necessary for the optimum air/fuel ratio. Some of these sensors and their corresponding ECU-controlled relays are not contained within EFI components, but are located throughout the engine compartment. This chapter includes the procedures for testing and replacing these devices. For further information regarding the ECU and its relationship to the engine electrical and ignition system, refer to Chapter 6.

2   General diagnosis

Warning: *Gasoline is extremely flammable, so extra precautions must be taken when working on any part of the fuel system. Do not smoke or allow open flames or bare light bulbs near the work area. Also, do not work in a garage if a natural gas-type appliance with a pilot light is present.*

The EFI system is not usually the source of engine problems. Trouble is usually caused by a bad contact in the wiring connectors. Always make sure that all connections are secure by tapping or wiggling the connectors to see if the signal changes. Make sure that the connector terminals are not bent and that the connectors are pushed completely together and locked.

Before troubleshooting the EFI system, always check the condition of the ignition system. Make sure that the battery, all fuses, fusible links and grounds, the igniter, the ignition coil, the high tension wire, the distributor, the plug wires and the spark plugs are all in good condition, properly connected and functioning correctly. Check the idle speed and the ignition timing. Never replace the ECU, which is an expensive component, until all other electrical devices have been eliminated as possible sources of trouble (with the exception of idle speed adjustment, which is in Chapter 1, information regarding all the above procedures is outlined in Chapter 5).

Check the air induction system for vacuum leaks. Removal of components such as

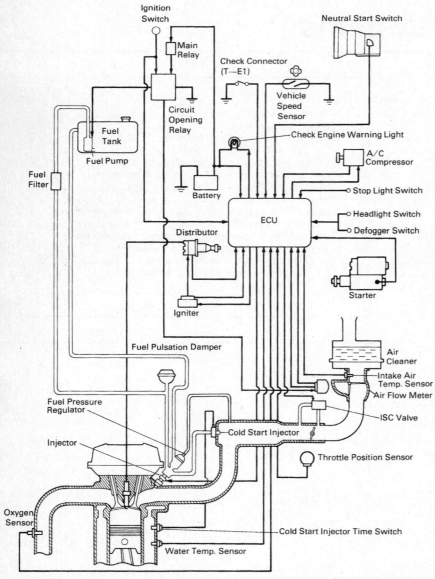

1.1a   The Toyota Computer Control System (TCCS) used on vehicles equipped with the 3S-FE four-cylinder engine

the engine oil dipstick, oil filler cap, PCV hose, etc. can cause the engine to run out of tune.

Check the fuel delivery system for fuel leaks. Make sure that the fuel filter and fuel pump are both operating properly.

3   Fuel pressure relief

Refer to illustration 3.2

Warning: *Gasoline is extremely flammable, so extra precautions must be taken when working on any part of the fuel system. Do not smoke or allow open flames or bare light bulbs near the work area. Also, do not work in a garage if a natural gas-type appliance with a pilot light is present.*

1   Always relieve the fuel pressure before disconnecting any fuel system component.
2   Locate the 15A EFI fuse in the fuse panel in the left front corner of the engine compartment. Pull this fuse **(see illustration)** and attempt to start the engine. Let it crank over five or six times. Reinstall the fuse.
3   Even though fuel pressure should now be safely relieved, it's always a good idea to place a shop rag over any fuel fitting before loosening it.

4   Fuel lines and fittings - general information

Refer to illustration 4.6

1   Check the fuel lines and all fittings and connections for cracks, leakage or deformation.
2   Check the fuel tank vapor vent system hoses and connections for looseness, sharp bends or damage.
3   Check the fuel tank for deformation, cracks, fuel leakage or tank band looseness.
4   Check the filler neck for damage or fuel leakage.
5   Repair or replace any damaged or deteriorated hoses or lines.
6   When attaching hoses to metal lines, overlap them as shown **(see illustration)**.

5   Fuel pump - check

Warning: *Gasoline is extremely flammable, so extra precautions must be taken when working on any part of the fuel system. Do not smoke or allow open flames or bare light bulbs in or near the work area. Also, don't work in a garage if a natural gas appliance such as a water heater or clothes dryer is present.*

3.2 To relieve the fuel pressure, locate the fuse panel next to the battery, lift off the cover, pull the EFI 15 amp fuse and crank the engine over four or five times

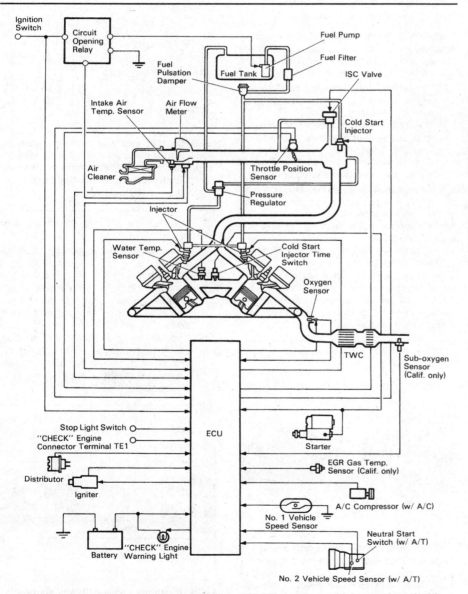

1.1b The Toyota Computer Control System (TCCS) used on vehicles equipped with the V6 engine

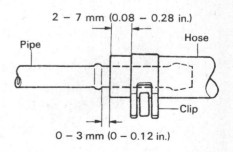

4.6 When attaching a section of rubber fuel hose to a metal fuel line, be sure to overlap the hose as shown and secure it to the line with a new hose clamp of the proper type

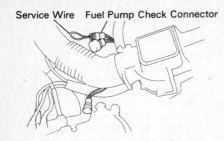

5.2a To check the fuel pump on 1983 and 1984 vehicles, turn on the ignition switch (but don't start the engine) and bridge both terminals of the fuel pump check connector with a jumper wire

Fuel pump operation check

Refer to illustrations 5.2a, 5.2b, 5.3a and 5.3b

1   Turn on the ignition switch (but do not start the engine).

2   On 1983 and 1984 vehicles, bridge both terminals of the fuel pump check connector with a jumper wire **(see illustration)**. On 1985 and later vehicles, bridge terminals +B and Fp of the service connector **(see illustration)**.

3   Listen for fuel return noises from the fuel pressure regulator and verify that there is pressure in the hose from the fuel filter **(see illustrations)**.

4   Remove the jumper wire. Close the cap on the service connector.

5   Turn the ignition switch off.

6   If there is no pressure, inspect the following components: the EFI 15-amp fuse and the ignition 7.5-amp fuse and/or the EFI main relay (all located in the fuse panel next to the battery); the circuit opening relay (see "Electronic Control System" in Chapter 6); the fuel pump; and the wiring and connectors (see the wiring diagrams at the end of the book).

Fuel pressure check

Refer to illustrations 5.7, 5.12, 5.13a, 5.13b, 5.16 and 5.18

7   A fuel pressure gauge equipped with an

5.7 If you don't have the special fuel pressure gauge and cannot find the required 8 mm banjo fitting for your own gauge, get an 8 mm bolt, place the bolt in a bench vise, cut the head off, drill out the bolt, add a locknut and coat the threads with Teflon tape

5.2b To check the fuel pump on 1985 and later vehicles, turn on the ignition switch (but don't start the engine) and bridge terminals +B and Fp of the service connector

8 mm banjo fitting on the end of the hose is required for the following procedure. There are a couple of alternatives to buying the special fuel pressure gauge setup:

a) *Simply buy an 8 mm banjo fitting and attach it to a fuel pressure gauge hose with a hose clamp.*

b) *If you can't find the correct size banjo fitting, buy an 8 mm bolt, cut the head off and drill it out. Add a locknut with the same thread pitch and seal the threads with Teflon tape* **(see illustration)**.

8   Relieve the fuel pressure (see Section 3).

9   Verify that the battery voltage is 12 volts or more (see Chapter 5).

10   Detach the cable from the negative terminal of the battery.

11   Detach the wiring connector from the cold start injector.

12   Put a metal container or shop towel under the cold start injector pipe banjo bolt at the fuel rail **(see illustration)**, then remove the banjo bolt and detach the cold start injector pipe from the fuel rail.

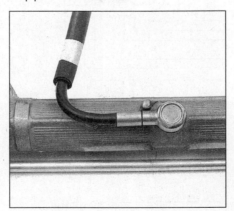

5.12 Remove this banjo bolt which attaches the lower end of the cold start injector pipe to the fuel rail and, using the banjo bolt and two crush washers, attach the banjo fitting of the fuel pressure gauge to the fuel rail (fuel rail removed from engine for clarity)

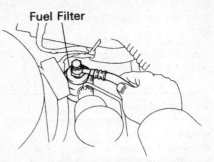

5.3a On 1983 and 1984 vehicles, listen for fuel return noise from the fuel pressure regulator and verify that there is pressure in the hose from the fuel filter by pinching it

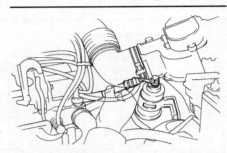

5.3b On 1985 and later vehicles, listen for fuel return noise from the fuel pressure regulator and verify that there is pressure in the hose from the fuel filter by pinching it

13   To attach the fuel pressure gauge to the fuel rail:

a) *If you are using the factory setup, or obtained an 8 mm banjo bolt for your pressure gauge kit, use the banjo bolt from the cold start injector pipe to attach the fuel pressure gauge to the fuel rail. Be sure to use crush washers on both sides of the banjo fitting.*

b) *If you are using a drilled out 8 mm bolt, attach the bolt to the fuel rail, tighten the locknut and attach the fuel pressure gauge hose with a hose clamp* **(see illustrations)**.

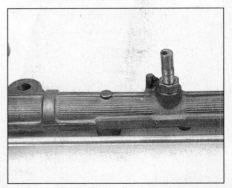

5.13a If you are using a makeshift adapter bolt, screw it into the fuel rail and tighten the locknut . . .

5.13b ... then attach the fuel pressure gauge hose with a hose clamp (fuel rail removed from engine for clarity)

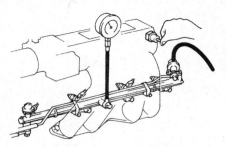

5.16 On 1983 through 19867 vehicles, start the engine, detach the vacuum sensing hose from the fuel vapor filter on the air intake plenum, plug it with your thumb and measure the fuel pressure at idle

5.18 On 1985 and later vehicles, bridge terminals +B and Fp of the check connector and measure the fuel pressure at idle

14   Wipe off any gasoline that has leaked out of the fuel delivery pipe and attach the cable to the negative terminal of the battery.
15   Place the transaxle in Neutral (manual) or Park (automatic) and apply the parking brake.
16   If your vehicle is a 1983 through 1986 model:

a) *Start the engine.*
b) *Detach the vacuum sensing hose between the fuel vapor filter on the air intake plenum and the pressure regulator.*
c) *Plug the filter with your thumb* **(see illustration)**.

17   If your vehicle is a 1987 or 1988 model:

a) *Bridge terminals +B and Fp of the check connector* **(see illustration 5.2b)**.
b) *Turn the ignition to On.*

18   Measure the fuel pressure at idle **(see illustration)** and compare it to the specified fuel pressure.

a) *If the pressure is high, replace the pressure regulator.*
b) *If the pressure is low, check the fuel hoses, lines and fittings, the fuel pump, the fuel filter and the pressure regulator.*

19   If your vehicle is a 1983 through 1986 model:

a) *Reattach the vacuum sensing hose between the pressure regulator and the fuel vapor filter on the plenum.*
b) *Measure the fuel pressure at idle and compare your reading to the specified fuel pressure.*
c) *Stop the engine.*
d) *If the pressure drops quickly, have the fuel pump, the pressure regulator and/or the fuel injectors checked out by a dealer service department (beyond listening to them to verify that they are operating, there's nothing that can be done by the home mechanic without special testing equipment).*

20   If your vehicle is a 1987 or later model:

a) *Remove the jumper wire from the service connector.*

b) *Start the engine.*
c) *Detach the vacuum sensing hose from the fuel pressure regulator.*
d) *Measure the fuel pressure at idle and compare your reading to the specified fuel pressure.*
e) *Reattach the vacuum sensing hose to the pressure regulator.*
f) *Measure the fuel pressure at idle and compare your reading to the specified fuel pressure.*
g) *If the pressure is not as specified, check the vacuum sensing hose and fuel pressure regulator.*
h) *Stop the engine. Verify that the fuel pressure remains at 24 psi or more for five minutes after the engine is turned off.*
i) *If the pressure is not as specified, have the fuel pump, the pressure regulator and/or the fuel injectors checked out by a dealer service department (beyond listening to them to verify that they are operating, there's nothing that can be done by the home mechanic without special testing equipment).*

21   Relieve the fuel pressure (see Section 3).
22   Detach the cable from the negative terminal of the battery.
23   Carefully remove the fuel pressure gauge.
24   Using new crush washers, reattach the cold start injector pipe banjo fitting to the fuel rail.
25   Reattach the wiring connector to the cold start injector. Be sure to wipe up any spilled gasoline.
26   Attach the cable to the negative terminal of the battery.
27   Start the engine and check for leaks.

6   Fuel tank - removal and installation

Refer to illustrations 6.1, 6.6, 6.8a, 6.8b and 6.9
Warning: *Gasoline is extremely flammable, so extra precautions must be taken when*

working on any part of the fuel system. Do not smoke or allow open flames or bare light bulbs near the work area. Also, do not work in a garage if a natural gas-type appliance with a pilot light is present. While performing any work on the fuel tank, wear safety glasses and have a dry chemical (Class B) fire extinguisher on hand. If you spill any fuel on your skin, rinse it off immediately with soap and water.

1   The following procedure is much easier to perform if the fuel tank is empty. Some tanks have a drain plug **(see illustration)** for this purpose. If your tank does not have a drain plug, simply run the engine until the tank is empty or see Step 4.
2   Remove the fuel filler cap to relieve fuel tank pressure. Relieve the fuel pressure (see Section 3).
3   Detach the cable from the negative terminal of the battery.
4   If the tank is full or nearly full, use a hand-operated pump to remove as much fuel through the filler tube as possible (if no such pump is available, you can drain the tank at the fuel feed line after raising the vehicle).
5   Raise the vehicle and place it securely on jackstands.

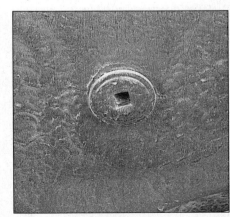

6.1 Remove the fuel filler cap, then drain the fuel from the fuel tank through the drain plug

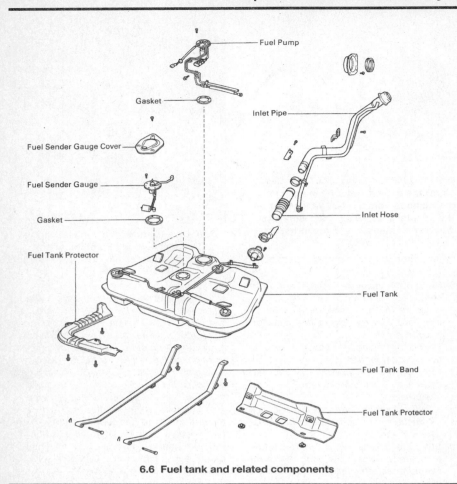

6.6 Fuel tank and related components

line are three different diameters, so reattachment is simplified. If you have any doubts, however, clearly label the three lines and their respective inlet or outlet pipes. Be sure to plug the hoses to prevent leakage and contamination of the fuel system.

12   Remove the tank from the vehicle.

13   Installation is the reverse of removal.

7   Fuel tank cleaning and repair - general information

1   Any repairs to the fuel tank or filler neck should be carried out by a professional who has experience in this critical and potentially dangerous work. Even after cleaning and flushing of the fuel system, explosive fumes can remain and ignite during repair of the tank.

2   If the fuel tank is removed from the vehicle, it should not be placed in an area where sparks or open flames could ignite the fumes coming out of the tank. Be especially careful inside garages where a natural gas-type appliance is located, because the pilot light could cause an explosion.

8   Fuel pump - removal and installation

Refer to illustrations 8.5a, 8.5b, 8.7, 8.9 and 8.12

Warning: *Gasoline is extremely flammable, so extra precautions must be taken when working on any part of the fuel system. Do not smoke or allow open flames or bare light bulbs near the work area. Also, do not work in a garage if a natural gas-type appliance with a pilot light is present.*

1   Relieve the fuel pressure (see Section 3).

2   Disconnect the cable from the negative terminal of the battery.

3   Remove the fuel tank (see Section 6) and place it on a workbench.

4   Remove any clamp bolts securing the

6   Study the accompanying exploded view drawing to familiarize yourself with the layout of the fuel tank assembly before proceeding **(see illustration)**.

7   Support the fuel tank with a floor jack. Place a sturdy plank between the jack head and the fuel tank to protect the tank.

8   Detach the fuel line bracket from the left fuel tank band and remove the two fuel tank protectors **(see illustrations)**.

9   Disconnect both fuel tank bands and pivot them down until they are hanging out of the way **(see illustration)**.

10   Lower the tank enough to disconnect the electrical wires and ground strap from the fuel pump/fuel gauge sending unit, if you have not already done so.

11   Disconnect the fuel lines, the vapor return line and the fuel inlet pipe. **Note:** *The fuel feed and return lines and the vapor return*

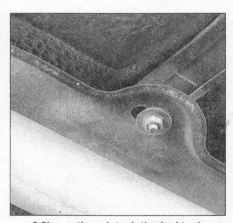

6.8a Remove the bracket nut (arrow) and detach the fuel line bracket from the left fuel tank retaining strap . . .

6.8b . . . then detach the fuel tank protector from the right fuel tank strap

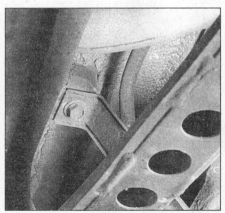

6.9 Remove the fuel tank band bolts (right shown) and swing the bands down out of the way

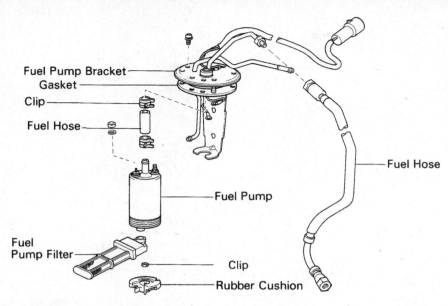

Fuel Pump Bracket
Gasket
Clip
Fuel Hose
Fuel Hose
Fuel Pump
Fuel Pump Filter
Clip
Rubber Cushion

8.5a An exploded view of the fuel pump assembly (1983 through 1986 vehicles)

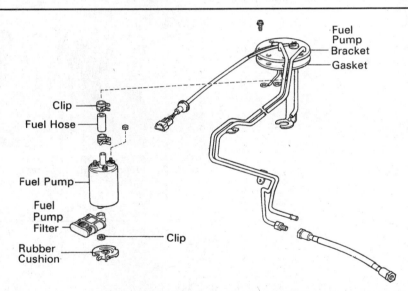

Fuel Pump Bracket
Gasket
Clip
Fuel Hose
Fuel Pump
Fuel Pump Filter
Clip
Rubber Cushion

8.5b An exploded view of the fuel pump assembly (1987 and later vehicles)

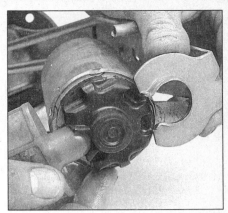

8.7 Pull the lower end of the fuel pump loose from the bracket and remove the rubber cushion that insulates the bottom of the pump

8.9 Pry off the clip that holds the filter to the fuel pump and pull the filter off—replace the clip if it's a loose fit

8.12 Pull the fuel pump loose from the hose far enough to get at the electrical lead near the bracket

fuel pump feed and return lines to the fuel tank.

5   Remove the fuel pump retaining screws **(see illustrations)**.

6   Carefully withdraw the fuel pump/bracket assembly from the fuel tank.

7   Pull the lower end of the fuel pump loose from the bracket **(see illustration)**.

8   Remove the rubber cushion from the lower end of the fuel pump.

9   Remove the clip securing the filter to the pump **(see illustration)**.

10   Pull out the filter and inspect it for contamination. If it is dirty, replace it.

11   If you are only replacing the fuel pump filter, install the new filter, the clip and the rubber cushion, push the lower end of the pump back into the bracket, install the pump/bracket assembly in the fuel tank and install the fuel tank (see Section 6).

12   If you are replacing the fuel pump, loosen the hose clamp at the upper end of the pump and disconnect the pump from the hose **(see illustration)**.

13   Disconnect the electrical wires from the pump terminals and remove the pump.

14   Installation is the reverse of removal.

9   Throttle cable - removal and installation

Refer to illustrations 9.2, 9.4a, 9.4b and 9.5
Note: *On cruise control equipped vehicles, the throttle cable is actually two cables, one*

between the accelerator pedal and the cruise control actuator and one between the actuator and the throttle linkage. Either can be replaced separately.

1   Detach the cable from the negative terminal of the battery.

9.2 To detach the throttle cable from the throttle lever arm, push down on the arm and rotate it in a clockwise direction to create some slack in the cable and slide the cable plug out of its slot in the arm (four-cylinder engine shown, V6 similar)

2   Grasp the throttle lever arm (see illustration) and rotate it to put some slack in the throttle cable, then slip the cable end out of its slot in the arm.

9.5 To detach the cable ferrule and mounting flange from the firewall, remove the bolts (arrows) from inside the vehicle

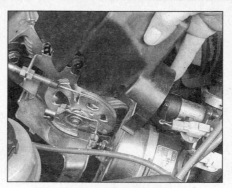

9.4a Remove the cruise control actuator cover

3   Trace the throttle cable to the firewall, detaching it from all brackets.
4   If the vehicle is equipped with cruise control, remove the cruise control actuator cover (see illustration) and detach the cables from the actuator (see illustration).
5   The cable is secured to the firewall with a flange and two mounting bolts (see illustration) that must be removed from inside the vehicle.
6   Detach the throttle cable from the accelerator pedal.
7   From inside the vehicle, pull the cable through the firewall.
8   Installation is the reverse of removal.

10   Air flow meter - check and replacement (1983 through 1986 models)

On-vehicle check

Refer to illustrations 10.2, 10.3a and 10.3b

1   Detach the cable from the negative ter-

9.4b Detach the cable(s) from the actuator

minal of the battery.
2   Unplug the electrical connector from the air flow meter (see illustration).
3   Using an ohmmeter, measure the resistance between each terminal (see illustrations).

10.2 Getting the wire spring lock loose on the air flow meter electrical connector can be tricky - the best way to remove it is to pry it loose with a pointed tool like a scribe

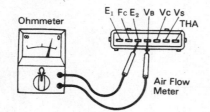

Between terminals	Resistance	Temperature
$E_2 - V_S$	20 – 400 Ω	–
$E_2 - V_C$	100 – 300 Ω	–
$E_2 - V_B$	200 – 400 Ω	–
$EE_2 - THA$	10 – 20 KΩ	–20°C (–4°F)
	4 – 7 KΩ	0°C (32°F)
	2 – 3 KΩ	20°C (68°F)
	0.9 – 1.3 KΩ	40°C (104°F)
	0.4 – 0.7 KΩ	60°C (140°F)
$E_1 - F_C$	Infinity	–

10.3a Refer to this terminal guide and resistance table when performing an on-vehicle check of the air flow meter on any 1983 through 1986 vehicle

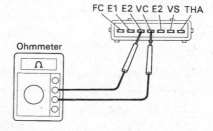

Between terminals	Resistance (Ω)	Temp. °C (°F)
E2 – VS	200 – 600	–
E2 – VC	200 – 400	–
E2 – THA	10,000 – 20,000	–20 (–4)
	4,000 – 7,000	0 (32)
	2,000 – 3,000	20 (68)
	900 – 1,300	40 (104)
	400 – 700	60 (140)
E1 – FC	Infinity	–

10.3b Refer to this terminal guide and resistance table when performing an on-vehicle check of the air flow meter on all 1987 and later vehicles

10.6a After removing the air cleaner housing upper half and air flow meter as an assembly, remove the four nuts . . .

10.6b . . . and the single bolt, then separate the two components

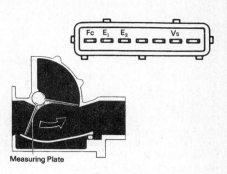

10.7a Refer to this terminal guide when bench testing the air flow meter on all vehicles

Between Terminals	Resistance Ω	Measuring plate opening
$E_1 - F_c$	Infinity	Fully closed
	Zero	Other than closed position
$E_2 - V_s$	20 – 400	Fully closed
	20 – 1000	Fully closed to fully open position

10.7b Resistance table for bench testing the air flow meter on 1983 through 1986 vehicles

Between Terminals	Resistance Ω	Measuring plate opening
E1 — FC	Infinity	Fully closed
	Zero	Other than closed
E2 — VS	200 — 600	Fully closed
	200 — 1,200	Fully closed to fully open

10.7c Resistance table for bench testing the air flow meter on 1987 and later models

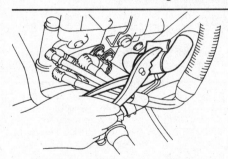

11.1 To check the operation of the air valve, start the engine, pinch the air hose and note what happens to engine rpm; it should drop during warm-up but should not drop more than 100 rpm after the engine is warmed up

a) *If the indicated resistance between the specified terminals falls within the specified resistance values, remove the air flow meter and bench test it (see Step 7).*

b) *If the indicated resistance between each terminal is not within the specified resistance value, replace the air flow meter.*

Removal

Refer to illustrations 10.6a and 10.6b

4   Loosen the hose clamps and detach the air intake duct between the air flow meter and the throttle body.

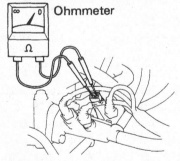

11.2 To check the resistance of the air valve heat coil, unplug the electrical connector and measure the resistance between the two terminals

5   Unsnap the spring clips that attach the upper and lower halves of the air cleaner housing, then remove the air flow meter and the air cleaner upper housing half as an assembly.

6   Remove the four nuts and single bolt **(see illustrations)** that attach the air cleaner upper housing half to the air flow meter and detach the air flow meter from the housing.

Bench test

Refer to illustrations 10.7a, 10.7b and 10.7c

7   Using an ohmmeter, measure the resistance between the specified terminals while moving the measuring plate the specified amount **(see illustrations)**.

a) *If the indicated resistance readings fall within the specified values, the air flow meter is okay.*

b) *If the indicated resistance readings do not fall within the specified resistance values, replace the air flow meter.*

Installation

8   Installation of the air flow meter is the reverse of removal. Be sure to use a new gasket.

11   Air valve - check and replacement (1983 through 1986 models)

On-vehicle check

Refer to illustrations 11.1 and 11.2

1   To check the operation of the air valve, start the engine and note the engine rpm while pinching the air hose **(see illustration)**:

a) *At low temperatures (during warm-up), the rpm should drop when the hose in pinched.*

b) *After the engine has warmed up, engine rpm should not drop more than 100 rpm when the hose is pinched.*

2   Unplug the electrical connector from the air valve. Using an ohmmeter, measure the resistance across the two terminals **(see**

illustration). This tells you the resistance of the air valve heat coil. The indicated resistance should be between 40 and 60 ohms.

3   If the air valve fails either of the above tests, replace it. If it passes both tests, remove it and bench test it.

Removal

Refer to illustration 11.6

4   If you have not already done so (if you are removing the air valve without already having checked it as described above), detach the cable from the negative terminal of the battery and unplug the electrical connector from the air valve.

5   Detach the air valve inlet and outlet hoses.

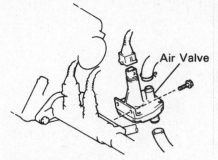

11.6 To remove the air valve, unplug the electrical connector, detach the inlet and outlet air hoses and remove the two mounting bolts

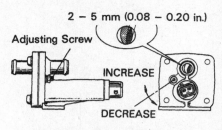

11.7 On the bench, verify that the air valve opens the specified amount when room temperature is about 68-degrees F - if it doesn't open the prescribed amount, adjust it by loosening the locknut and turning the adjusting screw

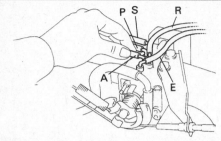

Port	At idling	Other than idling
A	No vacuum	Vacuum
P	No vacuum	Vacuum
E	No vacuum	Vacuum
S	Vacuum	No vacuum
R	No vacuum	No vacuum

12.2a Throttle body vacuum port guide (top) and vacuum table (bottom) for 1983 through 1986 vehicles

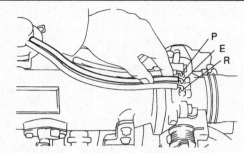

Port No.	At idling	Other than idling
E	No vacuum	Vacuum
P	No vacuum	Vacuum
R	No vacuum	No vacuum

12.2b Throttle body vacuum port guide (top) and vacuum table (bottom) for 1987 and later four-cylinder engines

6   Remove the mounting bolts and detach the air valve from the cylinder head rear cover **(see illustration).**

Bench test

Refer to illustration 11.7

7   Verify that the air valve opens the specified amount when room temperature is about 68-degrees F **(see illustration).** If it fails to open as shown, adjust it. If it can't be properly adjusted, replace it.

Installation

8   Installation of the air valve is the reverse of removal.

12   Throttle body, throttle position sensor and throttle - opener - check, removal, inspection and installation

On-vehicle check

Throttle body

Refer to illustrations 12.2a, 12.2b and 12.2c

1   Verify that the throttle linkage operates smoothly.

Port Name	At idling	Other than idling
Purge	No vacuum	Vacuum
EGR	No vacuum	Vacuum
R	No vacuum	Vacuum

12.2c Throttle body vacuum table for V6 engine (no port guide is necessary - the three ports are clearly identified on the casting)

2   Start the engine, detach each vacuum hose and, using your finger, check the vacuum at each port on the throttle body with the engine at idle and above idle, then compare your observations with the vacuum table which applies to your vehicle **(see illustrations).**

Throttle position sensor

Refer to illustrations 12.4a, 12.4b, 12.4c, 12.4d and 12.4e

Note: *On 1991 models, apply vacuum to the throttle opener.*

3   Unplug the electrical connector from the throttle position sensor.

4   Insert a feeler gauge of the specified thickness between the throttle stop screw and the stop lever **(see illustrations).**

12.4a To check the throttle position sensor, insert a feeler gauge of the specified thickness between the throttle stop screw and the stop lever

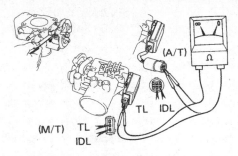

12.4b On-vehicle throttle position sensor check – terminal guide (top) and continuity table (bottom) (1983 through 1987 vehicles and 1988 and later vehicles without ECT)

Clearance between lever and stop screw		Continuity between terminals		
		IDL – TL	Psw – TL	IDL – Psw
0.50 mm	(0.0197 in.)	Continuity	No continuity	No continuity
0.90 mm	(0.0354 in.)	No continuity	No continuity	No continuity
Throttle valve fully opened position		No continuity	Continuity	No continuity

12.4c On-vehicle throttle position sensor check – terminal guide (left) and continuity table (right) (1988 and later vehicles with ECT)

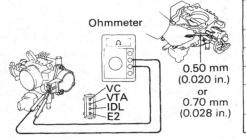

Clearance between lever and stop screw	Between terminals	Resistance
0 mm (0 in.)	VTA — E2	0.2 — 0.8 kΩ
0.50 mm (0.020 in.)	IDL — E2	Less than 2.3 kΩ
0.70 mm (0.028 in.)	IDL — E2	Infinity
Throttle valve fully opened	VTA — E2	3.3 — 10 kΩ
—	VC — E2	3 — 7 kΩ

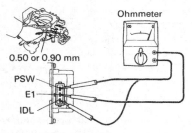

12.4d On-vehicle throttle position sensor check – terminal guide (top) and continuity table (bottom) (1988 and later vehicles without ECT)

Clearance between lever and stop screw	Continuity between terminals	
	IDL — E1	PSW — E1
0.50 mm (0.020 in.)	Continuity	No Continuity
0.90 mm (0.035 in.)	No Continuity	No Continuity
Throttle valve fully opened	No Continuity	Continuity

12.4e On-vehicle throttle position sensor check – terminal guide (left) and continuity table (right) (V6 engine)

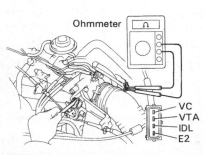

Clearance between lever and stop screw	Between terminals	Resistance
0 mm (0 in.)	VTA — E2	0.3 — 6.3 kΩ
0.30 mm (0.0118 in.)	IDL — E2	2.3 kΩ or less
0.70 mm (0.0276 in.)	IDL — E2	Infinity
Throttle valve fully opened	VTA — E2	3.5 — 10.3 kΩ
—	VC — E2	4.25 — 8.25 kΩ

12.8 To remove the throttle body from a V6 engine :

1   *Loosen the large hose clamp and detach the air cleaner duct*
2   *Disconnect the throttle cable (and the TV cable, if the vehicle has an automatic transaxle)*
3   *Detach the coolant hoses (other hose not visible)*
4   *Clearly label, then detach, all vacuum hoses*
5   *Remove the four mounting bolts (lower two bolts not visible*

12.13 Remove the four bolts (arrows) to detach the throttle body from the air intake chamber (four-cylinder engine shown, others similar - throttle body on automatic-equipped V6 engine has only three mounting bolts)

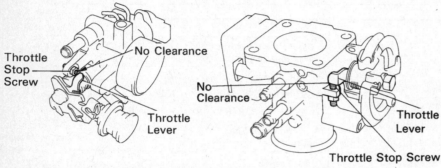

12.15 When inspecting the throttle body, verify that there is zero clearance between the throttle stop screw and the throttle lever when the throttle valve is closed (V6 engine - top; four-cylinder engine - bottom)

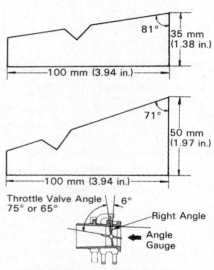

12.16 Before checking the throttle position sensor, fabricate two angle gauges (1983 through 1986 models and 1988 and later models without ECT)

5   Using an ohmmeter, check the continuity, or measure the resistance, between the indicated terminal pairs.

Removal

Refer to illustrations 12.8 and 12.13

6   If you have not already done so, detach the cable from the negative terminal of the battery.
7   Drain about a gallon of engine coolant from the radiator (see Chapter 1).
8   Loosen the hose clamps and remove the air intake duct between the air flow meter and the throttle body **(see illustration)**.
9   Detach the throttle cable from the throttle lever arm (see Section 9), then detach the throttle cable bracket and set it aside (it's not necessary to detach the throttle cable from the bracket).
10   If your vehicle is equipped with an automatic transaxle, detach the throttle valve (TV) cable from the throttle linkage (see Chapter 7B), detach the TV cable brackets from the engine and set the cable and brackets aside.
11   Clearly label, then detach, all vacuum and coolant hoses from the throttle body.
12   If you have not already done so, unplug the electrical connector from the throttle position sensor.
13   Remove the throttle body mounting

bolts **(see illustration)** and detach the throttle body and gasket from the air intake chamber.

Inspection

Throttle body

Refer to illustration 12.15

14   Using a soft brush and carburetor cleaner, thoroughly clean the throttle body casting, then blow out all passages with compressed air. **Caution:** *Do not clean the throttle position sensor with anything. Just wipe it off carefully with a clean soft cloth.*
15   Verify that there is zero clearance between the throttle stop screw and the throttle lever **(see illustration)** when the throttle valve is fully closed.

Throttle position sensor

Refer to illustrations 12.16, 12.17, 12.19a, 12.19b, 12.19c, 12.19d, 12.20a, 12.20b, 12.20c and 12.20d

16   If you have a 1987 model, a 1988 and later model with an Electronically Controlled Transaxle (ECT) or a V6 engine, proceed to Step 18. If you have a 1983 through 1986 model, or a 1988 and later model without ECT, make an angle gauge as shown **(see illustration)** to bench check the throttle position sensor.

17   Using the angle gauge, set the throttle valve opening angle to 81 degrees or 71 degrees (including the throttle valve fully closed angle of 6 degrees) from the vertical position. Using an ohmmeter, check the continuity between each pair of terminals and compare it to the specified continuity on the accompanying chart **(see illustration)**.
18   To bench check the throttle position sensor on 1987 and 1988 and later vehicles, refer to the procedure and accompanying illustrations described in Steps 4 and 5.
19   If the throttle position sensor needs to be adjusted:

a) *Loosen the two sensor screws and insert a feeler gauge of the specified thickness between the throttle stop screw and lever **(see illustrations)**.*

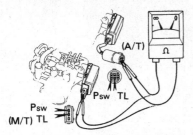

Throttle valve opening angle	Continuity		
	IDL – TL	Psw – TL	IDL – Psw
71° from vertical	No continuity	No continuity	No continuity
81° from vertical	No continuity	continuity	No continuity
Less than 7.5° from vertical	continuity	No continuity	No continuity

12.17 To check the throttle position sensor, use an ohmmeter to check the continuity between the indicated terminals with the throttle valve opening angle set at each of the specified angles

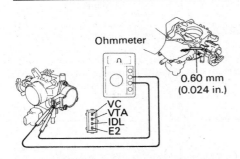

12.19b To adjust the throttle position sensor on all 1987 vehicles and 1988 and later four-cylinder models equipped with an Electronically Controlled Transaxle, use a 0.024-inch feeler gauge and connect the ohmmeter leads to terminals IDL and E2

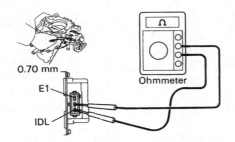

12.19c To adjust the throttle position sensor on 1988 and later four-cylinder models without an Electronically Controlled Transaxle, use a 0.028-inch feeler gauge and connect the ohmmeter leads to terminals IDL and E1

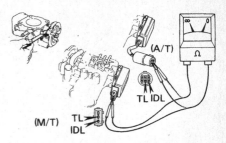

12.19a To adjust the throttle position sensor on 1983 through 1986 vehicles, use a 0.028-inch feeler gauge and connect the ohmmeter leads to terminals IDL and TL (note that the connectors are shaped differently depending on transaxle type)

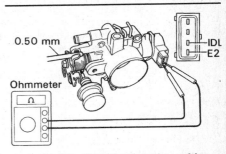

12.19d To adjust the throttle position sensor on V6 models, use a 0.020-inch feeler gauge and connect the ohmmeter leads to terminals IDL and E2

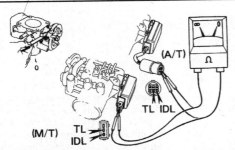

Clearance between lever and stop screw	Continuity (IDL – TL)
0.50 mm (0.0197 in.)	Continuity
0.90 mm (0.0354 in.)	No continuity

12.20a To recheck throttle position sensor continuity on 1983 through 1986 vehicles, use feeler gauges of 0.020-inch and 0.035-inch, respectively, while connecting the ohmmeter leads to terminals IDL and TL

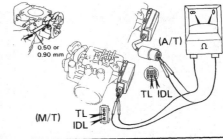

Clearance between lever and stop screw	Continuity (IDL – TL)
0.50 mm (0.0197 in.)	Continuity
0.90 mm (0.0354 in.)	No continuity

12.20b To recheck throttle position sensor continuity on all 1987 vehicles and 1988 and later four-cylinder models equipped with an Electronically Controlled Transaxle, use feeler gauges of 0.020-inch and 0.028-inch, respectively, while connecting the ohmmeter leads to terminals IDL and E2

b) *Connect the ohmmeter to the specified terminals.*
c) *Gradually turn the sensor counterclockwise until the ohmmeter deflects.*
d) *Secure the sensor by tightening the two screws.*

20   Using a feeler gauge, recheck the continuity between the specified terminals **(see illustrations)**.

Throttle opener (1991 four-cylinder models)

Refer to illustration 12.25

21   Start the engine and allow it to reach normal operating temperature and idle speed (if necessary, adjust idle speed) and place the transaxle in the Neutral range. Hook up a tachometer in accordance with the manufacturer's instructions.

22   Detach the vacuum hose from the throttle opener and plug the hose end.
23   Increase engine speed and maintain it at 2,500 rpm.
24   Release the throttle valve and check that the throttle opener is set. The throttle opener setting speed should be 1,300 to 1,500 rpm (with the cooling fan off).
25   Adjust, if necessary, by using an Allen wrench and turn the throttle opener adjusting

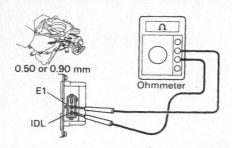

Clearance between lever and stop screw	Continuity IDL — E1
0.50 mm (0.002 in.)	Continuity
0.90 mm (0.035 in.)	No continuity

12.20c To recheck throttle position sensor continuity on 1988 and later four-cylinder models without an Electronically Controlled Transaxle, use feeler gauges of 0.020-inch and 0.028-inch, respectively, while connecting the ohmmeter leads to terminals IDL and E1

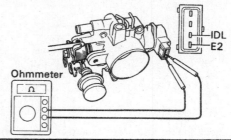

Clearance between lever and stop screw	Continuity (IDL — E2)
0.30 mm (0.0118 in.)	Continuity
0.70 mm (0.0276 in.)	No continuity

12.20d To recheck throttle position sensor continuity on V6 models, use feeler gauges of 0.012-inch and 0.028-inch, respectively, while connecting the ohmmeter leads to terminals IDL and E2

screw until 1,300 to 1,500 rpm is achieved **(see illustration)**.

26   Remove the plug and attach the vacuum hose to the throttle opener.

Installation

27   Installation of the throttle body is the reverse of removal. Be sure to tighten the throttle body mounting bolts to the specified torque.

13   Idle speed control (ISC) valve - check and replacement (1987 and later models)

On-vehicle check

Four-cylinder models (1988 and later only)

Refer to illustration 13.2

1   Start the engine and allow it to reach its normal operating temperature and idle speed (if necessary, adjust the idle speed) and place the transaxle in the Neutral range. Hook up a tachometer in accordance with the manufacturer's instructions (use the blue wire with the green connector at the distributor).

2   Using a jumper wire, bridge terminals T and E1 of the check connector **(see illustration)**. Engine speed should increase, to about 1000 to 1300 rpm.

3   Verify that the engine speed returns to idle speed after it has remained at 1000 to 1300 rpm for five seconds.

a) *If the engine speed changes as described, the ISC valve is okay.*

b) *If the engine speed does not change as described, measure the ISC valve resistance.*

4   Remove the jumper wire.

Four-cylinder models (1987 on)

Refer to illustration 13.6

5   Unplug the ISC valve electrical connector.

6   Measure the resistance between the ter-

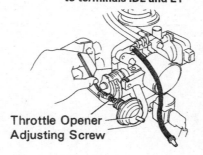

to terminals IDL and E1

Throttle Opener Adjusting Screw

12.25 Use an Allen wrench and turn the throttle opener adjusting screw

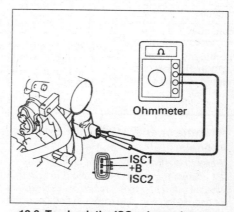

ISC1
+B
ISC2

13.6 To check the ISC valve resistance, unplug the electrical connector and verify that the resistance between terminal +B and each of the other two terminals (ISC1 and ISC2) is between 16.0 and 17.0 ohms - if it isn't, replace the ISC valve

minal +B and each of the other two terminals (ISC1 and ISC2) **(see illustration)**. It should be between 16.0 and 17.0 ohms.

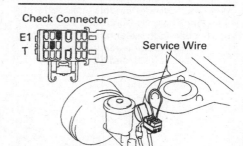

Check Connector

E1
T

Service Wire

13.2 To check the operation of the ISC valve, warm up the engine to its normal operating temperature and idle speed, bridge terminals T and E1 of the check connector, and the engine speed should increase to 1000 to 1300 rpm, then return to idle speed after five seconds - if it doesn't, check the ISC valve resistance

13.8 To check the operation of the ISC valve on a V6 model, start the engine and then turn it off and verify that the valve makes a clicking sound immediately after the engine is stopped - if the valve does not make a clicking sound, remove it for further testing

13.16 ISC valve terminal locations (V6 engine)

a) *If the resistance is as specified, the ISC valve is okay (but there may be a problem with the wiring or the ECU).*
b) *If the resistance is not as specified, replace the valve (see Step 20 below).*

7   Plug in the ISC valve electrical connector.

V6 models

Refer to illustration 13.8

8   Verify that the ISC valve **(see illustration)** makes a clicking sound immediately after the engine is stopped.

a) *If the valve makes a clicking sound, it is okay.*
b) *If the valve does not make a clicking sound, remove it for further inspection.*

Removal

Refer to illustrations 13.10 and 13.15

9   Remove the throttle body (see Section 12).
10   Remove the mounting screws and detach the ISC valve and gasket **(see illustration)**.

V6 models

11   Drain the engine coolant.
12   Unplug the ISC valve electrical connector.
13   Detach the air hose and the two water by-pass hoses.
14   Remove the nut and disconnect the wire harness clamp.
15   Remove the two bolts, the ISC valve and gasket **(see illustration)**.

Inspection (V6 models only)

Valve resistance

Refer to illustration 13.16

16   Using an ohmmeter, measure the resistance between terminals B1 and S1 and B1

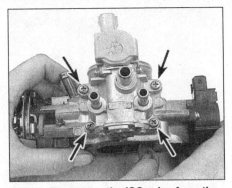

13.10 To remove the ISC valve from the throttle body of a four-cylinder engine, remove the throttle body from the engine, remove the four ISC valve mounting screws (arrows) from the underside of the throttle body, then detach the valve and gasket from the throttle body

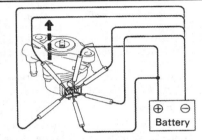

13.17 To check the operation of the ISC valve used on V6 models, apply battery voltage to terminals B1 and B2 while repeatedly grounding terminals S1, S2, S3 and S4 in sequence and verify that the valve moves toward its closed position . . .

and S3 **(see illustration)**. It should be 10 to 30 ohms. Measure the resistance between terminals B2 and S2 and B2 and S4. It should also be 10 to 30 ohms. If the indicated resistance values are not within the specified range, replace the ISC valve.

Valve operation

Refer to illustrations 13.17 and 13.18

17   While applying battery voltage to terminals B1 and B2, repeatedly ground terminals S1, S2, S3 and S4 in sequence (S1, S2, S3, S4, S1, S2, etc.) and verify that the valve moves toward its closed position **(see illustration)**.
18   While applying battery voltage to terminals B1 and B2, repeatedly ground terminals S4, S3, S2 and S1 in sequence (S4, S3, S2, S1, S4, S3, S2, etc.) and verify that the valve moves toward its open position **(see illustration)**.
19   If the ISC valve does not operate as described, replace it.

Installation

20   Installation of the ISC valve is the reverse of removal for all vehicles. Be sure to use a new gasket when installing the ISC valve.

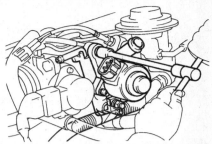

13.15 To remove the ISC valve from the throttle body of a V6 engine, unplug the ISC valve electrical connector, detach the air hose and the two water by-pass hoses, remove the nut, disconnect the wire harness clamp, remove the bolts and detach the ISC valve and gasket

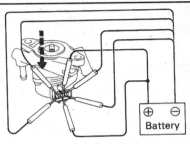

13.18 . . . then apply battery voltage to terminals B1 and B2 while repeated grounding terminals S4, S3, S2 and S1 in sequence and verify that the valve moves toward its open position - if the ISC valve fails either test, replace it

14.2a To check the resistance of the cold start injector on a four-cylinder engine, unplug the electrical connector and measure the resistance between the two terminals - it should be 3 to 5 ohms on 1983 vehicles or 2 to 4 ohms on 1984 and later vehicles

14   Cold start injector - check and replacement

On-vehicle check

Refer to illustrations 14.2a and 14.2b

1   Unplug the electrical connector from the cold start injector.
2   Using an ohmmeter, measure the resis-

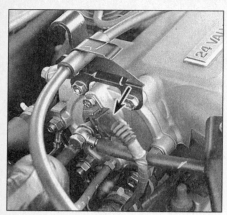

14.2b To check the resistance of the cold start injector on a V6 engine, unplug the electrical connector (arrow) and measure the resistance between the two terminals - it should be 2 to 4 ohms

14.7 To replace the cold start injector, unplug the electrical connector, remove the banjo bolt (bottom arrow) and crush washers, then remove the two mounting bolts (top arrows)

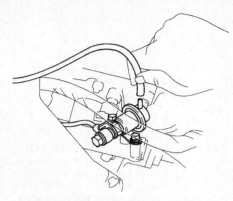

15.4a Detach the vacuum sensing hose from the fuel pressure regulator, which is located at the right end of the fuel rail (four-cylinder engines)

tance between the injector terminals **(see illustrations)**. On 1983 vehicles, it should be 3 to 5 ohms; on 1984 through 1988 and later vehicles, it should be 2 to 4 ohms.

a) *If the indicated resistance is within the specified range, the cold start injector is okay.*

b) *If the indicated resistance isn't within the specified range, replace the cold start injector.*

3   Plug in the cold start injector electrical connector.

Removal

Refer to illustration 14.7

4   Relieve the fuel pressure (see Section 3).
5   Detach the cable from the negative terminal of the battery.
6   Unplug the cold start injector electrical connector.

15.4b Detach the vacuum sensing hose (arrow) from the fuel pressure regulator, which is located at the left end of the front fuel rail (V6 engine) - to detach the regulator from the fuel frail, loosen the hose clamp, detach the fuel return line from the regulator, loosen the locknut (arrow) and pull the regulator from the end of the fuel rail

7   Place a metal container or shop towel under the banjo fitting at each end of the cold start injector line and remove the banjo bolt and crush washers **(see illustration)**. Discard the washers.
8   Remove the cold start injector mounting bolts, the injector and the gasket.

Bench test

9   The cold start injector can be bench tested (for spray pattern) but the test requires special equipment. If you are in any doubt as to the status of the cold start injector, take it to a dealer service department and have it tested.

Installation

10   Installation of the cold start injector is the reverse of removal. Be sure to use new crush washers with the banjo fittings at each end of the cold start injector pipe.

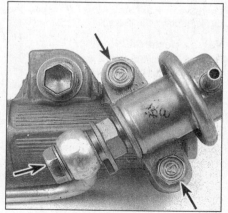

15.7 To detach the fuel pressure regulator from the fuel rail of a four-cylinder engine, remove the banjo bolt (left arrow) and crush washers, detach the fuel return line, remove the two regulator mounting bolts (right arrows), then separate the regulator from the fuel rail (fuel rail and regulator removed from vehicle for clarity)

15   Fuel pressure regulator - check and replacement

On-vehicle check

1   Refer to the fuel pressure check in Section 5.

Removal

Refer to illustrations 15.4a, 15.4b and 15.7

2   Relieve the fuel pressure (see Section 3).
3   Detach the cable from the negative terminal of the battery.
4   Detach the vacuum sensing hose **(see illustrations)**.
5   Place a metal container or shop towel under the fuel return line banjo fitting (four-cylinder engines) or the fuel return hose clamp (V6 engines).
6   Slowly loosen the banjo bolt, then remove it along with the crush washers and discard the crush washers (four-cylinder engines) or loosen the hose clamp and detach the fuel return hose from the regulator (V6 engines).
7   The remaining removal procedures for four-cylinder and V6 models differ:

a) *Four-cylinder models - Remove the pressure regulator mounting bolts* **(see illustration)** *and detach the pressure regulator from the fuel rail.*

b) *V6 models - Loosen the locknut* **(see illustration 15.4b)** *and remove the pressure regulator from the fuel rail. Note: Even if you are planning to install the same regulator, discard the old O-ring.*

Installation

Four-cylinder models

Refer to illustration 15.8

8   Installation is the reverse of removal. Be sure to use new crush washers and make sure that the pressure regulator is installed properly on the fuel rail **(see illustration)**.

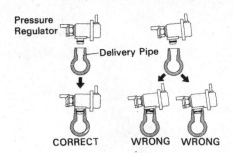

15.8 If the fuel pressure regulator on a four-cylinder engine is cocked during installation, it will not seal properly

15.10 On V6 models, make sure that you discard the old O-ring (even if you are reusing the same regulator) - coat the new O-ring with gasoline and install it on the shank (arrows) of the regulator

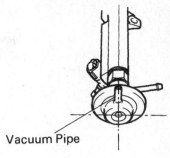

15.12 On V6 models, make sure that the fuel pressure regulator is aligned like this before you tighten the locknut (failure to do so will result in misalignment of the vacuum sensing hose and the fuel return hose)

V6 models

Refer to illustrations 15.10 and 15.12

9   Fully loosen the locknut of the pressure regulator.

10   Apply a light coat of gasoline to a new O-ring and install it on the (new or old) pressure regulator **(see illustration)**.

11   Insert the regulator into the end of the fuel rail by hand, as far as it will go.

12   Rotate the regulator counterclockwise until the vacuum pipe is aligned as shown **(see illustration)**.

13   Tighten the locknut securely.

14   The remainder of installation is the reverse of removal.

16   Fuel injector - check and replacement

On-vehicle check

1   With the engine running, or cranking, listen to the sound from each injector with an automotive stethoscope and verify that the injectors sound as if they are operating normally. If you don't have a stethoscope, touch each injector with your finger and, with the engine running, or cranking, try to determine whether the injector feels like it's operating smoothly. What is a "normal" sound or feel

for an injector? It should sound/feel smooth and uniform and its sound/feel should rise and fall with engine rpm. If no sound/feel, or an unusual sound/feel, is noted, inspect the wiring connector, the injector resistance, the signal from the computer and the injector itself.

2   To measure the injector resistance, unplug the wiring connector from the injector and, using an ohmmeter, measure the resistance between the two injector terminals. On 1983 through 1986 vehicles, it should be 1.5 to 3.0 ohms; on 1987 and later four-cylinder vehicles, it should be about 1.61 ohms; on V6 models, it should be about 13.8 ohms.

a) *If the resistance is within the specified range, but the injector is malfunctioning, remove the injector and have it bench tested by a dealer service department.*

b) *If the resistance is not within the specified range, replace the injector.*

Removal

3   Remove the fuel filler cap to relieve the fuel tank pressure.

4   Relieve the system fuel pressure (see

Section 3).

5   Detach the cable from the negative terminal of the battery.

6   If your vehicle is a four-cylinder model, proceed to Step 7; if your vehicle is a V6 model, go to Step 18.

Four-cylinder models

Refer to illustrations 16.10, 16.11, 16.13, 16.14, 16.15, 16.17a and 16.17b

7   Detach the accelerator cable from the throttle linkage and from its bracket on the air intake (see Section 9).

8   Detach the vacuum sensing hose from the fuel pressure regulator (see Section 15).

9   Unplug the cold start injector and remove the cold start injector pipe (see Section 14).

10   Unplug the four fuel injector electrical connectors **(see illustration)** and set the injector wire harness aside.

11   Remove the pulsation damper and detach the fuel feed line **(see illustration)**.

12   Remove the two fuel rail mounting bolts and detach the fuel rail/injector assembly from the cylinder head by pulling on it while wiggling it back and forth.

13   Remove the fuel injectors from the fuel

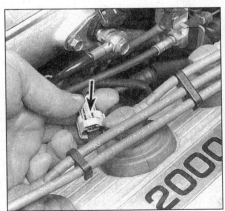

16.10 The injector connectors can be tricky to unplug - firmly depress the tang (arrow) to unlock each connector

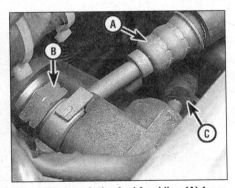

16.11 To detach the fuel feed line (A) from the fuel rail, remove the pulsation damper (B) - discard the crush washers - the fuel return line (C) is also visible in the lower right corner of this photo but you can't detach it until the fuel rail is detached from the head

16.13 Unless you are only removing one fuel injector at a time, it's a good practice to place the injectors in a clearly labeled container, like an egg carton, to prevent mixing up the injectors when it's time to install them in the fuel rail

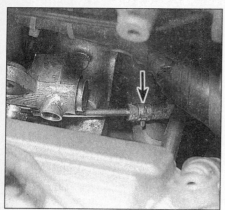

16.14 Once the fuel rail is detached from the head, you can remove the injectors and disconnect the fuel return line (arrow)

16.15 Carefully remove the fuel rail assembly through the space between the cam covers and the air intake chamber

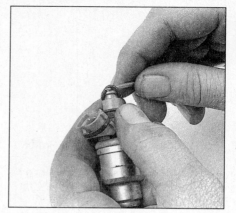

16.17a Even if you plan to reinstall the same injector(s), be sure to remove and discard the old O-rings and replace them with new ones

16.17b Also remove and discard the old grommets and replace them with new ones

16.20a On V6 models, remove the accelerator cable bracket bolt and detach the bracket . . .

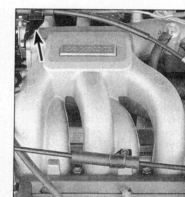

16.20b . . . then detach the throttle cable brackets (arrows) from the throttle body and the air intake chamber

rail and set them aside in a clearly labeled storage container **(see illustration)**.

14   Detach the hose from the fuel return line **(see illustration)**.

15   Remove the fuel rail **(see illustration)**.

16   Remove the four fuel rail insulators from the cylinder head and set them aside.

17   If you are replacing the injector(s), discard the old injector, the grommet and the O-ring. If you are simply replacing leaking injec-

tor O-rings, and intend to re-use the same injectors, remove the old grommet and O-ring **(see illustrations)** and discard them.

V6 models

Refer to illustrations 16.20a, 16.20b, 16.24, 16.29, 16.31, 16.35 and 16.36

18   Drain the engine coolant (see Chapter 1).

19   If your vehicle is equipped with an auto-

matic transaxle, detach the throttle valve (TV) cable from the throttle body and bracket (see Chapter 7B).

20   Detach the accelerator cable from the throttle linkage (see Section 9), then detach the throttle cable brackets from the throttle body and the air intake chamber **(see illustrations)**.

21   Remove the air cleaner cap and air flow meter (see Section 10).

22   Clearly label, then disconnect, all vacuum and water hoses.

23   Disconnect all electrical connectors from the throttle body.

24   Remove the mounting bolts and the No. 1 engine right hand mounting stay **(see illustration)**.

25   Unplug the cold start injector electrical connector and disconnect the cold start injector tube (see Section 14).

26   Clearly label, then detach, any remaining air and vacuum hoses.

27   Detach the ground strap connector.

28   Remove the wire harness clamp nut and clamp.

29   Disconnect the EGR pipe **(see illustration)**.

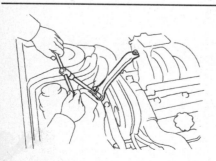

16.24 Remove the mounting bolts and the No. 1 engine right hand mounting stay (V6 models)

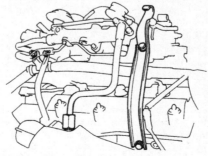

16.29 Disconnect the EGR pipe (on the left), then remove both bolts and the No. 1 engine hanger (on the right)

16.31 Remove the air intake chamber nuts and bolts and remove the air intake chamber and throttle body as an assembly

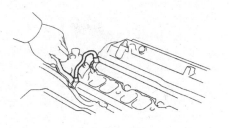

16.35 Remove the two banjo bolts, four crush washers and the No. 2 fuel pipe from the right end of the two fuel rails

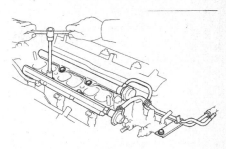

16.36 Remove the bolts and detach each fuel rail and its injectors as an assembly

30 Remove both bolts and the No. 1 engine hanger, then remove the bolt and disconnect the air intake chamber stay from the air intake chamber.

31 Remove the air intake chamber nuts and bolts **(see illustration)** and remove the air intake chamber and throttle body as an assembly. Discard the old air intake chamber gasket.

32 Disconnect the cold start injector connector, the water temperature sensor connector and all six injector connectors.

33 Disconnect the three wire harness clamps from the left fuel rail.

34 Disconnect the fuel return hose from the fuel pressure regulator (see Section 15) and the No. 1 fuel pipe and the fuel inlet hose from the fuel filter.

35 Remove the two banjo bolts, four crush washers and the No. 2 fuel pipe from the right end of the two fuel rails **(see illustration)**.

36 Remove the front fuel rail bolts **(see illustration)** and remove the fuel rail and its three injectors as an assembly. Then remove the rear fuel rail bolts, the fuel rail, its three injectors and the No. 1 fuel pipe as an assembly. Be careful not to drop the injectors when removing the fuel rails.

37 Pull the injector(s) from the fuel rails. Remove and discard the old grommet and O-ring from each injector **(see illustrations 16.17a and 16.17b)**.

38 Remove the six insulators and four spacers from the intake manifold.

Inspection

39 Further testing of the injector(s) is beyond the scope of the home mechanic. If you are in doubt as to the status of any injector(s), it can be bench tested for volume and leakage at a dealer service department.

Installation

40 Installation of the fuel injectors is the reverse of removal. Be sure to use new grommets and O-rings on the injector(s). Although it is not mandatory that you replace every grommet and O-ring on every injector when the fuel rail is removed (maybe you are only replacing one injector or replacing one leaking O-ring), it is a good practice to replace the O-rings and grommets on all the injectors just to save the time, labor and expense of tearing down the fuel system again to replace another leaky O-ring in a few months' time.

17 Exhaust system servicing - general information

Refer to illustrations 17.1, 17.6a, 17.6b and 17.6c

Warning: *Inspection and repair of exhaust system components should be done only after enough time has elapsed after driving the vehicle to allow the system components to cool completely. Also, when working under the vehicle, make sure it is securely supported on jackstands.*

1 The exhaust system consists of the exhaust manifold, catalytic converter, the muffler, the tailpipe and all connecting pipes, brackets, hangers and clamps. The exhaust system is attached to the body with mounting brackets and rubber hangers **(see illustration)**. If any of these parts are damaged or deteriorated, excessive noise and vibration will be transmitted to the body.

2 Regular inspections of the exhaust sys-

tem will keep it safe and quiet. Look for any damaged or bent parts, open seams, holes, loose connections, excessive corrosion or other defects which could allow exhaust fumes to enter the vehicle. Deteriorated exhaust system components should not be repaired - they should be replaced with new parts.

3 If the exhaust system components are extremely corroded or rusted together, they will probably have to be cut from the exhaust system. The convenient way to accomplish this is to have a muffler repair shop remove the corroded sections with a cutting torch. If, however, you want to save money by doing it yourself (and you don't have an oxy/acetylene welding outfit with a cutting torch), simply cut off the old components with a hacksaw. If you have compressed air, special pneumatic cutting chisels can also be used. If you do decide to tackle the job at home, be sure to wear eye protection to protect your eyes from metal chips and work gloves to protect your hands.

4 Here are some simple guidelines to apply when repairing the exhaust system:

a) *Work from the back to the front when removing exhaust system components.*

b) *Apply penetrating oil to the exhaust system component fasteners to make them easier to remove.*

c) *Use new gaskets, hangers and clamps when installing exhaust system components.*

d) *Apply anti-seize compound to the threads of all exhaust system fasteners during reassembly.*

e) *Be sure to allow sufficient clearance between newly installed parts and all points on the underbody to avoid overheating the floor pan and possibly damaging the interior carpet and insulation. Pay particularly close attention to the catalytic converter and its heat shield.* **Warning:** *The catalytic converter operates at very high temperatures and takes about 30 minutes to cool. Wait half an hour before attempting to remove the converter. Failure to do so could result in serious burns.*

5 The catalytic converter on 1983 through 1986 vehicles and on V6 models is under-

17.1 Every time the vehicle is raised for repairs, inspect all exhaust hangers (four or five, depending on the vehicle) - because they are subject to heat, vibration, road grit, etc., the rubber hangers deteriorate and break regularly

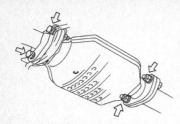

17.6a To detach an underbody converter from the exhaust system, apply penetrating oil to the front and rear flange bolts, allow it to soak in for a while, then remove the bolts

17.6b To remove an engine compartment converter, apply penetrating oil to the two studs and three bolts that attach the upper end of the converter to the exhaust manifold, allow it to soak in for a while, then remove the nuts and bolts (converter removed for clarity)

17.6c Apply penetrating oil to the three studs at the lower end of the converter and remove the three nuts

neath the vehicle; the converter on 1987 later four-cylinder models is in the engine compartment directly below the exhaust manifold.

6   To remove the converter:
a) *Raise the vehicle and place it securely on jackstands.*
b) *Make sure that the converter is cool.*
c) *Apply penetrating oil to the flange bolts at the front and rear converter flanges (underbody converter) or the upper and lower studs and bolts (engine compartment converter).*
d) *Remove the flange bolts from the front and the rear flanges of the underbody converter* **(see illustration)**, *or remove the studs and bolts from the upper and*

lower flanges of the engine compartment converter **(see illustrations)**.
e) *Remove the converter and gaskets. Discard the gaskets.*

7   If you are removing/replacing an underbody type converter, inspect the upper heat shield while the converter is removed. It should be firmly attached to the underside of

the vehicle and there should be adequate clearance between the shield and the converter.

8   If you are replacing an engine compartment type converter, remove the front and rear heat shields and the mounting bracket and switch them to the new converter.

9   Installation is the reverse of removal. Use new gaskets and coat the threads of all bolts/studs with anti-seize compound. Tighten the bolts securely. **Note:** *For further information regarding the catalytic converter, refer to Section 9 in Chapter 6.*

Chapter 5
Engine electrical systems

Contents

Specifications

Ignition coil

Primary coil resistance	
1983, 1987 and later four-cylinder models	0.38 to 0.46 ohms
1984 through 1986	0.3 to 0.5 ohms
V6	0.41 to 0.50 ohms
Secondary coil resistance	
1983, 1986 and later four-cylinder models	7.7 to 10.4 K ohms
1984 through 1985	7.5 to 10.5 K ohms
V6	7.7 to 10.4 K ohms

Distributor

Air gap	0.008 to 0.016 inch
Pick-up coil resistance	
1991 four-cylinder models	205 to 265 ohms
All other models	140 to 180 ohms

Charging system

Charging voltage	13.5 to 15.1 volts
Standard amperage	
No load	10 (or less) amperes
With a load	30 (or more) amperes
Alternator brush length	
Standard	10.5 mm (0.413 in)
Minimum	4.5 mm (0.177 in)

Ignition timing

1983 through 1986	
Vacuum advance disconnected	5-degrees BTDC at 950 rpm
Vacuum advance connected	16-degrees BTDC at 950 rpm
1987 on	
Four-cylinder engines	
Terminals T and E1 bridged	10-degrees BTDC at idle
Terminals T and E1 disconnected	13 to 22-degrees BTDC at idle
V6 engines	
Terminals T and E1 bridged	10-degrees BTDC at idle
Terminals T and E1 disconnected	13 to 27-degrees BTDC at idle

1   General information

The engine electrical systems include all ignition, charging and starting components.

Because of their engine-related functions, these components are considered separately from chassis electrical devices such as the lights, instruments, etc.

Safety related information on the engine electrical systems can be found in Safety first near the front of this manual. It should be referred to before beginning any operation included in this Chapter.

2 Battery - removal and installation

Refer to illustrations 2.1 and 2.2

1   Disconnect both cables from the battery terminals. **Caution:** *Always disconnect the negative battery cable first* **(see illustration)** *and hook it up last or the battery may be shorted by the tool being used to loosen the cable clamps.*

2   Remove the battery hold-down strap nut and bolt and the strap **(see illustration)**.

3   Lift out the battery. Use of a lifting strap is recommended - the battery is heavy.

4   While the battery is out, inspect the battery carrier (tray) for corrosion (see Chapter 1).

5   If you are replacing the battery, make sure that you get an identical battery, with the same dimensions, amperage rating, "cold cranking" rating, etc.

6   Installation is the reverse of removal.

3 Battery - emergency jump starting

Refer to the *Booster battery (jump) starting* procedure at the front of this manual.

4 Battery cables - check and replacement

1   Periodically inspect the entire length of each battery cable for damage, cracked or burned insulation and corrosion. Poor battery cable connections can cause starting problems and decreased engine performance.

2   Check the cable-to-terminal connections at the ends of the cables for cracks, loose wire strands and corrosion. The presence of white or green, fluffy deposits under the insulation at the cable terminal connection is a sign that the cable is corroded and should be replaced. Check the terminals for distortion, missing mounting bolts and corrosion.

3   When removing the cables, **always disconnect the negative cable first (see Section 2) and hook it up last** or the battery may be shorted by the tool used to loosen the cable clamps. Even if only the positive cable is being replaced, be sure to disconnect the negative cable from the battery first. (See Chapter 1 for further information regarding battery cable removal.)

4   Disconnect the old cables from the battery, then trace each of them to their opposite ends and detach them from the starter solenoid and ground. Note the routing of each cable to ensure correct installation.

5   If your are replacing either or both of the old cables, take them with you when buying new cables. It is vitally important that you replace the cables with identical parts. Cables have characteristics that make them easy to identify: positive cables are usually red, larger in cross-section and have a larger diameter battery post clamp; ground cables are usually black, smaller in cross-section and have a slightly smaller diameter clamp for the negative post.

6   Clean the threads of the solenoid or ground connection with a wire brush to remove rust and corrosion. Apply a light coat of battery terminal corrosion inhibitor, or petroleum jelly, to the threads to prevent future corrosion.

7   Attach the cable to the solenoid or ground connection and tighten the mounting nut/bolt securely.

8   Before connecting a new cable to the battery, make sure that it reaches the battery post without having to be stretched.

9   Connect the positive cable first, followed by the negative cable.

5 Ignition system - general information and precautions

The ignition system includes the ignition switch, the battery, the exciter, the coil, the primary (low voltage) and secondary (high voltage) wiring circuits, the distributor and the spark plugs. The ignition system is controlled by the Electronic Control Unit (ECU). Using data provided by information sensors which monitor various engine functions (such as rpm, intake air volume, engine temperature, etc.), the ECU ensures a perfectly timed spark under all conditions. This system is known as Electronic Spark Advance (ESA).

When working on the ignition system, take the following precautions:

a) *Do not keep the ignition switch on for more than 10 seconds if the engine will not start.*

b) *Always connect a tachometer in accordance with the manufacturer's instructions. Some tachometers may be incompatible with this ignition system. Consult your dealer before buying a tachometer for use with this vehicle.*

c) *Never allow the ignition coil terminals to touch ground. Grounding the coil could result in damage to the igniter and/or the ignition coil.*

d) *Do not disconnect the battery when the engine is running.*

e) *Make sure that the igniter is properly grounded.*

6 Ignition system - check

1   Attach an inductive timing light to each plug wire in sequence and crank the engine.

a) *If the light flashes each time the inductive pickup is attached to a wire and the engine is cranked, voltage is reaching the plugs.*

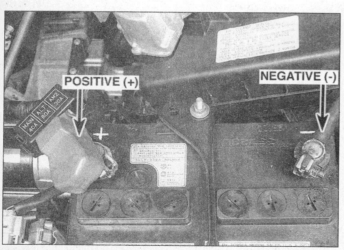

2.1 When detaching the cables from the terminals of the battery, be sure to ALWAYS disconnect the negative cable (the one with the minus sign) first - when reattaching the cables, hook up the positive cable (the one with the plus sign) first

2.2 To remove the battery, detach the negative and positive cables, then remove the hold-down strap bolt (arrow) and nut (arrow) and the strap, then carefully lift the battery out of the engine compartment

7.3a To check the primary resistance of the coil used on four-cylinder models, measure the resistance between the positive and negative terminals (arrows)

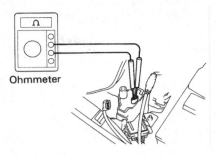

7.3b To check the primary resistance of the coil used on V6 models, measure the resistance between the positive and negative terminals

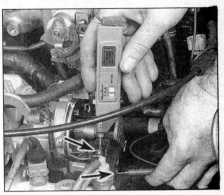

7.3c To check the secondary resistance of the coil used on four-cylinder models, measure the resistance between the positive and high-tension terminals (arrows)

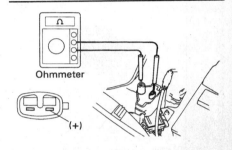

7.3d To check the secondary resistance of the coil used on V6 models, measure the resistance between the positive and high tension terminals

b) *If the light does not flash when the inductive pickup is hooked to a wire and the engine is cranked, proceed to the next Step.*

2   If the timing light indicates that no spark is getting to any of the plugs, check all connections at the ignition coil, the igniter and the distributor for a tight fit. If a loose connection is discovered, inspect it for corrosion, clean it if necessary and reconnect it securely (see Chapter 1).

3   If there is still no spark, check the resistance of the spark plug wires and the high tension cord (see Chapter 1). If any of the wires are over 25 K-ohms, replace them.

4   If there is still no spark, check the power supply to the ignition coil (see Section 8). If there isn't battery voltage at the ignition coil positive terminal, troubleshoot the wiring between the ignition switch and the ignition coil (see the wiring diagrams at end of this book).

5   If there is still no spark, check the resistance of the ignition coil (see Section 7). If the resistance is not within specification, replace the ignition coil.

6   If there is still no spark, check the resistance of the signal generator or pickup coil (see Section 10). If the resistance is not within the specified range, replace the distributor (or the pickup coil on pre-1987 Canadian models).

7   If there is still no spark, check the distributor air gap (see Section 10). If the air gap is not within specification, replace the distributor (or the pickup coil on pre-1987 Canadian models).

8   If there is still no spark, check the igniter (see Section 8). If the voltage is out of specification, replace the igniter (see Section 8). Note that in Section 8, on 1986 and later models, there is no specific test for the igniter. At this point, having eliminated all other possible causes of a "no spark" condition, the only alternative is to try another igniter.

7   Ignition coil - check and replacement

Check

Refer to illustrations 7.3a, 7.3b, 7.3c and 7.3d

1   Detach the cable from the negative terminal of the battery.

2   Remove the distributor cap (see Chapter 1).

3   Using an ohmmeter, check the coil:

a) *Measure the resistance between the positive and negative terminals* **(see illustrations)**. *Compare your reading with the specified primary coil resistance.*

b) *Measure the resistance between the positive terminal and high tension terminal* **(see illustrations)**. *Compare your reading with the specified secondary coil resistance.*

4   If either of the above tests yield resistance values outside the specified resistance, replace the coil.

Replacement

All vehicles except V6 models

Refer to illustration 7.8, 7.9 and 7.10

Note: *When replacing the ignition coil, refer to the exploded view of the distributor assembly for your vehicle in Section 9.*

5   Detach the cable from the negative terminal of the battery.

6   Remove the distributor (see Section 10).

7   If your vehicle is a 1983 through 1985 model or a 1986 Canada model, remove the igniter dust cover **(see illustration in Section 9)**.

8   Remove the ignition coil dust cover **(see illustration)**.

9   Disconnect the electrical wires from the coil terminals **(see illustration)**. Note that the

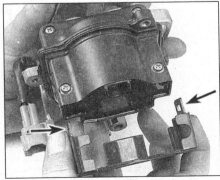

7.8 To remove the coil dust cover, spread the tangs (arrows) at each side and slide it off the coil

7.9 Label the coil primary leads, remove the negative and positive terminal nuts (arrows) and detach the wires

black and blue wires which go to the negative primary terminal are secured to the side of the coil by grooves which prevent them from touching the signal rotor shaft.

10   Remove the four coil mounting screws and the ignition coil (see illustration).

11   Installation is the reverse of removal. Be sure that the black and blue wires are correctly routed to the negative primary terminal - they should fit into their respective grooves on the side of the coil. Failure to route these wires properly could result in their interfering with the signal rotor.

V6 models

Refer to illustration 7.13

12   Detach the cable from the negative terminal of the battery.

13   Unplug the electrical connectors for the positive and negative leads to the primary side of the coil and for the high tension lead (see illustration).

14   Remove the coil mounting screws and detach the coil from its mounting bracket.

15   Installation is the reverse of removal.

7.10 Remove the four coil mounting screws to separate the coil from the distributor assembly

8   Igniter - check and replacement

Check

1   Turn the ignition switch to On.

Power source line voltage (all vehicles)

Refer to illustration 8.2

2   Using a voltmeter, connect the positive probe to the ignition coil positive terminal and the negative probe to body ground (see illustration). It should be about 12 volts.

Power transistor in igniter

1983 through 1985

Refer to illustrations 8.3, 8.4 and 8.5

3   Using a voltmeter, connect the positive probe to the ignition coil negative terminal and the negative probe to the body ground (see illustration). It should be about 12 volts.

4   Using a dry cell battery (1.5V), connect the positive pole of the battery to the pink wire terminal and the negative pole to the

7.13 To replace the coil on V6 models (located next to the battery, right above the igniter), detach the primary lead wires and the high tension lead (arrows), remove the four mounting screws and detach it from the mounting bracket - note the igniter immediately below the coil

white wire terminal (see illustration). Caution: *Do not apply voltage for more than five seconds or you could destroy the power transistor in the igniter.*

5   Using a voltmeter, connect the positive probe to the ignition coil negative terminal and the negative probe to the body ground (see illustration). Check the voltage reading. It should be about 8 to 10 volts.

6   If the voltage reading from either of these tests is not within the specified voltage, replace the igniter.

7   Turn the ignition switch off.

1986 on

8   There is no specific procedure for checking the power transistor in the igniter on 1986 and later vehicles - if a check of the ignition system (see Section 6) rules out all other possible malfunctions, replace the igniter. Make sure, however, that you eliminate all other possibilities before buying a new igniter.

Replacement

1983 through 1985 vehicles and 1986 Canadian models

Note: *Refer to the exploded views of various distributor assemblies in Section 9 when replacing the igniter.*

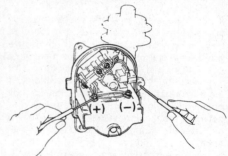

8.2 To check the power source line voltage to the igniter, connect the positive probe of a voltmeter to the coil positive terminal and the negative probe to body ground - it should be about 12 volts

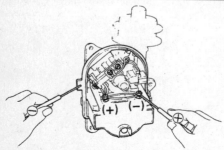

8.3 The first step in checking the power transistor in the igniter (1983 through 1985 vehicles) is to connect the positive probe of a voltmeter to the ignition coil negative terminal and the negative probe to the body ground and verify that there is about 12 volts

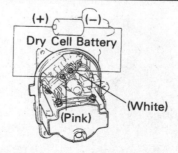

8.4 The next step is to connect the positive pole of a 1.5V dry cell battery to the pink wire terminal and the negative pole to the white wire terminal (don't apply voltage for more than five seconds or you could destroy the power transistor in the igniter) . . .

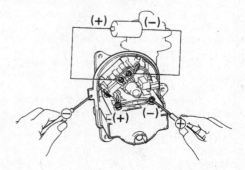

8.5 . . . then connect the positive probe of a voltmeter to the ignition coil negative terminal and the negative probe to the body ground - there should be about 8 to 10 volts

8.17 To remove the igniter from 1986 US models and all 1987 and later models, unplug the connector, remove the two mounting screws and detach the igniter from the mounting bracket

9   Detach the cable from the negative terminal of the battery.
10   Remove the distributor cap, packing and rotor (see Chapter 1).
11   Remove the igniter dust cover (1983 through 1985 vehicles and 1986 Canadian vehicles only).
12   Remove the ignition coil dust cover.
13   Remove the ignition coil (see Section 7).
14   Remove the igniter mounting screws and nuts, disconnect the wires from the igniter terminals and remove the two screws and the igniter.
15   Installation is the reverse of removal.

1986 US models and all 1987 and later vehicles

Refer to illustration 8.17
Note: *For V6 models, refer to illustration 7.13 in Section 7.*
16   Detach the cable from the negative terminal of the battery.

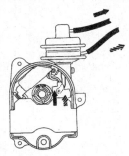

9.4 To check the vacuum advance unit, connect a vacuum pump to both diaphragms, apply vacuum and verify that the vacuum advancer moves

17   Unplug the electrical connector from the igniter **(see illustration)**.
18   Remove the mounting screws from the igniter and detach it from its mounting bracket.
19   Installation is the reverse of removal.

---

9   Vacuum and centrifugal advance - check and replacement (1983 through 1985 vehicles and 1986 Canada models)

Check

Vacuum advance

Refer to illustration 9.4
1   Detach the cable from the negative terminal of the battery.
2   Remove the distributor cap (see Chapter 1).
3   Disconnect the two vacuum hoses from the vacuum advance unit and, using a T-fit-

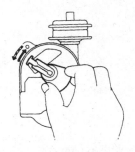

9.6 To check the centrifugal advance unit, turn the rotor shaft clockwise, release it and verify that the rotor returns slightly in a counterclockwise direction

ting and two hoses, connect a vacuum pump to both diaphragms.
4   Apply vacuum and verify that the vacuum advancer moves **(see illustration)**.
5   If the vacuum advancer does not work, replace it as necessary (see below).

Centrifugal advance

Refer to illustration 9.6
6   Turn the rotor shaft clockwise, release it and verify that the rotor returns slightly counterclockwise **(see illustration)**.
7   Verify that the rotor is not excessively loose.
8   If the centrifugal advance does not work as described, repair or replace it as necessary (see below).
9   Install the distributor cap on the distributor housing.
10   Attach the cable to the negative terminal of the battery.

Replacement

11   Detach the cable from the negative terminal of the battery.
12   Disconnect the electrical connector from the distributor.
13   Detach the vacuum hoses from the vacuum advance unit.
14   Disconnect the high tension wires from the spark plugs (see Chapter 1).
15   Remove the distributor (see Section 10).
16   Remove the distributor cap and rotor (see Chapter 1).
17   Remove the igniter dust cover (see Section 8).
18   Remove the ignition coil dust cover (see Section 7).
19   Remove the ignition coil (see Section 7).
20   Remove the igniter (see Section 8).
21   If you are replacing the vacuum advance unit, proceed to the next Step. Even if you are only replacing the centrifugal advance assembly, you must still remove the vacuum advance unit first, so perform Steps 22 and 23, then proceed to Step 25.

Vacuum advance unit

Refer to illustrations 9.22 and 9.23
22   Remove the retaining screw from the vacuum advance unit **(see illustration)**.
23   Disconnect the advancer link rod from

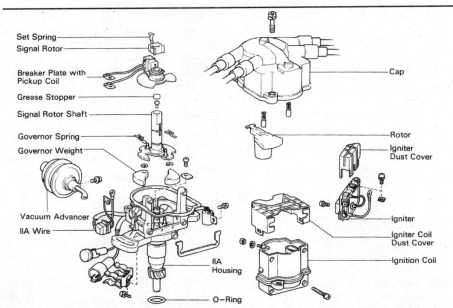

Set Spring
Signal Rotor
Breaker Plate with Pickup Coil
Grease Stopper
Signal Rotor Shaft
Governor Spring
Governor Weight
Vacuum Advancer
IIA Wire
Cap
Rotor
Igniter Dust Cover
Igniter
Igniter Coil Dust Cover
Ignition Coil
IIA Housing
O-Ring

9.22 Exploded view of the earlier Integrated Ignition Assembly (IIA) type distributor (1983 through 1985 vehicles and 1986 Canada models)

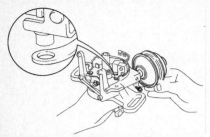

9.23 To detach the vacuum advance unit from the distributor, remove the small mounting screw (arrow) and disconnect the advancer link rod from the breaker plate

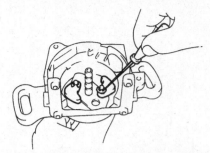

9.31 Using a small screwdriver, pop off the governor weight E-clips and remove the governor weights

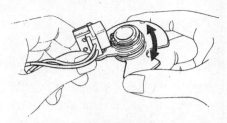

9.32 To inspect the breaker plate, turn it and make sure that there is a slight drag - if strong resistance or sticking is felt, replace the breaker plate and the pickup coil assembly

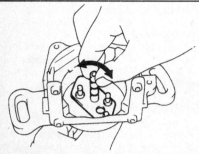

9.33 To inspect the governor shaft bearing, turn the governor shaft and verify that the bearing is neither rough nor worn - if it is, replace the distributor

the breaker plate **(see illustration)** and remove the advance unit.
24   Installation is the reverse of removal.

Centrifugal advance assembly

Refer to illustrations 9.31, 9.32, 9.33 and 9.38

25   Using a small screwdriver, pry out the signal rotor set spring, then pull out the signal rotor.
26   Remove the breaker plate screws and plate washers, then remove the breaker plate and pickup coil as a single assembly.
27   Remove the governor springs.
28   Remove the grease stopper.
29   Remove the screw at the top of the governor shaft.

10.3 Measure the air gap between the signal rotor and the pickup coil projection - if the gap is not within specification, replace the distributor

30   Pull out the signal rotor shaft.
31   Using a small screwdriver, pop off the governor weight E-clips **(see illustration)** and remove the governor weights.
32   Inspect the breaker plate **(see illustration)**. Turn it to make sure that there is a slight drag. If strong resistance or sticking is felt, replace the breaker plate and the pickup coil assembly.
33   Inspect the governor shaft bearing **(see illustration)**. Turn the governor shaft and verify that the bearing is neither rough nor worn. If necessary, replace the distributor.
34   Inspect the signal rotor shaft for signs of corrosion or a buildup of sludge (usually a combination of dirt and old grease). If any sludge is present, you might be able to revive the advance assembly by spraying it with carburetor cleaner or washing it with solvent, then lubricating it with high temperature grease. If corrosion is evident, clean the parts thoroughly, then remove any rust or pits with fine steel wool or emery cloth. Once the signal rotor shaft is clean and free of corrosion, temporarily install it onto the governor shaft and verify that both parts fit properly. If they bind because of advanced corrosion, either the signal rotor shaft or the distributor assembly, or both, must be replaced.
35   The governor springs may also be stretched, but it's difficult to assess their operation without specialized testing equipment. If you're in doubt, it's a good idea to replace them.
36   Install the governor weights. Using needle nose pliers, install the governor weight E-clips.

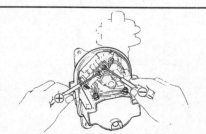

10.4a To check the pickup coil on 1983 through 1986 models, measure the resistance between the two terminals on top - it should be between 140 and 180 ohms

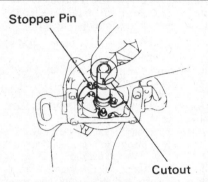

9.38 Make sure the signal rotor shaft is aligned like this when you install it

37   Lightly coat the governor shaft with high temperature grease.
38   Install the signal rotor shaft on the governor shaft as shown **(see illustration)**, install the screw, pack the inside of the shaft with high temperature grease, then push the grease stopper into place with your finger.
39   The remainder of installation is the reverse of removal. It's a good idea to check the air gap between the signal rotor and the pickup coil to be sure it's within specification.

10 Distributor - check, removal and installation

Check

1   Detach the cable from the negative terminal of the battery.
2   Remove the distributor cap (see Chapter 1).

Air gap

Refer to illustration 10.3

3   Using a feeler gauge, measure the gap between the signal rotor and the pickup coil projection **(see illustration)**. Compare your measurement to the specified air gap. If the air gap is not as specified, replace the distributor.

Signal generator (pickup coil) resistance

Refer to illustrations 10.4a and 10.4b

4   Using an ohmmeter, measure the resis-

10.4b To check the pickup coil on 1987 and later models, measure the resistance between terminals G and G- and between NE and G- - it should be as specified

tance between the terminals **(see illustrations)** and compare your measurement to the specified pickup coil resistance. If the resistance is not as specified, replace the distributor.

Removal

Refer to illustrations 10.6, 10.8a and 10.8b

5   Unplug the electrical connectors from the distributor.

6   Look for a raised "1" on the distributor cap **(see illustration)**. This marks the location for the number one cylinder spark plug wire terminal. If the cap does not have a mark for the number one spark plug, locate the number one spark plug and trace the wire back to its terminal on the cap.

7   Remove the distributor cap (see Chapter 1) and turn the engine over until the rotor is pointing toward the number one spark plug terminal (see locating TDC procedure in Chapter 2).

8   Make a mark on the edge of the distributor base directly below the rotor tip and in line with it **(see illustration)**. Also, mark the distributor base and the engine block to ensure that the distributor is reinstalled correctly **(see illustration)**.

9   Remove the distributor hold-down bolts, then pull the distributor straight out to remove it. Be careful not to disturb the intermediate driveshaft. **Caution:** *DO NOT turn the engine while the distributor is removed, or the alignment marks will be useless.*

10.6 Look for a raised "1" (arrow) on top of the distributor cap to find the number one spark plug terminal (if there is no raised "1" indicating the number one terminal, trace the plug lead from the number one spark plug back to its corresponding terminal)

Installation

Refer to illustrations 10.11, 10.12, 10.13a and 10.13b

Note: *If the crankshaft has been moved while the distributor is out, locate Top Dead Center (TDC) for the number one piston (see Chapter 2) and position the distributor and rotor accordingly.*

10   Insert the distributor into the engine in exactly the same relationship to the block that it was in when removed.

11   On SOHC four-cylinder engines, align the protrusion on the distributor housing with the protrusion on the spiral gear **(see illustration)**. To mesh the helical gears on the camshaft and the distributor, it may be necessary to turn the rotor slightly.

12   On DOCH four-cylinder engines, the lugs on the end of the distributor must fit into the slots on the end of the intake camshaft **(see illustration)**.

13   On V6 models, align the cutouts of the coupling and housing **(see illustration)**, then insert the distributor, aligning the line on the

10.8a Paint or scribe a mark (arrow) on the edge of the distributor housing immediately below the rotor tip to ensure that the rotor is pointing in the same direction when the distributor is reinstalled

10.8b Paint or scribe another mark across one of the distributor adjustment bolt flanges and the cylinder head (arrow) to ensure that the distributor is aligned correctly when it is reinstalled

housing with the cutout on the distributor attachment bearing cap **(see illustration)**.

14   If the distributor doesn't seat completely, recheck the alignment marks between the distributor base and the block to verify that the distributor is in the same posi-

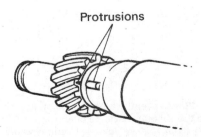

Protrusions

10.11 On SOHC four-cylinder engines, align the protrusion on the distributor housing with the one on the spiral gear before installing the distributor

10.12 On DOHC four-cylinder engines, the lugs on the end of the distributor must fit into the slots on the end of the intake crankshaft (arrow)

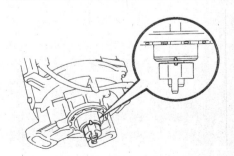

10.13a On V6 models, align the cutouts of the coupling and housing . . .

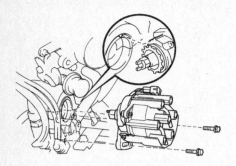

10.13b . . . then insert the distributor, aligning the line on the housing with the cutout on the distributor attachment bearing cap

11.1a On four-cylinder vehicles, locate the service connector at the distributor (blue wire with a green connector) and remove the cap

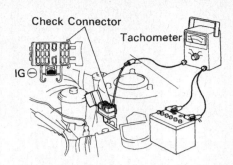

11.1b On V6 models, hook up the "TACH" lead of the tachometer to terminal IG- in the check connector next to the air flow meter

tion it was in before removal. Also check the rotor to see if it's aligned with the mark you made on the edge of the distributor base.

15   Loosely install the distributor hold-down bolts.

16   Install the distributor cap and tighten the cap screws securely.

17   Plug in the electrical connectors.

18   Reattach the spark plug wires to the plugs (if removed).

11.5 On 1986 and later vehicles, bridge terminals T and E1 of the check connector (four-cylinder model shown, V6 models similar)

11.6 Locate the timing notch (arrow) on the crankshaft pulley and the stationary timing marks on the timing cover (four-cylinder shown, V6 similar)

19   Connect the cable to the negative terminal of the battery.

20   Check the ignition timing (see Section 11), then tighten the distributor hold down bolts securely.

11 Ignition timing - check and adjustment

Refer to illustrations 11.1a, 11.1b, 11.5, 11.6, 11.7 and 11.12

Note: *The following ignition timing procedure should apply to all vehicles covered by this manual. However, if the procedure specified on the VECI label of your vehicle differs from this one, use the one contained on the VECI label.*

1   Hook up a tachometer in accordance with the manufacturer's instructions. Connect the "TACH" lead to the service connector of the distributor on four-cylinder vehicles **(see illustration)** or the IG-terminal of the check connector on V6 models **(see illustration)**.

2   Hook up a timing light in accordance with the manufacturer's instructions.

3   Warm up the engine and allow it to reach its normal operating temperature.

4   On 1983 through 1985 vehicles, detach

11.7 With the engine running, point the timing light at the timing notch and the timing marks, and compare your reading with the specified timing (four-cylinder engine shown)

the two vacuum hoses from the vacuum advance diaphragm on the distributor.

5   On 1986 and later vehicles, locate the service connector next to the air flow meter. Using a jumper wire, bridge terminals T and E1 of the check connector **(see illustration)**.

6   Locate the timing marks on the timing cover and crankshaft pulley **(see illustration)**.

7   Using the timing light, check the ignition timing **(see illustration)** and compare it to the specified timing.

8   If necessary, loosen the distributor hold-down bolts and turn the distributor slightly to align the timing marks.

9   Recheck the timing to make sure that the distributor did not move when the bolts were tightened.

10   On 1983 through 1985 vehicles, reattach the two vacuum hoses to the vacuum advance diaphragm.

11   On 1986 and later vehicles, remove the jumper wire from terminals T and E1 of the check connector.

12   Recheck the ignition timing **(see illustration)** and compare it to the specified timing.

13   Remove the timing light and tachometer.

11.12 After reattaching the vacuum hoses to the vacuum advance diaphragm (1983 through 1986 vehicles), or removing the jumper wire from terminals T and E1 (1986 and later vehicles), recheck the ignition timing and compare your reading to the specified timing (four-cylinder engine shown)

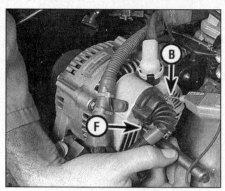

13.7 If the alternator is putting out less than standard voltage, ground terminal F, start the engine and check the voltage at terminal B - if the reading is greater than standard voltage, replace the regulator; if the reading is less than standard, check the alternator or have it checked by a qualified service outlet

12 Charging system - general information and precautions

The charging system includes the alternator, an internal voltage regulator, a charge indicator, the battery, a fusible link and the wiring between all the components. The charging system supplies electrical power for the ignition system, the lights, the radio, etc. The alternator is driven by a drivebelt at the front (right end) of the engine.

The purpose of the voltage regulator is to limit the alternator's voltage to a preset value. This prevents power surges, circuit overloads, etc., during peak voltage output.

The fusible link is a short length of insulated wire integral with the engine compartment wiring harness. The link is four wire gauges smaller in diameter than the circuit it protects. Production fusible links and their identification flags are identified by the flag color. See Chapter 12 for additional information regarding fusible links.

The charging system doesn't ordinarily require periodic maintenance. However, the drivebelt, battery and wires and connections should be inspected at the intervals outlined in Chapter 1.

The dashboard warning light should come on when the ignition key is turned to Start, then should go off immediately. If it remains on, there is a malfunction in the charging system (see Section 13). Some vehicles are also equipped with a voltage gauge. If the voltage gauge indicates abnormally high or low voltage, check the charging system (see Section 13).

Be very careful when making electrical circuit connections to a vehicle equipped with an alternator and note the following:

a) When reconnecting wires to the alternator from the battery, be sure to note the polarity.
b) Before using arc welding equipment to repair any part of the vehicle, disconnect

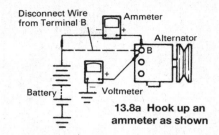

13.8a Hook up an ammeter as shown

the wires from the alternator and the battery terminals.
c) Never start the engine with a battery charger connected.
d) Always disconnect both battery leads before using a battery charger.
e) The alternator is driven by an engine drivebelt which could cause serious injury if your hand, hair or clothes become entangled in it with the engine running.
f) Because the alternator is connected directly to the battery, it could arc or cause a fire if overloaded or shorted out.
g) Wrap a plastic bag over the alternator and secure it with rubber bands before steam cleaning the engine.

13 Charging system - check

Refer to illustrations 13.7, 13.8a and 13.8b

1   If a malfunction occurs in the charging circuit, don't automatically assume that the alternator is causing the problem. First check the following items:

a) Check the drivebelt tension and its condition. Replace it if worn or deteriorated.
b) Make sure the alternator mounting and adjustment bolts are tight.
c) Inspect the alternator wiring harness and the connectors at the alternator and voltage regulator. They must be in good condition and tight.
d) Check the fusible link (if equipped) located between the starter solenoid and the alternator. If it's burned, determine the cause, repair the circuit and replace the link (the vehicle won't start and/or the accessories won't work if the fusible link blows).
e) Start the engine and check the alternator for abnormal noises (a shrieking or squealing sound indicates a bad bushing).
f) Check the specific gravity of the battery electrolyte. If it's low, charge the battery (doesn't apply to maintenance free batteries).
g) Make sure that the battery is fully charged (one bad cell in a battery can cause overcharging by the alternator).
h) Disconnect the battery cables (negative first, then positive). Inspect the battery posts and the cable clamps for corrosion. Clean them thoroughly if necessary (see Section 4 and Chapter 1). Reconnect the cable to the positive terminal.
i) With the key off, insert a test light

13.8b An inductive type ammeter like this one, which is available at most auto parts stores, is much cheaper than a professional ammeter, but it's accurate enough for a quick check of the charging system and is quite easy to use: Simply place it on the alternator output lead, start the engine and check charging amperage

between the negative battery post and the disconnected negative cable clamp.
1) If the test light does not come on, reattach the clamp and proceed to the next step.
2) If the test light comes on, there is a short in the electrical system of the vehicle. The short must be repaired before the charging system can be checked.
3) Disconnect the alternator wiring harness.
(a) If the light goes out, the alternator is bad.
(b) If the light stays on, pull each fuse until the light goes out (this will tell you which component is shorted).

2   Using a voltmeter, check the battery voltage with the engine off. It should be approximately 12 volts.
3   Start the engine and check the battery voltage again. It should now be approximately 13.5 to 15.1 volts.
4   Turn on the headlights. The voltage should drop and then come back up, if the charging system is working properly.
5   If the voltage reading is greater than the specified charging voltage, replace the voltage regulator (see Section 15).
6   If the voltmeter reading is less than standard voltage, check the regulator and alternator as follows.
7   Ground terminal F, start the engine, check the voltage at terminal B **(see illustration)** and compare your reading to the standard voltage.

a) If the voltmeter reading is greater than standard voltage, replace the regulator.
b) If the voltmeter reading is less than standard voltage, check the alternator (or have it checked by a dealer service department if you do not have an ammeter).

8   If you have an ammeter, hook it up to the charging system as shown **(see illustra-**

14.2 Before removing the alternator detach the cable from the negative terminal of the battery then unplug or disconnect the electrical connectors (arrows) from the alternator - to remove the drivebelt, loosen the adjustment bolts (arrows)

tion). If you don't have a professional ammeter, you can also use an inductive-type current indicator **(see illustration)**. This device is inexpensive, readily available at auto parts stores and accurate enough to perform simple amperage checks like the following test.
9   With the engine running at 2000 rpm, turn on the high beam headlights, turn the heater blower switch to the HI position, check the reading on the ammeter and compare your reading to the standard amperage.
10   If the ammeter reading is less than standard amperage, have the alternator repaired or replace it.

14 Alternator - removal and installation

Refer to illustrations 14.2 and 14.3
1   Detach the cable from the negative terminal of the battery.
2   Detach the electrical connectors from

15.2b Take the nut, washer and insulator off terminal B and remove the alternator end cover

14.3 To remove the alternator, loosen the adjustment bolts shown on other side of adjustment bracket in the previous illustration, then remove the adjustment bolt and pivot bolt (arrows) shown here

the alternator **(see illustration)**.
3   Loosen the alternator adjustment and pivot bolts **(see illustration)** and detach the drivebelt.
4   Remove the adjustment and pivot bolts and separate the alternator from the engine.
5   If you are replacing the alternator, take the old alternator with you when purchasing a replacement unit. Make sure that the new/rebuilt unit is identical to the old alternator. Look at the terminals - they should be the same in number, size and locations as the terminals on the old alternator. Finally, look at the identification markings - they will be stamped in the housing or printed on a tag or plaque affixed to the housing. Make sure that these numbers are the same on both alternators.
6   Many new/rebuilt alternators do not have a pulley installed, so you may have to switch the pulley from the old unit to the new/rebuilt one. When buying an alternator, find out the shop's policy regarding installation of pulleys - some shops will perform this service free of charge.
7   Installation is the reverse of removal.

15.3 Once the rear cover is removed, remove the five screws (arrows) that retain the voltage regulator and the brush holder

15.2a Remove the three nuts from the rear cover

8   After the alternator is installed, adjust the drivebelt tension (see Chapter 1).
9   Check the charging voltage to verify proper operation of the alternator (see Section 13).

15 Voltage regulator and alternator brushes - replacement

Refer to illustrations 15.2a, 15.2b, 15.3, 15.4a, 15.4b, 15.5 and 15.7
1   Remove the alternator (Section 14) and place it on a clean workbench.
2   Remove the three rear cover nuts, the nut and terminal insulator and the rear cover **(see illustrations)**.
3   Remove the five voltage regulator and brush holder mounting screws **(see illustration)**.
4   Remove the brush holder and the regulator from the rear end frame **(see illustration)**. If you are only replacing the regulator, proceed to Step 8, install the new unit, reassemble the alternator and install it on the engine (see Section 14). If you are going to replace the brushes, proceed with the next Step.
5   Measure the exposed length of each

15.4a Remove the brush holder

15.4b Remove the regulator

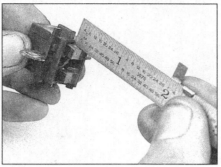

15.5 Measure the exposed length of the brushes and compare your measurements to the specified minimum length to determine whether they should be replaced

15.7 To facilitate installation of the brush holder, depress each brush with a small screwdriver to clear the shaft

brush **(see illustration)** and compare it to the specified minimum length. If the length of either brush is less than the specified minimum, replace the brushes.

6   Make sure that each brush moves smoothly in the brush holder.

7   Install the brush holder by depressing each brush with a small screwdriver to clear the shaft **(see illustration)**.

8   Install the voltage regulator and brush holder screws into the rear frame.

9   Install the rear cover and tighten the three nuts securely.

10   Install the terminal insulator and tighten it with the nut.

11   Install the alternator (see Section 14).

---

16   Starting system - general information and precautions

The sole function of the starting system is to turn over the engine quickly enough to allow it to start.

The starting system consists of the battery, the starter motor, the starter solenoid and the wires connecting them. The solenoid is mounted directly on the starter motor.

The solenoid/starter motor assembly is installed on the lower part of the engine, next to the transaxle bellhousing.

When the ignition key is turned to the Start position, the starter solenoid is actuated through the starter control circuit. The starter solenoid then connects the battery to the starter. The battery supplies the electrical energy to the starter motor, which does the actual work of cranking the engine.

The starter motor on a vehicle equipped with a manual transaxle can be operated only when the clutch pedal is depressed; the starter on a vehicle equipped with an automatic transaxle can be operated only when the transaxle selector lever is in Park or Neutral.

Always observe the following precautions when working on the starting system:

a)   *Excessive cranking of the starter motor can overheat it and cause serious damage. Never operate the starter motor for more than 30 seconds at a time without pausing to allow it to cool for at least two minutes.*

b)   *The starter is connected directly to the battery and could arc or cause a fire if mishandled, overloaded or shorted out.*

c)   *Always detach the cable from the negative terminal of the battery before working on the starting system.*

---

17   Starter motor - testing in vehicle

Note: *Before diagnosing starter problems, make sure that the battery is fully charged.*

1   If the starter motor does not turn at all when the switch is operated, make sure that the shift lever is in Neutral or Park (automatic transaxle) or that the clutch pedal is depressed (manual transaxle).

2   Make sure that the battery is charged and that all cables, both at the battery and starter solenoid terminals, are clean and secure.

3   If the starter motor spins but the engine is not cranking, the overrunning clutch in the starter motor is slipping and the starter motor must be replaced.

4   If, when the switch is actuated, the starter motor does not operate at all but the solenoid clicks, then the problem lies with either the battery, the main solenoid contacts or the starter motor itself (or the engine is seized).

5   If the solenoid plunger cannot be heard when the switch is actuated, the battery is bad, the fusible link is burned (the circuit is open) or the solenoid itself is defective.

6   To check the solenoid, connect a jumper lead between the battery (+) and the ignition switch terminal (the small terminal) on the solenoid. If the starter motor now operates, the solenoid is OK and the problem is in the ignition switch, Neutral start switch or in the wiring.

7   If the starter motor still does not operate, remove the starter/solenoid assembly for disassembly, testing and repair.

8   If the starter motor cranks the engine at an abnormally slow speed, first make sure that the battery is charged and that all terminal connections are tight. If the engine is partially seized, or has the wrong viscosity oil in it, it will crank slowly.

9   Run the engine until normal operating temperature is reached, then disconnect the coil wire from the distributor cap and ground it on the engine.

10   Connect a voltmeter positive lead to the battery positive post and connect the negative lead to the negative post.

11   Crank the engine and take the voltmeter readings as soon as a steady figure is indicated. Do not allow the starter motor to turn for more than 30 seconds at a time. A reading of 9 volts or more, with the starter motor turning at normal cranking speed, is normal. If the reading is 9 volts or more but the cranking speed is slow, the motor is faulty. If the reading is less than 9 volts and the cranking speed is slow, the solenoid contacts are probably burned, the starter motor is bad, the battery is discharged or there is a bad connection.

---

18   Starter motor - removal and installation

Refer to illustrations 18.2 and 18.3

1   Detach the cable from the negative terminal of the battery.

2   Detach the electrical connectors from the starter/solenoid assembly **(see illustration)**.

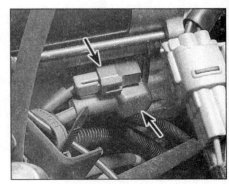

18.2 To remove the starter motor/solenoid assembly, detach the cable from the negative terminal of the battery, then disconnect the electrical connectors (arrows) from the starter/solenoid assembly

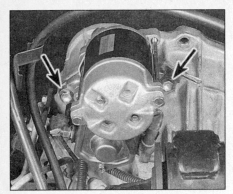

18.3 Remove the two mounting bolts (arrows), then separate the starter motor from the bellhousing

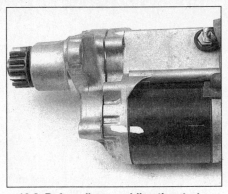

19.2 Before disassembling the starter motor, solenoid and gear reduction assembly, scribe or paint an alignment mark across the starter motor and the gear reduction assembly

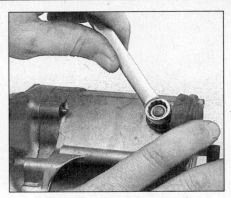

19.3 To disconnect the strap that connects the starter to the solenoid, remove this nut

19.4 To detach the solenoid from the starter motor, remove the screws (arrows) which secure the gear reduction assembly to the solenoid . . .

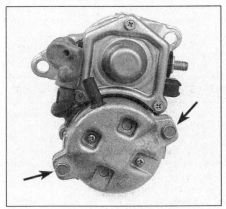

19.5 . . . then remove the through-bolts (arrows) which secure the starter motor to the gear reduction assembly

19.6a Separate the starter from the gear reduction assembly . . .

19.6b . . . then separate the solenoid from the gear reduction assembly (note the return spring protruding from the solenoid assembly - make sure that this spring is installed before reassembling the solenoid and the gear reduction assembly)

3   Remove the starter motor mounting bolts **(see illustration)**. Remove the starter.
4   Installation is the reverse of removal.

---

19 Starter solenoid - removal and installation

Refer to illustrations 19.2, 19.3, 19.4, 19.5, 19.6a and 19.6b

1   Remove the starter motor (see Section 18).
2   Scribe or paint a mark across the starter motor and gear reduction assembly **(see illustration)**.

3   Disconnect the strap from the solenoid to the starter motor terminal **(see illustration)**.
4   Remove the screws **(see illustration)** which secure the gear reduction assembly to the solenoid.
5   Remove the through-bolts **(see illustration)** which secure the starter motor to the gear reduction assembly.
6   Twist the solenoid in a clockwise direction to disengage the flange from the starter body **(see illustrations)**.
7   Installation is the reverse of removal. Be sure to align the paint or scribe mark.

Chapter 6
Emissions control systems

Contents

1 General information and precautions

Refer to illustrations 1.1a, 1.1b, 1.1c, 1.1d, 1.1e, 1.6a and 1.6b

To minimize pollution of the atmosphere from incompletely burned and evaporating gases and to maintain good driveability and fuel economy, a number of emission control systems are used on this vehicle **(see illustrations)**. They include the:

Positive Crankcase Ventilation (PCV) system - which reduces blowby gas (hydrocarbons)

Evaporative Emission Control (EVAP) system - which reduces evaporative hydrocarbons

Dashpot system - which reduces hydrocarbons and carbon monoxide

Exhaust Gas Recirculation (EGR) system - which reduces nitrous oxides

Three-way catalyst system - which reduces hydrocarbons, carbon monoxide and nitrous oxides

Electronic Fuel Injection (EFI) system - which reduces all exhaust emissions by regulating the operating conditions of the engine (see Chapter 4 for further information on the EFI system).

The sections in this chapter include general descriptions, checking procedures within the scope of the home mechanic and component replacement procedures (when possible) for each of the systems listed above.

Before assuming that an emissions control system is malfunctioning, check the fuel (see Chapter 4) and ignition (see Chapter 5) systems carefully. The diagnosis of some emission control devices requires specialized tools, equipment and training. If checking and servicing become too difficult or if a procedure is beyond the scope of your skills, consult your dealer service department.

This doesn't mean, however, that emission control systems are particularly difficult to maintain and repair. You can quickly and easily perform many checks and do most of the regular maintenance at home with common tune-up and hand tools. **Note:** *The most frequent cause of emissions problems is simply a loose or broken electrical connector or vacuum hose, so always check the electrical connectors and vacuum hoses first.*

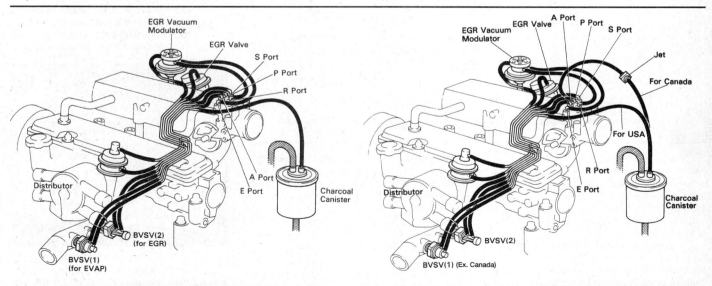

1.1a Emission control component layout and hose routing diagram (1983 vehicles)

1.1b Emission control component layout and hose routing diagram (1984 and 1985 vehicles)

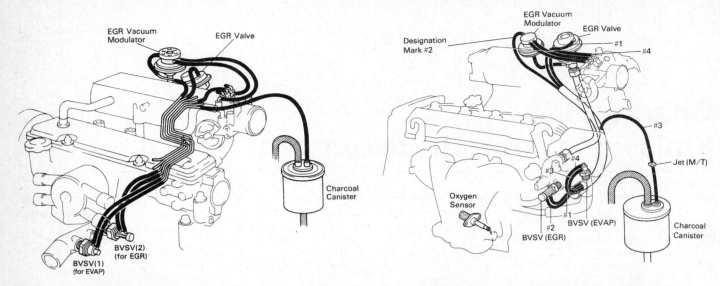

1.1c Emission control component layout and hose routing diagram (1986 vehicles)

1.1d Emission control component layout and hose routing diagram (1987 and later vehicles)

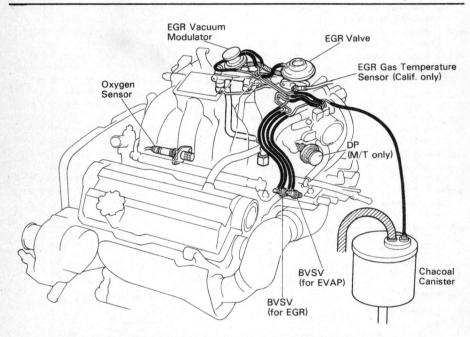

1.1e Emission control component layout and hose routing diagram (V6 models)

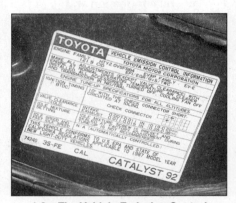

1.6a The Vehicle Emission Control Information (VECI) label, located on the left corner of the firewall, provides essential information regarding such topics as ignition timing and idle mixture setting

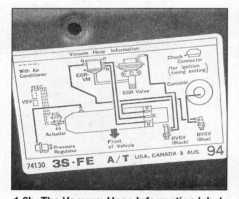

1.6b The Vacuum Hose Information label, located on the underside of the hood, shows the routing of all emissions-related vacuum hoses and identifies the emissions devices installed on the vehicle

Pay close attention to any special precautions outlined in this chapter. It should be noted that the illustrations of the various systems may not exactly match the system installed on your vehicle because of changes made by the manufacturer during production or from year-to-year.

Vehicle Emissions Control Information label and Vacuum Hose Information labels are located in the engine compartment **(see illustrations)**. These labels contain important emissions specifications and setting procedures, and a vacuum hose schematic with

emissions components identified. When servicing the engine or emissions systems, the VECI label in your particular vehicle should always be checked for up-to-date information.

2   Electronic control system - description and precautions

Description

The Toyota Computer Control System

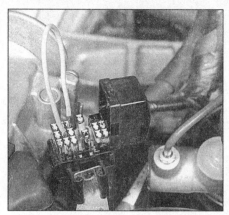

3.3 To activate the diagnostic portion of the computer's memory, bridge terminals E1 and T of the service connector (located in the engine compartment)

(TCCS) controls the fuel injection system, the spark advance system, the diagnosis system, the cooling fans, etc. by means of a microcomputer known as the Electronic Control Unit (ECU).

The ECU receives signals from various sensors which monitor changing engine operating conditions such as intake air volume, intake air temperature, coolant temperature, engine rpm, acceleration/deceleration, exhaust oxygen content, etc. These signals are utilized by the ECU to determine the correct injection duration and ignition timing.

The system is analogous to the central nervous system in the human body: The sensors (nerve endings) constantly relay signals to the ECU (brain), which processes the data and, if necessary, sends out a command to change the operating parameters of the engine (body).

Here's a specific example of how one portion of this system operates: An oxygen sensor, located in the exhaust manifold, constantly monitors the oxygen content of the exhaust gas. If the percentage of oxygen in the exhaust gas is incorrect, an electrical signal is sent to the ECU. The ECU takes this information, processes it and then sends a command to the fuel injection system, telling it to change the air/fuel mixture. This happens in a fraction of a second and it goes on continuously when the engine is running. The end result is an air/fuel mixture ratio which is constantly maintained at a predetermined ratio, regardless of driving conditions.

In the event of a sensor malfunction, a backup circuit will take over to provide driveability until the problem is identified and fixed (Section 3).

Precautions

a) *Always disconnect the power by either turning off the ignition switch or disconnecting the battery terminals before removing EFI wiring connectors.*

b) *When installing a battery, be particularly careful to avoid reversing the positive and negative battery cables.*

c) *Do not subject EFI or emissions related components or the ECU to severe impact during removal or installation.*

d) *Do not be careless during troubleshooting. Even slight terminal contact can invalidate a testing procedure and even damage one of the numerous transistor circuits.*

e) *Never attempt to work on the ECU or open the ECU cover. The ECU is protected by a government mandated extended warranty that will be nullified if you tamper with or damage the ECU.*

f) *If you are inspecting electronic control system components during rainy weather, make sure that water does not enter any part. When washing the engine compartment, do not spray these parts or their connectors with water.*

---

3 Diagnosis system - general information and obtaining diagnostic code output

Refer to illustrations 3.3, 3.4a through 3.4i, 3.7a and 3.7b

The ECU contains a built-in self-diagnosis system which detects and identifies malfunctions occurring in the network. When the ECU detects a problem, three things happen: the Check Engine light comes on, the trouble is identified and a diagnostic code is recorded and stored. The ECU stores the failure code assigned to the specific problem area until the diagnosis system is cleared by removing the AM2 fuse with the ignition switch off.

The Check Engine warning light, which is located on the instrument panel, comes on when the ignition switch is turned to On and the engine is not running. When the engine is started, the warning light should go out. If the light remains on, the diagnosis system has detected a malfunction in the system.

Obtaining diagnosis code output

1 To obtain an output of diagnostic codes, verify first that the battery voltage is above 11 volts, the throttle is fully closed, the transaxle is in Neutral, the accessory switches are off and the engine is at normal operating temperature.

2 Turn the ignition switch to On. Do not start the engine.

3 Use a jumper wire to bridge terminals T and E1 of the service connector **(see illustration)**.

4 Read the diagnosis code as indicated by the number of flashes of the "Check Engine" light **(see illustrations)**. Normal system operation is indicated by Code No. 1 (no malfunctions) for all models. The "Check Engine" light displays a Code No. 1 by blinking on and off at a constant rate. The duration of the light's on and off intervals, however, varies with the model year:

Code No.	Number of blinks "CHECK ENGINE"	System	Diagnosis	Trouble area
1		Normal	This appears when none of the other codes (2 thru 7) are identified	—
2		Air flow meter signal (V_c)	● Open circuit in V_c or $V_c - V_s$ short circuited. ● Open circuit in V_B	1. Air flow meter circuit (V_c, V_s) 2 Air flow meter 3. EFI computer
3		Air flow meter signal (V_s)	● Open circuit in V_s, or $V_s - E_2$ short circuited. ● Open circuit in V_B	1. Air flow meter circuit (V_B, V_c, V_s, E_3) 2 Air flow meter 3. EFI computer
4		Water thermo sensor signal (THW)	● Open circuit in coolant temperature sensor signal.	1. Coolant temperature sensor circuit 2. Coolant temperature sensor 3. EFI computer
5		Oxygen sensor signal	● Open or short circuit in Oxygen sensor signal (only lean or rich indication)	1. Oxygen sensor circuit 2. Oxygen sensor 3. EFI computer
6		Ignition signal	● No ignition signal	1. Ignition system circuit 2. IIA 3. EFI computer
7		Throttle position sensor signal	● IDL-Psw short circuited	1. Throttle position sensor circuit 2. Throttle position sensor 3. EFI computer

3.4a Trouble code chart for all 1983 through 1985 vehicles and 1986 Canadian vehicles

Code No.	Number of CHECK ENGINE blinks	System	Diagnosis	Trouble area
—	⎍⎍⎍⎍⎍⎍ ON/OFF	Normal	This appears when none of the other codes (11 thru 51) are identified.	—
11		ECU (+B)	Wire severence, however slight, in +B (ECU).	1. Main relay circuit 2. Main relay 3. ECU
12		RPM signal	No NE, G signal to ECU within several seconds after engine is cranked.	1. Distributor circuit 2. Distributor 3. starter signal circuit 4. ECU
13		RPM signal	No NE signal to ECU within several seconds after engine reaches 1,000 rpm.	Same as 12, above.
14		Ignition signal	No signal from igniter 4 — 5 times in succession.	1. Igniter circuit (+B, IGT, IGF) 2. Igniter 3. ECU
21		Oxygen sensor signal	Open circuit in oxygen sensor signal (only lean indication).	1. Oxygen sensor circuit 2. Oxygen sensor 3. ECU
22		Water temp. sensor signal	Open or short circuit in water temp. sensor signal (THW).	1. Water temp. sensor circuit 2. Water temp. sensor 3. ECU
24		Intake air temp. sensor signal	Open or short circuit in intake air temp. sensor (THA).	1. Intake air temp. sensor circuit 2. Intake air temp. sensor 3. ECU
31		Air flow meter signal	VC circuit open or VC–E2 short circuit.	1. Air flow meter circuit 2. Air flow meter 3. ECU
32		Air flow meter signal	E2 circuit open or VC–VS short circuited.	Same as 31, above.
41		Throttle position sensor signal	Open or short circuit in throttle position sensor signal (VTA).	1. Throttle position sensor circuit 2. Throttle position sensor 3. ECU
42		Vehicle speed sensor signal	Signal informing ECU that vehicle stopped has been input to ECU for 5 seconds while engine running between 2,500 — 5,500 rpm.	1. Vehicle speed sensor circuit 2. Vehicle speed sensor 3. ECU
43		Starter signal	No STA signal to ECU when vehicle stopped and engine running over 800 rpm	1. Main relay circuit 2. IG switch circuit 3. IG switch (starter) 4. ECU
51		Switch signal	Air conditioner switch ON, idle switch OFF or shift position other than P or N range during diagnosis check.	1. Air con. switch 2. Throttle position sensor circuit 3. Throttle position sensor 4. Neutral start switch 5. ECU

3.4c Trouble code chart for all 1987 through 1990 vehicles (four-cylinder engines)

Code No.	Number of "CHECK ENGINE" blinks	System	Diagnosis	Trouble area
1	ON/OFF	Normal	This appears when none of the other codes (2 thru 11) are identified.	—
2		Air flow meter signal	• Vc circuit open or Vs – E₂ short circuited. • E₂ circuit open or Vc – Vs short circuited.	1. Air flow meter circuit 2. Air flow meter 3. ECU
3		Ignition signal	No signal from igniter four times in succession.	1. Ignition circuit (+B, IGf, IGt) 2. Igniter 3. ECU
4		Water temp. sensor signal	Open or short circuit in water temp. sensor signal.	1. Water temp. sensor circuit 2. Water temp. sensor 3. ECU
5		Oxygen sensor signal	Open circuit in oxygen sensor signal (only lean indication).	1. Oxygen sensor circuit 2. Oxygen sensor 3. ECU
6		RPM signal	No Ne signal to ECU while cranking, or Ne value over 1,000 rpm in spite of no Ne signal to ECU.	1. Distributor circuit 2. Distributor 3. Igniter 4. Starter signal circuit 5. ECU
7		Throttle position sensor signal	Open or short circuit in throttle position signal.	1. Throttle position sensor circuit 2. Throttle position sensor 3. ECU
8		Intake air temp. sensor signal	Open or short circuit in intake air temperature sensor.	1. Air temp. sensor circuit 2. ECU
9		Vehicle speed sensor signal	Signal informing ECU that vehicle stopped had been input to ECU for 8 seconds with engine running between 2,400 – 5,000 rpm.	1. Vehicle speed sensor circuit 2. Vehicle sensor 3. ECU
10		Starter signal	No STA signal to ECU when vehicle stopped and engine running over 800 rpm.	1. Starter relay circuit 2. IG switch circuit (starter) 3. IG Switch 4. ECU
11		Switch signal	Air conditioner switch ON, idle switch OFF or shift position in any position other than P or N range during diagnosis check.	1. Air conditioner S/W 2. Throttle position sensor circuit 3. Throttle position sensor 4. Neutral start switch 5. ECU

3.4b Trouble code chart for 1986 US vehicles

Code No.	Number of blinks "CHECK" Engine Warning Light	System	"CHECK" Engine Warning Light	Diagnosis	Trouble Area
27		Sub-Oxygen Sensor Signal	ON	When sub-oxygen sensor is warmed up and full acceleration continued for 2 seconds, output of main oxygen sensor is 0.45 V or more (rich) and output of sub-oxygen sensor is 0.45 V or less (lean). (OX2) (2 trip detection logic)	• Short or open in sub-oxygen sensor circuit • Sub-oxygen sensor • ECU
31		Air Flow Meter Signal	ON	At idling, open or short detected continuously for 500 msec. or more in air flow meter circuit. • Open – VC • Short – VC-E2	• Open or short in air flow meter circuit • Air flow meter • ECU
32		Air Flow Meter Signal	ON	Open or short detected continuously for 500 msec. or more in air flow meter circuit. • Open – E2 • Short – VS-VC	
41		Throttle Position Sensor Signal	ON	Open or short detected in throttle position sensor signal (VTA) for 500 msec. or more. (Vehicle w/ECT) Low PSW signal is input continuously to the ECU for 500 msec. or more at idling (IDL contact is ON). (w/o ECT)	• Open or short in throttle position sensor circuit. • Throttle position sensor • ECU
42		Vehicle Speed Sensor Signal	OFF	SPD signal is not input to the ECU for at least 8 seconds during high load driving with engine speed between 2,500 rpm and 5,500 rpm.	• Open or short in vehicle speed sensor circuit • Vehicle speed sensor • ECU
43		Starter Signal	OFF	Starter signal (STA) is not input to ECU even once until engine reaches 800 rpm or more when cranking.	• Open or short in starter signal circuit • Open or short in IG SW circuit • ECU
71		EGR System Malfunction	ON	EGR gas temp. sensor signal (THG) is below 70°C (158°F) after driving for 50 seconds in EGR operation range. (2 trip detection logic)	• Open in EGR gas temp. sensor circuit • EGR gas temp. sensor • EGR vacuum hose disconnected, valve stuck • Clogged in EGR gas passage • ECU
51		Switch Condition Signal	OFF	Displayed when A/C is ON, IDL contact OFF or shift position in "R", "D", or "L" ranges with the check terminals E1 and TE1 connected.	• A/C switch circuit • Throttle position sensor • IDL circuit • Neutral start switch circuit • Accelerator pedal, cable • ECU

3.4e Trouble codes for 1991 vehicles (four-cylinder engines) (2 of 2)

Code No.	Number of blinks "CHECK" Engine Warning Light	System	"CHECK" Engine Warning Light	Diagnosis	Trouble Area
–		Normal	–	Output when no other code is recorded.	–
12		RPM Signal	ON	No G or NE signal is input to the ECU for 2 secs. or more after STA turns ON.	• Open or short in NE, G circuit • Distributor • Open or short in STA circuit • ECU
13		RPM Signal	ON	NE signal is not input to ECU for 50 msec. or more when engine speed is 1,000 rpm or more.	• Open or short in NE circuit • Distributor • ECU
14		Ignition Signal	ON	IGF signal from igniter is not input to ECU for 4 ~ 5 consecutive ignition.	• Open or short in IGF or IGT circuit from igniter to ECU • Igniter • ECU
16		ECT Control Signal	ON	Normal signal is not output from ECU of ECT.	• ECU
21		Main Oxygen Sensor Signal	ON	At normal driving speed (below 60 mph and engine speed is above 1,800 rpm), amplitude of main oxygen sensor signal OX1 is reduced to between 0.35 – 0.70 V continuously for 60 secs. or more.	• Open or short in main oxygen sensor circuit • Main oxygen sensor • ECU
22		Water Temp. Sensor Signal	ON	Open or short in water temp. sensor circuit for 500 msec. or more. (THW)	• Open or short in water temp. sensor circuit. • Water temp. sensor • ECU
24		Intake Air Temp. Sensor Signal	ON	Open or short in intake air temp. sensor circuit for 500 msec. or more. (THA)	• Open or short in intake air temp. circuit • Intake air temp. sensor • ECU
25		Air-Fuel Ratio Lean Malfunction	ON	(1) Oxygen sensor output is less than 0.45 V for at least 120 secs. when oxygen sensor is warmed up (racing at 2,000 rpm). – only for code 25 (2) When air-fuel ratio feedback correction value or adaptive control value continues at the upper (lean) or lower (rich) limit for a certain period of time and adaptive control value is not renewed for a certain period of time.	• Engine ground bolt loose • Open in E1 circuit • Open in injector circuit • Fuel line pressure (Injector blockage, etc.) • Open or short in oxygen sensor circuit • Oxygen sensor • Ignition system • Water temp. sensor • Air flow meter (air intake) • ECU
26		Air-Fuel Ratio Rich Malfunction	ON	(3) When the oxygen sensor feedback frequency is abnormally high during feedback condition. (2 trip detection logic) (1) ~ (3)	• Engine ground bolt loose • Open in E1 circuit • Short in injector circuit • Fuel line pressure (Injector leakage, etc.) • Open or short in cold start injector circuit • Cold start injector • Open or short in oxygen sensor circuit • Oxygen sensor • Water temp. sensor • Air flow meter • Compression pressure • ECU

3.4d Trouble codes for 1991 vehicles (four-cylinder engines) (1 of 2)

Code No.	Number of Check engine blinks	System	Diagnosis	Trouble area
*27		Sub-oxygen Sensor Signal	Open or short circuit in sub-oxygen sensor signal (OX2).	• Sub-oxygen sensor circuit • Sub-oxygen sensor • ECU
31		Air flow Meter Signal	Open circuit in VC signal or short circuit between VS and E2 when idle contacts are closed.	• Air flow meter circuit • Air flow meter • ECU
32		Air Flow Meter Signal	Open circuit in E2 or short circuit between VC and VS.	• Air flow meter circuit • Air flow meter • ECU
41		Throttle Position Sensor Signal	Open or short circuit in throttle position sensor signal (VTA).	• Throttle position sensor circuit • Throttle position sensor • ECU
42		Vehicle Speed Sensor Signal	No "SP1" signal for 8 seconds when engine speed is in between 2,500 rpm and 4,500 rpm and coolant temp. is below 80°C (176°F) except when racing the engine.	• No. 1 vehicle speed sensor (Meter side) circuit • No. 1 vehicle speed sensor (Meter side) • ECU
43		Starter Signal	No "STA" signal to ECU until engine speed reaches 800 rpm with vehicle not moving.	• Ignition switch circuit • Ignition switch • ECU
*71		EGR System Malfunction	EGR gas temp. below predetermined level during EGR operation.	• EGR valve • EGR hose • EGR gas temp. sensor circuit • EGR gas temp. sensor • BVSV circuit for EGR • BVSV for EGR • ECU
51		Switch Signal	No "IDL" signal, "NSW" signal or "A/C" signal to ECU, with the check terminals E1 and TE1 shorted.	• A/C switch circuit • A/C switch • A/C amplifire • Throttle position sensor circuit • Throttle position sensor • Neutral start switch circuit • Neutral start switch • Acceleration pedal and cable • ECU

* California vehicles only

3.4g V6 engine trouble code chart (1989 and 1990) (2 of 2)

Code No.	Number of Check engine blinks	System	Diagnosis	Trouble area
–		Normal	This appears when none of the other codes are identified.	–
11		ECU (+B)	Momentary interruption in power supply to ECU.	• Ignition switch circuit • Ignition switch • Main relay circuit • Main relay • ECU
12		PRM Signal	No "NE" or "G" signal to ECU within 2 seconds after engine has been cranked.	• Distributor circuit • Distributor • Starter signal circuit • ECU
13		RPM Signal	No "NE" signal to ECU when engine speed is above 1,000 rpm.	• Distributor circuit • Distributor • ECU
14		Ignition Signal	No "IGF" signal to ECU 6 – 8 times in succession.	• Igniter and ignition coil circuit • Igniter and ignition coil • ECU
21		Oxygen Sensor Signal	Detection of oxygen sensor. detrioration.	• Oxygen sensor circuit • Oxygen sensor • ECU
		Oxygen Sensor Heater Signal	Open or short circuit in oxygen sensor heater signal (HT).	• Oxygen sensor heater circuit • Oxygen sensor heater • ECU
22		Water Temp. Sensor Signal	Open or short circuit in water temp. sensor signal (THW).	• Water temp. sensor circuit • Water temp. sensor • ECU
24		Intake Air Temp. Sensor Signal	Open or short circuit in intake air temp. sensor signal (THA).	• Intake air temp. sensor circuit • Intake air temp. sensor • ECU
25		Air-fuel Ratio Lean Malfunction	(California vehicles) • When air-fuel ratio feed-back correction value or adaptive control value continues at the upper (lean) or lower (rich) limit for a certain period of time or adaptive control value is not renewed for a certain period of time. • When feedback frequency of air-fuel ratio feed-back correction or adaptive control is abnormally high during feedback condition. (ex. California vehicles) • Oxygen sensor outputs a lean signal continuosly for several seconds during air-fuel ratio feedback correction. • Open circuit in oxygen sensor signal (OX).	• Injector circuit • Injector • Fuel line pressure • Air intake system • Oxygen sensor circuits • Oxygen sensors • Ignition system • ECU
26		Air-fuel Ratio Rich Malfunction		• Injector circuit • Injector • Fuel line pressure • Air flow meter • Cold start injector • ECU

3.4f V6 engine trouble code chart (1989 and 1990) (1 of 2)

3.4i V6 engine trouble code chart (1991 models) (2 of 2)

Code No.	Number of blinks "CHECK" Engine Warning Light	System	"CHECK" Engine Warning Light	Diagnosis	Trouble Area
27		Sub-Oxygen Sensor Signal	ON	When sub-oxygen sensor is warmed up and full acceleration continued for 2 seconds, output of main oxygen sensor is 0.45 V or more (rich) and output of sub-oxygen sensor is 0.45 V or less (lean). (OX2) (2 trip detection logic)	• Short or open in sub-oxygen sensor circuit • Sub-oxygen sensor • ECU
31		Air Flow Meter Signal	ON	At idling, open or short detected continuously for 500 msec. or more in air flow meter circuit. • Open – VC • Short – VC-E2	• Open or short in air flow meter circuit • Air flow meter • ECU
32		Air Flow Meter Signal	ON	Open or short detected continuously for 500 msec. or more in air flow meter circuit. • Open – E2 • Short – VS-VC	• Open or short in air flow meter circuit • Air flow meter • ECU
41		Throttle Position Sensor Signal	ON	Open or short detected in throttle position sensor signal (VTA) for 500 msec. or more. IDL contact is ON and VTA output exceeds 1.45 V.	• Open or short in throttle position sensor circuit • Throttle position sensor • ECU
42		Vehicle Speed Sensor Signal	OFF	SPD signal is not input to the ECU for at least 8 seconds during high load driving with engine speed between 2,500 rpm and 4,500 rpm.	• Open or short in vehicle speed sensor circuit • Vehicle speed sensor • ECU
43		Starter Signal	OFF	Starter signal (STA) is not input to ECU even once until engine reaches 800 rpm or more when cranking.	• Open or short in starter signal circuit • Open or short in IG SW circuit • ECU
52		Knock Sensor Signal	ON	With engine speed between 1600 rpm – 5,200 rpm, signal from knock sensor is not input to ECU for 6 revolution. (KNK)	• Open or short in knock sensor circuit • Knock sensor (looseness etc.) • ECU
53		Knock Control Signal	ON	Engine speed is between 650 rpm and 5,200 rpm and engine control computer (for knock control) malfunction detected.	• ECU
71		EGR System Malfunction	ON	EGR gas temp. sensor signal (THG) is below 55°C (131°F) for M/T, 60°C (140°F) for A/T after driving for 60 seconds in EGR operation range. (2 trip detection logic)	• Open in EGR gas temp. sensor circuit • BVSV circuit for EGR • EGR vacuum hose disconnected, valve stuck • Clogged in EGR gas passage • ECU
51		Switch Condition Signal	OFF	Displayed when A/C is ON, IDL contact OFF or shift position in "R", "D", "2", or "1" ranges with the check terminals E1 and TE1 connected.	• A/C switch circuit • Throttle position sensor • IDL circuit • Neutral start switch circuit • Accelerator pedal, cable • ECU

3.4h V6 engine trouble code chart (1991 models) (1 of 2)

Code No.	Number of blinks "CHECK" Engine Warning Light	System	"CHECK" Engine Warning Light	Diagnosis	Trouble Area
–		Normal	–	Output when no other code is recorded.	—
12		RPM Signal	ON	No G or NE signal is input to the ECU for 2 secs. or more after STA turns ON.	• Open or short in NE, G circuit • Distributor • Open or short in STA circuit • ECU
13		RPM Signal	ON	NE signal is not input to ECU for 50 msec. or more when engine speed is 1,000 rpm or more.	• Open or short in NE circuit • Distributor • ECU
14		Ignition Signal	ON	IGF signal from igniter is not input to ECU for 6 consecutive ignition.	• Open or short in IGF or IGT circuit from igniter to ECU • Igniter • ECU
16		ECT Control Signal	ON	Normal signal is not output from ECU of ECT.	• ECU
21		Main Oxygen Sensor Signal	ON	(1) Open or short in heater circuit of main oxygen sensor for 500 msec. or more. (HT) (2) At normal driving speed (below 60 mph and engine speed is above 1,500 rpm), amplitude of oxygen sensor signal (OX1) is reduced to between 0.35 – 0.70 V continuously for 60 secs. or more. (2 trip detection logic) (2)	(1) Open or short in heater circuit of main oxygen sensor • ECU (2) Open or short in main oxygen sensor circuit • Main oxygen sensor • ECU
22		Water Temp. Sensor Signal	ON	Open or short in water temp. sensor circuit for 500 msec. or more. (THW)	• Open or short in water temp. sensor circuit • Water temp. sensor • ECU
24		Intake Air Temp. Sensor Signal	ON	Open or short in intake air temp. sensor circuit for 500 msec. or more. (THA)	• Open or short in intake air temp. circuit • Intake air temp. sensor • ECU
25		Air-Fuel Ratio Lean Malfunction	ON	(1) Oxygen sensor output is less than 0.45 V for at least 90 secs. when oxygen sensor is warmed up (racing at 2,000 rpm). – only for code 25 (2) When air-fuel ratio feedback correction value or adaptive control value continues at the upper (lean) or lower (rich) limit for a certain period of time or adaptive control value is not renewed for a certain period of time.	• Engine ground bolt loose • Open in E1 circuit • Open in injector circuit • Fuel line pressure (Injector blockage, etc.) • Open or short in oxygen sensor circuit • Oxygen sensor • Ignition system • Water temp. sensor • Air flow meter (air intake) • ECU
26		Air-Fuel Ratio Rich Malfunction	ON	(3) When the oxygen sensor feedback frequency is abnormally high during feedback condition. *6 (2 trip detection logic) (1) ~ (3)	• Engine ground bolt loose • Open in E1 circuit • Short in injector circuit • Fuel line pressure (Injector leakage, etc.) • Open or short in cold start injector circuit • Cold start injector • Open or short in oxygen sensor circuit • Oxygen sensor • Water temp. sensor • Air flow meter • Compression pressure • ECU

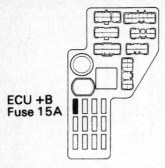

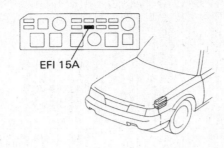

3.7a The "ECU +B" fuse (labeled "ECU -B" on 1986 vehicles) is located in the fuse panel behind the driver's side kick panel on all 1983 through 1986 vehicles

3.7b The ECU fuse is located in the fuse panel on the driver's side of the engine compartment on all 1987 and later vehicles

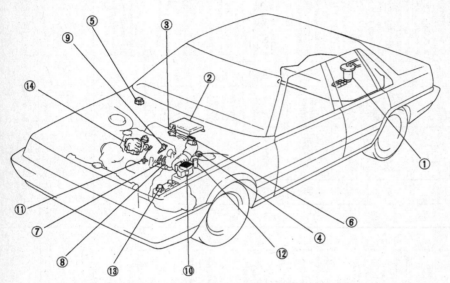

4.1a Electronic control system components (1983 through 1985 vehicles)

1	Fuel pump		8	Water thermo sensor
2	Electronic Control Unit (ECU)		9	injector
3	Cold start injector		10	Air flow, meter
4	Service connector		11	Oxygen sensor
5	Circuit opening relay		12	Solenoid resistor
6	Throttle position sensor		13	EFI main relay
7	Start injector time switch		14	IIA distributor assembly

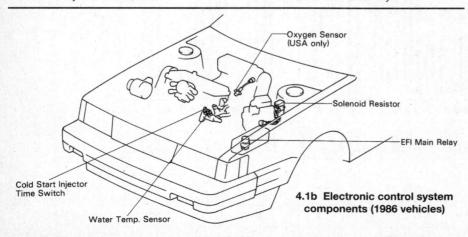

4.1b Electronic control system components (1986 vehicles)

a) On 1983 through 1985 vehicles, it blinks on for 0.3-second every 3.0 seconds.

b) On 1986 vehicles, it blinks on for 0.5-second every 4.5 seconds.

c) On 1987 and later four-cylinder vehicles, the light alternately blinks on for 0.25-second, then off for 0.25-second.

d) On the V6, the light blinks on for 0.26-second and off for 0.26-second.

5   If there are any malfunctions in the system, their corresponding trouble codes are stored in computer memory and the light indicates the numbers of these codes by blinking the same number of times as the number of the stored code(s).

a) On 1983 through 1986 vehicles, the number of blinks (any number between 1 and 11) indicates the number of the stored trouble code. For example, seven blinks indicates a Code No. 7, 11 blinks indicates a Code 11, etc. There is a 3.0-second pause between each trouble code displayed, then the next code stored in memory is displayed, then there is another 3.0-second pause, etc. If there is only one code stored, the "Check Engine" light will simply pause, then repeat the code already indicated. Whether there is one code - or several - stored in memory, the "Check Engine" light repeats its display as long as the service connector terminals are jumpered.

b) On 1987 and later vehicles, new codes were added and the code numbers were changed (from 11 to 51). Obviously, it wouldn't be practical to display a 51-blink trouble code, so the light blinks a number of times corresponding to each digit of the number. In other words, the first number of blinks indicates the first digit of the (two-digit) trouble code, there is a 1.5-second pause, then the next sequence of blinks indicates the second digit of the trouble code. For example, Code 21 is two blinks, pause, one blink; Code 42 is four blinks, pause, two blinks; etc.

6   To ensure correct interpretation of the blinking "Check Engine" light, watch carefully for the interval between the end of one code and the beginning of the next (otherwise, you will become confused by the apparent number of blinks and misinterpret the display). The length of this interval varies with the model year:

a) On all 1983 through 1985 vehicles and 1986 Canada vehicles, the interval between codes - between each code and between the end of the last code stored and the first of a sequence of codes previously displayed - is 3.0 seconds.

b) On 1986 US vehicles and all 1987 and later vehicles, the interval between codes is 2.5 seconds. After the last code, there is a 4.5-second interval before the light begins to repeat itself.

Canceling the diagnostic code

7   After the malfunctioning component has been repaired/replaced, the trouble code(s) stored in computer memory must be canceled. To accomplish this, simply remove the 15A ECU fuse for at least ten seconds with the ignition switch off (the lower the temperature, the longer the fuse must be left out). The location of this fuse varies with the model year:

a)   On 1983 through 1986 vehicles, the fuse is located in the fuse panel behind the driver's side kick panel. On 1983 through 1985 vehicles, it is labeled "ECU +B"; on 1986 vehicles, it is labeled "ECU -B" (**see illustration**).

b)   On all 1987 and later vehicles, the fuse is located in the fuse panel on the left side of the engine compartment (**see illustration**).

8   Cancellation can also be effected by removing the cable from the battery negative terminal, but other memory systems (such as the clock) will also be canceled.

9   If the diagnosis code is not canceled it will be stored by the ECU and appear with any new codes in the event of future trouble.

10   Should it become necessary to work on engine components requiring removal of the battery terminal, first check to see if a diagnostic code has been recorded.

INSERT THE ACCOMPANYING DIAGNOSIS CODE TABLE HERE

4/10/97 - There is not a diagnosis code table in the file.

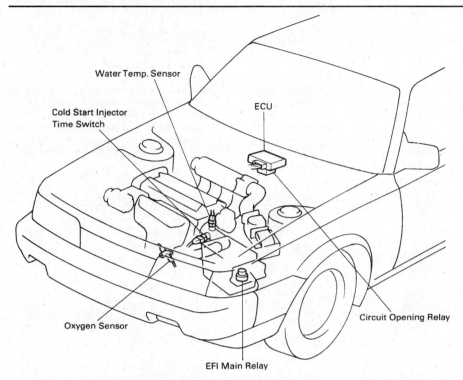

4.1c Electronic control system components (1987 and later four-cylinder vehicles)

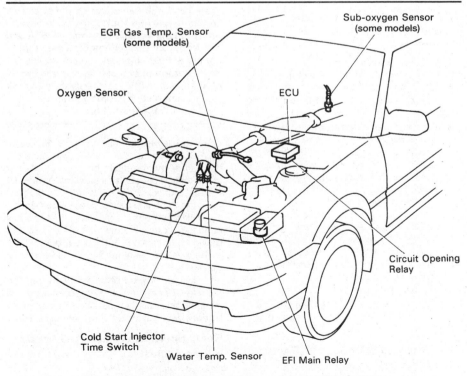

4.1d Electronic control system components (V6 models)

---

4   Electronic control system

Note: *All of the components described in this section are protected by a Federally-mandated extended warranty. See your dealer for the details regarding your vehicle. It therefore makes little sense to either check or replace any of these parts yourself as long as they are still under warranty. However, once the warranty has expired, most of them can be checked (the oxygen sensor and the ECU are the exceptions) and all of them can be easily replaced.*

EFI main relay

Refer to illustrations 4.1a, 4.1b, 4.1c, 4.1d and 4.1e

1   Remove the cover from the engine compartment fuse panel and locate the EFI main relay (**see illustrations**).

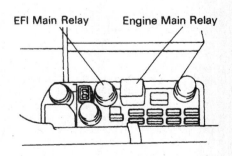

4.1e The EFI main relay is installed in the fuse panel located on the left front corner of the engine compartment

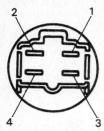

4.3 To check EFI relay continuity, verify that there is continuity between terminals 1 and 3 (40 to 60 ohms resistance) and no continuity between terminals 2 and 4

Relay operation check (1983 through 1987 vehicles)

Note: *On 1988 and later models, check relay continuity (see Step 3) first, then check relay operation (see Step 5).*

2   Turn on the ignition switch and listen carefully to the relay. It should make a clicking noise. **Note:** *The engine main relay must be removed first, because it makes the same noise as the EFI main relay next to it.*

a) *If the relay clicks, it is operating. The problem is elsewhere.*

b) *If the relay doesn't click, remove it and check it for continuity.*

Continuity check

Refer to illustration 4.3

3   Using an ohmmeter, verify that there is some continuity between terminals 1 and 3 (40 to 60 ohms resistance), but no continuity between terminals 2 and 4 **(see illustration)**.

4   If the EFI main relay fails either continuity check, replace it.

Relay operation check (1988 and later vehicles)

5   Apply battery voltage across terminals 1 and 3. Using an ohmmeter, verify that there is continuity between terminals 2 and 4. If there is no continuity, replace the relay.

Circuit opening relay

Relay operation check (1987 and later vehicles)

Refer to illustration 4.8

Note: *On 1987 and later vehicles, check relay continuity first, then check relay operation (see Step 12).*

6   On 1983 vehicles, the relay is located behind the right kick panel. On 1984 through 1986 vehicles, it's located behind the glove box.

7   If necessary - depending upon the orientation of the circuit opening relay electrical connector - remove the circuit opening relay from its mounting bracket so that the wiring side of the connector is facing you. Do not unplug the connector.

8   Using a voltmeter, verify that the meter indicates voltage at terminal Fp **(see illustration)** during engine cranking and starting.

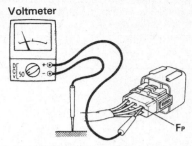

4.8 To check the operation of the circuit opening relay, use a voltmeter to verify that there is voltage at terminal Fp during engine cranking and starting (do not attempt to insert the voltmeter probe into the terminal from the face side of the plug - insert it from the back side as shown)

4.14 To remove the circuit opening relay from its mounting bracket, slide it off its mounting tang (unit shown in 1987 vehicle - ECU removed for clarity)

Relay continuity check (1983 through 1986 vehicles)

Refer to illustration 4.10

9   Unplug the electrical connector.

10   Using an ohmmeter, measure the resistance between each terminal **(see illustration)**.

a) *On 1983 and 1984 vehicles, the indicated resistance between terminals STA and E1 should be 30 to 60 ohms, the resistance between terminals B and Fc should be 80 to 120 ohms and the resistance between terminals B and Fp should be infinite.*

b) *On 1985 and 1986 vehicles, the indicated resistance between terminals STA and E1 should be 17 to 25 ohms, the resistance between terminals B and Fc should be 88 to 112 ohms and the resistance between terminals B and Fp should be infinite.*

11   If the resistance between the indicated terminals is not as specified, replace the relay.

Relay continuity check (1987 and later vehicles)

Refer to illustration 4.14

12   On 1987 and later vehicles, the circuit

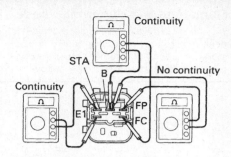

4.10 To check the continuity of the circuit opening relay, use an ohmmeter to measure the resistance between each terminal as shown (specified values for each pair of terminals in text)

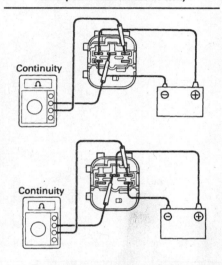

4.15 To check the operation of the circuit opening relay on 1987 and later vehicles, apply battery voltage to terminals STA and E1 and, with an ohmmeter, verify that there is continuity between terminals B and FP (top), then apply battery voltage to terminals B and FC and verify that there is continuity between terminals B and Fp (bottom)

opening relay is attached to the underside of the ECU mounting bracket, which is bolted to the pan below the dash, between the center console kick panels **(see illustration 4.1c or 4.1d)**. To check relay continuity, simply peel back the right side center console carpeting.

13   Using an ohmmeter, verify that there is continuity between terminals STA and E1 and between terminals B and FC but no continuity between terminals B and FP (see illustration 4.10).

14   If continuity is not as specified, replace the relay. Unplug the electrical connector and slide the relay off its mounting tab **(see illustration)**. Installation is the reverse of removal.

Relay operation check (1987 and later vehicles)

Refer to illustration 4.15

15   Apply battery voltage to terminals STA and E1 and, using an ohmmeter, verify that

4.18 A typical solenoid resistor - this unit, which is located on the left corner of the firewall, is on a 1987 vehicle (on 1983 through 1986 models, it's located near the air flow meter but looks just like this one)

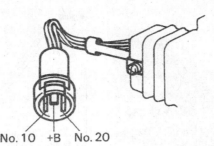

No. 10   +B   No. 20

4.19 To check the solenoid resistor, use an ohmmeter to measure the resistance between terminal +B and each of the other two terminals - on 1983 through 1985 vehicles, it should be 2.5 to 3.5 ohms; on 1986 and 1987 vehicles, it should be 2 to 3 ohms

4.21a The cold start injector time switch (A) and water temperature sensor (B) are located on this water outlet on all four-cylinder models (1987 model shown - 1988 and later models similar - on earlier models, however, the water temperature sensor is installed vertically, next to the cold start injector time switch)

there is continuity between terminals B and FP **(see illustration)**.

16 Apply battery voltage to terminals B and FC and verify that there is continuity between terminals B and FP.

17 If the relay does not operate as specified, replace it (see illustration 4.14).

Solenoid resistor (1983 through 1987 vehicles)

Refer to illustrations 4.18 and 4.19

18 Locate the resistor and unplug the resistor electrical connector. On 1983 through 1986 vehicles, the resistor is located next to the air flow meter **(see illustration 4.1a or 4.1b)**. On 1987 models, it's on the left side of the engine compartment firewall **(see illustration)**.

19 Using an ohmmeter, measure the resistance between terminal +B and the other two terminals **(see illustration)**. On 1983 through 1985 vehicles, there should be 2.5 to 3.5

ohms resistance between +B and each of the other terminals; on 1986 and 1987 vehicles, there should be 2 to 3 ohms.

20 If the resistance is not as specified, replace the resistor. Simply remove the single bracket bolt to detach the resistor from the left fender well or firewall, then remove the two Phillips screws from the resistor to separate it from its mounting bracket.

Cold start injector time switch

Refer to illustrations 4.21a, 4.21b and 4.23

21 The cold start injector time switch is located on the water outlet on all four-cylinder models and on the water bypass outlet on V6 models **(see illustrations)**.

22 Unplug the electrical connector.

23 Using an ohmmeter, measure the resistance between each terminal **(see illustration)**:

a) On 1983 and 1984 vehicles, the indicated resistance between terminals STA and STJ should be 30 to 50 ohms when the coolant temperature is below 95-

degrees F, and 70 to 90 ohms when the coolant exceeds 95-degrees F. The resistance between terminal STA and ground should be 30 to 90 ohms.

b) On 1985 on vehicles, except V6 models, the indicated resistance between terminals STA and STJ should be 20 to 40 ohms when the coolant temperature is below 86-degrees F, and 40 to 60 ohms when the coolant exceeds 104-degrees F. The resistance between terminal STA and ground should be 20 to 80 ohms.

c) On V6 models, the indicated resistance between terminals STA and STJ should be 25 to 45 ohms when the coolant temperature is below 59-degrees F, and 65 to 86 ohms when the coolant exceeds 86-degrees F. The resistance between terminal STA and ground should be 25 to 85 ohms.

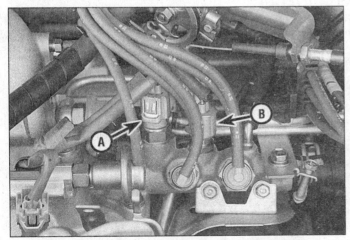

4.21b The cold start injector time switch (A) and water temperature sensor (B) are located on this water bypass outlet on V6 models

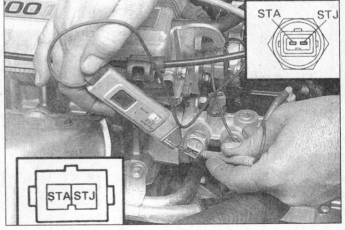

4.23 To check the cold start injector time switch, measure the resistance between the indicated terminals (terminals for 1983 and 1984 vehicles, above left; terminals for 1985 and later vehicles, above right)

4.27a To check the water temperature sensor, use an ohmmeter to measure the resistance between the two sensor terminals . . .

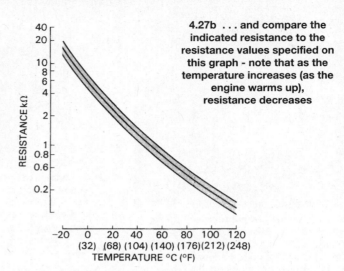

4.27b . . . and compare the indicated resistance to the resistance values specified on this graph - note that as the temperature increases (as the engine warms up), resistance decreases

24   If the indicated resistance is not as specified, replace the start injector time switch. Be sure to use Teflon tape or thread sealant on the threads of the new switch to prevent leaks.

Water temperature sensor

Refer to illustrations 4.27a and 4.27b

25   The water temperature sensor is located next to the cold start injector time switch on the water outlet of all four-cylinder models and on the water bypass outlet on V6 models **(see illustrations 4.21a and 4.21b)**.

26   Unplug the electrical connector.

27   Using an ohmmeter, measure the resistance between the two terminals **(see illustrations)**.

28   If the indicated resistance is not as specified, replace the water temperature sensor. Be sure to use Teflon tape or thread sealant on the threads of the new switch to prevent leaks.

Oxygen sensor

Refer to illustration 4.32

29   The oxygen sensor cannot be checked without special equipment. However, you can easily replace it yourself if a dealer service department diagnoses it as faulty.

30   Detach the cable from the negative terminal of the battery.

31   Locate the oxygen sensor. It's installed in the exhaust manifold on all vehicles (the rear manifold on V6 models). Follow the lead and unplug the electrical connector.

32   Remove the mounting nuts **(see illustration)**, the sensor and the old gasket. Discard the gasket. **Note:** *Some later California models have a second sensor mounted below the one shown.*

33   Installation is the reverse of removal. Be sure to coat the threads of the mounting nuts, or the studs, with anti-seize compound and use a new gasket.

Electronic Control Unit (ECU)

Refer to illustrations 4.37a and 4.37b

34   Because of the special tools necessary to check the ECU and the possibility of damage to the internal circuitry of the ECU if it is checked improperly, inspection is beyond the scope of the home mechanic. However, should a dealer service department determine that the ECU is faulty, you can easily replace it yourself.

35   Detach the cable from the negative terminal of the battery.

36   Remove the No. 1 and No. 2 under covers (the plastic panels under each side of the dash). Peel back the carpeting from the left and right sides of the front of the center console.

37   Remove the ECU mounting bracket bolts **(see illustrations)**.

38   Carefully pull the ECU rearward to release it from its forward mounting bracket, then slide it out to the right.

39   Unplug the electrical connectors from the right side of the ECU and, on 1987 and later vehicles, the circuit opening relay.

40   Installation is the reverse of removal.

4.32 To remove the oxygen sensor from the exhaust manifold, unplug the connector on the end of the electrical lead, remove the mounting nuts, the sensor and the old gasket (discard the gasket) - when installing the sensor, be sure to use a new gasket and coat the threads with anti-seize compound

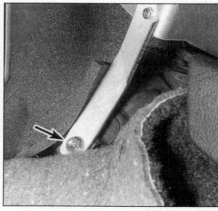

4.37a Left side ECU mounting bracket bolt (arrow)

4.37b Right side ECU mounting bracket bolt (arrow)

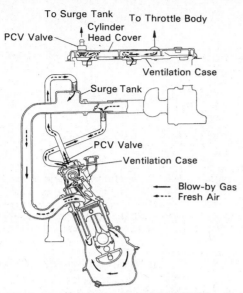

5.1 a The Positive Crankcase Ventilation (PCV) system used on 1983 through 1986 vehicles

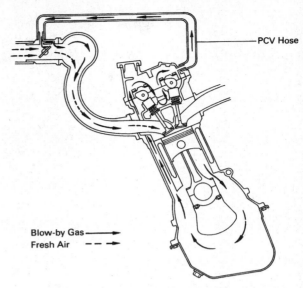

5.1b The Positive Crankcase Ventilation (PCV) system used on 1987 and later four-cylinder model vehicles (note that there is no PCV valve)

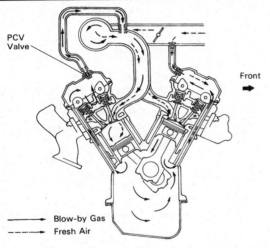

5.1c The Positive Crankcase Ventilation (PCV) system used on V6 models

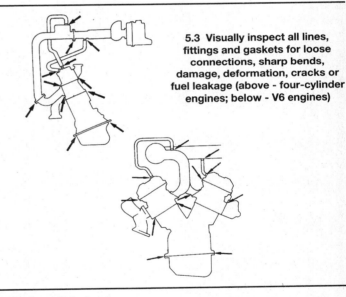

5.3 Visually inspect all lines, fittings and gaskets for loose connections, sharp bends, damage, deformation, cracks or fuel leakage (above - four-cylinder engines; below - V6 engines)

5 Positive crankcase ventilation (PCV) system

Refer to illustrations 5.1a, 5.1b, 5.1c, 5.3 and 5.5

1   To reduce hydrocarbon (HC) emissions, crankcase blow-by gas is routed to the intake manifold for combustion in the cylinders (**see illustrations**).

2   Check the PCV hose for cracks, leaks or damage. If any of these symptoms are evident, replace the hose.

3   Visually inspect the hoses, connections and gaskets (**see illustration**) that affect the PCV system. Tighten, repair or replace the causes of potential leaks.

4   Remove the PCV valve (the PCV systems on 1987 vehicles and 1988 four-cylinder models do not have a valve).

5   Attach a clean hose to the cylinder head side of the PCV valve and blow into it (**see illustration**). Air should pass through easily.

6   Blow through the valve from the intake manifold side. Air should pass through only with difficulty.

7   If the PCV valve fails either test, replace it.

6 Fuel Evaporative Emission Control (EVAP) system

Description

1   To reduce hydrocarbon emissions, evaporated fuel from the fuel tank is routed through the charcoal canister to the intake manifold for burning in the cylinders.

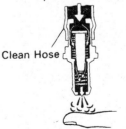

5.5 To check the PCV valve itself, first attach a clean section of hose to the cylinder head side of the valve and blow through it - air should pass through easily - then blow through the intake manifold side of the valve and verify that air passes through only with difficulty

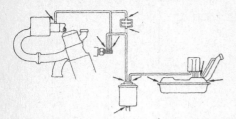

6.2 Periodically inspect the fuel vapor lines for loose fittings, sharp bends or damage; check the fuel tank hoses for deformation, cracks or fuel leakage

Check and replacement

Hoses

Refer to illustration 6.2

2   Periodically inspect the fuel vapor lines **(see illustration)** for loose connections, sharp bends or damage. Check the fuel tank plumbing for deformation, cracks or fuel leakage. Check the fuel filler cap for a damaged or deformed gasket.

Canister

Refer to illustrations 6.3, 6.5 and 6.6

3   Remove the charcoal canister **(see illustration)**.
4   Inspect the canister for cracks or damage.
5   Using low pressure compressed air, blow into the fuel tank pipe and verify that air flows without resistance from the other pipes **(see illustration)**. Blow into the purge pipe and verify that air does not flow from the other pipes. If the canister fails to perform as described, replace it.
6   Clean the canister filter by blowing compressed air (43 psi maximum) into the tank pipe while holding the other upper canister pipe closed **(see illustration)**. **Caution:** *Do not attempt to wash the canister.*
7   Installation of the canister is the reverse of removal.

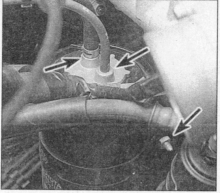

6.3 To remove the EVAP canister, detach the two hoses (top 2 arrows) from the top of the canister and a third hose from the underside (not visible) then loosen the mounting bracket pinch screw (bottom arrow) and lift the canister straight up

Bimetal Vacuum Switching Valve (BVSV)

Refer to illustrations 6.11 and 6.12

8   Locate the bimetal vacuum switching valve in the front of the thermostat **housing (see illustrations 1.1a through 1.1e)**.
9   Drain the coolant from the engine into a suitable container and remove the valve.
10   Cool the valve to below 35-degrees C (95-degrees F) with cold water.
11   Blow air into a pipe and verify that the valve is closed **(see illustration)**.
12   Heat the valve to above 54-degrees C (129-degrees F) with hot water **(see illustration)**.
13   Blow air into a pipe and verify that the valve is open.
14   If the valve fails either of these checks, replace it.
15   Apply sealer to the threads of the valve.
16   Install the valve, tighten it securely and reattach the vacuum hoses.
17   Fill the engine with coolant.

6.5 Using low pressure compressed air, blow into the fuel tank pipe and verify that air flows freely from the other pipes - then blow into the purge pipe and verify that air does not flow from the other pipes

Jet (1984 through 1986 Canada models; 1987 and four-cylinder models with manual transmissions)

18   Locate the jet **(see illustrations 1.1a through 1.1e)** in the EVAP hose between the canister and the throttle body.
19   Detach the jet from the EVAP hose and wipe it off.
20   Blow through the jet from each side and verify that air passes through.
21   If there is any blockage, replace the jet.

7   Dashpot (DP) system (V6 models with manual transaxles only)

Description

1   To reduce hydrocarbon and carbon monoxide emissions, the dashpot opens slightly more during deceleration than it does at idle, promoting a more complete burn of the air/fuel mixture.

Check and replacement

Dashpot

Refer to illustrations 7.4, 7.5 and 7.7

2   Warm up the engine.

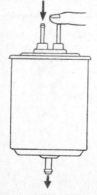

6.6 Clean the canister filter by blowing low pressure compressed air (no more than 43 psi maximum) into the tank pipe while holding the other upper canister pipe closed - DO NOT wash the canister

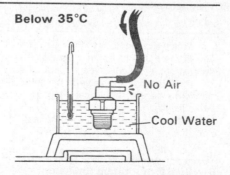

6.11 To check the bimetal vacuum switch valve (BVSV), remove the valve, attach a section of clean hose to the valve as shown and immerse the valve in a Pyrex-type container of cool water (below 95-degrees F), then blow air into the pipe and verify that air does not pass through (the valve is closed) . . .

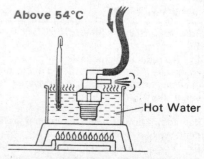

6.12 . . . then heat the water in the container to about 129-degrees F and blow into the hose again - this time, air should pass through (the valve should be open)

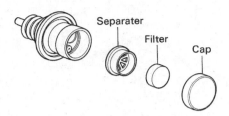

7.4 An exploded view of the dashpot separator, filter and cap - when reinstalling these parts, make sure that the coarser side of the filter faces towards atmosphere (outward)

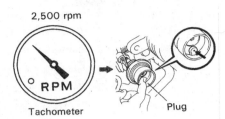

7.5 With the engine running at 2500 rpm, plug the vacuum transmitting valve (VTV) with your finger and verify that the engine speed drops to 2000 rpm

7.7 To adjust the dashpot, loosen the locknut and, while plugging the VTV hole with your finger, turn the adjusting screw with a hex wrench until the engine speed drops to the specified 2000 rpm, then tighten the locknut

8.2a To remove the EGR vacuum modulator, clearly label, then detach the vacuum hoses (arrows) and pull the modulator from its mounting bracket (unit shown on 1987 vehicle - others similar)

8.2b To remove the EGR vacuum modulator filters for cleaning, remove this cap . . .

8.2c . . . then pull out the two filters and blow them out with compressed air - be sure that the coarse side of the outer filter faces the atmosphere (outward) when reinstalling the filters

3   Check and, if necessary, adjust the idle speed (Chapter 1). It should be 700 rpm.
4   Remove the cap, filter and separator **(see illustration)** from the dashpot.
5   With the engine running at 2500 rpm, plug the VTV hole with your finger **(see illustration)**.
6   Release the throttle and verify that the engine speed drops to 2000 rpm. If it does, the dashpot is properly adjusted.
7   If engine speed does not drop to the specified rpm, adjust the dashpot adjusting screw **(see illustration)** and recheck.
8   Reinstall the dashpot separator, filter and cap. Make sure that the coarser side of

the filter faces outward (towards the atmosphere).

Vacuum Transmitting Valve (VTV)
9   With the engine running at 2500 rpm, release the throttle valve and verify that the engine drops to idle in a few seconds.

---

8   Exhaust Gas Recirculation (EGR) system

Description
1   To reduce nitrous oxide emissions, some of the exhaust gases are recirculated through the EGR valve to the intake manifold to lower combustion temperatures.

Check and replacement
EGR system
Refer to illustrations 8.2a, 8.2b, 8.2c, 8.3 and 8.7
2   Label and disconnect the vacuum hoses **(see illustration)**, remove the EGR vacuum modulator from its bracket, pull off the cover and check the filters **(see illustrations)** for contamination or damage. Clean them with compressed air. Reinstall the filters, the cover, the modulator and the vacuum hoses.
3   Using a three-way connector, connect a vacuum gauge to the hose between the EGR valve and the vacuum pipe **(see illustration)**.

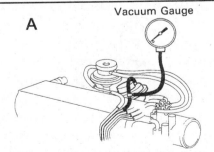

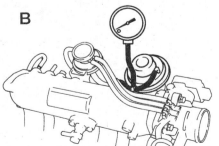

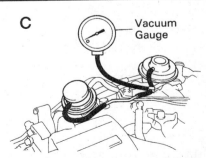

8.3 Using a three-way connector, connect a vacuum gauge to the hose between the EGR valve and the vacuum pipe

A   1983 through 1986 vehicles   *B   1987 and later vehicles*   *C   V6 models*

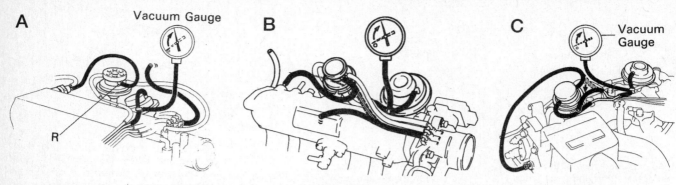

8.7 Disconnect the vacuum hose from port R of the EGR vacuum modulator and connect the R port directly to the intake manifold with another hose

A *1983 through 1986 vehicles*	*B* *1987 and later vehicles*	*C* *V6 models*

4   Start the engine and verify that the engine starts and runs at idle.

5   To determine whether the bimetal vacuum switching valve functions correctly when the engine is cold, note the vacuum gauge reading while the engine coolant temperature is still below 113-degrees F (four-cylinder models) or 104-degrees F (V6 models). It should indicate zero vacuum at 2500 rpm.

6   To determine whether the bimetal vacuum switching valve and EGR vacuum modulator function properly when the engine is hot, warm up the engine, then note the vacuum reading at 2500 rpm. The vacuum reading should be low.

7   Disconnect the vacuum hose from the R port of the EGR vacuum modulator and connect the R port directly to the intake manifold with another hose **(see illustration)**.

8   Verify that the vacuum gauge indicates high vacuum at 2500 rpm (four-cylinder models) or 3500 rpm (V6 models). **Note:** *As a large amount of EGR gas enters, the engine will misfire slightly.*

9   Disconnect the vacuum gauge and reconnect the vacuum hoses to the proper locations.

10   To check the EGR valve, apply vacuum directly to the EGR valve with the engine at idle. Verify that the engine runs roughly or dies. Reconnect the vacuum hoses to their respective ports.

11   If everything has checked out thus far, the EGR system is okay and no further testing is necessary. If any of the above system checks indicates a problem is present, the system must be checked part by part.

EGR valve

Refer to illustration 8.12

12   Disconnect the threaded fitting that attaches the EGR pipe to the EGR valve, remove the two EGR valve mounting bolts **(see illustration)**, remove the EGR valve from the cylinder head and check it for sticking and heavy carbon deposits. If the valve is sticking or clogged with deposits, replace it.

EGR vacuum modulator

Refer to illustration 8.14

13   Label and disconnect the hoses from ports P, Q and R of the vacuum modulator.

14   Plug ports P and R with your finger **(see illustration)**.

15   Blow air into port Q. Verify that air passes through freely to the air filter side.

16   Start the engine and, with the engine running at a constant 2500 rpm (four-cylinder models), or 3500 rpm (V6 models), repeat the above test. Verify that there is a strong resistance to air flow.

17   If the vacuum modulator fails either of the above checks, replace it.

Bimetal Vacuum Switching Valve (BVSV)

18   Drain the coolant from the engine into a suitable container.

19   Locate the bimetal vacuum switching valve **(see illustrations 1.1a through 1.1e)**.

20   Label and disconnect the vacuum hoses attached to the valve.

21   Remove the valve.

22   Cool the valve to below 113-degrees F (four-cylinder models) or 104-degrees F (V6 models) with cold water.

23   Blow air into the pipe and verify that the valve is closed **(see illustration 6.11)**.

24   Heat the valve to above 150-degrees F (four-cylinder models) or 129-degrees F (V6 models) in hot water.

25   Blow air into the pipe and verify that the valve is open **(see illustration 6.12)**.

26   If the valve fails either of the above tests, replace it.

27   Apply sealer to the threads of the valve and reinstall it.

28   Fill the engine with coolant.

8.12 To remove the EGR valve, unscrew the EGR pipe threaded fitting, remove both mounting bolts and detach the valve from the air intake (EGR and air intake removed from engine for clarity)

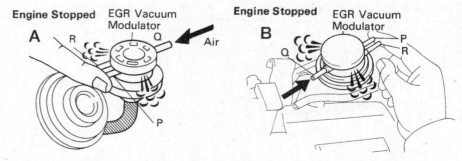

8.14 To check the EGR vacuum modulator, plug ports P and R with your finger, blow air into port Q and verify that air passes through freely to the air filter side

A Four-cylinder models	*B V6 models*

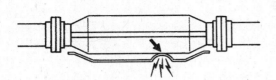

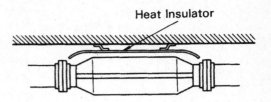

9.3 If the catalytic converter on your vehicle is mounted under the vehicle, periodically inspect the protector for dents or damage - if a dent is deep enough to touch the surface of the converter, replace the protector

9.4 If the catalytic converter on your vehicle is mounted under the vehicle, periodically inspect the heat insulator to make sure that there is adequate clearance between it and the converter

9   Catalytic converter

Refer to illustrations 9.3 and 9.4

Description

1   To reduce hydrocarbon and carbon monoxide emissions, 1984 through 1986 Canada vehicles are equipped with oxidation catalysts; to reduce hydrocarbon, carbon monoxide and nitrous oxide emissions, all US vehicles and 1987 and later Canada models are equipped with a three-way catalyst system which oxidizes and reduces these chemicals, converting them into harmless nitrogen, carbon dioxide and water.

Check

2   Periodically inspect the catalytic converter-to-exhaust pipe mating flanges and bolts. Make sure that there are no loose bolts and no leaks between the flanges.
3   Look for dents in or damage to the catalytic converter protector on underbody converters **(see illustration)**. If any part of the protector is damaged or dented enough to touch the converter, repair or replace it.
4   Inspect the heat insulator for damage. Make sure that there is adequate clearance between the heat insulator and the catalytic converter **(see illustration)**.

Replacement

5   To replace the catalytic converter, refer to "Exhaust system components - check and replacement" in Chapter 4.

Notes

Chapter 7 Part A
Manual transaxle

Contents

Specifications

General
Shift lever free play .... 0.1 to 0.2 lbs

Torque specifications   **Ft-lbs**
Transaxle-to-engine bolts
    10 mm bolt 32
    12 mm bolt 47
Engine mount center member bolt
    1983 through 1986 29
    1987 on 45
Front strut/stabilizer bar bracket-to-body bolts 45
Front suspension lower crossmember-to-body bolt (1987 on) 153

1 General information

The vehicles covered by this manual are equipped with either a 5-speed manual or a 4-speed automatic transaxle. Information on the manual transaxle is included in this Part of Chapter 7. Service procedures for the automatic transaxle are contained in Chapter 7, Part B.

The manual transaxle is a compact, two-piece, lightweight aluminum alloy housing containing both the transmission and differential assemblies.

Because of the complexity, unavailability of replacement parts and special tools necessary, internal repair procedures for the manual transaxle are not recommended for the home mechanic. For readers who wish to tackle a transaxle rebuild, exploded views and a brief *Manual transaxle overhaul - general information* Section are provided. The bulk of information in this Chapter is devoted to removal and installation procedures.

2 Oil seal replacement

1 Oil leaks frequently occur due to wear of the differential side gear shaft seals and/or the speedometer drive gear oil seal and O-rings. Replacement of these seals is relatively easy, since the repairs can usually be performed without removing the transaxle from the vehicle.

2 The differential side gear shaft oil seals are located at the sides of the transaxle, where the side gear shafts are attached. If leakage at the seal is suspected, raise the vehicle and support it securely on jackstands. If the seal is leaking, lubricant will be found on the side of the transaxle.

3 Refer to Chapter 8 and remove the driveaxles. Use a slide hammer to remove the side gear shafts. It will be necessary to replace the snap ring on the end of the side gear shafts.

4 Using a screwdriver or pry bar, carefully pry the oil seal out of the transaxle bore.

5 If the oil seal cannot be removed with a screwdriver or pry bar, a special oil seal removal tool (available at auto parts stores) will be required.

6 Using a large section of pipe or a large deep socket as a drift, install the new oil seal. Drive it into the bore squarely and make sure that it is completely seated. Lubricate the lip of the new seal with multipurpose grease.

7 Install the driveaxle(s) and side gear shaft(s). Be careful not to damage the lip of the new seal.

8 The speedometer cable and driven gear housing is located on the transaxle housing. Look for lubricant around the cable housing to determine if the seal and O-ring are leaking.

9 Disconnect the speedometer cable from the transaxle.

10 Using a hook, remove the seal.

11 Using a small socket of the appropriate diameter or other similar tool as a drift, install the new seal.

12 Install a new O-ring on the driven gear housing and reinstall the speedometer cable assembly on the housing.

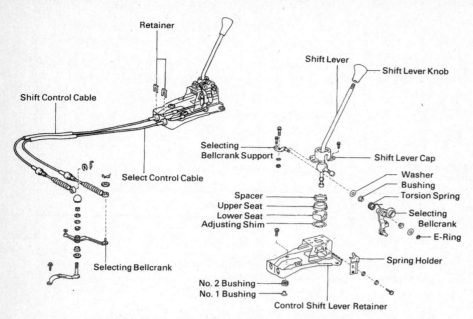

3.2 Manual transaxle shift lever and mechanism details

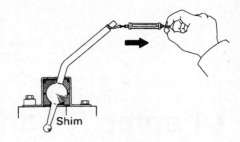

3.4 Use a spring scale to determine the shift lever free play

3   Shift lever - removal, installation and free play check and adjustment

Refer to illustrations 3.2 and 3.4

1   Remove the center console.
2   Remove the retaining bolts and detach the shift lever **(see illustration)**.
3   Installation is the reverse of removal.
4   Prior to installing the console, check the shift lever free play by connecting a spring scale to the top of the shift lever. Pull lightly on the spring scale to make sure the initial pressure required to move the lever is as specified **(see illustration)**.
5   If the free play is not as specified, remove the lever and install the proper adjusting shim (available at a dealer) and recheck the free play.
6   The remainder of installation is the reverse of removal.

4.1 Pry on the transaxle mount with a bar or large screwdriver to check for excessive movement

4   Transaxle mount - check and replacement

Refer to illustrations 4.1 and 4.3

1   Insert a large screwdriver or pry bar between the mount and the transaxle and pry up **(see illustration)**.
2   The transaxle should not move excessively away from the mount. If it does, replace the mount.
3   To replace a mount, support the transaxle with a jack, remove the nuts and bolts and remove the mount **(see illustration)**. It may be necessary to raise the transaxle slightly to provide enough clearance to remove the mount.
4   Installation is the reverse of removal.

5   Manual transaxle - removal and installation

Removal

1   Disconnect the negative cable from the battery. Place the cable out of the way so it cannot accidentally come in contact with the negative terminal of the battery, as this would once again allow power into the electrical system of the vehicle.
2   Working inside the vehicle, remove the shift lever (Section 3).
3   Raise the vehicle and support it securely on jackstands.
4   Disconnect the speedometer cable and electrical connections from the transaxle.
5   Remove the driveaxles and differential side gear shafts (Chapter 8).
6   Remove the exhaust system compo-

nents as necessary for clearance (Chapter 4).
7   Support the engine. This can be done from above by using an engine hoist, or by placing a jack (with a block of wood as an insulator) under the engine oil pan. The engine should remain supported at all times while the transaxle is out of the vehicle.
8   Support the transaxle with a jack - preferably a special jack made for this purpose. Safety chains will help steady the transaxle on the jack.
9   Remove any chassis or suspension components which will interfere with transaxle removal (Chapter 10).
10   Remove the transaxle mount bolts/nuts.
11   Remove the bolts securing the transaxle to the engine.
12   Make a final check that all wires and hoses have been disconnected from the transaxle and then move the transaxle and jack toward the side of the vehicle until the transaxle is clear of the engine. Keep the transaxle level as this is done.
13   Once the input shaft is clear, lower the transaxle and remove it from under the vehicle. **Caution:** *Do not depress the clutch pedal while the transaxle is removed from the vehicle.*
14   The clutch components can now be inspected (Chapter 8). In most cases, new clutch components should be routinely installed whenever the transaxle is removed.

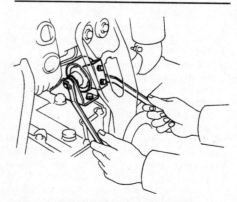

4.3 Use two wrenches to remove the transaxle mount through-bolt and nut

Installation

15   If removed, install the clutch components (Chapter 8).

16   With the transaxle secured to the jack as on removal, raise it into position and then carefully slide it forward, engaging the input shaft with the clutch splines. Do not use excessive force to install the transaxle - if the input shaft does not slide into place, readjust the angle of the transaxle so it is level and/or turn the input shaft so the splines engage properly with the clutch.

17   Install the transaxle-to-engine bolts. Tighten the bolts to the specified torque.

18   Install the transaxle mount nuts and bolts. Tighten all nuts and bolts securely.

19   Install the chassis and suspension components which were removed. Tighten all nuts and bolts securely.

20   Remove the jacks supporting the transaxle and the engine.

21   Install the various items removed previously, referring to Chapter 8 for the installation of the driveaxles and side gear shafts and Chapter 4 for information regarding the exhaust system components.

22   Make a final check that all wires, hoses and the speedometer cable have been connected and that the transaxle has been filled with the specified lubricant to the proper level (Chapter 1). Lower the vehicle.

23   Working inside the vehicle, connect the shift lever (see Section 3).

24   Connect the negative battery cable. Road test the vehicle to check for proper transaxle operation and check for leakage.

6   Manual transaxle overhaul - general information

Refer to illustrations 6.4a, 6.4b, 6.4c, 6.4d, 6.4e and 6.4f

Overhauling a manual transaxle is a difficult job for the do-it-yourselfer. It involves the disassembly and reassembly of many small parts. Numerous clearances must be precisely measured and, if necessary, changed with select fit spacers and snap-rings. As a

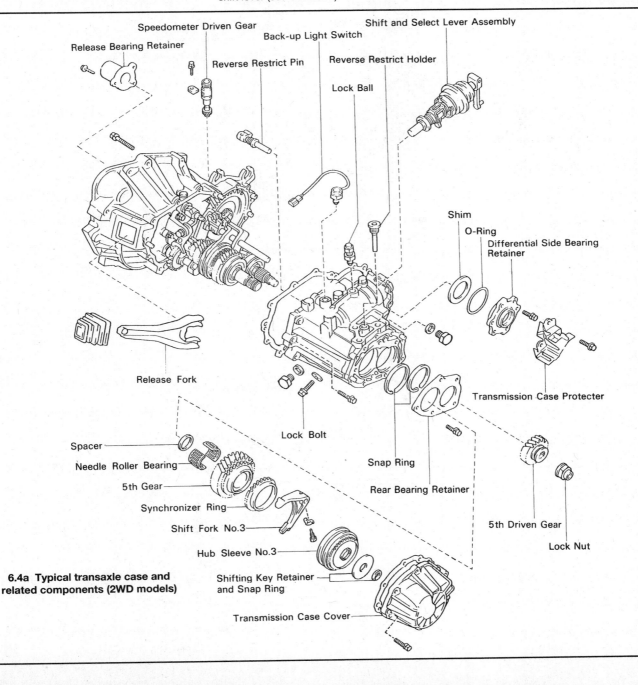

6.4a Typical transaxle case and related components (2WD models)

result, if transaxle problems arise, it can be removed and installed by a competent do-it-yourselfer, but overhaul should be left to a transmission repair shop. Rebuilt transaxles may be available - check with your dealer parts department and auto parts stores. At any rate, the time and money involved in an overhaul is almost sure to exceed the cost of a rebuilt unit.

Nevertheless, it's not impossible for an inexperienced mechanic to rebuild a transaxle if the special tools are available and the job is done in a deliberate step-by-step manner so nothing is overlooked.

The tools necessary for an overhaul include internal and external snap-ring pliers, a bearing puller, a slide hammer, a set of pin punches, a dial indicator and possibly a hydraulic press. In addition, a large, sturdy workbench and a vise or transaxle stand will be required.

During disassembly of the transaxle, make careful notes of how each piece comes off, where it fits in relation to other pieces and what holds it in place. Exploded views are included **(see illustrations)** to show where the parts go - but actually noting how they are installed when you remove the parts will make it much easier to get the transaxle back together.

Before taking the transaxle apart for repair, it will help if you have some idea what area of the transaxle is malfunctioning. Certain problems can be closely tied to specific areas in the transaxle, which can make component examination and replacement easier. Refer to the *Troubleshooting* section at the front of this manual for information regarding possible sources of trouble.

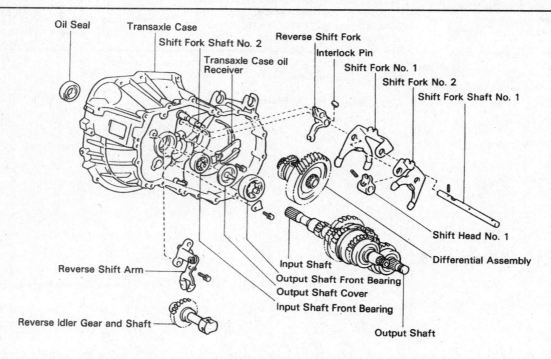

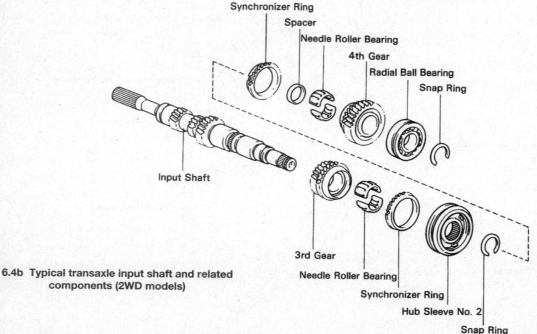

6.4b Typical transaxle input shaft and related components (2WD models)

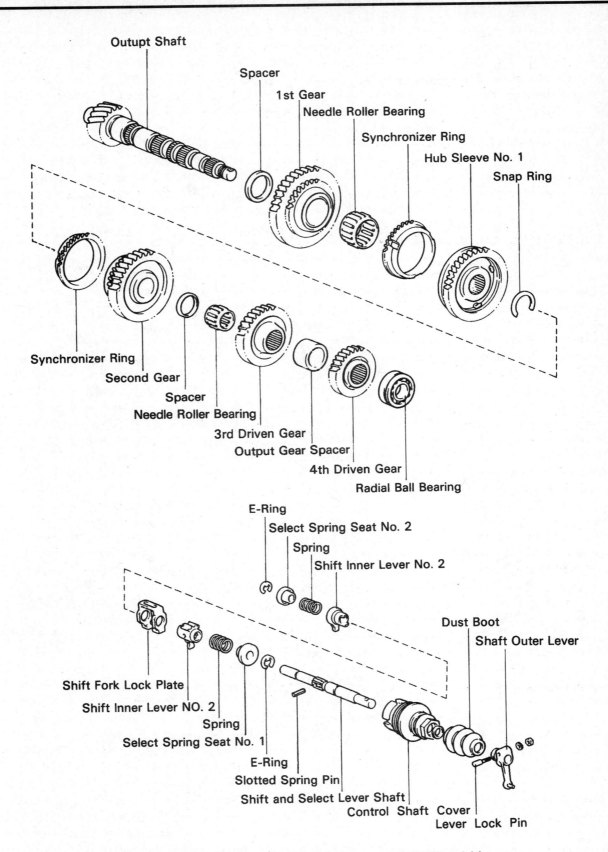

6.4c Typical transaxle output shaft and related components (2WD models)

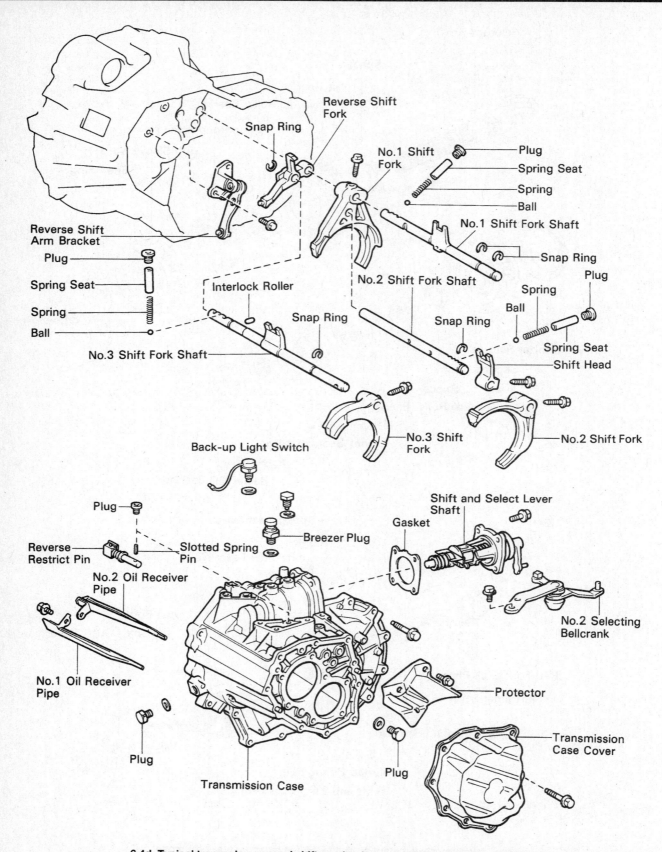

6.4d Typical transaxle case and shift mechanism components (All-Trac models)

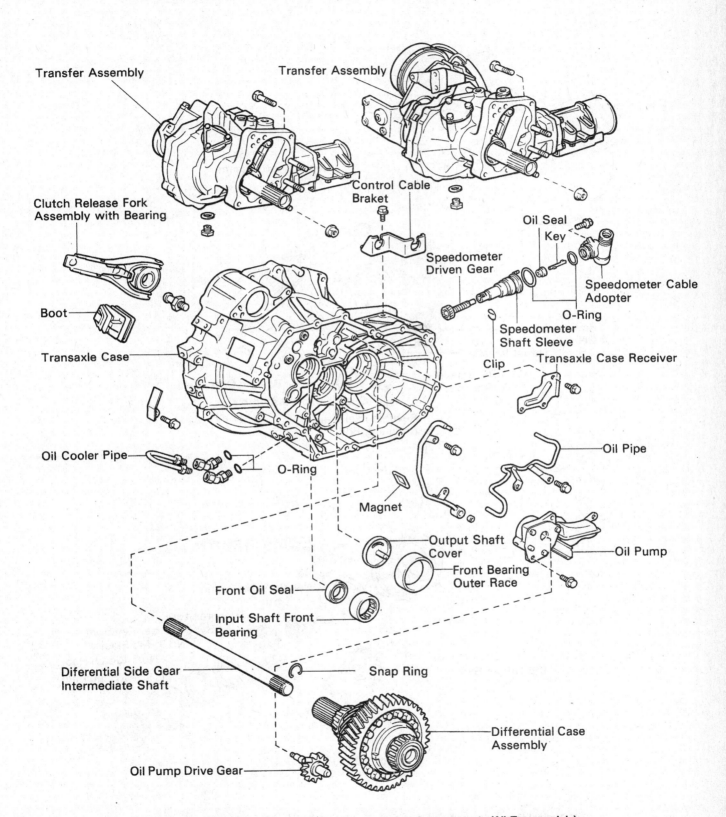

Transfer Assembly

Transfer Assembly

Clutch Release Fork
Assembly with Bearing

Control Cable
Braket

Oil Seal

Key

Speedometer
Driven Gear

Speedometer Cable
Adopter

Boot

O-Ring

Transaxle Case

Speedometer
Shaft Sleeve

Clip

Transaxle Case Receiver

Oil Cooler Pipe

O-Ring

Oil Pipe

Magnet

Output Shaft
Cover

Oil Pump

Front Bearing
Outer Race

Front Oil Seal

Input Shaft Front
Bearing

Diferential Side Gear
Intermediate Shaft

Snap Ring

Differential Case
Assembly

Oil Pump Drive Gear

6.4e Typical transaxle and transfer case and related components (All-Trac models)

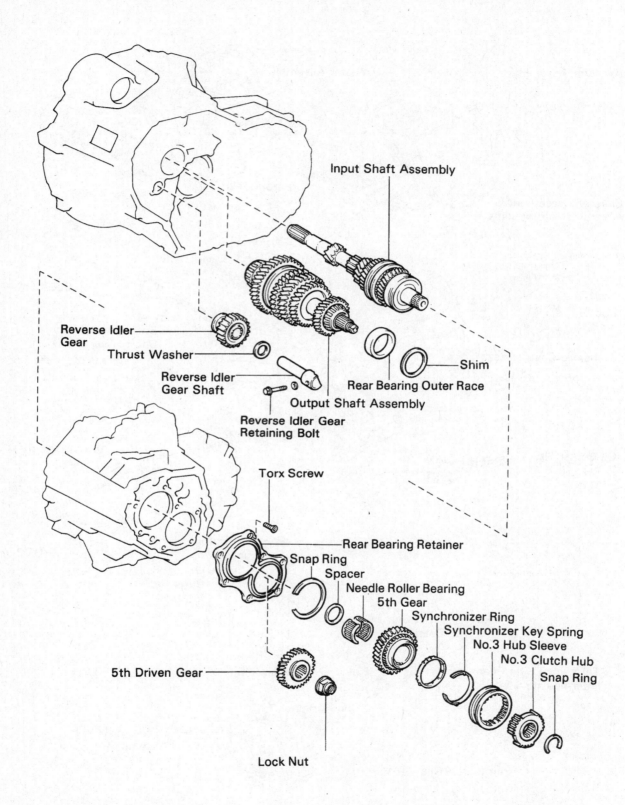

Input Shaft Assembly

Reverse Idler Gear

Thrust Washer

Reverse Idler Gear Shaft

Reverse Idler Gear Retaining Bolt

Output Shaft Assembly

Rear Bearing Outer Race

Shim

Torx Screw

Rear Bearing Retainer

Snap Ring

Spacer

Needle Roller Bearing

5th Gear

Synchronizer Ring

Synchronizer Key Spring

No.3 Hub Sleeve

No.3 Clutch Hub

Snap Ring

5th Driven Gear

Lock Nut

6.4f Typical transaxle input and output shafts and related components (All-Trac models)

Chapter 7 Part B
Automatic transaxle

Contents

Specifications

Torque specifications

	Ft-lbs
Transaxle-to-engine bolts	
10 mm	32
12 mm	47
Torque converter-to-driveplate bolts	
1983 through 1986 and 1989 on	20
1987 and 1988	13
Engine mounting center member bolt	
1983 through 1986	29
1987 on	45
Front strut/stabilizer bar bracket-to-body bolts	45
Front suspension lower crossmember-to-body	
bolt (1987 on)	153

---

1 General information

All vehicles covered in this manual come equipped with either a 5-speed manual or a 4-speed automatic transaxle. All information on the automatic transaxle is included in this Part of Chapter 7. Information for the manual transaxle can be found in Part A of this Chapter.

Due to the complexity of the automatic transaxles covered in this manual and to the specialized equipment necessary to perform most service operations, this Chapter contains only those procedures related to general diagnosis, routine maintenance, adjustment and removal and installation.

If the transaxle requires major repair work, it should be left to a dealer service department or an automotive or transmission repair shop. You can, however, remove and install the transaxle yourself and save the expense, even if the repair work is done by a transmission shop.

2 Diagnosis - general

Note: *Automatic transaxle malfunctions may be caused by five general conditions: poor engine performance, improper adjustments, hydraulic malfunctions, mechanical malfunctions or malfunctions in the computer or its signal network. Diagnosis of these problems should always begin with a check of the easily repaired items: fluid level and condition (Chapter 1), shift linkage adjustment and throttle linkage adjustment. Next, perform a road test to determine if the problem has been corrected or if more diagnosis is necessary. If the problem persists after the preliminary tests and corrections are completed, additional diagnosis should be done by a dealer service department or transmission repair shop. Refer to the Troubleshooting Section at the front of this manual for information on symptoms of transaxle problems.*

Preliminary checks

1   Drive the vehicle to warm the transaxle to normal operating temperature.

2   Check the fluid level as described in Chapter 1:

a) *If the fluid level is unusually low, add enough fluid to bring the level within the designated area of the dipstick, then check for external leaks (see below).*

b) *If the fluid level is abnormally high, drain off the excess, then check the drained fluid for contamination by coolant. The presence of engine coolant in the automatic transmission fluid indicates that a failure has occurred in the internal radiator walls that separate the coolant from the transmission fluid (see Chapter 3).*

c) *If the fluid is foaming, drain it and refill the transaxle, then check for coolant in the fluid, or a high fluid level.*

3   Check the engine idle speed. **Note:** *If the engine is malfunctioning, do not proceed with the preliminary checks until it has been repaired and runs normally.*

4   Check the throttle valve cable for freedom of movement. Adjust it if necessary (Section 4). **Note:** *The throttle cable may function properly when the engine is shut off and cold, but it may malfunction once the*

engine is hot. Check it cold and at normal engine operating temperature.

5　Inspect the shift control linkage (Section 3). Make sure that itÕs properly adjusted and that the linkage operates smoothly.

Fluid leak diagnosis

6　Most fluid leaks are easy to locate visually. Repair usually consists of replacing a seal or gasket. If a leak is difficult to find, the following procedure may help.
7　Identify the fluid. Make sure itÕs transmission fluid and not engine oil or brake fluid (automatic transmission fluid is a deep red color).
8　Try to pinpoint the source of the leak. Drive the vehicle several miles, then park it over a large sheet of cardboard. After a minute or two, you should be able to locate the leak by determining the source of the fluid dripping onto the cardboard.
9　Make a careful visual inspection of the suspected component and the area immediately around it. Pay particular attention to gasket mating surfaces. A mirror is often helpful for finding leaks in areas that are hard to see.
10　If the leak still cannot be found, clean the suspected area thoroughly with a degreaser or solvent, then dry it.
11　Drive the vehicle for several miles at normal operating temperature and varying speeds. After driving the vehicle, visually inspect the suspected component again.
12　Once the leak has been located, the cause must be determined before it can be properly repaired. If a gasket is replaced but the sealing flange is bent, the new gasket will not stop the leak. The bent flange must be straightened.
13　Before attempting to repair a leak, check to make sure that the following conditions are corrected or they may cause another leak. **Note:** *Some of the following conditions cannot be fixed without highly specialized tools and expertise. Such problems must be referred to a transmission shop or a dealer service department.*

Gasket leaks

14　Check the pan periodically. Make sure the bolts are tight, no bolts are missing, the gasket is in good condition and the pan is flat (dents in the pan may indicate damage to the valve body inside).
15　If the pan gasket is leaking, the fluid level or the fluid pressure may be too high, the vent may be plugged, the pan bolts may be too tight, the pan sealing flange may be warped, the sealing surface of the transaxle housing may be damaged, the gasket may be damaged or the transaxle casting may be cracked or porous. If sealant instead of gasket material has been used to form a seal between the pan and the transaxle housing, it may be the wrong sealant.

Seal leaks

16　If a transaxle seal is leaking, the fluid level or pressure may be too high, the vent

may be plugged, the seal bore may be damaged, the seal itself may be damaged or improperly installed, the surface of the shaft protruding through the seal may be damaged or a loose bearing may be causing excessive shaft movement.
17　Make sure the dipstick tube seal is in good condition and the tube is properly seated. Periodically check the area around the speedometer gear or sensor for leakage. If transmission fluid is evident, check the O-ring for damage.

Case leaks

18　If the case itself appears to be leaking, the casting is porous and will have to be repaired or replaced.
19　Make sure the oil cooler hose fittings are tight and in good condition.

Fluid comes out vent pipe or fill tube

20　If this condition occurs, the transaxle is overfilled, there is coolant in the fluid, the case is porous, the dipstick is incorrect, the vent is plugged or the drain back holes are plugged.

3　Shift linkage - adjustment

Refer to illustration 3.5

1　Raise the vehicle and support it securely on jackstands.
2　Loosen the swivel nut on the manual shift lever at the transaxle.
3　Push the lever toward the right side of the vehicle and then return it two notches to the Neutral position.
4　Move the shift lever inside the vehicle to the Neutral position.
5　While holding the lever with a slight pressure toward the Reverse position, tighten the swivel nut securely **(see illustration)**.
6　Check the operation of the transaxle in each shift lever position (try to start the engine in each gear - the starter should operate in the Park and Neutral positions only).

4　Throttle valve (TV) cable - check and adjustment

Refer to illustration 4.3

1　Remove the air cleaner duct assembly.
2　Have an assistant hold the throttle pedal down while you watch the TV link in the engine compartment to make sure it opens fully.
3　If the link does not open all the way, have the assistant continue to hold the pedal down, loosen the adjusting nuts and adjust the cable until the mark or stopper is the specified distance from the boot end **(see illustration)**.
4　Tighten the adjusting nuts securely, recheck the clearance and make sure the link opens all the way when the throttle is depressed.

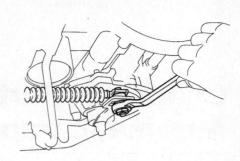

3.5 While pushing the lever lightly toward Reverse, tighten the swivel nut securely

---

5　Neutral start switch - replacement and adjustment

Replacement

1　Disconnect the negative cable from the battery. Place the cable out of the way so it cannot accidentally come in contact with the negative terminal of the battery, as this would once again allow power into the electrical system of the vehicle.
2　Shift the transaxle into Neutral.
3　Remove the nut and lift off the shift lever.
4　Unplug the electrical connector.
5　Remove the attaching bolts and lift the switch off the shift shaft.
6　To install, line up the flats on the shift shaft with the flats in the switch and push the switch onto the shaft.
7　Install the bolts, but leave them loose and follow the adjustment procedure below. The remainder of installation is the reverse of removal.

Adjustment

1983 through 1985

Refer to illustration 5.9

8　Make sure the switch connector is unplugged.

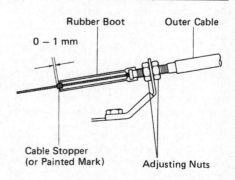

4.3 Loosen the adjusting nuts and adjust the cable housing position until the stopper or painted mark is the specified distance from the boot end

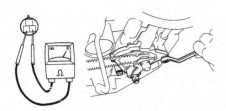

5.9 On 1983 through 1985 models, rotate the Neutral start switch until there is continuity between the switch terminals, then tighten the bolts

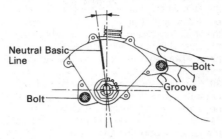

5.11 On 1986 and later models, align the neutral basic line on the housing with the groove in the shift shaft and tighten the bolts

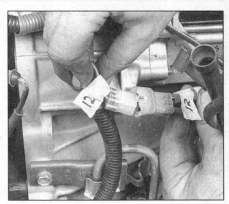

6.3 Tag the electrical connectors with marked pieces of tape before disconnecting them

9   Connect an ohmmeter to the switch terminals and rotate the switch until there is continuity between the terminals, indicating that it is now in the Neutral position **(see illustration)**. Tighten the switch bolts.

10   Connect the battery negative cable and verify that the engine will start only in Neutral or Park.

1986 on

Refer to illustration 5.11

11   Rotate the switch until the neutral basic line on the switch housing is lined up with the groove in the shift shaft and tighten the bolts securely **(see illustration)**.

---

6   Automatic transaxle - removal and installation

Refer to illustrations 6.3, 6.16 and 6.17

Removal

1   Disconnect the negative cable from the battery. Place the cable out of the way so it cannot accidentally come in contact with the negative terminal of the battery.

2   Remove the air cleaner assembly.

3   Disconnect the electrical connectors from the transaxle **(see illustration)**.

4   Disconnect any vacuum hoses connected to the transaxle.

5   Disconnect the throttle valve cable from the throttle lever.

6   Disconnect the shift linkage from the transaxle.

7   Disconnect the speedometer cable.

8   Remove the starter motor (see Chapter 5).

9   Raise the vehicle and support it securely on jackstands.

10   Drain the transmission fluid (see Chapter 1).

11   Disconnect both driveaxles from the transaxle (see Chapter 8A).

12   Remove any exhaust components which will interfere with transaxle removal (see Chapter 4).

13   Support the engine using a hoist from above or a jack and a block of wood under the oil pan to spread the load.

14   Support the transaxle with a jack; preferably with a special jack made for this purpose. Safety chains will help steady the transaxle on the jack.

15   Remove any chassis or suspension components which will interfere with transaxle removal. On All-wheel drive models, remove the rear driveshaft (see Chapter 8B).

16   Remove the torque converter cover **(see illustration)**.

17   Mark the torque converter and driveplate with white paint so they can be installed in the same position **(see illustration)**.

18   Remove the six torque converter-to-driveplate bolts. Turn the crankshaft for access to each one in turn.

19   Remove the transaxle mount bolts and nuts.

20   Remove the bolts securing the transaxle to the engine.

21   Lower the transaxle slightly and disconnect and plug the transaxle cooler lines.

22   Remove the transaxle fluid filler tube.

23   Move the transaxle to the side to disengage it from the engine block dowel pins and make sure the torque converter is detached from the driveplate. Secure the torque converter to the transaxle so it won't fall out during removal. Lower the transaxle from the vehicle.

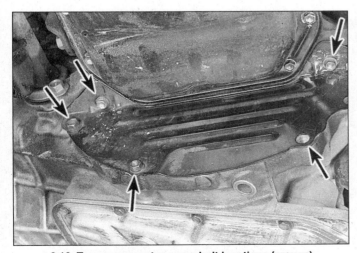

6.16 Torque converter cover bolt locations (arrows)

6.17 Mark the torque converter and driveplate with white paint so they can be reinstalled in the same relative position

Installation

24   Make sure the torque converter hub is securely engaged in the pump prior to installation.

25   With the transaxle secured to the jack, raise it into position. Be sure to keep it level so the torque converter does not slide forward. Connect the cooler lines.

26   Turn the torque converter to line up the bolt holes with the holes in the driveplate. The white paint marks on the torque converter and the driveplate made during Step 5 must line up.

27   Move the transaxle carefully into place until the dowel pins are engaged and the torque converter is engaged.

28   Install the transaxle housing-to-engine bolts and nuts. Tighten the bolts and nuts to the specified torque.

29   Install the torque converter-to-driveplate bolts. Tighten the bolts to the specified torque and install the cover.

30   Install any suspension and chassis components which were removed. Tighten the bolts and nuts to the specified torque.

31   Install the transaxle mounts and remove the jacks supporting the transaxle and the engine.

32   Connect the driveaxles.

33   Install the fluid filler tube.

34   Install any exhaust system components which were removed.

35   Lower the vehicle.

36   Install the starter.

37   Connect the vacuum hose(s) if equipped.

38   Connect the shift and TV linkage.

39   Plug in the transaxle electrical connectors.

40   Connect the speedometer.

41   Adjust the shift linkage (see Section 31).

42   Fill the transaxle (see Chapter 1), run the vehicle and check for fluid leaks.

Chapter 8 Part A
Clutch and driveaxles

Contents

Specifications

Note: *Refer to Chapter 8 Part B for Specifications related to all-wheel drive models.*

Clutch

Fluid type	See Chapter 1
Pedal free play	See Chapter 1
Pedal height..	See Chapter 1
Driveaxles - standard length	
Front wheel drive	
1986 and earlier	17.87 ± 0.20 in (454.0 ± 5 mm)
1987 and later	17.74 ± 0.20 in (450.0 ± 5 mm)
All-wheel drive	
Rear driveaxle	21.95 in (557 mm)
Intermediate shaft U-joint axial play (maximum)	Less than 0.0020 in (0.05 mm)
Intermediate shaft U-joint snap-ring thicknesses	
Plain..	0.0581 to 0.0600 in (1.475 to 1.525 mm)
Brown	0.0600 to 0.0620 in (1.525 to 1.575 mm)
Blue	0.0620 to 0.0640 in (1.575 to 1.625 mm)

Torque specifications

	Ft-lbs
Pressure plate-to-flywheel bolts..	14
Clutch master cylinder mounting nut	9
Clutch release cylinder mounting bolts	8
Driveaxle locknut	137
Driveaxle inner CV joint-to-side gear shaft	
Nuts (front wheel drive)	27
Bolts (all-wheel drive)	48
Driveaxle inner CV joint-to-intermediate driveshaft......................	27
Intermediate driveshaft bearing bracket-to-cylinder block	40
Center driveshaft bearing locknut	24

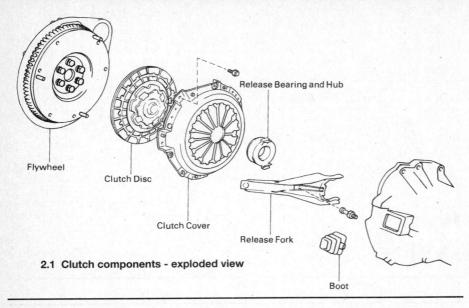

2.1 Clutch components - exploded view

Labels: Release Bearing and Hub, Flywheel, Clutch Disc, Clutch Cover, Release Fork, Boot

1 General information

The information in this Chapter deals with the components from the rear of the engine to the front wheels, except for the transaxle, which is dealt with in the previous Chapter. For the purposes of this Chapter, these components are grouped into two categories: clutch and driveaxles. Separate Sections within this Chapter offer general descriptions and checking procedures for both groups.

Since nearly all the procedures covered in this Chapter involve working under the vehicle, make sure it's securely supported on sturdy jackstands or on a hoist where the vehicle can be easily raised and lowered.

Where differences exist between front-wheel drive and all-wheel drive vehicles, references will be made at the beginning of these particular Sections, referring to Chapter 8 Part B.

2 Clutch - description and check

Refer to illustration 2.1

All vehicles with a manual transaxle use a single dry plate, diaphragm spring type clutch **(see illustration)**. The clutch disc has a splined hub which allows it to slide along the splines of the transaxle input shaft. The clutch and pressure plate are held in contact by spring pressure exerted by the diaphragm in the pressure plate.

The clutch release system is operated by hydraulic pressure. The hydraulic release system consists of the clutch pedal, a master cylinder and fluid reservoir, the hydraulic line, a slave cylinder which actuates the clutch release lever and the clutch release (or throwout) bearing.

When pressure is applied to the clutch pedal to release the clutch, hydraulic pres-

sure is exerted against the outer end of the clutch release lever. As the lever pivots, the shaft fingers push against the release bearing. The bearing pushes against the fingers of the diaphragm spring of the pressure plate assembly, which in turn releases the clutch plate.

Terminology can be a problem regarding the clutch components because common names have in some cases changed from that used by the manufacturer. For example e, the driven plate is also called the clutch plate or disc, the pressure plate assembly is sometimes referred to as the clutch cover, the clutch release bearing is sometimes called a throwout bearing, and the release cylinder is sometimes called the operating or slave cylinder.

Other than replacing components that have obvious damage, some preliminary checks should be performed to diagnose a clutch system failure.

a) *The first check should be of the fluid level in the clutch master cylinder (see Chapter 1). If the fluid level is low, add fluid as necessary and inspect the hydraulic clutch system for leaks. If the master cylinder reservoir has run dry, bleed the system as described in Section 7 and re-test the clutch operation.*

b) *To check "clutch spin down time," run the engine at normal idle speed with the transaxle in Neutral (clutch pedal up - engaged). Disengage the clutch (pedal down), wait nine seconds and shift the transaxle into Reverse. No grinding noise should be heard. A grinding noise would most likely indicate a problem in the pressure plate or the clutch disc.*

c) *To check for complete clutch release, run the engine (with the parking brake applied to prevent movement) and hold the clutch pedal approximately 1/2-inch from the floor. Shift the transaxle between 1st gear and Reverse several*

times. *If the shift is not smooth, component failure is indicated. Check the release cylinder pushrod travel. With the clutch pedal depressed completely the release cylinder pushrod should extend substantially. If it doesn't, check the fluid level in the clutch master cylinder.*

d) *Visually inspect the clutch pedal bushing at the top of the clutch pedal to make sure there is no sticking or excessive wear.*

e) *Under the vehicle, check that the clutch release lever is solidly mounted on the ball stud.*

3 Clutch components - removal, inspection and installation

Warning: *Dust produced by clutch wear and deposited on clutch components contains asbestos, which is hazardous to your health. DO NOT blow it out with compressed air and DO NOT inhale it. DO NOT use gasoline or petroleum-based solvents to remove the dust. Brake system cleaner should be used to flush the dust into a drain pan. After the clutch components are wiped clean with a rag, dispose of the contaminated rags and cleaner in a labeled, covered container.*

Removal

Refer to illustration 3.6

1   Access to the clutch components is normally accomplished by removing the transaxle, leaving the engine in the vehicle. If, of course, the engine is being removed for major overhaul, then the opportunity should always be taken to check the clutch for wear and replace worn components as necessary. However, the relatively low cost of the clutch components compared to the time and labor involved in gaining access to them warrants their replacement any time the engine or transaxle is removed, unless they are new or in near-perfect condition. The following procedures assume that the engine will stay in place.

2   Remove the release cylinder (see Section 6). Hang it out of the way with a piece of wire - it's not necessary to disconnect the hose.

3   Referring to Chapter 7 Part A, remove the transaxle from the vehicle. Support the engine while the transaxle is out. Preferably, an engine hoist should be used to support it from above. However, if a jack is used underneath the engine, make sure a piece of wood is used between the jack and oil pan to spread the load. **Caution:** *The pickup for the oil pump is very close to the bottom of the oil pan. If the pan is bent or distorted in any way, engine oil starvation could occur.*

4   The release fork and release bearing can remain attached to the transaxle for the time being.

5   To support the clutch disc during removal, install a clutch alignment tool through the clutch disc hub.

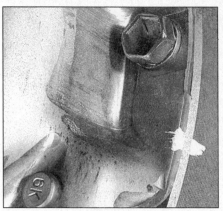

3.6 Mark the relationship of the pressure plate to the flywheel (in case you are going to reuse the same pressure plate)

3.10 Examine the clutch disc for evidence of excessive wear, such as smeared friction material, chewed up rivets, worn hub splines and distorted damper cushions or springs

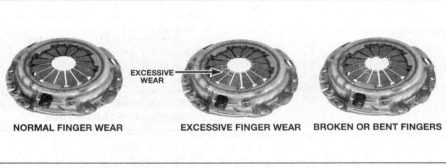

NORMAL FINGER WEAR   EXCESSIVE FINGER WEAR   BROKEN OR BENT FINGERS

EXCESSIVE WEAR

3.12a Replace the pressure plate it any of these conditions are noted

6   Carefully inspect the flywheel and pressure plate for indexing marks. The marks are usually an X, an O or a white letter. If they cannot be found, scribe marks yourself so the pressure plate and the flywheel will be in the same alignment during installation **(see illustration)**.

7   Turning each bolt only 1/2-turn at a time, slowly loosen the pressure plate-to-flywheel bolts. Work in a diagonal pattern and loosen each bolt a little at a time until all spring pressure is relieved. Then hold the pressure plate securely and completely remove the bolts, followed by the pressure plate and clutch disc.

Inspection

Refer to illustrations 3.10, 3.12a and 3.12b

8   Ordinarily, when a problem occurs in the clutch, it can be attributed to wear of the clutch driven plate assembly (clutch disc). However, all components should be inspected at this time.

9   Inspect the flywheel for cracks, heat checking, grooves or other signs of obvious defects. If the imperfections are slight, a machine shop can machine the surface flat and smooth, which is highly recommended regardless of the surface appearance. Refer to Chapter 2 for the flywheel removal and installation procedure.

10   Inspect the lining on the clutch disc. There should be at least 1/16-inch of lining above the rivet heads. Check for loose rivets, distortion, cracks, broken springs and other obvious damage **(see illustration)**. As mentioned above, ordinarily the clutch disc is replaced as a matter of course, so if in doubt about the condition, replace it with a new one.

11   The release bearing should be replaced along with the clutch disc (see Section 4).

12   Check the machined surface and the diaphragm spring fingers of the pressure plate **(see illustrations)**. If the surface is grooved or otherwise damaged, replace the pressure plate assembly. Also check for obvious damage, distortion, cracking, etc. Light glazing can be removed with medium grit emery cloth. If a new pressure plate is indicated, new or factory-rebuilt units are available.

Installation

Refer to illustration 3.14

13   Before installation, carefully wipe the flywheel and pressure plate machined surfaces clean. It's important that no oil or grease is on these surfaces or the lining of the clutch disc. Handle these parts only with clean hands.

14   Position the clutch disc and pressure plate with the clutch held in place with an alignment tool **(see illustration)**. Make sure it's installed properly (most replacement clutch plates will be marked "flywheel side" or something similar - if not marked, install the clutch disc with the damper springs or cushion toward the transaxle).

15   Tighten the pressure plate-to-flywheel bolts only finger tight, working around the pressure plate.

16   Center the clutch disc by ensuring the alignment tool is through the splined hub and into the pilot bearing in the crankshaft. Wiggle the tool up, down or side-to-side as needed to bottom the tool in the pilot bearing. Tighten the pressure plate-to-flywheel bolts a little at a time, working in a criss-cross pattern to prevent distorting the cover. After all of the bolts are snug, tighten them to the specified torque. Remove the alignment tool.

17   Using high temperature grease, lubricate the inner groove of the release bearing (refer to Section 4). Also place grease on the release lever contact areas and the transaxle input shaft bearing retainer.

18   Install the clutch release bearing as described in Section 4.

19   Install the transaxle, slave cylinder and all components removed previously, tightening all fasteners to the proper torque specifications.

3.12b Examine the pressure plate friction surface for score marks, cracks and evidence of overheating (blue spots)

3.14 Center the clutch disc in the pressure plate with a clutch alignment tool

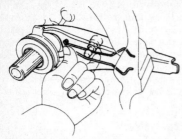

4.3 Reach behind the release lever and disengage the lever from the ball stud by pulling on the retention spring, then remove the lever and bearing

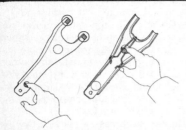

4.6 Apply high temperature grease to the release fork in the areas indicated

4   Clutch release bearing and fork - removal, inspection and installation

Warning: *Dust produced by clutch wear and deposited on clutch components contains asbestos, which is hazardous to your health. DO NOT blow it out with compressed air and DO NOT inhale it. DO NOT use gasoline or petroleum-based solvents to remove the dust. Brake system cleaner should be used to flush the dust into a drain pan. After the clutch components are wiped clean with a rag, dispose of the contaminated rags and cleaner in a labeled, covered container.*

Removal

Refer to illustration 4.3

1   Disconnect the negative cable from the battery.
2   Remove the transaxle (Chapter 7).

5.2 To release the clutch pushrod from the clutch pedal, remove the clip and clevis pin from the clutch pedal

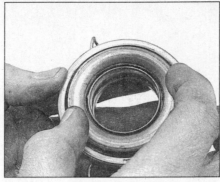

4.4 To check the operation of the bearing, hold it by the outer cage (hub) and rotate the inner race while applying pressure - the bearing should turn smoothly - if it doesn't, replace it

3   Remove the clutch release fork from the ball stud, then remove the bearing from the fork **(see illustration)**.

Inspection

Refer to illustration 4.4

4   Hold the bearing by the outer race and rotate the inner race while applying pressure **(see illustration)**. If the bearing doesn't turn smoothly or if it's noisy, replace the bearing/hub assembly with a new one. Wipe the bearing with a clean rag and inspect it for damage, wear and cracks. Don't immerse the bearing in solvent - it's sealed for life and to do so would ruin it. Also check the release lever for cracks and bends.

Installation

Refer to illustrations 4.5 and 4.6

5   Fill the inner groove of the release bearing with high temperature grease. Also apply a light coat of the same grease to the transaxle input shaft splines and the front bearing retainer **(see illustration)**.
6   Lubricate the release fork ball socket, fork ends and release cylinder pushrod socket with high temperature grease **(see illustration)**.
7   Attach the release bearing to the release fork.
8   Slide the release bearing onto the

5.5 The reservoir tank is attached to the master cylinder with a large nut in the bottom of the tank

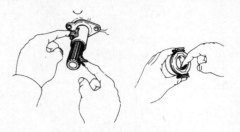

4.5 Apply a light coat of high temperature grease to the transaxle bearing retainer and also fill the release bearing groove

transaxle input shaft front bearing retainer while passing the end of the release fork through the opening in the clutch housing. Push the clutch release fork onto the ball stud until it's firmly seated.
9   Apply a light coat of high temperature grease to the face of the release bearing where it contacts the pressure plate diaphragm fingers.
10   The remainder of the installation is the reverse of the removal procedure, tightening all bolts to the specified torque.

5   Clutch master cylinder - removal, overhaul and installation

Note: *Before beginning this procedure, contact local parts stores and dealer service departments concerning the purchase of a rebuild kit or a new master cylinder. Availability and cost of the necessary parts may dictate whether the cylinder is rebuilt or replaced with a new one. If it's decided to rebuild the cylinder, inspect the bore as described in Step 12 before purchasing parts.*

Removal

Refer to illustration 5.2

1   Disconnect the negative cable from the battery.
2   Under the dashboard, disconnect the pushrod from the top of the clutch pedal. It's held in place with a clevis pin **(see illustration)**.
3   Disconnect the hydraulic line at the clutch master cylinder. If available, use a flare nut wrench on the fitting, which will prevent the fitting from being rounded off. Have rags handy as some fluid will be lost as the line is removed. **Caution:** *Don't allow brake fluid to come into contact with paint as it will damage the finish.*
4   From under the dash, remove the nut which secures the master cylinder to the engine firewall. Remove the master cylinder, again being careful not to spill any of the fluid.

Overhaul

Refer to illustrations 5.5, 5.6a, 5.6b and 5.8
5   Remove the reservoir cap and drain all fluid from the master cylinder. Remove the

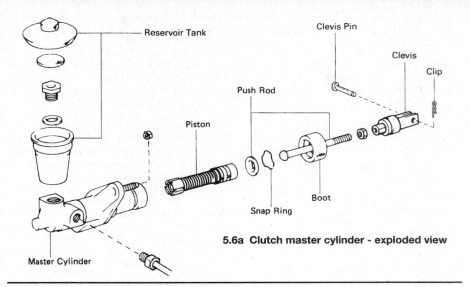

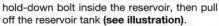

5.6a **Clutch master cylinder - exploded view**

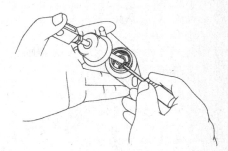

5.6b **Use a small screwdriver to pry the snap-ring from the cylinder bore**

hold-down bolt inside the reservoir, then pull off the reservoir tank **(see illustration)**.

6   Pull back the dust cover on the pushrod and remove the snap-ring **(see illustrations)**.

7   Remove the retaining washer and the pushrod from the cylinder.

8   Tap the master cylinder on a block of wood to eject the piston assembly from inside the bore **(see illustration)**. **Note:** *If the rebuild kit supplies a complete piston assembly, ignore the appropriate Steps.*

9   Separate the spring from the piston.

10   Remove the spring support, seal and shim from the pushrod.

11   Carefully remove the seal from the piston.

12   Inspect the bore of the master cylinder for deep scratches, score marks and ridges. The surface must be smooth to the touch. If the bore isn't perfectly smooth, the master cylinder must be replaced with a new or factory rebuilt unit.

13   If the cylinder will be rebuilt, use the new parts contained in the rebuild kit and follow any specific instructions which may have accompanied the rebuild kit. Wash all parts to be re-used with brake cleaner, denatured

alcohol or clean brake fluid. DO NOT use petroleum-based solvents.

14   Attach the seal to the piston. The seal lips must face away from the pushrod end of the piston.

15   Assemble the shim, spring support and spring on the other end of the piston.

16   Lubricate the bore of the cylinder and the seals with plenty of fresh brake fluid (DOT 3).

17   Carefully guide the piston assembly into the bore, being careful not to damage the seals. Make sure the spring end is installed first, with the pushrod end of the piston closest to the opening.

18   Position the pushrod and retaining washer in the bore, compress the spring and install a new snap-ring.

19   Apply a liberal amount of Girling Rubber Grease or equivalent to the inside of the dust cover and attach it to the master cylinder.

Installation

20   Position the master cylinder on the firewall, installing the mounting nut finger tight.

21   Connect the hydraulic line to the master

cylinder, moving the cylinder slightly as necessary to thread the fitting properly into the bore. Don't cross-thread the fitting as it's installed.

22   Tighten the mounting nut to the specified torque, then tighten the hydraulic line fitting.

23   Inside the vehicle, connect the pushrod to the clutch pedal.

24   Fill the clutch master cylinder reservoir with brake fluid conforming to DOT 3 specifications and bleed the clutch system as outlined in Section 7.

25   Check the clutch pedal height and freeplay and adjust if necessary, following the procedure in Chapter 1.

6   Clutch release cylinder - removal, overhaul and installation

Note: *Before beginning this procedure, contact local parts stores and dealer service departments concerning the purchase of a rebuild kit or a new release cylinder. Availability and cost of the necessary parts may dictate whether the cylinder is rebuilt or replaced with a new one. If it's decided to rebuild the cylinder, inspect the bore as described in Step 8 before purchasing parts.*

Removal

Refer to illustration 6.3

1   Disconnect the negative cable from the battery. Place the cable out of the way so it cannot accidentally come into contact with the terminal, which would again allow current to flow.

2   Raise the vehicle and support it securely on jackstands.

3   Disconnect the hydraulic line at the release cylinder. If available, use a flare nut wrench on the fitting, which will prevent the fitting from being rounded off **(see illustration)**. Have a small can and rags handy, as some fluid will be spilled as the line is removed.

4   Remove the release cylinder mounting nuts.

5   Remove the release cylinder.

5.8 **Invert the cylinder and tap it against a block of wood to eject the piston**

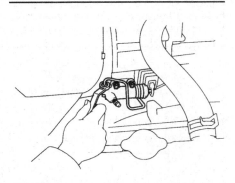

6.3 **Use a flare nut wrench when disconnecting the hydraulic fitting to prevent rounding off the corners of the tube nut**

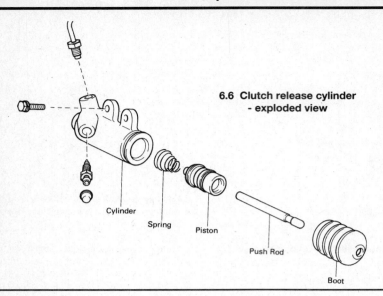

6.6 Clutch release cylinder - exploded view

Cylinder
Spring
Piston
Push Rod
Boot

Overhaul

Refer to illustration 6.6

6   Remove the pushrod and the boot **(see illustration)**.

7   Tap the cylinder on a block of wood to eject the piston and seal. Remove the spring from inside the cylinder.

8   Carefully inspect the bore of the cylinder. Check for deep scratches, score marks and ridges. The bore must be smooth to the touch. If any imperfections are found, the release cylinder must be replaced with a new one.

9   Using the new parts in the rebuild kit, assemble the components using plenty of fresh brake fluid for lubrication. Note the installed direction of the spring and the seal.

Installation

10   Install the release cylinder on the clutch housing. Make sure the pushrod is seated in the release fork pocket.

11   Connect the hydraulic line to the release cylinder. Tighten the connection.

12   Fill the clutch master cylinder with brake fluid (conforming to DOT 3 specifications).

13   Bleed the system as described in Section 7.

14   Lower the vehicle and connect the negative battery cable.

7   Clutch hydraulic system - bleeding

1   The hydraulic system should be bled of all air whenever any part of the system has been removed or if the fluid level has been allowed to fall so low that air has been drawn into the master cylinder. The procedure is very similar to bleeding a brake system.

2   Fill the master cylinder with new brake fluid conforming to DOT 3 specifications. **Caution:** *Do not re-use any of the fluid coming from the system during the bleeding operation or use fluid which has been inside an open container for an extended period of time.*

3   Raise the vehicle and place it securely on jackstands to gain access to the release cylinder, which is located on the left side of the clutch housing.

4   Remove the dust cap which fits over the bleeder valve and push a length of plastic hose over the valve. Place the other end of the hose into a clear container with about two inches of brake fluid. The hose end must be in the fluid at the bottom of the container.

5   Have an assistant depress the clutch pedal and hold it. Open the bleeder valve on the release cylinder, allowing fluid to flow through the hose. Close the bleeder valve when fluid stops flowing from the hose. Once closed, have your assistant release the pedal.

6   Continue this process until all air is evacuated from the system, indicated by a full, solid stream of fluid being ejected from the bleeder valve each time and no air bubbles in the hose or container. Keep a close watch on the fluid level inside the clutch master cylinder reservoir; if the level drops too low, air will be sucked back into the system and the process will have to be started all over again.

7   Install the dust cap and lower the vehicle. Check carefully for proper operation before placing the vehicle in normal service.

8   Clutch start system - inspection and adjustment

Refer to illustrations 8.4, 8.5, 8.8a and 8.8b

1   Check the pedal height, pedal free play and pushrod play (refer to Chapter 1).

2   Verify that the engine will not start when the clutch pedal is released.

3   Verify that the engine will start when the clutch pedal is fully depressed.

4   Measure clearance "A" **(see illustration)**. It must be a specified distance (see Step 8), but it must also be greater than 1 mm (0.04 in) when the clutch is fully depressed. If it is not, adjust or replace the clutch start switch.

5   Verify that there is continuity between the clutch start switch terminals when the switch is *On* **(see illustration)**.

6   Check that there is no continuity between the clutch start switch terminals when the switch is *Off*.

7   If the clutch start switch fails either of the above two tests, replace it. This is accomplished by removing the nut nearest the plunger end of the switch and sliding it from its bracket. Disconnect the electrical connector. Installation is the reverse of the removal procedure.

8   To adjust the clutch start switch, mea-

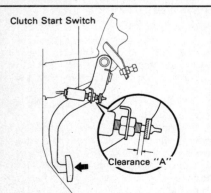

Clutch Start Switch

Clearance "A"

8.4 When the clutch pedal is fully depressed, clearance "A" must be greater than 1 mm (0.04 in). If it isn't, adjust or replace the switch

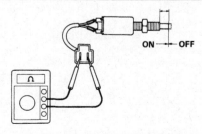

ON —|— OFF

8.5 Using an ohmmeter, check the continuity of the clutch switch - there should be continuity when the switch is On (pushed), but no continuity when it is Off (released)

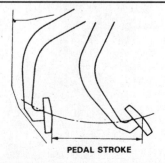

PEDAL STROKE

8.8a Pedal stroke is the distance between the position of the pedal at its full height and when fully depressed

sure the pedal stroke **(see illustration)** and calculate switch clearance "A" using the chart **(see illustration)**.
9   Loosen and adjust the switch position.
10   Verify again that the engine does not start when the clutch pedal is released.

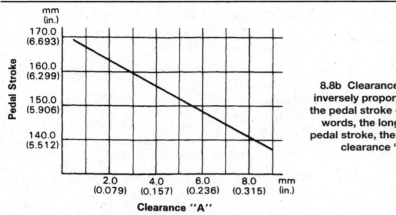

8.8b Clearance "A" is inversely proportional to the pedal stroke - in other words, the longer the pedal stroke, the closer is clearance "A"

9   Driveaxles - general information and check

Note: *For information pertaining to all-wheel drive vehicles, refer to Chapter 8 Part B.*
Power is transmitted from the transaxle to the wheels through a pair of driveaxles.

The inboard end of each driveaxle is connected to the transaxle by a side gear shaft (flanged stub axle) splined to the differential. The side gear shafts are lightly press fitted and can be easily driven out if it becomes necessary to replace the side gear shaft oil seals (Chapter 7A). The outboard ends of the driveaxles are splined to the axle hubs and locked in place by an axle nut.

The splined inboard ends of the driveaxles are fitted with sliding tripod joints, which are capable of both angular and axial motion. Each inboard joint assembly consists of a tripod bearing and a joint tulip (housing) in which the tripod is free to slide in and out as the driveaxle moves up and down with the wheel. The inboard joints are rebuildable (Section 12).

Each outer joint, which consists of ball bearings running between an inner race and an outer cage, is capable of angular but not axial movement. The outboard joints are neither rebuildable nor removable. Should one of them fail, a new driveaxle/outboard joint assembly must be installed.

The boots should be periodically inspected for damage, leaking lubricant and cuts. Damaged CV joint boots must be replaced immediately or the joints can be damaged. Boot replacement involves removal of the driveaxle (Section 10). **Note:** *Some auto parts stores carry "split" type replacement boots, which can be installed without removing the driveaxle from the vehicle. This is a convenient alternative; however, it's recommended that the driveaxle be removed and the CV joint disassembled and cleaned to ensure that the joint is free from contaminants such as moisture and dirt, which will accelerate CV joint wear.* The most common symptom of worn or damaged CV joints, besides lubricant leaks, is a clicking noise in turns, a clunk when accelerating from a coasting condition or vibration at highway speeds.

To check for wear in the CV joints and driveaxle shafts, grasp each axle (one at a time) and rotate it in both directions while holding the CV joint housings, inspecting for movement, indicating worn splines or sloppy CV joints. Also check the driveaxle shafts for cracks, dents, twisting and bending.

10   Driveaxle - removal and installation

Refer to illustrations 10.6a, 10.6b, 10.6c, 10.7, 10.8, 10.11a and 10.11b

1   Disconnect the cable from the negative terminal of the battery.
2   Set the parking brake.
3   Loosen but do not remove the front wheel lug nuts.
4   Raise the vehicle and place it securely on jackstands.
5   Remove the wheel.
6   Remove the cotter pin and bearing lock nut cap from the driveaxle lock nut **(see illustrations)**.

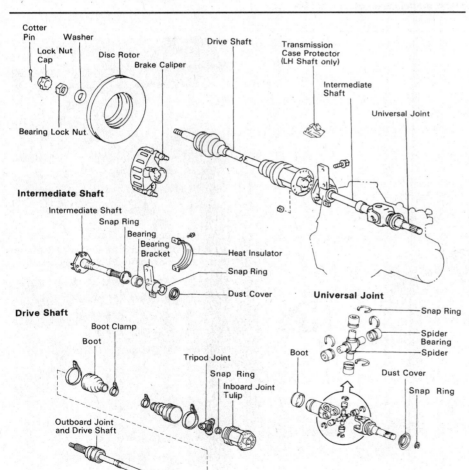

10.6a Driveaxle assembly details - 1983 and 1984 models

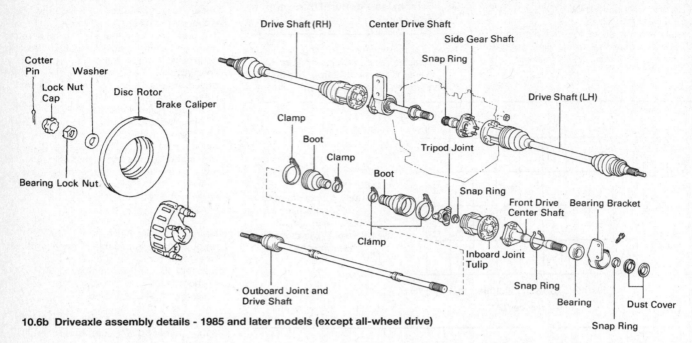

Cotter Pin
Lock Nut Cap
Washer
Lock Nut
Disc Rotor
Brake Caliper
Bearing Lock Nut
Drive Shaft (RH)
Center Drive Shaft
Side Gear Shaft
Snap Ring
Drive Shaft (LH)
Clamp
Boot
Clamp
Boot
Clamp
Clamp
Tripod Joint
Snap Ring
Front Drive Center Shaft
Bearing Bracket
Inboard Joint Tulip
Snap Ring
Bearing
Dust Cover
Snap Ring
Outboard Joint and Drive Shaft

10.6b Driveaxle assembly details - 1985 and later models (except all-wheel drive)

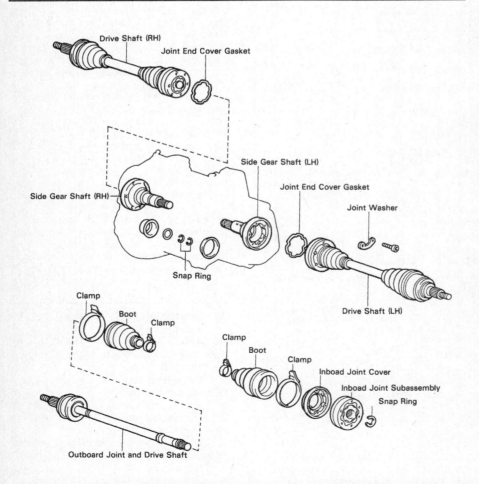

Drive Shaft (RH)
Joint End Cover Gasket
Side Gear Shaft (LH)
Side Gear Shaft (RH)
Joint End Cover Gasket
Joint Washer
Snap Ring
Drive Shaft (LH)
Clamp
Boot
Clamp
Clamp
Boot
Clamp
Inboad Joint Cover
Inboad Joint Subassembly
Snap Ring
Outboard Joint and Drive Shaft

10.6c Driveaxle assembly details - all-wheel drive models

10.7 Use a large pry bar to immobilize the hub while loosening the driveaxle locknut

10.8 The inner CV joint is attached to the side gear shaft (or intermediate shaft) flange with six nuts (front wheel drive models) or bolts (all-wheel drive and V6 models)

10.11a A two-jaw puller works well for pushing the driveaxle from the hub

7   Remove the driveaxle locknut. To prevent the hub from turning, wedge a pry bar between two of the wheel studs **(see illustration)**.
8   If you are working on the left driveaxle, remove the transaxle case protector. Remove the six nuts or bolts attaching the inner CV joint to the differential side gear shaft **(see illustration)** and detach the tripod joint from the side gear shaft. The driveaxle can be immobilized by using the same technique described in Step 7.
9   Remove the disc brake caliper, bracket and disc (Chapter 9).
10   Remove the balljoint-to-steering knuckle bolts and detach the balljoint from the steering knuckle (see Chapter 10).
11   Push the driveaxle from the hub with a two-jaw puller **(see illustration)** and remove the driveaxle. If removing an all-wheel drive or V6 model driveaxle, use bolts, nuts and washers to contain the inner joint **(see illustration)**. Do not push inward on the joint - it may separate. **Caution 1:** *Should it become necessary to move the vehicle while the driveaxle is removed, the hub bearing could be damaged when subjected to the vehicle weight. If it is absolutely necessary to place the vehicle weight on the hub bearing, support it first with a special tool and a large plate washer, available from most auto parts stores.*
Caution 2: *When removing the rear driveaxles on models equipped with the anti-lock brake system (ABS), be careful to not damage the sensor rotor serrations on the wheel end of the driveaxle.*
12   Installation is the reverse of removal.

11.5 Mark the relationship of the joint yoke to the shaft yoke before disassembly

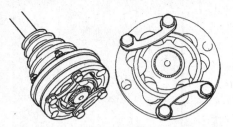

10.11b To contain the inner CV joint, use nuts/bolts of the proper size and reverse the washers to overlap the inner race and cage

11   Intermediate driveshaft (center driveshaft) - removal, overhaul and installation

1   Loosen the right front wheel lug nuts, raise the vehicle and support it securely on jackstands. Remove the wheel.
2   Remove the right side driveaxle (see Section 10).

Intermediate driveshaft and universal joint (1983 and 1984 models)

Refer to illustrations 11.3, 11.5, 11.6 and 11.8
3   Remove the two bolts securing the intermediate shaft bearing to the cylinder block **(see illustration)** and slide the shaft and bearing assembly from the universal joint. Before removing the universal joint assembly from the transaxle, check for signs of leakage around the side gear shaft oil seal. Refer to Chapter 7 for the replacement procedure, if necessary.
4   Position a drain pan under the transaxle. To remove the universal joint, carefully tap it out with a long drift and hammer. Check the joint for sticking, binding, roughness and excessive play, any of which will warrant replacement. Check the intermediate shaft bearing. If it requires replacement, take the assembly to a qualified shop to have a new

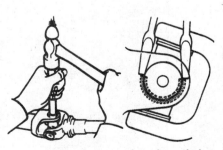

11.6 Drive the snap-rings from their grooves with a narrow screwdriver - if they are stubborn, tap on the ends of the bearing caps with a hammer and socket extension

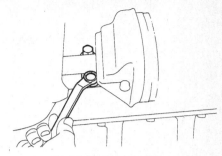

11.3 Unbolt the intermediate shaft bearing from the cylinder block

one installed, as special equipment is necessary.
5   To replace the universal joint spider and bearings, mark the relationship of the shaft yoke to the joint yoke to ensure correct reassembly **(see illustration)**.
6   Using a narrow screwdriver and hammer, knock the snap-rings from their grooves in the spider bearing caps **(see illustration)**.
7   To remove the bearings from the yokes, you will need two sockets. One should be small enough in diameter to fit inside the yoke boss (where the bearing caps are) and the other should have an inside diameter large enough for the bearing caps to fit into when they are forced out of the yoke.
8   Mount the universal joint in a vise with the large socket on one side of the yoke and the small socket on the other side, pushing against the bearing cap. Slowly tighten the vise until the bearing is pushed out of the yoke and into the large socket **(see illustration)**. If it can't be pushed out all the way, remove the assembly from the vise and use a pair of pliers to pull it out the rest of the way.
9   Reverse the sockets and push out the bearing on the other side of the yoke. This time, the small socket will be pushing against the cross-shaped universal joint spider end.
10   Repeat Steps 8 and 9 to remove the bearings from the other portion of the joint.
11   Check the splines for wear and damage.

11.8 Use a vise, a large socket (left) and a small socket (right) to press the bearing out of the universal joint

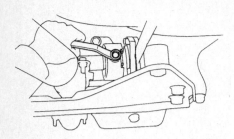

11.19 Loosen the center driveshaft lock bolt

11.20a Squeeze the snap-ring with a pair of pliers . . .

11.20b . . . then knock the center driveshaft out with a hammer and punch

Check the yoke ears for deformation and replace parts as necessary.

12   Before reassembly, pack each grease cavity in the bearing caps with a small amount of chassis grease. Apply a thin coat of grease to the dust seal lips and install the bearings and spider into the yoke using the vise and the sockets that were used to remove the old bearings (be sure to align the match marks that were applied previously). Work slowly and be very careful not to damage the bearings as they are being pressed into the yokes.

13   Press the bearings in until the snap-ring grooves are exposed an equal amount. They should be pressed in as far as possible, as well.

14   Install the snap-rings in the bearing cap grooves. Different width snap-rings are available, and the correct thicknesses should be selected to obtain an axial play of 0.0 to 0.002-inch. Refer to the Specifications section for the snap-ring thicknesses.

15   After the snap-rings have been installed, tap the yoke ears with a hammer to relieve any stress that may have set up in the joint. Check to see that the joint moves smoothly and that the axial play is within the 0.002-inch limit.

16   Replace the dust cover on the splined end of the U-joint shaft by prying it off and tapping a new one on with a plastic hammer. Replace the snap-ring on the splined portion.

17   To install the universal joint assembly, insert the splined shaft into the transaxle as far as possible, ensuring that the splines are lined up. Tap the yoke ears on the splined shaft portion (not the end of the joint assembly - the spider may be damaged) until the joint is seated.

18   The remainder of the installation procedure is the reverse of removal. Be sure to check the transaxle fluid level or differential oil, topping it up as necessary (Chapter 1).

Center driveshaft (1985 and later models)

Refer to illustrations 11.19, 11.20a and 11.20b

19   Position a drain pan underneath the transaxle. Loosen the center driveshaft lock bolt **(see illustration)**. Before removing the shaft, check the differential side gear shaft seal for evidence of leakage. Refer to Chapter 7 for the side gear shaft replacement procedure.

20   Remove the snap-ring from the bearing bracket and knock the center driveshaft out with a hammer and punch **(see illustrations)**.

21   Check the center driveshaft bearing for smooth operation. If it feels rough or sticky, it should be replaced. Take the assembly to a qualified repair shop, as special tools are needed to perform this job.

22   Installation is the reverse of the removal procedure.

12 Driveaxle boot replacement and CV joint overhaul

Refer to illustrations 12.2, 12.3, 12.5, 12.6, 12.7, 12.11, 12.12a, 12.12b and 12.14

Note: *If the CV joints exhibit signs of wear indicating need for an overhaul (usually due to torn boots), explore all options before beginning the job. Complete rebuilt driveaxles are available on an exchange basis, which eliminates much time and work. Whichever route you choose to take, check on the cost and availability of parts before disassembling your vehicle. See Chapter 8 Part B for the all-wheel drive boot replacement/CV joint overhaul procedure.*

1   Remove the driveaxle (refer to Section 10).

2   Paint a pair of match marks on the joint tulip and the driveaxle **(see illustration)**.

3   Pry the outer (larger) clamps loose with a small screwdriver **(see illustration)** and slide them off the ends of the driveaxle. Cut the inner (smaller) clamps and the damper clamp with a pair of diagonal cutters and discard them.

4   Separate the inboard joint tulip from the tripod joint.

5   Remove the tripod joint snap-ring with a pair of snap-ring pliers **(see illustration)**.

12.2 Paint (do not punch) match marks on the inboard joint tulip and the driveaxle

12.3 The large boot clamps can be pried open with a small screwdriver

12.5 Remove the snap-ring that retains the inboard joint tripod with a pair of snap-ring pliers

12.6 Use a centerpunch to place match marks (arrows) on the tripod and the driveaxle to ensure that they are reassembled properly

12.7 Drive the tripod joint from the driveaxle with a brass drift and hammer - be careful not to damage the bearing surfaces or the splines on the shaft

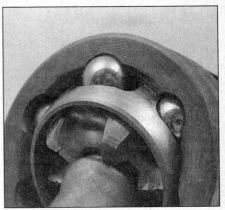

12.11 After the old grease has been rinsed away and the cleaning solvent has been blown out with compressed air, rotate the outboard joint through its full range of motion and inspect the bearing surfaces for wear or damage - if any of the balls, the race or the cage look damaged, replace the driveaxle/outboard joint assembly

12.12a To install the new clamps, bend the tang down and . . .

12.12b . . . tap the tabs over to hold it in place

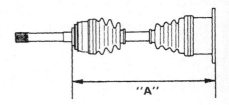

12.14 The driveaxle standard length (A) should be as specified

A   86 and earlier = 454 mm
      87 and later = 450 mm

6   Punch match marks on the tripod and the driveaxle **(see illustration)**.
7   Using a hammer and brass punch, drive the tripod joint from the driveaxle **(see illustration)**.
8   Slide the inboard joint boot and the outboard joint boot off the driveaxle.
9   Thoroughly wash the inboard and outboard CV joints in clean solvent and blow dry with compressed air, if available. **Note:** *Because the outboard joint cannot be disassembled, it is difficult to wash away all the old grease and to rid the bearing of solvent once it's clean. But it is imperative that the job be done thoroughly, so take your time and do it right.*
10   Inspect the inboard tripod joint for signs of wear or damage. If the tripod is obviously

worn or damaged, replace it, along with the tulip, as an assembly.
11   Bend the outboard CV joint housing at an angle to the driveaxle to expose the bearings, inner race and cage **(see illustration)**. Inspect the bearing surfaces for signs of wear. If the bearings are damaged or worn, replace the driveaxle.
12   Slide the new outboard boot onto the driveaxle. It's a good idea to wrap vinyl tape around the spline of the shaft to prevent damage to the boot. When the boot is in position, add the specified amount of grease (included in the boot replacement kit) to the outboard joint and the boot (pack the joint with as much grease as it will hold and put the rest into the boot). Slide the boot on the rest of the way and install the new clamps

(see illustrations).
13   Slide the inboard boot onto the driveaxle. Align the match marks you made before removing the joint and, using a brass bar and hammer, tap the tripod onto the driveaxle. Install the snap ring. Fill the inboard joint tulip with grease and install it over the tripod joint. Slide the boot into place and equalize the pressure inside the boot by inserting a small screwdriver between the boot and joint.
14   Measure the driveaxle standard length and make sure that the boot is not stretched, contracted or distorted in any way **(see illustration)**. Tighten the boot clamps.
15   Install the driveaxle (Section 10).

Notes

Chapter 8 Part B
All-wheel drive system

Contents

Specifications

Front driveaxle standard length	15.98 in (406 mm)
U-joint spider bearing play (max)	0.002 in (0.05 mm)

Torque specifications

	Ft-lbs
Intermediate driveshaft flange nut	
Initial torque	134
Final torque	51
Cross groove joint bolts	20
Driveshaft flange bolts	54
Center bearing bracket bolts	27
Differential mounting bolts	
Underside	70
Rear mount bolts	108

1   General information

This Chapter is devoted to the drivetrain components that are unique to the all-wheel drive models, with the exception of the transaxle/transfer case, which can be found in Chapter 7. Where similarities exist between all-wheel drive and front-wheel drive models, look for the appropriate Sections in Chapter 8 Part A.

In addition to the front driveaxles and related components, the all-wheel drive models employ a rear differential, a driveshaft which transmits power from the transfer case to the rear differential and two rear driveaxles that turn the rear wheels.

Although the front driveaxles on the all-wheel drive models perform in a similar manner to the driveaxles covered in Chapter 8 Part A, their constant velocity joints are of a different design. The inner joint is serviceable, but if a problem develops with the outer joint, it must be replaced along with the axleshaft. The driveaxle removal and installation procedure is very similar to that for front-wheel drive vehicles and can be found in Chapter 8 Part A, while the boot replacement and CV joint overhaul procedure can be found in this Chapter.

The rear driveaxles, as well as the rear CV joints, are similar in design to the driveaxles on the front-wheel drive models. All service procedures pertaining to the driveaxles on the front-wheel drive models also apply to the rear driveaxles on the all-wheel drive models.

2   Front driveaxle boot replacement and CV joint overhaul

Refer to illustrations 2.4, 2.6, 2.7, 2.9, 2.10, 2.11, 2.12a, 2.12b, 2.13, 2.15, 2.16, 2.17 and 2.21

Note: *If the CV joints exhibit signs of wear, indicating need for an overhaul (usually due to torn boots), explore all options before beginning the job. Complete rebuilt driveaxles are available on an exchange basis, which eliminates much time and work. Whichever route you choose to take, check on the availability of parts before disassembling your vehicle.*

1   Remove the driveaxle following the procedure described in Chapter 8, Part A. Be sure to contain the joint with the bolts and

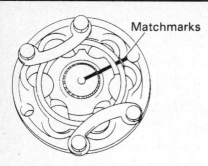

2.4 Apply match marks to the components of the CV joint to ensure correct reassembly - note how the washers have been turned around and the joint bolted together to prevent it from falling apart

washers as described in that Chapter, or the ball bearings will fall out.

2   Mount the driveaxle in a vise with wood-lined jaws (to prevent damage to the axleshaft). Check the CV joints for excessive play in the radial direction, which indicates worn parts. Check for smooth operation throughout the full range of motion of each CV joint. The inboard joint should slide smoothly in the

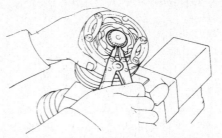

2.6 Remove the snap-ring with a pair of snap-ring pliers . . .

thrust direction (in and out). Check for damage to the boots - if a boot is torn, the recommended procedure is to disassemble the joint, clean the components and inspect them for damage due to loss of lubrication and the possible entrance of contaminants.

Inboard joint

3   Using a small screwdriver, pry the ends of the clamps up to loosen them **(see illustration 12.3 in Chapter 8 Part A)**.
4   Paint matchmarks on the end of the driveaxle, the inner race, the cage and the

outer race of the CV joint **(see illustration)**. Don't use a punch, as damage to the CV joint may occur.
5   Using a screwdriver and a hammer, knock the CV joint cover off the joint.
6   Using a pair of snap-ring pliers, remove the snap-ring from the end of the axleshaft **(see illustration)**.
7   Carefully drive the CV joint off the axleshaft with a brass bar and hammer **(see illustration)**. Strike the joint ONLY on the inner race, being careful not to damage the splines.
8   With the CV joint removed, the cover and the boot can now be removed from the axleshaft.
9   Tilt the inner race and cage assembly in the outer race and remove the balls one at a time. If the balls are difficult to remove, pry them out with a dull screwdriver, but don't scratch any of the components **(see illustration)**.
10   The inner race and cage can now be removed from the outer race by tilting them 90-degrees and aligning an opening in the cage with a land on the outer race **(see illustration)**.
11   Remove the inner race from the cage using the same technique **(see illustration)**.
12   Clean all of the components with solvent

2.7 . . . then carefully knock the joint off the shaft with a brass bar and hammer (be careful not to let the joint fall)

2.9 If necessary, pry the balls from the cage with a small screwdriver

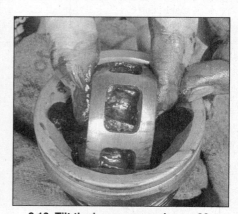

2.10 Tilt the inner race and cage 90-degrees, then align the windows in the cage with the lands and rotate the inner race up and out of the outer race

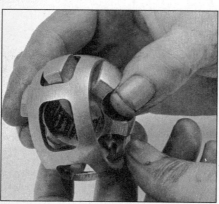

2.11 Align the inner race lands with the cage windows and rotate the inner race out of the cage

2.12a Check the inner race lands and grooves for score marks and pitting

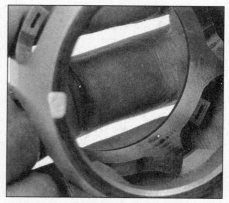

2.12b Check the cage for cracks, pitting and score marks (shiny spots are normal and don't affect operation)

2.13 Wrap the splined area of the axle with tape to prevent damage to the boot when installing it

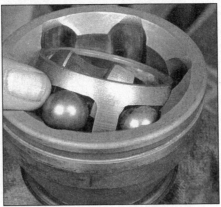

2.15 Align the cage windows and the inner and outer race grooves, then tilt the cage and inner race to insert the balls

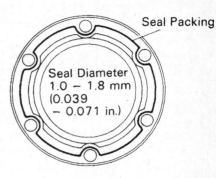

2.16 A bead of RTV sealer works well for sealing the joint cover. Install the cover while the sealer is still wet

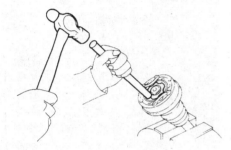

2.17 When tapping the joint back onto the axleshaft, apply force ONLY to the inner race

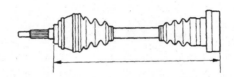

2.21 Before tightening the boot clamps, set the driveaxle to its standard length, listed in the Specifications

to remove all traces of grease. Check the cage and races for cracks, pitting, score marks and other signs of wear or damage (see illustrations). Shiny, polished spots are normal and will not adversely affect CV joint performance.

13 Wrap the axleshaft splines with tape to avoid damaging the boot (see illustration). Slide the small boot clamp on the axleshaft, followed by the axle boot and the large clamp. Remove the tape.

14 Assemble the inner race and cage then place them into the outer race by reversing the method used in Step 10. Make sure all of the match marks are aligned.

15 Tilt the inner race and cage to allow installation of the ball bearings. Press the balls into the cage windows one at a time (see illustration). When all of the balls are installed, lower the outer race and cage so the balls fit tightly within the inner race.

16 Apply a 1.0 mm bead of RTV sealant to the new inboard joint cover (see illustration). Align the bolt holes of the cover with the bolt holes of the CV joint and install the bolts. Using a plastic hammer, tap the cover onto the joint until it is fully seated.

17 Install the bolts, nuts and washers once again to contain the joint. Place the joint on

the axleshaft and tap it into position using a brass bar and hammer (see illustration).

18 Install the snap-ring in its groove on the end of the axleshaft. Make sure it is completely seated.

19 Using your fingers, thoroughly pack the joint with the grease supplied in the boot kit. Put the rest of the grease in the boot.

20 Slide the boot into position and install the large end onto the CV joint cover. The small end must be in the shaft groove. Don't tighten the clamps yet.

21 Adjust the driveaxle to the specified length by moving the inner joint in or out as necessary (see illustration), making sure the boot isn't stretched or compressed. With the driveaxle set to the proper length, relieve the pressure inside of the boot by inserting a small screwdriver between the boot and the outer race.

22 Tighten the boot clamps (see illustrations 12.12a and 12.12b in Chapter 8 Part A).

23 Install the driveaxle (Chapter 8 Part A).

Outboard joint

24 With the driveaxle removed from the vehicle, remove the inboard joint and boot following the above procedure. It will be nec-

essary to perform all of the Steps.

25 Follow the procedure described in Chapter 8 Part A, Section 12, Steps 9, 11 and 12 to clean, inspect, repack and reboot the outboard CV joint.

26 After the outboard joint is assembled, follow the above procedure and clean, repack and install the inboard joint.

27 Install the driveaxle (Chapter 8 Part A).

3 Driveline inspection

1 Raise the rear of the vehicle and support it securely on jackstands. Block the front wheels to prevent the vehicle from rolling.

2 Slide under the vehicle and visually inspect the condition of the driveshaft. Look for any dents or cracks in the tubing. If any are found, that particular portion of the driveshaft must be replaced.

3 Check for any oil leakage at the front and rear of the driveshaft. Leakage where the driveshaft enters the transaxle indicates a defective rear transaxle seal. Leakage where the driveshaft enters the differential indicates a defective pinion seal. For these repair operations refer to Chapters 7 Part B and 8 respectively.

4 While still under the vehicle, have an assistant turn the front wheel so the driveshaft will rotate. As it does, make sure that the universal joints are operating properly without binding, noise or looseness. Listen for any noise from the center bearings, indicating they are worn or damaged. Also check the rubber portion of the center bearings for cracking or separation, which will necessitate replacement.

5 The universal joints can also be checked with the driveshaft motionless, by gripping your hands on either side of the joint and attempting to twist the joint. Any movement at all in the joint is a sign of considerable wear. Lifting up on the shaft will also indicate movement in the universal joints. If the universal joints are worn, the portion of the driveshaft with the worn joint must be replaced.

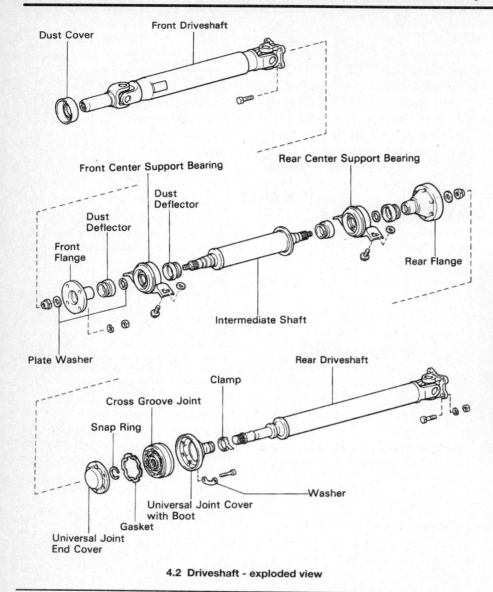

Dust Cover

Front Driveshaft

Front Center Support Bearing

Rear Center Support Bearing

Dust Deflector

Dust Deflector

Front Flange

Rear Flange

Plate Washer

Intermediate Shaft

Rear Driveshaft

Clamp

Cross Groove Joint

Snap Ring

Universal Joint Cover with Boot

Washer

Gasket

Universal Joint End Cover

4.2 Driveshaft - exploded view

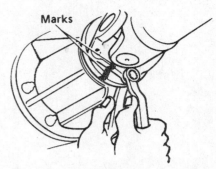

Marks

4.3 Place alignment marks on the two flanges, then remove the four bolts and nuts

4.4 A large socket, with the drive hole taped shut, can be used to prevent oil from leaking out of the transfer case

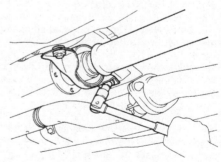

4.7 Unbolt the center support bearing bracket from the floor

6   Finally, check the driveshaft mounting bolts at the ends and intermediate shaft flanges to make sure they are tight.

4   Driveshaft - removal and installation

Refer to illustrations 4.2, 4.3, 4.4, 4.7 and 4.9

Removal

1   Raise the vehicle and support it securely on jackstands.
2   The driveshaft is comprised of three pieces: front shaft from the transfer case to the intermediate shaft; the intermediate shaft, which is supported by a front and rear center bearing; and a rear shaft from the intermediate shaft to the rear differential. The front shaft has a universal joint at either end, while the rear shaft has a universal joint at the rear

end and a constant velocity cross groove joint at the front **(see illustration)**.
3   Using white paint or a sharp scribe, place matchmarks on the front shaft U-joint flange to the intermediate shaft front flange, then remove the bolts **(see illustration)**. Separate the front shaft flange from the intermediate shaft front flange - a screwdriver or pry bar can be used to pry the two apart.
4   Pull the front driveshaft out of the transfer case. A large socket that fits snugly in the transfer case seal can be used to prevent lubricant leakage **(see illustration)**. Stick a piece of tape over the square drive hole in the socket.
5   Loosen, but do not remove the cross groove joint bolts using an Allen-head socket. Have an assistant depress the brake pedal to prevent the driveshaft from turning.
6   Apply matchmarks on the rear shaft flange to the differential companion flange. Remove the bolts, nuts and washers.

7   Remove the intermediate shaft front center support bearing mounting bolts **(see illustration)**.
8   While supporting the driveshaft with one hand so it doesn't fall, unbolt the rear center support bearing and lower the driveshaft. If the rear shaft flange sticks to the differential companion flange, pry the two apart with a screwdriver or pry bar.
9   Place matchmarks on the intermediate shaft rear flange to the outer race of the cross

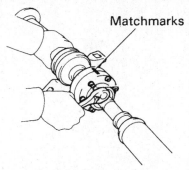

4.9 Use paint or a scribe to apply match marks to the cross groove joint and intermediate shaft flange - the use of a punch could damage the joint

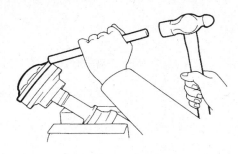

5.2 Carefully tap the end cover from the cross groove joint

5.3 Tap the inner cover off the joint with a hammer and screwdriver

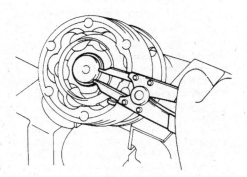

5.4 Remove the snap-ring from the end of the shaft with snap-ring pliers

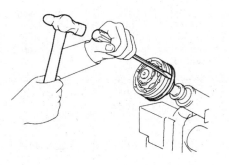

5.7 Tap the joint onto the driveshaft until it is seated - make sure the snap-ring groove is exposed

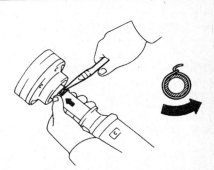

5.10 The cover boot clamp should be installed with the end of the clamp bent over against the direction of rotation of the driveshaft

groove joint, then remove the bolts **(see illustration)**. **Caution:** *Don't use a punch to apply the marks, as this could damage the cross groove joint.*

10   The spider bearings of the U-joints can now be inspected more thoroughly. Check for looseness of the joints, rough operation and/or sticking. If a joint is faulty, that portion of the driveshaft must be replaced, as the U-joints are not serviceable.

11   Inspect the cross groove joint for cracks, sticky or rough operation, grease leakage past the boot and other obvious damage, any of which will warrant replacement of the joint (the entire shaft doesn't have to be replaced). To replace the joint, see Section 5.

12   Check the center bearings for distorted rubber insulation, leaking seals and sloppy or rough bearing operation. If any of these conditions exist, replace the bearing following the procedure in Section 6.

Installation

13   Installation of the driveshaft is the reverse of the removal procedure. Be sure to align the matchmarks on the flanges and tighten the fasteners to the specified torque. Also, before tightening the center support bearing brackets, make sure they are at right angles to the driveshaft.

5   Cross groove joint - replacement

Refer to illustrations 5.2, 5.3, 5.4, 5.7 and 5.10

1   Remove the driveshaft from the vehicle as described in the preceding Section. Separate the rear driveshaft from the intermediate shaft.

2   Using a brass bar and a hammer, knock the joint end cover from the joint **(see illustration)**.

3   Using a hammer and screwdriver, knock the inner cover off the back of the joint **(see illustration)**.

4   Using a pair of snap-ring pliers, remove the snap-ring from the end of the shaft **(see illustration)**.

5   Tap the joint from the shaft using a brass bar and a hammer. Strike the joint only on the inner race, being extremely careful not to damage the driveshaft splines.

6   Loosen the clamp and slide the joint cover off the driveshaft.

7   To install the new joint, wrap the shaft splines with tape, place the rear cover and clamp on the shaft, then remove the tape. Apply a 1 mm bead of RTV sealer to the mating surface of the cover **(see illustration 2.16)**. Set the joint on the splined area of the

shaft and push it on as far as it will go. Using the brass bar and hammer, tap the joint onto the shaft completely, applying force to the inner race of the joint only **(see illustration)**.

8   Install the snap-ring to the end of the driveshaft, making sure it is completely seated in its groove.

9   Install two bolts through the top of the joint and through the cover to align the holes. Tap the cover onto the backside of the joint until it is completely seated. **Caution:** *Don't let the joint become separated - back it up with a block of wood or metal on the opposite side of the joint to take the shock.*

10   Install the cover boot clamp **(see illustration)**.

11   Using your fingers, thoroughly pack the joint with constant velocity joint grease. Install the new joint end cover and gasket, aligning it with two bolts. Tap it into place with a plastic faced hammer, if necessary, to keep it in place (it will be pressed on fully when the two shafts are joined and the bolts are tightened).

12   Assemble the rear driveshaft to the front driveshaft, tightening the bolts snugly.

13   Install the driveshaft (Section 4).

14   As an assistant depresses the brake pedal, tighten the cross groove joint bolts to the specified torque.

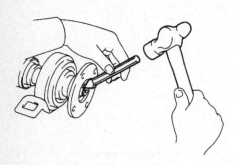

6.2 Use a hammer and chisel or punch to un-stake the nut

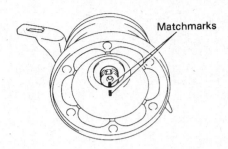

6.3 Place match marks from the driveshaft to the flange to insure correct realignment

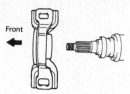
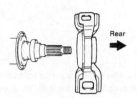

6.5 When installing either center support bearing, make sure it is installed in the correct direction

6   Center support bearing(s) - replacement

Refer to illustrations 6.2, 6.3 and 6.5
Note: *This procedure applies to the front or rear center support bearing.*
1   Remove the driveshaft following the procedure in Section 4. Separate the rear driveshaft from the intermediate shaft.
2   Using a hammer and chisel or punch, bend back the staked portion of the flange retaining nut **(see illustration)**. Remove the nut. To prevent the shaft from turning, thread two of the flange bolts back into the flange, wedge a screwdriver between them, then loosen the nut.
3   Place alignment marks on the flange and shaft **(see illustration)**, then slide the flange off the shaft. If it won't come off, use a two-jaw puller.
4   Slide the center support bearing off the shaft.
5   To install the center support bearing, slide it onto the shaft, making sure it is facing the correct direction **(see illustration)**, align the flange matchmarks and install the flange. Install a NEW nut and tighten it to the initial specified torque, using the method described in Step 2 to prevent the shaft from turning. If necessary, have an assistant to hold the shaft. Loosen the nut, then tighten it to the final specified torque. Using a hammer and

punch, stake the nut into the shaft groove.
6   Assemble the rear driveshaft to the intermediate shaft, making sure the matchmarks are aligned. Install the driveshaft as described in Section 4.

7   Rear differential carrier - removal and installation

Refer to illustrations 7.4, 7.7 and 7.8
1   Raise the rear of the vehicle and support it securely on jackstands. Block the front wheels to prevent it from rolling.
2   Drain the differential lubricant (Chapter 1).
3   Disconnect the driveaxles from the differential side gear shaft flanges (Chapter 8 Part A, Section 10) and hang the inner ends of the driveaxles out of the way with pieces of wire.
4   Remove the rear crossmember **(see illustration)**.
5   Mark the relationship of the driveshaft rear flange to the differential companion flange. Remove the driveshaft-to-differential companion flange bolts and nuts and disconnect the driveshaft from the differential. Support the driveshaft with a piece of wire - don't let it hang free, as this could damage the cross groove joint at the front of the rear driveshaft.
6   Support the differential carrier with a

floor jack.
7   Remove the two rear differential carrier mounting bolts **(see illustration)**.
8   Remove the four differential carrier mounting bolts and nuts from underneath the differential **(see illustration)**.
9   Carefully lower the differential to the ground.
10   Due to the complex nature, critical adjustments and special tools necessary to overhaul the differential assembly, it is recommended that the unit be taken to a qualified garage for repairs.
11   Installation is the reverse of the removal procedure. Be sure to tighten the mounting bolts to the specified torque and fill the differential with the recommended lubricant (Chapter 1).

8   Rear driveaxle boot replacement and CV joint overhaul

The rear driveaxles on all-wheel drive models are the same as the front driveaxles on front wheel drive models. Refer to Chapter 8, Part A, for the boot replacement and CV joint overhaul procedures. The removal and installation procedures are also the same as the procedures for the front driveaxles. See *General information* (Section 1) for additional information.

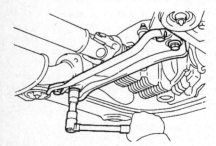

7.4 Unbolt the rear crossmember from the floor

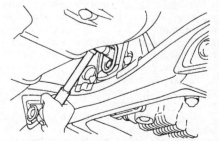

7.7 With the differential carrier supported by a floor jack, remove the two rear mounting bolts

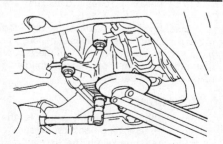

7.8 Make sure the differential carrier is balanced on the jack, then remove the bolts and nuts

Chapter 9 Brakes

Contents

Specifications

General

Brake fluid type	See Chapter 1
Brake pedal	
Pedal height - 1986 and earlier	7.36 to 7.75 in (187.0 to 197.0 mm)
Pedal height - 1987 and later	6.98 to 7.38 in (177.5 to 187.5 mm)
Pedal free play	0.12 to 0.24 in (3 to 6 mm)
Reserve distance (at 110 lbs, of force)	
1986 and earlier	3.54 in (90 mm) or more
1987 and later	3.35 in (85 mm) or more
Power brake booster pushrod-to-master cylinder piston clearance	0.0 in (0.0 mm)

Disc brakes

Minimum brake pad thickness	See Chapter 1
Front brake disc	
Standard thickness	
1987 and earlier	0.866 in (22.0 mm)
1988 and later	0.984 in (25.0 mm)
Minimum thickness*	
1987 and earlier	0.827 in (21.0 mm)
1988 and later	0.945 in (24.0 mm)
Front disc runout limit	
1987 and earlier	0.005 in (0.13 mm)
1988	0.003 in (0.08 mm)
Rear brake disc	
Standard thickness	0.394 in (10.0 mm)
Minimum thickness*	0.354 in (9.00 mm)
Rear disc runout limit	0.006 in (0.15 mm)

Refer to marks cast into the center of the disc (they supersede information printed here)

Drum brakes

Drum inside diameter	
Standard	
1986 and earlier	7.874 in (200.0 mm)
1987 and later	9.000 in (228.6 mm)
Maximum*	
1986 and earlier	7.913 in (201.0 mm)
1987 and later	9.079 in (230.6 mm)

Refer to marks cast into the drum (they supersede information printed here)

Torque specifications

	Ft-lbs (unless otherwise indicated)
Front disc brake caliper mounting bolts	
1986 and earlier	18
1987 and later	29
Front caliper torque plate-to-steering knuckle	
1986 and earlier	65
1987 and later	79
Rear disc brake caliper mounting bolts	14

Torque specifications (continued)   Ft-lbs (unless otherwise indicated)

Rear caliper torque plate-to-axle carrier.. 34
Brake hose-to-caliper union bolt 22
Wheel cylinder mounting bolts .... 84 in-lbs
Master cylinder-to-brake booster.. 108 in-lbs
Power brake booster mounting nuts .... 108 in-lbs
Wheel lug nuts 75

1   General information

The vehicles covered by this manual are equipped with hydraulically operated front and rear brake systems. The front brakes are disc type and the rear brakes are either drum or disc type. Both the front and rear brakes are self adjusting. The disc brakes automatically compensate for pad wear, while the drum brakes incorporate an adjustment mechanism which is activated as the parking brake is applied.

Hydraulic system

The hydraulic system consists of two separate circuits. The master cylinder has separate reservoirs for the two circuits and in the event of a leak or failure in one hydraulic circuit, the other circuit will remain operative. A load sensing proportioning valve (LSPV) regulates pressure to the rear brakes to prevent them from locking up under heavy braking conditions. Some later models are equipped with an anti-lock braking system (ABS).

Power brake booster

The power brake booster, utilizing engine manifold vacuum and atmospheric pressure to provide assistance to the hydraulically operated brakes, is mounted on the firewall in the engine compartment.

Parking brake

The parking brake operates the rear brakes only, through cable actuation. It's activated by a lever mounted in the center console.

Service

After completing any operation involving disassembly of any part of the brake system, always test drive the vehicle to check for proper braking performance before resuming normal driving. When testing the brakes, perform the tests on a clean, dry flat surface. Conditions other than these can lead to inaccurate test results.

Test the brakes at various speeds with both light and heavy pedal pressure. The vehicle should stop evenly without pulling to one side or the other. Avoid locking the brakes, because this slides the tires and diminishes braking efficiency and control of the vehicle.

Tires, vehicle load and front-end alignment are factors which also affect braking performance.

2   Anti-lock brake system (ABS) - general information

The anti-lock brake system was introduced in 1987 and is designed to maintain vehicle steerability, directional stability and optimum deceleration under severe braking conditions and on most road surfaces. It does so by monitoring the rotational speed of each wheel and controlling the brake line pressure to each wheel during braking. This prevents the wheel from lock up.

Components

Refer to illustrations 2.1 and 2.2

Actuator assembly

The actuator assembly consists of the master cylinder, an electric hydraulic pump and four solenoid valves **(see illustrations)**.

a) *The electric pump provides hydraulic pressure to charge the reservoirs in the actuator, which supply pressure to the braking system. The pump and reservoirs are housed in the actuator assembly.*
b) *The solenoid valves modulate brake line pressure during ABS operation. The valve body contains four valves - one for each wheel.*

Speed sensors

Refer to illustrations 2.3 and 2.4

These sensors are located at each wheel and generate small electrical pulsations when the toothed sensor rings are turning, sending a signal to the electronic controller indicating wheel rotational speed.

The front wheel sensors **(see illustration)** are mounted to the front spindles in close relationship to the toothed sensor rings, which are integral with the front hub assemblies.

The rear wheel sensors are bolted to the brake backing plates **(see illustration)**. The sensor rings are integral with the rear hub assemblies.

ABS computer

The ABS computer is mounted in the luggage compartment and is the "brain" for the ABS system. The function of the computer is to accept and process information received from the wheel speed sensors to control the hydraulic line pressure, avoiding wheel lock up. The computer also constantly monitors the system, even under normal driving conditions, to find faults within the system.

If a problem develops within the system, an "ANTILOCK" light will glow on the dashboard. A diagnostic code will also be stored in the computer, which, when retrieved by a service technician, will indicate the problem area or component.

Diagnosis and repair

If a dashboard warning light comes on and stays on while the vehicle is in operation, the ABS system requires attention. Although

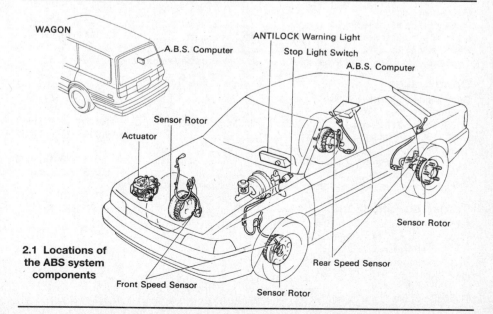

2.1 Locations of the ABS system components

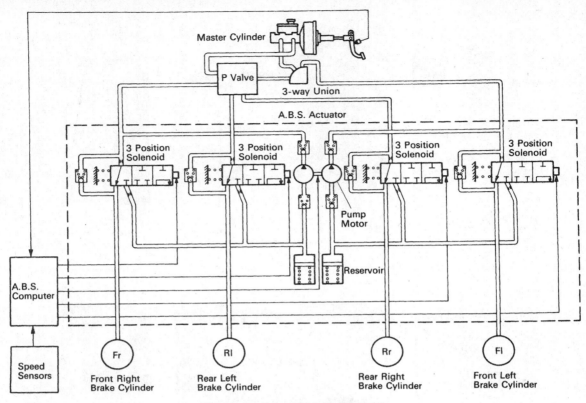

2.2 Schematic of the ABS hydraulic system

a special electronic ABS diagnostic tester is necessary to properly diagnose the system, the home mechanic can perform a few preliminary checks before taking the vehicle to a dealer service department which is equipped with this tester.

a) Check the brake fluid level in the reservoir.
b) Check that the computer master cylinder connectors are securely connected.
c) Check the electrical connectors at the actuator assembly.

d) Check the fuses.
e) Follow the wiring harness to each wheel and check that all connections are secure and that the wiring is not damaged.

If the above preliminary checks do not rectify the problem, the vehicle should be diagnosed by a dealer service department. Due to the complex nature of this system, all actual repair work must be done by a dealer service department.

3 Disc brake pads - replacement

Refer to illustrations 3.5 and 3.6a through 3.6h

Warning: *Disc brake pads must be replaced on both front or rear wheels at the same time - never replace the pads on only one wheel. Also, the dust created by the brake system may contain asbestos, which is harmful to your health. Never blow it out with compressed air and don't inhale any of it. An*

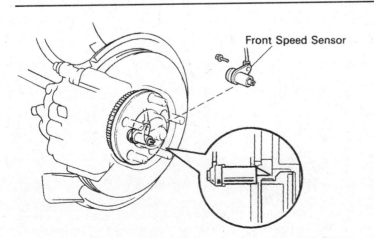

2.3 The front speed sensors bolt to the front brake backing plates

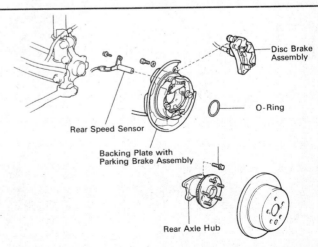

2.4 The rear brake sensors bolt to the rear brake backing plates

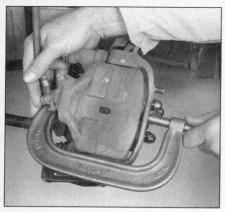

3.5 Using a large C-clamp, push the piston back into the caliper bore - note that one end of the clamp is on the flat area near the brake hose fitting and the other end (screw end) is pressing against the outer brake pad

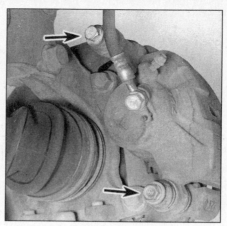

3.6a Remove the two caliper mounting bolts (arrows)

3.6b Pull the caliper straight up and off the disc

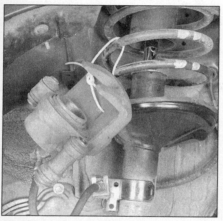

3.6c Once the caliper is removed from the torque plate, hang it from the coil spring with a piece of wire - DON'T let it hang by the brake hose!

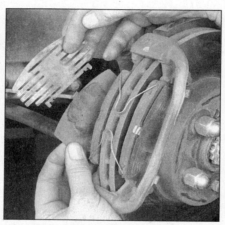

3.6d Remove the anti-squeal shims from the pads (note how they are positioned - some models have only one shim per pad, others utilize two on the inner pad and one on the outer pad)

3.6e Remove the anti-rattle springs from the brake pads

3.6f To remove the pads, slide them to the side then straight out of the torque plate

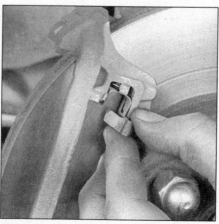

3.6g Remove the pad support plates from the torque plate - they should be replaced with new ones if distorted in any way

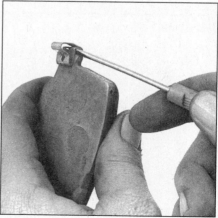

3.6h Pry the wear indicators off the brake pads and transfer them to the new pads - if they are worn or bent, replace them (the remainder of the brake pad replacement procedure is the reverse of removal)

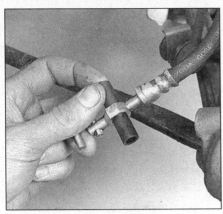

4.1 Using a piece of rubber hose of the appropriate size, plug the brake line

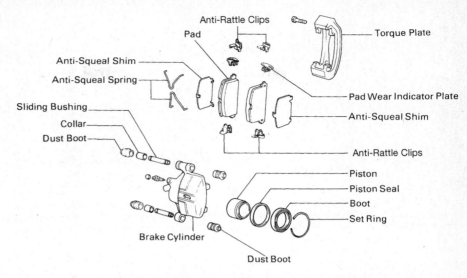

4.4a Exploded view of the caliper assembly

Labels in diagram:
Anti-Rattle Clips
Pad
Anti-Squeal Shim
Anti-Squeal Spring
Sliding Bushing
Collar
Dust Boot
Brake Cylinder
Dust Boot
Torque Plate
Pad Wear Indicator Plate
Anti-Squeal Shim
Anti-Rattle Clips
Piston
Piston Seal
Boot
Set Ring

approved filtering mask should be worn when working on the brakes. Do not, under any circumstances, use petroleum-based solvents to clean brake parts. Use brake cleaner or denatured alcohol only! When servicing the disc brakes, use only high quality, nationally recognized brand-name pads.
Note: *This procedure applies to both the front and rear disc brakes.*

1   Remove the cap from the brake fluid reservoir.

2   Loosen the wheel lug nuts, raise the front of the vehicle and support it securely on jackstands.

3   Remove the front wheels. Work on one brake assembly at a time, using the assembled brake for reference if necessary.

4   Inspect the brake disc carefully as outlined in Section 5. If machining is necessary, follow the information in that Section to remove the disc, at which time the pads can be removed from the calipers as well.

5   Push the piston back into its bore to provide room for the new brake pads. A C-clamp can be used to accomplish this **(see illustration)**. As the piston is depressed to the bottom of the caliper bore, the fluid in the master cylinder will rise. Make sure that it doesn't overflow. If necessary, siphon off some of the fluid.

4.4b Using a screwdriver, remove the cylinder boot set ring

6   Follow the accompanying photos, beginning with **illustration 3.6a**, for the actual pad replacement procedure. Be sure to stay in order and read the caption under each illustration.

7   When reinstalling the caliper, be sure to tighten the mounting bolts to the specified torque. After the job has been completed, firmly depress the brake pedal a few times to bring the pads into contact with the disc. Check the level of the brake fluid, adding some if necessary. Check the operation of the brakes carefully before placing the vehicle into normal service.

---

4   Disc brake caliper - removal, overhaul and installation

Refer to illustrations 4.1, 4.4a, 4.4b, 4.5, 4.7, 4.8a and 4.8b
Warning: *Dust created by the brake system may contain asbestos, which is harmful to your health. Never blow it out with compressed air and don't inhale any of it. An approved filtering mask should be worn when working on the brakes. Do not, under any circumstances, use petroleum-based solvents to clean brake parts. Use brake cleaner or denatured alcohol only!*
Note: *If an overhaul is indicated (usually because of fluid leakage) explore all options before beginning the job. New and factory rebuilt calipers are available on an exchange basis, which makes this job quite easy. If it's decided to rebuild the calipers, make sure that a rebuild kit is available before proceeding. Always rebuild the calipers in pairs - never rebuild just one of them.*

Removal

1   Disconnect the brake line from the caliper and plug it to keep contaminants out of the brake system and to prevent losing any

more brake fluid than is necessary **(see illustration)**.

2   Refer to Section 3 for either front or rear caliper removal procedures- it's part of the brake pad replacement procedure.

3   On the rear caliper, disconnect the parking brake by removing the clevis pin and the C-clip (see Section 13), then slide the caliper off the caliper guide pin.

Overhaul

4   To overhaul the caliper, remove the rubber boot retaining ring and the rubber boot **(see illustrations)**. Before you remove the piston, place a wood block between the piston and caliper to prevent damage as it is removed.

5   To remove the piston from the caliper, apply compressed air to the brake fluid hose connection on the caliper body **(see illustration)**. Use only enough pressure to ease the piston out of its bore. **Warning:** *Be careful not to place your fingers between the piston*

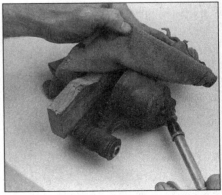

4.5 With the caliper padded to catch the piston, use compressed air to force the piston out of its bore. Make sure your hands or fingers are not between the piston and caliper

4.7   The piston seal should be removed with a plastic or wooden tool to avoid damage to the bore and seal groove. A pencil will do the job

4.8a On each side of the caliper, push the sliding bushing up through the boot and pull it free, then remove the dust boots

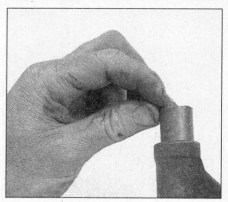

4.8b Push the bushing sleeve out of the caliper

and the caliper as the piston may come out with some force.

6   Inspect the mating surfaces of the piston and caliper bore wall. If there is any scoring, rust, pitting or bright areas, replace the complete caliper unit with a new one.

7   If these components are in good condition, remove the rubber seal from the caliper bore using a wooden or plastic tool **(see illustration)**. Metal tools may damage the cylinder bore.

8   Push the sliding bushings out of the caliper ears **(see illustration)** and remove the rubber boots from both ends. Slide the bushing sleeves out of the caliper ears **(see illustration)**.

9   Wash all the components in clean brake fluid or alcohol.

10   To reassemble the caliper, you should already have the correct rebuild kit for your vehicle. **Note:** *During reassembly apply silicone based grease (supplied with the rebuild kit) between the sliding bushing and the bushing sleeve.*

11   Submerge the new rubber seal and the piston in brake fluid and install them into the caliper bore. Do not force the piston into the bore, but make sure that it is squarely in

place, then apply firm (but not excessive) pressure to install it.

12   Install the new rubber boot and retaining ring.

13   Lubricate the sliding bushings and sleeves with silicone-based grease (supplied in the kit) and push them into the caliper ears. Install the dust boots.

Installation

14   Install the caliper by reversing the removal procedure. Remember to replace the copper sealing washer on the brake line union bolt (comes with the rebuild kit).

15   Bleed the brake circuit according to the procedure in Section 11.

---

5   Brake disc - inspection, removal and installation

Note: *This procedure applies to both the front and rear brake discs (on vehicles so equipped).*

Inspection

Refer to illustrations 5.2, 5.3, 5.4a, 5.4b, 5.5a and 5.5b

1   Loosen the wheel lug nuts, raise the

vehicle and support it securely on jackstands. Remove the wheel and install three lug nuts to hold the disc in place. If the rear brake disc is being worked on, release the parking brake.

2   Remove the brake caliper as outlined in Section 4. It is not necessary to disconnect the brake hose. After removing the caliper bolts, suspend the caliper out of the way with a piece of wire **(see illustration 3.6c)**. Remove the two torque plate-to-steering knuckle bolts **(see illustration)** and remove the torque plate.

3   Visually inspect the disc surface for scoring or damage. Light scratches and shallow grooves are normal after use and may not always be detrimental to brake operation, but deep scoring - over 0.015 inch (0.38 mm) - requires disc removal and refinishing by an automotive machine shop. Be sure to check both sides of the disc **(see illustration)**. If pulsating has been noticed during application of the brakes, suspect disc runout.

4   To check disc runout, place a dial indicator at a point about 1/2-inch from the outer edge of the disc **(see illustration)**. Set the indicator to zero and turn the disc. The indicator reading should not exceed the specified allowable runout limit. If it does, the disc should be refinished by an automotive

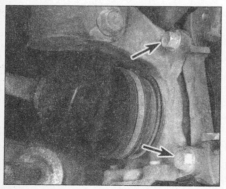

5.2 The torque plate (caliper mounting bracket) is secured to the steering knuckle with two bolts (arrows)

5.3 The brake pads on this vehicle were obviously neglected, as they wore down to the rivets and cut deep grooves into the disc - wear this severe will require replacement of the disc

5.4a Use a dial indicator to check disc runout - if the reading exceeds the maximum allowable runout limit, the disc will have to be machined or replaced

5.4b Using a swirling motion, remove the glaze from the disc surface with sandpaper or emery cloth

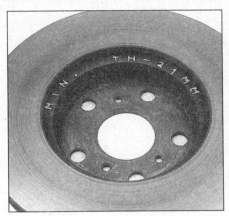

5.5a The minimum wear dimension is cast into the backside of the disc

5.5b Use a micrometer to measure disc thickness

machine shop. **Note:** *It is recommended that the discs be resurfaced regardless of the dial indicator reading, as this will impart a smooth finish and ensure a perfectly flat surface, eliminating any brake pedal pulsation or other undesirable symptoms related to questionable discs. At the very least, if you elect not to have the discs resurfaced, remove the glazing from the surface with emery cloth or sandpaper using a swirling motion* **(see illustration)**.
5   It is absolutely critical that the disc not be machined to a thickness under the specified minimum allowable disc refinish thickness. The minimum wear (or discard) thickness is cast into the inside of the disc **(see illustration)**. The disc thickness can be checked with a micrometer **(see illustration)**.

Removal

Refer to illustration 5.6
6   Remove the three lug nuts which were put on to hold the disc in place and remove the disc from the hub. If the disc is stuck to the hub and won't come off, thread three bolts into the holes provided **(see illustration)** and tighten them. Alternate between the

bolts, turning them a couple of turns at a time, until the disc is free.

Installation

7   Place the disc in position over the threaded studs.
8   Install the torque plate and caliper assembly over the disc and position it on the steering knuckle. Tighten the torque plate bolts to the specified torque.
9   Install the wheel, then lower the vehicle to the ground. Depress the brake pedal a few times to bring the brake pads into contact with the disc. Bleeding of the system will not be necessary unless the fluid hose was disconnected from the caliper. Check the operation of the brakes carefully before placing the vehicle into normal service.

6   Drum brake shoes - replacement

Refer to illustrations 6.4a through 6.4y and 6.5
Warning: *Drum brake shoes must be replaced on both wheels at the same time - never replace the shoes on only one wheel.*

Also, the dust created by the brake system may contain asbestos, which is harmful to your health. Never blow it out with compressed air and don't inhale any of it. An approved filtering mask should be worn when working on the brakes. Do not, under any circumstances, use petroleum-based solvents to clean brake parts. Use brake cleaner or denatured alcohol only!
Caution: *Whenever the brake shoes are replaced, the retractor and hold-down springs should also be replaced. Due to the continuous heating/cooling cycle that the springs are subjected to, they lose their tension over a period of time and may allow the shoes to drag on the drum and wear at a much faster rate than normal. When replacing the rear brake shoes, use only high quality nationally recognized brand-name parts.*
1   Loosen the wheel lug nuts, raise the rear of the vehicle and support it securely on jackstands. Block the front wheels to keep the vehicle from rolling.
2   Release the parking brake.
3   Remove the wheel. **Note:** *All four rear brake shoes must be replaced at the same time, but to avoid mixing up parts, work on only one brake assembly at a time.*
4   Follow the accompanying illustrations **(6.4a through 6.4y)** for the brake shoe replacement procedure. Be sure to stay in

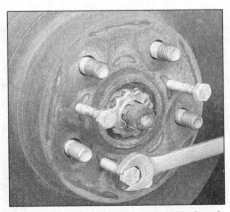

5.6 To help free the disc, thread bolts of the appropriate size into the three holes provided in the disc. Alternate between the bolts, turning them a little at a time, until the disc is free

6.4a Mark the relationship of the drum to the hub, so the adjuster hole in the drum will line up with the large hole in the hub upon installation

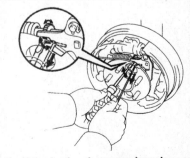

6.4b If the brake shoes are hanging up on the drum (because of excessive wear), pull the adjuster lever off the star wheel and turn the star wheel in the correct direction to retract the brake shoes

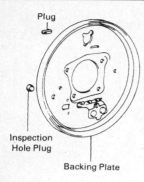

6.4c   Exploded view of the drum brake assembly

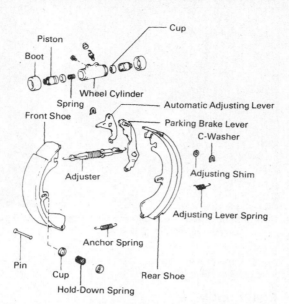

6.4d   Before removing anything, clean the brake assembly with brake cleaner and allow it to dry - position a drain pan under the brake to catch the fluid and residue - DO NOT USE COMPRESSED AIR TO BLOW THE DUST FROM THE PARTS!

6.4e   Unhook the return spring from the front brake shoe. A pair of locking pliers can be used to stretch the spring and pull the end out of the hole in the shoe

6.4f   Push the hold-down retainer (cup) down, turn it 90 degrees and release it. A pair of pliers will work, but this special hold-down spring remover tool makes this much easier. They are available at most auto parts stores and aren't very expensive

6.4g   Remove the front shoe from the backing plate and unhook the anchor spring from the end of the shoe

6.4h   Remove the hold-down spring from the rear shoe

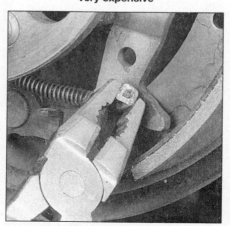

6.4i   Hold the end of the parking brake cable with a pair of pliers and pull it out of the parking brake lever

6.4j   Remove the rear shoe and adjuster assembly from the backing plate

6.4k Unhook the return spring from the shoe and slide the adjuster and spring off

6.4l Remove the adjusting lever spring

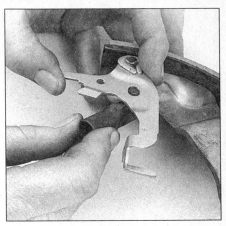

6.4m Remove the adjuster end from the automatic adjusting lever by rotating it out of the hole

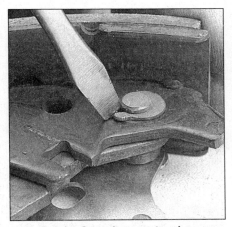

6.4n Pry the C-washer apart and remove it to separate the parking brake lever and adjusting lever from the rear shoe

6.4o Assemble the parking brake lever and adjuster lever to the new rear shoe and crimp the C-washer closed with a pair of pliers

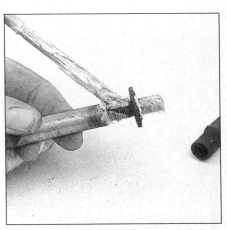

6.4p Lubricate the moving parts of the adjuster screw with a light coat of high-temperature grease

6.4q Install the adjuster assembly to the rear shoe, making sure the end fits properly into the slot of the shoe. Hook the spring into the opening in the shoe

6.4r Install the adjusting lever spring

6.4s Lubricate the brake shoe contact area with high-temperature grease

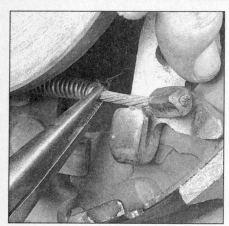

6.4t Pull the parking brake cable spring back and hold it there with a pair of pliers, then place the cable into the hooked end of the parking brake lever

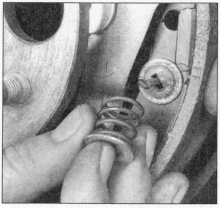

6.4u Place the rear shoe assembly against the backing plate and push the hold-down spring pin through the shoe. Install the cups (one on each side of the spring) and lock the outer cup to the pin by turning it 90 degrees after the spring has been compressed

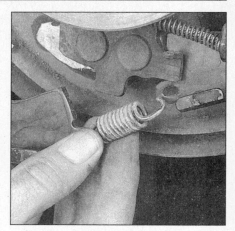

6.4v Connect the anchor spring to the bottom of each shoe and mount the front shoe to the backing plate. Install the hold-down spring and cups

6.4w Using a screwdriver, stretch the return spring into its hole in the front shoe

6.4x Pry the parking brake forward and check to see that the return spring didn't come unhooked from the rear shoe

6.4y Wiggle the assembly to make sure it is seated properly against the backing plate

order and read the caption under each illustration. **Note:** *If the brake drum cannot be easily pulled off the axle and shoe assembly, make sure that the parking brake is completely released, then squirt some penetrating oil around the center hub area. Allow the oil to soak in and install two bolts of the proper size and thread pitch into the threaded holes in the drum. Tighten the bolts a little at a time, alternating between them, until the drum is free. If the drum still cannot be pulled off, the brake shoes will have to be retracted. This is accomplished by first removing the plug from the drum. With the plug removed, pull the lever off the adjusting star wheel with a hooked tool while turning the adjusting wheel with a screwdriver, moving the shoes away from the drum* **(see illustration 6.4b)**. *The drum should now come off.*

5　Before reinstalling the drum it should be checked for cracks, score marks, deep scratches and hard spots, which will appear as small discolored areas. If the hard spots cannot be removed with fine emery cloth or if

any of the other conditions listed above exist, the drum must be taken to an automotive machine shop to have it turned. **Note:** *Professionals recommend resurfacing the drums whenever a brake job is done. Resurfacing will eliminate the possibility of out-of-round drums. If the drums are worn so much that they can't be resurfaced without exceeding the maximum allowable diameter (stamped into the drum), then new ones will be required* **(see illustration)**. At the very least, if you elect not to have the drums resurfaced, remove the glazing from the surface with emery cloth or sandpaper using a swirling motion.

6　Install the brake drum on the axle flange.

7　Mount the wheel, install the lug nuts, then lower the vehicle.

8　Make a number of forward and reverse stops to adjust the brakes until satisfactory pedal action is obtained.

9　Check the operation of the brakes carefully before placing the vehicle into normal service.

6.5 The maximum drum diameter is cast into the inside of the rear drums

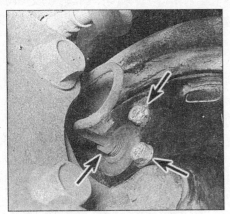

7.4 Disconnect the brake line fitting, (arrow) then remove the two wheel cylinder bolts (arrows)

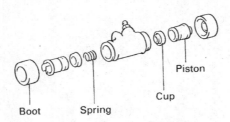

7.7 Exploded view of the wheel cylinder

Boot   Spring   Cup   Piston

8.4 Completely loosen the primary brake line fitting at the three-way union (arrow)

7 Wheel cylinder - removal, overhaul and installation

Note: *If an overhaul is indicated (usually because of fluid leakage or sticky operation) explore all options before beginning the job. New wheel cylinders are available, which makes this job quite easy. If it's decided to rebuild the wheel cylinder, make sure that a rebuild kit is available before proceeding. Never overhaul only one wheel cylinder- always rebuild both of them at the same time.*

Removal

Refer to illustration 7.4

1   Raise the rear of the vehicle and support it securely on jackstands. Block the front wheels to keep the vehicle from rolling.
2   Remove the brake shoe assembly (Section 6).
3   Remove all dirt and foreign material from around the wheel cylinder.
4   Disconnect the brake line with a flare-nut wrench, if available **(see illustration)**. Don't pull the brake line away from the wheel cylinder.
5   Remove the wheel cylinder mounting bolts.
6   Detach the wheel cylinder from the brake backing plate and place it on a clean workbench. Immediately plug the brake line to prevent fluid loss and contamination.

Overhaul

Refer to illustration 7.7

7   Remove the bleeder screw, cups, pistons, boots and spring assembly from the wheel cylinder body **(see illustration)**.
8   Clean the wheel cylinder with brake fluid, denatured alcohol or brake system cleaner. **Warning:** *Do not, under any circumstances, use petroleum-based solvents to clean brake parts!*
9   Use compressed air to remove excess fluid from the wheel cylinder and to blow out the passages.
10   Check the cylinder bore for corrosion and score marks. Crocus cloth can be used

to remove light corrosion and stains, but the cylinder must be replaced with a new one if the defects cannot be removed easily, or if the bore is scored.
11   Lubricate the new cups with brake fluid.
12   Assemble the brake cylinder components **(see illustration 7.7)**. Make sure the cup lips face in.

Installation

13   Place the wheel cylinder in position and install the bolts.
14   Connect the brake line and install the brake shoe assembly.
15   Bleed the brakes (Section 11).
16   Check the operation of the brakes carefully before placing the vehicle into normal service.

8 Master cylinder - removal, overhaul and installation

Note: *Before deciding to overhaul the master cylinder, check on the availability and cost of a new or factory rebuilt unit and also the availability of a rebuild kit.*

Removal

Refer to illustrations 8.4 and 8.6

1   The master cylinder is located in the engine compartment, mounted to the power

brake booster.
2   Remove as much fluid as you can from the reservoir with a syringe.
3   Place rags under the fluid fittings and prepare caps or plastic bags to cover the ends of the lines once they are disconnected. **Caution:** *Brake fluid will damage paint. Cover all body parts and be careful not to spill fluid during this procedure.*
4   Loosen the tube nuts at the ends of the brake lines where they enter the master cylinder. To prevent rounding off the flats on these nuts, the use of a flare nut wrench, which wraps around the nut, is preferred. Also unscrew the primary brake line tube nut at the three-way union **(see illustration)**.
5   Pull the brake lines slightly away from the master cylinder and plug the ends to prevent contamination.
6   Disconnect the electrical connector at the master cylinder, then remove the three nuts attaching the master cylinder to the power booster **(see illustration)**. Pull the master cylinder off the studs and out of the engine compartment. Again, be careful not to spill the fluid as this is done.

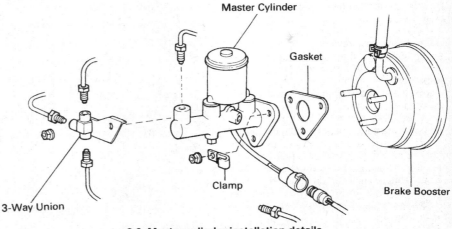

Master Cylinder

Gasket

3-Way Union

Clamp

Brake Booster

8.6 Master cylinder installation details

8.8a The brake fluid reservoir is retained by a set screw

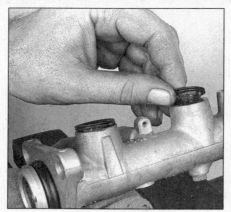

8.8b After the reservoir has been removed, pull the grommets from the cylinder body. If they are hardened, damaged or appear to have been leaking, replace them

8.9 Using a Phillips screwdriver, depress the pistons then remove the stop bolt. Be sure to replace the copper washer on the stop bolt when reassembling

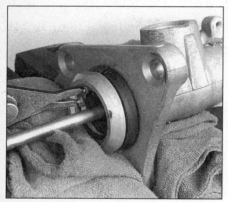

8.10 Depress the pistons again and remove the snap-ring with a pair of snap-ring pliers

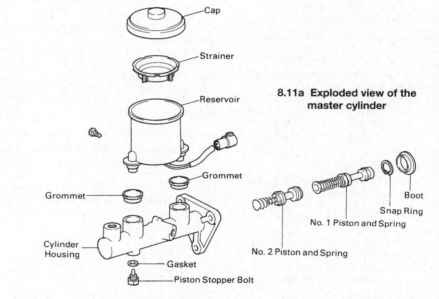

8.11a Exploded view of the master cylinder

Cap — Strainer — Reservoir — Grommet — Grommet — Cylinder Housing — Gasket — Piston Stopper Bolt — Boot — Snap Ring — No. 1 Piston and Spring — No. 2 Piston and Spring

Overhaul

Refer to illustrations 8.8a, 8.8b, 8.9, 8.10, 8.11a, 8.11b, 8.11c and 8.14

7   Before attempting the overhaul of the master cylinder, obtain the proper rebuild kit, which will contain the necessary replacement parts and also any instructions which may be specific to your model.

8   Remove the reservoir set screw, pull off the reservoir and remove the grommets **(see illustrations)**.

9   Place the cylinder in a vise and use a punch or Phillips screwdriver to fully depress the pistons until they bottom against the other end of the master cylinder **(see illustration)**. Hold the pistons in this position and remove the stop bolt on the side of the master cylinder.

10   Carefully remove the snap-ring at the end of the master cylinder **(see illustration)**.

11   The internal components can now be removed from the cylinder bore **(see illustrations)**. Make a note of the proper order of the components so they can be returned to their original locations. **Note:** *The two springs are of different tension, so pay particular attention to their order.*

12   Carefully inspect the bore of the master cylinder. Any deep scoring or other damage will mean a new master cylinder is required.

8.11b After the snap-ring has been removed, the primary piston assembly can be removed

8.11c Remove the cylinder from the vise and tap it against a block of wood until the secondary piston is exposed. Pull the piston assembly STRAIGHT out - if it becomes even slightly cocked, the bore may be damaged

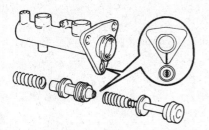 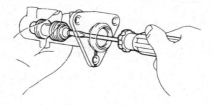

8.14 The secondary piston on an ABS equipped vehicle has a slot in the end of it - when installed, it must be aligned with the groove on the cylinder mounting flange. Be careful not to scratch the bore

8.27 Have an assistant pump the brake pedal several times, then hold it to the floorboard. Loosen the fitting nut, allowing the air and fluid to escape. Repeat this procedure on both fittings until the fluid is clear of air bubbles

DO NOT attempt to hone the master cylinder.

13   Replace all parts included in the rebuild kit, following any instructions in the kit. Clean all reused parts with clean brake fluid, brake parts cleaner or denatured alcohol. Do not use any petroleum-based cleaners. During assembly, lubricate all parts liberally with clean brake fluid. Be sure to tighten all fittings and connections to the specified torque.

14   Push the assembled components into the bore, bottoming them against the end of the master cylinder, then install the stop bolt. **Note:** *If the vehicle is equipped with ABS, align the slot in the secondary piston with the groove on the cylinder mounting flange* **(see illustration)**. *A screwdriver can be used, but be careful not to scratch the bore.*

15   Install the new snap-ring, making sure it is seated properly in the groove.

16   Install the reservoir grommets, reservoir and set screw.

17   Before installing the new master cylinder it should be bench bled. Because it will be necessary to apply pressure to the master cylinder piston and, at the same time, control flow from the brake line outlets, it is recommended that the master cylinder be mounted in a vise, with the jaws of the vise clamping on the mounting flange.

18   Insert threaded plugs into the brake line outlet holes and snug them down so that there will be no air leakage past them, but not

so tight that they cannot be easily loosened.

19   Fill the reservoir with brake fluid of the recommended type (see Chapter 1).

20   Remove one plug and push the piston assembly into the master cylinder bore to expel the air from the master cylinder. A large Phillips screwdriver can be used to push on the piston assembly.

21   To prevent air from being drawn back into the master cylinder, the plug must be replaced and snugged down before releasing the pressure on the piston assembly.

22   Repeat the procedure until only brake fluid is expelled from the brake line outlet hole. When only brake fluid is expelled, repeat the procedure with the other outlet hole and plug. Be sure to keep the master cylinder reservoir filled with brake fluid to prevent the introduction of air into the system.

23   Since high pressure is not involved in the bench bleeding procedure, an alternative to the removal and replacement of the plugs with each stroke of the piston assembly is available. Before pushing in on the piston assembly, remove the plug as described in Step 20. Before releasing the piston, however, instead of replacing the plug, simply put your finger tightly over the hole to keep air from being drawn back into the master cylinder. Wait several seconds for brake fluid to be drawn from the reservoir into the piston bore, then depress the piston again, removing your finger as brake fluid is expelled. Be sure to put your finger back over the hole each time before releasing the piston, and when the bleeding procedure is complete for that outlet, replace the plug and snug it before going on to the other port.

Installation

Refer to illustration 8.27

24   Install the master cylinder over the studs on the power brake booster and tighten the attaching nuts only finger tight at this time.

25   Thread the brake line fittings into the master cylinder and the junction block. Since the master cylinder is still a bit loose, it can be moved slightly in order for the fittings to thread in easily. Do not strip the threads as the fittings are tightened.

26   Fully tighten the mounting nuts and the brake fittings.

27   Fill the master cylinder reservoir with fluid, then bleed the master cylinder (only if

the cylinder has not been bench bled) and the brake system as described in Section 11. To bleed the cylinder on the vehicle, have an assistant pump the brake pedal several times and then hold the pedal to the floor. Loosen the fitting nut to allow air and fluid to escape. Repeat this procedure on both fittings until the fluid is clear of air bubbles **(see illustration)**. Test the operation of the brake system carefully before placing the vehicle in normal service.

---

9   Load Sensing Proportioning Valve (LSPV) - general information

Note: *This applies to wagon models only.*

1   Due to the fact that disc brakes are non-self-energizing, they require more hydraulic pressure than drum brakes to function properly. Added to the fact that, conversely, drum brakes require less hydraulic pressure to be efficient in an automotive system is the fact that they are usually fitted to the rear of vehicles, requiring even less pressure than the front discs because most of the vehicle's weight is transferred forward during braking.

2   If the hydraulic pressure were the same to the front and rear brakes, the rear drums would be locked up almost every time the brakes were applied with force. The load sensing proportioning valve (LSPV) allows a portion of the rear brake hydraulic pressure to be applied to the front brakes, thus providing for smoother, more controlled stops.

3   Due to the special tools, test equipment and skills required to service the LSPV system, it is not recommended that the home mechanic attempt the procedures. If servicing of the system becomes necessary, take the vehicle to a reputable, suitably equipped automotive repair shop.

---

10   Brake hoses and lines - inspection and replacement

Inspection

1   About every six months, with the vehicle raised and supported securely on jackstands, the rubber hoses which connect the steel brake lines with the front and rear brake assemblies should be inspected for cracks, chafing of the outer cover, leaks, blisters and other damage. These are important and vulnerable parts of the brake system and inspection should be complete. A light and mirror will be helpful for a thorough check. If a hose exhibits any of the above conditions, replace it with a new one.

Replacement

Front brake hose

Refer to illustrations 10.3 and 10.4

2   Loosen the wheel lug nuts, raise the vehicle and support it securely on jackstands. Remove the wheel.

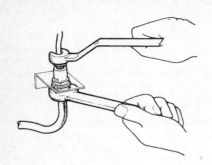

10.3 Hold the hose fitting with a wrench to prevent twisting the line, then loosen the tube nut with a flare nut wrench to prevent rounding off the corners of the nut

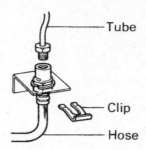

10.4 Once the tube nut has been completely loosened, remove the hose clip with a pair of pliers

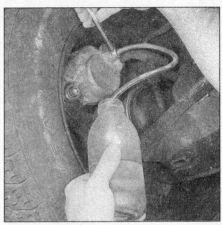

11.8 When bleeding the brakes, a hose is connected to the bleeder valve at the caliper or wheel cylinder and then submerged in brake fluid. Air will be seen as bubbles in the tube and container. All air must be expelled before moving to the next wheel

3   At the frame bracket, hold the hose fitting with an open end wrench and unscrew the tube nut from the hose **(see illustration)**. Use a flare nut wrench on the tube nut to prevent rounding off the corners.

4   Remove the U-clip from the female fitting at the bracket with a pair of pliers, then pass the hose through the bracket **(see illustration)**.

5   At the caliper end of the hose, remove the union bolt from the fitting, then separate the hose from the caliper. Note that there are two copper sealing washers on either side of the fitting - they should be replaced with new ones upon installation.

6   Remove the U-clip from the strut bracket, then feed the hose through the bracket.

7   To install the hose, pass the caliper fitting end through the strut bracket, then connect the fitting to the caliper with the union bolt and copper washers. Make sure that the locating lug on the fitting is engaged with the hole in the caliper, then tighten the fitting to the specified torque.

8   Push the metal support into the strut bracket and install the U-clip. Make sure that the hose isn't twisted between the caliper and the strut bracket.

9   Route the hose into the frame bracket, again making sure it isn't twisted, then connect the hydraulic line tube nut, starting the threads by hand. Install the U-clip then tighten the fitting securely.

10   Bleed the caliper as described in Section 11.

11   Install the wheel and lug nuts, lower the vehicle and tighten the lug nuts to the specified torque.

Rear brake hose

12   Perform Steps 2, 3 and 4 above, then repeat Steps 3 and 4 to the other end of the hose. Be sure to bleed the wheel cylinder (or caliper) as described in Section 11.

Metal brake lines

13   When replacing brake lines be sure to use the correct parts. Don't use copper tub-

ing for any brake system components. Purchase steel brake lines from a dealer or auto parts store.

14   Prefabricated brake line, with the tube ends already flared and fittings installed, is available at auto parts stores and dealers. These lines are also bent to the proper shapes.

15   When installing the new line make sure it's securely supported in the brackets and has plenty of clearance between moving or hot components.

16   After installation, check the master cylinder fluid level and add fluid as necessary. Bleed the brake system as outlined in the next Section and test the brakes carefully before driving the vehicle in traffic.

11   Brake hydraulic system - bleeding

Refer to illustration 11.8

Warning: *Wear eye protection when bleeding the brake system. If the fluid comes in contact with your eyes, immediately rinse them with water and seek medical attention.*

Note: *Bleeding the hydraulic system is necessary to remove any air that manages to find its way into the system when it's been opened during removal and installation of a hose, line, caliper or master cylinder.*

1   It will probably be necessary to bleed the system at all four brakes if air has entered the system due to low fluid level, or if the brake lines have been disconnected at the master cylinder.

2   If a brake line was disconnected only at a wheel, then only that caliper or wheel cylinder must be bled.

3   If a brake line is disconnected at a fitting located between the master cylinder and any of the brakes, that part of the system served by the disconnected line must be bled.

4   Remove any residual vacuum from the brake power booster by applying the brake several times with the engine off.

5   Remove the master cylinder reservoir cover and fill the reservoir with brake fluid. Reinstall the cover. **Note:** *Check the fluid level often during the bleeding operation and*

add fluid as necessary to prevent the fluid level from falling low enough to allow air bubbles into the master cylinder.

6   Have an assistant on hand, as well as a supply of new brake fluid, a clear container partially filled with clean brake fluid, a length of 3/16-inch plastic, rubber or vinyl tubing to fit over the bleeder valve and a wrench to open and close the bleeder valve.

7   Beginning at the right rear wheel, loosen the bleeder valve slightly, then tighten it to a point where it is snug but can still be loosened quickly and easily.

8   Place one end of the tubing over the bleeder valve and submerge the other end in brake fluid in the container **(see illustration)**.

9   Have the assistant pump the brakes slowly a few times to get pressure in the system, then hold the pedal firmly depressed.

10   While the pedal is held depressed, open the bleeder valve just enough to allow a flow of fluid to leave the valve. Watch for air bubbles to exit the submerged end of the tube. When the fluid flow slows after a couple of seconds, close the valve and have your assistant release the pedal.

11   Repeat Steps 9 and 10 until no more air is seen leaving the tube, then tighten the bleeder valve and proceed to the left rear wheel, the right front wheel and the left front wheel, in that order, and perform the same procedure. Be sure to check the fluid in the master cylinder reservoir frequently.

12   Never use old brake fluid. It contains moisture which will deteriorate the brake system components.

13   Refill the master cylinder with fluid at the end of the operation.

14   Check the operation of the brakes. The pedal should feel solid when depressed, with no sponginess. If necessary, repeat the entire process. **Warning:** *Do not operate the vehicle if you are in doubt about the effectiveness of the brake system.*

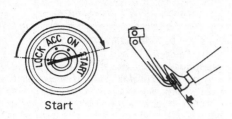

12.2 Push down on the brake pedal then start the engine - the brake pedal should go down slightly, indicating normal booster operation

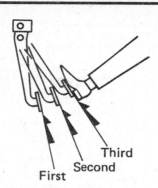

Third
Second
First

12.3 With the engine turned off, the pedal should build up with each pump if the booster is functioning properly

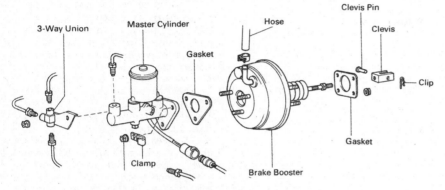

3-Way Union   Master Cylinder   Hose   Clevis Pin
Clevis
Gasket
Clip
Clamp   Gasket
Brake Booster

12.7 Power brake booster installation details

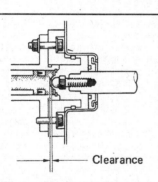

Clearance

12.14a The booster pushrod-to-master cylinder pushrod clearance must be as specified - if there is interference between the two, the brakes may drag; if there is too much clearance, there will be excessive brake pedal travel

12   Power brake booster - check, removal and installation

Operating check

Refer to illustration 12.2

1   Depress the brake pedal several times with the engine off and make sure that there is no change in the pedal reserve distance.
2   Depress the pedal and start the engine. If the pedal goes down slightly, operation is normal **(see illustration)**.

12.14b To adjust the length of the booster pushrod, hold the serrated portion of the rod with a pair of pliers and turn the adjusting screw in or out, as necessary, to achieve the desired setting

Air tightness check

Refer to illustration 12.3

3   Start the engine and turn it off after one or two minutes.
Depress the brake pedal several times slowly. If the pedal goes down farther the first time but gradually rises after the second or third depression, the booster is air tight **(see illustration)**.
4   Depress the brake pedal while the engine is running, then stop the engine with the pedal depressed. If there is no change in the pedal reserve travel after holding the pedal for 30 seconds, the booster is air tight.

Removal

Refer to illustration 12.7

5   Power brake booster units should not be disassembled. They require special tools not normally found in most automotive repair stations or shops. They are fairly complex and because of their critical relationship to brake performance it is best to replace a defective booster unit with a new or rebuilt one.
6   To remove the booster, first remove the brake master cylinder as described in Section 8.
7   Locate the pushrod clevis connecting the booster to the brake pedal **(see illustration)**. This is accessible from the interior in front of the driver's seat.
8   Remove the clevis pin retaining clip with pliers and pull out the pin.
9   Holding the clevis with pliers, disconnect the clevis locknut with a wrench. The clevis is now loose.
10   Disconnect the hose leading from the engine to the booster. Be careful not to damage the hose when removing it from the booster fitting.
11   Remove the four nuts and washers holding the brake booster to the firewall. You may need a light to see these, as they are up under the dash area.
12   Slide the booster straight out from the firewall until the studs clear the holes and pull the booster, brackets and gaskets from the engine compartment area.

Installation

Refer to illustrations 12.14a and 12.14b

13   Installation procedures are basically the reverse of those for removal. Tighten the clevis locknut securely and the booster mounting nuts to the specified torque.
14   If the power booster unit is being replaced, the clearance between the master cylinder piston and the pushrod in the vacuum booster must be measured. Using a depth micrometer or vernier calipers, measure the distance from the seat (recessed area) in the master cylinder to the master cylinder mounting flange. Next, measure the distance from the end of the vacuum booster pushrod to the mounting face of the booster (including gasket) where the master cylinder mounting flange seats. Subtract the two measurements to get the clearance **(see illustration)**. If the clearance is more or less than specified, turn the adjusting screw on the end of the power booster pushrod until the clearance is within the specified limit **(see illustration)**.
15   A second method to measure the pushrod-to-piston clearance is to install the master cylinder to the vacuum booster with a small piece of modeling clay placed on the end of the pushrod. Make sure the gasket is in place when making this trial fit. Remove the master cylinder and measure the resulting impression left in the clay. Again adjust as needed to meet the Specification. This

method may require several trial-and-error fits to reach the proper clearance.

16   After the final installation of the master cylinder and brake hoses and lines, the brake pedal height and free play must be adjusted and the system must be bled. See the appropriate Sections of this Chapter for the procedures.

13   Parking brake shoes (rear disc brakes only) - replacement

Refer to illustrations 13.3, 13.4, 13.5, 13.7, 13.8a, 13.8b, 13.10 and 13.15

Warning: *Dust created by the brake system may contain asbestos, which is hazardous to your health. Never blow it out with compressed air and don't inhale any of it. An approved filtering mask should be worn when working on the brakes. Do not, under any circumstances, use petroleum-based solvents to clean brake parts. Use brake cleaner or denatured alcohol only!*

1   Remove the brake caliper, torque plate and disc following the procedures outlined in Sections 4 and 5.

2   Inspect the thickness of the lining material on the shoes. If the lining has worn down to 1 mm or less, the shoes must be replaced.

3   Remove the parking brake shoe return springs from the anchor pin **(see illustration)**.

4   Remove the shoe strut from between the shoes **(see illustration)**.

5   Remove the front shoe hold-down spring, then remove the shoe and adjuster **(see illustration)**.

6   Remove the rear shoe hold-down spring, disconnect the parking brake cable from the lever and remove the shoe.

7   Spread the C-washer on the parking brake lever pivot pin with a screwdriver then remove the lever, shim and pin. Transfer the parts to the new rear shoe and crimp the C-washer to the pin using a pair of pliers **(see illustration)**.

8   Apply a thin coat of high temperature grease to the shoe contact surfaces of the backing plate and to the threads and sliding portion of the adjuster **(see illustrations)**.

9   Connect the parking brake cable to the lever and mount the rear shoe to the backing plate. Install the hold-down spring.

10   Connect the tension spring to the lower ends of both shoes and install the adjuster **(see illustration)**.

11   Position the front shoe on the backing plate and install the hold-down spring.

12   Install the parking brake strut, with the spring facing forward, between the two shoes.

13   Install the shoe return springs.

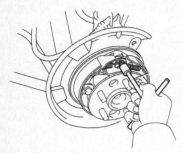

13.3 Unhook the parking brake shoe return springs - a special brake spring tool makes this much easier and is available at most auto parts stores

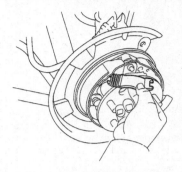

13.4 Remove the shoe strut and spring assembly

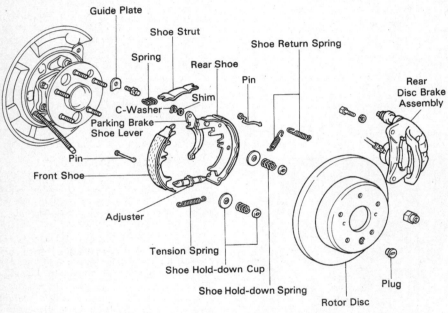

13.5 Exploded view of the parking brake assembly (rear disc brake models only)

Guide Plate
Shoe Strut
Spring
Rear Shoe
Shoe Return Spring
Pin
Shim
C-Washer
Parking Brake Shoe Lever
Pin
Front Shoe
Adjuster
Tension Spring
Shoe Hold-down Cup
Shoe Hold-down Spring
Rotor Disc
Plug
Rear Disc Brake Assembly

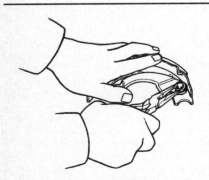

13.7 Use a pair of pliers to crimp the C-washer to the pivot pin

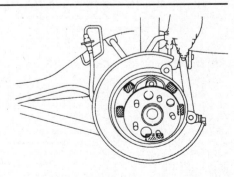

13.8a Apply a light coat of high-temperature grease to the parking brake shoe contact areas (shaded areas) on the backing plate

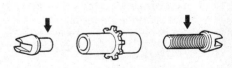

13.8b Clean the adjuster screw and apply high temperature grease to the indicated areas

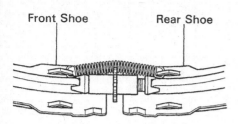

13.10 When assembled, the tension spring and adjuster screw should be arranged as shown

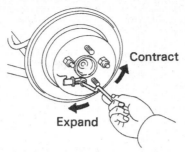

13.15 Turn the adjusting screw star wheel to expand the shoes until the disc can't be turned, then back it off eight clicks

14.3 Loosen the locknut then turn the adjusting nut until the desired handle travel is obtained

14   Install the brake disc. Temporarily thread three of the wheel lug nuts onto the studs to hold the disc in place.

15   Remove the hole plug from the brake disc. Adjust the parking brake shoe clearance by turning the adjuster wheel with a brake adjusting tool or screwdriver until the shoes contact the drum and the disc can't be turned **(see illustration)**. Back-off the adjuster eight clicks, then install the hole plug.

16   Install the torque plate and brake caliper (Section 4). Be sure to tighten the bolts to the specified torque.

17   Install the wheel and tighten the lug nuts to the specified torque.

18   Pull up on the parking brake handle and count the number of clicks that it travels. It should be between five and eight clicks - if it's not, adjust the parking brake as described in the next Section.

19   To bed the shoes to the drum, drive the vehicle at approximately 30 mph on a dry, level road. Push in on the parking brake release button and pull up slightly on the lever with about 20 pounds of force. Drive the vehicle for 1/4-mile with the parking brake applied like this.

20   Repeat this procedure two or three times, allowing the brakes to cool between applications.

14   Parking brake - adjustment

Refer to illustration 14.3

1   The parking brake lever, when properly adjusted, should travel five to eight clicks when a moderate pulling force is applied. If it travels less than five clicks, there is a chance that the parking brake might not be releasing completely and might be dragging on the drum. If the lever can be pulled up more than eight clicks, the parking brake may not hold adequately on an incline, allowing the car to roll.

2   To gain access to the parking brake cable adjuster, remove the center console.

3   Loosen the locknut (the upper nut) while holding the adjusting nut (lower nut) with a wrench **(see illustration)**. Tighten the adjust-

ing nut until the desired travel is attained. Tighten the locknut.

4   Install the console.

15   Parking brake cables - replacement

Equalizer-to-parking brake cable

Refer to illustration 15.4

1   Loosen the rear wheel lug nuts, raise the rear of the vehicle and support it securely on jackstands. Remove the wheel.

2   Make sure the parking brake is completely released, then remove the brake drum (or disc).

3   Remove the brake shoes and disconnect the cable from the parking brake lever (Section 6 for drum brakes, Section 13 for disc brakes).

4   Unbolt the cable casing from the backing plate **(see illustration)**.

5   Unbolt the cable bracket from the frame at the forward end of the strut rod.

6   Unbolt the cable bracket from the forward end of the fuel tank strap.

7   Follow the cable towards the front of the vehicle and locate the cable clamp. Loosen the clamp bolt and slide the cable casing out of the clamp.

8   Using a screwdriver, pry the cable and grommet out of the guide just to the rear of the equalizer.

9   Disconnect the cable end from the equalizer by aligning the cable with the slot in the top of the equalizer. Slide the cable end out of its hole.

10   To install the cable, reverse the removal procedure. Adjust the parking brake lever as outlined in the previous Section.

Equalizer-to-brake lever cable

11   Remove the center console (Chapter 11).

12   With the lever in the down (off) position, remove the locknut and the adjusting nut (Section 14) and detach the cable from the lever.

13   From underneath the vehicle, pull the

cable rearwards, turn it 90 degrees and pass it through the center of the equalizer.

14   Installation is the reverse of the removal procedure. Apply a light coat of grease to the portion of the cable end that contacts the equalizer. Adjust the parking brake lever as outlined in the previous Section.

16   Brake pedal - removal, installation and adjustment

Refer to illustrations 16.6, 16.11 and 16.13

Removal and installation

1   Remove the left side under-dash panel.

2   Disconnect the return spring from the outer groove in the pushrod clevis pin.

3   Remove the R-clip and extract the clevis pin.

4   Unscrew the pivot bolt nut, withdraw the bolt and remove the pedal. Inspect the bushings for wear, replacing them if necessary.

5   Install the brake pedal in the reverse order of removal. Lubricate the pivot with grease.

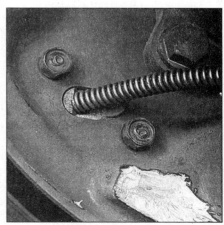

15.4 The parking brake cable casing is bolted to the brake backing plate

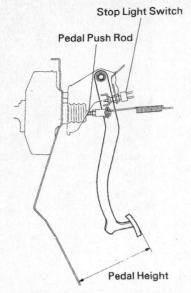

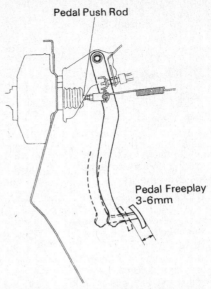

16.6 Measure the distance from the floor to the front of the pedal pad and compare your reading with the Specifications

16.11 The pedal free play is the distance the pedal moves before the pedal pushrod contacts the booster air valve

Adjustment

6   The pedal height is measured from the floorboard to the top of the pedal. Compare your measurement to the Specifications **(see illustration)**.

7   To adjust the pedal height, block the wheels and release the parking brake lever.

8   Loosen the locknut on the brake light switch and unscrew the switch until it no longer contacts the brake pedal shaft.

9   Depress the pedal a few times to remove any vacuum in the system.

10   Loosen the pushrod locknut and turn the rod in the desired direction to set the pedal.

11   Check the brake pedal free play **(see illustration)**. Press on the pedal with your fingers until initial resistance is felt. Compare the measurement to the Specifications.

12   If the free play of the pedal requires adjustment, recheck the pedal height and adjust accordingly.

13   Check brake pedal reserve travel **(see illustration)**. Start the engine, depress the brake pedal a few times and then press down hard and hold it.

14   Pedal reserve travel is measured from the floorboard to the top of the pedal while it is being depressed. Compare the measurement to the Specifications.

15   If the pedal reserve is less than specified, have the brakes adjusted by a qualified auto service department.

16   Readjust the brake light switch so that it is actuated when the pedal is up (not depressed) (refer to Section 17).

17   Brake light switch - removal, installation and adjustment

Removal and installation

1   The brake light switch is located on a bracket at the top of the brake pedal. The switch activates the brake lights at the rear of the vehicle whenever the pedal is depressed.

2   Disconnect the negative battery cable and secure it out of the way so that it cannot come into contact with the battery post.

3   Disconnect the wiring harness at the brake light switch.

4   Loosen the locknut and unscrew the switch from the pedal bracket.

5   Installation procedures are the reverse of removal.

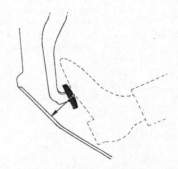

16.13 Measure the pedal reserve distance from the floorboard to the top of the pedal while the pedal is held depressed

Adjustment

6   Loosen the locknut, adjust the switch so that the threaded portion lightly contacts the pedal stopper, then tighten the locknut.

7   Connect the wiring at the switch and the battery. With an assistant, check that the rear brake lights are functioning properly.

Chapter 10
Suspension and steering systems

Contents

Specifications

Torque specifications

	Ft-lbs
Front suspension	
Suspension support-to-body	
1986 and earlier	27
1987 and later	47
Strut/shock absorber assembly damper shaft nut	34
Steering knuckle-to-strut bolts/nuts	
1986 and earlier	152
1987 and 1988	166
1989 and later	224
Stabilizer bar-to-control arm nut	
1986 and earlier	86
1987 and later	156
Stabilizer bar U-bracket bolts	
1986 and earlier	83
1987 and later	94
Balljoint-to-steering knuckle bolts	
1986 and earlier and 1989 and later	83
1987 and 1988	94
Balljoint-to-control arm	
1988 and earlier	67
1989 and later	90
Control arm-to-shaft bracket nut	
1986 and earlier	83
1987 and later	156
Control arm shaft bracket-to-body	153
Suspension crossmember	
Bolts and nuts (1983 through 1990)	153
Bolts (1991)	
Large (No. 10)	153
Small (No. 11)	112
Nuts (1991)	
Nut height of 0.51 inch	153
Nut height of 0.681 inch	112
Rear suspension	
Suspension support to body	
1988 and earlier	47
1989 and later	29
Strut/shock absorber assembly damper shaft nut	36

Rear suspension (continued)

Rear axle carrier-to-strut bolts/nuts
1983, 1984 105
1985, 1986 119
1987 and later 166
Rear suspension arm-to-frame
1986 and earlier... 64
1987 and later 83
Rear suspension arm-to-axle carrier
1986 and earlier... 64
1987 and later (exc. all-wheel drive)........................... 134
All-wheel drive 90
Strut rod-to-body
1986 and earlier... 64
1987 and later 83
Strut rod-to-axle carrier
1986 and earlier... 64
1987 and later 83
Rear hub and bearing assembly-to-axle carrier 59

Steering system

Steering wheel nut 25
Steering gear mounting bolts 43
Steering shaft universal joint-to-steering gear........................ 26
Tie-rod end-to-steering knuckle 36
Wheel lug nuts 75

1   General information

Refer to illustrations 1.1 and 1.2

The front suspension is a MacPherson strut design. The steering knuckle is located by a lower control arm, and both front control arms are connected by a stabilizer bar, which also controls fore-and-aft movement of the control arms **(see illustration)**.

The rear suspension also utilizes MacPherson struts. Lateral movement is controlled by two parallel control arms on each side, with longitudinally mounted strut rods between the body and the rear axle carriers **(see illustration)**.

The rack-and-pinion steering gear is located behind the engine/transaxle assem-bly on the firewall and actuates the steering arms, which are integral with the steering knuckles. Most vehicles are equipped with power steering. The steering column is designed to collapse in the event of an acci-dent.

Frequently, when working on the sus-pension or steering system components, you may come across fasteners which seem

1.1 Underside view of the front suspension and steering components

1 Stabilizer bar	3 Control arm	6 Suspension crossmember
2 Strut/shock absorber and coil spring assembly	4 Tie-rod 5 Balljoint	7 Engine center mounting member

1.2 Underside view of the rear suspension

1	Stabilizer bar	4	Strut rod
2	Strut/shock absorber and coil spring assembly	5	Rear axle carrier
3	Suspension arm		

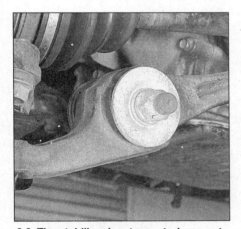

2.2 The stabilizer bar-to-control arm nuts and washers must be removed to separate the bar from the control arms

impossible to loosen. These fasteners on the underside of the vehicle are continually subjected to water, road grime, mud, etc., and can become rusted or "frozen," making them extremely difficult to remove. In order to unscrew these stubborn fasteners without damaging them (or other components), be sure to use lots of penetrating oil and allow it to soak in for a while. Using a wire brush to clean exposed threads will also ease removal of the nut or bolt and prevent damage to the threads. Sometimes a sharp blow with a hammer and punch is effective in breaking the bond between a nut and bolt threads, but care must be taken to prevent the punch from slipping off the fastener and ruining the threads. Heating the stuck fastener and surrounding area with a torch sometimes helps too, but isn't recommended because of the obvious dangers associated with fire. Long breaker bars and extension, or "cheater," pipes will increase leverage, but never use an extension pipe on a ratchet - the ratcheting mechanism could be damaged. Sometimes, turning the nut or bolt in the tightening (clockwise) direction first will help to break it loose. Fasteners that require drastic measures to unscrew should always be replaced with new ones.

Since most of the procedures that are dealt with in this chapter involve jacking up the vehicle and working underneath it, a good pair of jackstands will be needed. A hydraulic floor jack is the preferred type of jack to lift the vehicle, and it can also be used to support certain components during various operations. **Warning:** *Never, under any circumstances, rely on a jack to support the vehicle while working on it. Whenever any of the suspension or steering fasteners are loosened or removed they must be inspected and, if necessary, be replaced with new ones of the same part number or of original equipment quality and design. Torque specifications must be followed for proper reassembly and*

component retention. Never attempt to heat or straighten any suspension or steering components. Instead, replace any bent or damaged part with a new one.

2 Front stabilizer bar and bushings - removal and installation

Refer to illustrations 2.2, 2.3, 2.4, 2.5, 2.6 and 2.12
Warning: *Whenever any of the suspension or steering fasteners are loosened or removed they must be inspected, and if necessary replaced with new ones of the same part number or of original equipment quality and design. Torque specifications must be followed for proper reassembly and component retention.*
Note: *The stabilizer bar used on this vehicle is unique in that it also serves to prevent longitudinal movement of the control arms.*

Removal

1   Raise the vehicle and support it securely on jackstands. If only the stabilizer bar bushings are being replaced, proceed to Step 8, as it isn't necessary to unbolt the stabilizer bar from the control arms for bushing replacement.
2   Remove both large stabilizer-to-control arm nuts and retainers **(see illustration)**.

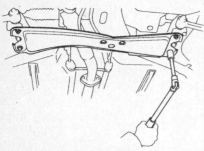

2.3 The suspension crossmember must be removed in order to unbolt the control arm shaft bracket from the body

3   Remove the suspension crossmember mounting bolts and nuts and lower the cross-member **(see illustration)**.
4   Loosen the shift control cable clamp bolts, then remove the engine center mounting member **(see illustration)**. The front and rear engine mounts will be unbolted from the engine center mounting member, but the left and right engine mounts will still be supporting the engine.
5   Unbolt the control arm shaft bracket from the body **(see illustration)**. Only one side must be removed.
6   Remove the four stabilizer bar U-bracket bolts. Support the bar while removing the last two bolts to prevent the stabilizer bar from falling **(see illustration)**.
7   Separate the stabilizer bar from the control arms (be careful not to lose the stabilizer bar-to-control arm spacers, if any are present).

Bushing replacement

8   Pull the U-bracket off the stabilizer bar and rubber bushing using a rocking motion.
9   Remove the rubber bushing from the bar and clean the bushing area with a stiff wire brush to remove any rust or dirt.
10   Lubricate the inside and outside of the new bushing with vegetable oil (used in cooking) to simplify reassembly. **Caution:** *Don't use petroleum or mineral-based lubricants or brake fluid - they will lead to deterioration of the bushing.*

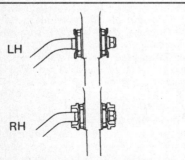

2.12 On the left end of the stabilizer bar, a dished retainer is installed on each side of the control arm rubber bushing - on the right end, a countersunk retainer is used

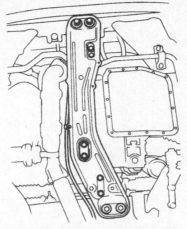

2.4 The engine center mounting member must be removed to allow stabilizer bar removal

11   Place the new bushing on the stabilizer bar and install the U-bracket, using a rocking motion if resistance is encountered.

Installation

12   Push the stabilizer bar-to-control arm spacers onto the bar. Install the retainers with the dished portion (left side) and hollow portion (right side) facing away from the control arm bushings.**(see illustration)**.
13   Insert the stabilizer bar ends into the control arms, install the retainers (see Step 12) and new nuts. Start the nuts on the threads by hand, but don't tighten them yet.
14   Attach the control arm shaft bracket to the body. Install the engine center mounting member and the suspension crossmember, tightening all fasteners to the specified torque. Position the shift cable and tighten the clamps.
15   Install new stabilizer bar U-bracket bolts, starting all four by hand before tightening any of them.
16   Tighten the U-bracket bolts to the specified torque.
17   Tighten the two large stabilizer bar-to-control arm nuts to the specified torque. Recheck your work, then lower the vehicle.
18   It's a good idea to drive the car to an alignment shop after this job has been performed, to have the front end alignment checked, and if necessary, adjusted.

---

3   Front strut/shock absorber and coil spring assembly - removal, inspection and installation

Refer to illustrations 3.2, 3.4, 3.6, 3.7a, 3.7a and 3.8

Removal

1   Loosen the wheel lug nuts, raise the vehicle and support it securely on jackstands. Remove the wheel.

2.5 The control arm shaft bracket may have to be pried from the body after the bolts and nuts are removed

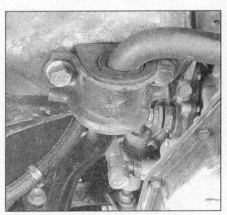

2.6 Remove the stabilizer bar U-bracket bolts - the nuts on the other side are welded in place and don't require a wrench to keep them from turning

2   Using white paint or a scribe, place a mark from the strut to the camber adjuster and steering knuckle and also around the strut-to-steering knuckle nuts **(see illustration)**.
3   Separate the tie-rod end from the steering arm as described in Section 18.

3.2 Mark the relationship of the steering knuckle and camber adjuster to the strut bracket

3.4 Pull the brake hose-to-strut bracket clip off with a pair of pliers

4   Unbolt the brake hose from the caliper (Chapter 9). Have some rags and a container handy to catch the brake fluid. Unclip the hose from the strut bracket and push it through **(see illustration)**.
5   Remove the caliper upper mounting bolt (Chapter 9) and swing the caliper forward.
6   Remove the strut-to-knuckle nuts and knock the bolts out with a hammer and punch **(see illustration)**.
7   Separate the strut from the steering knuckle **(see illustrations)**. Be careful not to overextend the inner CV joint. It's a good idea to wire the top of the steering knuckle to the body (where the tie-rod comes through) to prevent this from happening.
8   Support the strut and spring assembly with one hand and remove the three strut-to-shock tower nuts **(see illustration)**. Remove the assembly out from the fender well.

Inspection

9   Check the strut body for leaking fluid, dents, cracks and other obvious damage which would warrant repair or replacement.
10   Check the coil spring for chips or cracks in the spring coating (this will cause premature spring failure due to corrosion). Inspect the spring seat for cuts, hardness and general deterioration.

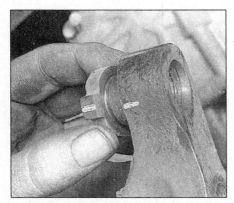

3.7b The camber adjuster slides into the upper hole in the steering knuckle - don't forget to install it

3.6 Remove the nuts from the steering knuckle-to-strut bolts and drive the bolts out with a hammer and punch

11   If any undesirable conditions exist, proceed to Section 4 for the strut disassembly procedure.

Installation

12   Guide the strut assembly up into the fender well and insert the three upper mounting studs through the holes in the shock tower. Once the three studs protrude from the shock tower, install the nuts so the strut won't fall back through. This is most easily accomplished with the help of an assistant, as the strut is quite heavy and awkward.
13   Insert the camber adjuster into the upper hole in the steering knuckle, if it fell out. Slide the steering knuckle into the strut flange and insert the two bolts. Install the nuts, align the previously applied marks and tighten them to the specified torque.
14   Swing the caliper up into position and install the mounting bolt. Tighten the bolt to the specified torque (Chapter 9). Reinstall the brake hose (Chapter 9).
15   Install the tie-rod end into the steering arm and tighten the castellated nut to the specified torque. Install a new cotter pin. If the cotter pin will not pass through, tighten the nut a little more, but just enough to align the hole in the stud with a castellation on the nut (do not loosen the nut).
16   Install the wheel, lower the vehicle and tighten the lug nuts to the specified torque.
17   Tighten the three upper mounting nuts to the specified torque.
18   Drive the vehicle to an alignment shop to have the front end alignment checked, and if necessary, adjusted.

---

4   Strut/shock absorber or coil spring - replacement

Refer to illustrations 4.3a, 4.3b, 4.4, 4.5, 4.6, 4.7, 4.12, 4.13a and 4.13b
Warning: *Whenever any of the suspension or steering fasteners are loosened or removed they must be inspected and if necessary, be replaced with ones of the same part number*

3.7a Pull the steering knuckle out of the strut bracket - be careful not to pull it out too far though, as the driveaxle inner CV joint may become overextended

or of original equipment quality and design. Torque specifications must be followed for proper reassembly and component retention.
1   If the struts or coil springs exhibit the telltale signs of wear (leaking fluid, loss of damping capability, chipped, sagging or cracked coil springs) explore all options before beginning any work. The strut/shock absorber assemblies are not serviceable and must be replaced if a problem develops. However, strut assemblies complete with springs may be available on an exchange basis, which eliminates much time and work. Whichever route you choose to take, check on the cost and availability of parts before disassembling your vehicle. **Warning:** *Disassembling a strut assembly is a potentially dangerous undertaking and utmost attention must be directed to the job at hand, or serious bodily injury may result. Use only a high quality spring compressor and carefully follow the manufacturer's instructions furnished with the tool. After removing the coil spring from the strut assembly, set it aside in a safe, isolated area (a steel cabinet is preferred).*
2   Remove the strut and spring assembly following the procedure described in the pre-

3.8 The upper end of the strut assembly is fastened to the shock tower with three nuts

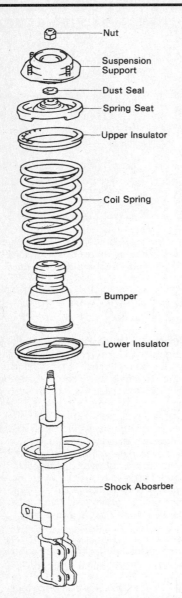

Nut

Suspension Support

Dust Seal

Spring Seat

Upper Insulator

Coil Spring

Bumper

Lower Insulator

Shock Abosrber

4.3a Exploded view of the strut/shock absorber and coil spring assembly

4.3b Install the spring compressor according to the tool manufacturer's instructions and compress the spring until all pressure is relieved from the upper spring seat

vious Section. Mount the strut assembly in a vise. Line the vise jaws with wood or rags to prevent damage to the unit and don't tighten the vise excessively.

3   Following the tool manufacturer's instructions, install the spring compressor (which can be obtained at most auto parts stores or equipment yards on a daily rental basis) on the spring and compress it sufficiently to relieve all pressure from the suspension support **(see illustrations)**. This can be verified by wiggling the spring.

4   Loosen the damper shaft nut with a socket wrench **(see illustration)**. To prevent the suspension support and damper shaft from turning, wedge a screwdriver or pry bar between one of the upper mounting studs and the socket.

5   Remove the nut and suspension support **(see illustration)**. Inspect the bearing in the suspension support for smooth operation. If it doesn't turn smoothly, replace the suspension support. Check the rubber portion of the suspension support for cracking and general deterioration. If there is any separation of the rubber, replace it.

6   Lift the spring seat and upper insulator

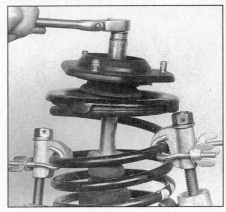

4.4 Remove the damper shaft nut

4.5 Lift the suspension support off the damper shaft

from the damper shaft **(see illustration)**. Check the rubber spring seat for cracking and hardness, replacing it if necessary.

7   Carefully lift the compressed spring from the assembly **(see illustration)** and set it in a safe place, such as a steel cabinet. **Warning:** *Never place your head near the end of the spring!*

8   Slide the rubber bumper and dust boot off the damper shaft.

9   Check the lower insulator for wear,

4.6 Remove the spring seat from the damper shaft

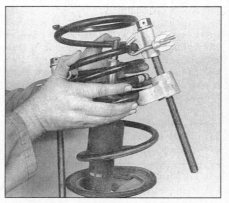

4.7 Remove the compressed spring assembly. Use extreme caution whenever handling the spring

4.12 When installing the spring, make sure that the lower end of the spring fits into the recessed portion of the lower seat (arrow)

4.13a The flats on the damper shaft (arrow) must match up with the flats in the spring seat

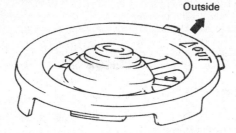

4.13b The "out" marking on the spring seat must face towards the strut bracket opening

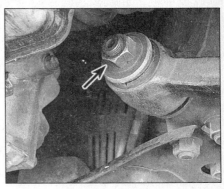

5.3 Remove the control arm shaft nut before loosening the bracket

cracking and hardness and replace it if necessary.

10   Assemble the strut beginning with the dust boot and rubber bumper - extend the damper rod as far as it will go and slide the boot and bumper down to the strut body.

11   If the lower insulator is being replaced, set it into position with the dropped portion seated in the lowest part of the seat.

12   Carefully place the coil spring onto the lower insulator, with the end of the spring resting in the lowest part of the insulator **(see illustration)**.

13   Install the upper insulator and spring seat, making sure that the flats in the hole in the seat match up with the flats on the damper shaft **(see illustration)**. Also make sure that the "out" marking on the spring seat faces toward the lower bracket, where the steering knuckle fits **(see illustration)**.

14   Install the dust seal and suspension support to the damper shaft.

15   Install the nut and tighten it to the specified torque.

16   Install the strut/shock absorber and coil spring assembly following the procedure outlined in the previous Section.

5   Control arm - removal, inspection and installation

Refer to illustrations 5.3 and 5.4

Warning: *Whenever any of the suspension or steering fasteners are loosened or removed they must be inspected and, if necessary, replaced with new ones of the same part number or of original equipment quality and design. Torque specifications must be followed for proper reassembly and component retention.*

Removal

1   Loosen the wheel lug nuts on the side to be dismantled, raise the front of the vehicle, support it securely on jackstands and remove the wheel.

2   Remove the stabilizer bar-to-control arm nut and retainer **(see illustration 2.2)**. Also remove the suspension crossmember (Section 2, Step 3).

3   Remove the nut from the control arm shaft **(see illustration)**.

4   Remove the balljoint stud cotter pin and loosen the nut a couple of turns (don't remove it yet). Separate the balljoint from the control arm **(see illustration)**. Remove the nut.

5   Unbolt the control arm shaft bracket from the body **(see illustration 2.5)**. Separate the bracket from the arm.

6   Pull the control arm off the stabilizer bar and remove it from the vehicle (be careful not to lose the stabilizer bar spacer, if equipped).

Inspection

7   Check the control arm for distortion and the bushings for wear, damage and deterioration. Replace a damaged or bent control arm with a new one. If the inner pivot bushing or stabilizer bar bushings are worn, take the control arm assembly to a dealer service department or a repair shop, as special tools are required to replace them.

Installation

8   Place the control arm balljoint stud into the steering knuckle. Install the nut but don't tighten it fully yet.

9   Push the stabilizer bar spacer (if equipped) and retainer onto the stabilizer bar (Section 2). Swing the control arm into position over the stabilizer bar end.

10   Install the control arm shaft bracket and nut to the control arm. Position the bracket

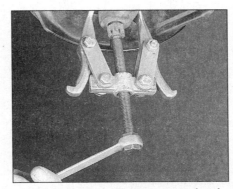

5.4 Loosen the balljoint-to-control and nut a couple of turns and push the balljoint stud from the control arm with a two-jaw puller - DON'T hit the end of the stud with a hammer!

on the body, install the suspension crossmember and fasteners (Section 2). Tighten all of the nuts and bolts to the specified torque.

11   Install the outside stabilizer bar-to-control arm retainer and nut (with the dished portion of the washer facing away from the rubber insulator- see Section 2). Tighten the nut to the specified torque. Also tighten the balljoint nut to the specified torque and install the cotter pin.

12   Install the wheel and lug nuts, lower the vehicle and tighten the lug nuts to the specified torque.

13   It's a good idea to have the front wheel alignment checked, and if necessary, adjusted after this job has been performed.

6   Balljoints - replacement

Refer to illustration 6.2

Warning: *Whenever any of the suspension or steering fasteners are loosened or removed, they must be inspected and, if necessary, replaced with new ones of the same part number or of original equipment quality and design. Torque specifications must be followed for proper reassembly and component retention.*

1   Loosen the wheel lug nuts, raise the vehicle and support it securely on jackstands. Remove the wheel.

2   Break the balljoint-to-steering knuckle bolts loose, but don't remove them yet **(see illustration)**.

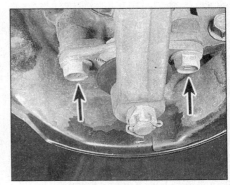

6.2 The balljoint is fastened to the steering knuckle with two bolts (arrows)

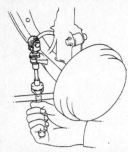

9.2 Unbolt the stabilizer bar from the control arm (1986 and earlier models)

3   Remove the cotter pin from the balljoint stud and loosen the nut a couple of turns. Separate the balljoint from the steering knuckle with a puller **(see illustration 5.4)**.

4   Unscrew the two balljoint-to-steering knuckle bolts and remove the balljoint. It may be necessary to pry downward on the stabilizer bar and control arm to provide clearance for removal.

5   To install the balljoint, position it on the steering knuckle and install the two bolts, but don't tighten them yet.

6   Insert the balljoint stud into the control arm and install the nut. Tighten the nut to the specified torque and install a new cotter pin. If the cotter pin hole doesn't line up with the slots on the nut, tighten the nut additionally until it does line up - don't loosen the nut to insert the cotter pin.

7   Tighten the balljoint-to-steering knuckle bolts to the specified torque.

8   Install the wheel and lug nuts. Lower the vehicle and tighten the lug nuts to the specified torque.

---

7   Steering knuckle and hub - removal and installation

Warning: *Whenever any of the suspension or steering fasteners are loosened or removed they must be inspected and, if necessary replaced with new ones of the same part number or of original equipment quality and design. Torque specifications must be followed for proper reassembly and component retention. Dust created by the brake system*

9.7 Remove the nuts from the lower end of the stabilizer bar links (arrow) (1987 and later models)

may contain asbestos, which is harmful to your health. Never blow it out with compressed air and don't inhale any of it. Do not, under any circumstances, use petroleum-based solvents to clean brake parts. Use brake cleaner or denatured alcohol only.

Removal

1   Loosen the wheel lug nuts, raise the vehicle and support it securely on jackstands. Remove the wheel.

2   Remove the brake caliper and support it with a piece of wire as described in Chapter 9. Separate the brake disc from the hub, then loosen the hub nut (Chapter 8).

3   Mark the relationship of the strut to the steering knuckle and camber adjuster **(see illustration 3.2)**. This will simplify reassembly.

4   Loosen, but do not remove the strut-to-steering knuckle bolts **(see illustration 3.6)**.

5   Separate the tie-rod from the steering knuckle arm as outlined in Section 18.

6   Remove the balljoint-to-steering knuckle bolts **(see illustration 6.2)**. The strut-to-knuckle bolts can now be removed.

7   Push the driveaxle from the hub as described in Chapter 8. Support the end of the driveaxle with a piece of wire.

8   Carefully separate the steering knuckle from the strut and balljoint.

Installation

9   Guide the knuckle and hub assembly into position, inserting the driveaxle into the hub.

10   Install the camber adjuster into the knuckle (if removed). Push the knuckle into the strut flange and install the bolts, but don't tighten them yet.

11   Pry down on the stabilizer bar then set the bottom of the steering knuckle on the balljoint. Install the bolts (don't tighten them yet).

12   Attach the tie-rod to the steering knuckle arm as described in Section 18. Tighten the strut bolt nuts, the balljoint bolts and the tie-rod nut to their specified torque settings.

13   Place the brake disc on the hub and install the caliper as outlined in Chapter 9.

14   Install the hub nut and tighten it to the specified torque (Chapter 9).

15   Install the wheel and lug nuts.

16   Lower the vehicle and tighten the lug nuts to the specified torque.

---

8   Front hub and bearing assembly - removal and installation

Due to the special tools and expertise required to press the hub and bearing from the steering knuckle, this job should be left to a professional mechanic. However, the steering knuckle and hub may be removed and the assembly taken to a local dealer service department or repair shop. Refer to Section 7 for steering knuckle and hub removal.

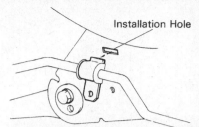

9.3 Unbolt the stabilizer bar brackets from the body - the tang on the other side of the bracket fits into a slot in the body (1986 and earlier models)

---

9   Rear stabilizer bar and bushings - removal and installation

1   Raise the vehicle and support it securely on jackstands.

1986 and earlier models

Refer to illustrations 9.2 and 9.3

2   Disconnect the stabilizer bar link from the suspension control arm **(see illustration)**. Take note as to how the bushings and spacers are situated.

3   Remove the stabilizer bar bracket-to-body bolts **(see illustration)**. Unhook the brackets from the body and remove the bar from the vehicle.

4   Check the bracket bushings for cracking, hardness and general deterioration, replacing them if necessary. Also check the link bushings for wear. Clean the areas where the bushings ride with a wire brush.

5   Installation is the reverse of the removal procedure. A light coat of vegetable oil will ease installation of the bushings and U-brackets (don't use petroleum-based lubricants or brake fluid - they will lead to premature failure of the bushing).

1987 and later models

Refer to illustrations 9.7 and 9.8

6   Disconnect the cable from the negative terminal of the battery.

7   Remove the stabilizer bar link-to-stabilizer bar nuts **(see illustration)**.

8   Unbolt the stabilizer bar bushing U-brackets from the body **(see illustration)**.

9.8 On 1987 and later models, the stabilizer bar brackets are retained by two bolts

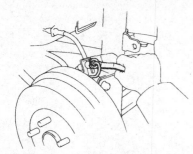

10.3 Use a flare nut wrench when disconnecting the brake line from the brake hose at the strut bracket

9   Using a floor jack and a block of wood, support the fuel tank and remove the two fuel tank band bolts (see Chapter 4). Allow the bands to hang down and lower the fuel tank about 1-1/2 to 2 inches.

10   The stabilizer bar can now be removed from the vehicle. Pull the U-brackets off the stabilizer bar (if they haven't fallen off already) using a rocking motion.

11   Check the bushings for wear, hardness, distortion, cracking and other signs of deterioration, replacing them if necessary. Also check the link bushings for these signs.

12   Using a wire brush, clean the areas of the bar where the bushings ride. Installation is the reverse of the removal procedure. If necessary, use a light coat of vegetable oil to ease bushing and U-bracket installation (don't use petroleum based products or brake fluid, as these will damage the rubber).

10   Rear strut/shock absorber and coil spring assembly - removal, inspection and installation

Warning: *Whenever any of the suspension or steering fasteners are loosened or removed they must be inspected and, if necessary, replaced with ones of the same part number or of original equipment quality and design. Torque specifications must be followed for proper reassembly and component retention.*

Removal

Refer to illustrations 10.3, 10.6, 10.8a and 10.8b

1   Loosen the wheel lug nuts, raise the vehicle and support it securely on jackstands. Remove the wheel.

2   Unscrew the brake line from the wheel cylinder (or caliper). Use a flare nut wrench to avoid rounding off the corners of the nut.

3   Disconnect the brake line from the flexible hose at the strut bracket **(see illustration)**. Again, the use of a flare nut wrench is recommended. Plug the hose end or wrap a plastic bag tightly around the end of the hose to prevent excessive leakage and contamination.

4   Remove the brake hose clip from the strut bracket with a pair of pliers, then pull the

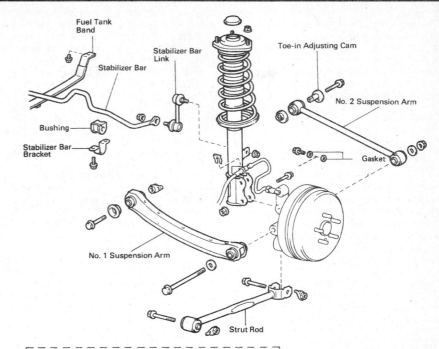

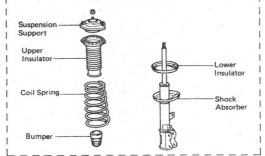

10.6 Exploded view of the rear suspension components

hose through the bracket.

5   Disconnect the stabilizer bar link from the strut bracket (1987 and later models only).

6   Support the axle carrier with a floor jack, then remove the two strut-to-axle carrier nuts and bolts **(see illustration)**.

7   Following the procedure outlined in Chapter 11, remove the rear seat back to gain access to the strut upper mounting nuts.

8   Remove the package tray support plate **(see illustration)** and unscrew the three strut upper mounting nuts **(see illustration)** while supporting the strut with your other hand, so it doesn't fall. Guide the strut out of the fenderwell.

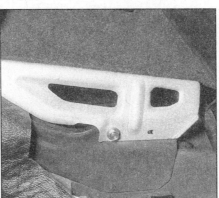

10.8a After removing the rear seat back, remove the package tray support plate

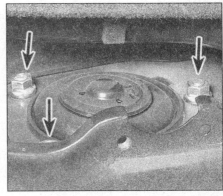

10.8b The strut is retained to the body by three nuts (arrows) under the package tray

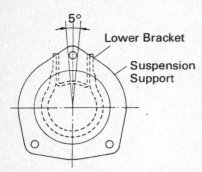

10.10 The bolt hole in the suspension support that is the farthest away from the other two must be aligned with the opening in the strut bracket

Inspection

Refer to illustration 10.10

9   Follow the inspection procedures described in Section 3. If it is determined that the strut assembly must be disassembled for replacement of the strut or the coil spring, refer to Section 4.

10   When reassembling the strut, make sure the suspension support is aligned with the lower bracket (where the axle carrier fits) **(see illustration)**.

Installation

11   Maneuver the assembly up into the fenderwell and insert the mounting studs through the holes in the body. Install the nuts.

12   Push the axle carrier into the strut lower bracket and install the bolts and nuts, tightening them to the specified torque.

13   Connect the stabilizer bar link to the strut bracket.

14   Route the brake hose through its bracket on the strut and connect the brake line, tightening it securely. Connect the other end of the line to the wheel cylinder (or caliper).

15   Install the wheel and lug nuts, lower the vehicle and tighten the lug nuts to the specified torque.

11.3b ... then drive the bolt through the axle carrier with a hammer and punch

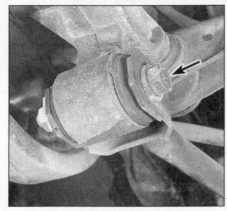

11.2 Remove the strut rod-to-axle carrier bolt (arrow)

16   Tighten the three strut upper mounting nuts to the specified torque.

17   Bleed the wheel cylinder (or caliper) following the procedure described in Chapter 9.

11   Rear suspension arms - removal and installation

Refer to illustrations 11.2, 11.3a, 11.3b, 11.4, 11.7, 11.9a and 11.9b

Warning: *Whenever any of the suspension or steering fasteners are loosened or removed they must be inspected and, if necessary replaced with new ones - discard the originals and don't reuse them. They must be replaced with new ones of the same part number or of original equipment quality and design. Torque specifications must be followed for proper reassembly and component retention.*

Removal

1   Raise the rear of the vehicle and support it securely on jackstands. Block the front wheels.

2   Disconnect the strut rod from the axle carrier **(see illustration)**.

3   Remove the suspension arm-to-spindle

11.4 Mark the relationship of the toe adjuster to the body on the inner end of the rear arm

11.3a Remove the suspension arm-to-rear axle carrier bolt nut ...

bolt and nut **(see illustrations)**.

4   If one of the rear suspension arms is being removed, mark the relationship of the toe adjuster wheel to the suspension arm inner mounting bracket **(see illustration)**. This will ensure that the toe adjustment will be returned to the same setting.

5   If one of the forward suspension arms is being removed, it will be necessary to remove the fuel tank protector first (see Chapter 4).

6   Using a screwdriver, pry the plastic plug from its hole in the subframe to gain access to the suspension arm inner mounting nuts.

7   Remove the inner mounting bolt and nut while supporting the suspension arm **(see illustration)**.

8   Remove the control arm from the vehicle.

Installation

9   Position the control arm with the slits in the bushings facing the rear. The stamped arms are marked L or R. The tubular arms have a small spot of paint that must be on the wheel end of the arm when installed **(see illustrations)**. Install the inner mounting bolt finger tight.

10   Insert the control arm-to-spindle bolt through the control arms and spindle from the front. Install the nut and washer and tighten the nut hand tight.

11   Connect the strut rod to the axle carrier,

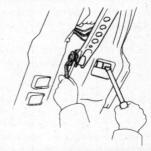

11.7 The inner mounting bolt nut is accessed by removing a plastic plug in the subframe

11.9a The stamped arms are marked as to which side of the vehicle they are installed on - the slits in the bushings also must face toward the rear

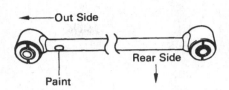

11.9b The tubular arms have a dot of paint that must be situated on the outer end of the arm - the slits in the bushings also face toward the rear

12.3 Remove the strut rod-to-frame bracket bolt (arrow)

tightening the nut hand tight only.

12   Place a jack under the axle carrier and raise it to simulate normal ride height.

13   Tighten the inner mounting bolt to the specified torque. Be sure to align the marks on the toe adjuster and body.

14   Tighten the outer nut to the specified torque.

15   Tighten the strut rod bolt to the specified torque.

16   Install the wheel and lug nuts, then lower the vehicle to the ground. Tighten the lug nuts to the specified torque.

17   Have the rear wheel alignment checked by a dealer service department or an alignment shop.

12   Strut rod - removal and installation

Refer to illustration 12.3

Warning: *Whenever any of the suspension or steering fasteners are loosened or removed they should be inspected, and if necessary, replaced with ones of the same part number or of original equipment quality and design. Torque specifications must be followed for proper reassembly and component retention.*

1   Loosen the wheel lug nuts, raise the

vehicle and support it securely on jackstands. Remove the wheel.

2   Remove the strut rod-to-axle carrier bolt **(see illustration 11.2)**. It isn't necessary to hold the nut with a wrench, because the nut has a tang attached to it to prevent rotation.

3   Remove the strut rod-to-body bracket bolt **(see illustration)**.

4   Installation is the reverse of the removal procedure. Be sure to tighten the bolts to the specified torque.

13   Rear hub and bearing assembly - removal and installation

Refer to illustrations 13.3 and 13.5

Warning: *Whenever any of the suspension or steering fasteners are loosened or removed they must be inspected, and if necessary replaced with new ones of the same part number or of original equipment quality and design. Torque specifications must be followed for proper reassembly and component retention. Dust created by the brake system contains asbestos, which is harmful to your health. Never blow it out with compressed air and don't inhale any of it. Do not, under any circumstances, use petroleum-based solvents to clean brake parts. Use brake cleaner*

or denatured alcohol only.

Note: *Due to the special tools required [to] replace the bearing, the hub and bear[ing] assembly should not be disassembled by [a] home mechanic. The assembly ca[n be] removed, however, and taken to a deale[r ser]vice department or repair shop to ha[ve the] bearing replaced. Also, this procedu[re does] not apply to all-wheel drive vehicles.*

Removal

1   Loosen the wheel lug nuts[, raise the] vehicle and support it securely o[n jackstands.] Remove the wheel.

2   Pull the brake drum (or [disc off the] hub. If difficulty is encoun[tered, refer to] Chapter 9 for the removal pr[ocedure.]

3   Remove the four hu[b mounting] bolts, accessible by turni[ng the hub so] that the large circular o[pening is over a] bolt **(see illustration)**.

4   Remove the hub [and bearing] from its seat, mane[uvering it past the] brake assembly.

Installation

5   Remove [the O-ring from the] seat and insta[ll a new one.]

6   Positio[n the hub and bearing] on the axle [carrier. Threading the] backing [plate bolts in first is] useful i[n aligning the bolt holes. The] flange [...] have [...] spe[...]

7   [...] L[...]

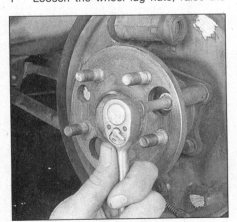

13.3 The rear hub and bearing assembly is held to the axle carrier with four bolts - turn the hub flange so the large hole lines up with a bolt, then remove it with a socket (brake shoes removed for clarity)

13.5 Be sure to replace this O-ring [in the] hub seat

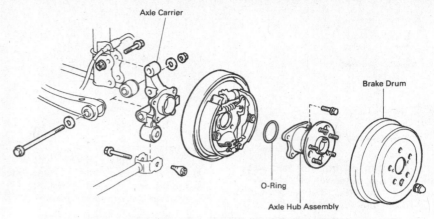

14.6 Installation details of the rear axle carrier and related components

Once the hub and bearing assembly been removed, slide the brake plate (with the brake hoes still off the axle carrier and hang it spring with a piece of wire

[text obscured] by the brake system which is harmful to your [text obscured] with compressed air [text obscured]. Do not, under any [text obscured]um-based sol- [text obscured]rake cleaner

[text obscured], raise the [text obscured] jackstands.

[text obscured]disc) from the [text obscured]ered, refer to [text obscured]ocedure. [text obscured] the [text obscured]k [text obscured]to-axle carrier [text obscured] the hub flange so [text obscured]out xposes each [text obscured] and bea assembly [text obscured]vering it ou ough the

6   Loosen, but don't remove the strut-to-axle carrier bolts **(see illustration)**.
7   Remove the suspension arm-to-axle carrier bolt, nut and washers **(see illustration 11.3b)**.
8   Remove the rear strut-rod bolt. **(see illustration 11.2)**.
9   Remove the previously loosened strut-to-axle carrier bolts while supporting the spindle so it doesn't fall.
10   Detach the axle carrier from the strut bracket. On all-wheel drive models, push the driveaxle out of the hub then support it with a piece of wire.

Installation

1   Inspect the carrier bushing for cracks, [text obscured]ormation and signs of wear. If it is worn [text obscured]take the carrier to a dealer service [text obscured]ent or repair shop to have the old [text obscured]t and a new one pressed in. If [text obscured]d with all-wheel drive, [text obscured]k the condition [text obscured]eness [text obscured]ice

when bending it back into place.
20   Install the rear brake drum (or disc) (Chapter 9).
21   Install the wheel and lug nuts.
22   Lower the vehicle and tighten the lug nuts to the specified torque.
23   On all-wheel drive models, tighten the hub nut to the specified torque and install a new cotter pin.

15   Steering system - general information

All models are equipped with rack-and-pinion steering. Most are power assisted. The steering gear is bolted to the firewall and operates the steering arms via tie-rods. The inner ends of the tie-rods are protected by rubber boots which should be inspected periodically for secure attachment, tears and leaking lubricant.

The power assist system consists of a belt-driven pump and associated lines and hoses. The power steering pump reservoir fluid level should be checked periodically (Chapter 1).

The steering wheel operates the steer-[text obscured]ft, which actuates the steering gear [text obscured]iversal joints. Looseness in the [text obscured]e caused by wear in the steer-[text obscured]versal joints, the steering gear, [text obscured]ends and loose retaining bolts.

[16] Steering wheel - removal and installation

Refer to illustrations 16.2, 16.3 and 16.4
1   Disconnect the cable from the negative terminal of the battery.
2   Remove the screws from the bottom of the horn pad and pull the pad from the steering wheel **(see illustration)**. Disconnect the wire to the horn switch.
3   Remove the steering wheel retaining nut, then mark the relationship of the steering shaft to the hub (if marks don't already exist

14 Rear axle carrier - removal and installation

Refer to illustrations 14.4 and 14.6
Warning: Whenever any of the suspension or steering fasteners are loosened or removed they must be inspected and, if necessary replaced with new ones of the same part number or of original equipment quality and design. Torque specifications must be followed for proper reassembly and component

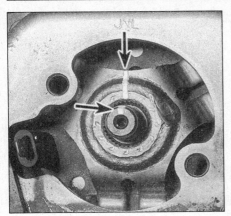

16.3 Paint or scribe alignment marks from the steering wheel hub to the steering shaft (arrows)

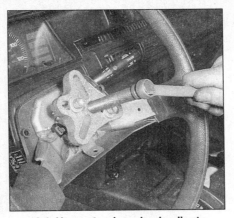

16.4 Use a steering wheel puller to separate the steering wheel from the shaft. DON'T attempt to remove the wheel with a hammer!

or don't line up) to simplify installation and ensure steering wheel alignment **(see illustration)**.

4   Use a puller to disconnect the steering wheel from the shaft **(see illustration)**.

5   To install the wheel, align the mark on the steering wheel hub with the mark on the shaft and slip the wheel onto the shaft. Install the hub nut and tighten it to the specified torque.

6   Connect the horn wire and install the horn pad.

7   Connect the negative battery cable.

17 Steering gear - removal and installation

Refer to illustrations 17.3 and 17.7

Note: *This procedure applies to both power and manual steering gear assemblies. When working on a vehicle equipped with a manual steering gear, ignore any references made to the power steering system.*

Removal

1   Loosen the front wheel lug nuts, raise the front of the vehicle and support it securely on jackstands. Apply the parking brake and remove the wheels. Remove the

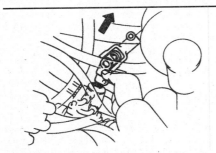

17.3 After the steering shaft universal joint has been marked to the steering gear input shaft and the bolt has been removed, slide it upward and off the shaft

engine undercovers on models so equipped.

2   Place a drain pan under the steering gear (power steering only). Remove the power steering pressure and return lines and cap the ends to prevent excessive fluid loss and contamination.

3   Mark the relationship of the lower universal joint to the steering gear input shaft. Remove the lower intermediate shaft pinch

bolt **(see illustration)**.

4   Separate the tie-rod ends from the steering knuckle arms (see Section 18).

5   Remove the suspension crossmember and the engine center mounting member (see Section 2).

6   Unbolt the engine rear mounting bracket from the engine (see Chapter 2).

7   Support the steering gear and remove the steering gear bracket-to-firewall mounting bolts **(see illustration)**. Lower the unit, separate the intermediate shaft from the steering gear input shaft and remove the steering gear from the vehicle.

8   Check the steering gear mounting grommets for excessive wear or deterioration, replacing them if necessary.

Installation

9   Raise the steering gear into position and connect the U-joint, aligning the marks.

10   Install the mounting brackets and bolts and tighten them to the specified torque.

11   Connect the tie-rod ends to the steering knuckle arms (Section 18).

12   Install the U-joint pinch bolt and tighten it to the specified torque.

13   Connect the power steering pressure and return hoses to the steering gear and fill the power steering pump reservoir with the recommended fluid (Chapter 1).

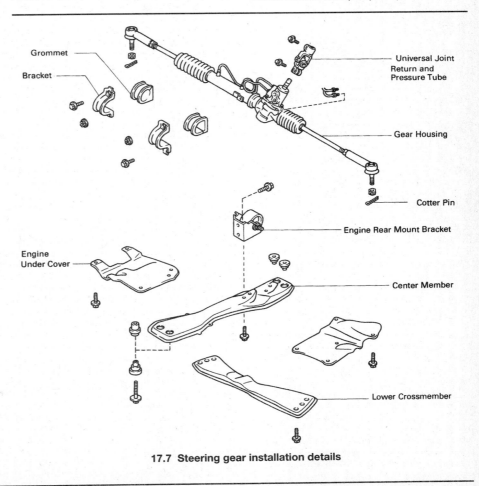

17.7 Steering gear installation details

18.2a Loosen the jam nut while holding the tie-rod with a wrench (or pair of locking pliers) on the flat portion of the rod to prevent it from turning

18.2b The relationship of the tie-rod end to the tie-rod can be marked with white paint

18.4 A two-jaw puller works well for separating the tie-rod end from the steering knuckle arm. Note that the nut hasn't been removed - it will prevent the two components from separating violently

14   Install the engine rear mounting bracket, tightening the bolts securely.
15   Install the engine center mounting member and suspension crossmember.
16   Lower the vehicle and bleed the steering system as outlined in Section 22.

18   Tie-rod ends - removal and installation

Refer to illustrations 18.2a, 18.2b and 18.4

Removal

1   Loosen the wheel lug nuts. Raise the front of the vehicle, support it securely, block the rear wheels and set the parking brake. Remove the front wheel.
2   Hold the tie-rod with a pair of locking pliers or wrench and loosen the jam nut enough to mark the position of the tie-rod end in relation to the threads **(see illustrations)**.
3   Remove the cotter pin and loosen the nut on the tie-rod end stud.
4   Disconnect the tie-rod from the steering knuckle arm with a puller **(see illustration)**.

Remove the nut and separate the tie-rod.
5   Unscrew the tie-rod end from the tie-rod.

Installation

6   Thread the tie-rod end on to the marked position and insert the tie-rod stud into the steering knuckle arm. Tighten the jam nut securely.
7   Install the castellated nut on the stud and tighten it to the specified torque. Install a new cotter pin.
8   Install the wheel and lug nuts. Lower the vehicle and tighten the lug nuts to the specified torque.
9   Have the alignment checked by a dealer service department or an alignment shop.

19   Steering gear boots - replacement

1   Loosen the lug nuts, raise the vehicle and support it securely on jackstands. Remove the wheel.
2   Refer to Section 18 and remove the tie-rod end and jam nut.

3   Remove the steering gear boot clamps and slide the boot off.
4   Before installing the new boot, wrap the threads and serrations on the end of the steering rod with a layer of tape so the small end of the new boot isn't damaged.
5   Slide the new boot into position on the steering gear until it seats in the groove in the steering rod and install new clamps.
6   Remove the tape and install the tie-rod end (Section 18).
7   Install the wheel and lug nuts. Lower the vehicle and tighten the lug nuts to the specified torque.

20   Power steering pump - removal and installation

Refer to illustration 20.6
Warning: *Whenever any of the suspension or steering system components are loosened or removed, they must be inspected and if, necessary, replaced with ones with the same part number or of original equipment quality and design.*

Removal

1   Disconnect the cable from the negative battery terminal.
2   Using a large syringe or suction gun, suck as much fluid out of the power steering fluid reservoir as possible. Place a drain pan under the vehicle to catch any fluid that spills out when the hoses are disconnected.
3   Loosen the right front wheel lug nuts, raise the vehicle and support it securely on jackstands. Remove the wheel.
4   Remove the suspension crossmember **(see illustration 2.3)**.
5   Loosen the clamps and pull the vacuum hoses off the air control valve (if equipped).
6   Loosen the clamp and disconnect the fluid return hose from the pump **(see illustration)**.
7   Remove   the   pressure   line-to-pump

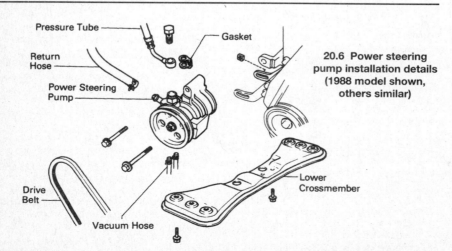

20.6 Power steering pump installation details (1988 model shown, others similar)

Pressure Tube
Gasket
Return Hose
Power Steering Pump
Drive Belt
Vacuum Hose
Lower Crossmember

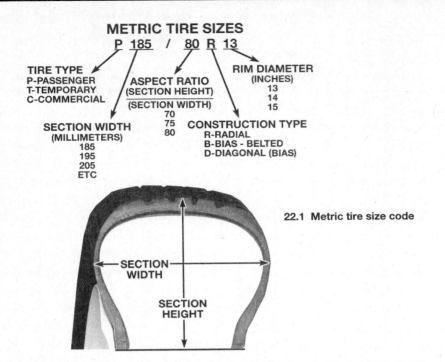

METRIC TIRE SIZES
P 185 / 80 R 13

TIRE TYPE
P-PASSENGER
T-TEMPORARY
C-COMMERCIAL

ASPECT RATIO
(SECTION HEIGHT)
――――――――――
(SECTION WIDTH)
70
75
80

RIM DIAMETER
(INCHES)
13
14
15

SECTION WIDTH
(MILLIMETERS)
185
195
205
ETC

CONSTRUCTION TYPE
R-RADIAL
B-BIAS - BELTED
D-DIAGONAL (BIAS)

SECTION WIDTH

SECTION HEIGHT

22.1 Metric tire size code

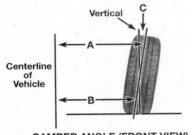

CAMBER ANGLE (FRONT VIEW)

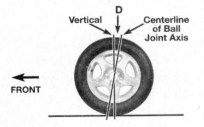

CASTER ANGLE (SIDE VIEW)

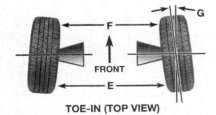

TOE-IN (TOP VIEW)

23.1 Front end alignment details - camber (top) and toe-in (bottom). The actual adjustment of these angles is beyond the scope of the home mechanic and must be performed by an alignment shop or service station

union bolt and separate the line from the pump. Remove the copper sealing washers on each side of the fitting - these should be replaced when installing the pump.

8   Remove the pivot and adjuster bolt and lower the pump from the vehicle.

Installation

9   To install the pump, reverse the removal procedure. Adjust the drivebelt tension following the procedure described in Chapter 1.

10   Top up the fluid level in the reservoir and bleed the system (see the following Section).

21   Power steering system - bleeding

1   Following any operation in which the power steering fluid lines have been disconnected, the power steering system must be bled to remove all air and obtain proper steering performance.

2   With the front wheels in the straight ahead position, check the power steering fluid level and, if low, add fluid until it reaches the Cold mark on the dipstick.

3   Start the engine and allow it to run at fast idle. Recheck the fluid level and add more if necessary to reach the Cold mark on the dipstick.

4   Bleed the system by turning the wheels from side to side, without hitting the stops. This will work the air out of the system. Keep the reservoir full of fluid as this is done.

5   When the air is worked out of the system, return the wheels to the straight ahead position and leave the vehicle running for several more minutes before shutting it off.

6   Road test the vehicle to be sure the steering system is functioning normally and noise free.

7   Recheck the fluid level to be sure it is up to the Hot mark on the dipstick while the engine is at normal operating temperature. Add fluid if necessary (see Chapter 1).

22   Wheels and tires - general information

Refer to illustration 22.1

All vehicles covered by this manual are equipped with metric-sized fiberglass or steel belted radial tires **(see illustration)**. Use of other size or type of tires may affect the ride and handling of the vehicle. Don't mix different types of tires, such as radials and bias belted, on the same vehicle as handling may be seriously affected. It's recommended that tires be replaced in pairs on the same axle, but if only one tire is being replaced, be sure it's the same size, structure and tread design as the other.

Because tire pressure has a substantial effect on handling and wear, the pressure on all tires should be checked at least once a month or before any extended trips (see Chapter 1).

Wheels must be replaced if they are bent, dented, leak air, have elongated bolt holes, are heavily rusted, out of vertical symmetry or if the lug nuts won't stay tight. Wheel repairs that use welding or peening are not recommended.

Tire and wheel balance is important in the overall handling, braking and performance of the vehicle. Unbalanced wheels can adversely affect handling and ride characteristics as well as tire life. Whenever a tire is installed on a wheel, the tire and wheel should be balanced by a shop with the proper equipment.

23   Front end alignment - general information

Refer to illustration 23.1

A front end alignment refers to the adjustments made to the front wheels so they are in proper angular relationship to the suspension and the ground. Front wheels that are out of proper alignment not only affect steering control, but also increase tire wear. The front end adjustments normally required are camber, caster and toe-in **(see illustration)**.

Getting the proper front wheel alignment is a very exacting process, one in which complicated and expensive machines are necessary to perform the job properly. Because of this, you should have a technician with the proper equipment perform these tasks. We will, however, use this space to give you a basic idea of what is involved with front end alignment so you can better understand the process and deal intelligently with the shop that does the work.

Toe-in is the turning in of the front wheels. The purpose of a toe specification is to ensure parallel rolling of the front wheels. In a vehicle with zero toe-in, the distance between the front edges of the wheels will be the same as the distance between the rear edges of the wheels. The actual amount of toe-in is normally only a fraction of an inch. Toe-in adjustment is controlled by the tie-rod end position on the inner tie-rod. Incorrect toe-in will cause the tires to wear improperly by making them scrub against the road surface.

Camber is the tilting of the front wheels from the vertical when viewed from the front of the vehicle. When the wheels tilt out at the top, the camber is said to be positive (+). When the wheels tilt in at the top the camber is negative (-). The amount of tilt is measured in degrees from the vertical and this measurement is called the camber angle. This angle affects the amount of tire tread which contacts the road and compensates for changes in the suspension geometry when the vehicle is cornering or traveling over an undulating surface.

Caster is the tilting of the front steering axis from the vertical. A tilt toward the rear is positive caster and a tilt toward the front is negative caster.

Caster is adjusted by inserting (or removing) spacers between the stabilizer bar and control arm.

Chapter 11 Body

Contents

1   General information

These models feature a "unibody" layout, using a floor pan with front and rear frame side rails which support the body components, front and rear suspension systems and other mechanical components.

Certain components are particularly vulnerable to accident damage and can be unbolted and repaired or replaced. Among these parts are the body moldings, bumpers, hood and trunk lids and all glass.

Only general body maintenance practices and body panel repair procedures within the scope of the do-it-yourselfer are included in this Chapter.

2   Body - maintenance

1   The condition of your vehicle's body is very important, because the resale value depends a great deal on it. It's much more difficult to repair a neglected or damaged body than it is to repair mechanical components. The hidden areas of the body, such as the wheel wells, the frame and the engine compartment, are equally important, although they don't require as frequent attention as the rest of the body.

2   Once a year, or every 12,000 miles, it's a good idea to have the underside of the body steam cleaned. All traces of dirt and oil will be removed and the area can then be inspected carefully for rust, damaged brake lines, frayed electrical wires, damaged cables and other problems. The front suspension components should be greased after completion of this job.

3   At the same time, clean the engine and the engine compartment with a steam cleaner or water soluble degreaser.

4   The wheel wells should be given close attention, since undercoating can peel away and stones and dirt thrown up by the tires can cause the paint to chip and flake, allowing rust to set in. If rust is found, clean down to the bare metal and apply an anti-rust paint.

5   The body should be washed about once a week. Wet the vehicle thoroughly to soften the dirt, then wash it down with a soft sponge and plenty of clean soapy water. If the surplus dirt is not washed off very carefully, it can wear down the paint.

6   Spots of tar or asphalt thrown up from the road should be removed with a cloth soaked in solvent.

7   Once every six months, wax the body and chrome trim. If a chrome cleaner is used to remove rust from any of the vehicle's plated parts, remember that the cleaner also removes part of the chrome, so use it sparingly.

3   Vinyl trim - maintenance

Don't clean vinyl trim with detergents, caustic soap or petroleum-based cleaners. Plain soap and water works just fine, with a soft brush to clean dirt that may be ingrained. Wash the vinyl as frequently as the rest of the vehicle.

After cleaning, application of a high quality rubber and vinyl protectant will help prevent oxidation and cracks. The protectant can also be applied to weatherstripping, vacuum lines and rubber hoses, which often fail as a result of chemical degradation, and to the tires.

4   Upholstery and carpets - maintenance

1   Every three months remove the carpets or mats and clean the interior of the vehicle (more frequently if necessary). Vacuum the upholstery and carpets to remove loose dirt and dust.

2   Leather upholstery requires special care. Stains should be removed with warm water and a very mild soap solution. Use a clean, damp cloth to remove the soap, then wipe again with a dry cloth. Never use alcohol, gasoline, nail polish remover or thinner to clean leather upholstery.

3   After cleaning, regularly treat leather upholstery with a leather wax. Never use car wax on leather upholstery.

4   In areas where the interior of the vehicle is subject to bright sunlight, cover leather seats with a sheet if the vehicle is to be left out for any length of time.

5   Body repair - minor damage

See photo sequence

Repair of minor scratches

1   If the scratch is superficial and does not penetrate to the metal of the body, repair is very simple. Lightly rub the scratched area with a fine rubbing compound to remove loose paint and built-up wax. Rinse the area with clean water.

2   Apply touch-up paint to the scratch, using a small brush. Continue to apply thin layers of paint until the surface of the paint in the scratch is level with the surrounding paint. Allow the new paint at least two weeks to harden, then blend it into the surrounding paint by rubbing with a very fine rubbing compound. Finally, apply a coat of wax to the scratch area.

3   If the scratch has penetrated the paint and exposed the metal of the body, causing the metal to rust, a different repair technique is required. Remove all loose rust from the bottom of the scratch with a pocket knife, then apply rust inhibiting paint to prevent the formation of rust in the future. Using a rubber or nylon applicator, coat the scratched area with glaze-type filler. If required, the filler can be mixed with thinner to provide a very thin paste, which is ideal for filling narrow scratches. Before the glaze filler in the scratch hardens, wrap a piece of smooth cotton cloth around the tip of a finger. Dip the cloth in thinner and then quickly wipe it along the surface of the scratch. This will ensure that the surface of the filler is slightly hollow. The scratch can now be painted over as described earlier in this section.

Repair of dents

4   When repairing dents, the first job is to pull the dent out until the affected area is as close as possible to its original shape. There is no point in trying to restore the original shape completely as the metal in the damaged area will have stretched on impact and

These photos illustrate a method of repairing simple dents. They are intended to supplement *Body repair - minor damage* in this Chapter and should not be used as the sole instructions for body repair on these vehicles.

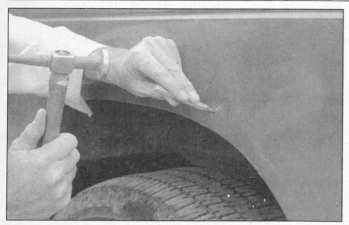

1   If you can't access the backside of the body panel to hammer out the dent, pull it out with a slide-hammer-type dent puller. In the deepest portion of the dent or along the crease line, drill or punch hole(s) at least one inch apart . . .

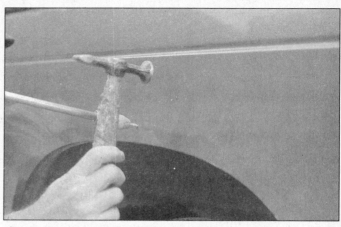

2   . . . then screw the slide-hammer into the hole and operate it. Tap with a hammer near the edge of the dent to help 'pop' the metal back to its original shape. When you're finished, the dent area should be close to its original contour and about 1/8-inch below the surface of the surrounding metal

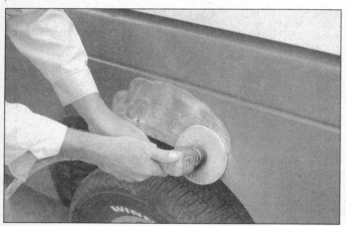

3   Using coarse-grit sandpaper, remove the paint down to the bare metal. Hand sanding works fine, but the disc sander shown here makes the job faster. Use finer (about 320-grit) sandpaper to feather-edge the paint at least one inch around the dent area

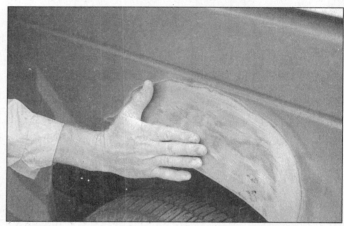

4   When the paint is removed, touch will probably be more helpful than sight for telling if the metal is straight. Hammer down the high spots or raise the low spots as necessary. Clean the repair area with wax/silicone remover

5   Following label instructions, mix up a batch of plastic filler and hardener. The ratio of filler to hardener is critical, and, if you mix it incorrectly, it will either not cure properly or cure too quickly (you won't have time to file and sand it into shape)

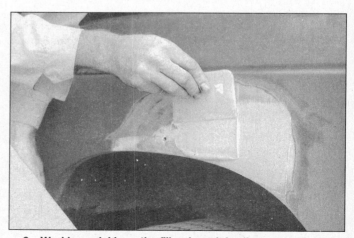

6   Working quickly so the filler doesn't harden, use a plastic applicator to press the body filler firmly into the metal, assuring it bonds completely. Work the filler until it matches the original contour and is slightly above the surrounding metal

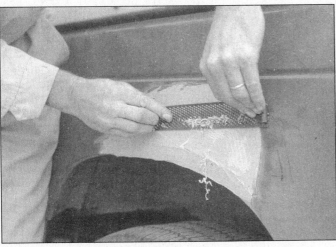

7 Let the filler harden until you can just dent it with your fingernail. Use a body file or Surform tool (shown here) to rough-shape the filler

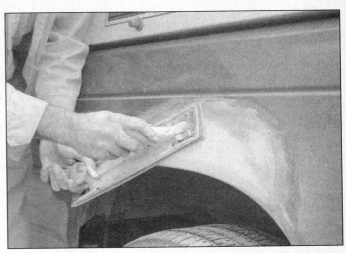

8 Use coarse-grit sandpaper and a sanding board or block to work the filler down until it's smooth and even. Work down to finer grits of sandpaper - always using a board or block - ending up with 360 or 400 grit

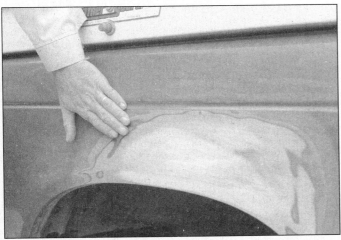

9 You shouldn't be able to feel any ridge at the transition from the filler to the bare metal or from the bare metal to the old paint. As soon as the repair is flat and uniform, remove the dust and mask off the adjacent panels or trim pieces

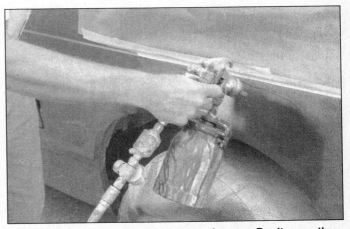

10 Apply several layers of primer to the area. Don't spray the primer on too heavy, so it sags or runs, and make sure each coat is dry before you spray on the next one. A professional-type spray gun is being used here, but aerosol spray primer is available inexpensively from auto parts stores

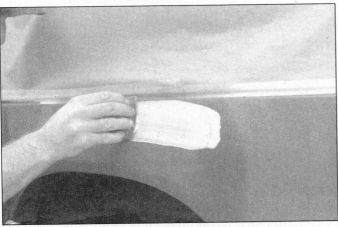

11 The primer will help reveal imperfections or scratches. Fill these with glazing compound. Follow the label instructions and sand it with 360 or 400-grit sandpaper until it's smooth. Repeat the glazing, sanding and respraying until the primer reveals a perfectly smooth surface

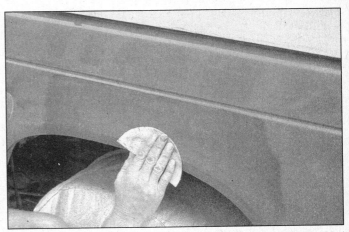

12 Finish sand the primer with very fine sandpaper (400 or 600-grit) to remove the primer overspray. Clean the area with water and allow it to dry. Use a tack rag to remove any dust, then apply the finish coat. Don't attempt to rub out or wax the repair area until the paint has dried completely (at least two weeks)

cannot be restored to its original contours. It is better to bring the level of the dent up to a point which is about 1/8-inch below the level of the surrounding metal. In cases where the dent is very shallow, it is not worth trying to pull it out at all.

5   If the back side of the dent is accessible, it can be hammered out gently from behind using a soft-face hammer. While doing this, hold a block of wood firmly against the opposite side of the metal to absorb the hammer blows and prevent the metal from being stretched.

6   If the dent is in a section of the body which has double layers, or some other factor makes it inaccessible from behind, a different technique is required. Drill several small holes through the metal inside the damaged area, particularly in the deeper sections. Screw long, self-tapping screws into the holes just enough for them to get a good grip in the metal. Now the dent can be pulled out by pulling on the protruding heads of the screws with locking pliers.

7   The next stage of repair is the removal of paint from the damaged area and from an inch or so of the surrounding metal. This is done with a wire brush or sanding disk in a drill motor, although it can be done just as effectively by hand with sandpaper. To complete the preparation for filling, score the surface of the bare metal with a screwdriver or the tang of a file, or drill small holes in the affected area. This will provide a good grip for the filler material. To complete the repair, see the subsection on filling and painting later in this Section.

Repair of rust holes or gashes

8   Remove all paint from the affected area and from an inch or so of the surrounding metal using a sanding disk or wire brush mounted in a drill motor. If these are not available, a few sheets of sandpaper will do the job just as effectively.

9   With the paint removed, you will be able to determine the severity of the corrosion and decide whether to replace the whole panel, if possible, or repair the affected area. New body panels are not as expensive as most people think and it is often quicker to install a new panel than to repair large areas of rust.

10   Remove all trim pieces from the affected area except those which will act as a guide to the original shape of the damaged body, such as headlight shells, etc. Using metal snips or a hacksaw blade, remove all loose metal and any other metal that is badly affected by rust. Hammer the edges of the hole inward to create a slight depression for the filler material.

11   Wire brush the affected area to remove the powdery rust from the surface of the metal. If the back of the rusted area is accessible, treat it with rust inhibiting paint.

12   Before filling is done, block the hole in some way. This can be done with sheet metal riveted or screwed into place, or by stuffing the hole with wire mesh.

13   Once the hole is blocked off, the af-

fected area can be filled and painted. See the following subsection on filling and painting.

Filling and painting

14   Many types of body fillers are available, but generally speaking, body repair kits which contain filler paste and a tube of resin hardener are best for this type of repair work. A wide, flexible plastic or nylon applicator will be necessary for imparting a smooth and contoured finish to the surface of the filler material. Mix up a small amount of filler on a clean piece of wood or cardboard (use the hardener sparingly). Follow the manufacturer's instructions on the package, otherwise the filler will set incorrectly.

15   Using the applicator, apply the filler paste to the prepared area. Draw the applicator across the surface of the filler to achieve the desired contour and to level the filler surface. As soon as a contour that approximates the original one is achieved, stop working the paste. If you continue, the paste will begin to stick to the applicator. Continue to add thin layers of paste at 20-minute intervals until the level of the filler is just above the surrounding metal.

16   Once the filler has hardened, the excess can be removed with a body file. From then on, progressively finer grades of sandpaper should be used, starting with a 180-grit paper and finishing with 600-grit wet-or-dry paper. Always wrap the sandpaper around a flat rubber or wooden block, otherwise the surface of the filler will not be completely flat. During the sanding of the filler surface, the wet-or-dry paper should be periodically rinsed in water. This will ensure that a very smooth finish is produced in the final stage.

17   At this point, the repair area should be surrounded by a ring of bare metal, which in turn should be encircled by the finely feathered edge of good paint. Rinse the repair area with clean water until all of the dust produced by the sanding operation is gone.

18   Spray the entire area with a light coat of primer. This will reveal any imperfections in the surface of the filler. Repair the imperfections with fresh filler paste or glaze filler and once more smooth the surface with sandpaper. Repeat this spray-and-repair procedure until you are satisfied that the surface of the filler and the feathered edge of the paint are perfect. Rinse the area with clean water and allow it to dry completely.

19   The repair area is now ready for painting. Spray painting must be carried out in a warm, dry, windless and dust free atmosphere. These conditions can be created if you have access to a large indoor work area, but if you are forced to work in the open, you will have to pick the day very carefully. If you are working indoors, dousing the floor in the work area with water will help settle the dust which would otherwise be in the air. If the repair area is confined to one body panel, mask off the surrounding panels. This will help minimize the effects of a slight mismatch in paint color. Trim pieces such as chrome strips, door handles, etc., will also need to be

masked off or removed. Use masking tape and several thicknesses of newspaper for the masking operations.

20   Before spraying, shake the paint can thoroughly, then spray a test area until the spray painting technique is mastered. Cover the repair area with a thick coat of primer. The thickness should be built up using several thin layers of primer rather than one thick one. Using 600-grit wet-or-dry sandpaper, rub down the surface of the primer until it is very smooth. While doing this, the work area should be thoroughly rinsed with water and the wet-or-dry sandpaper periodically rinsed as well. Allow the primer to dry before spraying additional coats.

21   Spray on the top coat, again building up the thickness by using several thin layers of paint. Begin spraying in the center of the repair area and then, using a circular motion, work out until the whole repair area and about two inches of the surrounding original paint is covered. Remove all masking material 10 to 15 minutes after spraying on the final coat of paint. Allow the new paint at least two weeks to harden, then use a very fine rubbing compound to blend the edges of the new paint into the existing paint. Finally, apply a coat of wax.

6   Body repair - major damage

1   Major damage must be repaired by an auto body shop specifically equipped to perform unibody repairs. These shops have the specialized equipment required to do the job properly.

2   If the damage is extensive, the body must be checked for proper alignment or the vehicle's handling characteristics may be adversely affected and other components may wear at an accelerated rate.

3   Due to the fact that all of the major body components (hood, fenders, etc.) are separate and replaceable units, any seriously damaged components should be replaced rather than repaired. Sometimes the components can be found in a wrecking yard that specializes in used vehicle components, often at considerable savings over the cost of new parts.

7   Hinges and locks - maintenance

Once every 3000 miles, or every three months, the hinges and latch assemblies on the doors, hood and trunk should be given a few drops of light oil or lock lubricant. The door latch strikers should also be lubricated with a thin coat of grease to reduce wear and ensure free movement. Lubricate the door and trunk locks with spray-on graphite lubricant.

8   Fixed glass - replacement

Replacement of the windshield and

fixed glass requires the use of special fast-setting adhesive/caulk materials and some specialized tools. It is recommended that these operations be left to a dealer or a shop specializing in glass work.

9   Hood - removal, installation and adjustment

Refer to illustrations 9.2, 9.9, 9.10a, 9.10b and 9.11

Note: *The hood is heavy and somewhat awkward to remove and install - at least two people should perform this procedure.*

Removal and installation

1   Use blankets or pads to cover the cowl area of the body and fenders. This will protect the body and paint as the hood is lifted free.
2   Scribe or paint alignment marks around the bolt heads to ensure proper alignment upon installation **(see illustration)**.
3   Disconnect any cables or electrical connectors which will interfere with removal.
4   Have an assistant support the weight of the hood. Remove the hinge-to-hood screws or bolts.
5   Lift off the hood.
6   Installation is the reverse of removal.

Adjustment

7   Fore-and-aft and side-to-side adjustment of the hood is made by moving the hinge plate slot after loosening the bolts or nuts.
8   Scribe a line around the entire hinge plate so you can judge the amount of movement **(see illustration 9.2)**.
9   Loosen the bolts or nuts and move the hood into correct alignment **(see illustration)**.

9.10b Squeeze all of the clips in (arrows) and then pull the grille out for access to the latch

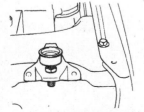

9.11 Turn the hood bumpers with a screwdriver to adjust the hood so that it is flush with the fenders when closed

Move the hood only a little at a time. Tighten the hinge bolts or nuts and carefully lower the hood to check the position.
10   If necessary after installation, the entire hood latch assembly can be adjusted up-and-down as well as side-to-side on the radiator support so the hood closes securely, with the hood flush with the fenders. To perform this adjustment, scribe a line around the hood latch mounting screws to provide a reference point, then loosen them and reposition the latch assembly, as necessary **(see illustration)**. If necessary, remove the grille for access by squeezing the grille retaining clips and pulling out sharply to detach it **(see illustration)**. Press the grille into place until the clips lock to reinstall it. Following adjustment, retighten the mounting bolts.
11   Finally, adjust the hood bumpers on the radiator support so that the hood, when

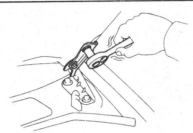

9.9 After loosening the hinge-to-hood bolts, the hood position can be adjusted

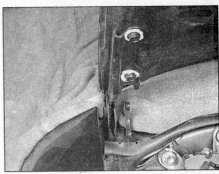

9.2 Use white paint or a scribe to mark the hood bolt locations - note the cloths protecting the windshield and body from damage if the hood should swing back

9.10a Loosen the bolts with a wrench, reposition the latch and retighten the bolts before checking the hood alignment

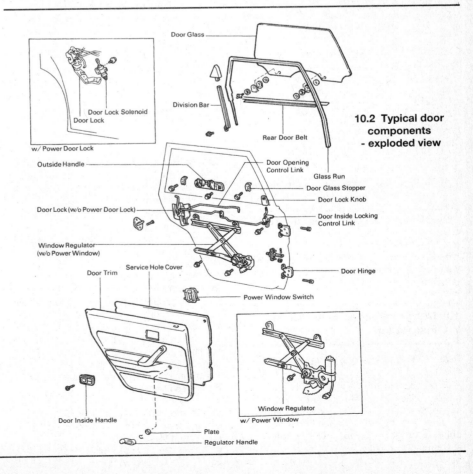

10.2 Typical door components - exploded view

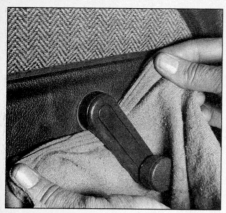

10.3a Work a cloth up behind the regulator handle and move it back and forth . . .

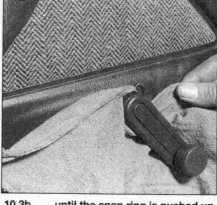

10.3b . . . until the snap ring is pushed up so you can remove it

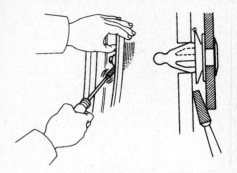

10.4 Pry under the clips to detach the trim panel

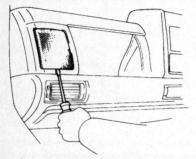

11.1a On earlier models the instrument panel speaker panels can be pried loose with a screwdriver

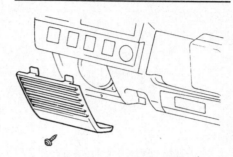

11.1b Later model speaker panels are held in place by a screw

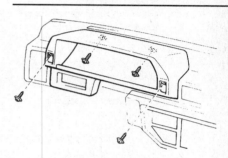

11.2a After prying the switch cover loose, the instrument cluster finish panel can be detached after removing the four retaining screws (1983 through 1986 models)

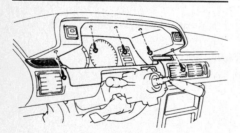

11.2b 1987 and 1988 instrument cluster finish panel details

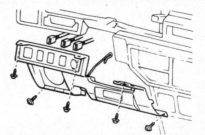

11.3a Remove the five retaining screws, detach the lower finish panel, unplug the connectors and remove the panel (1983 through 1986 models)

closed, is flush with the fenders (see illustration).

12   The hood latch assembly, as well as the hinges, should be periodically lubricated with white lithium base grease to prevent sticking or jamming.

10   Door trim panel - removal and installation

Refer to illustrations 10.2, 10.3a, 10.3b and 10.4

1   Disconnect the negative cable from the battery. Place the cable out of the way so it cannot accidentally come in contact with the negative terminal of the battery, as this would once again allow power into the electrical system of the vehicle.

2   Remove any door trim panel retaining screws and door pull/armrest assemblies (see illustration).

3   On manual window regulator equipped models, remove the window crank by working a cloth back and forth behind the handle to dislodge the snap-ring (see illustrations). On power regulator models, pry off the control switch assembly and unplug it.

4   Insert a large putty knife or a thin pry bar between the trim panel and the door and disengage the retaining clips, working around the outer edge until the panel is free of the door (see illustration).

5   Once all of the clips are disengaged, detach the trim panel, lift it away, unplug any electrical connectors and remove the trim panel from the vehicle.

6   For access to the inner door, peel back

the plastic service hole cover, taking care not to tear it. To install, place the service hole cover in position and press it in place.

7   Prior to installation of the door panel, make sure to reinstall any clips in the panel which may have come out during the removal procedure and remain in the door itself.

8   Plug in any electrical connectors and place the panel in position in the door. Press the door panel into place until the clips are seated and install any retaining screws and armrest/door pulls. Install the manual regulator window crank or power switch assembly.

11   Instrument panel finish panels - removal and installation

Speaker panels

Refer to illustrations 11.1a and 11.1b

1   Remove any screws and pry the panel(s) free with a screwdriver (see illustrations). Installation is the reverse of removal.

Instrument cluster finish panel

Refer to illustrations 11.2a and 11.2b

2   Remove the retaining screws, rotate the panel down and lower it from the instrument panel (see illustrations). Installation is the reverse of removal.

Lower finish panel

Refer to illustrations 11.3a and 11.3b

3   Remove the retaining screws, pull the

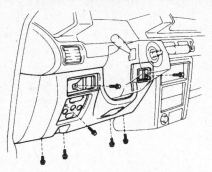

11.3b 1987 and 1988 lower finish panel details

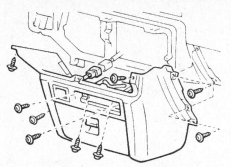

11.4a 1983 through 1986 model instrument panel center lower finish panel details

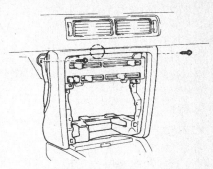

11.4b Instrument panel center lower finish panel details (1987 and 1988 models)

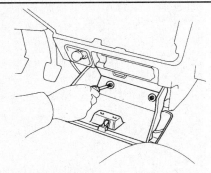

11.5a Open the glove compartment for access to the retaining screws (1983 through 1986 models)

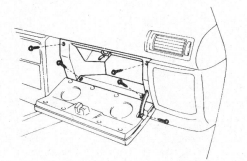

11.5b 1987 and 1988 glove compartment details

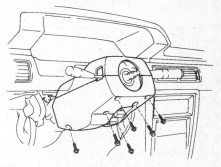

12.1 The steering column cover screws are accessible from under the column

panel down, unplug any electrical connectors and detach the panel **(see illustrations)**. Installation is the reverse of removal.

Center lower panel

Refer to illustrations 11.4a and 11.4b

4   Remove the retaining screws, detach the panel and lower it from the instrument panel **(see illustrations)**. Installation is the reverse of removal.

Glove compartment

Refer to illustrations 11.5a and 11.5b

5   Open the glove compartment for access, remove the retaining screws and pull the assembly down out of the instrument panel **(see illustrations)**. Installation is the reverse of removal.

12   Steering column cover - removal and installation

Refer to illustration 12.1

1   Remove the retaining screws **(see illustration)**.
2   Carefully pry the halves of the cover apart. Unplug any electrical connectors and remove the cover halves from the steering column.
3   Installation is the reverse of removal.

13   Door - removal, installation and adjustment

Refer to illustrations 13.2, 13.3, 13.5a, 13.5b, 13.5c, 13.5d and 13.5e

1   Remove the door trim panel. Disconnect any electrical connectors and push them through the door opening so they won't interfere with door removal.
2   Either place a jack or stand under the door or have an assistant on hand to support

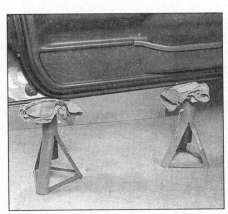

13.2 Use two jackstands padded with rags (to protect the paint) to support the door during the removal and installation procedures

it when the hinge bolts are removed **(see illustration)**. **Note:** *If a jack or stand is being used, place a rag between it and the door to protect the door's painted surfaces.*
3   Scribe around the door bolts **(see illustration)**.
4   Remove the hinge-to-door bolts and carefully lift off the door. Installation is the reverse of removal.
5   Following installation of the door, check that it is in proper alignment and adjust it if necessary as follows:

13.3 Before loosening or removing them, scribe or paint around the door bolts

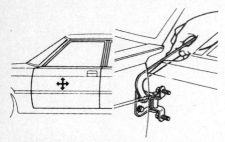

13.5a When adjusting the front door forward or backward, up or down, a special cranked wrench such as this one, available at most auto parts stores, or equivalent will make the job easier

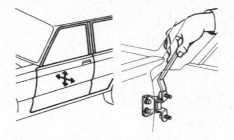

13.5b Adjust the front door up and down or in and out after loosening the hinge to door bolts with a box end wrench

13.5c Use a socket with extension to loosen the bolts when making rear door adjustments

13.5d Use a box end wrench to loosen the rear door side hinge bolts (left/right and vertical adjustment)

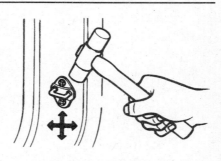

13.5e Adjust the door lock striker by loosening the retaining screws and tapping the striker in the desired direction

14.3 Scribe or paint around the trunk lid bolts before removing them

a) *Up-and-down and forward-and-backward adjustments are made by loosening the hinge-to-body bolts and moving the door, as necessary. A special cranked tool may be required to reach some of the bolts* **(see illustrations).**

b) *The door lock striker can also be adjusted both up-and-down and sideways to provide a positive engagement with the locking mechanism. This is done by loosening the screws and moving the striker, as necessary* **(see illustration).**

14   Trunk lid - removal, installation and adjustment

Refer to illustrations 14.3, 14.6, 14.7a and 14.7b

1   Open the trunk lid and cover the edges of the trunk compartment with pads or cloths to protect the painted surfaces when the lid is removed.

2   Disconnect any cable or electrical connectors which are attached to the trunk lid and would interfere with removal.

3   Scribe or paint alignment marks around the hinge bolt mounting flanges **(see illustration).**

4   While an assistant supports the lid, remove the lid-to-hinge bolts on both sides and lift off the lid.

5   Installation is the reverse of removal. **Note:** *When reinstalling the trunk lid, align the lid-to-hinge bolts with the marks made during removal.*

6   After installation, close the lid and check that it is in proper alignment with the surrounding panels. Fore-and-aft and side-to-side adjustments of the lid are controlled by the position of the hinge bolts in their slots. To adjust, loosen the hinge bolts, reposition the lid and retighten the bolts **(see illustration).**

7   The height of the lid in relation to the surrounding body panels when closed can be adjusted by loosening the lock and/or striker bolts, repositioning the striker and tightening the bolts **(see illustrations).**

14.6 Use a wrench to loosen the trunk lid bolts so the lid position can be adjusted

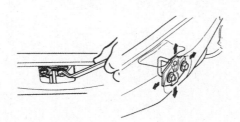

14.7a On 1983 through 1986 models, the trunk lid lock striker position can be adjusted after loosening the retaining bolts

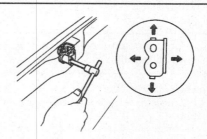

14.7b On 1987 and 1988 models, loosen the trunk lid lock striker bolts and use a punch and hammer to tap the striker into the proper position

15 Liftgate - removal, installation and adjustment

Refer to illustrations 15.4, 15.5 and 15.8

1   Open the liftgate and cover the upper body area around the opening with pads or cloths to protect the painted surfaces when the liftgate is removed.

2   Disconnect any cables, hoses or electrical connectors which would interfere with removal of the liftgate.

3   Paint or scribe around the mounting bolts.

4   While an assistant supports the liftgate, detach the support struts **(see illustration)**.

5   Remove the hinge bolts and detach the liftgate from the vehicle **(see illustration)**.

6   Installation is the reverse of removal.

7   After installation, close the liftgate and check that the door is in proper alignment with the surrounding panels. Adjustments to the liftgate are made by moving the position

15.4 Use an open end wrench to unscrew the liftgate support strut nuts

of the hinge bolts in their slots. To adjust, loosen the hinge bolts and reposition them either side-to-side or fore-and-aft the desired amount and retighten the bolts.

8   The engagement of the liftgate can be adjusted by loosening the lock striker screws, repositioning the striker and tightening the screws **(see illustration)**.

16 Door lock, lock cylinder and handle - removal and installation

1   Remove the door trim panel and service hole cover (Section 10).

2   Remove the door window glass (Section 17).

Door lock

Refer to illustrations 16.4a, 16.4b and 16.5

3   Reach in through the door service hole and disconnect the control link from the lock (see illustration 10.2).

4   Remove the three door lock retaining screws from the end of the door **(see illustration)**. Remove the door lock and (if equipped) solenoid **(see illustration)**.

5   Installation is the reverse of removal. When connecting the outside door handle control link to the lock on 1983 through 1986 models, raise the link 0.020 to 0.039 inch (0.5

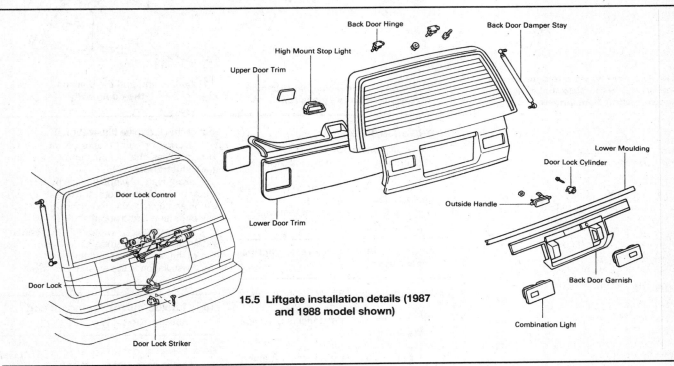

15.5 Liftgate installation details (1987 and 1988 model shown)

15.8 To adjust the liftgate lock striker, loosen the retaining screws and move the striker in the desired direction by tapping on it

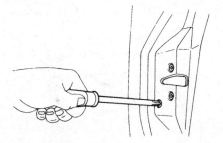

16.4a Use a Phillips head screwdriver to remove the door lock retaining screws located in the end of the door

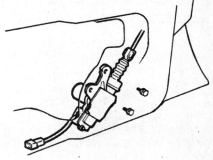

16.4b Door lock solenoid installation details

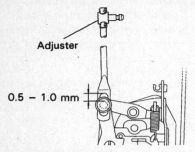

16.5 To adjust the outside handle during installation on 1983 through 1986 models, raise the control link with the adjuster and fit the pin into the hole

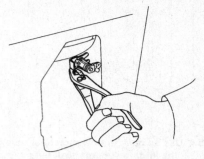

16.7 Use pliers to pull off the lock cylinder retaining clip

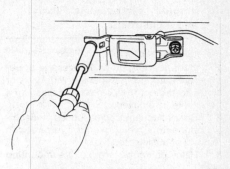

16.9 Use a screwdriver or nut driver to remove the inside door handle screws

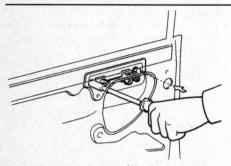

16.13 Remove the outside door handle retaining nuts from inside the door, using a socket with extension or nut driver

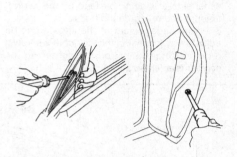

17.3a Remove the division bar retaining screws. pull out the glass run . . .

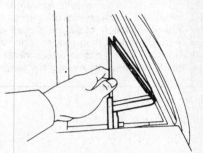

17.3b . . . and pull the division bar out of the door cavity

to 1.0 mm) and insert the pin into the lock hole by turning the adjuster **(see illustration)**.

Lock cylinder

Refer to illustration 16.7

6   Disconnect the control link and electrical connector (if equipped) from the lock cylinder.
7   Use pliers to slide the retaining clip off and remove the lock cylinder from the door **(see illustration)**.
8   Installation is the reverse of removal.

Inside handle

Refer to illustration 16.9

9   Remove the retaining screw(s) **(see illustration)**.
10   Rotate the handle away and detach it from the door.
11   Installation is the reverse of removal.

Outside handle

Refer to illustration 16.13

12   Disconnect the control link from the handle.
13   Remove the nuts and detach the handle from the door **(see illustration)**.
14   Installation is the reverse of removal.

---

17   Door window glass - removal and installation

Refer to illustrations 17.3a, 17.3b, 17.4 and 17.5

1   Remove the door trim panel and service hole cover (Section 10).
2   Lower the window glass.
3   On rear doors, remove the retaining screws and pull the glass run and division bar

out of the door **(see illustrations)**.
4   Scribe or paint marks on the two window-to-glass channel nuts and remove them **(see illustration)**.
5   Remove the window glass by tilting it to detach the glass from the glass channel studs and then sliding the glass up and out of the door **(see illustration)**.
6   If necessary, remove the regulator retaining bolts and then slide the regulator out of the opening in the door.
7   Installation is the reverse of removal.

---

18   Outside mirror - removal and installation

Refer to illustrations 18.1 and 18.3

1   Use a screwdriver to pry off the trim cover **(see illustration)**.

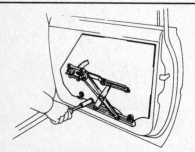

17.4 After marking their positions, remove the two window glass retaining nuts

17.5 Lift the door glass up and angle it out, toward the outside of the door

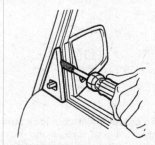

18.1 Pry off the outside mirror trim cover with a screwdriver

18.3 Use a Phillips head screwdriver to remove the three mirror retaining screws (arrows)

2   On power mirrors unplug the electrical connector.
3   Remove the three retaining screws and lift off the mirror **(see illustration)**.
4   Installation is the reverse of removal.

19   Seats - removal and installation

Refer to illustrations 19.1a, 19.1b and 19.1c
1   Remove the retaining bolts, unplug any electrical connectors and lift the seats from the vehicle **(see illustrations)**.
2   Installation is the reverse of removal.

20   Fender apron seal - removal and installation

Refer to illustration 20.2
1   Raise the vehicle, support it securely and remove the front wheel(s).
2   Pry out the retaining clips with a screwdriver, remove the bolts and lower the seal from the fender well **(see illustration)**.
3   Installation is the reverse of removal.

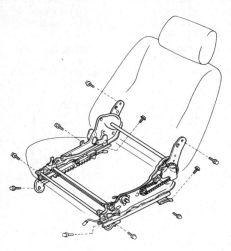

19.1b Typical front seat installation details (1987 and 1988 models)

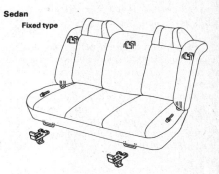

Sedan
Fixed type

Separate type

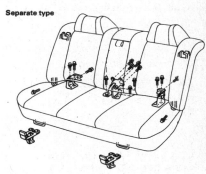

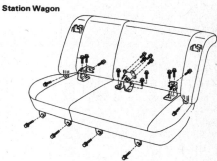

Station Wagon

19.1c Typical rear seat installation details (1987 and 1988 models)

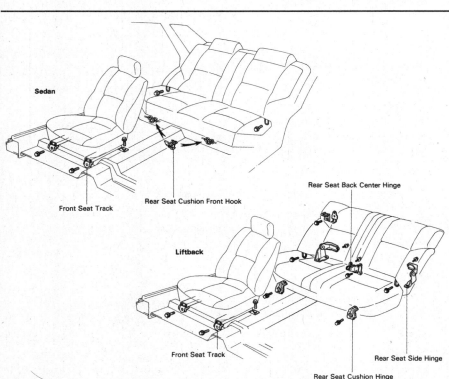

Sedan

Front Seat Track

Rear Seat Cushion Front Hook

Rear Seat Back Center Hinge

Liftback

Front Seat Track

Rear Seat Side Hinge

Rear Seat Cushion Hinge

19.1a Typical 1983 through 1986 model seat installation details

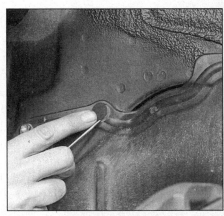

20.2 Pry out the fender apron seal plastic retaining pins with a small screwdriver

21 Seat belt check

1   Check the seat belts, buckles, latch plates and guide loops for any obvious damage or signs of wear.
2   Check that the seat belt reminder light comes on when the key is turned to the Run or Start positions. A chime should also sound.
3   The seat belts are designed to lock up during a sudden stop or impact, yet allow free movement during normal driving. Check that the retractors return the belt against your chest while driving and rewind the belt fully when the buckle is unlatched.
4   If any of the above checks reveal problems with the seat belt system, replace parts as necessary.

22 Automatic shoulder harnesses - general information

Many late model vehicles are equipped with automatic front seat shoulder harnesses. They are termed automatic because you don't have to buckle them - the shoulder harness automatically positions itself when the door is closed and the key is turned on. An emergency release lever allows the harness to be manually removed for exit in an emergency. **Warning:** *Be sure to fasten the manual seatbelt as well. The automatic shoulder harness will not work properly unless the seatbelt is fastened.*

Most systems have a warning light and buzzer that indicate the emergency release lever has been pulled up, releasing the shoulder harness. Make sure the release lever is down and the light/buzzer are off to ensure proper operation of the automatic shoulder harness. Also, if you disconnect any wires or remove any automatic shoulder harness components when performing repair procedures on other vehicle components, be sure to reinstall everything and check the harness for proper operation when the repairs are complete.

Since the automatic shoulder harness is operated by several electrical switches and is computer controlled, diagnosis and repair must be done by a dealer service department. Do not jeopardize the safety of front seat occupants - if the automatic shoulder harness malfunctions, or you have questions regarding the proper use or operation of the system, contact a dealer service department.

Chapter 12
Chassis electrical system

Contents

1 General information

The electrical system is a 12-volt, negative ground type. Power for the lights and all electrical accessories is supplied by a lead/acid-type battery which is charged by the alternator.

This Chapter covers repair and service procedures for the various electrical components not associated with the engine. Information on the battery, alternator, distributor and starter motor can be found in Chapter 5.

It should be noted that when portions of the electrical system are serviced, the cable should be disconnected from the negative battery terminal to prevent electrical shorts and/or fires.

2 Electrical troubleshooting - general information

A typical electrical circuit consists of an electrical component, any switches, relays, motors, fuses, fusible links or circuit breakers related to that component and the wiring and connectors that link the component to both the battery and the chassis. To help you pinpoint an electrical circuit problem, wiring diagrams are included at the end of this book.

Before tackling any troublesome electrical circuit, first study the appropriate wiring diagrams to get a complete understanding of what makes up that individual circuit. Trouble spots, for instance, can often be narrowed down by noting if other components related to the circuit are operating properly. If several components or circuits fail at one time, chances are the problem is in a fuse or ground connection, because several circuits are often routed through the same fuse and ground connections.

Electrical problems usually stem from simple causes, such as loose or corroded connections, a blown fuse, a melted fusible link or a bad relay. Visually inspect the condition of all fuses, wires and connections in a problem circuit before troubleshooting it.

If testing instruments are going to be utilized, use the diagrams to plan ahead of time where you will make the necessary connections in order to accurately pinpoint the trouble spot.

The basic tools needed for electrical troubleshooting include a circuit tester or voltmeter (a 12-volt bulb with a set of test leads can also be used), a continuity tester, which includes a bulb, battery and set of test leads, and a jumper wire, preferably with a circuit breaker incorporated, which can be used to bypass electrical components. Before attempting to locate a problem with test instruments, use the wiring diagram(s) to decide where to make the connections.

Voltage checks

Voltage checks should be performed if a circuit is not functioning properly. Connect one lead of a circuit tester to either the negative battery terminal or a known good ground. Connect the other lead to a connector in the circuit being tested, preferably nearest to the battery or fuse. If the bulb of the tester lights, voltage is present, which means that the part of the circuit between the connector and the battery is problem free. Continue checking the rest of the circuit in the same fashion. When you reach a point at which no voltage is present, the problem lies between that point and the last test point with voltage. Most of the time the problem can be traced to a loose connection. **Note:** *Keep in mind that some circuits receive voltage only when the ignition key is in the Accessory or Run position.*

Finding a short

One method of finding shorts in a circuit is to remove the fuse and connect a test light or voltmeter in its place to the fuse terminals.

There should be no voltage present in the circuit. Move the wiring harness from side to side while watching the test light. If the bulb goes on, there is a short to ground somewhere in that area, probably where the insulation has rubbed through. The same test can be performed on each component in the circuit, even a switch.

Ground check

Perform a ground test to check whether a component is properly grounded. Disconnect the battery and connect one lead of a self-powered test light, known as a continuity tester, to a known good ground. Connect the other lead to the wire or ground connection being tested. If the bulb goes on, the ground is good. If the bulb does not go on, the ground is not good.

Continuity check

A continuity check is done to determine if there are any breaks in a circuit - if it is passing electricity properly. With the circuit off (no power in the circuit), a self-powered continuity tester can be used to check the circuit. Connect the test leads to both ends of the circuit (or to the "power" end and a good ground), and if the test light comes on the circuit is passing current properly. If the light doesn't come on, there is a break somewhere in the circuit. The same procedure can be used to test a switch, by connecting the continuity tester to the power in and power out sides of the switch. With the switch turned On, the test light should come on.

Finding an open circuit

When diagnosing for possible open circuits, it is often difficult to locate them by sight because oxidation or terminal misalignment are hidden by the connectors. Merely wiggling a connector on a sensor or in the wiring harness may correct the open circuit condition. Remember this when an open circuit is indicated when troubleshooting a circuit. Intermittent problems may also be caused by oxidized or loose connections.

Electrical troubleshooting is simple if you keep in mind that all electrical circuits are basically electricity running from the battery, through the wires, switches, relays, fuses and fusible links to each electrical component (light bulb, motor, etc.) and to ground, from which it is passed back to the battery. Any electrical problem is an interruption in the flow of electricity to and from the battery.

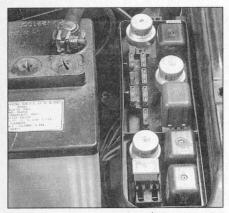

3.1 The engine compartment fuse block is located next to the battery, under a cover

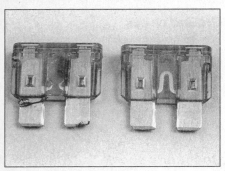

3.3 When a fuse blows, the element between the terminals melts - the fuse on the left is blown, the fuse on the right is good

4.3a The fusible links are protected by a cover which is marked with the link circuit and amperage

3 Fuses - general information

Refer to illustrations 3.1 and 3.3

The electrical circuits of the vehicle are protected by a combination of fuses, circuit breakers and fusible links. The fuse blocks are located under the instrument panel on the left side of the dashboard and next to the battery in the engine compartment **(see illustration)**.

Each of the fuses is designed to protect a specific circuit, and the various circuits are identified on the fuse panel itself.

Miniaturized fuses are employed in the fuse block. These compact fuses, with blade terminal design, allow fingertip removal and replacement. If an electrical component fails, always check the fuse first. A blown fuse is easily identified through the clear plastic body. Visually inspect the element for evidence of damage **(see illustration)**. If a continuity check is called for, the blade terminal tips are exposed in the fuse body.

Be sure to replace blown fuses with the correct type. Fuses of different ratings are physically interchangeable, but only fuses of the proper rating should be used. Replacing a fuse with one of a higher or lower value than specified is not recommended. Each electrical circuit needs a specific amount of protection. The amperage value of each fuse is molded into the fuse body.

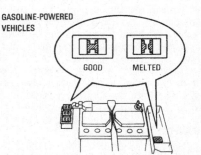

4.2 Fusible links can be checked visually to determine if they are melted

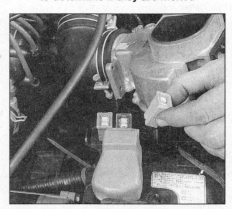

4.3b Unplug the fusible link and replace it with a new one - always determine the cause of the circuit overload before replacement

If the replacement fuse immediately fails, don't replace it again until the cause of the problem is isolated and corrected. In most cases, this will be a short circuit in the wiring caused by a broken or deteriorated wire.

4 Fusible links - general information

Refer to illustrations 4.2, 4.3a and 4.3b

Some circuits are protected by fusible links. The links are used in circuits which are not ordinarily fused, such as the ignition circuit.

The fusible links on these models are similar to fuses in that they can be visually checked to determine if they are melted **(see illustration)**.

To replace a fusible link, first disconnect the negative cable from the battery. Unplug the burned out link and replace it with a new one (available from your dealer) **(see illustrations)**. Always determine the cause for the overload which melted the fusible link before installing a new one.

5 Circuit breakers - general information

Refer to illustration 5.3

Circuit breakers protect components such as power windows, power door locks and headlights. Some circuit breakers are located in the fuse box.

Because on some models the circuit breaker resets itself automatically, an electrical overload in a circuit breaker protected system will cause the circuit to fail momentarily, then come back on. If the circuit does not come back on, check it immediately. Note, however, that some circuit breakers must be reset manually. Once the condition is corrected, the circuit breaker will resume its normal function.

To reset a manual circuit breaker, first

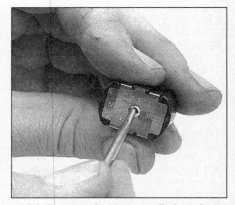

5.3 Insert a pin or paper clip into the circuit breaker reset hole and push in to reset it

disconnect the cable from the negative battery terminal. Remove the circuit breaker, insert a pin into the reset hole and push in **(see illustration)**. Reinstall the circuit breaker.

6   Relays - general information

Refer to illustrations 6.2a and 6.2b

Several electrical accessories in the vehicle use relays to transmit the electrical signal to the component. If the relay is defective, that component will not operate properly.

The various relays are grouped together in several locations under the dash for convenience in the event of needed replacement **(see illustrations)**.

If a faulty relay is suspected, it can be removed and tested by a dealer or other qualified shop. Defective relays must be replaced as a unit.

7   Turn signal/hazard flashers - check and replacement

1   The turn signal/hazard flasher, a small canister shaped unit located under the dash **(see illustrations 6.2a and 6.2b),** flashes the turn signals.
2   When the flasher unit is functioning properly, and audible click can be heard during its operation. If the turn signals fail on one side or the other and the flasher unit does not make its characteristic clicking sound, a faulty turn signal bulb is indicated.
3   If both turn signals fail to blink, the problem may be due to a blown fuse, a faulty flasher unit, a broken switch or a loose or open connection. If a quick check of the fuse box indicates that the turn signal fuse has blown, check the wiring for a short before installing a new fuse.
4   To replace the flasher, simply pull it out of the fuse block or wiring harness.
5   Make sure that the replacement unit is identical to the original. Compare the old one to the new one before installing it.
6   Installation is the reverse of removal.

8   Ignition switch and lock cylinder - removal and installation

1   Disconnect the negative cable at the battery. Place the cable out of the way so it cannot accidentally come in contact with the negative terminal of the battery, as this would once again allow power into the electrical system of the vehicle.
2   Remove the steering wheel (Chapter 10).
3   Remove the lower finish panel and the steering column cover (Chapter 11).

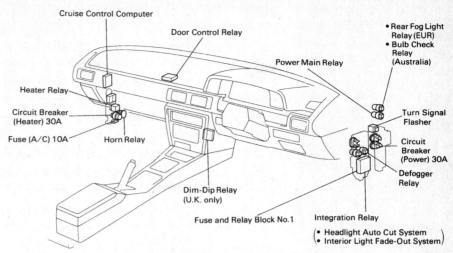

6.2a 1987 and 1988 model relay locations

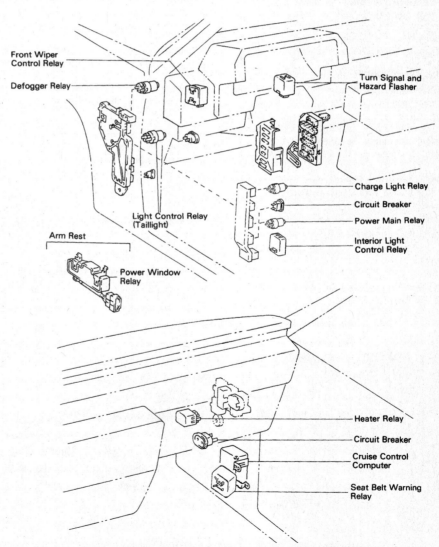

6.2b Typical relay locations (1983 through 1986 models)

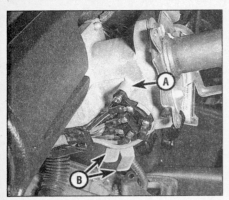

8.4 Remove the retaining screw (A), bend the wiring tabs (B) back and withdraw the ignition switch from the housing

Ignition switch

Refer to illustration 8.4

4   Remove the retaining screw and bend back the wiring retainer **(see illustration)**.
5   Unplug the electrical connector and lift the switch from the steering column.
6   Installation is the reverse of removal.

Lock cylinder

Refer to illustration 8.7

7   With the key in the Accessory position, insert a pin in the hole in the casting, pull the lock cylinder straight out and remove it from the steering column **(see illustration)**.
8   Installation is the reverse of removal.

---

9   Combination switch - removal and installation

Refer to illustrations 9.4 and 9.5

1   Disconnect the negative cable at the battery. Place the cable out of the way so it cannot accidentally come in contact with the negative terminal of the battery, as this would once again allow power into the electrical system of the vehicle.
2   Remove the steering wheel (Chapter 10).

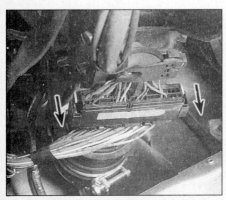

9.5 Release the harness clamp, swing it out of the way (arrow) and unplug the connector

8.7 Insert a pin or paper clip into the casting hole (a bent tool should be used due to limited clearance) and with the key in the Accessory position, pull the lock cylinder sharply in the direction shown to remove it

3   Remove the lower finish panel and steering column cover (Chapter 11).
4   Remove the retaining screws **(see illustration)**.
5   Trace the wiring harness down the steering column to the connector. Release the wiring retainer clamp (if equipped), unplug the connector and slide the switch up off the column **(see illustration)**.
6   Installation is the reverse of removal.

---

10   Steering column switches - removal and installation

1   Remove the combination switch (Section 9).

Turn signal/headlight control switch

Refer to illustration 10.2

2   Disconnect the wiring harness clips and pry off the switch cover with a small screwdriver **(see illustration)**.
3   Remove the retaining screws and lift the switch off.
4   Disconnect the switch wiring terminals

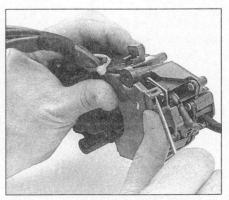

10.2 Use a small screwdriver to pry off the switch cover

9.4 Combination switch retaining screw locations (arrows)

from the combination switch connector plug (Steps 13 through 16).
5   Installation is the reverse of removal.

Wiper/washer/cruise control switch

Refer to illustration 10.6

6   Remove the retaining screws, detach the switch and lift it off the combination switch **(see illustration)**.
7   Disconnect the switch wiring terminals from the combination switch connector plug (Steps 13 through 16).
8   Installation is the reverse of removal.

Hazard warning flasher switch

Refer to illustration 10.10

9   Remove the turn signal/headlight control switch.
10   Remove the retaining screws, detach the switch and lift it off the combination switch **(see illustration)**.

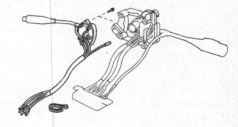

10.6 Wiper/washer switch details

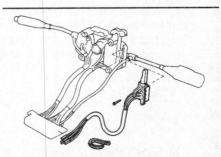

10.10 Hazard warning switch details

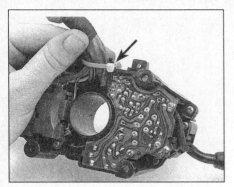

10.13 Cut or disconnect any wiring ties (arrow) or straps to make the job of tracing the switch wires to the combination switch connector easier

11   Disconnect the switch wiring terminals from the combination switch connector plug (Steps 13 through 16).
12   Installation is the reverse of removal.

Wiring connectors

Refer to illustrations 10.13, 10.14, 10.15a, 10.15b and 10.16

13   Trace the wiring harness from the switch be disconnected to the combination switch connector. It may be necessary to detach or cut some of the wiring ties or straps to separate the wires of a particular switch from the harness **(see illustration)**. Mark the wires and combination switch terminals with pieces of tape so that only the wires involved with a specific switch are disconnected.
14   Use a small screwdriver or punch to pry the combination switch cover up for access to the terminals **(see illustration)**.
15   Insert a small screwdriver or punch into the connector and pry the locking lug down, disconnect the terminal and then pull it out to remove it **(see illustrations)**.
16   To connect the terminal, insert it into the connector and push in with a small screwdriver until the locking lug snaps into place **(see illustration)**.
17   Snap the connector cover shut to lock the terminals.

---

11   Radio and speakers - removal and installation

1   Disconnect the negative cable at the battery. Place the cable out of the way so it cannot accidentally come in contact with the negative terminal of the battery, as this would once again allow power into the electrical system of the vehicle.

Radio

Refer to illustration 11.3

2   Remove the instrument panel center lower finish panel (Chapter 11).
3   Remove the radio mounting screws or bolts **(see illustration)**.

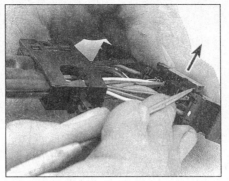

10.14 Use a small screwdriver or punch to push the combination switch connector up (arrow) for access to the terminals

4   Pull the radio out, reach behind it and unplug the electrical connector and the antenna lead.
5   Lift the radio from the instrument panel.
6   Installation is the reverse of removal.

Speakers

Refer to illustration 11.8

7   Remove the speaker cover(s) (Chapter 11).
8   Remove the retaining screws or bolts, unplug the connector and lower the speaker from the instrument panel **(see illustration)**.
9   Installation is the reverse of removal.

---

12   Headlights - removal and installation

1   Disconnect the negative cable from the battery. Place the cable out of the way so it cannot accidentally come in contact with the negative terminal of the battery, as this would once again allow power into the electrical system of the vehicle.

Sealed-beam type

Refer to illustration 12.2

2   Loosen the retaining screws, insert a screwdriver blade into the clips at the base to release them and detach the headlight bezel **(see illustration)**.
3   Remove the headlight retainer screws, taking care not to disturb the adjustment screws.

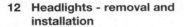

11.8 Instrument panel mounted speaker details

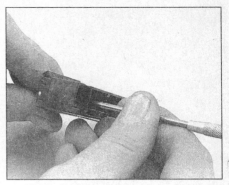

10.15a Insert a small screwdriver or punch into the connector . . .

10.15b . . . and pry the locking lug down so the terminal can be disconnected

10.16 Push in on the connector collar until the connector snaps in place

11.3 Typical radio installation details

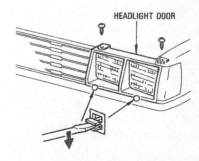

12.2 After loosening the screws, insert a flat screwdriver blade into the clips and turn to unlock the bezel so it can be lifted off (sealed beam headlights)

12.8 Press in on the locking tab and unplug the connector from the bulb-type headlight housing

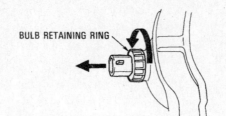

12.9 Turn the bulb retaining ring counterclockwise and withdraw the assembly from the housing

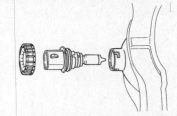

12.11 Bulb housing installation details - align the tab with the slot on the headlight housing, push in and turn clockwise to lock it

4   Remove the retainer and pull the headlight out sufficiently to allow the connector to be unplugged.

5   Remove the headlight.

6   To install, plug the connector securely into the headlight, place the headlight in position and install the retainer and screws. Tighten the screws securely.

7   Place the headlight bezel in position, press it into place and tighten the retaining screws.

Bulb type

Refer to illustrations 12.8, 12.9 and 12.11

Warning: *The halogen gas filled bulbs used on these models are under pressure and may shatter if the surface is scratched or the bulb is dropped. Wear eye protection and handle the bulbs carefully, grasping only the base whenever possible. Do not touch the surface of the bulb with your fingers because the oil*

from your skin could cause it to overheat and fail prematurely. If you do touch the bulb surface, clean it with rubbing alcohol.

8   Open the hood. Unplug the electrical connector **(see illustration)**.

9   Reach behind the headlight assembly, grasp the bulb holder and turn it counterclockwise to remove it **(see illustration)**. Lift the holder assembly out for access to the bulb.

10   Push in and rotate the bulb counterclockwise to remove it.

11   Insert the new bulb into the holder and turn it clockwise to seat it in the holder **(see illustration)**.

12   Install the bulb holder in the headlight assembly.

13   Headlights - adjustment

Refer to illustrations 13.6a and 13.6b

Note: *It is important that the headlights be aimed correctly. If adjusted incorrectly they*

could blind the driver of an oncoming vehicle and cause a serious accident or seriously reduce your ability to see the road. The headlights should be checked for proper aim every 12 months and any time a new headlight is installed or front end body work is performed. It should be emphasized that the following procedure is only an interim step which will provide temporary adjustment until the headlights can be adjusted by a properly equipped shop.

1   Headlights have two adjusting screws, one on the top controlling up and down movement and one on the side controlling left and right movement.

2   There are several methods of adjusting the headlights. The simplest method requires a blank wall 25 feet in front of the vehicle and a level floor *(see illustration)*.

3   Position masking tape vertically on the wall in reference to the vehicle centerline and the centerlines of both headlights.

4   Position a horizontal tape line in reference to the centerline of all the headlights.

Note: *It may be easier to position the tape on the wall with the vehicle parked only a few inches away.*

5   Adjustment should be made with the vehicle sitting level, the gas tank half-full and no unusually heavy load in the vehicle.

6   Starting with the low beam adjustment, position the high intensity zone so it is two inches below the horizontal line and two inches to the right of the headlight vertical line. Adjustment on sealed beam equipped models is made by turning the top adjusting screw clockwise to raise the beam and counterclockwise to lower the beam **(see illustra-**

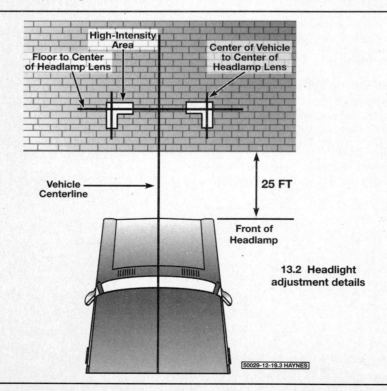

13.2 Headlight adjustment details

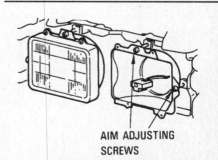

AIM ADJUSTING SCREWS

13.6a Sealed beam headlight adjusting screw locations

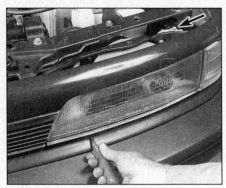

13.6b On bulb-type headlights, the upper adjusting screw (arrow) moves the beam horizontally and the lower screw (accessible under the housing with a Phillips head screwdriver) moves it vertically

tion). The adjusting screw on the side should be used in the same manner to move the beam left or right. On bulb-type headlights, the top adjusting screw moves the headlight assembly right or left and the lower one moves it up and down **(see illustration)**.

7   With the high beams on, the high intensity zone should be vertically centered with the exact center just below the horizontal line. **Note:** *It may not be possible to position the headlight aim exactly for both high and low beams. If a compromise must be made, keep in mind that the low beams are the most used and have the greatest effect on driver safety.*

8   Have the headlights adjusted by a dealer service department at the earliest opportunity.

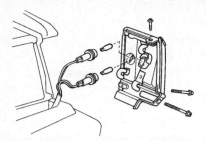

14.2a Parking and front side marker light details (1983 through 1986 models)

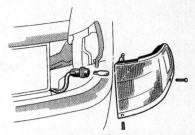

14.2b Parking light details (1987 through 1988 models)

14.2c Front turn signal light details

14   Bulb replacement

Refer to illustrations 14.2a through 14.2o and 14.4

1   The lenses of many lights are held in place by screws, which makes it a simple procedure to gain access to the bulbs.

2   On some lights the lenses are held in place by clips. On these, the lenses can either be removed by unsnapping them or by using a small screwdriver to pry them off **(see illustrations)**.

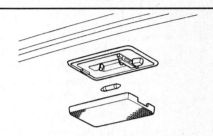

14.2d Typical interior light details

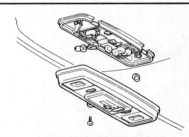

14.2e Personal light bulb installation details

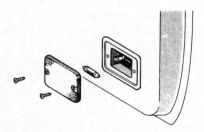

14.2f Typical door courtesy light details

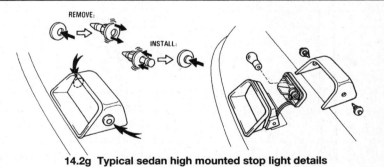

14.2g Typical sedan high mounted stop light details

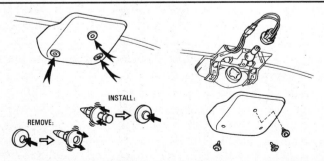

14.2h 1983 through 1986 liftback model high mounted stop light details

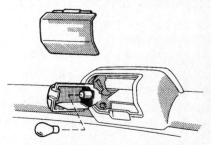

14.2i Station wagon high mounted stop light details

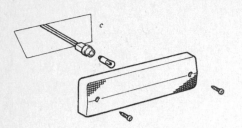

14.2j Rear side marker light details

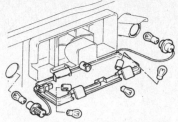

14.2k 1983 through 1986 sedan model rear turn signal, stop, tail, backup and license plate light details

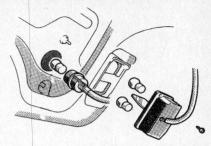

14.2l 1987 and 1988 model sedan stop, tail, backup and license plate light details

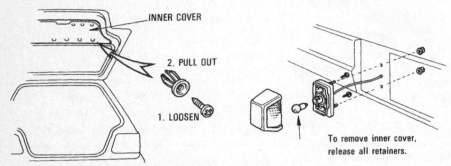

14.2m Liftback license plate light details

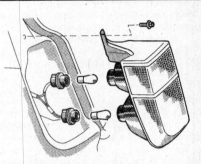

14.2n Station wagon rear turn signal, stop and tail light details

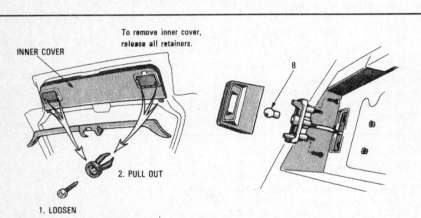

14.2o Station wagon license plate lights

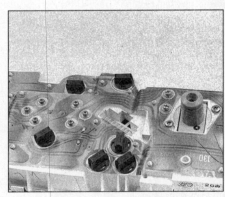

14.4 After removing the instrument cluster, turn the bulb holders, lift them out and withdraw the bulbs

15.2 Unplug the electrical connector (A), remove the bolts (B) and lift the wiper motor off

3   Several types of bulbs are used. Some are removed by pushing in and turning counterclockwise. Others can simply be unclipped from the terminals or pulled straight out of the socket.

4   To gain access to the instrument panel illumination lights **(see illustration)**, the instrument cluster will have to be removed as described in Section 16.

15   Windshield wiper motor - removal and installation

Refer to illustration 15.2

1   Disconnect the negative cable at the battery. Place the cable out of the way so it cannot accidentally come in contact with the negative terminal of the battery, as this would

once again allow power into the electrical system of the vehicle.

2   Unplug the electrical connector, remove the retaining bolts and lift the wiper motor from the engine compartment **(see illustration)**.

3   Installation is the reverse of removal.

16   Instrument cluster - removal and installation

Refer to illustration 16.5

1   Disconnect the negative cable at the battery. Place the cable out of the way so it cannot accidentally come in contact with the negative terminal of the battery, as this would once again allow power into the electrical system of the vehicle.

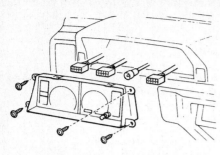

16.5 Instrument cluster details

2   Remove the steering column covers (Chapter 11).

3   Remove the screws holding the cluster finish panel in place, then remove the finish panel (Chapter 11).

4   On some models it will be necessary to grasp the speedometer cable collar and pull it toward the cluster to detach the cable. On later models, the cable unlocks automatically when the cluster is pulled out.

5   Remove the retaining screws, then pull out the instrument cluster and disconnect the wiring connectors **(see illustration)**.

6   To replace any faulty components within the cluster, simply unbolt or unscrew them and replace them with new units.

7   Installation is the reverse of removal.

---

17   Instrument panel - removal and installation

Refer to illustrations 17.3a, 17.3b, 17.4a and 17.4b

1   Disconnect the negative cable at the

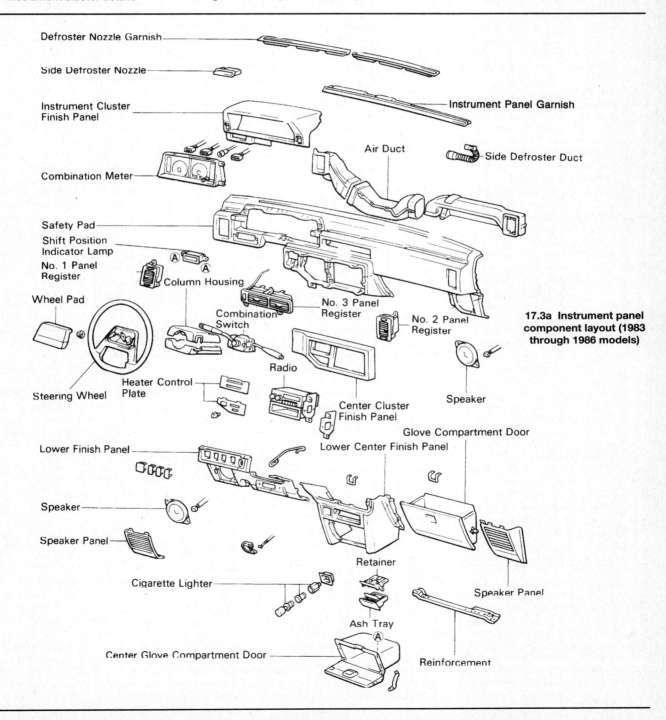

17.3a Instrument panel component layout (1983 through 1986 models)

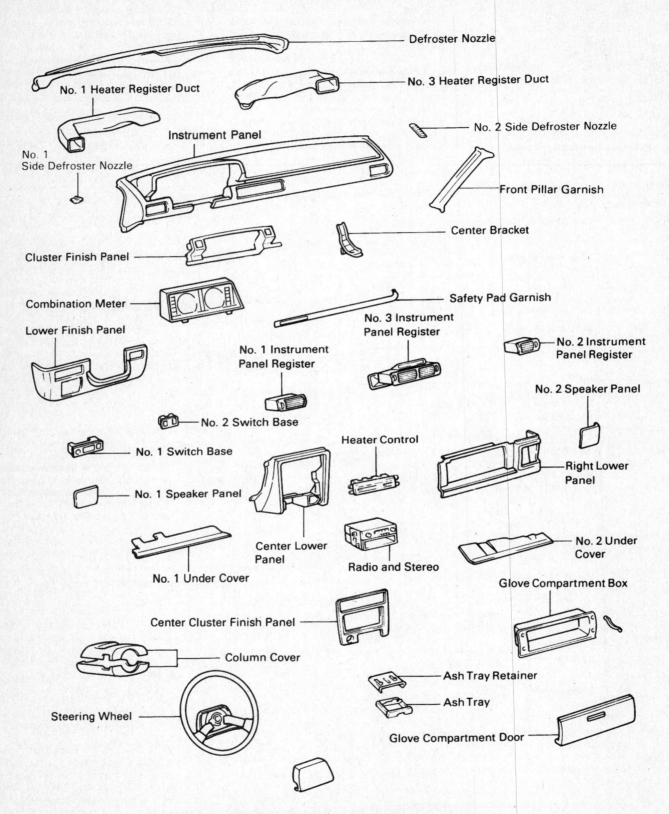

17.3b 1987 and 1988 instrument panel component layout

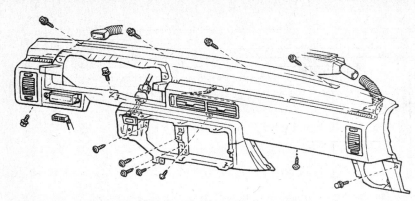

17.4a 1983 through 1986 instrument panel retaining bolt and screw locations

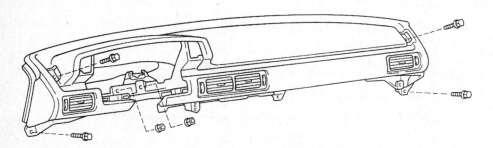

17.4b 1987 and 1988 instrument panel retaining bolt and nut locations

battery. Place the cable out of the way so it cannot accidentally come in contact with the negative terminal of the battery, as this would once again allow power into the electrical system of the vehicle.

2   Remove the steering wheel (Chapter 10).

3   Remove the steering column covers, instrument panel finish panels, instrument cluster, heater register ducts, radio, heater controls and any other components which would interfere with removal **(see illustrations)**.

4   Remove the retaining bolts, nuts and screws, unplug any electrical connectors and pull the instrument panel up and to the rear to detach it from the clips on the back **(see illustrations)**.

5   Installation is the reverse of removal.

18   Cruise control system - description and checking

The cruise control system maintains vehicle speed by means of a vacuum actuated servo motor located in the engine compartment which is connected to the throttle linkage by a cable. The system consists of the servo motor, clutch switch, stoplight switch, control switches, a relay and associated vacuum hoses.

Because of the complexity of the cruise control system and the special tools and techniques required for diagnosis and repair, this should be left to a dealer or properly equipped shop. However, it is possible for the home mechanic to make simple checks of the wiring and vacuum connections for minor faults which can be easily repaired. These include:

a) *Inspecting the cruise control actuating switches and wiring for broken wires or loose connections.*

b) *Checking the cruise control fuse.*

c) *Checking the hoses in the engine compartment for tight connections, cracked hoses and obvious vacuum leaks. The cruise control system is operated by a vacuum so it is critical that all vacuum switches, hoses and connections be secure.*

19   Power door lock system - description and checking

The power door lock system operates the door lock actuators mounted in each door. The system consists of the switches, actuators and associated wiring. Special tools and techniques are required to fully diagnose this system, and this should be left to a dealer or properly equipped shop. However, it is possible for the home mechanic to make simple checks of the wiring connections and actuators for minor faults which can be easily repaired. These include:

a) *Checking the system fuse and/or circuit breaker.*

b) *Checking the switch wiring for damage or loose connections.*

c) *Checking the switches for continuity.*

d) *Removing the door panel(s) and checking the actuator wiring connections for looseness or damage. Inspect the actuator rods (if equipped) to make sure they are not bent, damaged or binding. The actuator can be checked by applying battery power momentarily. A solid click indicates the solenoid is operating properly.*

20   Power window system - description and checking

The power window system operates the electric motors mounted in the doors which lower and raise the windows. The system consists of the control switches, the motors (regulators), glass mechanisms and associated wiring.

Because of the complexity of the power window system and the special tools and techniques required for diagnosis and repair, this should be left to a dealer or properly equipped shop. However, it is possible for the home mechanic to make simple checks of the wiring connections and motors for minor faults which can be easily repaired. These include:

a) *Inspecting the power window actuating switches and wiring for broken wires or loose connections.*

b) *Checking the power window fuse and/or circuit breaker.*

c) *Removing the door panel(s) and checking the power window motor wiring connections for looseness and damage, and inspecting the glass mechanisms for damage which could cause binding.*

21   Wiring diagrams - general information

Since it isn't possible to include all wiring diagrams for every year covered by this manual, the following diagrams are those that are typical and most commonly needed.

Prior to troubleshooting any circuits, check the fuse and circuit breakers (if equipped) to make sure they are in good condition. Make sure the battery is properly charged and has clean, tight cable connections (Chapter 1).

When checking the wiring system, make sure that all connectors are clean, with no broken or loose pins. When unplugging a connector, do not pull on the wires, only on the connector housings themselves.

Refer to the accompanying illustration for the wire color codes applicable to your vehicle.

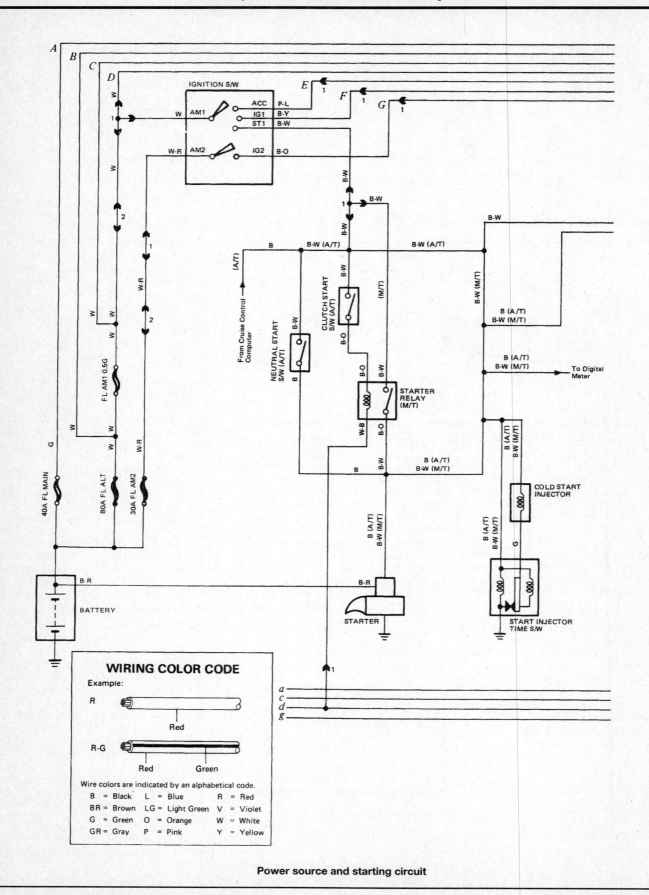

Power source and starting circuit

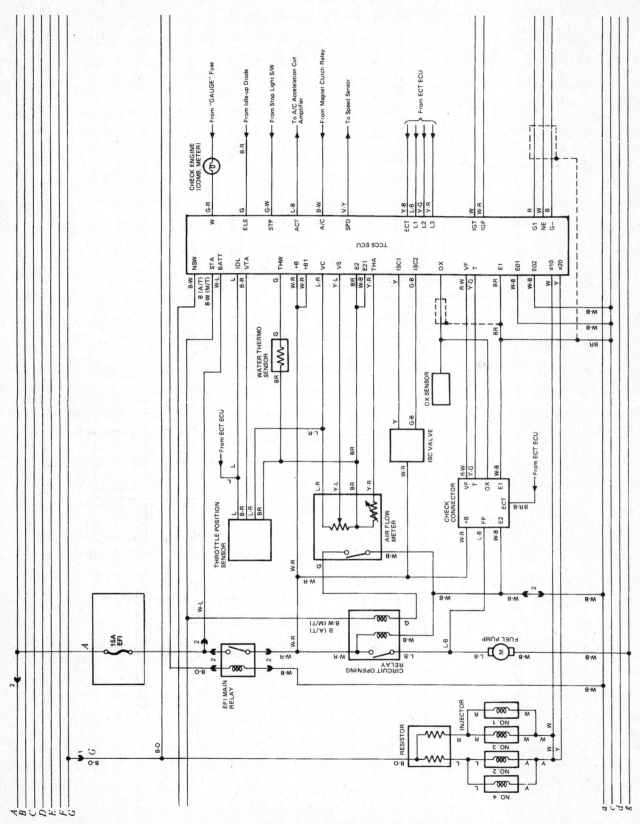

Toyota Computer Control System (TCCS) system circuit

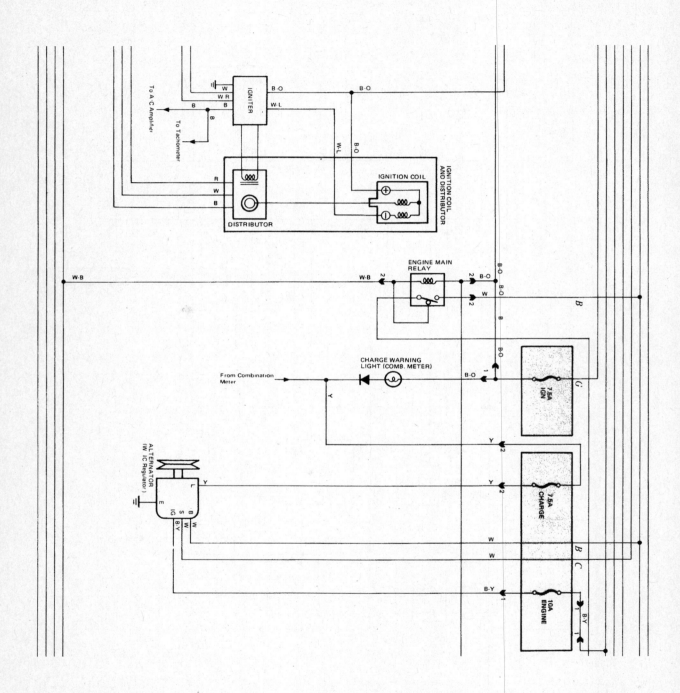

Starting and ignition system circuit

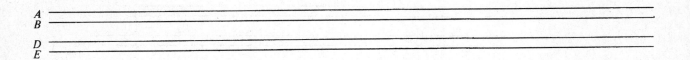

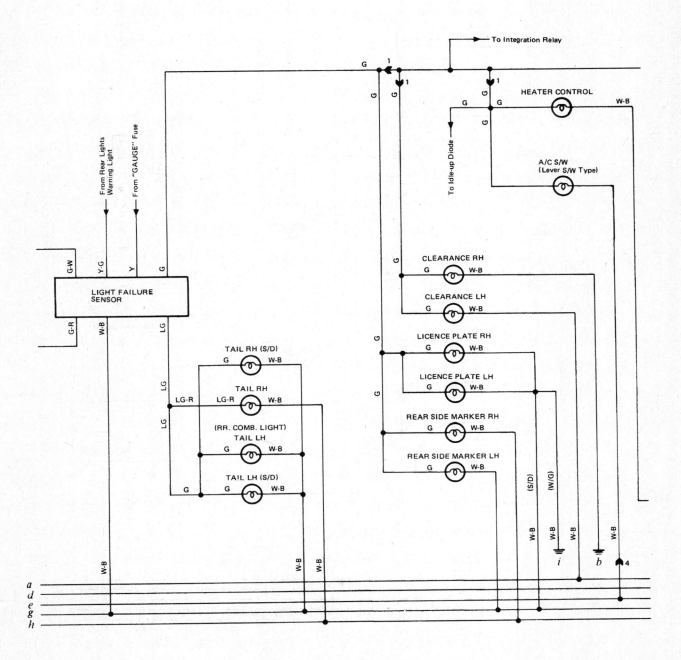

Tail light and rear illumination circuit

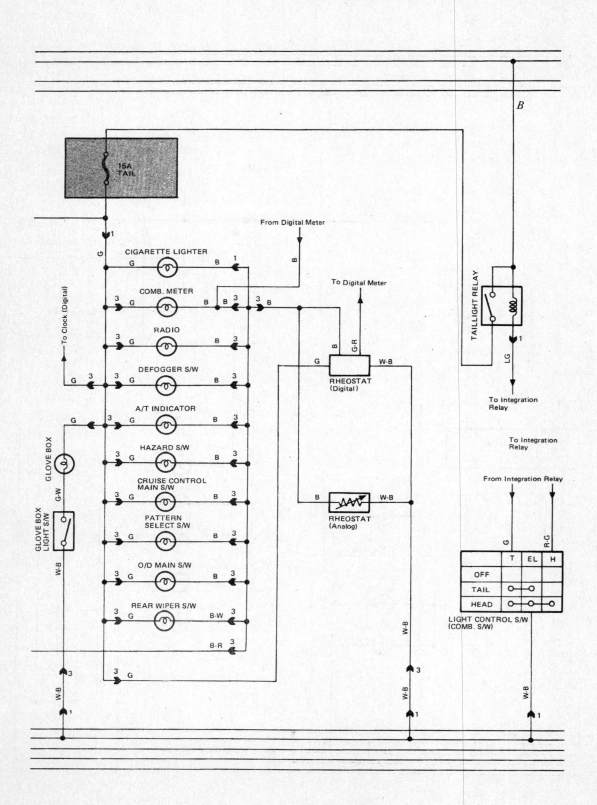

Tail light and rear illumination circuit (cont.)

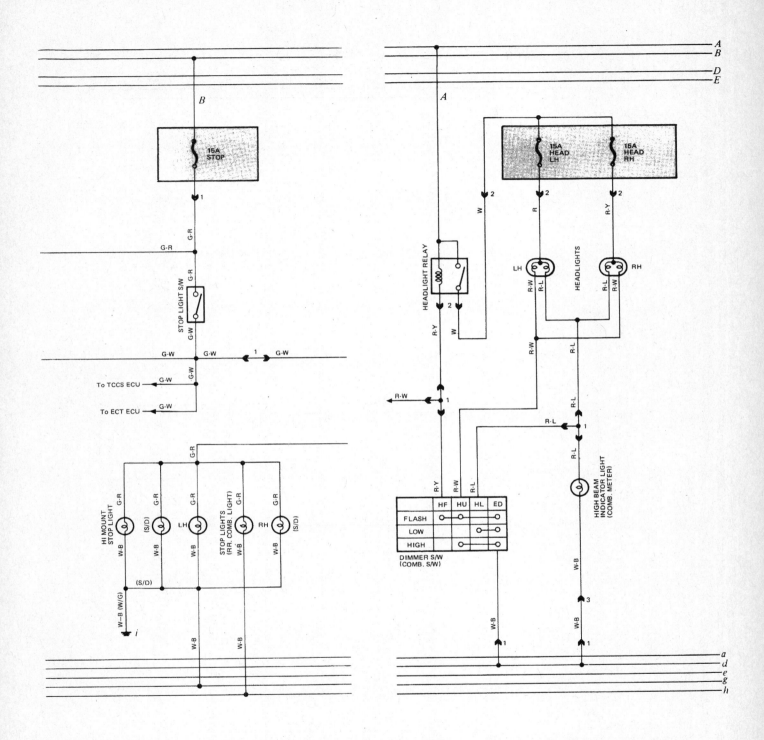

Stop light system circuit

Headlight circuit

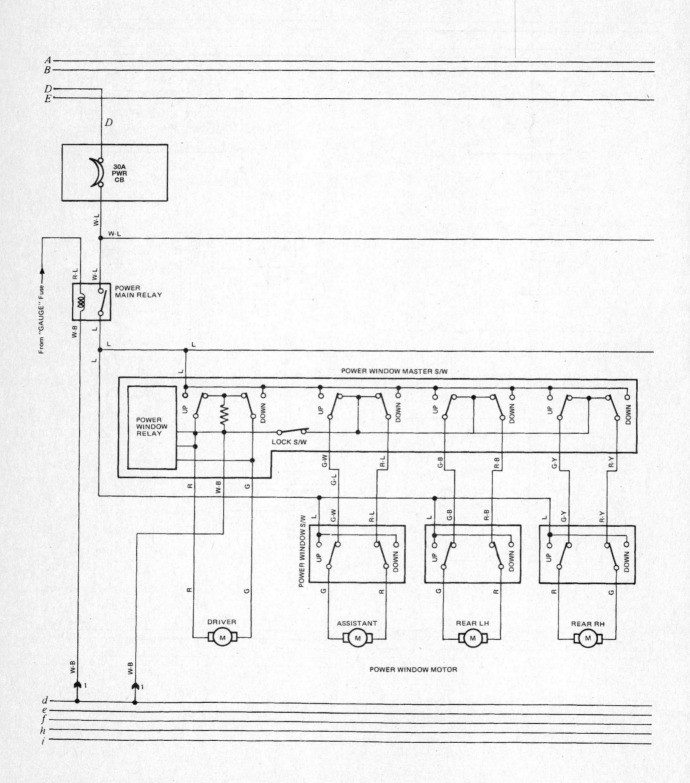

Power window circuit

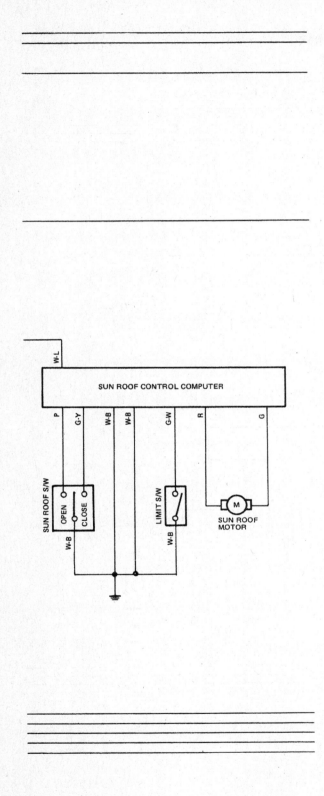

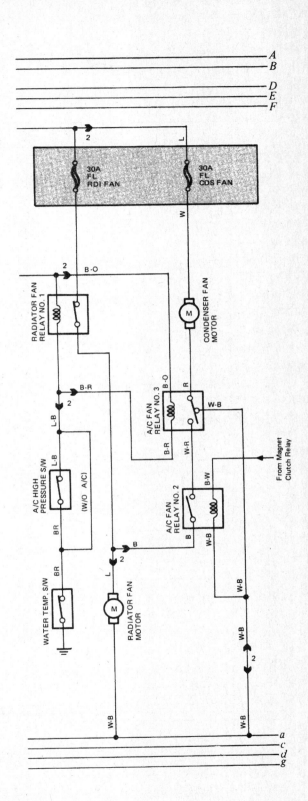

Sunroof circuit

Radiator fan circuit

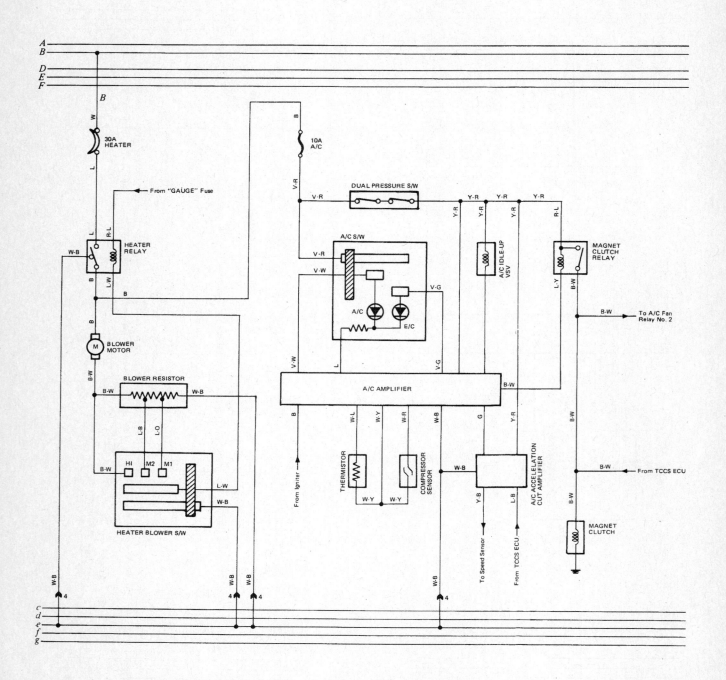

Air conditioning and heater system circuit

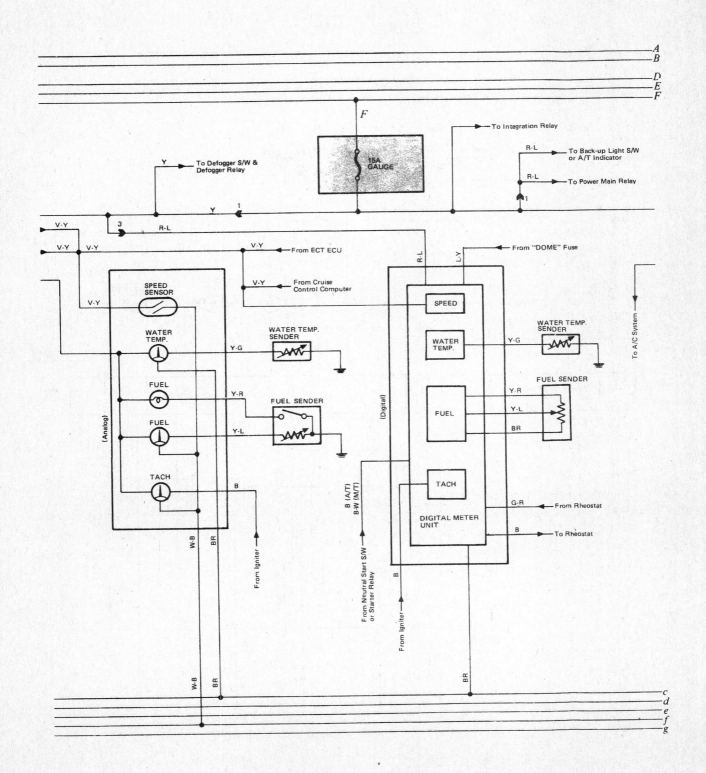

Instrument cluster circuit

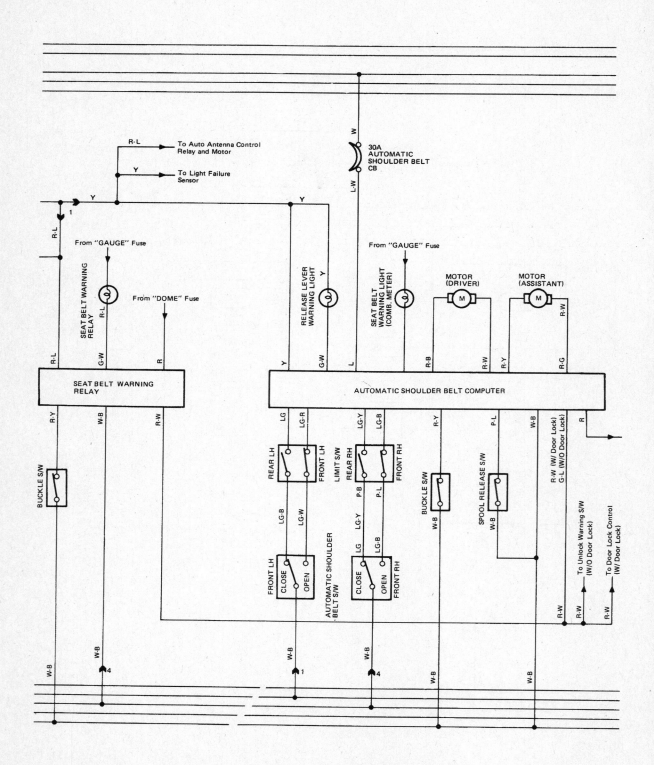

Seat belt warning system circuit

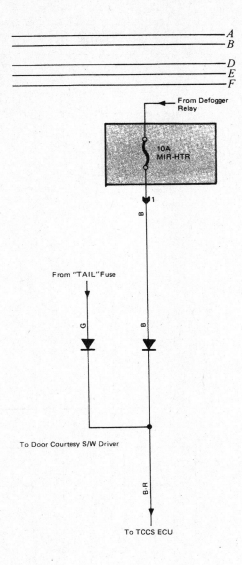

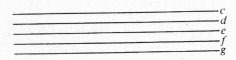

Idle-up system circuit

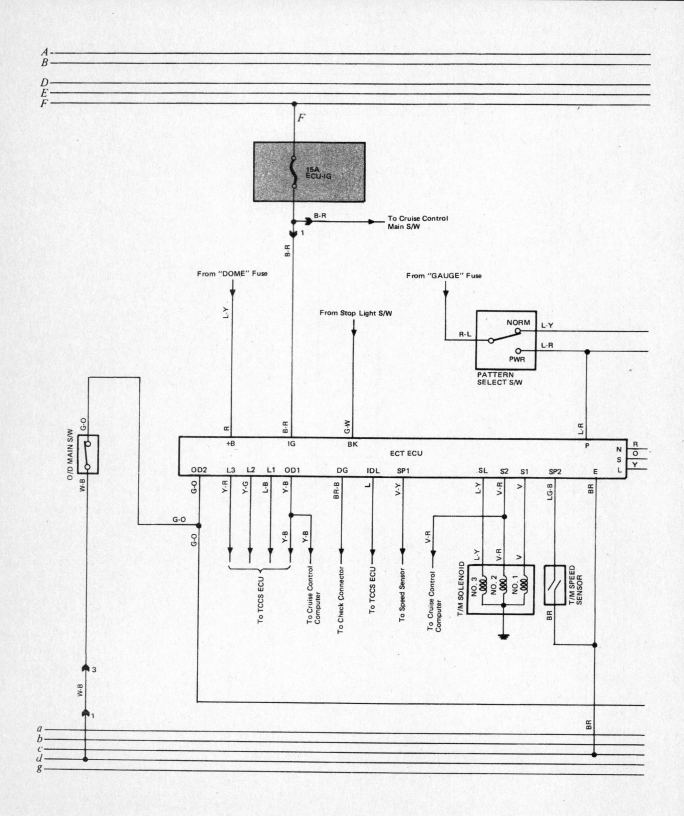

Overdrive and electronically controlled transaxle circuit

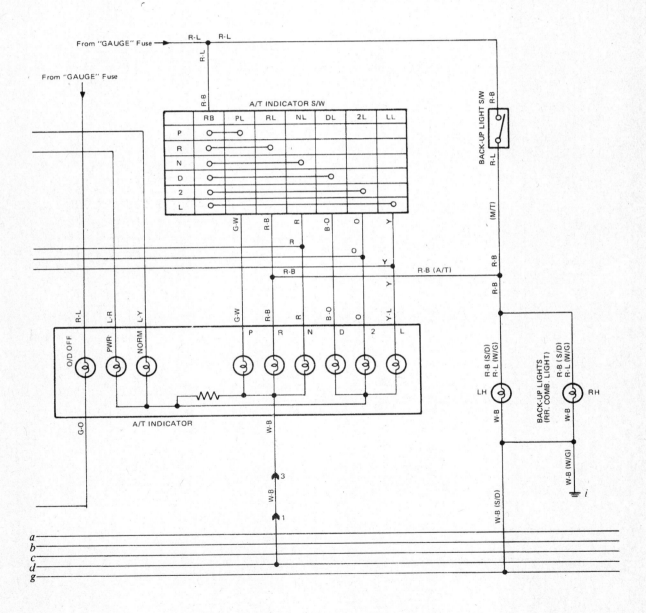

Automatic transaxle indicator and backup light circuit

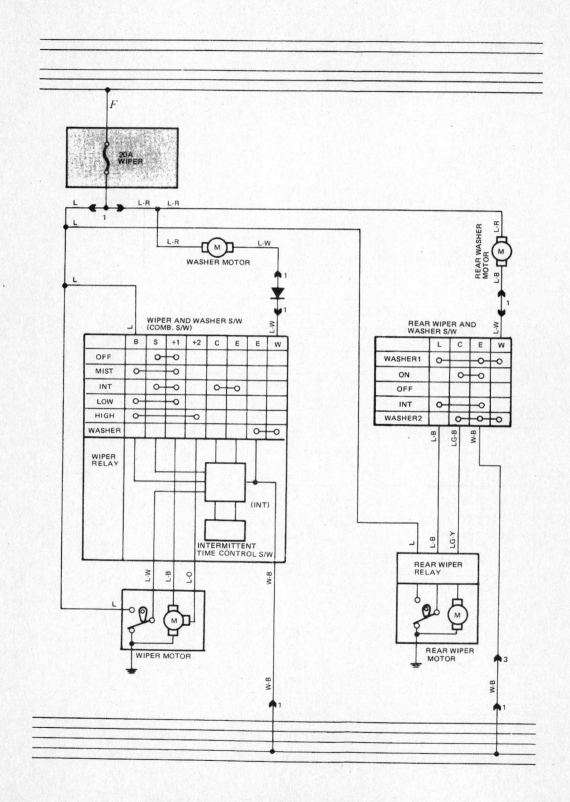

Front and rear wiper/washer system circuit

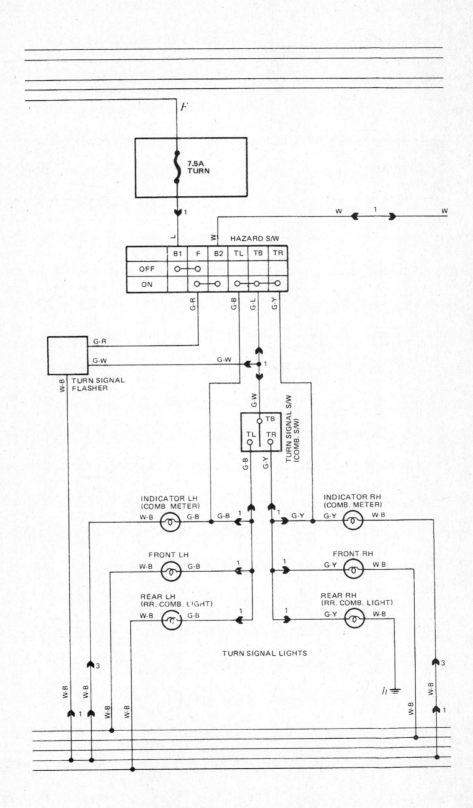

Turn signal/hazard flasher circuit

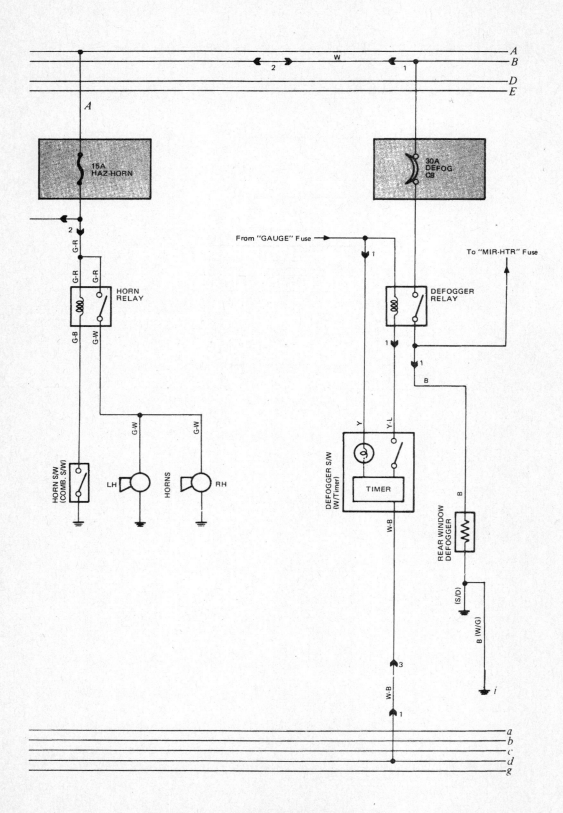

Horn and rear window defogger circuit

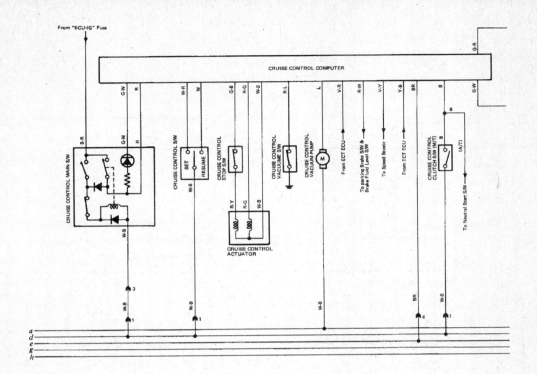

Cruise control circuit

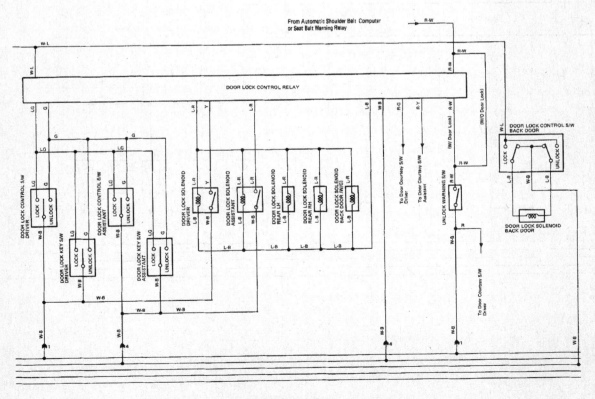

Door lock circuit

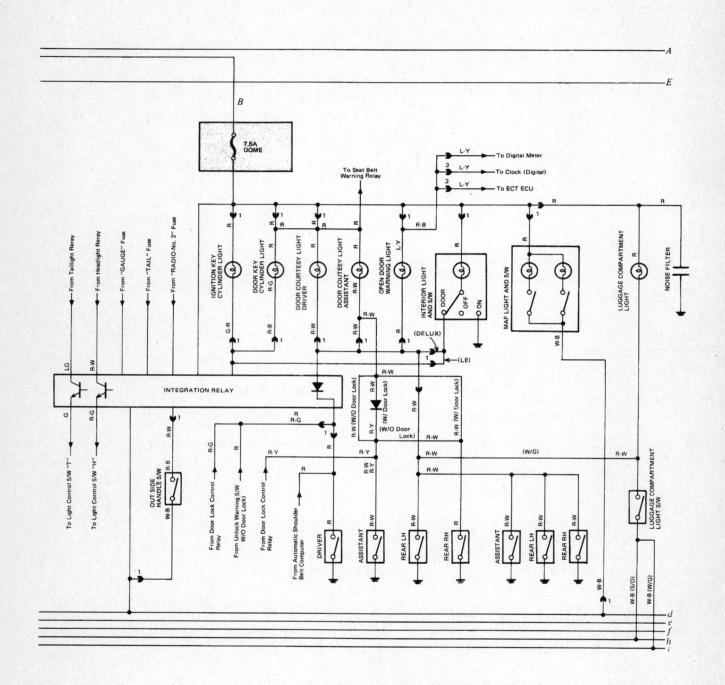

Interior light circuit

Index

Haynes Automotive Manuals

NOTE: If you do not see a listing for your vehicle, consult your local Haynes dealer for the latest product information.

Haynes Xtreme Customizing
11101 Sport Compact Customizing
11102 Sport Compact Performance
11110 In-car Entertainment
11150 Sport Utility Vehicle Customizing
11213 Acura
11255 GM Full-size Pick-ups
11314 Ford Focus
11315 Full-size Ford Pick-ups
11373 Honda Civic

ACURA
12010 Integra '86 thru '89 & Legend '86 thru '90
12021 Integra '90 thru '93 & Legend '91 thru '95

AMC
Jeep CJ - see JEEP (50020)
14020 Concord/Hornet/Gremlin/Spirit '70 thru '83
14025 (Renault) Alliance & Encore '83 thru '87

AUDI
15020 4000 all models '80 thru '87
15025 5000 all models '77 thru '83
15026 5000 all models '84 thru '88

AUSTIN
Healey Sprite - see MG Midget (66015)

BMW
18020 3/5 Series '82 thru '92
18021 3 Series including Z3 models '92 thru '98
18025 320i all 4 cyl models '75 thru '83
18050 1500 thru 2002 except Turbo '59 thru '77

BUICK
19010 Buick Century '97 thru '02
Century (FWD) - see GM (38005)
19020 Buick, Oldsmobile & Pontiac Full-size (Front wheel drive) '85 thru '02
19025 Buick Oldsmobile & Pontiac Full-size (Rear wheel drive) '70 thru '90
19030 Mid-size Regal & Century '74 thru '87
Regal - see GENERAL MOTORS (38010)
Skyhawk - see GM (38030)
Skylark - see GM (38020, 38025)
Somerset - see GENERAL MOTORS (38025)

CADILLAC
21030 Cadillac Rear Wheel Drive '70 thru '93
Cimarron, Eldorado & Seville - see GM (38015, 38030, 38031)

CHEVROLET
10305 Chevrolet Engine Overhaul Manual
24010 Astro & GMC Safari Mini-vans '85 thru '03
24015 Camaro V8 all models '70 thru '81
24016 Camaro all models '82 thru '92
Cavalier - see GM (38015)
Celebrity - see GM (38005)
24017 Camaro & Firebird '93 thru '02
24020 Chevelle, Malibu, El Camino '69 thru '87
24024 Chevette & Pontiac T1000 '76 thru '87
Citation - see GENERAL MOTORS (38020)
24032 Corsica/Beretta all models '87 thru '96
24040 Corvette all V8 models '68 thru '82
24041 Corvette all models '84 thru '96
24045 Full-size Sedans Caprice, Impala, Biscayne, Bel Air & Wagons '69 thru '90
24046 Impala SS & Caprice and Buick Roadmaster '91 thru '96
Lumina '90 thru '94 - see GM (38010)
24048 Lumina & Monte Carlo '95 thru '03
Lumina APV - see GM (38035)
24050 Luv Pick-up all 2WD & 4WD '72 thru '82
Malibu - see GM (38026)
24055 Monte Carlo all models '70 thru '88
Monte Carlo '95 thru '01 - see LUMINA
24059 Nova all V8 models '69 thru '79
24060 Nova/Geo Prizm '85 thru '92
24064 Pick-ups '67 thru '87 - Chevrolet & GMC, all V8 & in-line 6 cyl, 2WD & 4WD '67 thru '87; Suburbans, Blazers & Jimmys '67 thru '91
24065 Pick-ups '88 thru '98 - Chevrolet & GMC, all full-size models '88 thru '98; C/K Classic '99 & '00; Blazer & Jimmy '92 thru '94; Suburban '92 thru '99; Tahoe & Yukon '95 thru '99
24066 Pick-ups '99 thru '02 - Chevrolet Silverado & GMC Sierra '99 thru '05; Suburban/Tahoe/Yukon/Yukon XL '00 thru '05
24070 S-10 & GMC S-15 Pick-ups '82 thru '93
24071 S-10, Sonoma & Pick-ups '94 thru '04
24072 Chevrolet TrailBlazer & TrailBlazer EXT, GMC Envoy & Envoy XL, Oldsmobile Bravada '02 and '03
24075 Sprint '85 thru '88, Geo Metro '89 thru '01
24080 Vans - Chevrolet & GMC '68 thru '96
24081 Chevrolet Express & GMC Savana Full-size Vans '96 thru '05

CHRYSLER
10310 Chrysler Engine Overhaul Manual
25015 Chrysler Cirrus, Dodge Stratus, Plymouth Breeze, '95 thru '98
25020 Full-size Front-Wheel Drive '88 thru '93
K-Cars - see DODGE Aries (30008)
Laser - see DODGE Daytona (30030)
25025 Chrysler LHS, Concorde & New Yorker, Dodge Intrepid, Eagle Vision, '93 thru '97
25026 Chrysler LHS, Concorde, 300M, Dodge Intrepid '98 thru '03
25030 Chrysler/Plym. Mid-size '82 thru '95
Rear-wheel Drive - see DODGE (30050)
25035 PT Cruiser all models '01 thru '03
25040 Chrysler Sebring/Dodge Avenger '95 thru '02

DATSUN
28005 200SX all models '80 thru '83
28007 B-210 all models '73 thru '78
28009 210 all models '78 thru '82
28012 240Z, 260Z & 280Z Coupe '70 thru '78
28014 280ZX Coupe & 2+2 '79 thru '83
300ZX - see NISSAN (72010)
28018 510 & PL521 Pick-up '68 thru '73
28020 510 all models '78 thru '81
28022 620 Series Pick-up all models '73 thru '79
720 Series Pick-up - NISSAN (72030)
28025 810/Maxima all gas models, '77 thru '84

DODGE
400 & 600 - see CHRYSLER (25030)
30008 Aries & Plymouth Reliant '81 thru '89
30010 Caravan & Ply. Voyager '84 thru '95
30011 Caravan & Ply. Voyager '96 thru '02
30012 Challenger/Plymouth Sapporo '78 thru '83
Challenger '67-'76 - see DART (30025)
30016 Colt/Plymouth Champ '78 thru '87
30020 Dakota Pick-ups all models '87 thru '96
30021 Durango '98 & '99, Dakota '97 thru '99
30022 Dodge Durango models '00 thru '03
Dodge Dakota models '00 thru '03
30025 Dart, Challenger/Plymouth Barracuda & Valiant 6 cyl models '67 thru '76
30030 Daytona & Chrysler Laser '84 thru '89
Intrepid - see Chrysler (25025, 25026)
30034 Dodge & Plymouth Neon '95 thru '99
30035 Omni & Plymouth Horizon '78 thru '90
30036 Dodge and Plymouth Neon '00 thru '03
30040 Pick-ups all full-size models '74 thru '93
30041 Pick-ups all full-size models '94 thru '01
30042 Dodge Full-size Pick-ups '02 thru '05
30045 Ram 50/D50 Pick-ups & Raider and Plymouth Arrow Pick-ups '79 thru '93
30050 Dodge/Ply./Chrysler RWD '71 thru '89
30055 Shadow/Plymouth Sundance '87 thru '94
30060 Spirit & Plymouth Acclaim '89 thru '95
30065 Vans - Dodge & Plymouth '71 thru '03

EAGLE
Talon - see MITSUBISHI (68030, 68031)
Vision - see CHRYSLER (25025)

FIAT
34010 124 Sport Coupe & Spider '68 thru '78
34025 X1/9 all models '74 thru '80

FORD
10355 Ford Automatic Transmission Overhaul
10320 Ford Engine Overhaul Manual
36004 Aerostar Mini-vans '86 thru '97
Aspire - see FORD Festiva (36030)
36006 Contour/Mercury Mystique '95 thru '00
36008 Courier Pick-up all models '72 thru '82
36012 Crown Victoria & Mercury Grand Marquis '88 thru '00
36016 Escort/Mercury Lynx '81 thru '90
36020 Escort/Mercury Tracer '91 thru '00
36022 Expedition - see FORD Pick-up (36059)
36024 Explorer & Mazda Navajo '91 thru '01
36025 Ford Explorer & Mercury Mountaineer '02 and '03
36028 Fairmont & Mercury Zephyr '78 thru '83
36030 Festiva & Aspire '88 thru '97
36032 Fiesta all models '77 thru '80
36034 Focus all models '00 thru '05
36036 Ford & Mercury Full-size '75 thru '87
36044 Ford & Mercury Mid-size '75 thru '86
36048 Mustang V8 all models '64-1/2 thru '73
36049 Mustang II 4 cyl, V6 & V8 '74 thru '78
36050 Mustang & Mercury Capri '79 thru '86
36051 Mustang all models '94 thru '03
36054 Pick-ups and Bronco '73 thru '79
36058 Pick-ups and Bronco '80 thru '96
36059 Pick-ups, Expedition & Lincoln Navigator '97 thru '02
36060 Super Duty Pick-ups, Excursion '99 thru '02
36062 Pinto & Mercury Bobcat '75 thru '80
36066 Probe all models '89 thru '92
36070 Ranger/Bronco II gas models '83 thru '92
36071 Ford Ranger '93 thru '05 & Mazda Pick-ups '94 thru '05
36074 Taurus & Mercury Sable '86 thru '95
36075 Taurus & Mercury Sable '96 thru '01
36078 Tempo & Mercury Topaz '84 thru '94
36082 Thunderbird/Mercury Cougar '83 thru '88
36086 Thunderbird/Mercury Cougar '89 thru '97
36090 Vans all V8 Econoline models '69 thru '91
36094 Vans full size '92 thru '01
36097 Windstar Mini-van '95 thru '03

GENERAL MOTORS
10360 GM Automatic Transmission Overhaul
38005 Buick Century, Chevrolet Celebrity, Olds Cutlass Ciera & Pontiac 6000 '82 thru '96
38010 Buick Regal, Chevrolet Lumina, Oldsmobile Cutlass Supreme & Pontiac Grand Prix front wheel drive '88 thru '02
38015 Buick Skyhawk, Cadillac Cimarron, Chevrolet Cavalier, Oldsmobile Firenza Pontiac J-2000 & Sunbird '82 thru '94
38016 Chevrolet Cavalier/Pontiac Sunfire '95 thru '04
38020 Buick Skylark, Chevrolet Citation, Olds Omega, Pontiac Phoenix '80 thru '85
38025 Buick Skylark & Somerset, Olds Achieva, Calais & Pontiac Grand Am '85 thru '98
38026 Chevrolet Malibu, Olds Alero & Cutlass, Pontiac Grand Am '97 thru '03
38030 Cadillac Eldorado & Oldsmobile Toronado '71 thru '85, Seville '80 thru '85, Buick Riviera '79 thru '85
38031 Cadillac Eldorado & Seville '86 thru '91, DeVille & Buick Riviera '86 thru '93, Fleetwood & Olds Tornado '86 thru '92
38032 DeVille '94 thru '02, Seville '92 thru '02
38035 Chevrolet Lumina APV, Oldsmobile Silhouette & Pontiac Trans Sport '90 thru '96
38036 Chevrolet Venture, Olds Silhouette, Pontiac Trans Sport & Montana '97 thru '01
General Motors Full-size Rear-wheel Drive - see BUICK (19025)

GEO
Metro - see CHEVROLET Sprint (24075)
Prizm - see CHEVROLET (24060) or TOYOTA (92036)
40030 Storm all models '90 thru '93
Tracker - see SUZUKI Samurai (90010)

GMC
Vans & Pick-ups - see CHEVROLET

HONDA
42010 Accord CVCC all models '76 thru '83
42011 Accord all models '84 thru '89

42012 Accord all models '90 thru '93
42013 Accord all models '94 thru '97
42014 Accord all models '98 thru '02
42015 Honda Accord models '03 thru '05
42020 Civic 1200 all models '73 thru '79
42021 Civic 1300 & 1500 CVCC '80 thru '83
42022 Civic 1500 CVCC all models '75 thru '79
42023 Civic all models '84 thru '91
42024 Civic & del Sol '92 thru '95
42025 Civic '96 thru '00, CR-V '97 thru '01, Acura Integra '94 thru '00
Passport - see ISUZU Rodeo (47017)
42026 Civic '01 thru '04, CR-V '02 thru '04
42035 Honda Odyssey '99 thru '04
42040 Prelude CVCC all models '79 thru '89

HYUNDAI
43010 Elantra all models '96 thru '01
43015 Excel & Accent all models '86 thru '98

ISUZU
Hombre - see CHEVROLET S-10 (24071)
47017 Rodeo '91 thru '02, Amigo '89 thru '02, Honda Passport '95 thru '02
47020 Trooper '84 thru '91, Pick-up '81 thru '93

JAGUAR
49010 XJ6 all 6 cyl models '68 thru '86
49011 XJ6 all models '88 thru '94
49015 XJ12 & XJS all 12 cyl models '72 thru '85

JEEP
50010 Cherokee, Comanche & Wagoneer Limited all models '84 thru '01
50020 CJ all models '49 thru '86
50025 Grand Cherokee all models '93 thru '04
50029 Grand Wagoneer & Pick-up '72 thru '91
50030 Wrangler all models '87 thru '03
50035 Liberty '02 thru '04

KIA
54070 Sephia '94 thru '01, Spectra '00 thru '04

LEXUS
ES 300 - see TOYOTA Camry (92007)

LINCOLN
Navigator - see FORD Pick-up (36059)
59010 Rear Wheel Drive all models '70 thru '01

MAZDA
61010 GLC (rear wheel drive) '77 thru '83
61011 GLC (front wheel drive) '81 thru '85
61015 323 & Protegé '90 thru '00
61016 MX-5 Miata '90 thru '97
61020 MPV all models '89 thru '94
Navajo - see FORD Explorer (36024)
61030 Pick-ups '72 thru '93
Pick-ups '94 on - see Ford (36071)
61035 RX-7 all models '79 thru '85
61036 RX-7 all models '86 thru '91
61040 626 (rear wheel drive) '79 thru '82
61041 626 & MX-6 (front wheel drive) '83 thru '92
61042 626 '93 thru '01, MX-6/Ford Probe '93 thru '01

MERCEDES-BENZ
63012 123 Series Diesel '76 thru '85
63015 190 Series 4-cyl gas models, '84 thru '88
63020 230, 250 & 280 6 cyl sohc '68 thru '72
63025 280 123 Series gas models '77 thru '81
63030 350 & 450 all models '71 thru '80

MERCURY
64200 Villager & Nissan Quest '93 thru '01
All other titles, see FORD listing.

MG
66010 MGB Roadster & GT Coupe '62 thru '80
66015 MG Midget & Austin Healey Sprite Roadster '58 thru '80

MITSUBISHI
68020 Cordia, Tredia, Galant, Precis & Mirage '83 thru '93
68030 Eclipse, Eagle Talon & Plymouth Laser '90 thru '94
68031 Eclipse '95 thru '01, Eagle Talon '95 thru '98
68035 Mitsubishi Galant '94 thru '03
68040 Pick-up '83 thru '96, Montero '83 thru '93

NISSAN
72010 300ZX all models incl. Turbo '84 thru '89
72015 Altima all models '93 thru '04
72020 Maxima all models '85 thru '92
72021 Maxima all models '93 thru '01
72030 Pick-ups '80 thru '97, Pathfinder '87 thru '95
72031 Frontier Pick-up '98 thru '01, Xterra '00 & '01, Pathfinder '96 thru '01
72040 Pulsar all models '83 thru '86
72050 Sentra all models '82 thru '94
72051 Sentra & 200SX all models '95 thru '99
72060 Stanza all models '82 thru '90

OLDSMOBILE
73015 Cutlass '74 thru '88
For other OLDSMOBILE titles, see BUICK, CHEVROLET or GM listings.

PLYMOUTH
For PLYMOUTH titles, see DODGE.

PONTIAC
79008 Fiero all models '84 thru '88
79018 Firebird V8 models except Turbo '70 thru '81
79019 Firebird all models '82 thru '92
79040 Mid-size Rear-wheel Drive '70 thru '87
For other PONTIAC titles, see BUICK, CHEVROLET or GM listings.

PORSCHE
80020 911 Coupe & Targa models '65 thru '89
80025 914 all 4 cyl models '69 thru '76
80030 924 all models incl. Turbo '76 thru '82
80035 944 all models incl. Turbo '83 thru '89

RENAULT
Alliance, Encore - see AMC (14020)

SAAB
84010 900 including Turbo '79 thru '88

SATURN
87010 Saturn all models '91 thru '02
87020 Saturn all L-series models '00 thu '04

SUBARU
89002 1100, 1300, 1400 & 1600 '71 thru '79
89003 1600 & 1800 2WD & 4WD '80 thru '94
89100 Legacy all models '90 thru '98

SUZUKI
90010 Samurai/Sidekick/Geo Tracker '86 thru '01

TOYOTA
92005 Camry all models '83 thru '91
92006 Camry all models '92 thru '96
92007 Camry/Avalon/Solara/Lexus ES 300 '97 thru '01
92008 Toyota Camry, Avalon and Solara & Lexus ES 300/330 all models '02 thru '05
92015 Celica Rear Wheel Drive '71 thru '85
92020 Celica Front Wheel Drive '86 thru '99
92025 Celica Supra all models '79 thru '92
92030 Corolla all models '75 thru '79
92032 Corolla rear wheel drive models '80 thru '87
92035 Corolla front wheel drive models '84 thru '92
92036 Corolla & Geo Prizm '93 thru '02
92040 Corolla Tercel all models '80 thru '82
92045 Corona all models '74 thru '82
92050 Cressida all models '78 thru '82
92055 Land Cruiser FJ40/43/45/55 '68 thru '82
92056 Land Cruiser FJ60/62/80/FZJ80 '80 thru '96
92065 MR2 all models '85 thru '87
92070 Pick-up all models '69 thru '78
92075 Pick-up all models '79 thru '95
92076 Tacoma '95 thru '00, 4Runner '96 thru '00, T100 '93 thru '98
92078 Tundra '00 thru '02, Sequoia '01 thru '02
92079 Previa all models '91 thru '95
92080 RAV4 all models '96 thru '02
92082 Tercel all models '87 thru '94
92085 Tercel all models '87 thru '94
92090 Toyota Sienna all models '98 thru '02

TRIUMPH
94007 Spitfire all models '62 thru '81
94010 TR7 all models '75 thru '81

VW
96008 Beetle & Karmann Ghia '54 thru '79
96009 New Beetle '98 thru '00
96016 Rabbit, Jetta, Scirocco, & Pick-up gas models '75 thru '92 & Convertible '80 thru '92
96017 Golf, GTI & Jetta '93 thru '98, Cabrio '95 thru '98
96018 Golf, GTI, Jetta & Cabrio '99 thru '02
96020 Rabbit, Jetta, Pick-up diesel '77 thru '84
96023 Passat '98 thru '01, Audi A4 '96 thru '01
96030 Transporter 1600 all models '68 thru '79
96035 Transporter 1700, 1800, 2000 '72 thru '79
96040 Type 3 1500 & 1600 '63 thru '73
96045 Vanagon air-cooled models '80 thru '83

VOLVO
97010 120, 130 Series & 1800 Sports '61 thru '73
97015 140 Series all models '66 thru '74
97020 240 Series all models '76 thru '93
97040 740 & 760 Series all models '82 thru '88

TECHBOOK MANUALS
10205 Automotive Computer Codes
10206 OBD-II & Electronic Engine Management Systems
10210 Automotive Emissions Control Manual
10215 Fuel Injection Manual, 1978 thru 1985
10220 Fuel Injection Manual, 1986 thru 1999
10225 Holley Carburetor Manual
10230 Rochester Carburetor Manual
10240 Weber/Zenith/Stromberg/SU Carburetor
10305 Chevrolet Engine Overhaul Manual
10310 Chrysler Engine Overhaul Manual
10320 Ford Engine Overhaul Manual
10330 GM and Ford Diesel Engine Repair
10340 Small Engine Repair Manual
10345 Suspension, Steering & Driveline
10355 Ford Automatic Transmission Overhaul
10360 GM Automatic Transmission Overhaul
10405 Automotive Body Repair & Painting
10410 Automotive Brake Manual
10415 Automotive Detailing Manual
10420 Automotive Electrical Manual
10425 Automotive Heating & Air Conditioning
10430 Automotive Reference Dictionary
10435 Automotive Tools Manual
10440 Used Car Buying Guide
10445 Welding Manual
10450 ATV Basics
10452 Scooters, Automatic Transmission 50cc to 250cc

SPANISH MANUALS
98903 Reparación de Carrocería & Pintura
98904 Carburadores para los modelos Holley & Rochester
98905 Códigos Automotrices de la Computadora
98910 Frenos Automotriz
98913 Electricidad Automotriz
98915 Inyección de Combustible 1986 al 1999
99040 Chevrolet & GMC Camionetas '67 al '87
99041 Chevrolet & GMC Camionetas '88 al '98
99042 Chevrolet/GMC Camionetas Cerradas '68 al '95
99055 Dodge Caravan/Ply. Voyager '84 al '95
99075 Ford Camionetas y Bronco '80 al '94
99077 Ford Camionetas Cerradas '69 al '91
99088 Ford Modelos de Tamaño Mediano '75 al '86
99091 Ford Taurus & Mercury Sable '86 al '95
99095 GM Modelos de Tamaño Grande '70 al '90
99100 GM Modelos de Tamaño Mediano '70 al '88
99106 Jeep Cherokee, Wagoneer & Comanche '84 al '00
99110 Nissan Camionetas '80 al '96, Pathfinder '87 al '95
99118 Nissan Sentra '82 al '94
99125 Toyota Camionetas y 4-Runner '79 al '95

Over 100 Haynes motorcycle manuals also available

9-05

Haynes North America, Inc., 861 Lawrence Drive, Newbury Park, CA 91320 • (805) 498-6703